Rise of the Plebeians?

Exploring the Political in South Asia

Series Editor: Mukulika Banerjee
Reader in Anthropology, University College London.

Exploring the Political in South Asia is devoted to the publication of research on the political cultures of the region. The books in this Series will present qualitative and quantitative analyses grounded in field research, and will explore the cultures of democracies in their everyday local settings, specifically the workings of modern political institutions, practices of political mobilisation, manoeuvres of high politics, structures of popular beliefs, content of political ideologies and styles of political leadership, amongst others. Through fine-grained descriptions of particular settings in South Asia, the studies presented in this Series will inform, and have implications for, general discussions of democracy and politics elsewhere in the world.

Also in this Series

The Vernacularisation of Democracy: Politics, Caste and Religion in India
Lucia Michelutti
ISBN: 978-0-415-46732-2

Rise of the Plebeians?

The Changing Face of Indian Legislative Assemblies

Editors

Christophe Jaffrelot
Sanjay Kumar

Routledge
Taylor & Francis Group
LONDON   NEW YORK   NEW DELHI

First published 2009
by Routledge
912 Tolstoy House, 15–17 Tolstoy Marg, New Delhi 110 001

in association with

Centre de Sciences Humaines
2 Aurangzeb Road, New Delhi 110 011

Centre for the Study of Developing Societies
29 Rajpur Road, Delhi 110 054

SciencesPo. | CERI/CNRS
Centre d'études et de recherches internationales
Centre d'Etudes et de Recherches Internationales
56 rue Jacob 75006 Paris

Simultaneously published in the UK
by Routledge
2 Park Square, Milton Park, Abingdon, OX14 4RN

Routledge is an imprint of the Taylor & Francis Group, an informa business

© 2009 Christophe Jaffrelot and Sanjay Kumar

Typeset by
Star Compugraphics Private Limited
5–CSC, First Floor, Near City Apartments
Vasundhara Enclave, Delhi 110 096

Printed and bound in India by
D.K. Fine Art Press (P) Ltd.
An ISO 9001-2000 Certified Company
A-6, Nimri Commercial Centre,
Ashok Vihar, Phase-IV, Delhi-110052

British Library Cataloguing-in-Publication Data
A catalogue record of this book is available from the British Library

ISBN 978-0-415-46092-7

For *Elisabeth Theunissen and Rajendra Vora*
IN MEMORIAM

Contents

List

List of Figures

Maps

List of Tables

List of Abbreviations

ABVKA	Akhil Bharatiya Vanavasi Kalyan Ashram
ADMK	Anna Dravida Munnetra Kazhagam
AIADMK	All India Anna Dravida Munnetra Kazhagam
AJSU	All Jharkhand Student Union
AM	Adivasi Mahasabha
BC	Backward Classes
BCP	Bangla Congress Party
BJP	Bharatiya Janata Party
BJS	Bharatiya Jana Sangh
BKD	Bharatiya Kranti Dal
BPKS	Bihar Pradesh Kisan Sabha
BSP	Bahujan Samaj Party
CAS	Chhattisgarh Asmita Sangathan
CERI	Centre d'Etudes et de Recherches Internationales
CFSA	Congress Forum for Socialist Action
CM	Chief Minister
CMM	Chhattisgarh Mukti Morcha
CNUS	Chhotanagpur Unnati Samaj
CPI	Communist Party of India
CPI(M)	Communist Party of India (Marxist)
CRSM	Chhattisgarh Rajya Sangharsh Morcha
CSDS	Centre for the Study of Developing Societies
CSP	Congress Socialist Party
DC	Denotified Communities
DCC	District Congress Committees
DK	Dravida Kazhagam
DMDK	Desiya Murpokku Dravida Kazhagam
DMK	Dravida Munnetra Kazhagam
DPI	Dalit Panthers of India
EBC	Extremely Backward Castes
FBL	Forward Bloc
FBM	Forward Bloc (Marxist)
GKS	Gujarat Kshatriya Sabha
GNLF	Gorkha National Liberation Front
HDI	Human Development Index

HT	Hindustan Times
INC	Indian National Congress
JAAC	Jharkhand Area Autonomous Council
JD	Janata Dal
JMM	Jharkhand Mukti Morcha
JNP	Janata Party
KLP	Krishikar Lok Party
KMPP	Kisan Mazdoor Praja Party
KRRS	Karnataka Rajya Raitha Sangha
KS	Kisan Sabha
LJP	Lok Janshakti Party
LTTE	Liberation Tigers of Tamil Eelam
MBC	Most Backward Classes
MBT	Majlis Bachao Tahreek
MDMK	Marumalarchi Dravida Munnetra Kazhagam
MGJP	Maha Gujarat Janata Parishad
MIM	Majlis-e-Ittehadul Muslimeen
MLA	Member of Legislative Assembly
MP	Member of Parliament
NCO	National Congress Organisation
NCP	Nationalist Congress Party
NDA	National Democratic Alliance
NTR	Nandamuri Taraka Rama Rao
OBC	Other Backward Classes
PCC	Pradesh Congress Committee
PDF	Progressive Democratic Front
PLA	Punjab Legislative Assembly
PMK	Pattali Makkal Katchi
PSP	Praja Socialist/Samajwadi Party
PWP	Peasants and Workers Party
RPI	Republican Party of India
RRP	Ram Rajya Parishad
RSP	Revolutionary Socialist Party
RSS	Rashtriya Swayamsevak Sangh
SAD	Shiromani Akali Dal
SC	Scheduled Castes
SCF	Scheduled Castes Federation
SDF	Secular Democratic Front
SGPC	Shiromani Gurdwara Parbandhak Committee

SMS	Samyukta Maharashtra Samiti
SNDP	Sree Narayana Dharma Paripalana
SP	Samajwadi Party
SP	Socialist Party
SRC	States Reorganisation Commission
SS	Shiv Sena
SSP	Samyukta Socialist Party
ST	Scheduled Tribes
SUCI	Socialist Unity Centre of India
SVD	Samyukta Vidhayak Dal
TDP	Telugu Desam Party
TMC	Tamil Manila Congress
TMC	Trinamul Congress
TPS	Telengana Praja Samithi
UGDP	United Goans Democratic Party
UP	Uttar Pradesh
UPCC	Uttar Pradesh Congress Committee
VHP	Vishwa Hindu Parishad
WBLA	West Bengal Legislative Assembly

Glossary

Amma:	Mother
archakas:	Temple priests
asmita:	Identity
bhadralok:	The 'respected people' are an urban elite, defined by their upper caste status, English education and employment in the higher professions; in the 19th century, most of them were landlords and dominated Bengal's public life
bhagat:	Reform and classical movements during the 19th and 20th centuries
darbar:	Eminent owner of the lands in the state during the Mughal era and in British India; also the court of rulers
Delhiwala:	A native of Delhi
dvija:	Twice-born
hindutva:	The Hindu nationalist ideology as codified by V.D. Savarkar in his book *Hindutva: Who is a Hindu?* (1923), and its followers including the RSS
izzat:	Dignity
jagir:	Estates of varying value and size controlled by the kings' sardars
jagirdari:	A system of agricuture based on *jagirs*
jati:	Caste
jhuggi-jhonpri:	Slums
kanthi:	Tuft
khalsa:	Crown lands under the direct rule and control of the central owner of the lands in the state
Kisan Sabha:	Farmer's association
kisan:	Farmer
kulak:	A rich, landed farmer
mudal:	The first
munsif:	A judge at the lowest local level of court (district munsif court)
nawab:	Muslim rulers (princes) who became independent after the disintegration of the Mughal empire

pracharak:	Full-time cadre of the Rashtriya Swayamsevak Sangh (RSS)
Praja Mandal:	Political association active in the princely states during the British Raj
punjabiyat:	The defining characteristic of what constitutes the ethno-cultural identity of the people of Punjab
Ram shila:	Bricks marked with Lord Rama's name to be used in the building of the Ayodhya temple
sadaan:	Permanent non-tribal settlers in the region of Jharkhand
sardar:	Title from Persian origin; it applied to native nobles in British India
savarna:	The higher castes; the twice-born
taluqdar:	Landlords who belonged to the United Provinces (today's Uttar Pradesh), and especially Oudh during the British Raj
varna:	Any of the four Hindu castes — Brahmin, Kshatriya, Vaishya and Shudra
Vidhan Sabha:	Legislative Assembly at the state level

Foreword

In this book, the second in the series *Exploring the Political in South Asia*, we present a collection of essays on one of the most important aspects of modern Indian democracy, namely, the caste and community backgrounds of its elected representatives. The essays primarily focus on the caste membership of the members of state-level legislative assemblies of India and the data covers a period of several decades since 1950. By systematically charting this basic, but hitherto unexplored, facet of India's electoral representation, the volume adds a valuable insight into the nature of India's experiments with representative democracy.

As observers of South Asia are aware, the nature of electorates has been a contentious issue since the colonial period and the very first experiments with democracy in this region. The British colonial government sought to create electorates in the image of its own model in Britain which sought to represent like by like. Therefore, in India it created electorates and reserved seats on the basis of caste, community and religion. This move has continued to shape South Asia's political map to this day. In India, at the time of independence, the Constituent Assembly debated the wisdom of this model and decided against its continuation except for certain castes and tribes. As a result, the Indian Constitution asserted its commitment to equality by introducing universal adult franchise and implemented its commitment to reform India's social structure through the reservation and positive discrimination of only the weaker sections of society, the Scheduled Caste and Scheduled Tribe seats. But this arrangement was put in place for the first four decades until 1990 when the utility of this policy was to be re-examined. This constitutional commitment to equality of opportunity for all in the long term, through an emphasis on collective identities in the short term, has been arguably one of the most important aspects of the creation of contemporary India. Further, as we know, India's states have had considerable flexibility in the adoption of policies of positive discrimination in their particular milieux, and therefore the career of caste groups in each of the Indian states has varied giving rise to very specific political arrangements in each setting. This volume attempts to chart this diversity in a systematic and comparative framework.

As the editor, Christophe Jaffrelot, points out in his Introduction of this volume:

> The main objective of the present book is to study how India's caste-based social diversity translated into politics in a dynamic perspective, over more than 50 years, at the state level. In India's state politics, caste plays a major part today. But if its importance is increasing, it has always been a significant factor. This is why the relation between caste and politics needs to be scrutinised in a historical perspective.

The book is largely the result of Jaffrelot's initiative in broadening the scope of his work on the social profile of MPs in the northern states. The result was a collaboration between Indian and French scholars who brought to bear their expertise in particular regions into comparative perspective to explore common themes. Consequently, the important category of state-level MLAs have also been covered in this study, as have states beyond those of the north. Each essay in this volume utilises quantitative data from the National Sample Survey, state-level *Who's Who* and the National Election Survey of CSDS. The first conclusion this study reveals is that 'the arithmetic of caste is very different from one region to another'. Further, caste and class do not coincide, but they greatly overlap and caste membership has direct bearing on one's standard of living. Examining the caste background of India's MLAs it is clear from these essays that in some parts of India caste has emerged as more transformative factor than in other states.

The editors therefore offer a typology to cluster some broad trends that emerge across the 16 states studied across the country. Jaffrelot sums up the key findings thus:

> The Hindi belt pattern is marked by the rise of the OBC at the expense of the upper castes; the north-western trajectory is a variant of the previous one since the main beneficiaries of the erosion of the upper castes, here, are dominant castes; the Deccan distinguishes itself with the continuation of the dominant castes in command; so-called 'tribal states' of the Hindi belt have, in fact, not let the Adivasis seize power (which remains in the hands of upper castes); states with a communist tradition — West Bengal and Kerala — epitomise a typical resilience of the uppper castes. Such a domination is also evident from the social profile of the MLAs elected in Himachal Pradesh and Delhi, but this is a case of proportionality; Tamil Nadu is a similar case, but in favour of plebeian groups which have had to struggle to gain their share of power.

Overall, it emerges that the rise of the OBC in formal parliamentary politics has been most robust in the three states characterised as the 'Hindi belt' — Bihar, Uttar Pradesh and Madhya Pradesh. Here, the growth of the OBC representation among MPs is the most phenomenal, from 4.45 per cent in 1952 to 25.3 per cent in 2004. Among MLAs too, their numbers have doubled.

Each essay also takes into account historical and qualitative analyses of caste available from related disciplines, thereby providing an explanatory framework for the observed trends. For instance, significant divergences are noted even when the adoption of the official taxonomy of caste has occurred in particular states through political pressures by particular castes, for example, the ownership of the 'OBC' label by Vokkaligas in Karnataka. Where the rise of the OBC is consistently high, such as the states of the Hindi belt, the authors identify the different reasons behind this overall phenomenon. To give an example, it is argued that while in Bihar it is the influence of Lohia's socialist politics which mobilised backward castes from early on in Madhya Pradesh, it was more the result of Congress strategy.

The volume also raises a number of broader themes for future research on Indian politics. For instance, the figures clearly show that while there is a variation in jostling for position among upper and backward castes, the rates of representation among SC, ST and Muslims remain the same. In states where Muslims have gained in representation, there is need for further probing into their caste backgrounds too. Further, as the authors themselves acknowledge, representation in the legislature by MLAs is no guarantee for the representation of the interests of the groups who put them in power. As the authors recognise, representations of interests need to be made consistently across different levels of government, and some of the essays begin to examine the posts which low caste people may occupy in the state government and party organisation. Also, as emerging work by other scholars is beginning to show, elected or bureaucratic officials, who are in positions of influence through political mobilisation and policies of affirmative action, do not necessarily see their role as representatives of any particular group, but rather in more universal and abstract terms of citizenship and as servants of the state. In this, the tension between the different moments of representation — representation through disinterested moral authority (e.g., the CPI(M) leadership), representing the interests of those whom you belong to (e.g., Laloo Prasad Yadav), and representing yourself through sheer presence in the political space on the basis of the authenticity of your experience (e.g., some Dalit leaders) — is highlighted. This begs the questions: is representation of identity generating a new kind of politics; is there a growing realm of subaltern parliamentary politics versus the more established political styles of older elites? Further, it is also worth noting that in recent decades, there has been a growth of several simultaneous trends. On the one hand, there is a growing popular disillusion with political manifestoes and the inability of most political parties to achieve any radical social agenda. Yet at the same time, there is a consistent enthusiasm for political participation among the same category of the electorate. What seems to hold sway in the voters' mind, however, is political style over political subtance. Thus, in the light of similar political agendas, it is the political style of particular political leaders and their influence in reshaping the visual, symbolic realm of the public sphere through their politics, that has greater political mileage than complex manifestoes. Mayawati's rise in U.P. is the best exemplar of this phenomenon, but of course, there are others. This forces scholars of Indian politics, and specially those who have been sceptical of the importance of the symbolic in politics, to treat these phenomena with greater seriousness.

It is hoped that this book will inspire further studies and analysis of Indian politics around these important and emergent issues.

Mukulika Banerjee
London
June 2008

Preface

The 1990s decade or so has witnessed an intense interpretative dispute concerning the present and the future course of Indian democracy. This dispute can be described as a contest between two influential stories of Indian democracy. A story of the 'decline and fall' of Indian democracy dominates the readings offered by a wide range of commentaries — popular and journalistic. On this reading, democracy made a decent beginning in India, especially in the first two decades after independence, but suffered a steady decline since then. It experienced a particularly steep erosion in the last decade-and-a-half, facing bleak prospects today. Over the last few years, many voices have questioned this reading from different vantage points. Commentators have drawn attention to the elitist (upper class or upper caste) bias in this reading and have argued that the story would look very different from a subaltern, especially Dalit, vantage point. They, in fact, suggest that there has been something of a participatory upsurge notwithstanding claims of popular apathy. These counter-readings offer a variety of diagnoses of the current situation and varying prescriptions of what is to be done.

Such an intense and rich dispute involves a deep difference of theoretical perspectives, and cannot thus be solved in a simple factual manner. However, there is one aspect of this dispute that admits of an empirical answer. This aspect relates to the question of the nature and implications of the changing profile of the political elite. The dominant story of the 'decline and fall' draws upon the presumption that there has been a decline in the 'quality' of political leadership in India. Those who challenge this story build on the idea that political leadership is more representative now than was the case before and thus we may have, in fact, been witnessing a process of democratisation. To be sure, even this narrow difference is not simply a factual dispute; the reference to 'quality' implies a normative angle here. Yet, we are dealing with a subject where a systematic empirical enquiry can effectively throw light and serve to recast the larger interpretative dispute. This is what the present volume seeks to attempt. This introductory essay draws upon the findings of the state-specific papers collected in this volume and offers a preliminary answer to some of the general questions.

There are three sets of general questions that are addressed here. The first question is a factual one in the narrow sense, something that every essay in this volume takes up. What is the social profile of political representatives in the Indian states? The contributors to this volume focus on just one, though, arguably, the most crucial variable, namely, the caste–community profile of the elected representatives. A meaningful answer to this question involves going beyond a bland statement of numbers; the numbers need to be put in perspective through a series of comparisons. First of all, the social profile of the representative invites a comparison with the profile of the citizens: do the two profiles stand in a relationship of a certain proportionality or are we looking at systemic skews? Second, we need to compare these figures with similar figures of the past: are we looking at a gradual process of deepening representativeness? Third, figures from different states invite mutual comparison: how similar are the patterns across different states, especially across the north/south divide? And fourth, the figures need to be informed with figures from different levels: does the pattern that we describe for the state legislative assemblies hold at the higher (Lok Sabha) and the lower (panchayat or municipality) levels?

The second set of questions is causal in nature, something that many, though not all, chapters in this volume attend to. Why do we have the kind of profile that we find in different states? Why is it that 'mandalisation' has taken different trajectories in different states? Why did south Indian states march ahead of their north Indian counterparts? Why do some states continue to defy the seemingly inevitable all-India pattern? Why do we have 'mandalisation' at different stages of political history? There are two set of explanatory variables that may help us develop an explanation. There are, on the one hand, socio–demographic variables that can explain these differences: the profile of political representatives differs across states; similarly, periods for the initial conditions by way of the social composition of the population were different in different parts of India. On the other hand, one could seek to explain these differences not with reference to the initial conditions but with the help of differences in political dynamics thereafter, such as the existence of political movements and the nature of party political competition.

The third question relates to the significance or the implications of the changes that are described here. In part, it is an empirical question that seeks to understand the pattern of the consequences of changes in the social profile of political representatives: how does it affect distribution of material resources through state policies? Besides material goods, are there non-material consequences as regards identity, security and dignity that accrue to those sections of society that experience a change in their share of political power? But partly, this is a normative question: so, what if the profile of the leadership changes? Is this something to look forward to? Is this good news for democracy, especially if the change comes about in terms of 'primordial' identities?

Yogendra Yadav
Centre for the Study of Developing Societies, Delhi

Acknowledgements

This book has a long history that needs to be recalled here. While researching on the Hindu nationalist movement in the Hindi belt in the 1990s, and, subsequently, the rise of the lower castes in the same area, Christophe Jaffrelot developed an interest in the social profile of the political personnel of India at the state level. He gathered data on the Lok Sabha MPs of the Hindi belt, which are now available on the website of the Centre des Données Socio-Politiques (CDSP), Sciences Po, Paris (http://cdsp.sciences-po.fr). He began to undertake a similar exercise for the Members of the Legislative Assemblies of the Indian states, but immediately realised that such an enterprise had to be collective.

Luckily, the then director of the French Centre for Social Humanities, Frédéric Grare, and his counterpart at the Centre for the Study of Developing Societies (CSDS), V. B. Singh, showed interest in what came to be known as the 'MLAs project'. At the CSDS, Yogendra Yadav and Sanjay Kumar supported this project. Three institutions — Centre de Sciences Humaines (CSH), CSDS and the Centre d'Études et de Recherches Internationales (CERI) — signed a Memorandum of Understanding in 1999 which made possible the research presented in this book.

This exercise has been painful and time-consuming since we intended to cover most of the Indian states from the 1950s onwards. Yet, we were in a position to present our preliminary findings at CSDS during a fascinating conference entitled 'The Sociological Profile of the Indian MLAs'. The present volume stems from the proceedings of this colloquium, with some substantial additions which have enabled us to cover 16 states.

In the course of the making of this book, which took 10 years, two of its contributors have left us. In France, Elisabeth Theunissen, who worked so hard on the processing of the data, passed away in 2006. In India, two years later, Rajendra Vora, who has authored the chapter on Maharashtra in this book, had a sudden demise a few weeks after we discussed the introduction of the book in Pune University. This volume is dedicated to them both.

We are especially grateful to Anil Majumdar for the Eklavya painting that he has specially created for the cover of the book. Finally, we are grateful to Rimina Mohapatra, from Routledge India, who has enabled us to finalise this book; without her patient and painstaking work, this book would have possibly not seen the light of the day.

Introduction

Christophe Jaffrelot

Political theories tell us that there are two kinds of representation— one which is based on the election of individual deputies by abstract citizens, and the other which emphasises the social identities of the represented and the representatives, namely, mirror-representation (Pitkin 1967). Historically, the former has been epitomised by the French experience since 1789: in post-revolutionary France, any elected member of the national assembly was supposed to represent the nation as a whole. The link between the representatives and their local electors was so tenuous that when France lost Alsace-Lorraine to Germany, the members elected in this province continued to participate in the deliberations as part of the 'représentation nationale'. The French parliamentary system relied on territorial constituencies, but the way it operated calls to mind the 'scrutin de liste'.

The second ideal-type of representation is best exemplified, among the democratic trajectories of the world, by the British case. Here, in contrast to the French tradition, the social identity of the represented and the representative — and the relationship between both — mattered so much that, originally, groups were entitled to forms of statutory representation (Beer 1957). In the 19th century, the British tradition of representation took for granted that the people at the university, the gentry, the merchants, etc., were entitled to some political representation. In a way, this approach harked back to the medieval form of representation — which was based on guilds and orders — that the French Revolution had deliberately attempted to eradicate.

Unsurprisingly, the British tended to introduce a group-based form of representation in India when they began to democratise the institutions of the Raj. Not only did universities, landlords and merchants get their special representatives, but religious minorities (Muslims, Sikhs) as also caste groups (non-Brahmins, Marathas, Scheduled Castes, etc.) got separate electorates or reserved seats. Naturally, these special representations were granted to these groups by the government as a result of their political pressures as interest groups. But the British tradition laid themselves to such pressures and predisposed the government to be responsive. This policy was of course in tune with the Raj's strategy of 'divide and rule'.

However, these special representations did not cover the majority of the electorate; they were compensatory schemes since the abstract citizen remained the basis of the political system. And, this embryonic form of mirror-representation was further reduced after independence. The debates in the Constituent Assembly bear testimony to the fact that any system of separate electorates had become illegitimate simply because the partition of India was attributed to the original privilege that the Muslims got in terms of such separate electorates. But other schemes were abolished too: non-Brahmins, Marathas and other non-Dalit castes lost their reserved seats. The Scheduled Castes and Scheduled Tribes alone continued to benefit from quotas in the assemblies.[1]

The removal of institutional provisions which were intended, under the British, to improve the representation of non-elite groups was justified in the name of universalistic values. The Indian Constituent Assembly attempted to erase socio-economic distinctions on behalf of the fundamental equality of all the citizens. However, under the cover of such ideological commitments, this orientation reflected the hegemonic design of the dominant classes which occupied the upper layers of the Congress party. Be they from the state bureaucracy, the capitalist milieu or from the landowners, these 'dominant proprietary classes' (Bhardan 1984) were keen to establish, as much as they could, their monopoly over the political representation of India. The Congress party, therefore, came to consist of huge clientelistic networks through which these groups maintained their domination by resorting to vote bank politics: the party fielded candidates from these social categories at the time of elections and had them returned to the assemblies largely because of their local influence as notables — be they big merchants (and moneylenders) or landowners (and moneylenders). The common point of all these elite groups was their social background: they all belonged to the upper castes.

---

[1] However, post-independence reservations were not likely to mirror the interests of these groups as much as before, under the British, since the system of primaries had gone. Till 1947, the Scheduled Caste citizens had to vote in order to select the three candidates who would be allowed to stand before the general electorate. But after independence, just any candidate could contest elections for those reserved seats provided he or she was a member of the Scheduled Castes.

The domination of the upper castes over the Indian society traditionally relied on several factors. In ritual terms, the upper varnas — Brahmins, Kshatriyas and Vaishyas — are known as the *dvijas* (twice-born) or *savarnas*, and therefore enjoy the reputation of being purer than the varna below, the Shudras and, of course, the untouchables (or Scheduled Castes), better known as Dalits today. In the Hindu worldview, as codified in the Sanskrit literature by the Brahmins themselves, these three groups which are ordered in a ritual hierarchy are supposed to exert a moral authority over the rest of society — at least, they expect greater respect because of the caste into which they are born.

While the caste system is obviously organised according to the notion of status, what Max Weber called 'stand' (2003: 110–27), the domination of the upper castes did not rely on their ritual position alone. It had also much to do with their social position in socio-economic terms and their occupation which were largely related to the ritual status of each caste: Brahmins, as literati, were bound to administer power; Kshatriyas, as warriors, exerted power — at least as landlords or maharajas in the territory they (or their ancestors) had conquered and Vaishyas, as merchants and moneylenders, became industrialists who largely controlled the economy.

Certainly, caste and class (defined in socio-economic terms) never coincided. But they have always broadly overlapped and they still do, as evident from the National Sample Survey 2000 which shows a remarkable correlation between caste and one's standard of living. According to this survey, more than 60 per cent of the urban upper caste Hindus had a per capita monthly consumption expenditure of Rs 775 or more, whereas less than 25 per cent of the urban Other Backward Classes (OBC) and less than 18 per cent of the urban Scheduled Castes (SC) were in such a position. Similarly, among the urban rich whose per capita consumption expenditure is more than Rs 1,500, 59.8 per cent were from the upper caste Hindus, 14.6 per cent from the OBC and 3.8 per cent from the SC (Deshpande 2003: 112–13). Unsurprisingly, castes and occupations coincide to a large extent. According to a survey achieved thanks to the Centre for the Study of Developing Societies (CSDS) database, 24.5 per cent of the upper castes belong to the 'salariat' and 20.4 per cent to 'business', as against 9.5 and 10.1 per cent respectively for the OBC and 10.9 and 5.3 per cent respectively for the SC (Kumar 2002: 4095).

However, Shudras have also exerted power in the past, when they could assert their authority and even rule society. The case in point is the dominant castes, peasant Shudras, who have occasionally risen to power because of their hold over land and their sheer number.[2] In history, the dominant castes which were the most successful in their attempt at conquering power managed to be recognised as Kshatriyas by Brahmins who invented genealogies for them. According to M. N. Srinivas, the Kshatriya category was the most open of the caste system (1978: 238). The very existence of the 'dominant' castes show that the brahminical view of society may describe (or prescribe) an ideal-type in the Weberian sense, but not the reality of power relations: *savarnas* may not be at the top of the socio-political hierarchy. But, sometimes, ritual status and power position coincide when a savarna group is also a dominant caste, like the Rajputs in several regions of the Hindi belt. For us, the main point to bear is that caste remains a key variable of the Indian social structure, and especially so when compared to class, for instance.

Regional Contrasts and Systemic Evolutions

Caste groups are not equally distributed in every region. In fact, the varna system never existed in a full-fledged manner outside the Hindi belt. Elsewhere, there is always a missing category, like the Kshatriyas (in Bengal or Maharashtra) or the Vaishyas (in Maharashtra). As a result, the arithmetic of caste is very different from one region to another. In the Hindi belt where savarnas are all represented, the upper castes form about one-fifth of the society with the Brahmins topping 10 per cent of the total population in Uttar Pradesh, for instance. By contrast, in the south of the Vindhyas, the upper castes represent a very small minority of less than 10 per cent — with the Brahmins, the largest of all the upper castes, culminating at about 3 per cent of society.

Besides, anthropologists and sociologists have shown that the ritual dimension of caste hierarchies based on the notion of the pure and the impure was eroding quickly, especially in urban settings as also in the countryside (see Srinivas 1996 and Gupta 2000). And political scientists have joined hands with them to explain, with the help of qualitative

---

[2] The notion of dominant caste has been introduced in the vocabulary of Indian studies by M. N. Srinivas (1995).

methods, the changing socio-political landscape of India.[3] As argued by Rajni Kothari: 'It is not politics that gets caste-ridden; it is caste that gets politicised' (1970: 20). The Kshatriyas of Gujarat are a case in point since this new category — bearing an old name — was born out of the need that some caste leaders (Rajputs, who are upper castes, and Kolis, who are Shudras) felt to add up their demographic strength in order to play a more effective role in the political arena, especially at the time of elections.[4]

The main objective of the present book is to study how India's caste-based social diversity translated into politics in a dynamic perspective, over more than 60 years, at the state level. Indeed, in India's state politics, caste plays a major part today. But if its importance is increasing, it has always been a significant factor. This is why the relation between caste and politics needs to be scrutinised in a historical perspective. The timeframe of this book follows post-independent India and, especially, the successive electoral rounds ranging from the 1950s to the 2000s.

In some regions, caste has been a vehicle for socio-political change; in others, it has preserved a deep-rooted *status quo*. Our survey helps to build a typology based on most of the large states of the Indian Union, some of the case studies being more detailed and comprehensive than others.

The contributors to this book have closely studied the individual trajectory of 16 Indian states according to one dominant parameter — the evolution of the caste background of the Members of the Legislative Assemblies (MLAs). Though it is mainly a quantitative exercise, this approach has a strong qualitative dimension since each of the contributors has had to study the caste composition of 'his/her' state in order to evolve relevant analytical tools. Certainly, the official taxonomy has been respected in most cases, but sometimes the state has applied politically-motivated categories. For instance, it has sometimes bowed to the pressures of the Vokkaligas in Karnataka and to the Jats in Rajasthan to give them the label of OBC whereas these are dominant landowning castes in both states — a status the authors of the chapters in question have retained instead of the official categorisation.

---

[3] The two-volume book edited by F. Frankel and M. S. A. Rao (1989 and 1990) remains a landmark in this respect.

[4] As Ghanshyam Shah showed in his seminal work (1975).

This typology of the Indian states based on the social background of their MLAs studied over more than half a century has led us to identify seven categories to which we shall now turn.

A Hindi Belt Pattern

The region which has always attracted a lot of attention so far as politics is concerned in India, is the Hindi belt. That is fair enough since it was weighted more than any other: about 40 per cent of the total population of the country lived there; as a result, the same proportion of Members of Parliament (MPs) was returned from this area. For decades, the prime minister of India invariably came from this area, and more precisely from Uttar Pradesh, the largest state of the country.

For decades too, the Hindi belt was the stronghold of conservative Congressmen from the upper castes who cultivated a clientelistic *modus operandi*. The opposition parties were hardly more plebeian. This is well reflected in the caste background of the MPs returned in Uttar Pradesh, the Hindi-speakers-dominated constituencies of Punjab as also Haryana, Chandigarh, Madhya Pradesh, Rajasthan, Bihar and Delhi. In 1952, the upper caste MPs represented 64 per cent of the total (Table 1). They remained in majority till 1977, when the defeat of the Congress for the first time was the occasion of a significant decline of the percentage of the upper castes among the Hindi belt MPs — from almost 54 per cent to about 48 per cent. Then they remained above 40 per cent till 1989 — the date of the second defeat of the Congress at the centre and the second milestone in terms of the caste background of the MPs. This turning point, which was due to the success of the Janata Dal — a peasant and low caste-oriented party — was reconfirmed during the 1990s: election after election, the percentage of the upper caste MPs continued to decrease (to end up with 33 per cent in 2004) whereas the share of the OBC continued to grow. While the percentage of the OBC MPs had increased by only 3 percentage points in 1977, the first milestone, it almost doubled in 1989, from 11 to 21 per cent and continued to grow afterwards — whichever party be in office. This change was largely due to the impact of the Mandal affair, when upper caste students (and others) opposed the granting of a quota of 27 per cent of the posts in the administration to the OBC. OBC leaders orchestrated counter-mobilisations and their followers started to vote for candidates

Table 1
Caste and Community of MPs in the Hindi Belt, 1952–2004 (%)

Castes and Communities	1952	1957	1962	1967	1971	1977	1980	1984	1989	1991	1996	1998	1999	2004
Upper Castes	64.00	58.60	54.90	55.50	53.90	48.20	40.88	46.90	38.20	37.11	35.30	34.70	35.40	33.00
Intermediate Castes	1.00	1.43	1.88	2.75	4.11	6.64	5.33	5.31	8.00	5.43	7.53	8.90	7.90	7.10
OBC	4.45	5.24	7.98	9.64	10.10	13.30	13.74	11.10	20.87	22.60	24.80	23.60	24.00	25.30
SC	15.76	18.10	19.72	18.35	18.26	17.70	17.78	17.26	17.78	18.10	18.14	18.20	18.60	17.80
ST	5.42	6.90	7.04	7.80	7.31	7.08	7.56	7.52	7.56	8.14	7.52	7.60	7.50	8.40
Muslims	5.42	4.76	4.23	3.67	4.57	5.75	11.56	9.73	5.78	4.52	3.54	5.30	5.00	7.10
TOTAL	96.05	95.03	95.75	97.71	98.25	98.67	96.85	97.82	98.19	95.90	96.83	98.30	98.40	98.70

Source: Survey by author.

from their own milieu in order to defend their interests and also simply because they got politicised and were eager to emancipate themselves from the vertical, old clientelistic system of the Congress party.

V. P. Singh, who decided to implement the recommendations of the Mandal report, called this process a silent revolution, and I borrowed the term from him because a non-violent transfer of power had indeed begun to take place — plebeians dislodging elite groups from power.[5]

Figure 1
Castes and Communities of MPs in the Hindi Belt, 1952–2004

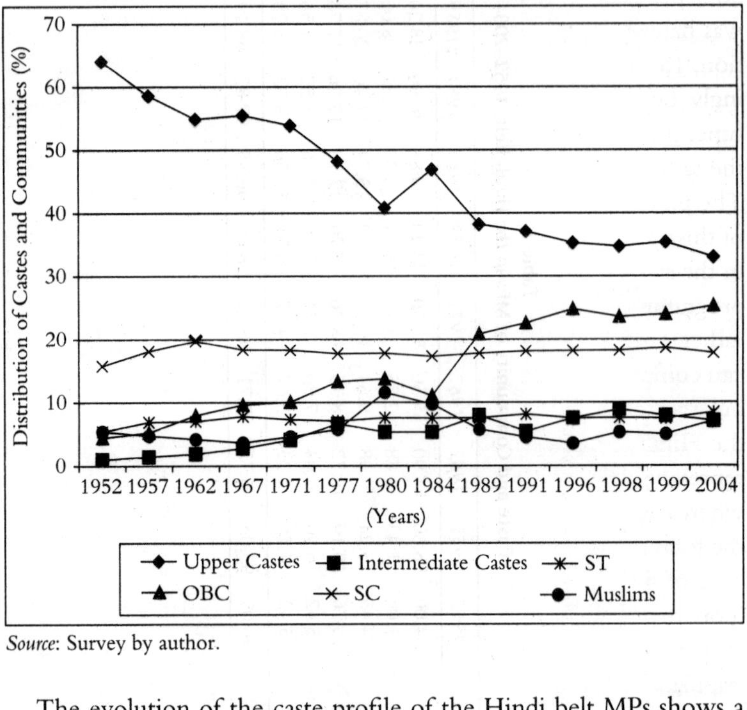

Source: Survey by author.

The evolution of the caste profile of the Hindi belt MPs shows a distinctive pattern: the growing politicisation of the OBC, largely due to their mobilisation in favour of reservations, resulted in a transfer of power from upper castes to OBC politicians.

This process is even more pronounced at the state level among some of the largest states of the Hindi belt. Indeed, the state assemblies of the

---

[5] For more details on this process, see Jaffrelot (2003).

core of the Hindi belt formed by Uttar Pradesh, Madhya Pradesh and Bihar emulate the development mentioned above regarding the MPs. In all these states, the proportion of the upper caste MLAs has steadily declined from about 40–55 per cent in the 1950s to about 25–35 per cent today while the share of the OBC grew from 10–20 per cent to about 20–40 per cent.

Here, Bihar shows the way: between 1952 and 2005, the proportion of OBC MLAs has doubled from 20 to 42 per cent — slightly more than their share in the population according to the 1931 Census, 38.5 per cent — whereas the percentage of the upper caste MLAs was halved, from 46 to 26 per cent (twice their share in the population, 13.7 per cent).[6] The trends are exactly symmetrical and, interestingly, both graphs crossed each other in 1990, the Mandal year. At that time, the proportions of OBC MLAs and upper caste MLAs were still the same at 35 per cent and then the pace of change got accelerated. The pioneering role of Bihar, as Cyril Robin points out in Chapter 2 of this volume, was partly due to the long tradition of socialist politics in the state: Lohia's socialists were keen to promote affirmative action programmes for the OBC in Bihar and mobilised the lower castes rather early in this very perspective. No other state in the Hindi belt can compete with Bihar so far as the rise of OBC MLAs is concerned, but two of them, Uttar Pradesh and Madhya Pradesh, comply with the Hindi belt pattern anyway. In both states, upper caste MLAs still represented more than one-third of the assemblies in the late 1990s, whereas the OBC represented between one-fifth and one-fourth of the total. In Madhya Pradesh, where the upper castes represent 13 per cent of the population, the share of the upper caste MLAs was still more than 37 per cent in 2003, whereas the OBC MLAs were less than 20 per cent in a state where they form more than 41 per cent of the population. But the OBC have jumped in 1977 and have continued to grow steadily since as early as 1980 because of the Congress strategy, as I explain in Chapter 3. In Uttar Pradesh, where the upper caste represent more than 20 per cent of the population, 'their' MLAs represented more than 35 per cent of the population after the 2002

---

[6] In this Introduction, the 1931 Census is the source I have used to present the share of caste groups in state population, except for Delhi and Tamil Nadu.

elections, and the OBC MLAs reached 27.5 per cent in a state where OBC are almost 42 per cent of the population. However, figures do not vary significantly according to which party wins the election, as Jasmine Zérinini shows in Chapter 1. When the BJP performs well, the upper castes display a great resilience whereas the OBC — and the Muslims — surge when the Samajwadi Party and/or the Bahujan Samaj Party get good results.

A North-western Pattern

On the western border of this core group — Uttar Pradesh, Madhya Pradesh and Bihar — three states, namely, Punjab, Rajasthan and Gujarat, introduce a variant to the so-called Hindi belt pattern. There, upper castes are almost at the same level among the MLAs as those in the Hindi belt (between one-fifth and one-third), but the dominant castes, the Jats in Punjab and Rajasthan and the Patidars in Gujarat, are as strong as the upper caste MLAs and on the rise in most cases. In contrast with the Hindi belt, the OBC remain rather low, except in Gujarat.

In Punjab, where the Jats represented 21.3 per cent of the state in 1931, they have always represented between 35 and 52 per cent of the MLAs over the last 15 years. This domination of the Jats went on par with the erosion of the upper castes (from 27 per cent in 1992 to 19.7 per cent in 2002) and the embryonic mobilisation of the OBC whose MLAs never represented more than 5 per cent of the MLAs! The Dalit MLAs form a large contingent thanks to a quota of 25 per cent of the seats for the Scheduled Castes. But they are not in a position to compete with the Jats, as Ashutosh Kumar and T. R. Sharma show in Chapter 4.

In Rajasthan — a Hindi-speaking state which, from our point of view here, does not belong to the Hindi belt but to north-west India because of the growing role played by the Jats — the upper castes (who represent about 20 per cent of the population) have met the same fate as those in Uttar Pradesh and Madhya Pradesh. 'Their' MLAs fell from 51 per cent in 1952 to 32 per cent in 2003, but the OBC (about 40 per cent of society) have not benefited from their decline; they still represented less than 10 per cent of the MLAs in 2003. The Jats, less than 10 per cent of the population, on the contrary, have been able to assert themselves. In 1995, they peaked at 30 per cent of the

MLAs and remained around 29 per cent in 2003. Jats — a dominant caste — and upper castes remain in command of Rajasthan politics as Cyril Robin and I point out in Chapter 5.[7]

This pattern is closely followed by Gujarat, one of Rajasthan's neighbouring states. Here too, a dominant caste, that of the Patidars, 13 per cent of the population, established its strength as early as the 1960s. Like the Jats in Rajasthan, the Patidars of Gujarat represent between one-fifth and one-third of the MLAs since the 1963 elections. And like in Rajasthan, the upper castes — also 13 per cent of the population — show a strong resilience. In both states; their representation has declined by 15 percentage points since the early 1960s but they were still 20–30 per cent of the MLAs — till 2007 when their share declined in Gujarat. The main difference between Gujarat and Rajasthan concerns the OBC which have mobilised early in the former, as Kiran Desai and Ghanshyam Shah explain in Chapter 6. As a result, the proportion of OBC in the State Assembly has jumped from 8 to 34 per cent between 1962 and 2007.

Where the Dominant Castes Alone Run the Show:
The Deccan Pattern

Three states of the Deccan plateau — Maharashtra, Karnataka and Andhra Pradesh — show the unchallenged rule of the dominant castes. In these three states, peasant proprietary castes have always represented between 40 and 60 per cent of the MLAs and their share is not on the decline.

In Maharashtra, as Rajendra Vora shows in Chapter 7, the Marathas — who represent 32 per cent of the population — remain in control, though they have never won more than 45 per cent of the seats. While Maharashtra belongs to western India, it can be included in the Deccan belt owing to the major role traditionally played by the Marathas, a dominant caste comparable to those in Andhra Pradesh and Karnataka. In this state, the Maratha MLAs are slightly less numerous than their alter egos of the dominant castes in the bordering Dravidian states, but they tend to increase from 39 per cent in 1985 to almost 45 per cent

---

[7] Although the Jats were classified as OBC before the 2003 elections, they have been included in the Intermediary Castes category in our statistical surevy in order to compare figures over a longer period of time.

in 2004. Correlatively, the share of the upper castes — less than 7 per cent of the population — is eroding, but it has always been very low anyway: from less than 6 per cent in 1967 to less than 3 per cent in 2004. Maharashtra is the only state of this group where the OBC (almost 30 per cent of the population) represent more than 20 per cent of the MLAs; but this percentage remains the same since the 1960s.

In Karnataka, Lingayats and Vokkaligas — who represent 26 per cent of the population — have always been in majority in the State Assembly, as Sandeep Shastri shows in Chapter 8. In 1999, they still represented 58.9 per cent of the MLAs, 0.6 percentage points more than in 1952! Certainly, the share of the OBC — 32.5 per cent of the population — was almost doubled in the meantime, but it remained very low, passing from 7 per cent to about 12 per cent. The share of the upper castes — 3.5 per cent of the population — remained almost stable but also very low; it decreased from 9 to 8 per cent.

In Andhra Pradesh, Kammas and Reddys — who represent also 26 per cent of the population — are increasingly more prominent since 1990 — they represent more than 50 per cent of the MLAs since this date — at the expense of the upper castes and the OBC, 6 and 36 per cent respectively of the population, as Anne Vaugier-Chatterjee demonstrates in Chapter 9. From the 1970s to the 2000s, they have jumped from 42.5 per cent of the MLAs to 59.2 per cent. At the same time, the share of the upper caste MLAs dropped from more than 9 per cent to 2 per cent and that of the OBC MLAs declined from 19.5 per cent to 18.3 per cent.

The Forgotten Adivasi

In 2000, three new states were carved out in the Indian Union: Uttaranchal (now Uttarakhand), Jharkhand and Chhattisgarh. The last two resulted partly from the demands of tribal movements which were eager to give the local Adivasi states that they could call their own. Indeed, the percentages of Scheduled Tribes in Jharkhand and in Chhattisgarh are among the highest in India (with the exception of the north-east) with 26.3 per cent and 31.8 per cent respectively according to the 2001 Census. In both states, tribals represent 36–39 per cent of the MLAs but the upper castes are still very influential. In Jharkhand, they represent 4 per cent of the population and 11 per cent of the MLAs whereas in Chhattisgarh they represent 3.3 per cent of the population and 25.5 per cent of the MLAs. The main difference lies in the share of the OBC who are only 20 per cent of the Jharkhand population but represent 30 per cent of the MLAs whereas they form 50 per cent of the population of Chhattisgarh, but only 23.3 per cent of the MLAs. More importantly, Cyril Robin for Jharkhand (Chapter 10) and Samuel Berthet for Chhattisgarh (Chapter 11) show that in neither state the tribals could really seize power owing to their marginalisation within the apparatus of the main parties and within state governments.

While the four patterns that we have just identified can be associated with regions — the Hindi belt, the north-west, the Deccan and the tribal belt of central India — the other ones are found in states which are not at all contiguous.

Where the Upper Castes Resist Well: West Bengal and Kerala

The fifth group is made of two states — West Bengal and Kerala — which have no borders in common but have something else in common: a remarkable share of upper caste MLAs in their assemblies. In none of these states, this percentage is below 37 per cent whereas in fact, upper castes are not present in large numbers in the population.

West Bengal and Kerala are strongholds of communism for years. Kerala was the first state where the Communist Party of India (CPI) rose to power in 1957 and West Bengal is governed by the Communist Party of India (Marxist) or CPI(M) since 1977. There is probably no contradiction between the upper caste social profile of the political personnel of these two states and their communist leanings simply because the upper caste communist elites believe more in class than caste and have implemented socio-economic reforms accordingly. They have managed to retain power — or to stage repeated comebacks — not mainly by opening up to the lower castes, but by being associated with progressive measures like land reforms.

West Bengal represents a trajectory on its own. This is the only state where the percentage of the upper castes MLAs has increased over the last 20 years, from 38 per cent in 1972 to 50 per cent in 1996. Lately, the trend has been reverted in 2001, when the percentage of the upper caste MLAs fell just below 38 per cent, but upper caste ministers were still more than 51 per cent in the state government, as Stéphanie Tawa Lama shows in Chapter 12. This very uncommon route is partly due to the fact that over the same period, the Congress and the CPI(M) — two upper caste dominated parties — remained the main political forces. But it is also due to the sheer absence of OBC movements in this region.

The situation of Kerala is very similar, as Gopa Kumar points out in Chapter 13. Here, the percentage of the upper caste MLAs decreased from 49 per cent in 1957 to 38 per cent after the last elections. Kerala, however, has a large number of OBC MLAs due, mainly, to the sizeable Izhavas community and their well-established organisation, the Shree Narayana Dharma Paripalana Yogam (SNDP) which has strong relations with the communist movement. Indeed, the CPI(M) is more plebeian than the Congress, one of the most elitist state branches of the party in India.

The Reign of Proportionality

In Himachal Pradesh and Delhi too, upper caste MLAs represent the largest share of the state assemblies. In Himachal, their share is slightly eroding, from 68 per cent in 1967 to 61.8 per cent after the last elections; but it remains quite comfortable, as Ramesh K. Chauhan, S. N. Ghosh and T. R. Sharma argue in Chapter 14. The OBC, by contrast, have never represented more than 10 per cent of the MLAs. Delhi tells a similar story. In this state, for which data are available for only three elections — 1993, 1998 and 2003 — the upper caste MLAs are not in majority any more since their share fell from 54 per cent to 46 per cent, but this is a rare achievement anyway, as shown by Sanjay Kumar in Chapter 15, especially because the Jats are still below 10 per cent of the MLAs since the 2003 elections and the OBC at 7 per cent.

However, this trajectory is different from that of West Bengal and Kerala for the simple reason that in these two states, small elites were over-represented at the top whereas in Himachal Pradesh and Delhi they are represented in a quasi-proportional way. Indeed, upper castes represent 48 per cent of the population of Himachal Pradesh according to the 1931 Census and 38 per cent of Delhi population according to surveys conducted by the Centre for the Study of Developing Societies (CSDS) in the state.

Tamil Nadu: The Subalternist Tradition

Tamil Nadu is another case of quasi-proportionality. According to the Backward Classes Commission, the OBC represent 67 per cent of the population and, indeed, the OBC MLAs have never been less than 56 per cent of the state assembly and have reached 66 per cent once. But it is a very different situation from that of Himachal Pradesh and Delhi for the obvious reason that it is easier for a large elite group to retain power than for plebeian groups — even when they are large groups — since, to begin with, they were not in office. The Tamil trajectory clearly harks back to the history of the region, as Jean-Luc Racine shows in Chapter 16. In the Madras Presidency, during the British Raj, the plebeians mobilised early against the Brahmin power and organised social movements such as the non-Brahmin movement and established political parties such as the Justice Party — which seized power in the 1920s. As a result, programmes of positive discrimination have been implemented in a big way for the upliftment of the lower castes. After independence, the Congress was obliged to promote a low-caste leader, Kamaraj, as replacement for C. Rajagopalachari, a conservative Brahmin, but it was not sufficient for defusing the rising popularity of the Dravidian parties which had inherited some of their legitimacy from the non-Brahmin movement.

To sum up, the sociology of the political personnel has followed several different routes in India. The Hindi belt pattern is marked by the rise of the OBC at the expense of the upper castes; the north-western trajectory is a variant of the previous one since the main beneficiaries of the erosion of the upper castes, here, are dominant castes; the Deccan distinguishes itself with the continuation of the dominant castes in command; so-called 'tribal states' of the Hindi belt have, in fact, not let the Adivasis seize power (which remains in the hands of upper castes); states with a communist tradition — West Bengal and Kerala — epitomise a typical resilience of the upper castes. Such a domination is also evident from the social profile of the MLAs elected in Himachal Pradesh and Delhi, but this is a case of proportionality; Tamil Nadu is a similar case, but in favour of plebeian groups which have had to struggle to gain their share of power.

The great variety of trajectories reflected in this typology suggests that the 'silent revolution pattern' largely identified with the Hindi belt, is not that dominant. Certainly, the states embodying this pattern — Uttar Pradesh, Bihar, Madhya Pradesh — are among the largest in India. But one must recognise that beyond the Hindi belt, there are other dynamics at work. The dominant caste-oriented trajectory is indeed a strong challenger because it does not only prevail south of the Vindhyas but also in Punjab, Rajasthan and Gujarat although to a lesser extent. In fact, one may argue that the south and the west have become less progressive than some of the northern states in terms of the lower caste people's rise to power.

Such a view needs to be qualified though. First, the state which has played a really pioneering role is Tamil Nadu, a southern state par excellence. Second, the increase of the OBC MLAs in state legislatures does not necessarily mean that the influence of the OBC has increased. To measure this influence, one must not contend oneself with studying the MLAs but must also look at the posts low-caste people may occupy within the apparatus of the parties and in state governments; some portfolios carry more weight than other. This issue is addressed in several chapters. Third, caste does not say everything. Therefore, this book does not focus on the caste background of the MLAs alone. It also takes into account variables like gender, age, education and occupation. The data which have been gathered together in this respect are often less systematic because of the limitations of the sources used by the contributors of this book, the state-specific volumes of the *Who's Whos* in the state assemblies. For instance, the *Who's Whos* do not always have information on the occupation or education of MLAs. But the data show anyway that, by and large, peasants are increasingly becoming numerous in the assemblies, that the level of education of the MLAs is rising, and that women tend to be more numerous in the assemblies now.

Appendix 1

Evolution of the Upper Caste MLAs (state-wise %)

States	Percentage in the State Population[a]	1952	1955–57	1960–63	1967	1969–70	1971–74	1975–79	1980–83	1984–85	1987–90	1991–92	1993–95	1996–2000	2001–05	2007
Type 1																
Utar Pradesh[b]	20.5	58.0	55.0	58.0	45.3	43.9	37.8	35.2	41.3	39.7	35.7	39.0	26.7	34.6	35.4[i]	–
Madhya Pradesh[b]	12.9	–	41.2	48.4	44.9	–	49.6	46.6	40.3	40.7	40.9	–	37.1	35.6	37.7	–
Bihar[b]	13.7	46.1	46.1	46.1	44.8	42.0	42.8	40.6	36.6	38.5	34.6	–	21.8	25.1	25.9	–
Type 2																
Punjab	14.7	–	–	–	–	–	–	17.9	–	–	–	27.4	–	15.4	19.7	–
Rajasthan	20.6	51.2	47.1	45.6	45.6	–	42.1	32.5	31.9	35.7	22.0	–	32.5	31.1	32.1	–
Gujarat	13.0	–	–	34.0	40.0	–	30.0	27.0	21.0	25.0	25.0	–	21.0	21.0	20.0	14.0
Type 3																
Maharashtra	6.6	–	–	–	5.9	–	6.6	6.9	5.2	4.8	4.5	–	4.1	2.7	3.4	–
Karnataka	3.5	9.4	10.0	9.1	8.8	–	7.7	9.8	8.2	7.3	5.8	–	5.2	5.4	–	–
Andhra Pradesh	6.0	–	9.1	9.3	5.9	–	9.4	6.1	4.8	4.4	4.4	–	3.2	3.4	2.0	–
Type 4																
Jharkhand[c]	3.9	–	–	–	–	–	–	–	–	–	–	–	–	17.3[e]	11.1[f]	–
Chhattisgarh[d]	3.3	–	–	–	–	–	–	–	–	–	–	–	–	–	25.5[g]	–

(*Appendix 1 continued*)

(*Appendix 1 continued*)

States	Percentage in the State Population[a]	1952	1955–57	1960–63	1967	1969–70	1971–74	1975–79	1980–83	1984–85	1987–90	1991–92	1993–95	1996–2000	2001–05	2007
Type 5																
West Bengal	5.7	45.4	50.0	49.2	40.0	41.8	38.2/38[j]	45.9	43.2	45.2	45.3	45.0	–	50.0	37.5	–
Kerala	–	–	49.0	46.0	42.0	43.0	–	52.0	41.0	42.0	44.0	43.0	–	40.0	38.0	–
Type 6																
Himachal Pradesh	48.0	–	–	–	68.3	–	67.6	66.2	64.7	66.2	61.8	–	61.8	58.8	61.8	–
Delhi	38.0[h]	–	–	–	–	–	–	–	–	–	–	–	54.0	46.0	46.0	–
Type 7																
Tamil Nadu	–	–	–	–	17.9	–	18.8	17.9	20.5	18.4	11.9	12.4	–	11.6	–	–

Source: Survey by author.

Note: [a] Based on Census 1931.

[b] As till year 2000.

[c] Scheduled Tribes (ST) represent 26.3 per cent of the population according to Census 2001.

[d] ST represent 31.8 per cent of the population according to Census 2001.

[e] ST represented 35.8 per cent of the MLAs.

[f] ST represented 37 per cent of the MLAs.

[g] ST represented 38.9 per cent of the MLAs.

[h] Based on surveys of the CSDS Data unit.

[i] Source: Jaffrelot (2007).

[j] The two percentages refer to the two elections held in 1971 and 1972 respectively.

Appendix 2

Evolution of the Intermediate/Dominant Caste MLAs (state-wise %)

States	Percentage in the State Population[a]	1952	1955–57	1960–63	1967	1969–70	1971–74	1975–79	1980–83	1984–85	1987–90	1991–92	1993–95	1996–2000	2001–05	2007
Type 1																
Uttar Pradesh[b]	2.0	3.0	3.0	2.0	0	–	1.4	1.2	1.2	2.1	2.6	3.1	3.1	3.7	4.7[f]	–
Madhya Pradesh[b]	1.1	–	1.1	0.6	0.6	–	0.3	0.9	0.9	0.3	0.3	–	0.6	0.9	2.6	–
Bihar[b]	–	0	0	0	0	–	0	0	0	–	0	–	0	0	–	–
Type 2																
Punjab	21.3	–	–	–	–	–	–	47.9	–	–	–	39.3	–	52.2	35.9	–
Rajasthan	9.2	15.9	17.7	23.3	16.7	–	17.2	40.0	20.7	14.3	26.0	–	29.9	18.5	28.6	–
Gujarat	13.0	–	–	27.0	21.0	–	23.0	27.0	21.0	21.0	25.0	–	24.0	22.0	25.0	28.0
Type 3																
Maharashtra	32.0	–	–	–	43.1	–	43.1	40.9	42.7	39.2	44.7	–	45.4	43.0	44.7	–
Karnataka	26.1	58.3	50.8	55.8	58.5	–	53.2	52.6	57.5	60.4	54.8	–	60.2	59.8	–	–
Andhra Pradesh	26.0	–	53.6	47.7	48.4	–	42.5	45.2	47.6	46.9	52.0	–	58.5	56.8	59.2	–
Type 4																
Jharkhand[c]	–	–	–	–	–	–	–	–	–	–	–	–	0	0	0	–
Chhattisgarh[d]	0.2	–	–	–	–	–	–	–	–	–	–	–	0	–	0	–

(*Appendix 2 continued*)

(*Appendix 2 continued*)

States	Percentage in the State Population[a]	1952	1955–57	1960–63	1967	1969–70	1971–74	1975–79	1980–83	1984–85	1987–90	1991–92	1993–95	1996–2000	2001–05	2007
Type 5																
West Bengal	35.0	4.6	7.5	5.9	6.0	8.2	7.5/6.5[g]	9.5	7.5	–	7.5	5.0	3.0	–	5.0	–
Kerala	–	0	0	0	0	0	0	0	0	0	0	0	0.7	–	–	–
Type 6																
Himachal Pradesh	0	–	–	–	0	–	0	0	0	0	0	–	0	0	0	–
Delhi	5.0[c]	–	–	–	–	–	–	–	–	–	–	–	9.0	13.0	9.0	–
Type 7																
Tamil Nadu	–	–	–	–	0	–	0	0	0	0	0	0	0	–	–	–

Source: Survey by author.

Note: [a] Based on Census 1931.

[b] As till year 2000.

[c] Scheduled Tribes (ST) represent 26.3 per cent of the population according to Census 2001.

[d] ST represent 31.8 per cent of the population according to Census 2001.

[e] Based on surveys of the CSDS Data unit.

[f] Source: Jaffrelot (2007).

[g] The two percentages refer to the two elections held in 1971 and 1972 respectively.

Appendix 3

Evolution of the OBC MLAs (state-wise %)

States	Percentage in the State Population[a]	1952	1955–57	1960–63	1967	1969–70	1971–74	1975–79	1980–83	1984–85	1987–90	1991–92	1993–95	1996–2000	2001–05	2007
Type 1																
Uttar Pradesh[b]	41.7	9.0	12.0	13.0	29.2	26.8	18.3	16.8	13.4	19.6	24.2	27.1	32.4	24.8	27.5[i]	–
Madhya Pradesh[b]	41.5	–	4.7	9.1	9.4	–	9.5	14.3	16.1	18.6	18.7	–	22.7	22.0	19.5	–
Bihar[b]	38.5	20.6	19.4	24.4	26.6	27.9	25.7	28.3	30.4	–	34.9	–	46.8	40.3	42.0	–
Type 2																
Punjab	–	–	–	–	–	–	–	3.4	–	–	–	5.1	–	3.4	3.4	–
Rajasthan	40.0	3.7	2.5	4.4	2.2	5.5	2.5	7.4	8.0	12.0	–	5.2	–	6.6	8.9	–
Gujarat	40.0	–	–	8.0	11.0	–	16.0	15.0	24.0	24.0	26.0	–	21.0	21.0	29.0	34.0
Type 3																
Maharashtra	29.8	–	–	–	22.3	–	21.4	23.2	19.7	24.6	26.0	–	23.2	23.6	23.9	–
Karnataka	32.5	7.3	13.1	14.1	11.2	–	12.6	13.0	13.0	10.1	13.9	–	12.8	12.5	–	–
Andhra Pradesh	36.0	–	8.7	13.0	14.3	–	19.5	19.0	20.7	20.1	11.9	–	12.9	11.9	18.3	–
Type 4																
Jharkhand[c]	19.7	–	–	–	–	–	–	–	–	–	–	–	–	27.2[e]	29.7[f]	–
Chhattisgarh[d]	50.4	–	–	–	–	–	–	–	–	–	–	–	–	–	23.3[g]	–

(*Appendix 3 continued*)

(*Appendix 3 continued*)

States	Percentage in the State Population[a]	1952	1955–57	1960–63	1967	1969–70	1971–74	1975–79	1980–83	1984–85	1987–90	1991–92	1993–95	1996–2000	2001–05	2007
Type 5																
West Bengal	—	0	0	0	0	0	0	0	0	0	0	0	0	—	—	—
Kerala	—	—	27.0	26.0	33.0	30.0	—	20.0	26.0	27.0	28.0	25.0	—	29.0	31.0	—
Type 6																
Himachal Pradesh	10.5	—	—	—	1.7	—	2.9	5.9	7.4	5.9	7.4	—	10.3	7.4	7.4	—
Delhi	14.0[h]	—	—	—	—	—	—	—	—	—	—	—	7.0	7.0	7.0	—
Type 7																
Tamil Nadu	63.6	—	—	—	66.2	—	61.6	59.0	57.7	56.9	61.5	62.4	—	62.0	—	—

Source: Survey by author.

Note: [a] Based on the Census 1931.

[b] As till year 2000.

[c] Scheduled Tribes (ST) represent 26.3 per cent of the population according to the Census 2001.

[d] ST represent 31.8 per cent of the population according to the Census 2001.

[e] ST represented 35.8 per cent of the MLAs.

[f] ST represented 37 per cent of the MLAs.

[g] ST represented 38.9 per cent of the MLAs.

[h] Based on surveys of the CSDS Data unit.

[i] Source: Jaffrelot (2007).

References

Beer, S. H. 1957. 'The Representation of Interests in British Government: Historical Background', *The American Political Science Review*, 51 (3): 613–50.

Bhardan, Pranab. 1984. *The Political Economy of Development in India*. Oxford: Blackwell.

Census of India, 1931. 1933. Government of India, Rajputana Agency, Nagpur.

Deshpande, Satish. 2003. *Contemporary India: A Sociological View*. New Delhi: Penguin Books.

Frankel, F. and M. S. A. Rao (eds). 1989, 1990. *Dominance and State Power in Modern India*, 2 vols. Delhi: Oxford University Press.

Gupta, D. 2000. *Interrogating Caste: Understanding Hierarchy and Difference in Indian Society*. New Delhi: Penguin Books.

Jaffrelot, C. 2003. *India's Silent Revolution: The Rise of the Lower Castes in North Indian Politics*. Delhi: Permanent Black.

———. 2007. 'Caste and the Rise of Marginalized Groups', in S. Ganguly, L. Diamond and M. Plattner (eds), *The State of Indian Democracy*, pp. 67–88. Baltimore and Washington: The Johns Hopkins University Press.

Kothari, R. 1970. 'Introduction: Caste in Indian Politics', in R. Kothari (ed.), *Caste in Indian Politics*, pp. 3–25. New Delhi: Orient Longman.

Kumar, S., A. Heath and O. Heath. 2002. 'Changing Patterns of Social Mobility: Some Trends over Time', *Economic and Political Weekly*, 37 (40): 4091–96.

Pitkin, H. F. 1967. *The Concept of Representation*. Berkeley: University of California Press.

Shah, G. 1975. *Caste Association and Political Process in Gujarat*. Bombay: Popular Prakashan.

Srinivas, M. N. 1978. 'The Future of the Caste System', *Economic and Political Weekly*, 14 (7–8): 238.

———. 1995. *Social Change in Modern India*. New Delhi: Orient Longman.

——— (ed.). 1996. *Caste: Its Twentieth Century Avatar*. New Delhi: Viking.

Weber, Max. 2003. *Hindouisme et Bouddhisme*. Paris: Flammarion.

Part I

The Hindi Belt towards Social Engineering

Part 1

The Hindi Belt towards
Social Engineering

1

The Marginalisation of the *Savarnas* in Uttar Pradesh?

Jasmine Zérinini

Over the last 50 years, the political history of Uttar Pradesh has borne the consequences of three major events: the agrarian revolution (i.e., land reforms and the Green Revolution), the Mandal reservation policy and the dispute over the Babri Masjid in Ayodhya. These events resulted from national politics but had deep local consequences. Their impact has gone beyond the triggering of political change in the state; they have got to be reflected in the nature of the political operators.

After India achieved its independence from the British, the educational project in politics was put aside. Politics had become too important a game for parties to find time to educate the voters to help distance themselves from primary identity associations. Since then, to quote Sudipto Kaviraj, elections have 'constantly reconfirmed ordinary people's community orientation instead of undermining it' (2000). Parties, in their search for majority in India's plural society, have constantly put forward primary identity factors as bases of identification with a candidate or a party. Of these community orientations, the much-villained criterion of caste is primordial in the understanding of the evolution of politics and, through politics, of society. Today still, caste, more than party identification, remains central in determining who to vote for. In Uttar Pradesh (U.P.), in particular, as a result of agrarian reform and quota politics, caste identities have not receded but evolved under the influence of political parties. The relationship between the political and the social spheres has passed through caste from the 1950s onwards. At that time, parties had to find a new basis for mobilisation once the all-embracing goal of independence was reached. As ideological politics withered away and no new ideological orientations were offered, the opportunity was seized to fill the gap. Caste provided with an easy, ready-to-use mobilisational social basis.

In democratic societies, the relations between social groups and the polity are bi-dimensional and reciprocal. Parties influence and shape society about as much as society shapes political parties. Considering the space still occupied by caste in Indian society, it would be a mistake not to take into account those transformations which have led to a re-structuring of political parties, both national and regional, on the basis of social, caste-based dynamics. In fact, if caste is present in the Indian electoral politics from its very beginning as a democratic, open-to-all, system, it has taken various forms reflected in turn through vote. Over the length of what Yogendra Yadav has named India's three 'electoral systems' (Yadav 1999), the evolution has been from *jati*-based vote via cross-sectional mobilisation in a vertical clientelistic system, to what we witness today: a wide participation of marginal sections of society and a new form of cross-sectional alignment. Going back to the data which is at the core of our study, one can expect the two-way link between society and politics to be reflected in the evolution of the political elite. Here, as we will see, the primacy of caste as a criterion for mobilisation can be ascertained through the fact that, more than other social indicators (education and occupation), the caste composition of the Assembly was the one subject to registering the deepest and most significant changes. The bulk in the evolution of the political elite of U.P. was made through changes in its caste composition with parties both adapting to and promoting changes. The 'third electoral system' is still in the process of change, with the arrival of new social groups and the introduction of new political rules by them. Its consequences cannot be fully assessed today. Over the whole period considered (1952–2002), U.P. has evolved from having a political system dominated by upper castes and relying on co-optation to a less rigid form of mobilisation where previously co-opted groups of the electorate now have representatives more generally coming from their own socio-economic milieu.

This does not mean that political representation has only evolved in terms of community orientation. As we will see, the years since independence have seen a gradual rise in the education and a less marked change in the occupations of MLAs. But contrary to caste, which is endowed with its own dynamics rooted in local systems, education and occupation have changed in a more continuous manner and reflect the general evolution of Indian society. In addition, these other two factors can be considered on a secondary level of change. They are part of the overall evolution of U.P.'s political elite from an upper caste, white-collar group to a more socially and economically mixed lot.

Religion and religious community do not fall into the same explanations. In U.P., but for three exceptional electoral years, the representation of Muslim MLAs, in a state where the community accounts for 18 per cent of the population, has remained below the 10 per cent barrier. In addition, no Muslim leadership has emerged in U.P. either in the years after independence or more recently. While once-marginalised Hindu groups have benefited from the context of social change to assert themselves, the Muslim community does not appear to have been able to do the same.

The Social Bases of Congress Ascendancy

From independence until the mid-1980s, the political life of U.P. was linked to the Congress party. The Congress was founded by an intelligentsia of urban English-educated professionals. They came from the upper castes since these were already in a social and economic position that enabled them to take advantage of the new educational opportunities. After independence, the party's ascendency relied on a patronage system which developed with the economic resources made available. The Congress politicians who had led the country during the early 20th century became the social pillars of that system. Locally speaking, they were the dominant castes: Brahmins and Thakurs, endowed with a high social rank and wide-ranging economic power. In a sense, the system reproduced and developed that which already prevailed during the Raj, with zamindars and *taluqdars* being the intermediaries of the political power. For the whole of U.P. in the years after independence, the Congress selected candidates coming from the upper castes because these castes were widespread throughout the state and had the largest influence in the rural zones. From the economic point of view too, it chose candidates with an established influence, such as ex-zamindars who brought to the party entire vote banks made of those economically dependent on them — from Scheduled Castes agricultural labourers to backward castes sub-tenants. The period was characterised by the twin phenomena of patronage and co-optation as the engines of political mobilisation. They accounted for the above average numbers of upper castes sent to the Assembly and for the below average numbers of backward castes and Muslims. The position of Scheduled Castes (SC) very similar to that of Muslims, was nevertheless guaranteed by the reserved constituencies. Indeed, as in the case of the Muslims, the approach of the party's leadership to SC was one of distrust and condescension. Because of B. R. Ambedkar's radicalism during the colonial period, the Congress leaders expected SC to repent and follow the upper caste leadership blindfoldedly. To quote a speech Sardar Vallabhbhai Patel delivered in 1947: 'Let us forget what Dr Ambedkar and his group have done. Let us forget what you did' (quoted in Jaffrelot 2003: 95).[1] This was very much the prevailing attitude as far as the Muslim community was concerned. For those who had chosen to stay in India, the question was now to assimilate and be content with being represented by the Congress. Yet compared to Muslims, SC were in a more favourable position due to the reserved constituencies which made it legal to have a minimal number of such legislators in the Assembly. In the idea of the 'coalition of extremes' put forward by Paul Brass (1980), Muslims and SC were in a similar position by being an inherent part of power structures inside the party as MLAs, ministers and cadres but nevertheless in a secondary position to upper castes.

The Congress had a policy of selecting members of society which belonged to specifically prominent groups, namely castes, either numerically important throughout the whole of U.P. or in one of its subregions, or castes whose socio-economic weight is heavy. In the first category fell Chamars, Pasis, Dhobis and Bhumihars. In the second, were Brahmins and Rajputs. Baniyas, also largely represented in the Congress' ranks after independence, were between those two categories. In fact, their socio-economic weight has been heavy but only in the urban zones. In a city like Bareilly, for instance, the Congress, as also the Jana Sangh and the Bharatiya Janata Party (BJP), selected candidates of the Baniya caste who in fact managed to get elected in two to three of the area's constituencies (Aonla, Baheri and Bareilly city). The case was similar in many cities of the doab and Rohilkhand (Moradabad, Bahraich, Pilibhit, etc.) where, from 1952 onwards, Baniyas were elected in the urban areas on either the Congress' or Hindu nationalists' tickets.

---

[1] The speech was delivered on 28 August 1947.

Though Chamars, Pasis and Dhobis belong to the SC, whose cultural and economic capital is weak, their numeric strength is still an advantage. Therefore, they are unavoidable for most political parties in the quota system. Since SC have to be nominated because of reservations, candidates are then selected in view of the numerical advantage of some castes over others. An additional factor is the attempt at fostering political consciousness in some of these castes, as expressed in the colonial period through caste associations (see Rudolph and Rudolph 1987). Chamars are certainly the best example of this in U.P. In 1931, Chamars, Pasis and Dhobis accounted for 81.9 per cent of the SC population in U.P., with Chamars alone constituting 60.5 per cent of the total. In addition, we will see later that many of the SC candidates and MLAs recruited by the Congress belonged to an advanced economic category. Apart from the hills subregion, SC cover the whole of U.P. Again according to the 1931 Census, if we exclude Uttaranchal and the district of Gonda, Chamars accounted for a minimum of 6.4 per cent (Pilibhit) and a maximum of 19.6 per cent (Azamgarh and Ballia) of each district's population. Though little represented in two regions (around Meerut district and around Varanasi), Dhobis can be found in rest of the others between 1 per cent and 1.8 per cent. Pasis are concentrated in the centre of the state but are not negligible in the south and west (Schwartzberg 1965).

As far as Brahmins and Rajputs are concerned, their advantage over other upper castes lies in their well-established presence over the state, with an additional zone of absolute numerical domination, namely, Uttaranchal. This is also increased by their cultural and economic capital since Rajputs were the main landholders during the colonial period and Brahmins were the first to benefit from the new English-medium educational system, in addition to having some hold on land.

In the same manner, the few backward castes which are being recruited and selected as candidates for the Assembly elections come from the most important of their categories: Yadavs, Kurmis, Kacchis, Mallahs and Gujjars. These are numerically important and economically rising after independence. Yadavs in particular had developed caste associations before 1947 and were most politicised of the group. If their cultural capital remained lower than upper castes', these backward castes have nevertheless been characterised by their upward mobility since the 1950s. Their numbers in the ranks of MLAs had to be compared with that of the Jats, whose low percentage in the population of the state cannot account for their political representation. In 1931, Jats were only 1.6 per cent of the state's population but had at least six MLAs in 1957, five of them from the Congress, and three of them coming from the single district of Meerut. Compared to most

Table 1.1
Castes and Communities in Uttar Pradesh, 1931 (%)

Castes and Communities	
Upper Castes	**20.5**
Brahmin	9.2
Rajput	7.2
Bhumihar	0.4
Baniya/Jain	2.5
Kayastha	1.0
Khatri	0.1
Tyagi	0.1
Intermediary Castes	**2.0**
Jat	2.0
Other Backward Classes (OBC)	**41.7**
Yadav	8.7
Kurmi	3.5
Lodhi	2.2
Teli	2.0
Koeri/Kacchi	3.1
Kewat/Murao	2.4
Gujjar	0.7
Others	19.1
Scheduled Castes (SC)	**21.0**
Chamar	12.7
Pasi	2.9
Dhobi	1.6
Bhangi	1.0
Others	2.8
Scheduled Tribes (ST)	**less than 1.0**
Muslims	**15.0**
Sikhs	**less than 0.5**
Anglo-Indians	**less than 0.1**
TOTAL	100.0

Source: Census 1931, United Provinces of Agra and Awadh, Part 2, Provincial and Imperial Tables, 1933, reproduced in Hasan 1989.

other castes, Jats have both the advantages in western U.P. — a high economic capital because of the *bhaichara* system which enabled them, even before the land reforms of the 1950s, to cultivate and own their own lands, and a numerical advantage as they are concentrated in the northern doab. According to the 1931 Census, Jats accounted for 7.2 per cent of population in the Meerut division and 1.7 per cent in the Agra division, further south. Also, together with Chamars and Yadavs, their political commitment dates back to the colonial period.

Political Change in the Assembly: From Upper Caste Dominance to Contestation

Three distinct periods emerge from the figures shown in Tables 1.2 to 1.6: the immediate post-independence years (from 1952 until 1967) marked by upper caste ascendency, a second phase from 1967 until 1989, following the first decrease in upper caste representation and the years from 1989 onwards, with a marked and sustained rise of OBC numbers in the Assembly.

In terms of overall caste composition in the Assembly, the years 1952–67 are quite similar in nature. The period is characterised by the domination of upper castes, not all of them Congress-oriented as we will see. The numbers of upper caste MLAs in the Assembly go from 58 per cent at its highest in 1952 to around 45 per cent in 1967 and 1969. The lowest number is still more than twice their representation in the state's population. Though most of these MLAs came from the Congress Legislative Party, the other parties also recruited such suitable candidates to fight the elections. For the Jana Sangh, in 1969, at least 47 per cent of the party's MLAs were upper castes, with Brahmin or Baniyas constituting the highest percentage. But it also must be noted that more than 10 per cent of the MLAs were backward castes, with Lodhis already the most numerous caste among them, a trend that was to be continued in the BJP. The socialist parties were in a more balanced position despite having a large share of their MLAs also coming from the upper castes. In fact, 25 per cent of the socialists' legislators were backward-castes middle tenants. The factor was acknowledged by Paul Brass who wrote that 'one of the weaknesses of the left parties is that their leaders and their support partly come from the same elements

Figure 1.1
Caste and Community in the U.P. Assembly, 1952–96

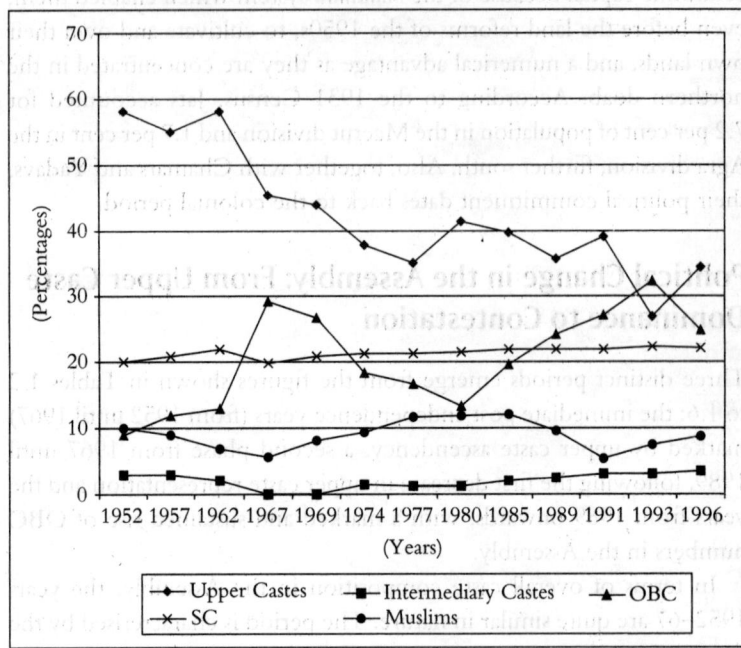

Source: Prepared by author.

Note: Hindu MLAs whose caste could not be identified have not been represented in
the graph.

which support the Congress. The MLAs come from the middle peasantry and zamindars' (1985: 255).

The cross-sectional mobilisation of the years 1969–89 can be seen
in the evolution of the caste composition of the U.P. Assembly. The
number of castes represented multiplied, smaller castes appeared
within the SC group and the castes of the middle peasantry assumed a
more important role. The years 1969–89 also come out as a transitory
period. The slow erosion of the traditional social order is translated
politically in the Assembly's representation. In the political arena, space
was made available for new groups that had become more assertive,
better organised and which could draw on their numbers. Yet that
space remained limited as upper castes tried to remain in control of
political power.

Table 1.2
Caste and Community Composition of the U.P. Assembly,
1952–69 (%)

Castes and Communities	1952	1957	1962	1967	1969
Upper Castes	**58.0**	**55.0**	**58.0**	**45.3**	**43.9**
Brahmin	27.0	21.0	21.0	21.5	19.0
Rajput	15.0	17.0	20.0	14.0	16.2
Bhumihar	2.0	2.0	2.0	4.9[a]	4.9[a]
Baniya/Jain	7.0	7.0	7.0	4.9[b]	3.8[b]
Kayastha	5.0	5.0	4.0	–	–
Khatri	1.0	1.0	1.0	–	–
Tyagi	1.0	1.0	1.0	–	–
Others		1.0	2.0	–	–
Intermediary Castes	**3.0**	**3.0**	**2.0**	–	–
Jat	3.0	3.0	2.0	–	–
OBC	**9.0**	**12.0**	**13.0**	**49.2**	**26.8**
Yadav	4.0	6.0	5.0	16.5[b]	17.6[c]
Kurmi	2.0	3.0	4.0	–	–
Lodhi	–	1.0	1.0	–	–
Gujjar	–	–	–	12.7	–
Others	3.0	2.0	3.0	19.8	9.2
SC	**20.0**	**21.0**	**22.0**	–	**20.9**
Muslims	**10.0**	**9.0**	**7.0**	**5.6**	**8.2**
TOTAL	100.0	100.0	100.0	100.0	100.0
	(N=430)	(N=430)	(N=430)	(N=425)	(N=425)

Source: Meyer (1969: 189); reproduced in Hasan (1989: 176).
Note: [a] Includes Bhumihar, Jat and Tyagi.
   [b] Includes Baniya, Kayastha and Khatri.
   [c] Includes Yadav, Kurmi, Lodhi and Gujjar.

Table 1.3
Caste Composition of the Congress MLAs in U.P., 1952–62 (%)

	1952	1957	1962
Upper Castes	58	56	61
Intermediate Castes	3	2	2
Backward Castes	7	6	6
SC	21	24	22
Muslims	11	10	8
TOTAL	100	100	100
	(N=390)	(N=286)	(N=249)

Source: Meyer (1969) adapted by Jaffrelot (2003: 66).

Table 1.4
Caste and Community Composition of the U.P. Assembly, 1974–96 (%)

Castes and Communities	1974	1977	1980	1985	1989	1991	1993	1996	2002*
Upper Castes	**37.80**	**35.18**	**41.31**	**39.70**	**35.68**	**39.05**	**26.98**	**34.55**	**35.38**
Baniya	2.58	2.56	1.41	1.40	2.82	4.52	4.46	3.71	4.42
Bhumihar	1.88	1.16	1.41	0.93	0.94	0.48	–	0.69	1.72
Brahmin	17.84	17.48	19.72	18.69	15.02	15.00	8.68	10.90	9.83
Kayastha	0.94	0.93	0.70	1.40	0.94	1.19	0.70	1.62	0.74
Khatri	–	0.23	0.47	0.23	0.47	0.95	0.94	0.93	1.47
Rajput	12.21	10.49	15.02	16.35	15.02	16.43	11.97	16.00	16.95
Tyagi	–	–	0.47	–	0.47	0.48	0.23	0.70	–
Others	2.35	2.33	2.11	0.70	–	–	–	–	–
Intermediary Castes	**1.41**	**1.16**	**1.17**	**2.10**	**2.58**	**3.09**	**3.05**	**3.71**	**4.67**
Jat	1.41	1.16	1.17	2.10	2.58	3.09	3.05	3.71	4.67
OBC	**18.30**	**16.78**	**13.36**	**19.60**	**24.14**	**27.14**	**32.39**	**24.83**	**27.52**
Bind	0.23	–	–	0.23	0.23	0.24	0.23	–	–
Gadariya	–	–	–	–	0.23	1.19	0.94	1.39	0.74
Gujjar	0.47	0.23	0.70	1.40	1.87	1.19	1.64	0.93	1.47
Jaiswala	–	0.23	–	–	–	–	0.23	–	–
Kacchi	0.23	0.47	0.94	0.47	0.70	0.95	0.47	2.55	0.74
Kewat	0.47	0.47	0.23	1.17	0.47	0.95	0.93	1.62	–
Kurmi	2.82	2.10	2.82	3.50	4.22	6.66	6.81	4.64	6.88
Lodhi	1.41	0.93	0.47	0.93	1.88	3.33	2.82	3.02	1.72
Mallah	0.23	–	0.23	0.70	0.47	0.24	0.47	–	–
Rajbhar	–	–	0.23	–	–	0.48	0.47	0.93	0.74
Rawat	0.23	0.23	–	–	0.23	–	–	–	–
Saini	0.47	0.70	0.23	0.23	0.70	1.90	1.41	0.70	0.49
Sainthwar	–	–	–	–	–	0.48	0.23	0.23	–
Yadav	7.75	6.29	3.52	7.94	8.92	8.33	12.21	7.66	9.09
Unidentified	3.99	5.13	3.99	2.80	4.22	1.19	3.52	1.16	5.65
SC	**21.35**	**21.42**	**21.58**	**21.94**	**22.02**	**22.14**	**22.30**	**22.07**	**21.87**
Bahelia	–	–	–	–	–	0.24	0.23	–	–
Baiswar	–	–	–	–	0.23	0.24	0.23	–	–
Berya	–	–	–	–	0.23	0.24	0.23	–	–
Chamar	2.35	2.80	4.46	6.54	5.16	4.28	5.87	6.03	12.29
Dhanuk	–	–	–	–	–	–	0.23	–	0.49
Dharkar	–	–	–	–	–	0.24	–	–	–
Dhobi	0.94	0.23	1.17	0.70	1.17	2.38	0.47	1.62	0.98
Dohare	–	–	0.47	0.23	0.23	0.24	0.23	0.23	–
Dom	0.23	0.23	–	0.23	0.70	–	0.70	0.70	–
Dusadh	–	–	–	0.23	–	–	–	–	–
Gond	–	–	0.23	0.23	0.47	0.71	0.93	0.70	–

(Table 1.4 continued)

(*Table 1.4 continued*)

Castes and Communities	1974	1977	1980	1985	1989	1991	1993	1996	2002*
Khatik	0.47	0.23	0.47	1.17	0.70	0.95	0.47	1.62	1.23
Kori	0.47	0.93	0.70	1.17	1.17	1.90	1.41	1.39	–
Kureel	0.23	0.70	0.47	0.23	0.23	0.48	0.23	0.23	–
Pasi	2.11	2.33	5.16	5.84	4.46	4.05	3.76	3.71	4.42
Shilpkar	0.70	0.70	0.70	0.70	0.70	0.71	0.70	0.70	–
Valmiki	0.23	0.47	–	0.70	0.23	0.48	0.47	0.46	–
Unidentified	13.62	12.80	7.75	3.97	6.34	4.76	6.10	4.64	2.46
ST	**0.23**	**0.23**	**0.23**	**0.23**	**0.23**	**0.24**	**0.23**	**0.23**	**–**
Muslims	**9.38**	**11.66**	**11.97**	**12.15**	**9.62**	**5.48**	**7.51**	**8.82**	**10.57**
Sikhs	**0.94**	**0.23**	**0.93**	**0.70**	**0.23**	**0.24**	**0.70**	**0.46**	**–**
Nominated	**0.23**	**0.23**	**0.23**	**0.23**	**0.23**	**0.24**	**0.23**	**0.23**	**–**
Unidentified	**10.33**	**13.05**	**9.15**	**3.27**	**5.16**	**2.38**	**6.57**	**5.34**	**–**
TOTAL	99.97	99.94	99.93	99.92	99.89	100.00	99.97	100.00	100.00

Source: Author's fieldwork.
Note: *Source*: Jaffrelot (2007).

The Social and Political Contest: 1967–89

The party-wise breakdown (Table 1.5) shows that after the 1967 turning point, representation in the Legislative Assembly or the Vidhan Sabha remained altered on lines set by Chaudhury Charan Singh. It may seem inappropriate to discuss the topic in terms of caste when Chaudhury's *kisan* politics actually relied on class and the bringing together of the backward castes and the Jats. In fact, the second period is marked by just this attempt at beating the Congress by aggregating small and middle landowners regardless of their caste. But the approach had its limits. One of them is that it was limited to landowners, and excluded agrarian workers and petty landowners. There was no room in Charan Singh's ideology for petty landowners or landless workers from the Scheduled Castes. They were co-opted in very much the same manner as the Congress had co-opted them before. Another point is that although the emphasis was on class and not caste, the monopoly of upper castes, in particular Brahmins, over the Congress and the state's institutions, was at the root of Charan Singh's revolt and of his claim for change. In the Congress, in 1969 and 1974, the proportion of upper castes, already reduced compared to the post-independence years, remains around 45 per cent and the rise of OBC which had marked the arrival of Charan Singh in 1967 is stabilised. Among OBC,

Table 1.5
Caste and Community in the 1974, 1977, 1980 and 1985 Assemblies of U.P. (party-wise) (%)

	1974			1977		1980	1985		
	Congress	Jana Sangh	BKD	Congress	Janata Party	Congress	Congress	BJP	Lok Dal
Upper Castes	**47.63**	**44.25**	**14.82**	**45.83**	**34.56**	**46.88**	**44.12**	**56.25**	**18.19**
Baniya	2.83	6.55	0.93	–	2.83	1.55	1.10	12.50	7.80
Bhumihar	1.89	–	2.78	–	1.42	1.55	0.37	6.25	–
Brahmin	25.94	9.83	5.55	22.92	17.00	22.98	22.06	6.25	–
Kayastha	0.94	–	0.93	–	1.13	0.62	1.47	12.50	–
Khatri	–	–	–	–	0.28	0.62	0.37	–	–
Rajput	14.62	18.03	3.70	14.58	10.20	16.15	17.65	18.75	10.39
Tyagi	–	–	–	–	–	0.62	1.10	–	–
Others	1.41	9.84	0.93	8.33	1.70	2.79	–	–	–
Intermediary Castes	**0.94**	**0.94**	**3.70**	–	**1.13**	–	**1.47**	–	**5.19**
Jat	0.94	–	3.70	–	1.13	–	1.47	–	5.19
OBC	**8.01**	**21.32**	**35.20**	**12.49**	**16.97**	**9.61**	**12.86**	**31.25**	**38.97**
Bind	–	–	0.93	–	–	–	0.37	–	–
Gujar	0.47	–	0.93	2.08	–	0.62	0.37	–	5.19
Jaiswala	–	–	–	–	0.28	–	–	–	–
Kacchi	–	–	–	–	0.56	0.62	0.37	–	1.30
Kewat	–	–	1.85	–	0.56	0.31	1.47	–	–
Khirwar/Khairaha	–	–	–	–	–	–	0.37	–	–
Kurmi	1.41	4.92	4.63	2.08	1.70	1.24	4.04	–	3.90
Lodhi	0.47	4.92	0.93	–	1.13	0.62	0.73	12.50	–
Mallah	–	–	0.93	–	–	0.31	0.73	–	1.30

	(N=212)	(N=61)	(N=108)	(N=48)	(N=353)	(N=322)	(N=272)	(N=16)	(N=77)
Rajbhar	–	–	–	–	–	0.31	–	–	–
Rawat	–	0.93	0.93	–	0.28	–	–	–	1.30
Saini	0.47	1.64	18.52	8.33	0.85	0.31	–	–	–
Yadav	2.83	6.56	5.55	–	6.23	2.17	3.31	12.50	22.08
Others	2.36	3.28	–	–	5.38	3.10	1.10	6.25	3.90
SC	**23.10**	**22.95**	**24.08**	**16.66**	**23.22**	**22.98**	**27.58**	**12.50**	**16.88**
Chamar	3.77	–	1.85	2.08	3.12	4.66	8.46	–	–
Dhobi	1.89	–	–	2.08	–	1.24	1.10	–	–
Dohare	–	–	–	–	–	0.62	0.37	–	–
Dom	–	–	0.93	–	0.28	–	0.37	–	–
Dusadh	–	–	–	–	–	–	0.37	–	–
Gond	–	–	–	–	–	0.31	0.37	–	–
Khatik	0.94	–	–	–	0.28	0.62	1.47	–	1.30
Kori	–	3.28	–	–	1.13	0.93	1.84	–	–
Kureel	–	–	0.93	–	0.85	0.62	–	–	1.30
Pasi	2.36	–	3.70	–	2.55	4.66	6.62	–	6.49
Shilpkar	1.41	–	–	–	0.85	0.62	1.10	–	–
Valmiki	0.47	–	–	2.08	0.28	–	0.73	6.25	–
Others	12.26	19.67	16.67	10.42	13.88	8.70	4.78	6.25	–
ST	**0.47**	–	–	–	**0.28**	**0.31**	**0.37**	–	–
Muslims	**10.38**	**9.26**	**10.42**	**10.42**	**11.33**	**10.87**	**11.03**	–	**15.58**
Sikhs	**1.41**	–	**2.08**	**2.08**	–	**0.93**	**1.10**	–	–
Unidentified	**8.02**	**11.47**	**12.96**	**12.50**	**12.46**	**8.38**	**1.10**	–	**5.19**
TOTAL	100.00	100.00	100.01	100.00	100.00	99.96	99.63	100.00	100.00

Source: Author's fieldwork.

Yadavs, and to a lesser extent, Kurmis and Lodhis are most numerous. But smaller, less organised castes also appear, for instance Kewat, Gujjar and Rawat. Their support to the successive *kisan* parties then, since the early 1990s, to the BJP, would guarantee them representation in the Assembly. In the case of SC, there is also a diversification. Castes which were not represented in the parliament in the 1950s and early 1960s now send one or two MLAs. One of the reasons for the fall in upper caste MLAs is to be found in the fact that the electoral rise of the Bharatiya Kranti Dal (BKD) was made at the expense of the socialists. The socialist parties were virtually wiped out between 1969 and 1974. It has to be said that they never really took roots in U.P., except in Poorvanchal. They lacked the organisational skills and money of the Congress and the mass appeal of the BKD. When the latter arrived on the political scene, it infringed upon much of the socialist vote in the eastern rural districts. Paradoxically enough, more than the socialists, whose avowed aim was to change the traditionally oppressive bases of U.P. society, it was the BKD (whose socio-economic programme was more limited) which drew votes from the weaker sections of the electorate. The BKD took on the socialists' SC vote bank as well as the backward castes'. But while the socialist parties were, as we saw earlier, led by upper caste politicians, the BKD's representation dwelt on OBC and Jats. As a result, the number of upper caste MLAs fell down while that of intermediary castes and OBC rose.

One hypothesis can be advanced for the more varied representation of SC in the period from 1967 to 1989. Due to the counter-mobilisation of Chamars in the 1960s, the Congress realised the fragility of basing its electoral success in reserved constituencies on this caste mainly. It must then have started looking for new SC partners. It could not do without Chamars; no mainstream party can, yet it was trying to expand its vote banks among other castes. Dhobi and Khatik are two such castes whose representation in the Assembly rose in the late 1960s and 1970s.

In 1969 and 1974, the Jana Sangh was clearly an upper caste-dominated party but, interestingly, with a good return in reserved constituencies. In 1969, 22.5 per cent of its MLAs were SC. The proportion of the Congress SC MLAs was then 22 per cent. In 1974, the figure rose to nearly 24 per cent for the Jana Sangh, while in the same year, the Congress SC MLAs were just above 23 per cent. Considering the Jana Sangh's conservative outlook on Indian social structures, these results are primarily due to the choice of consensual SC candidates who were suitable to the party's upper caste constituency. In fact, in 1974, the Congress party and the Jana Sangh's representation in the Assembly have in common their proportion of SC MLAs and the large percentage of upper castes. On the contrary, the BKD stands out for its small proportion of upper caste MLAs.

In 1974, the percentage of OBC in the Congress party and the Jana Sangh is underevaluated. It is likely that a vast proportion of the MLAs whose caste could not be identified in fact comprises the OBC. This would be in line with the trend of increased recruitment of this social group by the Congress party from the mid-1960s onwards. In 1962 already, 6 per cent of the Congress MLAs came from the backward castes. The 1967 experiment had led the party to recruit some more and the case was quite similar in the Jana Sangh as well. This is partly visible in 1974. The attempt to rely on OBC support in the Jana Sangh — which had already had more than 20 per cent of its MLAs coming from the back-ward castes in 1974 — was a long-term trend confirmed in the BJP, even before the Mandal Commission submitted its report.

In 1977, the Janata Party coalition government was split between upper castes (represented by the Jana Sangh) and backward castes (coming from the BKD). Upper caste representation in our table stands at 34.5 per cent, but it is likely to be underestimated because of the large number of MLAs whose caste could not be identified. So, in fact, we can expect this figure to be closer to 40 per cent, which would hardly be a change from the previous years under the Congress. In 1977, the Congress managed to maintain some of its MLAs in general consti-tuencies but lost in all but eight reserved seats. It was caught between the Jana Sangh's base among upper castes in reserved constituencies, helping it win the decisive votes, and in eastern and western U.P., the alliance between backward castes and SC. Two factors were at work. First was that SC were drawn away from the Congress because of the party's inability to implement its 'Garibi Hatao' ('Remove Poverty') agenda and more importantly, the violent family planning measures it had submitted them to. The second was that, by the late 1970s, Jats, Kurmis, Yadavs, etc., had replaced upper castes at the head of many middle-sized land properties in western and central U.P. and they were now in a position to tell SC agricultural workers who to vote for. In many cases, the forms taken by this alliance were probably just as coercive as in the case of the Congress' own upper castes–SC alliance and collapsed in favour of the Congress in 1980. The Janata Party did not provide a long-term solution for a form of SC mobilisation acceptable to SC themselves. In that sense, its failure can be seen as a prerequisite to the rise of the BSP.

The Muslim community had voted massively for the Janata Party, which had put up quite a high number of Muslim candidates. Their representation in the Assembly during the Janata government went up in a noticeable manner with them constituting 11.3 per cent of the Janata Party's legislators and 11.6 per cent of the entire Vidhan Sabha, with a few having been elected on the Congress tickets (10.4 per cent of all the Congress MLAs still). During the 1960s and early 1970s, they had accounted for between 5.5 and 10 per cent of all MLAs in the Assembly.

The fragility of the Janata Party was inherent because it brought together communities, both political and social, whose common interests were merely limited to defeating the Congress.

When the Congress returned to power in 1980, it was able to regain the support it had lost in reserved constituencies, with SC votes turning to the party's candidates again and upper castes massively coming back to their previous allegiance. The defection of SC to the Janata Party had not gone unnoticed and during the 1980 election campaign, Mrs Indira Gandhi did her best to win them back. The campaign was, very much like in 1974, pro-SC and pro-poor, but with a greater care not to offend upper castes and Muslims. The results show in terms of caste and community representation in the Assembly and within the party. While the Congress won over 75 per cent of the Vidhan Sabha seats in 1980, 80 per cent of reserved seats went to the Congress candidates. More than 23 per cent of its MLAs were elected in reserved constituencies. The figures also show that it won back the Muslim community. In fact, 66 per cent of Muslim MLAs in the Assembly belonged to the Congress; the remaining 33 per cent were split between various other parties.

The two elections won by the Congress in 1980 and 1985 are characteristic by the high percentage of upper castes, the balancing between Rajputs and Brahmins among the party's MLAs and the reduced share of OBC MLAs. They are the last attempts at a clear upper caste ascendency in the state's political life. The upper caste–SC alliance had been eroded by the 1960s and the 1977 experiment and its revival did not amount to much. In addition, because the Congress had remained a factional party, real power was concentrated in the hands of the upper castes. The SC and OBC were allotted positions in the various institutions controlled by the party, but they carried little or no real power. The 1980s' functioning style of the Congress cannot be said to have changed since the 1960s, with the real question still being: how to ac-commodate castes and communities, without delegating power.

The Rise of OBC and SC and the Attempt at Accommodation: 1989–2002

One of the defining characteristics of the period starting in 1989 is the fact that the erosion in the number of upper caste MLAs was for the first time matched by proportionately rising numbers of OBC MLAs. On a long-term basis, the fall in the number of upper caste legislators is very clear: from nearly 60 per cent in 1952 to less than 40 per cent in the 1990s. But it is not until the Mandal Commission and the 1990s that the rise of OBC remained a stable factor from one election to another. One could have expected the number of OBC in the Assembly to have varied with each party in power. Yet, such is not the case. There are changes from one party to the other but they only help explaining the smaller changes in the percentage points. For instance, the electoral success of the Samajwadi Party (SP)–Bahujan Samaj Party (BSP) alliance in 1993 explains the comparatively smaller proportion of the upper caste MLAs and the record percentage of OBC MLAs. The explanation does not hold for the deepest changes of the period from 1989 to 2002. That is, even if we assumed that in parties traditionally built around upper caste cadres (such as the Congress or the BJP), the number of upper caste MLAs would be higher, the figures indicate a different picture. In the years following 1990, the number of OBC under these very parties remained high. This is because though the rise has not been steadfast, it is nevertheless indisputably clear that whichever party has come to power after Mandal, it has maintained a high level of OBC MLAs. This is evident from the rather large proportion of OBC MLAs in 1991 and 1996, when the BJP came first. Charan Singh's 1967 experiment had made it necessary to give room to rural backward castes. Mandal now made it necessary to widen that political space. In that sense, Mandal opened the power-sharing era. In fact, in the three elections that span the 1990s, the proportion of OBC MLAs in the Assembly's main party, the BJP, remains around 20 per cent. It is higher than in the Congress (more OBC are nominated by the BJP than the Congress) but much less than the openly pro-OBC or pro-Dalit parties, the SP and the BSP.

With more than 40 per cent of OBC MLAs, the SP and the BSP in 1993 are the main contributors to the introduction of a new political personnel in U.P. In 1993 in particular, though both parties show specific trends — more OBC in the SP and more SC in the BSP — their common peculiarity is the drastically reduced share of upper caste MLAs in their ranks. In fact, in 1993, the BSP whose positioning was then aggressively anti-Brahmin invested no upper caste candidate at all. More interestingly, the SP came out with just 10 per cent of upper caste MLAs, elected in rural constituencies dominated by OBC in Oudh and the lower doab. In the same year, Yadavs alone, with 35 per cent of the party's MLAs, amounted to more than SC and upper caste MLAs put together.

Both parties changed their stance in the following election and introduced upper caste candidates to a larger extent. As a result, the share of OBC and SC in the SP and the BSP went down in 1996 compared to 1993, though it remains to be seen if their power really increased in the parties' machines. The dilution of the BSP's anti-Brahmin discourse was a result of the alliance entered with the Congress and it did yield fruit as some 15 per cent of the party's MLAs were upper castes. The Congress was pushed into presenting a mockery of its former self with over 63 per cent of upper caste MLAs, just about 15 per cent of OBC and 9 per cent of SC. Its lack of adaptation is visible when compared to the BJP, which although perceived as an upper caste party nevertheless has over 21 per cent of its MLAs coming from the backward castes.

In terms of political representation, the main phenomenon of U.P.'s political scene since the late 1960s is the rise of the OBC. But contrary to Bihar where they are at the core of the main parties and control the political agenda, U.P.'s political parties have resisted this rise. Their co-optation into the BJP and, to a much smaller extent, the Congress, has to be seen as a necessity that clashes with either the ideological leanings or the power structure of these parties. It remains limited in numbers and, as we will see in the last section of this chapter, in power too.

Education and Occupation: A Secondary Level of Change

The question which has to be answered here is whether the changes discussed so far in terms of caste representation are also visible in terms

Table 1.6
Caste and Community in the Vidhan Sabha of U.P. (party-wise), 1989–96 (%)

	1989				1991				1993				1996			
	INC	BJP	JD	BSP	INC	BJP	JD	BSP	INC	BJP	SP	BSP	INC	BJP	SP	BSP
Upper Castes	46.23	55.16	28.43	0	53.19	49.83	19.78	–	53.57	46.07	9.17	–	63.63	48.60	15.60	14.92
Baniya	2.15	10.34	0.47	–	4.25	6.82	1.10	–	3.57	8.43	1.83	–	3.03	6.08	2.75	–
Bhumihar	2.15	–	0.95	–	–	0.45	1.10	–	25.00	14.61	2.75	–	–	0.55	0.92	1.49
Brahmin	21.50	22.41	12.80	–	27.66	20.90	1.10	–	–	1.68	–	–	24.24	16.56	2.75	4.48
Kayastha	–	5.17	0.47	–	–	2.27	–	–	–	2.25	–	–	–	2.21	0.92	1.49
Khatri	–	3.45	–	–	–	1.81	–	–	25.00	18.54	4.59	–	–	2.21	–	–
Rajput	20.43	13.79	13.27	–	19.15	17.13	16.48	–	–	0.56	–	–	33.33	20.44	7.34	7.46
Tyagi	–	–	0.47	–	2.13	0.45	–	–	–	–	–	–	3.03	0.55	0.92	–
Others	–	–	–	–	–	–	–	–	–	–	–	–	–	–	–	–
Intermediary Castes	2.15	–	4.26	0	–	3.18	6.59	–	3.57	3.93	–	–	–	5.52	0.92	1.49
Jat	2.15	–	4.26	–	–	3.18	6.59	–	3.57	3.93	–	–	–	4.97	0.92	1.49
Others	–	–	–	–	–	–	–	–	–	–	–	–	–	0.55	–	–
OBC	16.11	20.67	28.89	23.07	19.16	19.53	31.88	83.31	14.28	21.34	54.12	40.59	15.15	21.51	31.19	37.30
Bind	–	–	0.47	–	–	–	1.10	–	–	–	–	1.45	–	–	–	–
Gadariya	–	–	0.47	–	–	–	2.20	16.66	–	–	1.83	2.90	–	0.55	–	5.97
Gujjar	1.07	–	3.32	–	2.13	0.91	2.20	–	10.71	1.68	–	–	3.03	1.10	0.92	–
Jaiswala	–	–	–	–	2.13	–	–	–	–	–	–	–	–	–	–	–
Kacchi	–	–	0.95	7.69	2.13	–	2.20	–	–	0.56	–	2.90	3.03	2.21	0.92	7.46
Kewat	–	1.72	0.47	–	2.13	0.91	–	8.33	–	0.56	–	4.35	–	1.10	0.92	4.48

(Table 1.6 continued)

(Table 1.6 continued)

	1989				1991				1993				1996			
	INC	BJP	JD	BSP	INC	BJP	JD	BSP	INC	BJP	SP	BSP	INC	BJP	SP	BSP
Kurmi	1.07	5.17	4.74	7.69	2.13	5.45	7.69	25.00	3.57	5.62	7.34	8.70	3.03	4.97	1.83	11.94
Lodhi	1.07	5.17	1.90	–	2.13	5.0	–	–	–	5.06	1.83	1.45	–	5.52	1.83	1.49
Mallah	1.07	–	0.47	–	–	0.45	–	8.33	–	0.56	0.92	–	–	–	–	–
Rawat	–	–	0.47	–	–	0.45	–	–	–	–	–	–	–	–	–	2.98
Rajbhar	–	–	–	–	–	–	–	–	–	–	–	2.90	–	1.10	–	–
Saini	2.15	1.72	–	–	–	3.18	1.10	–	–	2.81	–	1.45	–	1.10	0.92	–
Sainthwar	–	–	–	–	–	0.91	–	–	–	0.56	–	–	–	0.55	–	–
Yadav	9.68	1.72	11.37	7.69	6.38	2.27	12.09	16.66	–	1.12	34.86	13.04	3.03	2.76	22.93	1.49
Others	–	5.17	4.26	–	2.13	–	3.30	8.33	–	2.81	7.34	1.45	3.03	0.55	0.92	1.49
SC	**21.50**	**22.41**	**23.66**	**38.46**	–	–	–	–	**21.42**	**19.64**	**20.19**	**39.13**	**9.09**	**22.08**	**16.52**	**29.84**
Bahelia	–	–	–	–	–	0.45	–	–	–	0.56	–	–	–	–	–	–
Baiswar	–	1.72	–	–	–	0.45	–	–	–	0.56	–	–	–	–	–	–
Berya	–	–	0.47	–	–	–	–	–	–	–	0.92	–	–	–	–	–
Chamar	2.15	5.17	7.58	–	4.25	4.54	6.59	–	3.57	4.49	5.50	13.04	–	4.97	1.83	20.89
Dhanuk	–	–	–	–	–	–	–	–	–	–	0.92	–	–	–	–	–
Dharkar	–	–	–	–	–	0.45	–	–	–	–	–	–	–	–	–	–
Dhobi	2.15	3.45	0.47	–	2.13	4.09	–	–	–	0.56	–	1.45	–	2.76	0.92	1.49
Dohare	–	–	0.47	–	–	0.45	–	–	–	0.56	–	–	–	0.55	–	–
Dom	1.07	–	0.95	–	–	–	–	–	7.14	–	–	–	3.03	–	0.92	–
Gond	–	–	–	–	–	0.91	1.10	–	–	1.12	0.92	–	–	1.10	0.92	–
Khatik	–	–	1.42	–	–	1.36	2.20	–	–	1.12	0.92	–	–	1.66	0.92	1.49
Kori	–	6.90	0.47	–	–	3.18	1.10	–	–	3.37	–	–	–	3.31	–	–

Kureel	–	–	0.47	–	–	0.45	0.10	–	–	0.56	–	–	–	0.55	–	–
Pasi	9.68	–	3.79	7.69	10.64	3.18	1.10	3.57	–	1.12	6.42	7.25	3.03	2.21	4.59	5.97
Shilpkar	2.15	–	0.47	–	–	1.36	–	7.14	8.33	–	0.92	–	–	1.66	–	–
Valmiki	–	–	0.47	–	–	0.45	–	–	8.33	0.56	0.92	–	–	0.55	0.92	–
Others	4.30	5.17	6.63	30.77	6.38	4.54	8.79	–	–	5.06	2.75	17.39	3.03	2.76	5.50	–
ST	**1.07**	–	–	–	–	–	–	**3.57**	–	–	–	–	–	–	**0.92**	–
Muslims	**11.83**	–	**6.63**	**38.46**	**8.51**	**13.18**	**1.10**	**3.57**	**8.33**	–	**11.01**	**17.39**	**9.09**	–	**19.27**	**16.41**
Sikhs	–	**1.72**	–	–	–	–	–	–	–	**0.56**	**0.92**	–	–	**1.10**	–	–
Unidentified	**8.06**	–	**8.06**	–	**2.13**	**0.45**	**5.49**	–	–	**8.43**	**4.59**	**2.90**	**3.03**	**1.10**	**15.59**	–
TOTAL	99.96	99.99	99.93	100.00	99.97	99.98	99.97	99.00	99.93	99.99	100.00	100.00	99.99	99.90	100.00	99.96
	(N=93)	(N=58)	(N=211)	(N=13)	(N=47)	(N=220)	(N=91)	(N=28)	(N=12)	(N=178)	(N=109)	(N=69)	(N=33)	(N=181)	(N=109)	(N=67)

Source: Author's fieldwork.

of socio-economic profile. In other words, do the new MLAs also hold different positions from their predecessors? Have they received a different education? Education and occupation are a way to assess more fully the change which has been taking place since the late 1960s.

Land and Knowledge as Primary Economic Assets

In spite of there being a large number of MLAs whose education and occupation could not be ascertained in the 1957–69 period, some trends are visible. For one, the high number of legislators who have been to university, though overestimated because of the proportion of MLAs whose education could not be identified, is still representative of a certain trend noticeable from the 1960s onwards. The recruitment of these individuals was synonymous with the transformation of the Congress from a mass mobilisation movement to a real political party whose structures they controlled. Though the Congress had acquired democratic credit through contact with the masses, it had little democratised in its organisation and structures. Hence we see a double-standard between the language and the rhetoric of electoral mobilisation directed to the masses and its selection of candidates (who had to be chosen for their personal wealth or social network to be able to defeat their opponents). A university education leading to a well-paid or influential white-collar job was a good pre-requisite for this. Coming from the landed or enterprising classes was even more useful and acceptable to the Congress in its quest for candidates. The intelligentsia was the Congress' choice representative until 1969. It does not mean that in 1957, 1962 and 1969, the proportion of legislators with a pre-university education was negligible. On the contrary, it was probably roughly similar to that of MLAs educated with a B.A. or more, which is more in keeping with the socio-educational profile in U.P. after independence. But the most telling fact is the development of the political elite on very much the same terms as before independence: English-medium educated professionals whose links with the masses were only limited to their socio-economic influence. Another telling fact is that among university graduates, LLB diplomas are most current. This is again consistent with the pre-independence pattern where, apart from periods of mass mobilisation like the Non-Cooperation movement, lawyers accounted for more than 50 per cent of the Congress delegates at the All India Congress Committee (AICC) (Jaffrelot 2002: 178).

That trend was not limited to the Congress. In the 1953 plenary meeting of the Praja Socialist Party (PSP), Ashoka Mehta, its General Secretary, circulated questionnaires aimed at determining the members' socio-economic background. The results were very similar to those found in the case of the Congress. It emerged that 18 per cent of the PSP's members had received primary education, about 30 per cent secondary education and more than 52 per cent were university graduates. This shows the difficulty for political parties to recruit members but also candidates from non-privileged social milieux.

Before more conclusions can be drawn, the figures have to be compared with the occupational data (see Table 1.7).

Throughout the period, agriculture is the single largest category, but the group of self-employed professionals (lawyers and medical practitioners) remains close behind. If we add another white-collar group — teachers — then the percentages in both categories are roughly similar.

'Agriculturists' is a vague term which includes here both agricultural labourers and ex-zamindars. In the 1950s, in the Congress in particular, the category was rather mixed with prominent Hindu, Brahmins, Thakurs — in one case, even Kacchi — and Muslim landowners being elected on the Congress tickets. Just to quote a few instances, Amaresh Chandra Pandey, elected from Mirzapur in 1952 and 1957, was a member of the U.P. Zamindars' Union and the general secretary of the Mirzapur branch. He had joined the Congress in 1950. In 1957 in Jhansi district, Laxman Rao Kadam, the Congress MLA was also an ex-zamindar. Members of *nawab* families were also courted by the Congress as they presented the twin advantage of being able to take on the Muslim component of the electorate as well as the Hindu rural vote. In most cases, ex-zamindars had been elected as independent candidates but also at times on Jana Sangh tickets, for instance in Jaunpur constituency where the Brahmin Raja of Jaunpur was elected in 1957.

As far as the Congress is concerned, the main reason behind the decision seems to be the choice made between ideology and on-the-field necessities. This is best illustrated by Rafi Ahmed Kidwai's well-known judgement that 'in the legislatures, we want political goondas' (quoted in Graham 1986). Kidwai was a shrewd political operator in charge of the campaigning in U.P. and he does not seem to have had the same

Table 1.7

Occupation of Congress MLAs in U.P., 1952–93 (%)

Occupation	1952	1957	1962	1980	1985	1989	1991	1993
Agriculture	38.7	37.8	42.2	48.12	52.82	47.77	40.00	38.03
Teaching	7.4	10.8	11.2	7.51	4.46	6.09	9.52	9.62
Law	22.1	17.1	15.7	18.30	17.60	18.50	17.14	15.49
Medicine	2.8	3.1	1.6	2.11	2.35	2.58	2.14	1.41
Business	13.8	14.3	13.3	7.04	7.98	7.02	11.43	15.73
Public Work	3.9	3.8	3.6	–	–	–	–	–
Labour	2.3	1.7	2.4	–	–	–	–	–
Others*	9.0	11.2	10.0	3.76	5.63	6.23	5.71	7.28
Unknown	–	–	–	13.38	9.15	11.71	14.05	12.44
TOTAL	100.0	99.8	100.0	100.22	99.99	99.90	99.99	100.00
	(N=390)	(N=286)	(N249)	(N=426)	(N=426)	(N=427)	(N=420)	(N=427)

Source: Meyer (1969); author's adaptation from *Who's Who in the U.P. Vidhan Sabha.*

Note: *Government service, housewives, unknown.

ideologically rigourous approach to candidate selection as Jawaharlal Nehru had. He had accepted the necessity to recruit individuals who could win elections thanks to prestige, money or coercion. These MLAs came from a more traditionalist milieu than the lawyers and teachers mentioned before. They contributed to the conservative turn taken by the Congress governments in U.P. after independence, their rejection of large-scale land reforms, their emphasis on the conflicting dimensions of Hinduism and Islam and rejection of Urdu. The question we may ask as a result of the data of the 1950s is whether this recruitment was only due to the influence of such operators in the U.P. of the times, the socio-economic structures of which favoured them. Or did it go beyond that and last even in the 1960s, 1970s, etc., when the traditional social order was declining and new groups asserted themselves on the political scene? The political elite of U.P in the 1950s had a foothold in the past. This went on along the mobilisation lines drawn during the colonial period. In fact, there is not much difference between the legislators elected during the 1920s and 1930s (people in the services, tradesmen, upper caste rural landlords) and those elected in the 1950s. But gradually this style of functioning was to become ill adapted to U.P.'s changing social scene.

In the following years, the resilience of agriculture might at first sight seem puzzling. But if we cross caste and occupation data, we see that most of the resilience of agriculture is engineered by the entrance of OBC in the Assembly. For instance, in 1980, 72.7 per cent of all OBC MLAs were agriculturists. The figure had fallen to 57.89 per cent in 1989, but was still then higher than the Assembly's average. The caste dimension is also important in the occupational polarisation between the group of agriculturists (mostly backward castes) and the group of professionals (mostly upper castes). One can note a resilience of agriculture-based occupations, which vary around 50 per cent throughout the 1980s, with a climax to 61 per cent in 1985. Other distinguishing features are the remarkably stable percentage of law professionals and medical practicians. Those features are linked to the changes in the caste composition in the Assembly in the sense that the rise of backward caste MLAs is synonymous with the maintaining of a large proportion of agriculturists. In contemporary U.P., land tenancy remains a factor of political assertion. In the 1990s, though the proportion of agriculturists declines as compared to the previous decades, it remains as high as between 38 to 40 per cent. Most of the

MLAs engaged in agriculture are tenants and, to a smaller extent, labourers, while about 27 per cent are professionals (lawyers, educationists and doctors). The evolution since the 1980s seems to have stabilised in the 1990s around those two poles: agriculture and knowledge-based professions.

An Increasingly Educated Political Elite

Table 1.8 alludes to deeper variations in terms of education than caste. The tendency is towards an increasingly educated political elite after 1980, with around 60 per cent of MLAs comprising university graduates or postgraduates.

Table 1.8
Education of U.P. MLAs, 1980–89 (%)

	1980	1985	1989	1991	1993	1991	1993
Up to Class VIII	6.57	3.76	4.68	3.57	2.81	3.57	2.81
Class IX to Intermediate	25.59	26.76	23.89	23.24	21.12	23.24	21.12
Graduation	15.72	20.19	23.42	25.23	35.70	25.23	35.70
Postgraduation	36.39	39.67	36.06	32.38	25.35	32.38	25.35
PhD	0.23	0.23	0.23	0.24	1.88	0.24	1.88
Non-conventional	0.23	0	0.23	0.24	0	0.24	0
Unknown	15.25	9.39	11.47	15.00	13.14	15.00	13.14
TOTAL	99.97	100.00	99.98	100.00	99.97	100.00	99.97
	(N=426)	(N=426)	(N=427)	(N=420)	(N=426)	(N=420)	(N=426)

Source: Adapted from the *Who's Who in U.P. Vidhan Sabha*.

One interesting phenomenon is that these changes affect all castes but not all parties in the same manner. In 1985 and 1989 for instance, SC account for 12.6 per cent and 16 per cent of all MLAs with a first university diploma. A further 37.2 per cent of postgraduates are SC (72.4 per cent of which are the Congress MLAs) in 1985. Out of the total 36.4 per cent of postgraduate MLAs, SC account for 17.4 per cent in 1985. In 1989, the proportion of SC postgraduate MLAs falls down to 16.9 per cent of which 23.1 per cent are the Congress MLAs and 53.8 per cent were elected on a Janata Dal ticket.

In 1989, an additional 41.7 per cent of OBC MLAs were postgraduates. The proportion had risen from 30.1 per cent in the previous Assembly.

It amounted to 27.9 per cent of the whole number of postgraduates in the Assembly.

This global rise in the educational level should be considered as the chief development. It crystallised in the 1980s with the appearance of an increasingly educated political elite, belonging to previously marginalised sections of society.

As is the case with occupation, the trend set in the 1980s appears to be confirmed by the figures of the 1990s, in particular, regarding the general rise in the educational level of legislators.

A large share of SC MLAs are then again university graduates. In 1991, the proportion was 18.5 per cent. In 1993, in a BSP–SP dominated Assembly, it was also 18.5 per cent. SC elected on the Congress or on BJP tickets have a more educated profile than the ones elected on BSP. This is an interesting factor considering the BSP's rejection of the Congress and the BJP on the ground that they are ignorant of their constituency's living conditions and act as simple pawns in the hands of the upper castes. In addition, these figures also tend to confirm our hypothesis that the Congress' recruitment of more than average educationally qualified personnel was a flaw. The BSP, whose quick growth and stabilisation among the Dalits is based on a better adequation between those represented and those who represent them, must have benefited from it.

OBC were similarly affected by the rise in the educational level with 35.1 per cent of graduates being OBC in 1993, when most of them were elected on SP or BSP tickets. It is slightly less than the 38.7 per cent peak reached in 1991 (a BJP-dominated Assembly).

To conclude this analysis of educational and occupational change, the growing access to education since the 1960s appears not to have gone hand in hand with the developement of blue-collar occupations. Though U.P.'s economy has changed, the control of resources still goes through land tenancy. In a patronage-based society such as U.P.'s, land still gives access to more resources, both political and economic. The fact that most MLAs still declare being agriculturists, even when they actually have another job, is an indication of the importance of owning land. It is an illustration of the circle of what can be called 'global dominance': land ownership and education are resources pulled together in the ultimate aim of political power, which in turn gives access to more economic resources and power. Considering that the main political fact of last 50 years is the mass entry of OBC in the Assembly, one can venture as far as to say that the political rise of the OBC has displaced the old patronage system based on land and controlled by upper castes and introduced a new one, very similar in its economic style of functioning but with OBC at its helm.

This fact seem to go contrary to the usual view that a global democratisation process is underway, making it easier for the once marginal sections of society to win power thanks to parties which, in various degrees, contest the traditional social order. In fact, though this assertion is indeed valid, the consolidation of an OBC-controlled patronage system is also taking place.

Behind this general evolution, one must point to the fact that the BJP, a party usually seen as conservative, has also played a part in the changing profile of the Assembly. In fact, in 1991 and 1996, two years when the BJP was the single largest party in the Assembly, OBC accounted for 27.1 per cent and 24.8 per cent of all MLAs. In the perspective that the BJP's leaders are not in favour of drastic changes in the social order of the state, how can one account for their selecting so many OBC candidates? And why, when the SP, or even the BSP in the early 1990s, were seen as favouring OBC, did voters elect OBC candidates on BJP tickets? A look at the Congress policy of power-sharing points to the reasons the BJP might have had and the factors of its relative success within the OBC community.

Beyond the Assembly: Cabinet and Party Machines

Congress' Road to Political Suicide

If we consider that representation in the Assembly is partly dictated by factors exterior to the party's real stakes (numbers in state population, reservations, politicisation of castes), we can argue that intra-party positions answer a different logic. The following tables show that the position of castes or caste-groups in governments, the core of power in the state, was not the same as in the Assembly. The results show that upper castes, in particular, Brahmins and Baniyas, are about as dominant in governments than in the Assembly. On the contrary, Muslims and SC are more represented in governments than in the Assembly, while middle castes are absent from them all together until the 1990s.

Table 1.9
Caste and Community in the U.P. Governments*, 1952–63 (%)

	1952	1954	1957	1960	1962	1963
Upper Castes						
Brahmin	36.84	31.25	–	17.64	19.04	31.25
Rajput	15.79	6.25	6.25	11.76	14.28	12.50
Bhumihar	–	–	–	5.88	–	–
Kayastha	10.53	12.50	12.50	5.88	4.76	–
Khatri	–	–	–	–	4.76	–
Baniya	10.53	18.75	12.50	29.41	23.81	18.75
Sindhi	–	–	–	5.88	–	–
Other Upper Castes	–	–	–	–	4.76	–
Jat	5.26	–	6.25	5.88	4.76	6.25
Scheduled Castes	**5.26**	**12.50**	**12.50**	**11.76**	**14.28**	**12.50**
Muslims	**15.79**	**18.75**	**18.75**	**11.76**	**9.52**	**12.50**
TOTAL	100.00	100.00	100.00	99.97	99.97	100.00
	(N=19)	(N=16)	(N=16)	(N=18)	(N=21)	(N=16)

Source: Adapted from Government of Uttar Pradesh (1977).
Note: * Only ministerial and state secretarial positions.

Table 1.9 covers two different phases in the history of the U.P. Congress. From 1952 to 1960, power was organised around G. B. Pant, until his inclusion in Nehru's Cabinet in Delhi, and then Dr Sampurnanand. The former was a Brahmin, the second a Kayastha. Through the succeeding governments, we get a good insight into the construction of factional coalitions. The predominance of members of Pant and Dr Sampurnanand's castes is striking. Brahmins occupy a minimum of 30 per cent of the seats in all governments. Except in 1963, Kayasthas, a negligable caste in terms of numbers but an educated and influential one, also occupy two berths in each government, representing between 4.8 per cent and 12.5 per cent. Between 1960 and 1963, with the emergence of Chandra Bhan Gupta, a Baniya, at the head of the strongest faction in the Uttar Pradesh Congress Committee (UPCC), the proportion of Brahmins falls while the number of Baniyas rises. However, Baniyas do not assert themselves in the same proportion as Brahmins, occupying 'only' between 18.75 and 29.41 per cent of the seats in the various governments. In spite of the fall of the Gupta government in 1963, Baniyas maintain a strong influence in government, in particular because Sucheta Kripalani, the next Chief Minister and an outsider to the state, was Gupta's ally. Factions are a well-documented phenomena and we know that the rivalries inside the Congress made it necessary for faction leaders to expand their circle beyond their castemen. However, these other faction members did not constitute the inner circle and were endowed with limited power. The important number of Muslims throughout the period is not reflected by the simultaneous rise of a Muslim leadership inside the party. As far as SC are concerned, their co-optation in the party and to positions in the U.P. executive goes hand in hand with the recognition that they are to adopt mainstream positions. But the most striking feature is clearly the complete lack of backward caste ministers throughout the period. In fact, it is only in 1967, with Charan Singh's government that two Yadavs and one Kurmi were allotted cabinet ministerial portfolios in the U.P. government.

This power-sharing is visible in the Congress governments through-out the 1980s also. The proportion of SC and Muslims in government bears witness to an attempt to revive the 'coalition of extremes', in the late 1980s when together with upper castes, Muslims and SC are again the poles around which power is distributed. But there is no comparison between the share of power attributed to upper castes and other groups. In all three governments shown in Table 1.10, upper castes amount to more than 50 per cent, going as high as 64.4 per cent under Sripat Misra in 1984. On the contrary, Muslims and SC ministers are present in a number more proportionate with their population size.

Table 1.10
Caste and Community Composition of
Congress Governments in U.P., 1982–87 (%)

	1984	1985	1987
Upper Castes	64.4	51.3	57.1
OBC	8.9	13.5	8.6
SC	15.6	21.6	20.0
Muslims	8.9	10.8	14.3
Unknown	2.2	2.7	0
TOTAL	100.0	100.0	100.0
	(N=45)	(N=37)	(N=35)

Source: Author's fieldwork.

While the UPCC shows a more balanced image, with the propor-tion of upper castes and backward castes widely varying from one com-mittee to the other, the real locus of ground-power, district units, were controlled by upper castes throughout the 1970s and 1980s. In the context of backward castes assertion of the period and with a view to the re-partition of castes in U.P., this amounts to little short of political suicide. Throughout the 1970s and 1980s, OBC appear to have been excluded from the core decision-making organs of the Congress party as well as from its policy-making branches. In 1982–84, the U.P. Parliamentary Board of Congress contained only about 7 per cent of OBC, as against 57 per cent of upper castes.

Table 1.11
Composition of the UPCC, 1976–88 (%)

	1976–79	1980–81	1981–82	1982–84	1985–88
Upper Castes	37.5	49.8	40.0	52.4	39.5
Intermediary Castes	–	–	–	–	2.1
OBC	18.7	17.2	16.0	14.3	24.1
SC and ST	25.0	10.3	8.0	4.8	6.2
Muslims	18.7	10.3	20.0	14.3	12.5
Others	–	3.4	–	–	2.1
Unknown	–	6.9	16.0	14.3	12.5
TOTAL	100.0	99.9	100.0	100.1	100.0
	(N=16)	(N=29)	(N=25)	(N=21)	(N=48)

Source: Author's fieldwork.

Table 1.12
Caste and Community of Congress Party District Unit Presidents, 1976–88 (%)

	1976–79	1980–81	1981–82	1982–84	1985–88
Upper Castes	63.6	33.3	52.4	55.1	43.75
Intermediary Castes	–	5.5	–	–	6.25
OBC	18.2	27.7	12.7	14.5	6.25
SC	9.1	5.5	6.3	4.3	18.75
Muslims	9.1	22.2	17.5	14.5	6.25
Others	–	5.5	1.6	1.4	–
Unknown	–	5.5	9.5	10.1	12.50
TOTAL	11.0	99.9	100.0	100.0	100.00
	(N=11)	(N=18)	(N=63)	(N=69)	(N=16)

Source: Author's fieldwork.

We also find here a partial explanation of the failure of the Congress to grow back. One part of the explanation lies in the fact that having patronage slipped out of its hands, the party has progressively lost all means to maintain its cadres and apparatus alive. But its inability to adapt, quite the opposite of the BJP case, is a major factor in its decline.

The Congress is limited by its lack of resources, ideas and leaders to be able to mobilise the electorate, and it has not really attempted to reform yet. Apart from 1990, the year the propositions of the Mandal Commission were implemented, upper caste percentage in the party's executive remained near or over 50 per cent. And even then, the U.P. Congress Parliamentary Board was packed with as many as 61.5 per cent of upper castes, and just 7.7 per cent of OBC.

Throughout the 1990s, the share of OBC remained particularly low, yet higher than that of SC or Muslims. Table 1.13 gives an indication of the lack of evolution of power-sharing in the Congress.

Table 1.13
Composition of the Congress State Executive
(vice-presidents and general secretaries), 1991–2000 (%)

	1991–94	1994–95	1999–2000
Upper Castes	57.8	63.2	50.0
Intermediary Castes	1.1	–	1.4
OBC	14.4	15.8	15.3
SC and ST	17.8	5.3	22.2
Muslims	8.9	10.5	9.7
Unknown	–	5.3	–
TOTAL	100.0	100.1	100.0
	(N=90)	(N=19)	(N=72)

Source: Author's fieldwork.

The Post-Congress Political Scene or
How to Resist the Rise of OBC and SC

Representation in the Assembly is only one form of political change and to understand it fully, we need to be able to identify various types of commitment to the process of power-sharing. In fact, though all winning parties have increased OBC representation in the Vidhan Sabha, they have not raised OBC representation in the Cabinet in a similar manner. Here the 'party variable' comes to light again as one of the limits to the dynamics of OBC rise in Uttar Pradesh.

Looking back to 1990 and the first Mulayam Singh-led government, we can analyse the changes since then in the various castes present in governments ranging from the Congress, the Janata Dal, the SP, the BSP and the BJP (see Table 1.14).

Table 1.14
Caste Composition of Some Governments in U.P. since 1990 (%)

	1990	1991	1993	1995	1997	1999	2001
	JD	BJP	SP–BSP	SP–BSP	BSP–BJP	BJP	BJP
Upper Castes	50.00	51.61	6.66	6.25	17.39	47.01	50.00
Intermediary Castes*	–	3.22	0	6.25	8.69	0.85	1.00
OBC	14.30	19.35	40.00	43.75	26.08	29.91	21.00
SC and ST	14.30	16.13	33.33	31.25	30.43	8.55	12.00
Muslims	21.40	0	0	0	0	4.27	1.00
Unknown	0	9.67	20.00	12.50	17.39	8.55	4.00
TOTAL	100.00	99.98	99.99	100.00	99.98	99.99	100.00
	(N=14)	(N=31)	(N=15)	(N=16)	(N=23)	(N=117)	(N=100)

Source: Author's fieldwork.
Note: * Includes Jats and Bhumihars.

The change that came with the victory of the Janata Dal in 1989 was not as marked as one would have expected it to be. Though the percentage of upper castes fell to 50 per cent, the proportion of OBC was not marked by a corresponding rise. The main factor for that probably is that the Janata Dal government was indebted to the BJP for its support. In addition, it still relied on the legacies of Charan Singh and the socialists, each leading it in two opposite directions: the Jats and the upper castes. Nevertheless, Mulayam Singh's government constitutes the first foray of the backward castes into power politics since Charan Singh. In the long run, this government provided a model for other parties to apply with more or less conviction. After 1989, the percentage of OBC in government did not go back to the pre-Janata Dal numbers.

In U.P., much of the political assertion of the backward castes is due to the Yadav caste's mobilisation. The rise to power of Mulayam Singh Yadav in 1989 and again in 1993 was largely due to the support of his own caste. It was a support he was quick to acknowledge by promoting an openly pro-Yadav reservation policy in the administration (see Jaffrelot and Zérinini-Brotel 2004). A one-caste man, Mulayam Singh can be held responsible both for centralising the Yadav political mobilisation and alienating other backward castes displeased by his one-sided favouritism. Kurmis in particular, in spite of the token-like presence of Beni Prasad Verma, are not strong supporters of the SP. In 1993, they accounted for 7.3 per cent of the party's MLAs as against 34.5 per cent for Yadavs. At that time, there were more Kurmis elected on BJP tickets than on SP's. The fact was confirmed in 1996 when even the BSP had more Kurmi MLAs than the SP. The centrality of the Yadavs in the development of the SP's base has in turn provided the BJP with an answer to the rise of OBC, and in that process to the dominance of Yadavs.

One of the reasons for the success of the BJP in U.P. is the division of the OBC, and to a lesser extent of the SC. In 1991, the BJP allotted portfolios to as many as 19.35 per cent of OBC. This is reminiscent of the share of OBC in the Jana Sangh. The 1991 campaign was dominated by the issue of the Babri Masjid and by the communal mobilisation generated by the BJP. Out of the whole of the BJP's OBC candidates, only 46.3 per cent were elected. The figures compares badly to the 51.5 per cent of Brahmin, 61.5 per cent of Baniya or even 47.1 per cent of Rajput BJP candidates returned. While the situation changed in the mid-1990s, with more OBC candidates returned than upper castes, in 1991, the BJP's nomination of several backward caste legislators in the government cannot be interpreted as a necessity but as an attempt to placate them and keep them part of the Hindutva flock.

After 1991, the hypothesis that all parties had to give increased political space to OBC is confirmed by the two BJP governments of 1997–99, led by Kalyan Singh; then, the one led in 2000–02 by the former BJP State Executive President, Rajnath Singh, a Thakur. The dismissal of Kalyan Singh has not meant that the BJP is turning its back on the OBC. In fact, the one lesson all parties have had to learn since the late 1960s is that the evolution of U.P.'s political scene has made it compulsory for any party hopeful of winning the elections to nominate OBC candidates and integrate them inside the party within the limits of its own ideological set-up. In 1993 and 1996, the proportion of OBC MLAs in the Assembly was about 25 per cent and 33 per cent respectively. The share of OBC ministers in Rajnath Singh's government was of 21 per cent.

The core issue of power-sharing must be examined beyond the acknowledged position of OBC in representational politics (as MLAs or as ministers) to see the impact, if any, that power-sharing has on the structure of political parties.

While the Congress has not been able to take advantage of the divisions within the OBC 'social category', the BJP has made an effort through its policy of 'social engineering' to bring into its fold other backward castes which resent the position of Yadavs as also the Jats, and who are unhappy to have been excluded from the OBC category. More recently, Rajnath Singh's announcement that reservations would be introduced for Most Backward Castes (MBC) within the global OBC quota must be seen as another attempt to expand among this sub-group. MBCs are little represented in other parties, including the BSP, and do not side either with SC or with OBC. The BJP has targeted them as a potential vote bank since the early 1990s, a strategy which has paid good returns.

In other words, the divisions inside the OBC category in U.P. have had a twofold, virtually contradictory, impact on politics. On the one hand, they have helped to increase the representation of the lower castes by having a dominant OBC community — the Yadavs — spur counter-mobilisation — from Kurmis and Lodhis — through somewhat unexpected vehicles as the BJP. On the other hand, the competitive mobilisation exacerbated the cleavages between the backward castes, and the BJP instrumental-ised their rivalries with a view to divide and rule.

The BJP has promoted non-Yadav OBC leaders — and more especially, a Lodhi, Kalyan Singh — in order to broaden its base (in the post-Mandal context when the low-caste mobilisation was at its peak) and in order to hinder the formation of an OBC front. Kalyan Singh was promoted as an OBC leader and he became the architect of the BJP's strategy of relative mandalisation in U.P. Yet the changes did not go as deep as the composition of the party machine.

While the upper caste dimension of the BJP of U.P. clearly comes out of the social profile of its MLAs, it is even more obvious from that of its cadres, which shows an even more upper caste profile than the Congress in the 1990s. The gap is best seen in the case of the executive committee in charge at the time of Kalyan Singh's chief ministership. While OBC had gained visibility as cabinet ministers and even more as state secretaries, during the same period their presence in the party's decision-making organs remained minimal.

In 1998–99, it was considered in the BJP that Kalyan Singh's growing freedom towards the party and establishment of an OBC-lobby had to be controlled. The figures in Table 1.15 tend to show that Kalyan Singh's

Table 1.15
Composition of the BJP's State Executive in U.P., 1998–99 (%)

Upper Castes	Intermediary Castes	OBC	SC	Muslims	Sikhs	Sadhus	Unidentified	TOTAL
65.5	3.8	21.9	6.1	1.1	0.5	0.5	0.5	100 (N=183)

Source: Author's fieldwork.

freedom was anything but complete, with more than 65 per cent of the positions in the party given to upper caste members. In the BJP, the rise of the backward castes has been circumscribed to positions that are endowed with visibility but are not at the centre of the party's decision-making process.

Intra-party positions are crucial to the endurance of a party's identity. They can certainly be considered as more critical than the designation of election candidates. With the increased competition in politics and the necessity for large private campaign funding, parties have selected candidates notable for their personal wealth or aura rather than for long-term (ideological or organisational) association with the party they come to represent. On the opposite, party workers are in direct relation to the higher authorities and need to be ideologically closer. This distinction is especially important in the case of the BJP whose key party workers come from the Rashtriya Swayam Sevak Sangh (RSS). The dismissal of Kalyan Singh and the removal of the high-profile Dalit Governor, Suraj Bhan, who had been hailed by the BJP in an attempt to counter the BSP, are both setbacks to the democratisation of the BJP. They reaffirm the party's limits in its integration of backward and SC. In fact, the BJP's attitude can be compared to the Congress' pragmatism towards Muslims and SC in the 1950s and 1960s. The necessity to nominate them and have them inside the party is recognised but this in turn conflicts with the control of power.

The future of the BJP — as well as the Congress' — in U.P. remains tied to their ability to open their inner political space to backward castes and SC. The BJP is in a less fragile position. The Congress has very little chance of success until it comes face to face with the urge to reform.

The SP and the BSP are in a different position with a hardcore of voters likely to side with the party whichever the circumstances. Their future is therefore linked to their expanding beyond this group and being recognised as the dominant component of future governmental coalitions. SP's opposition to the BJP makes it more difficult for it to find suitable partners than for the BSP, whose 'practical' side has made it side with the BJP three times already. In addition, from a sociological point of view, the association of OBC with upper castes or with SC remains problematic because of their often tense relations in the countryside. In fact, BSP's path seems more prone to changes than the SP's. Since 1993, the caste and community identity of BSP's MLAs has widely varied. In fact, while the SP has remained centred around its Yadav–Muslim axis, BSP has tried to put together various alliances, reflected in the choice of its candidates.

In fact, in 1993, BSP had no upper caste MLAs. Its representatives came, virtually in the same proportions, from the OBC and the SC. By the next elections, its alliance with the Congress party and the departure of Kurmis had made it change its strategy and nominate upper caste candidates. That year, nearly 15 per cent of the party's MLAs were from upper castes. The proportion of OBC MLAs had remained almost the same at 37 per cent. The rise in upper caste MLAs had been achieved at the expense of SC whose share in the party's representation in the Assembly had gone down to 30 per cent. The BSP's adaptation to the post-Congress dominance in U.P. pushes it to evolve tactical changes virtually with each election. Its hold on the SC electorate makes it possible for upper caste or OBC candidates to be elected simply because they have received BSP tickets. In comparison, the SP appears to be more rigid and with less possibilities of expansion or association with other parties. In a long-term perspective, the BSP seems to be endowed with the greatest potential, both because of its hold on its electorate and because of its ability to adapt.

The constraints of the BJP's ideological frame have been apparent since 1993. The party is now in a difficult situation and has only two solutions: a return to religious mobilisation or a dilution of Hindutva in order to appeal to larger sections of the electorate. The Gujarat elections in December 2002 and the turn taken by the Rajasthan and Madhya Pradesh electoral campaigns in early 2003 point to the first path.

References

Brass, Paul R. 1980. 'The Politicization of the Peasantry in a North Indian State — Part II', *Journal of Peasant Studies*, 8(1): 3–36.

———. 1985. *Caste, Faction, and Party in Indian Politics*, vol. 1. New Delhi: Chanakya Press.

Government of Uttar Pradesh. 1977. 'Sabse Pichre Varg Ayog ki Sanstutiyan ka Sankshipta Vivran'. Lucknow: Most Backward Classes Commission.

Graham, Bruce. 1986. 'The Candidate-Selection Policies of the INC, 1952–1969', *Journal of Commonwealth and Comparative Politics*, 24(2): 197–218.

Hasan, Zoya. 1989. 'Power and Mobilization: Patterns of Resilience and Change in Uttar Pradesh', in Francine Frankel and M. S. A. Rao (eds), *Dominance and State Power in Modern India*, pp. 133–203. Delhi: Oxford University Press.

Jaffrelot, C. 2003. *India's Silent Revolution: The Rise of the Lower Castes*. London: Hurst.

———. 2007. 'Caste and the Rise of Marginalized Groups', in S. Ganguly, L. Diamond and M. Plattner (eds), *The State of Indian Democracy*, pp. 67–88. Baltimore and Washington: The Johns Hopkins University Press.

Jaffrelot, C. and Jasmine Zérinini-Brotel. 2004. 'Post-"Mandal" Politics in Uttar Pradesh and Madhya Pradesh', in Rob Jenkins (ed.), *Regional Reflections: Comparing Politics Across India's States*, pp. 139–74. New Delhi: Oxford University Press.

Kaviraj, S. 2000. 'Democracy and Social Inequality', in F. Frankel, R. Bhargava, Zoya Hasan and B. Arora (eds), *Transforming India: Social and Political Dynamics of Democracy*, pp. 89–119. Delhi: Oxford University Press.

Meyer, Richard. 1969. 'The Political Elite in an Under-Developed Society: The Case of Uttar Pradesh in India'. PhD dissertation. Department of Political Science, University of Pennsylvania.

Rudolph, Lloyd and Suzanne Hoeber Rudolph. (1969) 1987. *The Modernity of Tradition: Political Development in India*. Chicago: University of Chicago Press.

Schwartzberg, J. 1965. 'The Distribution of Selected Castes in the North Indian Plains', *The Geographical Review*, 55: 477–95.

Who's Who in U.P. Vidhan Sabha. 1952–2002. Lucknow: Vidhan Sabha Secretariat.

Yadav, Y. 1999. 'Electoral Politics in the Time of Change: India's Third Electoral System, 1989–99', *Economic and Political Weekly*, 34 (34–35): 2393–99.

2

Bihar: The New Stronghold of OBC Politics

Cyril Robin

In the Hindi belt, Bihar has experienced, as any other state, the crucial role played by the electoral system in loosening the rigid hierarchical structure of status and power in the traditional social order and promoting political integration within the framework of secular authority (Krishna 1967). But, observers pay less attention to changes within the Bihar society (known as the poorest, most criminalised and most backward state in India), than to indicators of persisting under-development.

Yet, from the point of view of the gradual political empowerment of the backward classes, Bihar can be considered as the most 'progressive' state of the Hindi belt.[1] The percentage of upper caste MPs returned from Bihar has declined from 56.4 in 1952 to 27.5 per cent in 2004 whereas the share of the OBC MPs has jumped from 5.5 in 1952 to 37.5 per cent in 2004. As a result, Bihar is the only state of India whose government has been headed by an OBC leader for more than 15 years without any major interruption.[2]

This chapter attempts to explain the rise of the lower castes in Bihar starting with the historical trajectory of the state. As a result, it deals with Bihar in its two successive incarnations, before and after the creation of Jharkhand in 2000.

Yadavs of Bihar and Tribals of Jharkhand: A Peculiar Social Profile

In Bihar, according to the Census of 1931, the upper castes constitute 13.7 per cent of the state population (5 per cent Brahmins, 3 per cent

---

[1] In this chapter, the terms 'Backward Classes', and 'lower castes', refer only to the Other Backward Classes (OBC) (see Verna 2005).

[2] During the 15 years of Laloo–Rabri regime, two spells of President's Rule have been imposed from 28 March 1995 to 4 April 1995, and subsequently from 12 February 1999 to 9 March 1999.

Bhumihars, 4.4 per cent Rajputs and 1.2 per cent Kayasthas). So far as the lower castes are concerned, two groups need to be distinguished. The upper OBC represented 20.3 per cent of the state population (11.7 per cent Yadavs, 4.4 per cent Koeris, 3.5 per cent Kurmis and 0.6 per cent Baniyas).[3] Their significance derived from their numbers, from their control over small and medium landholdings and from their not so low standing in the caste hierarchy: they therefore form the elite of the OBC. The lower OBC represent 18.2 per cent of the state population, but they are more fragmented than the Backward Castes. Finally, the Scheduled Castes (SC) represented 16 per cent of the state population and the Scheduled Tribes (ST), 10.1 per cent.

The relative numerical weakness of the upper castes is compensated by their ritual and socio-economic status: Brahmins, Kayasthas, Rajputs and Bhumihars still today own most of the land. They are also well-represented in the bureaucracy and continue to play a significant role in politics.

Bihar stands as an exception in terms of caste arithmetic in the entire range of the Hindi belt because of the large proportion of the Yadavs. In no other state of north India does an OBC caste represent more than 11 per cent of the population. And Yadavs are ever in a larger number in post-2000 Bihar with almost 15 per cent of the total population.

In comparison, the Jats in Rajasthan represent 9.2 per cent of the Rajasthani population and the Yadavs of Uttar Pradesh and Madhya Pradesh 8 and 5 per cent of the population respectively. By contrast, the SC account for about 10 per cent and are very fragmented: none of the castes of this category represented even 5 per cent of the state population in 1931. Yet, in north Bihar, the Chamars and the Dusadhs respectively accounted for 5.5 per cent and 5.7 per cent of the population;[4] in south Bihar the Dusadhs represented 6.9 per cent of the population.[5]

---

[3] The term 'upper OBC' (OBC (U)) corresponds to the Backward Castes (BC) listed in the Annexure II of the Mungeri Lal Commission report on Backward Classes in Bihar. The term 'lower OBC' (OBC (L)) corresponds to the Extremely Backward Castes (EBC) listed in the Annexure I of the Mungeri Lal Commission report.

[4] North Bihar, in the year 2001, comprised the districts of Saran, East Champaran, West Champaran, Muzaffarpur, Darbhanga, Bhagalpur, Purnea, Gopalganj, Siwan, Vaishali, Saharsa, Madhepura, Araria, Kishanganj, Katihar, Banka, Supaul, Sheohar, Sitamarhi, Samastipur and Madhubani.

[5] South Bihar, in the year 2001, comprised the districts of Patna, Gaya, Monghyr, Buxar, Bhabhua, Rohtas, Aurangabad, Jehanabad, Nalanda, Jamui, Sheikhpura, Nawada, Khagaria, Bhojpur, Begusarai and Lakhisarai.

Table 2.1
Caste Composition of Bihar (subregion-wise) (%)

Castes and Communities	Bihar in 1931				
	North Bihar	South Bihar	First Total	Chhota Nagpur Plateau[b]	TOTAL
Upper Caste	**16.1**	**19.9**	**17.7**	**3.9**	**13.7**
Brahmin	6.7	5.8	6.4	1.7	5.0
Bhumihar	3.0	6.2	4.1	0.4	3.0
Rajput	5.0	6.2	5.7	1.3	4.4
Kayastha	1.4	1.7	1.5	0.5	1.2
Backward Castes	**24.3**	**27.4**	**24.8**	**9.4**	**20.2**
Yadav	14.0	15.7	14.6	4.7	11.7
Kurmi	3.5	4.4	3.8	2.9	3.5
Koeri	5.3	6.3	5.7	1.4	4.4
Baniya	0.5	1.0	0.7	0.4	0.6
Extremely Backward Castes	**22.2**	**20.3**	**21.3**	**10.2**	**18.2**
Barhi	0.9	1.7	1.2	0.6	1.0
Dhanuk	2.9	2.0	2.6	0.2	1.9
Ghatwar	0	0	0	0.6	0.2
Kahar	0.7	4.3	2.0	1.1	1.7
Kamar/Lohar	1.5	1.0	1.3	1.5	1.4
Kandu, Kanu	2.3	2.4	2.4	0.2	1.7
Kewat	1.4	0	0.9	0.1	0.7
Khetauri[a]	0	0	0	0.3	0.1
Kumhar	1.3	1.5	1.4	1.3	1.4
Mali	0.3	0.3	0.3	0.1	0.2
Mallah	3.0	0.7	2.1	0.2	1.6
Nai	1.6	1.9	1.7	0.9	1.5
Tanti	2.6	1.6	2.2	0.7	1.8
Teli	3.4	2.9	3.2	2.2	2.9
Tharu[a]	0.3	0	0.2	0	0.1
Scheduled Castes	**16.9**	**20.8**	**18.3**	**10.6**	**15.9**
Bhogta	0	0.1	0	0.7	0.2
Bhuiya[a]	0.2	2.2	1.0	3.0	1.6
Bhumij[a]	0	0	0	0.8	0.2
Chamar	5.5	4.9	5.3	1.9	4.3
Dhobi	1.1	0.9	1.0	0.5	0.9
Dom	0.4	0.3	0.3	0.7	0.4
Dusadh	5.7	6.2	5.8	0.9	4.4
Ghasi	0	0	0	0.5	0.1
Hari	0.3	0	0.2	0.1	0.1
Musahar	3.2	3.7	3.4	0.2	2.4
Pasi	0.3	1.6	0.8	0.1	0.6
Rajwar	0	0.8	0.3	0.3	0.3

(Table 2.1 continued)

(*Table 2.1 continued*)

Castes and Communities	Bihar in 1931				
	North Bihar	South Bihar	First Total	Chhota Nagpur Plateau[b]	TOTAL
Turi	0	0	0	0.5	0.2
Others	0.2	0.1	0.2	0.4	0.2
Scheduled Tribes	**0.8**	**0.4**	**0.6**	**32.3**	**9.9**
Chero	–	–	–	0.2	0.1
Chik Baraik	–	–	–	0.3	0.1
Gond	–	–	–	0.2	0.1
Ho	–	–	–	3.9	1.2
Kharia	–	–	–	0.9	0.3
Kharwar	–	–	–	0.7	0.2
Khetauri	–	–	–	0.3	0.1
Mahli	–	–	–	0.5	0.2
Mal Paharia	–	–	–	0.4	0.1
Munda	0	0	0	5.4	1.6
Oraon	0.2	0	0.1	6.1	1.9
Santhal	0.6	0.4	0.5	11.9	3.9
Sauria Paharia	–	–	–	0.7	0.2
Others	–	0	0	0.8	0.2
Religious Minorities	**20.5**	**11.1**	**17.0**	**32.4**	**21.3**
Muslims	20.3	10.9	16.8	6.6	13.8
Christians	0.1	0.1	0.1	3.6	1.1
Sikhs	0	0	0	0	0
Others[d]	0.1	0.1	0.1	22.2	6.6
Unidentified	–	–	–	**0.9**	**0.3**
TOTAL	99.8	99.9	99.9	98.9	99.6

Source: Census of India 1931.

Note: [a] Considered as Tribes in the Census 1931.

[b] Chhota Nagpur Plateau (it corresponds to the state of Jharkhand in the year 2001 plus the Manbhum district): Hazaribagh, Ranchi, Palamau, Garhwa, Lohardaga, Kodarma, Giridih, Godda, Sahibganj, Gumla, Pakaur, Chatra, Bokaro, Dhanbad, Deoghar, Dumka, East Singhbhum, West Singhbhum, Saraikela-Kharsawan[c]

[c] Both Saraikela and Kharsawan were former feudatory states and formed a single district only in 1931.

[d] Jains, Buddhists, Zoroastrians, tribal religions.

The most striking difference between post-2000 Bihar and Jharkhand is naturally due to the high proportion of ST in the latter. In 1991, the ST represented 31.3 per cent of the population in the districts which were to form Jharkhand. As a result, the social profile of Jharkhand is even more tribal-dominated than Chhattisgarh; naturally, the upper castes lag behind with a meagre 4 per cent, while the OBC are less than 20 per cent and the SC just above 10 per cent.

Historical Legacies: Peasants' Movements and Semi-feudalism

Post-independence Bihar has inherited from a tradition of mass agitations, many a times in the framework of the freedom movement, or in the form of rural jacqueries. It was witness to numerous isolated cases of peasant uprisings in the 19th and 20th centuries such as the Santhal insurrection of 1855–56 and Indigo riots of 1867, 1877 and 1907. And it is only after the First World War that the radicalisation of the nationalist movement began to draw the rural masses into its fold. Peasants were brought into the nationalist movement in order to make it more broad-based but the movement became also more radical as a result of this addition.

From the late 1920s onwards, peasant movements developed and committed themselves to class struggle against the brazen exploitation of the peasants by the zamindars who were mainly upper caste landowners. In 1929, after having established its presence all over the province, the Kisan Sabha (started in west Patna district in 1927) got upgraded to become the Bihar Pradesh Kisan Sabha (BPKS). It was led by Swami Sahajanand who belonged to the Bhumihar caste and for whom class struggles were the only method to emancipate the masses from bonded labour and other forms of slavery.[6] Under the increasing influence of socialists over the BPKS, Swami Sahajanand developed a more radical discourse against zamindars and declared that 'zamindars formed a parasitic class' (Sharma 1994: 78).

By the late 1930s, when the condition of the cultivators in Bihar had dramatically deteriorated due to a sharp fall in the prices of stable food crops, the BPKS mainly comprised the upper layers of middle peasantry.

---

[6] Before leading the BPKS, between 1914 and 1929, Swami Sahajanand was the Chief of the Bhumihar Brahman Mahasabha, a caste-association for the self-respect and status recognition of Bhumihars as true Brahmins. From 1920, he was also a member of the All Indian Congress Committee and later the Working Committee of the Bihar Provincial Congress Committee.

However it gained momentum and its leaders launched struggles in several districts. Dispossessed tenants forcibly attempted to regain their land. Moreover, as the scope of the struggle widened, it focussed more on economic issues like rent and forced labour. Eventually, it dealt with the much broader issue of the abolition of zamindari system.[7]

The abolition of this system also appeared a necessity to the Congress intelligentsia in order to introduce a new agrarian ethos. Indeed, zamindars neither invested capital for increasing agricultural production nor did they do anything to improve the standard of production. They failed to play the role of rural entrepreneurs, so they were considered to be the main obstacle to progress in agriculture.

In 1950, the abolition of the zamindari system was the first major legislative step achieved by the Congress government in Bihar.[8] The professed objective of this measure was the elimination of all inter-mediaries between the tiller of the land and the state. But, though it altered the agrarian structure of the state, the elimination of the inter-mediaries did not fully take place. Indeed, ex-zamindars were allowed to retain considerable parts of their land. Nevertheless, a significant pro-portion of the tenants of the zamindars emancipated themselves and emerged as middle peasants. Many of them were from the Backward Castes, mostly Yadavs and Kurmis. But in spite of the development of this category of intermediate peasants, land reforms have tended to polarise the society of rural Bihar. Before and after the Land Reform Act was voted, landlords evicted numerous tenants on the ground that they needed the land for 'personal cultivation'. Consequently, 'land reforms have resulted in an increase in the proportion of poor peasants working part-time for wages, of landless labourers and of both rural and urban casual workers and unemployed' (Gough 1974). While the Land Reform Act abolished the intermediaries, it failed to abolish the rent-receiving class. Still today, the ex-zamindars of Bihar are at the helm of the biggest holdings.

---

[7] The zamindars were powerful landowners, recognised as such by the British in exchange for the right to collect taxes in the rural areas, who functioned as inter-mediaries between the peasants and the state. The abolition of the zamindari system sought to do away with their role as tax collecting intermediaries and promote the development of peasant proprietors.

[8] Bihar was the first state to abolish the zamindari system under the Bihar Land Reform Act.

The Rise of the OBC: The Unintended Consequence of Congress Upper Caste Factionalism

Undoubtedly, the freedom movements were instrumental in bringing into the Congress diverse social groups and in integrating them in the pursuit of a common cause. However, the prospect of capturing the power apparatus of the society divided these elements into factions contending for positions of power. The outcome of this factionalism was indiscipline and the emergence of parochial interests in the party (Roy 1966: 707).

As early as the 1920s, the formation of alliances and coalitions emerged as a dominating feature of the party in Bihar and factional rivalries became manifest when the Bihar Congress decided to fight elections in local bodies (*ibid.*: 708).[9] Then, castes became the most important base for formation of these political alignments.

The factional structure of the Bihar Congress relied on caste with, on the one hand, a faction dominated by the Bhumihars, and on the other hand, a faction dominated by the Rajputs. With the elections of 1952, 1957 and 1962, the intensity of factional conflicts among caste-based coalitions gathered momentum: the selection of candidates, the contest for the leadership of the Bihar Congress Legislature Party or the formation of the government constantly giving rise to new groups' rivalries. For instance, after the 1952 elections, the inclusion of M. P. Sinha (a Bhumihar) in the Congress government headed by S. K. Sinha (a Bhumihar) led to the formation of a non-Bhumihar group from the S. K. Sinha faction.

Also, the succession to the leadership of a faction led to the emergence of new groups. For instance, soon after the 1957 elections were over, the death of Anugrah Narain Sinha left his Rajput faction without a leader capable of appealing to and winning support from other communities (*ibid.*: 712). As a consequence, the non-Rajput castes — mainly Brahmin and Kayastha — emerged from it and were reorganised under the leadership of B. N. Jha, a Brahmin.

---

[9] In 1926, Swami Sahajanand commented on the Council elections: 'I can never forget the highly improper behaviour I witnessed at the time of that election. Among other things, factionalism of the most blatant kind characterised all party politics. Even the most prominent Congress leaders were talking and mobilising themselves in terms of caste' (see Swami Sahajanand 1952: 479–80).

However, given the nature of the Congress party system, the swelling factional conflicts never prevented the party from winning the large majority of seats in the elections and, certainly, the upper castes were still able to maintain their dominant position in the state Congress.

Table 2.2
Caste and Community of the Congress MLAs and all MLAs
(in parentheses) in Bihar (%)

	1952		1957		1962	
Upper Castes	**51.1**	**(46.1)**	**46.2**	**(46.1)**	**49.1**	**(46.1)**
Brahmin	13.6	(12.1)	10.1	(10.0)	16.2	(13.8)
Bhumihar	12	(10.0)	13.5	(12.5)	12.4	(8.8)
Bengali	1.2	(1.5)	1.0	(0.6)	1.1	(0.9)
Rajput	13.6	(14.2)	16.8	(17.2)	15.1	(19.1)
Kayastha	10.7	(8.2)	4.8	(5.6)	4.3	(3.4)
Backward Castes	**18.0**	**(19.4)**	**19.6**	**(18.8)**	**23.8**	**(23.5)**
Yadav	6.6	(7.9)	5.3	(6.6)	7.6	(9.4)
Kurmi	4.1	(3.6)	3.8	(3.8)	5.4	(4.4)
Koeri	3.7	(4.5)	6.7	(5.3)	6.5	(6.0)
Baniya	4.5	(3.3)	3.8	(3.1)	4.3	(3.8)
Extremely Backward Castes	**0.8**	**(1.2)**	**0.5**	**(0.6)**	**0.5**	**(0.9)**
Scheduled Castes	**16.1**	**(13.9)**	**18.3**	**(14.7)**	**16.8**	**(13.2)**
Scheduled Tribes	**2.4**	**(10.9)**	**3.8**	**(11.3)**	**1.6**	**(9.1)**
Santhal	1.2	(2.7)	1.4	(2.2)	0.5	(0.6)
Munda	–	(1.2)	–	(0.9)	–	(0.6)
Oraon	–	(0.6)	–	(0.9)	–	(0.6)
Others	1.2	(6.4)	2.4	(7.2)	1.1	(7.2)
Religious Minorities	**9.9**	**(7.6)**	**11.1**	**(8.2)**	**8.1**	**(7.2)**
Muslims	9.9	(7.6)	11.1	(7.8)	8.1	(6.6)
Christian	–	–	–	(0.3)	–	(0.6)
Unidentified	**0.4**	**(0.9)**	**0.5**	**(0.3)**	**–**	**–**
TOTAL	98.8		100		99.9	
	(N=242 (330))		(N=208 (319))		(N=185 (319))	

Source: Survey by author.

But, the representation of the higher castes among Congress MLAs declined from 51.2 per cent in 1952 to 49.2 per cent in 1962. In the Vidhan Sabha, the percentage of these caste groups was 46.1 per cent of all the MLAs.

The lower castes remained a neglected lot which was used to fill in the lack of numerical strength of the upper caste dominated factions in a clientelistic framework: their leaders were co-opted to mobilise various caste groups in favour of the ruling castes especially at the time of elections. But this arrangement contributed to their promotion, especially when faction fights became more intense within the Congress.

The percentage of upper OBC MLAs increased by 4.1 percentage points between 1957 and 1962. This was an indication of the new strategy of Krishna Ballabh Sahay, the Kayastha leader, at the helm of the former Sinha faction who incorporated in it prominent lower caste leaders like Ram Lakhan Singh Yadav. Indeed, 'as competition for political power intensified, the contending groups (the political factions) had necessarily to look beyond their own caste groups' (Roy 1970: 238) and to co-opt members of castes which were numerically important. Gradually, low caste political leaders built support structures and began to ask for more power.

This tendency of increasing representation of the lower castes in the party may be referred to as a trend towards 'dispersal of inequality' (*ibid.*: 227). This change prepared the ground for the polarisation of Bihar politics between the Forwards and the Backwards. This was especially so after the OBC caste groups understood the advantages they could derive from the introduction of universal suffrage, and, later, from the publication of the Backward Classes Commission Report in 1955, which got the OBC elite to change its emphasis from social activities to political mobilisation (Frankel 1989).[10]

1967: The First Socialists-dominated OBC Mobilisation

In the 1960s, the Socialists were in a position to cash in on the political awareness of the OBC. Socialist leaders of the Kisan Sabha, like Jayaprakash Narayan, Ganga Sharan Sinha, Awadheshwar Prasad Sinha and others, had played a key role in bringing about new consciousness among the peasantry in the decades through 1930s and 1940s. Bihar was the crucible of the socialist movement in India: it was not just by

---

[10] This report which was the result of the appointment of the Kalelkar Commission by the Government of India in January 1953 recommended preferential treatment for members of the Other Backward Classes, especially reservations in professional and technical institutions and the higher ranks of the government services.

chance that the Congress Socialist Party (CSP) was founded in Patna in May 1934. The CSP leaders wanted to focus on the peasants' condition, when the Congress leadership was still rather urban-oriented. According to Narendra Deva, who was one of the prominent Socialist leaders before and after independence, this sociological difference justified the foundation of the CSP: the Congressmen's 'social basis being very narrow they really feel stronger by entertaining the belief that they are acting in interests of society as a whole', but the Congress, according to Deva, badly needed to promote 'an alliance between the lower middle class and the masses' (cited in Jaffrelot 2003: 256–57). For the leaders of the CSP, the masses in question were primarily to be found in the village.

The alliance between the Congress Socialists and the Kisan Sabha then resulted in a strong, class-oriented peasant movement and the two started agitating for the complete abolition of the zamindari system considered as 'an obstacle in the way of economic and social advancement of society' (Sharma 1994: 78). As a consequence, the socialist ideological influence over the Kisan Sabha enhanced the cause of class struggle within the peasant movement and transformed it from a *kisan*-dominated resistance movement into an emancipatory movement for workers of the whole village (Nathan 1996). With the creation of the Socialist Party in 1948, this ideological framework reached its logical political conclusion and allowed people who did not belong to the traditional elite to integrate the political class of the state and to strengthen the democratisation process. Moreover, the Socialists gradually highlighted the importance of caste when it appeared that land reform might not solve all the problems of rural India and that 'in the framework of a democratic system certain sections of the society had to be mobilised' (Jaffrelot 2003: 259).

The first turning point of this process took place during the 1967 elections, as evident from the social profile of the MLAs who were then returned in Bihar. Whereas the percentage of the upper caste MLAs decreased from 46.1 per cent to 44.8 per cent for the first time since 1952, that of the OBC MLAs rose from 23.5 per cent to 26 per cent. This new state of things manifested in the defeat of the Congress,[11]

---

[11] For the first time, the Congress lost elections in as many as nine states, including all northern Indian states.

Table 2.3
Caste and Community of the Congress and of the Samyukta Socialist Party MLAs, and of all MLAs in Bihar in 1967, and in 1969 (in parentheses) (%)

	Congress		Samyukta Socialist Party		Vidhan Sabha	
Upper Castes	**43.8**	**(41.8)**	**42.8**	**(33.3)**	**44.8**	**(42)**
Brahmin	14.1	(15.5)	8.6	(9.3)	11.0	(9.4)
Bhumihar	11.7	(8.2)	11.4	(7.4)	11.6	(10.3)
Bengali	–	–	1.4	(0)	1.9	(2.5)
Rajput	13.3	(17.3)	21.4	(14.8)	17.2	(17.6)
Kayastha	4.7	(0.9)	0	(1.9)	3.1	(2.2)
Backward Castes	**22.7**	**(29.1)**	**40.0**	**(37.0)**	**26.0**	**(27.9)**
Yadav	7.8	(18.2)	22.9	(22.2)	11.6	(15.0)
Kurmi	6.3	(4.5)	1.4	(1.9)	4.1	(2.8)
Koeri	2.3	(0.9)	11.4	(5.6)	4.7	(2.8)
Baniya	6.3	(5.5)	4.3	(7.4)	5.6	(6.3)
Extremely Backward Castes	**0**	**(0.9)**	**1.4**	**(3.7)**	**0.6**	**(0.9)**
Scheduled Castes	**17.2**	**(12.7)**	**12.9**	**(24.1)**	**13.5**	**(14.1)**
Scheduled Tribes	**10.1**	**(5.5)**	**1.4**	**(0)**	**9.1**	**(8.8)**
Santhal	0.80	–	–	–	1.3	(0.9)
Munda	2.3	(0.9)	–	–	1.3	(0.6)
Oraon	–	–	–	–	0.3	(1.3)
Other	7.0	(4.5)	1.4	(0)	6.3	(6.0)
Religious Minorities	**6.3**	**(10)**	**1.4**	**(1.9)**	**5.9**	**(6.3)**
Muslim	6.3	(10)	1.4	(0.9)	5.6	(6.0)
Christian	–	–	–	–	0.3	(0.3)
TOTAL	100.1		99.9		99.9	
	(N=128 (110))		(N=70 (54))		(N= 319 (319))	

Source: Survey by author.

which was able to secure only 128 seats instead of 185 in 1962, and by the rise of the Samyukta Socialist Party (SSP) which won 70 seats out of which 28 were secured by (upper) Shudras.[12]

The architect of the success of the political mobilisation of the OBC and the emergence of the SSP as a strong political force was Ram Manohar Lohia. Unlike the Praja Socialist Party (PSP), which showed little interest in uplifting the lower castes, the SSP, under the leadership of Lohia, had already recognised that the Backward Classes could

---

[12] The Samyukta Socialist Party was created in 1964 after the reunification of the Praja Socialist Party founded in 1954 and the Socialist Party launched in 1956 by Lohia.

provide an important source of support in the opposition's efforts to unseat the Congress because caste conflicts have as much relevance as class struggles in the Indian context.

In 1967, the OBC MLAs constituted 40 per cent of the SSP's elected members and among them 22.9 per cent were Yadavs. Within the Vidhan Sabha, the Yadavs emerged as the second largest group, equal to Bhumihars, with 11.6 per cent, after the Rajputs (17.2 per cent). The largest groups of OBC MLAs, comprising the Yadavs, the Koeris and the Kurmis, belonged to the upper layer of the OBC; they were the ones who had benefited from the land reforms and had become landowners.

In spite of their increasing share in the Vidhan Sabha, the MLAs of the OBC category were more under-represented in the Samyukta Vidhayak Dal government[13] headed by Mahamaya Prasad Sinha (a Kayastha) than in the K. B. Sahay government formed after B. N. Jha's resignation in 1963 under the Kamaraj Plan.[14] But, given the instability of the Samyukta Vidhayak Dal (SVD) due to coalition politics based on narrow political gains, the first non-Congress government fell in January 1968. Thus, a Congress-backed Shoshit Dal government was formed in February with Bindeshwari Prasad Mandal (a Yadav) as chief minister.[15] For the first time, a ministry was characterised by a number of OBC larger than that of the upper castes. But, a group of defectors from the Congress, headed by B. N. Jha (a Brahmin), led to the fall of the Shoshit Dal government. Finally, the upper caste MLAs tended to restore the old 'coalition of extremes' pattern at the expense of the OBC with the formation of a new Congress-supported government under the chief ministership of Bhola Paswan Shastri (a Harijan); after three months and new acts of defection, Bihar was placed under President's Rule from June 1968 to February 1969.

---

[13] None of the opposition parties was in a position to form a government on its own strength. The result was the formation of a ruling coalition led by the Samyukta Socialist Party, the Samyukta Vidhayak Dal, or United Legislators' Party.

[14] The Kamaraj Plan refers to the strategy under which senior leaders holding offices of power were asked to quit and take up organisational work. This plan meant to strengthen and reform the Congress party, to checkmate Nehru's rivals in the Congress.

[15] The Shoshit Dal was created by B. P. Mandal in 1967 and was constituted, in the very beginning, by 25 former members of the Samyukta Vidhayak Dal.

Table 2.4
Caste Category Composition of Nine Major Successive Governments in Bihar (%)

Caste Categories	B. N. Jha 1962	K. B. Sahay 1963	M. P. Sinha 1967–68	B. P. Mandal 1968	B. P. Shastri 1968	Harihar Singh 1969	D. P. Rai 1970	Karpoori Thakur 1970–71	B. P. Shastri 1971
Upper Castes	58	40	57	23	54	42	26	36	45
Backward Castes	8	20	20	31	14	25	35	28	20
Extremely Backward Castes	0	0	5	3	0	0	3	4	0
Scheduled Castes	14	15	5	9	8	9	13	9	17
Scheduled Tribes	7	10	0	17	8	15	16	9	9
Muslims	10	10	5	11	8	9	6	8	9
Unidentified	3	5	8	6	8	0	0	6	0
TOTAL	(N=28)	(N=20)	(N=21)	(N=35)	(N=13)	(N=33)	(N=31)	(N=53)	(N=35)

Source: Blair (1980) and Rai and Pandey (1981: 55).

After the first phase of 'non-Congressism' from March 1967 to June 1968 and a spell of President's Rule, a mid-term poll was held in February 1969. If the elections failed to provide a stable majority government, the political empowerment of Backward Castes reached a new threshold. In the aftermath of the Socialists' OBC mobilisation in the 1967 elections, the Congress party nominated a larger number of OBC. As a result, the candidate share of the party MLAs belonging to the OBC increased by 7.3 percentage points, from 22.7 per cent to 30 per cent, and in the Vidhan Sabha the representation of the OBC MLAs rose by 2.2 percentage point, from 26.6 per cent to 28.8 per cent. This siseable presence of the Backward Castes in the Vidhan Sabha, and in the Congress, resulted in the rise of the number of OBC in the Congress-led coalition government headed by Harihar Singh (a Rajput).

But, the continuous political instability in Bihar entailed the collapse of the Harihar Singh ministry and the imposition of a second spell of President's rule from June 1969 to February 1970.[16] Then, a Congress(R)-led coalition comprising six parties headed by Daroga Prasad Rai (a Yadav) formed the government and, for the second time, the share of OBC ministers was larger than the proportion of the upper castes.[17] Indeed, the split in the Indian National Congress created new opportunities for the Backward Classes after K. B. Sahay, M. P. Sinha and S. N. Sinha left Mrs Gandhi's Congress(R) to join the 'Syndicate'-led Congress(O) (Frankel 1989). Besides, the Daroga Prasad Rai government appointed a Backward Classes Commission which was to put forward recommendations for reservations in educational institutions and government services in favour of the OBC.[18] Therefore, out of 23 Congress(R) ministers, 10 belonged to the Backward Castes and only five were from the upper castes. Thus, the new strategy of the Congress played a very significant role during and after the 1969 mid-term elections in increasing the number of OBC both in the Legislative Assembly and in the government.

---

[16] Between the fall of the Harihar Singh government and the second President's Rule, Bhola Paswan Shastri formed a nine-day government with an equal number of backward castes and upper castes (see Mishra 1986: 155–57).

[17] The Congress (R) ('R' for ruling) and the Congress (O) ('O' for Organisation) emerged from the Congress party after the split of the Congress Working Committee in November 1969.

[18] This Commission was headed by Mungeri Lal, a former general secretary of the BPCC and minister who belonged to the Dusadh community (Scheduled Castes).

But, the fall of the seventh government since the fourth General Elections, and the third after the mid-term poll, led to the formation of another non-Congress(R) government. This fourth, Samyukta Vidhayak Dal ministry, in spite of the appointment of Karpoori Thakur (a Nai, from Extremely Backward Castes) as chief minister, was characterised by a new drop in the representation of the Backward Classes as evident from Table 2.4. This new downward trend for the OBC increased in the Congress(R)-led Progressive Vidhayak Dal government headed by Bhola Paswan Shastri and was to the benefit of the upper castes and the Scheduled Castes. This return of the 'coalition of extremes' was consummated by the comeback of the Congress in 1972 and the strengthening of the Brahmins' position inside the party (the Congress(R)).

Table 2.5
Caste and Community of the Congress MLAs and of all the MLAs in Bihar, 1972 (%)

	Congress Party	Vidhan Sabha
Upper Castes	41.6	42.8
Brahmin	14.4	11.0
Bhumihar	9.4	10.4
Rajput	16.1	17.6
Kayastha	1.1	1.3
Others	0.6	2.5
Backward Castes	22.2	24.9
Yadav	8.3	11.0
Kurmi	5.6	6.0
Koeri	3.9	4.1
Baniya	4.4	3.8
Extremely Backward Castes	1.1	0.9
Scheduled Castes	15.0	13.8
Scheduled Tribes	9.5	8.9
Santhal	0.6	1.3
Munda	1.1	1.3
Oraon	0.6	0.6
Others	7.2	5.7
Religious Minorities	10.6	8.5
Muslim	10.6	8.2
Christian	–	0.3
Unidentified	–	0.3
TOTAL	99.9	100.1
	(N=180)	(N=318)

Source: Survey by author.

After the victory of the Congress in the 1972 elections, the share of the Brahmin MLAs rose from 9.4 to 11 per cent whereas the share of the OBC MLAs declined by 3 percentage points. The Brahmins came to represent the second largest group in the Vidhan Sabha, after the Rajputs (17.6 per cent) and equalled with the Yadavs who lost 4 percentage points compared to 1967.

This over-domination of the upper castes in the Legislative Assembly was also found at the governmental level. The successive chief ministers — Kedar Pandey (a Brahmin), Abdul Ghafoor (a Muslim) and Dr Jagannath Mishra (a Maithil Brahmin) — circumvented the Backward Classes by building up representation for the Forwards at the same time as the proportion of Muslims, SC and ST in the Cabinets increased (Frankel 1989: 101). As a result, the percentage of the (upper) Backward Classes did not exceed 25 per cent and the share of the upper castes always remained above 40 per cent in the different Cabinets till 1977 and the victory of the Janata Party.

The Janata Phase: The Second Milestone

Following the student-led Gujarat uprising in January 1974 for the resignation of the Congress chief minister, students in Bihar mobilised for the resignation of the Ghafoor ministry and dissolution of the state Assembly for their failure to maintain law and order (Frankel 1989: 102). After Jayaprakash Narayan (also known as J.P.) assumed the leadership of the movement, large-scale demonstrations and huge protest meetings were organised in several states. In Bihar, as in other states, the central government deployed thousands of security forces and finally imposed an internal Emergency on 26th June 1975.

During the 19 months of Emergency, an anti-Congress wave grew in most parts of India. This feeling transcended rivalries between Forward Castes and Backward Classes who joined together in an 'all-out war' against Mrs Indira Gandhi (Frankel 1989: 106). Moreover, in Bihar, the then Chief Minister Jagannath Mishra ignored the final report of the (Mungeri Lal) Backward Classes Commission and opposed the introduction of reservations for OBC. In the state, this attitude resulted in an unprecedented alienation of the masses from the ruling party.

With the announcement on 18th January 1977 that elections to the Lok Sabha would be held in March, the J. P. movement (Congress(O), the Jana Sangh, the Bharatiya Lok Dal and the Socialists) constituted a joint electoral party: the Janata Party (Frankel 1989: 105). The same year, in June, the Janata won 212 out of 325 seats in the Bihar Legislative Assembly. Ten years after the SVD victory, the year 1977 marked the second turning point in the democratisation of the social profile of the Bihar Vidhan Sabha: with 40.6 per cent of the total, the upper caste MLAs reached their lowest percentage since 1952 while the share of the (upper) Backwards reached 27.7 per cent, one of their highest percentages.

Table 2.6
Caste and Community of the Opposition Parties, of the Janata Party MLAs and of all the MLAs in Bihar, 1977 (%)

	Opposition Parties*	Janata Party	Vidhan Sabha
Upper Castes	35.4	43.4	40.8
Brahmin	11.5	4.7	7.1
Bhumihar	9.7	10.4	10.2
Rajput	12.4	21.7	18.5
Kayastha	–	4.2	2.8
Other	1.8	2.4	2.2
Backward Castes	34.6	24.0	27.7
Yadav	20.4	12.7	15.4
Kurmi	5.3	2.8	3.7
Koeri	6.2	3.8	4.6
Baniya	2.7	4.7	4
Extremely Backward Castes	0.9	0.5	0.6
Scheduled Castes	8.0	17.0	13.8
Scheduled Tribes	8.9	8.5	8.5
Santhal	0.9	1.4	1.2
Munda	1.8	–	0.6
Oraon	0.9	1.4	1.2
Other	5.3	5.7	5.5
Religious Minorities	11.5	6.1	8
Muslim	10.6	6.1	7.7
Christian	0.9	–	0.3
Unidentified	0.9	0.5	0.6
TOTAL	100.2	100.0	100.0
	(N=113)	(N=212)	(N=325)

Source: Survey by author.

Note: * Opposition parties include Akhil Bharatiya Jharkhand Party, Communist Party of India, Communist Party of India (Marxist), Indian National Congress, Independent, Jharkhand, Samyukta Socialist Dal.

However, in contrast to what happened in Uttar Pradesh, the Janata Party's MLAs did not appear as more plebeian than the average. Indeed, the caste composition of the party MLAs was characterised by the over-representation of the upper castes with 43.4 per cent. So the decline of the upper castes' representation among the MLAs was largely due to the opposition parties.

Yet, the Janata Party appointed Karpoori Thakur as chief minister and formed an OBC-oriented government. Indeed, his government was constituted by 34 per cent of Backward Castes (40 per cent for all the OBC), 32 per cent of upper castes, 6 per cent of Muslims, 11 per cent of SC and 6 per cent of ST. In addition, Karpoori Thakur decided to implement the recommendation of the State Backward Classes Commission regarding reservations of 25 per cent of the administrative posts for the OBC.

As a result, the upper caste supporters of the Janata Party, who came massively from the Jana Sangh, tried to destabilise Thakur's government. They succeeded in overthrowing it in April 1979. Subsequently, Ram Sundar Das, a Dalit, was promoted by the Congress For Democracy party of Jagjivan Ram and Jana Sangh leaders to restore the old 'coalition of extremes'. In this government, the upper castes received 40 per cent of the ministerial posts, while the Backward Castes were pushed back to 22 per cent.

Congress Domination in the 1980s: The Triumph of the Coalition of Extremes

While the percentage of the upper castes MLAs decreased by 4 percentage points between 1977 and 1980 and that of the Backward Castes increased by 1.2 percentage points in the Vidhan Sabha, the caste composition of the Congress(I) MLAs was over-dominated by the upper castes with 44.2 per cent of the total as against 17.9 per cent for the upper OBC.

In that way, as in 1977, it was not the caste structure of the winning party which influenced the caste composition of the Vidhan Sabha but that of the major parties of the opposition with 44.4 per cent of upper OBC and only 25.9 per cent of upper caste MLAs.

Indeed, the caste composition of two of the three principal parties of the opposition, the Janata Party (Secular) (JP(S)) and the Communist Party of India (CPI), shows that the share of the Backward Castes among their MLAs was larger than in Congress(I) (see Table 2.7). However, we can observe some disparities between the caste composition in the Bharatiya Janata Party and that of the CPI and JP(S) especially regarding the share of the Backward Castes.

Table 2.7
Caste and Community of the Opposition Parties MLAs, the Congress MLAs, and all the MLAs in Bihar, 1980 (%)

	Opposition Parties*	Congress	Vidhan Sabha
Upper Castes	**25.9**	**44.2**	**36.5**
Brahmin	4.4	17.9	12.3
Bhumihar	5.9	12.6	9.8
Rajput	10.4	12.1	11.4
Kayastha	3	1.1	1.8
Other	2.2	0.5	1.2
Backward Castes	**44.4**	**17.8**	**29.0**
Yadav	23.7	6.8	13.8
Kurmi	9.6	3.7	6.2
Koeri	5.9	0.5	2.8
Baniya	5.2	6.8	6.2
Extremely Backward Castes	**0.7**	**2.1**	**1.5**
Scheduled Castes	**11.9**	**16.3**	**14.5**
Scheduled Tribes	**8.9**	**8.5**	**8.6**
Santhal	2.2	1.1	1.5
Munda	–	0.5	0.3
Oraon	–	1.1	0.6
Other	6.7	5.8	6.2
Religious Minorities	**7.3**	**11.1**	**9.5**
Muslim	5.9	11.1	8.9
Christian	0.7	–	0.3
Sikh	0.7	–	0.3
Unidentified	**0.7**	**–**	**0.3**
TOTAL	99.8	100.1	99.9
	(N=135)	(N=190)	(N=325)

Source: Survey by author.

Note: * Opposition parties include Bharatiya Janata Party, Indian National Congress (U), Communist Party of India, Communist Party Marxist, Janata Party (Secular)-Charan Singh, Independent, Janata Party (JP), Jharkhand Mukti Morcha, Janata Party (Secular)-Raj Narain.

Table 2.8
Caste and Community of the BJP, CPI and JP(S) MLAs in Bihar, 1980 (%)

	Bharatiya Janata Party	Communist Party of India	Janata Party (Secular)	Total
Upper Castes	39.0	21.6	9.3	19.2
Brahmin	16.7	4.3	2.3	6.0
Bhumihar	–	13.0		3.6
Rajput	16.7	–	4.7	6.0
Kayastha	5.6	–	2.3	2.4
Other	–	4.3	–	1.2
Backward Castes	27.9	47.7	62.8	51.3
Yadav	16.7	21.7	41.9	31.0
Kurmi	5.6	4.3	11.6	8.3
Koeri	5.6	13.0	2.3	6.0
Baniya	–	8.7	7.0	6.0
Extremely Backward Castes	–	–	2.3	1.2
Scheduled Castes	5.6	21.7	16.3	15.5
Scheduled Tribes	22.3	4.3	–	6.0
Santhal	5.6	4.3	–	2.4
Other	16.7	–	–	3.6
Religious Minorities	5.6	4.3	9.3	7.2
Muslim	–	4.3	9.3	6.0
Sikh	5.6	–	–	1.2
TOTAL	100.4	99.6	100.0	100.3
	(N=18)	(N=23)	(N=43)	(N=84)

Source: Survey by author.

As it is evident from Table 2.8, the Janata Party (Secular) had become an OBC-dominated party after the 1979 split. Unlike the JP(S), headed by Charan Singh, the Bharatiya Janata Party, formed by a breakaway faction of former members of the Jana Sangh, was still dominated by the upper castes.

But, as Francine Frankel noted about the OBC during the 1980 electoral campaign, 'individual Backward Classes politicians withdrew from almost all parties to assert their own claim to power without considering the effect on the strength of OBC as a group. Once again, members of the OBC competed against each other' (1989: 114). As a result, their lack of sense of belonging to one group, their division among themselves and diverse political parties principally benefited the upper castes. Moreover, in the aftermath of the large victory of the Congress(I), the formation of the Congress government, headed by Jagannath Mishra, reasserted their dominant position.

In the late 1980s, the Janata Dal took shape in Bihar as the political heir of the Janata Party. The victory of the Janata Dal under the leadership of Ram Sundar Das and Laloo Prasad Yadav in Bihar in 1990 was revealing of the disintegration of long-established patterns of vertical mobilisation and highlighted the coalescence of disadvantaged social groups.

The very fact that in 1990 even the Congress(I), notoriously associated with the upper castes, had to nominate a record number of 105 Backward Classes candidates (to confront the Janata Dal OBC candidates), including 80 candidates from the upper OBC, gave an unmistakable signal to the upper castes that the days of their reign were numbered.

The Rise of the Janata Dal to Power: The Third Landmark

The Fall of the Congress Party: Political Power Transferred to the OBC

Although the Congress party won 196 seats out of 325 in the 1985 elections, taking advantage of the sympathy wave for Rajiv Gandhi after the assassination of Indira Gandhi in October 1984, its political future in Bihar was already on a downward trend. Indeed, the Congress leaders in Bihar were unable to substantially modify the caste structure of their party and to select more OBC candidates. As a result, the percentage of the Congress MLAs belonging to the OBC reached its lowest mark since 1952 with 17.3 per cent.

In the early 1990s, the implementation by the V. P. Singh government of the Mandal Commission report regarding reservations for the Socially and Economically Backward Classes led to the polarisation of the Indian society between the pro-Mandal versus the anti-Mandal, i.e., Backwards versus Forwards.[19]

In Bihar, the Mandal affair strengthened the emergence of a secular alternative to the Congress party in the form of the Janata Dal as the

---

[19] Appointed in 1978 by the Janata Party government, and completed two years later and implemented in 1990, the Mandal Commission report called for reserving 27 per cent of all services and public sector undertakings under the central government and 27 per cent of all admissions to institutions of higher education (except in states that have reserved higher percentages for Other Backward Classes members).

Table 2.9

Caste and Community of the Congress MLAs in 1985, of the Janata Dal MLAs in 1990 and 1995, and of all the MLAs (in parentheses) in Bihar (%)

	Congress 1985		Janata Dal 1990		Janata Dal 1995	
Upper Castes	**41.8**	**(38.5)**	**25.6**	**(34.6)**	**16.1**	**(21.8)**
Brahmin	14.3	(10.8)	5.8	(8.3)	2.3	(3.1)
Bhumihar	10.2	(10.5)	5.8	(11.1)	4.0	(5.8)
Rajput	15.3	(14.5)	13.2	(12.7)	9.8	(9.5)
Kayastha	0.5	(1.5)	0.8	(1.2)	0	(2.2)
Other	1.5	(1.2)	0	(1.2)	0	(1.2)
Backward Castes	**17.4**	**(25.2)**	**43.9**	**(34.3)**	**52.6**	**(43.7)**
Yadav	9.2	(14.5)	29.8	(19.1)	36.4	(25.8)
Kurmi	4.6	(5.2)	5.0	(4.9)	3.5	(5.8)
Koeri	1.0	(2.8)	5.0	(4)	8.1	(6.8)
Baniya	2.6	(2.8)	4.1	(6.2)	4.6	(5.2)
Extremely Backward Castes	**2.0**	**(1.8)**	**0.8**	**(0.6)**	**2.3**	**(3.1)**
Scheduled Castes	**16.8**	**(14.8)**	**19**	**(14.8)**	**18.5**	**(15.1)**
Scheduled Tribes	**7.1**	**(8.9)**	**1.7**	**(9)**	**0.6**	**(8.3)**
Santhal	1.0	(0.9)	0	(0.6)	0	(0.9)
Munda	0.5	(1.2)	0	(0.9)	0	(0.9)
Oraon	1.0	(0.6)	0	(0.9)	0	(0.6)
Other	4.6	(6.2)	1.7	(6.5)	0.6	(5.8)
Religious Minorities	**14.3**	**(10.8)**	**9.1**	**(6.8)**	**9.8**	**(7.7)**
Muslim	14.3	(10.2)	9.1	(6.2)	9.2	(7.1)
Christian	0	(0.3)	0	(0.3)	0	(0.3)
Sikh	0	0	(0.3)	0.6	(0.3)	–
Unidentified	**0.5**	**(0.3)**	**0**		**0**	**(0.3)**
TOTAL	99.9		100.1		99.9	
	(N=196 (325))		(N=121 (324))		(N=173 (325))	

Source: Survey by author.

former was not able to build an OBC leadership.[20] Besides, due to the Bhagalpur riots of October–November 1989, Muslims felt that Congress had acted decisively against them by permitting Ram *shila* processions to pass through sensitive areas.[21] These two events accelerated the decline in the popular vote of the Congress party in the eve of the 1990 Bihar Legislative Assembly elections.

---

[20] Interview with Digvijay Singh, New Delhi, 10 January 2006. Digvijay Singh is member of the Congress Working Committee, General Secretary of the All India Congress Committee and ex-Chief Minister of Madhya Pradesh.

[21] The Bhagalpur communal riots broke out as provocative slogans, denouncing Muslims, their religion and their 'suspect' patriotism — such as 'Hindi, Hindu,

As a result, for the first time in Bihar, OBC MLAs were in a larger number than the upper caste MLAs in the 1990 Vidhan Sabha (34.9 against 34.6 per cent), largely because of the share of the OBC MLAs returned on a JD ticket. The upper castes represented only 25.6 per cent of the JD MLAs whereas the percentage of the Backward Castes constituted 43.8 per cent of the party MLAs, including 29.8 per cent of Yadavs. As a consequence, the Yadavs represented the largest caste group in the Legislative Assembly (19.1 per cent). The 1995 elections reconfirmed this trend towards a plebeian — and rustic — brand of politics.

Moreover, for the first time, the rural poor who were victims of a semi-feudal order cast their votes in very large numbers, resisting intimidations. They were obviously galvanised by the speeches of Laloo Prasad Yadav against the upper caste landlords, giving the Dalits a new sense of *Izzat* (dignity). The OBC MLAs now represented 46.8 per cent of all the MLAs, including 25.8 per cent of Yadavs (the 36.4 per cent Yadavs of the JD constituted 75 per cent of all the Yadav MLAs). While the lower Backward Castes represented about 2 per cent of the JD MLAs, the share of the Dalits reached 18.5 per cent of the party MLAs. The JD Dalit MLAs represented 67 per cent of all the Dalits MLAs. The JD, therefore, became an OBC–Dalit–Muslim party (the Muslim MLAs represented 9.2 per cent of the JD MLAs and 7.1 per cent of the Bihar MLAs). In contrast, the upper castes were marginalised within the Janata Dal with only 16.2 per cent of the MLAs (despite 9.8 per cent of Rajputs who represented the second largest caste group among the party MLAs). As a consequence, they constituted only 21.8 per cent of all the MLAs, less than the percentage of the Yadavs. The 1995 elections, therefore, marked an acceleration of change in the social composition of the political personnel of Bihar with the upper caste MLAs representing less than half of the OBC MLAs in the Vidhan Sabha.

Laloo Prasad Yadav, by then, was projecting himself as the leader of the rural poor, while his adversaries' strategy of concentrating their fire against his malpractices and corruption ideally suited the game plan of a man who ranked high in image-building and low in performances.

Hindustan, Mullah Bhago Pakistan' ('India is for Hindi-speaking Hindus; Muslims must go to Pakistan') — were renting the air. More than 1,000 people lost their lives, mostly Muslims.

Laloo Prasad belongs to the category of politicians who think that development has no electoral value. As a result, the 1995 election was more a referendum on the personality of Laloo Prasad than issue-based.

The Weakening of the 'Social Justice' Factor: The Limits of Caste Mobilisation

Elections 2000: Crumbling Laloo's Vote Banks

After his 1995 electoral victory, Laloo's government sought to cash in on the ideology of 'social justice' to mobilise the OBC, Dalits and women. But the demands of the peasants as a social class continued to be ignored, and their agitations were suppressed in different areas like Bhojpur, Jehanabad or Palamau. The Rashtriya Janata Dal (RJD), the new name of Laloo's party, could secure only 124 seats out of 325, 49 seats less than in 1995.[22] The orientation of the party towards the upper OBC, the Dalits and the Muslims became even more pronounced. The share of the upper OBC MLAs increased from 52.6 to 53.2 per cent among the party MLAs. And within this category, the share of the Yadavs rose from 36.4 per cent to 37.9 per cent. The same phenomenon was in evidence so far as the SC were concerned. Their share reached 21 per cent of the RJD MLAs. Simultaneously, the share of the RJD upper castes MLAs was reduced to 10.5 per cent. The decline of the RJD went on at par with the decline of the OBC in the Assembly. Their share decreased by 6.4 percentage points to reach 40.4 per cent (including 20.7 per cent Yadavs).[23]

Similarly, the share of the SC MLAs dropped from 15.1 to 14.8 per cent of the Vidhan Sabha members. These trends benefited the upper castes. The proportion of the upper castes MLAs increased by 1.3 percentage points to reach 23.1 per cent. The Bhumihars and the Rajputs respectively represented 7.1 and 11.4 per cent (+ 2.3 per cent for the former and + 1.9 per cent for the latter) of the Vidhan Sabha.

---

[22] RJD was formed when Laloo Prasad Yadav broke away from the Janata Dal in 1997.

[23] It is noteworthy that this decline only concerned the upper backward classes. In fact, the share of the upper OBC MLAs decreased by 8.5 per cent points to reach 35.2 per cent whereas the lower backward classes rose from 3.1 per cent to 5.2 per cent.

Table 2.10
Caste and Community of all the MLAs of the NDA and RJD, 2000 (%)

	Vidhan Sabha	NDA*	Rashtriya Janata Dal
Upper Castes	**23.1**	**31.2**	**10.5**
Brahmin	3.1	4.1	0.8
Bhumihar	7.1	9.0	2.4
Bengali	0.3	–	–
Rajput	11.4	14.8	7.3
Kayastha	1.2	3.3	–
Backward Castes	**35.2**	**31.1**	**53.2**
Yadav	20.7	13.9	37.9
Kurmi	4.6	7.4	3.2
Koeri	5.9	4.1	8.1
Baniya	4.0	5.7	4.0
Extremely Backward Castes	**5.2**	**9.8**	**0.8**
Scheduled Castes	**14.8**	**10.7**	**21.0**
Scheduled Tribes	**8.9**	**12.4**	**–**
Santhal	0.9	–	–
Munda	1.2	3.3	–
Oraon	0.9	2.5	–
Other	5.9	6.6	–
Religious Minorities	**9.6**	**2.4**	**13.7**
Muslims	9.3	1.6	13.7
Sikhs	0.3	0.8	–
Unidentified	**3.1**	**2.5**	**0.8**
TOTAL	99.9	100.1	100.0
	(N=324)	(N=122)	(N=124)

Source: Survey of author.
Note: * National Democratic Alliance (NDA): Bharatiya Janata Party won 67 seats, Samata Party won 34 seats and Janata Dal (United) won 21 seats.

This slight resurgence of the upper castes was due to the increasing presence of the Bharatiya Janata Party MLAs in the Vidhan Sabha. But the BJP targeted also the OBC. Its strategy to woo the Yadavs paid rich dividends: the Yadav MLAs represented 10.4 per cent of the BJP MLAs, which formed the second largest group of the party MLAs after the Rajputs (at this time, the BJP state president was a Yadav). More importantly, the BJP also targeted the Extremely Backward Castes, a neglected category, by assuring them that it would provide adequate reservation programmes. As a result, the BJP MLAs from this group represented 10.4 per cent of the party MLAs.

With the creation of Jharkhand out of unified Bihar in November 2000, the representation of political parties has significantly changed in the Bihar Legislative Assembly as the Jharkhand region constituted an electoral stronghold for some parties.

The most striking feature of Figure 2.1 is the strong increase of the RJD's proportion within the Assembly when other parties like the BJP and the Congress experienced a slight decrease. But, as the NDA is concerned, the percentages of its two other components — the Janata Dal (United) and the Samata Party — show a small growth.

Figure 2.1
Representation of Main Political Parties in Bihar Legislative Assembly, 2000

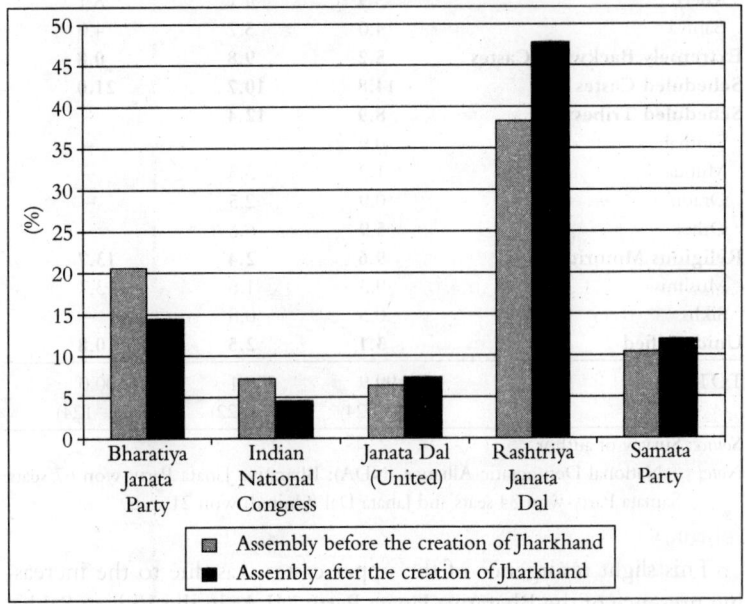

Source: Prepared by author.

In terms of castes, Figure 2.2 shows the complete disappearance of ST from the Vidhan Sabha since all the ST reserved constituencies of the undivided Bihar were now located in the new Jharkhand. This resulted in the progression of all the caste groups proportion except for the Extremely Backward Castes.

The two groups that mainly benefited from the creation of Jharkhand have been the Backward Caste MLAs and the upper caste MLAs whose share rose from 35.2 to 41.2 per cent and from 23.1 to 24.7 per cent

Figure 2.2
Representation of Caste Groups in the Bihar Legislative Assembly, 2000

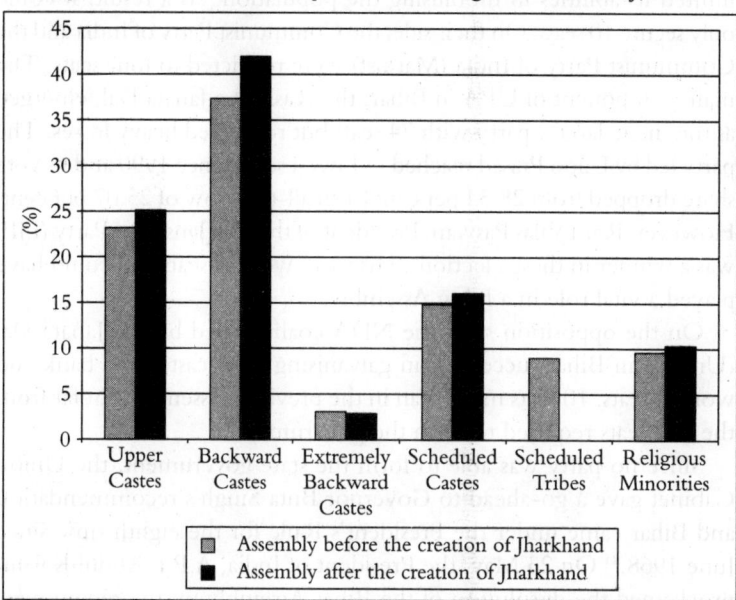

Source: Prepared by author.

respectively (see Appendix 1). The creation of Jharkhand strengthened both the grasp of Backward Castes over Bihar politics and political polarisation between these Backward Castes and the upper castes.

The Two 2005 Assembly Elections: Two Votes for Change

February 2005: A First Warning Shot for the United Progressive Alliance (UPA)

During the electoral campaign of the first elections held after the creation of Jharkhand, the Congress-led coalition at the centre broke up in Bihar as some of its components decided to contest the elections separately. The relations between the allies — Laloo Prasad and Ram Vilas Paswan — worsened as electoral campaign gained momentum. The latter called to the Congress party to distance itself from the RJD as Laloo Prasad was expected to offer only 25 seats to Congress in the then approaching Assembly polls (Kaushal 2004) and because the RJD supremo still believed that his wife Rabri Devi, the then Chief Minister, was the only UPA candidate for chief ministership.

Besides, the Congress party's inability to break out of its stagnation limited its abilities in mobilising the population. As a result, it could only secure 10 seats. On their side, the Communist Party of India and the Communist Party of India (Marxist) were restricted to four seats. The main component of UPA in Bihar, the Rashtriya Janata Dal, emerged as the single largest party with 74 seats but registered heavy losses. The party led by Laloo Prasad reached its lowest score since 1990 and its vote share dropped from 28.34 per cent to an all-time low of 25.07 per cent. However, Ram Vilas Paswan, President of the Lok Janshakti Party (LJP) was a winner in these elections. His party won 29 seats and could have played a vital role in a hung Assembly.

On the opposition side, the NDA coalition led by the Janata Dal (United) in Bihar succeeded in galvanising their caste vote bank and won 92 seats, 10 seats more than in the previous Assembly but far from the 122 seats required to form the government.

Since no party was able to form the state government, the Union Cabinet gave a go-ahead to Governor Buta Singh's recommendation and Bihar came under the President's Rule for the eighth time since June 1968.[24] On 23 May, the President of India, A.P.J. Abdul Kalam, proclaimed the dissolution of the Bihar Assembly on the recommendation of the Union Cabinet in order to prevent horse-trading and formation of government through foul means.[25] New elections were planned for October–November 2005.

Regarding the castes' representation, the results of the February confirmed the trend of the 2000 elections; namely, the increase of the proportion of upper caste MLAs by 4.9 percentage points to reach their highest level since year 1990. The noteworthy feature of Figure 2.3 is that the upper caste MLAs were the only ones to reflect an upward trend. Moreover, with the decrease of the proportion of the Backward Castes, the gap between this group and the upper castes dramatically narrowed.

The main factor in this new castes' set-up was the caste structure of the Lok Janshakti Party (LJP) MLAs. Indeed, despite his strong desire for clubbing together a Muslim–Dalit combination to take on RJD leader Laloo Prasad Yadav, Ram Vilas Paswan nominated about 30 per cent

---

[24] On 29 June 1968, Bihar was first put under President's Rule for a record 243 days during the regime of Mr Bhola Paswan Shastri, who was the Chief Minister then and Mr Nityanand Kanoongo, the Governor.

[25] See 'Prez Nod for Bihar Assembly Dissolution', 23 May 2005, http://www.rediff.com/news/2005/may/23bihar.htm.

Figure 2.3
Representation of Caste Groups in the Bihar Legislative Assembly,
2000 and 2005

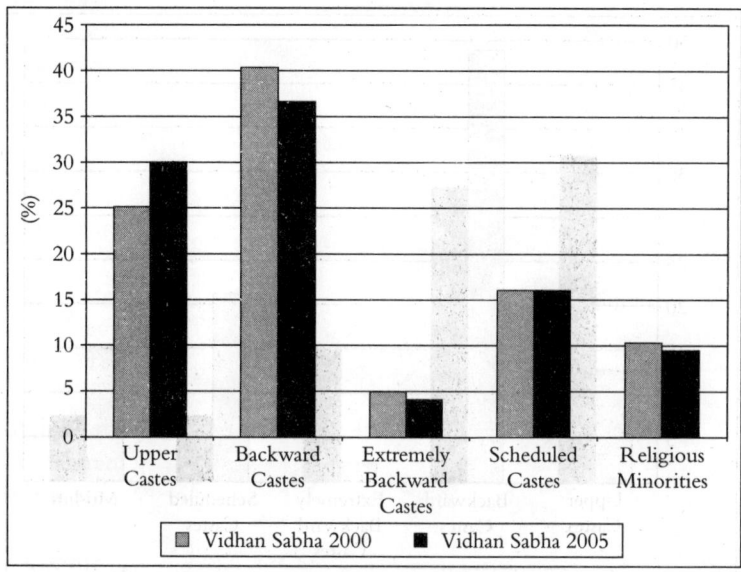

Source: Prepared by author.

upper castes as candidates, and Muslims and Dalits together accounted only for 20 per cent of the candidates. Therefore, the percentage of the upper castes reached 55.2 per cent of the LJP MLAs and none of its Muslim candidates had been elected (see Appendix 2).

November 2005: The Beginning of the Post-Mandal Era Electoral Politics; the End of Laloo–Rabri Regime

Unlike the February 2005 elections, the NDA obtained a clear majority — 144 seats out of 243 seats — in November Assembly elections and formed the new government. Living up to his promise, the new Chief Minister, Nitish Kumar (a Kurmi), gave adequate representation to members of the EBC by inducting four of them in his government, around 15 per cent of the cabinet members. This presence is all the more sizeable, at least proportionately, as the EBC only represented 2.1 per cent in the former Rabri Devi government and 4.9 per cent of the MLAs. As Figure 2.4 shows, an increasing representation is also observed for the upper castes whereas the share of the other caste groups, mainly the Backward Castes and the SC, has clearly declined.

Figure 2.4
Caste and Community of Members of Rashtriya Janata Dal and Janata Dal (United) Governments in Bihar

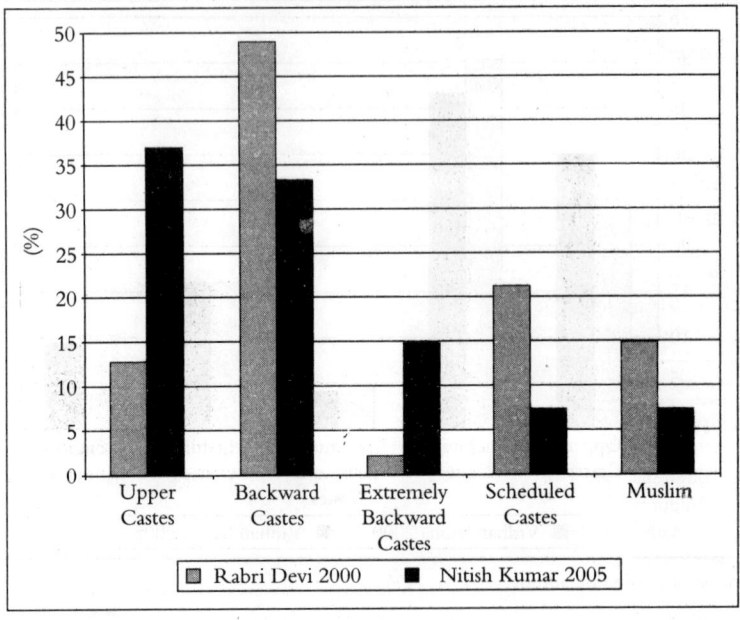

Source: Prepared by author.

This caste readjustment shows Nitish's willingness to give more adequate representation to all caste groups than Laloo–Rabri did regarding the EBC and the non-Backward Castes. But, the most striking aspect of this new caste management is the reallocation of power in favour of the upper castes, mainly from the JD(U), as they represent 37 per cent of the government's members. This is also a sign that Nitish Kumar does not want to lose the support he got from the upper castes as they are usually aligned with the BJP but voted for JD(U) candidates for political convenience.

At the same time, 'the coming together of upper castes, upper backward and lower backward castes including dalits has been necessitated more for political exigency that was to dethrone the family rule of the Laloo Yadav–Rabri Devi duo than for convergence of ideological and policy interests' (Pankaj 2005: 25–26).

Within the Vidhan Sabha, the new balance of power between the political coalitions had a limited impact on the representation of the caste categories. Compared with the Legislative Assembly in year 2000, the share of each caste groups has slightly changed. As Table 2.11 shows, Muslim MLAs are the only group who experienced a sharp decrease of its share. This evolution of the Muslim percentage is mainly linked with the loss of seats of the RJD as for the last 15 years this party represented the best opportunity for a Muslim to get a ticket and to be elected. The fall of the Laloo-led RJD also had an impact on the number of Yadav MLAs as most of them were returned on the RJD ticket in the previous elections. However, Yadavs still represent the most numerous group with 20.6 per cent.

Table 2.11
Caste and Community of the Members of the Bihar Vidhan Sabha, 2000 and 2005 (%)

Caste and Community	*2000*	*2005*
Upper Castes	**25.0**	**25.9**
Brahmin	3.7	3.7
Bhumihar	8.6	11.1
Rajput	11.5	9.9
Kayastha	1.2	1.2
Backward Castes	**40.3**	**41.9**
Yadav	24.7	20.6
Kurmi	4.9	7.8
Koeri	6.6	8.6
Baniya	4.1	4.9
Extremely Backward Castes	**4.9**	**5.3**
Scheduled Castes	**16.0**	**16.0**
Muslim	**10.3**	**7.4**
Unidentified	**3.3**	**3.3**
TOTAL	99.8	99.9
	(N=243)	(N=243)

Source: Survey by author.

Unlike the Yadav MLAs, Kurmis and Koeris have reached their highest percentage in the Bihar Vidhan Sabha from 1952 onwards. As these two castes constitute the core of the JD(U) electorate, they benefited from the victory of the JD(U)-led NDA.

The coming to power of the JD(U)-led NDA did not challenge the 15 years old monopoly of the OBC over Bihar politics. Moreover, the results of these elections show the strengthening of the Backwards at the forefront of the politics in Bihar. As Figure 2.5 shows, the Backward Caste members represent the majority in the Janata Dal (United), the

Rashtriya Janata Dal — two OBC based parties — and the Bharatiya Janata Party in which the share of the OBC MLAs is for the first time, since 1962, bigger than that of the upper caste MLAs. Unlike the Congress party, the BJP leaders have understood that no political party could survive in Bihar without nominating a large number of Backward Classes' candidates for elections.

Figure 2.5
Caste Categories of the MLAs of the BJP, JD(U) and RJD, 2005

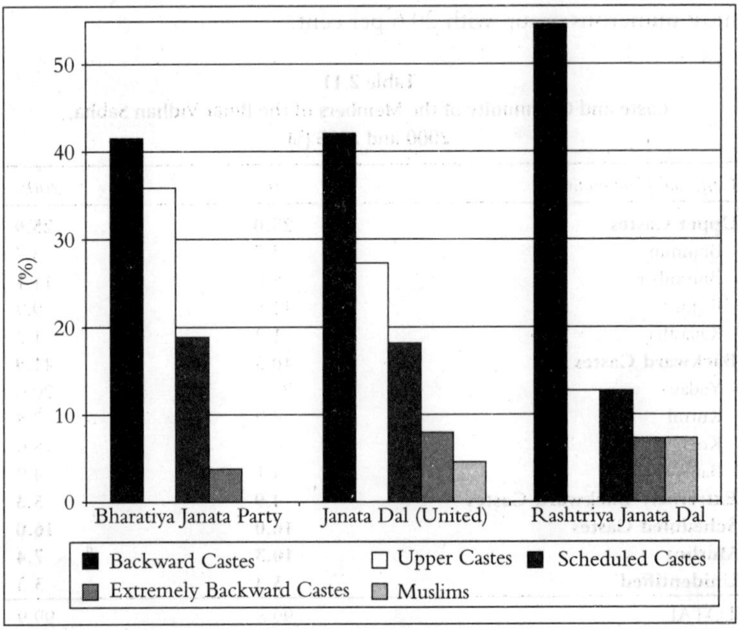

Source: Prepared by author.

Conclusion

The process of party political democratisation in Bihar has had a substantial impact on the representation of the OBC in the Vidhan Sabha. After the Janata Dal came to power in 1990, Bihar became the first stronghold for OBC politics. Moreover, this identity of Backward Classes in Bihar politics has been strengthened after the creation of Jharkhand (on 15 November 2000) since the tribal element of undivided Bihar disappeared.

However, the OBC are a very heterogeneous category, and, in Bihar, the castes which benefited from this political empowerment belong to the upper strata of the OBC. They are mainly Yadavs from the small middle landowners' class, thereby comprising the economic elite of the category. The gradual political empowerment is therefore confined to a very limited section of the OBC experiencing some upward social mobility, and, small labourers and landless peasants have been left out of any social upliftment. Indeed, Laloo Prasad has better understood than any other political leader that 'politics organised around interests do not have the benefit of the kind of popular mobilisation that electoral and party politics produce' (Katzenstein et al. 2001: 251). He has instrumentalised the Backward movement so that the main goal was not the elimination of caste discrimination but the coming to power by the instrumentalisation of this discrimination. The way Laloo Prasad reached power was indeed due to the mobilisation of caste through the 'backward' identity. The notion of social justice only corresponded to the removal of the upper caste from government in favour of the Backward Castes, mainly the Yadavs. Thus, the idea of social development was not contained in the concept of 'social justice'. Social justice meant the identity movement for the political upliftment of some Backward Castes.

As a result, the social coalition of OBC, SC and Muslims that supported RJD from 1990 onwards fell apart as the government did not take any economic and social measures in favour of the non-elite categories.[26] Therefore, the RJD-led Secular Democratic Front (SDF) — RJD, INC, NCP and CPI-M — lost the elections in November 2005 in favour of the JD(U)–BJP combine. This new era in the politics of Bihar probably announces a new kind of caste politics, less exclusive than the one carried out for the 15 years of Laloo–Rabri regime, but still working, for caste, although it is not an autonomous factor, is one of the most relevant criteria for candidate nomination that no political party can deny.

---

[26] See Appendix 3 for a comparison of the caste coalitions of the major parties in Bihar since 1952.

Appendix 1

Bihar Vidhan Sabha before and after November 2000, and Jharkhand Vidhan Sabha after the Creation of Jharkhand, November 2000 (%)

Caste and Community	Bihar before November 2000	Bihar after November 2000	Jharkhand
Upper Castes	**23.1**	**24.6**	**17.3**
Brahmin	3.1	3.7	1.2
Bhumihar	7.1	8.2	1.2
Rajput	0.3	11.5	11.1
Kayastha	11.4	1.2	2.5
Other	1.2	–	1.2
Backward Castes	**35.2**	**41.2**	**22.2**
Yadav	20.7	24.7	7.4
Kurmi	4.6	6.2	4.9
Koeri	5.9	5.8	4.9
Baniya	4	4.5	4.9
Extremely Backward Castes	**5.2**	**5.3**	**3.7**
Scheduled Castes	**14.8**	**16.5**	**9.9**
Scheduled Tribes	**9.0**	**0**	**37.0**
Muslim	**9.3**	**10.3**	**4.9**
Sikh	**0.3**	**0**	**1.2**
Unidentified	**3.1**	**2.1**	**3.7**
TOTAL	100.0	100.0	100.0
	(N=324)	(N=243)	(N=81)

Source: Survey by author.

Appendix 2

Caste and Community of all the MLAs (NDA and RJD), February 2005 (%)

	BJP–JD(U) Alliance*	Rashtriya Janata Dal	Lok Janshakti Party
Upper Castes	**30.1**	**12.0**	**55.2**
Brahmin	6.5	2.7	0.0
Bhumihar	7.5	0.0	27.6
Bengali	0.0	8.0	0.0
Rajput	14.0	0.0	27.6
Kayastha	2.2	1.3	0.0
Backward Castes	**32.3**	**45.3**	**27.6**
Yadav	15.1	38.7	13.8
Kurmi	10.8	1.3	0.0
Koeri	4.3	2.7	10.3
Baniya	2.2	2.7	3.4
Extremely Backward Castes	**6.5**	**4.0**	**3.4**

(*Appendix 2 continued*)

(Appendix 2 continued)

	BJP–JD(U) Alliance*	Rashtriya Janata Dal	Lok Janshakti Party
Scheduled Castes	**16.1**	**18.7**	**13.8**
Religious Minorities	**4.3**	**13.3**	**0.0**
Muslim	4.3	13.3	0.0
Unidentified	**10.8**	**6.7**	**0.0**
TOTAL	100.0	100.0	100.0
	(N=92)	(N=75)	(N=29)

Source: Survey by author.

Note: * Bharatiya Janata Party won 37 seats while Janata Dal (United) won 55 seats.

Appendix 3

Caste and Community of the Communist, Socialist, Congress, RJD, Janata Party and BJP MLAs in Bihar, 1952–2005 (%)

	Communist Parties	Socialist Parties	Congress	JD/RJD	Janata Party	BJS/BJP
Upper Castes	**40.7**	**47.9**	**45.1**	**16.8**	**43.4**	**35.7**
Brahmin	7.2	10.4	14.4	2.9	4.7	9.0
Bhumihar	18.0	12.1	11.8	3.5	10.4	5.4
Rajput	9.0	21.8	14.4	10	21.7	13.0
Kayastha	1.1	3.2	3.6	0.4	4.2	4.3
Other	5.4	0.4	0.9	–	2.4	4.0
Backward Castes	**33.1**	**33.2**	**20.7**	**50.1**	**24.0**	**29.5**
Yadav	17.3	19.6	8.7	35.9	12.7	10.7
Kurmi	3.6	2.5	4.4	3.5	2.8	4.7
Koeri	9.7	7.9	3.3	6.6	3.8	3.7
Baniya	2.5	3.2	4.4	4.1	4.7	10.4
Extremely Backward Castes	**0.4**	**3.2**	**1.0**	**1.8**	**0.5**	**4.3**
Scheduled Castes	**15.9**	**12.1**	**15.5**	**19.5**	**17.0**	**14.7**
Scheduled Tribes	**2.2**	**0.7**	**6.5**	**0.6**	**8.5**	**14.4**
Santhal	1.1	–	0.8	–	1.4	0.7
Munda	–	–	0.7	–	–	1.3
Oraon	–	–	0.4	–	1.4	3.0
Other	1.1	0.7	4.6	0.6	5.7	9.4
Religious Minorities	**6.0**	**2.9**	**11.0**	**11.3**	**6.1**	**0.7**
Muslim	6.0	2.9	10.9	11.1	6.1	–
Parsi	–	–	0.1	–	–	–
Sikh	–	–	–	0.2	–	0.7
Unidentified	**1.1**	**–**	**0.1**	**0.2**	**0.5**	**0.3**
TOTAL	99.4	100.0	98.9	100.3	100.1	99.6
	(N=266)	(N=280)	(N=1629)	(N=418)	(N=212)	(N=267)

Source: Survey by author.

Appendix 4

Caste and Community of the MLAs in Bihar (%)

	1952	1957	1962	1967	1969	1972	1977	1980	1985	1990	1995	2000	2005	TOTAL
Upper Castes	**46.0**	**45.9**	**46.2**	**44.8**	**42.0**	**42.8**	**40.8**	**36.5**	**38.5**	**34.5**	**21.8**	**23.1**	**30.0**	**38.1**
Brahmin	12.1	10.0	13.8	11.0	9.4	11.0	7.1	12.3	10.8	8.3	3.1	3.1	4.9	9.1
Bhumihar	10.0	12.5	8.8	11.6	10.3	10.4	10.2	9.8	10.5	11.1	5.8	7.1	9.5	9.8
Bengali	1.5	0.6	0.9	1.9	2.5	2.5	2.2	1.2	1.2	1.2	1.2	0.3	–	1.4
Rajput	14.2	17.2	19.1	17.2	17.6	17.6	18.5	11.4	14.5	12.7	9.5	11.4	14.0	15.0
Kayastha	8.2	5.6	3.4	3.1	2.2	1.3	2.8	1.8	1.5	1.2	2.2	1.2	1.6	2.8
Backward Castes	**19.3**	**18.8**	**23.6**	**26.0**	**27.9**	**24.9**	**27.7**	**29.0**	**25.3**	**34.2**	**43.6**	**35.2**	**34.5**	**28.4**
Yadav	7.9	6.6	9.4	11.6	15.0	11.0	15.4	13.8	14.5	19.1	25.8	20.7	22.6	14.8
Kurmi	3.6	3.8	4.4	4.1	3.8	6.0	3.7	6.2	5.2	4.9	5.8	4.6	4.5	4.7
Koeri	4.5	5.3	6.0	4.7	2.8	4.1	4.6	2.8	2.8	4.0	6.8	5.9	4.9	4.5
Baniya	3.3	3.1	3.8	5.6	6.3	3.8	4.0	6.2	2.8	6.2	5.2	4.0	2.5	4.4
Extremely Backward Castes	**1.2**	**0.6**	**0.9**	**0.6**	**0.9**	**0.9**	**0.6**	**1.5**	**1.8**	**0.6**	**3.1**	**5.2**	**5.3**	**1.7**
Scheduled Castes	**13.9**	**14.7**	**13.2**	**13.5**	**14.1**	**13.8**	**13.8**	**14.5**	**14.8**	**14.8**	**15.1**	**14.8**	**16.9**	**14.4**
Scheduled Tribes	**10.9**	**11.2**	**9.0**	**9.2**	**8.8**	**8.9**	**8.5**	**8.6**	**8.9**	**9.0**	**8.2**	**8.9**		**8.7**
Santhal	2.7	2.2	0.6	1.3	0.9	1.3	1.2	1.5	0.9	0.6	0.9	0.9	–	1.2
Munda	1.2	0.9	0.6	1.3	0.6	1.3	0.6	0.3	1.2	0.9	0.9	1.2	–	0.9
Oraon	0.6	0.9	0.6	0.3	1.3	0.6	1.2	0.6	0.6	0.9	0.6	0.9	–	0.7
Others	6.4	7.2	7.2	6.3	6.0	5.7	5.5	6.2	6.2	6.5	5.8	5.9	–	5.9

Religious Minorities	7.6	8.1	7.2	5.9	6.3	8.5	8.0	9.5	10.8	6.8	7.7	9.6	9.5	8.1
Muslims	7.6	7.8	6.6	5.6	6.0	8.2	7.7	8.9	10.2	6.2	7.1	9.3	9.5	7.7
Christians	–	0.3	0.6	0.3	0.3	0.3	0.3	0.3	0.3	0.3	0.3	–	–	0.3
Parsis	–	–	–	–	–	–	–	–	0.3	–	–	–	–	0
Sikhs	–	–	–	–	–	–	–	0.3	–	0.3	0.3	0.3	–	0.1
Unidentified	0.9	0.3	–	–	–	0.3	0.6	0.3	–	–	0.3	3.1	3.7	0.7
TOTAL	99.8	99.7	100.1	100.0	100.0	100.1	100.0	99.9	100.1	99.9	99.8	99.9	99.9	100.0
	(N=330)	(N=319)	(N=319)	(N=319)	(N=319)	(N=318)	(N=325)	(N=325)	(N=325)	(N=324)	(N=325)	(N=324)	(N=243)	(N=4115)

Source: Survey by author.

References

Blair, H. W. 1980. 'Rising Kulaks and Backward Classes in Bihar', *Economic and Political Weekly*, 15 (2): 64–74.

Census of India, 1931. 1933. Government of India, Rajputana Agency, Nagpur.

Frankel, Francine R. 1989. 'Caste, Land and Dominance in Bihar: Breakdown of the Brahmanical Social Order', in F. R. Frankel and M. S. A. Rao (eds), *Dominance and State Power in Modern India: Decline of a Social Order*, pp. 46–132. Delhi: Oxford University Press.

Gough, Kathleen E. 1974. 'Peasant Uprisings in India', *Economic and Political Weekly*, 9 (13): 1391–412.

Jaffrelot, Christophe. 2003. *India's Silent Revolution: The Rise of the Low Castes in North Indian Politics*. New Delhi: Permanent Black.

Katzenstein, Mary, Smitu Kothari and Uday Mehta. 2001. 'Social Movements Politics in India: Institutions, Interests, and Identities', in Atul Kohli (ed.), *The Success of India's Democracy*, pp. 242–69. Cambridge: Cambridge University Press.

Kaushal, Pradeep. 2004. 'Congress Worries over Laloo, Paswan Spat', *The Indian Express*, 30 November.

Krishna, Gopal. 1967. 'Electoral Participation and Political Integration', *Economic and Political Weekly*, 2(3–5): 179–90.

Mishra, Upendra. 1986. *Caste and Politics in India: A Study of Political Turmoil in Bihar, 1967–1977*. New Delhi: Uppal Publishing House.

Nathan, Dev. 1996. *Agricultural Labour and the Poor Peasant Movement in Bihar*, in T. V. Sathyamurthy (ed.), *Class Formation and Political Transformation*, pp. 151–78. Delhi: Oxford University Press.

Pankaj, Ashok Kumar. 2005. 'Dream Bihar', *Hardnews*, December, pp. 25–26.

Rai, Haridwar and Jawaharlal Pandey. 1981. 'State Politics in Bihar: A Crisis of Political Institutionalisation', *The Indian Journal of Political Science*, 42 (4): 45–64.

Roy, Ramashray. 1966. 'Intra-party Conflict in the Bihar Congress', *Asian Survey*, 6 (12): 706–15.

———. 1970. *Caste and Political Recruitment in Bihar*, in Rajni Kothari (ed.), *Caste in Indian Politics*, pp. 215–42. New Delhi: Orient Longman.

Sharma, Gayatri. 1994. 'Contributions of the Socialists to the Kisan Movement in Bihar, 1931–1950', in K. Munirathna Naidu (ed.), *Peasant Movements in India*, pp. 71–89. New Delhi: Reliance Publishing House.

Swami Sahajanand. 1952. *Mera Jivan Sangharsh*. Patna: Shri Sitaram Ashram.

Verna, H. S. (ed.). 2005. *The OBCs and the Ruling Classes in India*. New Delhi: Rawat Publications.

3
The Uneven Rise of Lower Castes in the Politics of Madhya Pradesh

Christophe Jaffrelot

In the late 1980s, the very systematic survey edited by F. Frankel and M. S. A. Rao on 'the decline of a social order' (that was its subtitle) in India almost eluded Madhya Pradesh — and more or less rightly so because in this state the old 'social order' then showed strong resilience. In particular, the Other Backward Classes (OBC) had not emerged as a significant force on the political scene. One of the appendixes of the first volume of the book showed that in 1984, Madhya Pradesh had the lowest proportion of MPs from this category in India, namely, 5 per cent (Frankel and Rao 1989: 422). However, things changed very rapidly since the late 1980s and in 12 years, from 1984 to 1996, the proportion of the OBC MPs jumped from 7.5 to 25 per cent.

Yet, so far as the changing profile of its MPs is concerned, the pattern of Madhya Pradesh is slightly different from the pattern I presented in the Introduction of this volume on the basis of the Hindi belt MPs at large. There is a time lag between the crossing of most of the thresholds simply because the rise of the OBC has been more rapid in the major states of the Hindi belt, that is, U.P. and Bihar. While the share of the upper castes among the Hindi belt MPs fell below 50 per cent in 1977, it remained exactly at 50 in Madhya Pradesh where it fell below 50 only in 1984. And while it fell below 40 per cent in the Hindi belt in 1989, in Madhya Pradesh it remained exactly at 40 and fell below that figure only in 1991, this date being the real turning point when the Mandal effect impacted the state. But then the share of the upper caste MPs started to rise again in 1999 and this unprecedented trend continued in 2004, when their figure took Madhya Pradesh back to 1980. Similarly, while the share of the OBC MPs reached 10 per cent among the Hindi belt MPs in 1971, it did so in Madhya Pradesh only in 1977; and while it crossed the 20 per cent threshold in 1989 in the Hindi belt, it took until 1991 for this to happen in Madhya Pradesh. And then it accomplished an invert U-curve which meant that in 2004 Madhya Pradesh was back to the 1991 situation, a unique development in the

Table 3.1

Caste and Community of the Madhya Pradesh MPs, 1957–2004 (%)

Castes and Communities	1957	1962	1967	1971	1977	1980	1984	1989	1991	1996	1998	1999	2004
Upper Castes	**52.80**	**52.80**	**50.00**	**56.80**	**50.00**	**50.00**	**47.50**	**40.00**	**33.30**	**32.50**	**35.00**	**37.50**	**41.40**
Brahmin	30.60	36.10	25.00	32.40	22.50	30.00	22.50	15.00	10.26	15.00	15.00	17.50	20.69
Rajput	5.56	8.33	13.90	13.50	10.00	7.50	12.50	10.00	15.38	10.00	10.00	12.50	13.79
Baniya/Jain	13.90	8.33	11.10	10.80	15.00	10.00	10.00	12.50	2.56	5.00	5.00	7.50	3.45
Kayastha	2.78	–	–	–	–	–	2.50	2.50	5.13	2.50	5.00	–	–
Khatri	–	–	–	–	2.50	2.50	–	–	–	–	–	–	3.45
Intermediary Castes	–	–	–	**2.70**	**5.00**	**2.50**	**2.50**	**2.50**	**2.56**	**2.50**	**2.50**	**2.50**	**3.45**
Maratha	–	–	–	2.70	5.00	2.50	2.50	2.50	2.56	2.50	2.50	2.50	3.45
OBC	**5.56**	**2.78**	**8.34**	**5.40**	**10.00**	**5.00**	**7.50**	**15.00**	**20.50**	**25.00**	**22.50**	**22.50**	**20.70**
Bairagi	–	–	–	–	–	–	2.50	–	–	–	–	–	–
Kacchi	–	–	–	–	–	–	–	–	–	2.50	–	–	–
Kirar	–	–	–	–	–	–	–	–	–	2.50	2.50	2.50	3.45
Kurmi	2.78	–	2.78	2.70	7.50	2.50	2.50	7.50	15.38	10.00	12.50	7.50	6.90
Lodhi	–	–	–	–	–	–	–	7.50	2.56	5.00	2.50	5.00	–
Pankha	–	–	–	–	–	–	–	–	–	–	–	2.50	–
Panwar	2.78	–	2.78	2.70	–	–	–	–	2.56	2.50	–	–	–
Paradhi	–	2.78	–	–	–	–	–	–	–	–	–	–	–
Teli	–	–	–	–	–	–	–	–	–	2.50	5.00	–	–
Yadav	–	–	2.78	–	2.50	2.50	2.50	–	–	–	–	–	–
Others	–	–	2.78	–	–	–	–	–	–	–	–	–	10.34

SC	16.70	13.90	13.90	13.50	12.50	15.00	15.00	15.38	15.00	15.00	15.00	15.00	15.00	13.80
ST	19.40	22.20	25.00	21.60	22.50	22.50	22.50	23.08	22.50	22.50	22.50	22.50	22.50	17.24
Muslims	2.78	2.78	–	–	2.50	5.00	5.00	2.56	2.50	–	–	–	–	–
Parsis	–	–	–	–	–	–	–	–	–	–	–	–	–	–
Sikhs	2.78	2.78	2.78	–	–	–	2.50	2.56	2.50	2.50	2.50	2.50	–	3.45
Unidentified	–	–	–	–	–	–	–	–	–	–	–	–	–	–
TOTAL	100.00	100.00	100.00	100.00	100.00	100.00	100.00	100.00	100.00	100.00	100.00	100.00	100.00	100.00
	(N=36)	(N=36)	(N=36)	(N=37)	(N=40)	(N=40)	(N=40)	(N=40)	(N=40)	(N=40)	(N=40)	(N=40)	(N=40)	(N=29*)

Source: Survey by author.

Note: * In 2000, the number of MPs was reduced to 29 because of the creation of Chhattisgarh.

whole of the Hindi belt. I shall try to explain this unprecedented trajectory by taking a socio-historical perspective.

Till the last decade, the elitist social profile of the MPs returned to the Lok Sabha could be explained from different points of view. First, Madhya Pradesh is characterised by both an extreme fragmentation of the lower castes and the large size of the princely states whose ex-rulers continued to play an important role after 1947, giving a conservative overtone to the clientelistic brand of politics that the Congress system developed in the state from the 1950s to the 1970s. As a result, the lower castes were marginalised in the Vidhan Sabha and the state government. In contrast to her socialist rhetoric, Indira Gandhi did not succeed in promoting low caste Congressmen in the 1970s — in fact she hardly tried to do so, as evident from the social profile of the Congress candidates to the state Assembly. However, there is a tradition of low caste politics that has been represented by the socialist parties for decades in Madhya Pradesh and things began to change in the late 1970s, with the Janata Party victory in 1977. The inclusion of an increasingly large number of low caste people in the Vidhan Sabha was then part of a larger democratisation process, which is also evident from the growing number of agriculturists and women in the Assembly. In the 1980s, interestingly, the rise of the low castes was largely due to the strategy of the local Congress. But the promotion of low caste people in the political arena was primarily an electoral strategy of the upper caste leaders of the party. Unsurprisingly, therefore, the apparatus of the Congress and the other major party in the state, the BJP, remains very much elitist.

In this chapter, I focus on Madhya Pradesh in its post-1956 frontiers. Indeed, this state was born in 1956 by agglomerating three Part C states (Madhya Bharat, Vindhya Pradesh and Bhopal) and the Hindi-speaking part of the old Central Provinces — renamed Madhya Pradesh after independence. In the year 2000, Chhattisgarh was carved out from Madhya Pradesh (see Chapter 11 of this volume).

The Socio-political Background

The Inhibiting Impact of the Caste Composition

According to the 1931 Census — the last census that included detailed questions about castes — the upper castes represented 12.9 per cent of the state population of the post–1956 Madhya Pradesh (5.7 per cent Brahmins, 5.3 per cent Rajputs and 2 per cent Baniyas), the lower castes, 42 per cent; the Scheduled Castes (SC), 14 per cent; and the Scheduled Tribes (ST), an exceptionally high 22 per cent. Yet, one must not content oneself in regarding Madhya Pradesh as a whole; it is important to look at the subregions composing the state. The domination of the upper castes — in terms of numbers at least — was especially strong in Vindhya Pradesh (where one could find one of the highest concentrations of Brahmins in India, about 14 per cent) and Madhya Bharat (where the proportion of Rajputs is higher than in Rajasthan with about 9 per cent). In these two subregions, the upper castes represented 22 and 19 per cent respectively of the total population. In contrast, they formed only 11.7 per cent of Mahakoshal and a meagre 3.25 per cent in Chhattisgarh where the (ST) were in large numbers — 32.5 per cent according to the 2001 Census and the OBC in majority (with 50.3 per cent of the total).

Besides the demographic weight of the upper castes, Table 3.2 shows the fragmentation of the lower castes, which was bound to stunt feelings of caste solidarity. With the exception of the Ahirs (or Yadavs), none of the OBC represented more than 5 per cent of the state population. The Kurmis came second with 2.6 per cent. Once again, the subregional differences are very significant but reinforce the feeling of fragmentation since none of these castes is evenly spread over the whole state. While the Ahirs accounted for more than 5 per cent of the population in Chhattisgarh (8.4 per cent) and Vindhya Pradesh (6.1 per cent), they were weaker in Mahakoshal (4.7 per cent) and Madhya Bharat (2.6 per cent). In fact, each subregion had a different OBC-leading caste in demographic as well as political terms: in Chhattisgarh they were the Telis (9.35 per cent), who accounted for less than 3 per cent of the population of the other regions; in Vindhya Pradesh the Kacchis (6.1 per cent), who formed about 3 per cent of the population of Madhya Bharat and were absent from the rest of the state; in Mahakoshal, besides the Ahirs, the Lodhis (4.4 per cent) who represented less than 3 per cent of the population elsewhere.[1] This fragmentation was also in evidence

---

[1] The fragmentation is also linguistic since Madhya Pradesh 'speaks' many dialects. That might not have been an obstacle for the educated elite but it certainly hindered the interactions between members of the few OBC who are spread over the whole state.

Table 3.2
Social Composition of Madhya Pradesh, post-1956 and post-2000 (subregion-wise) (%)

Castes and Communities	Madhya Bharat	Vindhya Pradesh	Mahakoshal	Chhattisgarh	Post-1956 Madhya Pradesh	Post-2000 Madhya Pradesh
Upper Castes	**18.60**	**21.67**	**11.69**	**3.25**	**12.88**	**16.77**
Brahmin	6.55	13.85	4.57	1.67	5.66	7.27
Rajput	9.05	4.71	5.64	0.94	5.29	7.04
Baniya/Jain	2.22	2.30	1.00	0.49	1.44	1.81
Kayastha	0.68	0.81	0.48	0.15	0.49	0.63
Intermediary Castes	**0.87**	**0.34**	**2.96**	**0.17**	**1.11**	**1.48**
Maratha	0.42	–	0.57	0.11	0.31	0.39
Kunbi	0.45	0.34	2.39	0.06	0.80	1.09
OBC	**37.30**	**41.03**	**36.25**	**50.34**	**41.44**	**37.71**
Jat	0.73	–	–	–	0.11	0.34
Ahir	2.63	6.06	4.79	8.40	5.29	4.00
Kurmi	1.60	4.75	2.58	2.88	2.64	2.50
Gujjar	2.88	0.04	1.09	0.02	1.23	1.71
Lodhi	2.04	2.70	4.37	0.94	2.25	2.96
Kacchi	3.25	6.08	–	–	1.91	2.68
Kirar	1.52	0.09	–	–	0.51	0.72
Gadaria	1.87	2.12	–	–	0.91	1.27
Kumhar	1.57	1.74	0.88	0.75	1.19	1.36
Mali	1.02	0.12	2.27	2.88	1.73	1.27
Teli	1.56	2.90	2.30	9.35	4.02	2.07
Bairagi	0.69	0.04	0.15	0.44	0.93	0.37
Khati	1.58	–	–	–	0.52	0.73
Lohar, Luhar	0.79	1.50	1.26	1.07	1.08	1.08

	(N=7,161,901)	(N=2,969,437)	(N=5,279,634)	(N=6,228,959)	(N=21,639,931)	(N=15,410,972)
Nai	1.40	1.76	1.24	0.80	1.24	1.41
Sondhya	1.10	–	–	–	0.36	1.99
Bhoi, Dhimar Kahar	1.14	2.92	2.64	0.79	1.65	0.51
Dangi	0.54	0.21	–	–	0.21	0.29
Deswali	0.30	0	–	–	0.10	0.13
Dhakad	0.91	0	–	–	0.30	0.42
Darzi	0.57	0.52	0.40	0.06	0.38	0.50
Sutar, Barhai	0.56	0.95	0.80	0.02	0.52	0.71
Sonar, Sunar	0.62	0.88	0.99	0.35	0.67	0.79
Dhobi	0.90	1.07	0.95	1.35	1.06	0.94
Mankad	0.31	–	–	–	0.10	0.14
Banjara	0.86	0.46	0.49	0.24	0.47	0.56
Barai, Tamboli	0.20	0.68	–	–	0.13	0.17
Kotwai	0.12	1.00	–	–	0.13	0.18
Kalal	0.47	0.55	–	–	0.29	0.40
Khangar	0.28	–	0.22	–	0.22	0.31
Kalar	–	–	1.07	1.52	0.70	0.36
Panka	–	–	–	3.20	0.91	–
Kewat	–	–	–	2.92	0.84	–
Others	3.29	2.16	7.76	12.37	6.84	4.59
SC	**16.68**	**14.70**	**11.90**	**12.54**	**14.05**	**14.65**
ST	**13.10**	**14.48**	**25.05**	**31.74**	**21.62**	**17.46**
Muslims	**6.30**	**2.64**	**4.42**	**1.11**	**3.85**	**4.96**
Sikhs	**0.02**	**0.006**	**0.03**	–	**0.02**	**0.02**
Christians	**0.13**	**0.02**	–	**0.02**	**0.05**	**0.06**
Others	**7.08**	**4.84**	**7.67**	**0.80**	**4.70**	**6.85**
TOTAL	**100.00**	**100.00**	**100.00**	**100.00**	**100.00**	**100.00**

Source: Censuses of Central Provinces and Central India agencies (1931).

regarding the Scheduled Castes. The Chamars represented 9–10 per cent of the population in Madhya Bharat and Vindhya Pradesh but less than 5 per cent of the total in the other subregions.

In addition to these factors, in contrast with Rajasthan and Uttar Pradesh where the Jats form the dominant caste in several districts of the state, in Madhya Pradesh, the intermediate (and locally dominant) castes who could have acted as the spearhead of anti-establishment move-ments are neither prosperous nor large or assertive enough. The Jats, who have always been classified as OBC in Madhya Pradesh, represent only 0.1 per cent of the population. And the Marathas, who are also an almost negligible quantity, often belonged to the elite of the princely states, whose ruling families came from the same milieu, or related to them. They have therefore tended to emulate the Rajputs.[2]

The strength of the upper castes does not rely on this demographic advantage alone but, precisely, on the resilience of the princely elite because of the persistence of old kingdoms during the British Raj. In 1947, they were 35 in Vindhya Pradesh, 25 in Madhya Bharat and a dozen in today's Chhattisgarh. In Madhya Bharat and Vindhya Pradesh demographic weight and socio-political domination were concomitant. As mentioned above, the Rajputs represent, for instance, the largest caste in Madhya Bharat with more than 9 per cent of the regional popu-lation. Rajas and maharajas (sometimes with Maratha background in the western part of the state) headed networks of Rajput zamindars and jagirdars. In the post-1956 Madhya Pradesh, it was estimated that 170 out of 296 Assembly constituencies and 20 out of 37 parliamen-tary constituencies were located in part or in totality on the territory of former princely states (Jaffrelot 1999: 215).

The political history of Madhya Pradesh and Chhattisgarh has been over-dominated by the Congress largely because of its links with these caste groups and the princely elite. The party has ruled pre-2000 Madhya Pradesh continuously since its formation in 1956 except for two short periods: in 1977–79 (the Janata phase) and 1990–92 (when the BJP briefly took over).

---

[2] This 'kshatriyaisation' process was well illustrated by several marital alliances such as that of Jivaji Rao Scindia — a Maratha ruler — with Vijaya Raje Scindia, a Rana Rajput from Nepal.

The steady erosion of the Congress party — and of the socialists — gradually gave birth to a two-party system with the Jana Sangh (JS) and, subsequently, the Bharatiya Janata Party (BJP) gaining momentum from the 1960s onwards.

Table 3.3
Share of Votes of the Two Main Parties of Madhya Pradesh, 1957–2003 (%)

Year	1957	1962	1967	1972	1977	1980	1985	1990	1993	1998	2003
Congress	49.8	38.5	40.7	47.9	35.9	47.5	48.9	33.5	40.8	40.60	31.6
JS/BJP	9.9	16.7	28.3	28.7	–	30.3	32.4	39.0	38.8	39.28	42.6
TOTAL	59.7	55.2	69.0	76.6	–	77.8	81.3	72.5	79.6	79.88	74.2

Source: Survey by author.

The domination of the Congress party, to begin with, was partly due to its capacity to co-opt former princes, a process which is well illustrated by the case of the Scindias. This dynasty was, in 1947, at the helm of one of the largest princely states of northern India and it controlled, thanks to its own power and prestige as well as the network of its former jagirdars, nearly one-fifth of the Assembly constituencies. In 1952, 'the Palace', the name under which the Scindias are known in Gwalior, discreetly supported the Hindu Mahasabha which emerged as the main rival to the Congress in Madhya Bharat. Nehru realised that this party might pose a threat to his camp in this area. He therefore requested Maharaja Jivaji Rao to side with Congress just before the elections of 1957. The Maharaja declined the invitation but the Maharani, Vijaya Raje Scindia was persuaded to contest the elections under the Congress banner (see Scindia and Malgonkar 1988: 172–73). She won with a large margin against the Hindu Mahasabha candidate. The Mahasabha lost ground in the whole area of Madhya Bharat whereas Congress established a domination which remained unrivalled till 1967 when 'the Palace' left the ruling party and joined the Hindu nationalist opposition once again.

Until 1967, the princely families of Madhya Pradesh, when they participated actively in politics, sided with Congress, either because they were anxious to find themselves in the camp of those in government, or because they did not dare oppose the solicitations of the ruling party. In Madhya Bharat, in addition to Vijaya Raje Scindia, the Congress benefited from the support of Bhanu Prakash Singh (ex-Maharaja of Narsingarh) who became a minister in the Indira Gandhi government in the late 1960s. In Vindhya Pradesh, the Congress received the backing of the former Raj Pramukh (governor of the province immediately after independence), the Maharaja of Rewa, a state equal in size to all the others of this region. Another Congress Rajput landowner, Siva Bahadur Singh, a prominent zamindar, was a minister in the first Cabinet of Vindhya Pradesh. His son, Arjun Singh, was first elected MLA in 1957 as an independent but then he joined Congress in March 1960. Interestingly, he had asked Nehru for an interview to submit him his intention of joining his party and Nehru had given him 'his blessings'.[3] In Chhattisgarh, the Congress obtained, from 1952 onwards, the support of the Maharajas of Sarangarh (district of Raigarh) and Surguja, who contested elections under its banner, and the support of the Rani of Khairagarh (Padmavati Devi) and of the Maharaja of Kanker (see *Hitavada* 1952). Thus, the Congress established its domination over Madhya Pradesh by aggregating 'vote banks' owned by former princes or jagirdars. This 'feudal' brand of clientelism partly explains the over-representation of the upper castes among the Congress MLAs, and more generally speaking, in the Vidhan Sabha itself from the 1950s to the 1960s.

The evolution of the social profile of the Madhya Pradesh Assembly is similar to that of the state's MPs, a clear indication of a distinctive regional pattern. The thresholds are almost the same: the share of the upper caste declined significantly, for the first time, in 1977 for the MPs and in 1980 for the MLAs; and then, again, in 1991 for the MPs and 1993 for the MLAs before the recent increase which put the clock back by several years. Similarly, the share of the OBC crossed the double digit in 1977 for the MPs and the MLAs and then the 20 per cent figure in 1991 for the MPs and in 1993 for the MLAs before declining in 2003–04.

The recent comeback of the upper castes at the expense of the OBC is largely due to the creation of Chhattisgarh which has left Madhya Pradesh with a larger share of upper caste population and less of OBC. In the pre-2000 Madhya Pradesh, the upper castes represented less than 13 per cent of society and the OBC more than 41 per cent, whereas they are now 16.8 per cent and 37.8 per cent respectively. Inevitably, this change has been reflected in the distribution of tickets by the political parties and the voting pattern of the electorate.

---

[3] Arjun Singh, interview by author, 18 November 1997, New Delhi.

Table 3.4

Castes and Communities of the Madhya Pradesh MLAs, 1957–2003 (%)

Castes and Communities	1957	1962	1967	1972	1977	1980	1985	1990	1993	1998	2003
Upper Castes	**41.2**	**48.4**	**44.9**	**49.6**	**46.6**	**40.3**	**40.7**	**40.9**	**37.1**	**35.6**	**37.7**
Brahmin	20.4	21.5	21.8	24.7	21.3	19.7	16.9	15.9	15.3	12.2	12.6
Rajput	8.1	14.2	10.9	12.3	10.6	11.3	15.0	12.5	12.8	15.3	16.5
Baniya/Jain	10.6	8.3	8.2	9.6	10.0	5.9	7.2	10.0	7.5	6.9	7.4
Kayastha	2.1	3.8	3.4	2.7	3.1	2.5	1.3	1.3	0.9	0.6	0.4
Khatri	–	–	–	0.3	1.3	0.6	0.3	0.6	0.3	–	0.4
Other	–	0.6	0.6	–	0.3	0.3	–	0.6	0.3	0.6	0.4
Intermediary Castes	**1.1**	**0.6**	**0.6**	**0.3**	**0.9**	**0.9**	**0.3**	**0.3**	**0.6**	**0.9**	**2.6**
Maratha	0.7	0.3	0.3	0.3	0.9	0.3	0.3	0.3	0.6	0.9	0.9
Patel	–	–	–	–	–	0.6	–	–	–	–	–
Raghuvanshi	0.4	0.3	0.3	–	–	–	–	–	–	–	1.7
OBC	**4.7**	**9.1**	**9.4**	**9.5**	**14.3**	**16.1**	**18.6**	**18.7**	**22.7**	**22.0**	**19.5**
Jat	–	–	–	0.3	0.3	0.3	–	0.3	0.3	–	0.4
Yadav	–	0.3	–	–	1.6	0.9	1.9	2.5	2.5	2.8	3.0
Kurmi	0.7	1.0	2.4	1.7	3.1	4.4	4.1	3.1	5.0	6.3	1.3
Kirar	–	–	0.7	0.3	–	0.3	0.3	1.3	0.6	0.9	0.4
Lodhi	0.4	–	–	–	0.6	0.9	0.9	1.3	1.6	2.2	2.2

(*Table 3.4 continued*)

(*Table 3.4 continued*)

Castes and Communities	1957	1962	1967	1972	1977	1980	1985	1990	1993	1998	2003
Mali	–	–	–	0.3	–	0.3	0.6	0.3	0.6	–	–
Teli	–	0.3	1.0	1.4	1.6	0.9	1.6	1.9	2.2	1.6	0.9
Panwar	2.1	1.7	1.4	2.1	2.2	1.9	2.2	2.5	1.6	0.3	2.2
Other	1.5	5.8	3.9	3.4	4.9	6.2	7.0	5.5	8.3	7.8	9.1
SC	**15.9**	**14.4**	**12.8**	**13.0**	**13.4**	**14.0**	**13.3**	**13.7**	**14.3**	**14.7**	**14.7**
ST	**18.3**	**20.1**	**20.4**	**22.2**	**20.4**	**24.4**	**24.4**	**23.7**	**23.4**	**23.4**	**19.1**
Muslims	**1.8**	**4.3**	**1.0**	**2.1**	**0.9**	**1.9**	**1.6**	**0.9**	**–**	**1.6**	**0.4**
Other Minorities	**0.8**	**–**	**–**	**0.35**	**0.3**	**0.6**	**0.3**	**0.6**	**1.2**	**1.2**	**0.9**
Unidentified	**16.5**	**4.2**	**10.6**	**2.7**	**3.1**	**1.6**	**0.6**	**0.3**	**0.3**	**0.6**	**4.8**
TOTAL	100.3 (N=284)	100.1 (N=289)	99.7 (N=293)	99.75 (N=292)	99.9 (N=320)	99.8 (N=320)	99.8 (N=320)	99.1 (N=320)	99.6 (N=320)	100.0 (N=320)	99.7 (N=230)

Source: Survey by author.

Occupation: More Agriculturists, Less Professionals

Even if the caste composition of the Madhya Pradesh Assembly is not changing as fast as in other North Indian states, the *savarna* MLAs of today do not belong to the same segment of the elite as 10 or 20 years ago, as evident from the occupation of the MLAs. Certainly, the rise of the agriculturists (from 48 per cent of the MLAs in 1977 to 63 per cent in 1993) and the decline of the lawyers (from 23 per cent in 1977 to 10 per cent in 1993) and the teachers (from 5 to 1 per cent) goes along with the assertion of the OBC and the decreasing number of the upper castes, but it goes also with the political emergence of a different kind of upper castes: Brahmins and Baniyas are making room for Rajputs.[4]

Table 3.5
Occupation of the MLAs Returned in Madhya Pradesh, 1977–93 (%)

Occupation	1977	1980	1985	1990	1993
Agriculturist	48.29	54.41	57.72	52.75	62.78
Lawyer	22.81	19.61	15.77	14.89	10.41
Medical Practitioner	4.56	3.92	4.70	3.88	5.68
Businessman	7.22	11.76	10.39	14.24	12.61
Labourer	0.38	–	1.01	1.94	1.26
Employee/Former Civil Servant	1.14	1.47	–	1.62	–
Ex-armyman	–	0.49	0.67	–	0.32
Teacher	5.32	0.98	2.68	2.91	0.95
Journalist	2.66	1.96	3.36	1.94	1.26
Student	–	–	–	0.32	–
Political/Social Worker	6.46	3.43	2.35	3.56	2.52
Artist	0.76	0.98	0.67	1.29	0.63
Unknown	0.38	0.98	0.67	0.65	1.58
TOTAL	99.98	99.99	94.99	99.34	100.00
	(N=263)	(N=204)	(N=298)	(N=309)	(N=317)

Sources: *Madhya Pradesh Vidhan Sabha Sadasyon ka Sankshipt Parichay*, for the years 1977, 1980; *Madhya Pradesh Vidhan Sabha Sadasya-Parichay* for the years 1985, 1990, 1993.

---

[4] The data concerning the occupation of the MLAs have been compiled on the basis of *Who's Who in Vidhan Sabha* which were not available or fully documented except for the years 1977–93.

Table 3.6

Occupation of the MLAs Returned in Madhya Pradesh by Caste and Community, 1977–93 (%)

Occupation	Upper Castes	Intermediary Castes	OBC	SC	ST	Religious Minorities	Unidentified Caste and Community
Agriculturist	39.45	50.00	64.91	45.65	81.85	42.86	50.00
Lawyer	22.42	10.00	17.74	12.50	7.14	9.52	25.00
Medical Practitioner	5.43	10.00	3.40	8.15	1.79	9.52	–
Businessman	19.44	30.00	3.02	14.13	1.20	23.81	25.00
Labourer	1.60	–	2.88	1.09	0.30	4.76	–
Employee/Former Civil Servant	0.18	–	0.75	1.63	1.19	–	–
Ex-armyman	0.70	–	–	–	–	–	–
Teacher	2.80	–	2.64	2.17	2.38	4.76	–
Journalist	3.50	–	2.64	1.63	–	4.76	–
Student	–	–	–	–	0.30	–	–
Political/Social Worker	4.38	–	1.51	6.52	2.68	–	–
Artist	–	–	0.75	4.89	0.30	–	–
Unknown	0.70	–	0.75	1.63	0.89	–	–
TOTAL	100.55	100.00	100.99	99.99	98.02	99.99	100.00
	(N=571)	(N=10)	(N=265)	(N=184)	(N=336)	(N=21)	(N=4)

Source: See Table 3.5.

The former represented about 30 per cent of the MLAs in 1962, they are 10 percentage points less today; the latter were about 8 per cent of the MLAs in 1957, they are twice this figure today. Many of these rural notables are registered as agriculturists in the *Who's Who in Vidhan Sabha* even if they are absentee landlords; but many of them do till their land. The share of the agriculturists is also much larger than that of the OBC because there are many non-OBC agriculturists who are, in fact, labourers (mostly in the case of SC/ST).

The Level of Education Goes up

Though the number of agriculturists increased, the general level of education of the MLAs of Madhya Pradesh has significantly improved between 1972 and 1993. In 20 years, the percentage of graduates almost doubled from less than 16 per cent to almost 32 per cent of the total, so much so that the sum of PhD holders, postgraduates and graduates has reached 68 per cent (as against less than 50 per cent in 1972). This is the outcome of a very steady increase of the 'Graduates', as is evident in Table 3.7.

Table 3.7
Level of Education of the Madhya Pradesh MLAs, 1972–93 (%)

Education	1972	1977	1980	1985	1990	1993
PhD	–	–	–	–	0.34	0.95
Postgraduate	33.57	35.16	38.02	37.92	35.84	35.96
Graduate	15.88	22.66	21.88	26.85	27.30	30.91
Matriculate	14.44	16.02	15.63	16.78	17.75	10.09
Intermediate	10.11	11.33	11.46	9.06	6.48	8.83
Middle School	10.47	7.81	10.42	7.38	7.85	9.46
Below Class V	1.08	0.39	–	–	1.37	0.32
Primary School	7.94	5.86	2.60	2.01	3.07	2.52
Ayurved	0.36	–	–	–	–	–
Shastri/Vaidya	–	0.39	–	–	–	0.32
Unknown	6.14	0.39	–	–	–	0.63
TOTAL	99.99	100.01	100.01	100.00	100.00	99.99
	(N=277)	(N=256)	(N=192)	(N=298)	(N=293)	(N=317)

Source: See Table 3.5; and *Madhya Pradesh Vidhan Sabha Sadasyon ka Sankshipt Parichay* for the year 1972.

Women and Muslim MLAs: Still Minuscule Minorities

While the OBC and the agriculturists have benefited from the demo-cratisation of the Indian polity in Madhya Pradesh, the women and the religious minorities have not, if one goes by their representation in the state Assembly. The average proportion of women among the MLAs over the years 1957–98 is below 6 per cent and it is not possible to identify any real upward trend. While the women MLAs were al-most 12 per cent of the total in 1957, their representation subsequently oscillated between 3 and 9 per cent. During the 1990s, their share has risen from 3.75 per cent to 7.19 per cent but it is too early to say whether this is an enduring process.

The women MLAs from Madhya Pradesh have come from two social milieus, the upper castes and the Scheduled Tribes. Till the 1980s, the women from upper castes have been in majority. Since then, the repartition is more balanced. In a way, this equi–repartition epitomises the 'coalition of extremes' pattern that the Congress has established in Madhya Pradesh in the 1990s as we shall see shortly. This pattern explains why Congressmen might be interested in carving out quotas for women in the assemblies: they expect that it will not foster the representation of the OBC, but that of the upper castes.

The Congress party matters more, here, than the BJP simply be-cause the latter has remained for a long time an overwhelmingly male-dominated party whereas the Congress has made room for women earlier. Still in 1998, whereas the Congress had twice more women MLAs than the BJP, it was far from having twice more MLAs. Things changed, of course, after the huge defeat that the Congress met in 2003: at that time 14 women MLAs were returned on a BJP ticket and only two on the Congress one.

Besides women, minorities have not benefited a great deal from the democratisation of politics either. Muslims remain under-represented in the Madhya Pradesh Assembly, so much so that it does not make any sense to calculate the percentage of Muslim MLAs. Unsurprisingly, the Congress accounts for most of them; there were only a handful on the BJP side.

In the present section of the chapter we have been gradually dragged into party politics. Indeed, the attitude of the leaders of political parties towards the process of the selection of candidates for state elections is a major explanation for the evolution of the social profile of the Assembly in Madhya Pradesh as elsewhere.

Table 3.8

Men and Women in the Legislative Assembly of Madhya Pradesh, 1957–2003 (%)

Year	1957	1962	1967	1972	1977	1980	1985	1990	1993	1998	2003
Females	11.62	4.15	3.07	4.45	3.13	5.63	9.38	3.75	4.06	7.19	6.90
Males	88.38	95.85	96.93	95.55	96.88	94.38	90.63	96.25	95.94	92.81	93.10
TOTAL	100.00	100.00	100.00	100.00	100.00	100.00	100.00	100.00	100.00	100.00	100.00
	(N=284)	(N=289)	(N=293)	(N=292)	(N=320)	(N=320)	(N=320)	(N=320)	(N=320)	(N=320)	(N=230)

Source: Survey of author.

Table 3.9
The Female MLAs of Madhya Pradesh, by Caste and Community, 1957–2003 (%)

Castes and Communities	1957	1962	1967	1972	1977	1980	1985	1990	1993	1998	2003
Upper Castes	**42.42**	**49.99**	**66.66**	**69.23**	**80.00**	**61.12**	**36.66**	**66.66**	**38.45**	**39.13**	**31.25**
Brahmin	24.24	33.33	44.44	30.77	40.00	33.33	16.67	25.00	15.38	21.74	12.50
Rajput	12.12	8.33	11.11	23.08	30.00	16.67	13.33	33.33	15.38	13.04	6.25
Baniya/Jain	3.03	–	–	–	–	5.56	3.33	–	7.69	4.35	12.50
Kayastha	3.03	8.33	11.11	7.69	10.00	5.56	3.33	–	–	–	–
Khatri	–	–	–	7.69	–	–	–	8.33	–	–	–
Intermediary Castes	–	–	–	–	–	–	–	–	–	**4.35**	**6.25**
Maratha	–	–	–	–	–	–	–	–	–	4.35	6.25
OBC	–	**16.67**	–	–	–	**5.56**	**6.66**	**8.33**	**15.38**	**8.70**	**12.50**
Dangi	–	–	–	–	–	–	–	–	–	4.35	–
Lodhi	–	–	–	–	–	–	–	8.33	–	4.35	12.50
Teli	–	–	–	–	–	–	3.33	–	–	–	–
Yadav	–	–	–	–	–	–	–	–	7.69	–	–
Other	–	16.67	–	–	–	5.56	3.33	–	7.69	–	–
SC	**12.12**	–	**11.11**	–	–	**11.11**	**13.33**	–	**7.69**	**4.35**	**25.00**
ST	**27.27**	**25.00**	**22.22**	**23.08**	**20.00**	**22.22**	**40.00**	**25.00**	**38.46**	**43.48**	**25.00**
Unidentified	**18.18**	**8.33**	–	**7.69**	–	–	**3.33**	–	–	–	–
TOTAL	100.00	100.00	100.00	100.00	100.00	100.00	100.00	100.00	100.00	100.00	100.00
	(N=33)	(N=12)	(N=9)	(N=13)	(N=10)	(N=18)	(N=30)	(N=12)	(N=13)	(N=23)	(N=16)

Source: Survey by author.

Table 3.10
Muslim Representation in the Madhya Pradesh Assembly, 1957–2003

Year	1957	1962	1967	1972	1977	1980	1985	1990	1998	2003
Muslim MLAs	5	7	3	6	3	6	5	3	5	1
Congress Muslim MLAs	4	6	1	5	–	5	4	1	5	1
BJP Muslim MLAs	–	–	–	–	–	–	1	1	–	–

Source: Survey by author.

The Contrasting Social Profile of the Congress, BJP, Socialist and BSP MLAs

As mentioned earlier, Madhya Pradesh is known for its resilience to a two-party system based on the competition between the Congress and the Jana Sangh/BJP. While the following discussion is largely devoted to these two political forces, it will pay attention to the emergence of a third actor, the BSP which, indeed, is asserting itself in places where the Left was strong through the 1950s to1960s.

The Congress Party: Stability and Change in the 'Coalition of Extremes Pattern'

From 1957 to 1967, the proportion of the Congress upper caste MLAs remained between 40–51 per cent. The highest figures, which correspond to the 1962 election, are more reliable given the fact that the percentage of those whose caste could not be identified is much lower for this election (1.4 per cent of the Congress MLAs), than for the elections of 1957 (14 per cent) and 1967 (10.1 per cent). The share of the intermediate castes and low castes Congress representatives in the Madhya Pradesh Assembly grew from about 5 per cent to about 11 per cent in 10 years, which reflects a massive under-representation. The most important non-upper castes groups were the Dalits and tribals. But these MLAs, who were often uneducated, did not form powerful lobbies. In fact, they had been co-opted because of the reservation system — they were very few in the state government where there was no reservation (as we shall see later) — and they were part of a 'coalition of extremes pattern', to use the phrase Paul Brass has coined to describe the situation prevailing in Uttar Pradesh (Brass 1980). According to him, the coalition supporting the Congress could be qualified in such terms because its constitutive groups were poles apart in the social structure. However, this terminology is rather misleading since it suggests that the groups in question might possess the same influence, while, in fact, the Dalits in Congress depended on the upper caste leaders who were really in command — one more indication that the Congress system is truly a clientelistic arrangement.

Table 3.11
Caste and Community of the Congress MLAs in Madhya Pradesh, 1957–67 (%)

Castes and Communities	1957	1962	1967
Upper Castes	**40.1**	**51.2**	**44.5**
Brahmin	20.5	27.7	23.7
Rajput	7.4	12.1	10.7
Baniya/Jain	10.0	6.4	7.1
Kayastha	2.2	4.3	2.4
Other	–	0.7	0.6
Intermediary Castes	**0.4**	**0.7**	**0.6**
Maratha	0	0	0.6
Raghuvanshi	0.4	0.7	0
OBC	**4.7**	**8.5**	**10.2**
Lodhi	0.4	–	–
Dangi	–	0	–
Gujjar	–	0	0.6
Jaiswal	–	0.7	1.2
Kirar	–	–	0
Kurmi	0	1.4	2.4
Pawar	2.6	2.1	2.4
Teli	–	0	0.6
Yadav	–	0	–
Sondhia Rajput	–	0	0
Soni	0.4	–	–
Baghel	–	–	0.6
Other	1.3	4.3	2.4
SC	**18.2**	**17.0**	**11.9**
ST	**20.5**	**17.0**	**22.5**
Muslims	**1.7**	**4.3**	**0.6**
Unidentified	**14.0**	**1.4**	**10.1**
TOTAL	99.6	100.1	100.7
	(N= 229)	(N= 141)	(N= 169)

Sources: Fieldwork interviews on the basis of the official results of the Madhya Pradesh Election Commission and the biodata of the relevant *Who's Who in Vidhan Sabha*.

In 1969, the scission of the Congress prepared the ground for a major shift in the social profile of the ruling party: while the Congress(O) ('O' for 'Organisation' or for 'Old', as its detractors called it) represented the traditional notables, Indira Gandhi's Congress(R) ('R' for 'Requisitionist') pretended to epitomise a new, more people-oriented political programme. Indira Gandhi broke away from the traditional Congress style during the 1971 mid-term election campaign. She tried to short-circuit the local notables at the helm of 'vote banks' by presenting her socio-economic programme directly to the people. Indira Gandhi tried to establish a bipolar political scene where forces of progress would be confronted to conservatives. The Congress Forum for Socialist Action (CFSA) exerted much pressure in that direction too.

The CFSA was very particular about the social profile of the candidates for the 1972 state assemblies' elections (Awana 1988: 207). However, the 1972 elections showed that the Congress(R) did not break from the age-old collaboration between an upper caste-educated intelligentsia and the notables from the merchant and agricultural classes. The caste profile of the Congress(R) MLAs is even more upper caste-dominated than those of the 1967 Congress group.

On the top of it, the Congress(R) relied on princes during the 1972 elections. In 1967, princes had begun to leave Congress because they were worried about the authoritarianism of the new Chief Minister, D. P. Mishra. Most of these defectors had joined the Bharatiya Jana Sangh in the wake of Vijaya Raje Scindia who had, by then, returned to Hindu nationalism. In spite of these defections, out of the 36 princes that had stood for the 1967 elections, 17 had still contested under the banner of Congress(R), and the Maharaja of Rewa had continued to support the ruling party (Purohit 1970: 304). But defections multiplied in the early 1970s when Indira Gandhi put into question the pensions and privileges that the princes had obtained after independence in exchange for the merger of their states with the Indian Union. The Maharaja of Rewa himself left the Congress. At the time of the 1971 elections, the Jana Sangh had presented half-a-dozen of princes as its candidates to the Lok Sabha. However, once the abolition of their privileges and pensions had been voted by parliament after Indira Gandhi's electoral success in 1971, most of the princes, who had no more interest in supporting the

Table 3.12
Caste and Community of the Congress MLAs in Madhya Pradesh, 1972 (%)

Castes and Communities	1972
Upper Castes	**51.0**
Brahmin	27.1
Rajput	11.5
Baniya/Jain	10.1
Kayastha	1.8
Khatri	0.5
Intermediary Castes	**0.5**
Maratha	0.5
OBC	**9.7**
Baghel	0.5
Gujjar	0.5
Jaiswal	0.9
Jat	0.5
Kurmi	1.8
Pawar	2.3
Rawat	0.5
Teli	0.9
Others	1.8
SC	**12.4**
ST	**21.1**
Muslims	**2.3**
Unidentified	**3.2**
TOTAL	100.2
	(N=218)

Source: Survey by author.

opposition, returned to the Congress(R) fold. The Maharaja of Rewa was amongst them and he was instrumental in having eight Congress(R) MLAs returned in the 1972 Assembly elections. Of the 37 princes who contested in the 1972 state elections, 24 stood on the Congress(R) ticket, and 17 of them were allotted Congress(R) tickets in Madhya Pradesh (Narain and Sharma 1973: 325).

The elitist bias of the Congress was gradually put into question after the party returned to power in 1980. Already in 1977, in facing its worse defeat since independence, the party had a record number of OBC MLAs returned. But the decline of the upper caste MLAs was not evident before 1980 when their share dropped below 39 per cent. Arjun Singh, the Chief Minister from 1980 to 1985 arguably tried to project himself as the spokesperson of the plebeians. At that time, the OBC of Madhya Pradesh continued to lack political organisation of their own (the socialist movement, the main advocate for the OBC in states like Bihar and Uttar Pradesh, was very much divided and dominated by upper caste leaders). The proponents of *kisan* politics were also very weak, largely because of the absence of a strong middle-caste milieu, like the Jats in Uttar Pradesh. There was, therefore, room for manoeuvre for the Congress. In 1981, Arjun Singh appointed a commission named after its Chairman, Ramji Mahajan, a former state minister and himself a Mali (OBC), to establish a list of the OBC and to identify their needs in the state. The Mahajan Commission report was submitted in late 1983. It identified 80 OBC castes which represented 48.08 per cent of the state's population (including 2.08 per cent Muslims). The Commission's report recommended that 35 per cent seats be reserved for the OBC seeking admission in educational institutions (see Mahajan 1983), and in all governmental, semi-governmental and public sector services. However, Arjun Singh did not really promote low caste leaders as Assembly candidates; hence the low level of Congress OBC MLAs who remained around 14–15 per cent over the 1980s.

Things really changed in the 1990s, with the decreasing number of upper caste MLAs and the rise of the OBC. The 1990 election however stands as an interesting aberration: more than 50 per cent of the Congress MLAs who were returned then were from the upper castes, something that had never occurred in the 1980s and which was not repeated in the 1990s. Now, 1990 was in fact, the worst election year for the Congress since the 1977 post-Emergency rout. This suggests that when the party faced defeat this time, its upper caste candidates performed better than the others, probably because they were better entrenched in their constituency. This interpretation is substantiated by the 2003 elections, when the Congress underwent an even worse defeat and registered more than 50 per cent of upper caste MLAs once again — but this rise occurred at the expense of the ST, the OBC remaining above 22 per cent as if their share had reached a point of no return.

The most striking aspect of Table 3.13 lies, indeed, in the sudden increase in the number of Congress OBC MLAs in the 1993 and their subsequent relative stability. The 1993 shift of about 7 percentage points compared to the 1980s is unprecedented. The percentage of the

Table 3.13
Castes and Communities of the Congress MLAs in the Madhya Pradesh
Legislative Assembly, 1977–2003 (%)

Castes and Communities	1977	1980	1985	1990	1993	1998	2003
Upper Castes	**41.5**	**38.7**	**41.3**	**51.0**	**35.0**	**35.5**	**52.5**
Brahmin	20.7	17.3	17.0	24.6	13.3	12.8	5.0
Rajput	12.2	12.3	17.0	15.8	15.1	18.0	47.5
Baniya/Jain	3.7	5.8	6.1	8.8	6.0	4.1	–
Kayastha	3.7	2.9	0.8	–	0.6	0.6	–
Khatri	1.2	0.4	0.4	1.8	–	–	–
Intermediary Castes	**1.2**	**1.2**	**1.6**	–	**0.6**	**1.8**	**5.0**
Raghuvanshi	1.2	0.4	1.2	–	0.6	1.2	2.5
Maratha	–	–	0.4	–	–	0.6	–
Patidar	–	0.8	–	–	–	–	2.5
OBC	**24.2**	**14.2**	**15.2**	**14.2**	**23.4**	**19.2**	**22.5**
Bairagi	–	0.8	–	–	–	–	–
Dangi	–	–	–	–	–	1.2	–
Baghel	1.2	0.4	0.4	–	0.6	–	–
Gujjar	–	–	0.4	–	2.4	1.7	2.5
Jaiswal	2.4	0.4	0.8	1.8	–	0.6	–
Kacchi	–	–	0.4	–	–	–	–
Kirar	–	–	0.4	–	0.6	0.6	–
Kunbi	–	–	–	–	–	0.6	–
Kurmi	7.3	4.9	3.6	3.5	5.4	7.6	2.5
Lodhi	1.2	0.4	0.4	–	1.2	1.7	–
Mali	1.2	0.4	0.8	1.8	1.2	–	–
Pankha	–	0.4	0.4	–	0.6	–	–
Pawar	2.4	0.8	1.2	3.5	1.2	–	2.5
Rawat	–	–	–	–	0.6	–	2.5
Tamoli	–	0.4	–	–	–	–	–
Teli	1.2	0.8	0.8	1.8	2.4	1.7	–
Yadav	1.2	0.8	2.4	–	3.0	2.3	2.5
Other	6.1	3.7	2.8	1.8	4.2	1.2	10.0
SC	**9.8**	**13.6**	**13.0**	**3.5**	**8.4**	**11.6**	**10.0**
ST	**21.9**	**26.7**	**26.3**	**29.8**	**30.1**	**27.9**	**5.0**
Christians	–	**0.4**	–	–	–	**0.6**	–
Muslims	–	**2.1**	**2.0**	**1.8**	–	**2.9**	**2.5**
Sikhs	–	**0.4**	**0.4**	–	**1.2**	–	–
Unidentified	**1.2**	**2.5**	–	–	**1.2**	**0.6**	**2.5**
TOTAL	99.8	99.8	99.8	100.3	99.9	100.1	100.0
	(N=82)	(N=243)	(N=247)	(N=57)	(N=166)	(N=172)	(N=40)

Source: Survey by author.

Congress OBC MLAs rose from about 14–15 per cent during 1980–90 to about 19–23 per cent during 1993–2003. The largest group was made of the Kurmis who represented 7.6 per cent of the Congress(I) MLAs in 1998 while they formed only 3.7 per cent of the state population according to the Mahajan Commission report. Another interesting figure concerns the ST which represented the second largest group among the Congress(I) MLAs after the upper castes with 26–30 per cent of the MLAs in the years 1993–98, whereas only 23.4 per cent of the seats are reserved for them. So far as the upper castes are concerned, the weight of the Brahmins tended to decline whereas that of the Rajputs increased, probably because of the attractiveness of Digvijay Singh, the new Congress leader and Chief Minister, over his caste fellows. One can, at last, see the Mandal impact in this social transformation. Indeed, these figures reflect the responsiveness of the party — and of its president, Digvijay Singh, whose mentor, at that time, was Arjun Singh — to the Mandal phenomenon as evident from the social profile of the candidates nominated by the Congress in the years 1993–2003.

The social profile of the Congress governments is rather different from that of the party's MLAs. Certainly, the share of the upper castes among the ministers tended to decline, but this change occurred very unevenly. For instance, while the 1985 elections sent a smaller number of upper caste candidates and a larger number of OBC to the Assembly, the 1985 Congress government was massively dominated by upper caste people. But here again, things changed in the 1990s. In fact, the transformation of the caste profile of the Congress was especially pronounced in the governments formed by Digvijay Singh. In 1993, his Cabinet was much less upper caste-dominated than the Congress governments of the 1980s. While the upper caste members represented 45–57 per cent of the governments in the decade 1980–90, in 1993, their percentage fell to about 33 per cent and remained below 40 per cent in the 1990s (except in 1998). The Rajputs, once again, 'resisted' more effectively than the other upper castes, especially the Brahmins and the Baniyas who had been especially well-represented in the BJP government of S. Patwa from 1990 to 1992 — one more indication that the Congress tended to be associated with the Rajputs while the BJP remained a 'Baniya/Brahmin' party. In the years 1993–99, the main beneficiaries of the decline of the upper castes were not primarily the OBC (who represented about one-fifth of the ministers, with the Kurmis still much

Table 3.14
Castes and Communities of the Congress Candidates in the Madhya Pradesh
Legislative Assembly, 1993–2003 (%)

Castes and Communities	1993	1998	2003
Upper Castes	**38.1**	**35.7**	**34.5**
Brahmin	17.6	13.9	11.7
Rajput	12.6	14.6	15.7
Baniya/Jain	6.3	4.4	4.9
Kayastha	1.3	1.6	0.9
Khatri	0.3	0.9	0.9
Sindhi	–	0.3	–
Other	–	–	0.4
Intermediary Castes	**0.6**	**1.2**	**1.3**
Raghuvanshi	0.3	0.9	1.3
Maratha	0.3	0.3	–
OBC	**17.8**	**20.4**	**23.9**
Bairagi	0.3	–	–
Dangi	–	0.6	2.2
Darzi	0.3	0.3	–
Baghel	0.3	0.3	–
Gujjar	1.3	2.5	2.2
Jaiswal	0.9	0.3	–
Kallar	–	0.3	–
Kirar	0.3	0.6	0.4
Khushwaha/Kacchi	–	0.6	0.9
Kunbi	–	0.6	–
Kurmi	3.8	5.1	2.2
Lodhi	0.9	1.9	0.9
Mali	0.6	0.3	–
Pankha	0.3	–	–
Pawar	0.6	–	1.8
Rawat	0.3	–	–
Teli	1.6	2.2	0.4
Yadav	1.9	3.2	3.6
Other	4.4	1.6	9.3
SC	**13.5**	**14.4**	**14.2**
ST	**23.9**	**23.1**	**18.8**
Christians	–	**0.3**	**0.4**
Muslims	**1.9**	**1.9**	**2.2**
Sikhs	**0.9**	**0.3**	**0.4**
Unidentified	**3.1**	**2.2**	**3.6**
TOTAL	99.8	99.5	99.1
	(N=318)	(N=316)	(N=223)

Source: Survey by author.

Table 3.15
Castes and Communities of the Members of Madhya Pradesh Governments, 1980–2004 (%)

Castes and Communities	1980–84 Congress	1985–86 Congress	1990–92 BJP	1993–95 Congress	1997 Congress	1998 Congress	1999 Congress	2000 Congress	2003 BJP	2004 BJP
Upper Castes	**43.1**	**57.1**	**51.7**	**33.4**	**37.8**	**42.9**	**38.7**	**39.5**	**61.2**	**48.6**
Brahmin	18.2	33.3	19.4	11.1	13.2	8.6	7.8	7.9	11.1	18.9
Rajput	13.6	23.8	6.5	16.7	15.1	20.0	18.0	18.4	22.2	13.5
Baniya/Jain	9.0	–	19.4	5.6	5.7	11.4	10.3	10.5	16.7	10.8
Khatri	–	–	3.2	–	–	–	–	–	5.6	2.7
Kayastha	2.3	–	3.2	–	3.8	2.9	2.6	2.6	–	–
Other	2.3	–	–	–	–	–	–	–	5.6	2.7
Intermediary Castes	**2.3**	–	–	**2.8**	–	**2.9**	**2.6**	**2.6**	–	–
Raghuvanshi	2.3	–	–	–	–	2.9	2.6	2.6	–	–
Other	–	–	–	2.8	–	–	–	–	–	–
OBC	**20.4**	**14.3**	**22.6**	**22.3**	**28.4**	**14.3**	**18.1**	**18.3**	**22.3**	**18.9**
Jat	–	–	3.2	–	–	–	–	–	–	–
Gujjar	–	–	–	–	1.9	–	2.6	2.6	–	2.7
Kirar	–	–	3.2	–	1.9	–	–	–	–	–
Kurmi	6.8	4.8	6.5	2.8	11.3	11.4	10.3	10.5	–	2.7
Lodhi	–	–	3.2	–	3.8	2.9	2.6	2.6	5.6	2.7
Mali	–	–	–	2.8	–	–	–	–	–	–

(Table 3.15 continued)

(Table 3.15 continued)

Castes and Communities	1980–84 Congress	1985–86 Congress	1990–92 BJP	1993–95 Congress	1997 Congress	1998 Congress	1999 Congress	2000 Congress	2003 BJP	2004 BJP
Pawar	4.5	–	–	–	–	–	–	–	5.6	2.7
Teli	–	–	3.2	2.8	1.9	–	2.6	2.6	–	–
Yadav	2.3	4.8	3.2	8.3	5.7	–	–	–	11.1	5.4
Other	6.8	4.8	–	5.6	1.9	–	–	–	–	2.7
SC	**13.6**	**9.5**	**9.7**	**8.3**	**3.8**	**8.6**	**10.3**	**13.2**	**5.6**	**13.5**
ST	**15.9**	**9.5**	**9.7**	**25.0**	**26.4**	**25.7**	**25.7**	**21.0**	**11.1**	**13.5**
Christians	–	–	–	2.8	–	2.9	–	2.6	–	–
Muslims	2.3	4.8	3.2	2.8	1.9	2.9	2.6	2.6	–	–
Sikhs	2.3	4.8	3.2	2.8	1.9	–	2.6	–	–	–
Unidentified	–	–	–	–	–	–	–	–	–	**5.5**
TOTAL	100.0	100.0	100.0	100.0	100.0	100.0	100.0	100.0	100.0	100.0
	(N=44)	(N=21)	(N=31)	(N=36)	(N=53)	(N=35)	(N=38)	(N=38)	(N=18)	(N=37)

Source: Survey by author.

more numerous than any other caste group) or the SC (who remained largely under-represented), but the ST, whose representation jumped to 25–26 per cent. These trends suggest, once again, that the traditional pattern of 'coalition of extremes' is surviving while being reshaped. An interesting variant of this pattern is emerging since the components of these vertical arrangements are not so much the Brahmins and the SC — as in the case of Uttar Pradesh — but the Rajputs and tribals.

In addition to diluting the domination of the upper castes over the state government, Digvijay Singh tried to promote non-elite groups within the machinery of the Congress party. However, comparing the caste composition of the Congress group of MLAs in the Vidhan Sabha and the Congress governments with the party apparatus immediately shows that while the upper caste Congress leaders may be willing to give tickets to low caste candidates for wooing their social milieu at the time of elections, and may resign themselves to appoint ministers from the non-upper castes groups with the same objectives in mind, they are not prepared to let the plebeians gain control over the party machinery.

In the Pradesh Congress Committee appointed in 1993, not only its president, Digvijay Singh was a Rajput, but the upper castes represented 55 per cent of the members. Once again, the OBC formed a small minority (15.5 per cent) whereas the SC were almost as numerous with about 14 per cent. The share of the upper castes — especially, that of the Brahmins and the Baniyas — decreased by 10 percentage points in 1996 to the advantage, not of the OBC, but of the ST and the Muslims. But in the post-Digvijay Singh era, which began after his defeat in 2003, the upper castes — especially the Brahmins and the Baniyas — have recovered their previous position.

The evolution of the District Congress Committees (DCC) was rather similar. The percentage of the upper caste presidents of DCC remained very important over the 1990s — between 50 and 61.5 per cent — since the decline of the Brahmins was partially compensated, once again, by the rise of the Rajputs. However, the trend was in favour of the OBC since they rose from 15–17 per cent in the years 1994–96 to 23–26 per cent in the late 1990s. The post-Digvijay Singh era witnessed the comeback of the upper castes (especially of the Brahmins) and the correlative decline of the subaltern groups (to the extent that there was not even one SC left as DCC president!).

Table 3.16
Castes and Communities of the Members of the Madhya Pradesh
Congress Committee, 1993–2004 (%)

Castes and Communities	1993	1996	2004
Upper Castes	**55.17**	**44.57**	**54.6**
Brahmin	27.59	20.65	23.8
Rajput	12.07	11.41	13.1
Baniya/Jain	10.34	8.70	13.8
Kayastha	3.45	1.09	3.1
Khatri	1.72	1.63	–
Sindhi	–	1.09	0.8
Intermediary Castes	**3.44**	**0.54**	**–**
Maratha	1.72	–	–
Patidar	1.72	0.54	–
OBC	**15.49**	**15.19**	**16.3**
Bairagi	1.72	0.54	–
Jat	–	–	0.8
Kirar	1.72	0.54	0.8
Kurmi	5.17	3.26	–
Mali	1.72	0.54	–
Pankha	1.72	–	–
Yadav	1.72	2.72	2.3
Other	1.72	7.59	12.4
SC	**13.79**	**8.70**	**6.2**
ST	**6.90**	**9.24**	**6.9**
Muslims	**3.45**	**6.52**	**9.2**
Christians	**–**	**0.54**	**0.8**
Sikhs	**–**	**1.09**	**1.5**
Unidentified	**1.72**	**13.59**	**4.6**
TOTAL	99.96	99.98	100.1
	(N=58)	(N=184)*	(N=130)*

Source: Survey by author.
Note: * Including 'special invitees'.

To sum up, the Congress of Madhya Pradesh has been slower than most of the large state units of the Hindi belt (except Rajasthan) to become more plebeian. Even though Digvijay Singh's strategy of 'social engineering' was designed in order to adjust to the post-Mandal context, it was still biased in favour of the SC and, even more, the ST, initiating a new variant of the old pattern of 'coalition of extremes'. In this framework, the Rajputs tended to replace the Brahmins, and the ST substituted the SC, but the rationale of this arrangement was based on the logic of clientelism. Digvijay Singh candidly admitted that his

Table 3.17
Castes and Communities of the Presidents of the Congress District
Committees in Madhya Pradesh, 1994–2004 (%)

Castes and Communities	1994	1996	1997	1999	2004
Upper Castes	**61.6**	**53.8**	**49.9**	**56.6**	**63.8**
Brahmin	30.8	32.7	18.3	18.3	36.2
Rajput	13.5	9.6	15.0	18.3	12.1
Baniya/Jain	17.3	11.5	13.3	15.0	12.1
Kayastha	–	–	–	1.7	–
Khatri	–	–	3.3	3.3	3.4
Intermediary Castes	**5.8**	**5.8**	**3.3**	**3.4**	**–**
Maratha	5.8	5.8	3.3	1.7	–
Others	–	–	–	1.7	–
OBC	**17.1**	**15.2**	**26.7**	**23.6**	**17.1**
Bairagi	–	–	–	1.7	–
Dangi	–	–	–	1.7	–
Dhobi	–	–	–	1.7	–
Gosain	–	–	–	1.7	–
Gujjar	–	–	3.3	3.3	3.4
Jaiswal	–	–	–	1.7	–
Kirar	3.8	1.9	1.7	–	–
Kori	–	–	–	1.7	–
Kurmi	3.8	3.8	1.7	1.7	6.9
Panwar	–	1.9	3.3	1.7	1.7
Teli	1.9	1.9	–	–	–
Yadav	3.8	1.9	1.7	1.7	–
Others	3.8	3.8	15.0	5.0	5.1
SC	**–**	**1.9**	**3.3**	**1.7**	**–**
ST	**5.8**	**7.7**	**5.0**	**3.3**	**5.2**
Muslims	**7.7**	**7.7**	**10.0**	**10.0**	**10.3**
Sikhs	**–**	**–**	**–**	**1.7**	**3.4**
Unidentified	**1.9**	**7.7**	**1.7**	**–**	**–**
TOTAL	99.9	99.8	99.9	100.3	99.8
	(N=52)	(N=52)	(N=60)	(N=60)	(N=60)

Source: Survey by author.

strategy of promoting tribal leaders has partly failed because none of them displayed statesman's qualities.[5] After the creation of Chhattisgarh, this strategy was put into question because of the decreasing influence of the tribals whose share had gone down from 23.27 per cent according

---

[5] Digvijay Singh, interview by author, November 1997, Bhopal. According to Jamuna Devi, one of the tribal leaders sidelined by Singh, his pro-Adivasi strategy had failed because he had not promoted the right persons lest they took his place (interview with Jamuna Devi, 20 February 2004, Bhopal).

to the 1991 Census to less than 20 per cent according to the 2001 Census. Digvijay Singh then promoted a 'Dalit agenda' that was intended to counter the BSP which he considered to be more dangerous than the BJP.[6]

Digvijay Singh, in fact, asked, Chandra Bhan Prasad, a Dalit journalist, to prepare a report on the living conditions of the Dalit and the reforms needed.[7] He then wrote the preface, entitled 'Transforming India through a Dalit Paradigm', where he advocated the cause of the Dalits and the Adivasis in a rather emotional manner (Singh 2002: 5). Subsequently, he convened a large conference in Bhopal in January 2002 where a 'Dalit Agenda' made of 21 recommendations was evolved. This document emphasised the need for land reform and reservations for the Dalits in the private sector, as well as in the army and the judiciary. By year 2000, Singh had already redistributed 250,000 acres to 68,000 Dalit families and 47,000 Adivasi families (ibid.: 110–11). He also recruited 1200 teachers and 2700 policemen from among these two groups (ibid.: 122) This policy was counterproductive. First, it alienated the tribals who resented the fact that they were called 'Dalits' and bracketed together with this group, at a time when they asserted a new identity — as evident from the rise of a new Gond party, the Gondwana Ganatantra Party which won 22 to 39 per cent of the valid votes in six Gond constituencies in 2003 (Dhar 2004). Second, it was not sufficient for wooing the Dalits who protested that they could not buy the so-called 'redistributed land' with the 75,000 rupees offered by the state (Central Chronicle 2003a). Third, the Dalit Agenda infuriated the OBC and the upper caste notables, including those within the Congress party. The OBC were also embittered by Digvijay Singh's inability to secure the 27 per cent quota he had promised in the state administration. Though this measure was voted by the Vidhan Sabha in the summer 2003, the governor, and then the High Court, objected that such a decision was illegal because it would push the sum of the quotas to 63 per cent, whereas the limit had to be below 50 per cent. The fiasco of the Dalit Agenda in political terms was one of the reasons for the defeat of the Congress in 2003 (Manor 2004).

---

[6] Digvijay Singh, interview by author, March 2007, New Delhi.

[7] Chandra Bhan Prasad, interview by author, October 2002, Madison.

The BJP in Madhya Pradesh, An OBC-friendly Party?

The Jana Sangh was known in Madhya Pradesh as a 'Baniya/Brahmin' party, not only because its electoral strongholds were made of the urban upper caste middle class (see Graham 1990: Chapter 6), but also because the party was over-dominated by leaders coming from this social milieu (see Jaffrelot 1999: 172–78). Indeed, an overwhelming majority of the party MLAs were from social background and, in 1972, from the Rajput caste-group.

Table 3.18
Castes and Communities of the Jana Sangh MLAs in Madhya Pradesh, 1957–72 (%)

Castes and Communities	1957	1962	1967	1972
Upper Castes	66.66	39.03	45.57	47.92
Brahmin	11.11	26.83	18.99	14.58
Rajput	11.11	2.44	8.86	18.75
Baniya/Jain	44.44	9.76	10.13	10.42
Kayastha	–	–	7.59	4.17
Intermediary Castes	11.11	4.88	1.27	–
Maratha	–	4.88	–	–
Raghuvanshi	–	–	1.27	–
OBC	–	12.22	11.40	8.32
Dangi	–	2.44	–	–
Gujjar	–	2.44	2.53	2.08
Kirar	–	–	1.27	2.08
Kurmi	11.11	–	2.53	–
Pawar	–	–	–	2.08
Rawat	–	–	1.27	–
Sondhia Rajput	–	2.44	1.27	–
Teli	–	2.44	2.53	2.08
Yadav	–	2.44	–	–
SC	11.11	17.08	18.99	18.74
ST	11.11	21.95	15.19	22.92
Unidentified	–	4.88	7.59	2.08
TOTAL	(N=9)	(N=41)	(N=79)	(N=48)

Source: Survey by author.

To begin with, the BJP — which was founded in 1980 to take over from the Jana Sangh — was not different from its predecessor so far as its social profile was concerned. However, the share of the upper caste MLAs — mostly Brahmins and Baniyas — underwent a steady, though limited, erosion over the years 1993–2003, from 42.3 per cent to 35.8 per cent. This change benefited the OBC — who crossed the 20 per cent threshold in 1998 and remained at this level in 2003 — and to the ST — who jumped from 15.3 to 22.8 per cent. While this last development was not due to the fielding of a larger number of ST candidates, the party displayed a more voluntarist policy vis-à-vis the OBC. It gave tickets to 23.1 per cent OBC in 2003 — almost 4 percentage points more than in 1993. And after its electoral success — unprecedented in the annals of the state — the BJP MLAs voted to power an OBC Chief Minister, Uma Bharti (a Lodhi), who was succeeded by two other OBC chief ministers, Babulal Gaur (a Yadav) and Shivraj Singh Chouhan (a Kirar).

Table 3.19

Castes and Communities of the BJP MLAs in Madhya Pradesh, 1980–2003 (%)

Castes and Communities	1980	1985	1990	1993	1998	2003
Upper Castes	**39.3**	**40.7**	**36.8**	**42.3**	**35.9**	**35.7**
Brahmin	14.8	18.6	13.8	17.8	14.2	13.4
Rajput	4.9	8.5	8.9	10.2	7.5	12.3
Baniya/Jain	13.1	11.9	11.6	11.9	11.7	7.6
Kayastha	3.3	1.7	1.3	0.8	0.8	0.6
Khatri	1.6	–	0.4	0.8	–	0.6
Sindhi	1.6	–	0.4	0.8	1.7	1.2
Other	–	–	0.4	–	–	–
Intermediary Castes	**1.6**	**–**	**1.7**	**0.8**	**1.7**	**1.8**
Raghuvanshi	–	–	1.3	–	–	1.2
Maratha	1.6	–	0.4	0.8	1.7	0.6
OBC	**19.4**	**27.2**	**19.2**	**16.6**	**21.7**	**19.9**
Bairagi	–	1.7	0.4	–	–	–
Dangi	–	1.7	0.4	1.7	1.7	–
Gujjar	1.6	–	–	–	–	0.6
Jat	1.6	–	0.4	0.8	–	0.6
Kallar	–	–	0.4	–	0.8	0.6
Kasar	–	1.7	–	–	–	–
Khati	–	1.7	0.4	0.8	0.8	0.6
Kirar	1.6	–	1.8	0.8	0.8	–
Kurmi	3.3	5.1	4.0	3.4	4.2	2.3
Lodhi	1.6	3.4	0.9	0.8	2.5	2.9
Pawar	3.3	5.1	2.2	1.7	0.8	2.3
Rawat	1.6	–	0.4	–	–	0.6
Sondhia Rajput	–	–	0.4	0.8	–	0.6
Soni	–	–	0.4	–	–	–
Tamoli	–	–	0.4	–	–	–
Teli	1.6	3.4	1.8	2.5	1.7	0.6

(Table 3.19 continued)

(*Table 3.19 continued*)

Castes and Communities	1980	1985	1990	1993	1998	2003
Yadav	1.6	1.7	3.1	2.5	4.2	3.5
Other	1.6	1.7	1.8	0.8	4.2	4.7
SC	**21.3**	**13.6**	**15.9**	**21.9**	**18.3**	**16.4**
ST	**16.4**	**16.9**	**24.4**	**15.3**	**19.2**	**22.8**
Muslims	–	**1.7**	**0.4**	–	–	–
Sikhs	–	–	**0.9**	**0.8**	**2.5**	**1.2**
Unidentified	**1.6**	–	–	**1.7**	**0.8**	**1.2**
TOTAL	99.6	100.1	99.3	99.4	100.1	99.0
	(N=61)	(N=59)	(N=225)	(N=118)	(N=120)	(N=171)

Source: Survey by author.

Table 3.20
Castes and Communities of the Candidates of the BJP to the State Assembly
Elections of Madhya Pradesh, 1993–2003 (%)

Castes and Communities	1993	1998	2003
Upper Castes	**39.7**	**36.6**	**38.8**
Brahmin	15.8	14.4	16.2
Rajput	9.5	8.8	12.7
Baniya/Jain	12.0	10.6	8.7
Kayastha	0.9	0.9	0.4
Khatri	0.6	0.6	0.4
Sindhi	0.9	1.3	0.4
Intermediary Castes	**0.3**	**1.5**	**2.6**
Maratha	0.3	0.9	1.3
Raghuvanshi	–	0.6	1.3
OBC	**19.3**	**20.8**	**23.2**
Dangi	0.6	0.9	–
Gujjar	–	0.3	–
Jat	0.6	0.3	–
Kacchi	–	0.3	–
Kallar	0.3	1.3	–
Khati	0.3	0.3	–
Kirar	0.6	0.6	1.3
Kolahar	0.3	–	–
Kunbi	0.6	–	–
Kurmi	5.1	5.3	1.7
Lodhi	1.9	2.5	4.4
Mina	–	0.3	0.9
Pawar	0.9	0.3	1.7
Sondhia Rajput	0.3	0.3	0.9
Soni	0.3	–	–
Tamoli	–	0.3	–

(*Table 3.20 continued*)

(*Table 3.20 continued*)

Castes and Communities	1993	1998	2003
Teli	2.5	2.2	0.9
Yadav	1.9	2.5	3.1
Other	3.1	3.1	8.3
SC	**13.6**	**14.1**	**14.4**
ST	**23.7**	**23.1**	**18.8**
Muslims	**0.3**	**0.3**	**0**
Sikhs	**0.6**	**0.9**	**0.9**
Unidentified	**1.9**	**2.5**	**1.3**
TOTAL	99.4	99.8	100.0
	(N=316)	(N=320)	(N=229)

Source: Survey by author.

While the BJP has nominated an increasing number of non-upper caste candidates at the time of elections in the wake of the Mandal affair for benefiting from the mobilisation of the lower castes, the composition of Patwa's government between 1990 and 1992 was a good indication of the persisting domination of the upper castes within the BJP in the early 1990s. As shown in Table 3.15, out of 31 Cabinet members, 17 belonged to the upper castes, seven to the OBC, three to the ST and two to the SC; there was also one Muslim. Similarly, in 2003, when the BJP came back to power, the share of the upper castes in the government jumped from 39.5 per cent to 61.2 per cent: the chief minister may have been from the OBC, but his team was not at all plebeian. Things changed in 2004 when the proportion of the upper caste ministers fell to 48.6 per cent — still about 10 percentage points more than in the Digvijay Singh's governments of the 1990s.

The BJP's party machinery remains also over-dominated by upper caste dignitaries, with a significant over-representaton of the Brahmins and the Baniyas. Between 1991 and 2003, the share of the upper castes in the BJP Madhya Pradesh State Executive Committee oscillated between 57 per cent and 67 per cent whereas the OBC were never more than about 20 per cent, the SC, never more than about 5 per cent and the ST never exceeding about 14 per cent.

The same picture emerges from the social profile of the presidents of the BJP district units in Madhya Pradesh. Once again, the upper caste members oscillate between 58 and 68 per cent over the years 1990–2003, with a striking over-representation of the Brahmins and the Baniyas. While the OBC represent a significant minority with 20–28 per cent of the total, the SC and ST are completely marginalised.

Table 3.21
Castes and Communities of the Members of the BJP State Executive
Committee of Madhya Pradesh, 1991–2003 (%)

Castes and Communities	1991	1994	1995	1997	2000	2003
Upper Castes	**65.1**	**56.9**	**66.6**	**61.2**	**59.6**	**67.5**
Brahmin	30.3	26.4	27.5	27.8	26.2	28.2
Rajput	10.1	10.7	14.5	13.9	9.5	11.1
Baniya/Jain	15.6	11.6	20.3	11.1	17.9	18.8
Kayastha	6.1	6.6	4.3	4.2	2.4	5.1
Khatri	–	0.8	–	1.4	–	0.9
Other	3.0	0.8	–	2.8	3.6	3.4
Intermediary Castes	**2.0**	**1.7**	**2.9**	**2.8**	**2.4**	**0.9**
Raghuvanshi	–	–	–	2.8	–	–
Maratha	1.0	1.7	2.9	–	2.4	0.9
OBC	**13.0**	**20.2**	**12.8**	**19.6**	**14.4**	**19.8**
Gujjar	–	–	–	1.4	–	0.9
Jat	1.0	0.8	1.4	–	1.2	2.6
Kirar	–	0.8	1.4	–	1.2	–
Kacchi/Kucchwaha	1.0	0.8	–	–	–	0.9
Kurmi	–	2.5	2.9	4.2	4.8	1.7
Lodhi	2.0	4.1	1.4	4.2	2.4	1.7
Nai	–	0.8	–	–	–	–
Sondhia Rajput	1.0	0.8	–	–	–	–
Soni	–	0.8	–	1.4	–	–
Teli	2.0	3.3	1.4	1.4	2.4	–
Yadav	3.0	1.7	1.4	1.4	1.2	1.7
Other	3.0	4.1	2.9	5.6	1.2	10.3
SC	**4.0**	**5.0**	**4.3**	**1.4**	**4.8**	**3.4**
ST	**8.1**	**8.3**	**2.9**	**13.9**	**9.5**	**2.6**
Christians	–	**1.7**	**1.4**	–	**1.2**	**0.9**
Muslims	**4.0**	**1.7**	**1.4**	**1.4**	**1.2**	**1.7**
Sikhs	**1.0**	**0.8**	**1.4**	–	–	**1.7**
Unidentified	**4.0**	**3.3**	**5.8**	–	**7.1**	**0.9**
TOTAL	100.2	99.6	99.5	100.3	100.2	99.4
	(N=99)	(N=121)	(N=69)	(N=72)	(N=84)	(N=117)

Source: Survey by author.

The over-representation of the upper castes among the BJP cadres stems from the conjunction of two factors. First, the party apparatus comprises many former *pracharaks* who have been seconded by the RSS to the BJP for organisational tasks; and most of the RSS *pracharaks*, till recently, came from the upper castes, particularly from the Brahmin *jatis*, often with a Maharashtrian background. Second, the traditional elitist profile continues because the party establishment has not undergone

Table 3.22
Castes and Communities of the Presidents of the BJP District Units in
Madhya Pradesh, 1990–2003 (%)

Castes and Communities	1990	1994	1999	2003
Upper Castes	**63.4**	**67.9**	**58.0**	**64.2**
Brahmin	26.8	23.2	14.0	26.4
Rajput	7.3	19.6	14.0	9.4
Baniya/Jain	19.5	19.6	21.1	20.8
Kayastha	2.4	5.4	1.8	3.8
Khatri	4.9	–	1.8	3.8
Other	2.4	–	5.3	–
Intermediary Castes	–	–	**1.8**	**1.9**
Raghuvanshi	–	–	–	1.9
Maratha	–	–	1.8	–
OBC	**22.0**	**19.6**	**28.1**	**26.5**
SC	**2.4**	–	**1.8**	–
ST	**2.4**	**8.9**	**5.3**	–
Sikhs	–	**1.8**	**3.5**	**7.5**
Unidentified	**9.8**	**1.8**	**1.8**	–
TOTAL	100.0	100.0	100.0	100.0
	(N=41)	(N=56)	(N=57)	(N=53)

Source: Survey by author.

any significant renewal in the last decades, which means that the traditional base of the Hindu nationalist movement among the Brahmins and the Baniyas remain over-represented. Though the BJP tries to project a plebeian image by promoting OBC chief ministers and appointing SC leaders within the party apparatus (since May 2006, for instance, the President of the State Executive Committee is a Dalit, Satyanarayan Jatia), upper caste leaders remain very much in control, more than what the erosion of their share among the party MLAs may suggest.

To sum up: the two mainstream parties of Madhya Padesh, the Congress and the BJP are still in the hands of upper caste politicians, even though they have pretended to plebeianise themselves, the former by revisiting the old 'coalition of extremes' pattern, the latter by promoting OBC leaders. But these two parties do not represent the same segments of the elite. While the BJP is still, to a large extent, a 'Baniya/Brahmin' party, the Congress, in the 1990s, has relied more on the Rajputs — something which has changed after Digvijay Singh left the scene.

This difference in terms of castes is well reflected in the occupation of the MLAs. While the agriculturists represented about 60–70 per cent of the Congress MLAs in the years 1980–93, they were about 10 percentage points less on the BJP side. Symmetrically, the businessmen represented an average of 19 per cent of the BJP MLAs over this period — that is, more than twice the Congress average.

Table 3.23
Occupation of the Congress MLAs of Madhya Pradesh, 1977–93 (%)

Occupation	1977	1980	1985	1990	1993	TOTAL
Agriculturist	62.67	60.14	59.40	66.67	71.51	63.57
Lawyer	24.00	19.58	16.24	16.67	9.88	16.22
Medical Practitioner	–	3.50	5.13	–	3.49	3.39
Businessman	4.00	7.70	10.26	5.56	6.98	7.81
Labourer	–	–	0.43	–	–	0.15
Employee/Ex-Civil Servant	1.33	2.10	–	–	–	0.59
Ex-Armyman	–	0.70	0.85	–	0.58	0.59
Teacher	1.33	0.70	2.14	–	–	1.03
Journalist	4.00	2.80	2.99	5.56	2.33	3.10
Political/Social Worker	2.67	1.40	1.71	5.56	2.91	2.36
Unidentified	–	1.40	0.85	–	2.33	1.18
TOTAL	100.00 (N=75)	100.02 (N=143)	100.00 (N=234)	100.02 (N=54)	100.04 (N=172)	99.99 (N=678)

Source: See Table 3.5.

Table 3.24
Occupation of the BJP MLAs of Madhya Pradesh, 1980–93 (%)

Occupation	1980	1985	1990	1993	TOTAL
Agriculturist	40.35	52.73	48.37	50.86	48.53
Lawyer	19.30	12.73	13.49	12.07	13.77
Medical Practitioner	5.26	3.64	5.12	6.03	5.19
Businessman	21.05	12.73	17.68	22.4	18.73
Labourer/Technician	–	3.64	2.79	3.44	2.71
Employee/Ex-Civil Servant	–	–	1.86	–	0.9
Education	1.75	5.45	3.26	2.59	3.16
Journalist	–	3.64	0.93	–	0.9
Student	–	–	0.47	–	0.23
Political/Social Worker	8.77	1.82	3.26	–	2.93
Artist	3.51	3.64	1.86	1.72	2.26
Unidentified	–	–	0.93	0.86	0.68
TOTAL	99.99 (N=57)	100.02 (N=55)	100.02 (N=215)	99.97 (N=116)	99.99 (N=443)

Source: See Table 3.5.

From the Socialists to the BSP:
A Tradition to (Re)invent

In contrast to Uttar Pradesh and Bihar, Madhya Pradesh has no solid tradition of '*kisan* politics' or 'quota politics'. There is no equivalent here to Charan Singh and Devi Lal — possibly because there is no equivalent to the Jats — or to Ram Manohar Lohia and Karpoori Thakur. Yet, the socialists had made some inroads in the state after independence, so much so that their party had become the second largest one in the Vidhan Sabha in 1962. It was especially strong in Vindhya Pradesh, because of the virulence of caste conflicts in this area and because of the political influence of the socialists in the bordering state of U.P. But the socialist leaders of this region were mostly from the upper castes — mainly Brahmins, like their chief leader, Yamuna Prasad Shastri — and the MLAs of this school of thought too.

Since the socialist MLAs have never been in large numbers, I have looked at the performances of their parties together for calculating the aggregated percentages which follow. In Table 3.25, the Socialist Party, the Samyukta Socialist Party, the Praja Socialist Party, the Janata Party and the Janata Dal have been amalgated. The election year 1977 has not been taken into account because the Janata Party, at that time, gathered together very different political groups, ranging from the socialists to the Jana Sangh (which, in fact, dominated the party group in the Vidhan Sabha).

Table 3.25 shows that the upper castes have always been in majority among the socialist MLAs except in 1993; however, we cannot draw any conclusion from this election year because there were only four socialist MLAs in the Vidhan Sabha at that time! In 1962, when the socialists formed the largest opposition group in the Vidhan Sabha — and in 1990, when they made inroads in the wake of V. P. Singh's victory at the centre — they were more numerous. But in both cases, the OBC MLAs were marginal — even non-existent in 1990 — and the upper caste MLAs remained in majority, with the Rajputs representing between one-fifth and one-third of the total. However, the socialists prepared the ground for the Bahujan Samaj Party (BSP) — and at the same time, because of their upper caste profile could not compete with it vis-à-vis the plebeian voters.

Indeed, in Madhya Pradesh, the BSP has primarily developed pockets of influence in the districts of Vindhya Pradesh and Madhya Bharat

Table 3.25
Castes and Communities of the Socialist MLAs of Madhya Pradesh, 1957–98 (%)

Castes and Communities	1957	1962	1967	1972	1980	1985	1990	1993	1998
Upper Castes	**28.57**	**52.07**	**53.33**	**55.55**	**33.33**	**60**	**57.14**	**25**	**100**
Brahmin	28.57	14.58	33.33	44.44	–	20	17.86	25	20
Rajput	–	20.83	13.33	11.11	33.33	–	32.14	–	80
Baniya/Jain	–	8.33	6.67	–	–	–	3.57	–	–
Kayastha	–	6.25	–	–	–	40	3.57	–	–
Khatri	–	2.08	–	–	–	–	–	–	–
OBC	**7.14**	**12.50**	–	**11.11**	**33.33**	**40**	**17.85**	**50**	–
Kurmi	7.14	2.08	–	11.11	–	–	–	–	–
Lodhi	–	–	–	–	–	20	–	–	–
Pawar	–	4.17	–	–	33.33	20	3.57	25	–
Yadav	–	–	–	–	–	–	10.71		–
Others	–	6.25	–	–	–	–	3.57	25	–
SC	**7.14**	**10.42**	–	**11.11**	–	–	**10.71**	–	–
ST	**7.14**	**20.83**	**26.67**	**11.11**	**33.33**	–	**10.71**	**25**	–
Christians	**7.14**	–	–	–	–	–	–	–	–
Muslims	–	–	**6.67**	**11.11**	–	–	–	–	–
Unidentified	**42.86**	**4.17**	**13.33**	–	–	–	**3.57**	–	–
TOTAL	99.99	99.99	100.00	99.99	99.99	100	99.98	100	100
	(N=14)	(N=48)	(N=15)	(N=9)	(N=3)	(N=5)	(N=28)	(N=4)	(N=5)

Source: Survey by author.

bordering Uttar Pradesh where the socialists used to be strong. During the 1996 Lok Sabha elections, it polled 19.6 per cent in Vindhya Pradesh and progressed in the districts of Morena, Bhind and Gwalior in northern Madhya Bharat. These areas have been familiar with low caste politics for decades since they were already the strongholds of the Janata Dal and, before that, of the socialists of the 1950s and the 1960s.[8] Moreover, in 1993, the BSP had snatched four MLA seats from the Janata Dal and one from the CPI, all of them in Rewa and Morena districts.

The BSP of Madhya Pradesh has tried to broaden its base beyond the SC in a systematic manner. First, the party has nominated an increasing number of OBC candidates, from 23.7 in 1993 to 50.5 per cent

---

[8] In 1997, the then Vice President of the Madhya Pradesh unit of the BSP, I. M. P. Verma pointed out that the 'OBC votes were automatically transferred from the socialists to the BSP when it emerged as a force in Rewa division' (I. M. P. Verma, interview by author, 15 February 1997, Bhopal).

in 1998 (Table 3.26). In 1998, the BSP OBC candidates 'represented' 27 different castes. Among them, the Kurmis stood prominent with 12.4 per cent of the party candidates — the largest group. The decision to nominate more than half of the OBC candidates was not made at the expense of the SC (whose percentage was stable around 30 per cent with the Chamars and the Satnamis remaining the largest groups) but to the Muslims and the ST. Acknowledging their strength in a state where they represented one-fourth of the population, the BSP nominated almost 26 per cent tribal candidates in 1993 but reduced this percentage to 16 per cent in 1998.

Table 3.26
Castes and Communities of the BSP Candidates in the 1993 and 1998
Assembly Elections in Madhya Pradesh (%)

Castes and Communities	1993	1998
Upper Castes	**0.4**	**1.2**
Rajput	–	0.6
Baniya/Jain	0.4	0.6
OBC	**23.7**	**50.5**
Aghariya	–	0.6
Bari	–	1.2
Bhoi	–	0.6
Chaurasia	0.4	–
Dangi	–	1.2
Dhiwar	–	0.6
Dhobi	–	0.6
Gadariya	0.4	1.8
Gujjar	0.7	5.3
Kacchi	3.2	4.7
Kallar	–	0.6
Kenwat	–	2.4
Kirar/Dhakad	0.7	3.0
Kolta	–	0.6
Kosta	–	0.6
Kumhar	–	0.6
Kurmi	5.7	12.4
Lodhi	0.4	1.8
Mali	0.4	1.8
Marar	0.4	0.6
Mina	–	0.6
Nai	0.7	0.6
Panwar	–	0.6
Rawat	0.4	0.6

(Table 3.26 continued)

(*Table 3.26 continued*)

Castes and Communities	1993	1998
Teli	3.9	5.3
Yadav	3.2	1.8
Others	3.2	–
SC	**30.8**	**30.7**
Ahirwar	0.7	1.8
Bagri	–	0.6
Balai	0.7	2.9
Balmiki	0.7	1.2
Basor	–	0.6
Chamar	10.6	10.6
Khangar	–	0.6
Kori	0.4	1.2
Mahar	4.2	1.2
Rawat	0.4	–
Satnami	7.8	8.2
Shakwar	–	0.6
Suryawansi	–	1.2
Others	5.3	–
ST	**25.8**	**16.1**
Barela	–	0.6
Bhilala	–	1.2
Gond	2.1	4.7
Kanwar	–	1.8
Kol	0.4	2.4
Kotwar	–	0.6
Muriya	–	0.6
Panika	–	1.2
Oraon	–	1.2
Others	23.3	1.8
Muslims	**8.5**	**1.8**
Sikhs	–	**0.6**
Unidentified	**11.3**	–
TOTAL	100.5	100.9
	(N=283)	(N=170)

Source: Survey by author.

Even though the BSP registered a setback during the 1998 election (its percentage of valid votes dropping from about 8 in 1993 to 6.3 per cent), the party's strategy of attracting OBC voters, beyond its Dalit base — as is evident from its nomination of OBC candidates in large numbers — might have posed a threat to the mainstream parties and obliged them to further 'democratise' themselves. However, the BSP changed its strategy in 2003 when it gave tickets to a larger number of upper caste candidates at the expense of the OBC in order that its list of candidates should reflect the general social structure. Out of 146 candidates, 17.8 per cent were from the upper castes, 34.2 per cent from the OBC, 34.9 per cent from the SC, 19.2 per cent from the ST and 7.5 per cent from the Muslim community (*Central Chronicle* 2003b and 2003c). This strategy bore fruit since the party polled 7.6 per cent of the valid votes; interestingly, its two MLAs were both returned in non-reserved constituencies.

Conclusion

In contrast to other states of the Hindi belt where non-upper castes have been in a position to take the lead against the *savarna* — like the Jats in U.P. and Rajasthan or the Yadavs in U.P. and Bihar — post-1956 Madhya Pradesh was characterised by the domination of large groups of upper castes and the fragmentation of the lower castes. This state of things was further aggravated by the resilience of the princely elite which reinforced the conservative overtone of Madhya Pradesh politics. Till the 1960s, the Congress party — which was fully in control till 1967 — relied on a clientelistic arrangement in which the lower castes were marginalised, as evident from the social profile of the party's MLAs. Indira Gandhi's (timid or hypocritical) efforts at democratising the party did not bear fruit in Madhya Pradesh.

However, things began to change in the 1970s, especially after the victory of the Janata Party and more clearly during the following decades when the rise of the OBC MLAs was steadier. This gradual change went hand in hand with the rise of agriculturists in the Vidhan Sabha. Interestingly, this process of democratisation did not mean that the level of education declined because the non-elite MLAs have in fact improved their level of education. Women and Muslims, however, did not benefit from these trends.

This slow but steady process of democratisation was largely due to the social elevation of castes who had been massively under-educated and economically marginal so far, but it was also due to the political strategy of the dominant party in the state, the Congress. In contrast to the traditional attitude of the party leaders, Arjun Singh paid more attention to the OBC in the 1980s — partly to cash in on their new, relative prosperity and assertiveness. More importantly, his former 'disciple', Digvijay Singh, was somewhat responsive to social change. However, he was especially interested in establishing a new coalition of extremes between the upper castes on the one hand — primarily Rajputs — who retained control of the party apparatus, and tribals and Dalits on the other hand, in order to circumvent OBC leaders of the BJP (and, possibly, of the Congress, such as Subhash Yadav, a rival Congressman) and to defuse the rise of the BSP.

The OBC were given a more important role on the BJP side, as is evident from the castes of the party's chief ministers after 2003. However, once again, the upper castes were keen to keep power for themselves within the party apparatus.

This trend seemed to be irreversible before the creation of Chhattisgarh as a separate state. It may still be so, but this event has certainly modified the balance of power between the different groups by increasing the proportion of the upper castes at the expense of the OBC and tribals. By the end of Digvijay Singh's era, this new picture has led the Congress to reshape its strategy of the 'coalition of extremes' by co-opting SC instead of tribals. However, it failed to make an impact, and with the BJP, a *savarna*-dominated party is back in office.

The Congress and the BJP may be forced to further democratise themselves under pressures from the BSP and also, possibly, from the Samajwadi Party, another heir of the local socialist tradition which made its entry in the Madhya Pradesh Vidhan Sabha with seven MLAs in 2003.

References

Awana, Ram Singh. 1988. *Pressure Politics in Congress Party: A Study of the Congress Forum for Socialist Action*. New Delhi: Northern Book Centre.

Brass, P. 1980. 'The Politicization of the Peasantry in a North Indian State', *Journal of Peasant Studies*, 8 (1): 3–36.

Censuses of Central Provinces and Central Agencies, 1931.

Central Chronicle. 2003a. 22 September.

———. 2003b. 7 November.

———. 2003c. 6 December.

Dhar, A. 2004. 'Tribal Party Woos Gond Vote in M.P.', *The Hindu*, 21 March.

Frankel, F. and M. S. A. Rao (eds). 1989. *Dominance and State Power in Modern India*. Delhi: Oxford University Press.

Graham, B. D. 1990. *Hindu Nationalism and Indian Politics: The Origins and Development of the Bharatiya Jana Sangh*. Cambridge: Cambridge University Press.

Hitavada, The. 1952. 5 January.

————. 1956. 10 November.

Jaffrelot, C. 1999. *The Hindu Nationalist Movement and Indian Politics*. New Delhi: Penguin Books India.

Madhya Pradesh Chronicle. 1963. 1 May, p. 3.

————.1962. 19 January, p. 6.

Madhya Pradesh Vidhan Sabha Sadasyon ka Sankshipt Parichay, 1957. 1961. Bhopal: Madhya Pradesh Sabha Sachivalay.

Madhya Pradesh Vidhan Sabha Sadasyon ka Sankshipt Parichay, 1962. 1964. Bhopal: Madhya Pradesh Sabha Sachivalay.

Madhya Pradesh Vidhan Sabha Sadasyon ka Sankshipt Parichay, 1967. 1970. Bhopal: Madhya Pradesh Sabha Sachivalay.

Madhya Pradesh Vidhan Sabha Sadasyon ka Sankshipt Parichay, 1972. 1972. Bhopal: Madhya Pradesh Sabha Sachivalay.

Madhya Pradesh Vidhan Sabha Sadasyon ka Sankshipt Parichay, 1977. 1977. Bhopal: Madhya Pradesh Sabha Sachivalay.

Madhya Pradesh Vidhan Sabha Sadasyon ka Sankshipt Parichay, 1980. 1980. Bhopal: Madhya Pradesh Sabha Sachivalay.

Madhya Pradesh Vidhan Sabha Sadasya-Parichay, 1985. 1985. Bhopal: Madhya Pradesh Sabha Sachivalay.

Madhya Pradesh Vidhan Sabha Sadasya-Parichay, 1990. 1991. Bhopal: Madhya Pradesh Sabha Sachivalay.

Madhya Pradesh Vidhan Sabha Sadasya-Parichay, 1993. 1995. Bhopal: Madhya Pradesh Sabha Sachivalay.

Mahajan, Ramji. 1983. '*Madhya Pradesh Rajya Picchra Varg Ayog — Antim Prativedan*' (Hindi). Bhopal: Government of Madhya Pradesh.

Manor, J. 2004. 'The Congress Defeat in Madhya Pradesh', *Seminar*, February, 534: 18–24.

Narain, I. and M. L. Sharma. 1973. 'The Fifth State Assembly Elections in India', *Asian Survey*, 13 (3): 318–35.

Purohit, B. R. 1970. 'General Elections in Madhya Pradesh', in S. P. Varma and I. Narain (eds), *Fourth Elections in India*. Bombay: Orient Longman.

Scindia, V. and M. Malgonkar. 1988. *Princess: The Autobiography of the Dowager Maharani of Gwalior*. New Delhi: Time Book International.

Singh, D. 2002. 'Transforming India through a Dalit Paradigm', in *The Bhopal Document: Charting a New Course for Dalits for the 21st Century*, pp. 1–6. Bhopal: Government of Madhya Pradesh.

Singh, P. 1973. 'Haryana State Assembly Polls of 1968 and 1972', *Indian Journal of Political Science*, 7: 143–64.

The Bhopal Declaration: Charting a New Course for Dalits for the 21st Century. 2002. Bhopal, Madhya Pradesh, 12–13 January, pp. 1–4.

Part II

The North-western Pattern

4

Legislative Elite in Punjab:
A Socio-political Study

Ashutosh Kumar and *T. R. Sharma*

According to the 'mirror approach', the legislature in a representative democracy should be the microcosm of the populace. In this sense, a legislature does not merely reflect horizontal representation; it also mirrors vertical representation of the citizenry. This means that every social group is represented in the house proportionate to its share in the total population although many social groups cannot be represented through elections due to not having the critical number. One of the bases of such argument is that in a society consisting of intensely diverse population in terms of caste, ethnicity, religion, language and so on, if public institutions, especially elected assemblies, are dominated by one particular group or the other, the future of democracy is uncertain, for such a situation has the potential to create serious political tensions. This chapter is an attempt to trace how broad-based the representation of Punjab Legislative Assembly (PLA) has been with two salient objectives: (*a*) to assess the trend in the social composition of PLA over the periods of time, and (*b*) to analyse underlying factors that have caused the change in the social composition of PLA.

The chapter is broadly structured along two parts. The first part deals with the basic determinants of electoral politics in Punjab: the demographic composition and evolving nature of communal/caste cleavages as well as other socio-political cleavages, like the regional, rural–urban and caste–class linkages. It also refers to the emergence of politics of ethno-religious identity that found expression in the *Punjabi Suba* movement as well as in the Anandpur Sahib resolutions. The second part of the chapter attempts to capture the changes in the social composition of PLA.

I

Changing Political Demography

The partition of the erstwhile Punjab meant that the state lost two-thirds of the territory and half of its population to Pakistan. State reorganisation in 1966 resulted in a further loss of more than half of the territory of the post-partition Punjab (Akbar 1985: 155–56). The changed territorial boundaries created a new kind of identity politics as the Muslims ceased to exist in any significant number in post-partition Punjab. After partition, as per the 1951 Census, 61 per cent of the total population of Punjab was made up of Hindus, whereas the Sikhs constituted 35 per cent. In pre-partition Punjab, Muslims had constituted half of the population. After reorganisation into Himachal Pradesh, Haryana and Punjab, post-1966 Punjab became a Sikh majority state with exactly the reverse: Sikh community constituting 60 per cent and the Hindus constituting 37 per cent of the population (Deol 2000: 2–3).

Emergence of Identity Politics

While partition and the resulting riots momentarily witnessed the rise of anti-Muslim sentiments, the demand for the creation of a Punjabi Suba on linguistic basis contributed a great deal to shape Sikh identity politics. The Akalis demanded a state that would satisfy the aspirations to uphold *punjabiyat*. Notions of 'punjabiyat', however, got inextricably linked to the dictums of 'Khalsa ka Bolbala' or 'Raj Karega Khalsa'. Mobilisation of Hindu segments by the Arya Samaj, its appeal to Hindus to register Hindi as their mother tongue, emphasis on the Vedic tradition and attempts to distance the Hindus from Sikh tradition contributed to the crystallisation of Sikh identity as the basis of punjabiyat sowing the seeds of communal identity and politics based on that identity. Thus, the language controversy was symptomatic of a 'deeper quest for recognition and power' (Deol 2000: 94). The fall out of these developments was the concern on the part of both the communities (Hindu and Sikh) for their distinct identity (Oberoi 1994: 416). This is not to say that Sikh identity politics emerged only after independence. Shiromani Akali Dal (SAD) had come into existence in January 1921, as an institutional–political arm of the Shiromani Gurdwara Prabandhak Committee (SGPC), that was formed earlier to undertake the task of managing all the Sikh gurdwaras in the province after the passage of the Sikh Gurdwara Act by the British. Significantly, when the Muslim League's demand for Pakistan, which was mainly based on communal identity, began to gather momentum during the late 1930s and early 1940s, a segment of Sikh leadership had asked for a separate homeland for the Sikhs. Their contention was that before the British rule in India, three religious communities were ruling the country: the Hindus (mainly the Marathas); the Muslims (in Bengal, Mysore and the Mughal empire); and the Sikhs (in Punjab) under Maharaja Ranjit Singh. Now when the British were leaving it was only fair that Sikhs (like Hindus and Muslims) should have got separate homeland in Punjab. However, while there were clearly identifiable Hindu and Muslim majority provinces in colonial India, there was no province where the Sikhs were in majority. They were not in majority even in any district of pre-partition Punjab. It must be added that there was not much of a popular support for secession among the Sikh community.

Punjabi Suba movement was formally launched in August 1950, spanning over two decades following the refusal of the central political leadership to concede to the Akali leadership's demands for separate communal electorates and reservations of seats for the Sikhs in the legislature. Though the Punjabi Suba movement was launched ostensibly on the linguistic basis, the Akali leadership never concealed its real intention to form a Sikh-majority state. The Sikhs led by the Akalis asserted their identity on the grounds that their culture and language was distinct from the Hindus. While dubbing the rejection of Punjabi as mother tongue by the non-Sikhs as 'an overt and deliberate political act designed to undercut linguistic basis of Punjabi Suba demand', Brass has significantly argued that 'the dominant Hindu majority, unable to assimilate the Sikhs, adopted the tactic of avoiding their language so that the Sikhs, a minority people by religion, might become a minority by language as well' (1974: 327). While the slogan of 'Hindi, Hindu, Hindustan' found support among the Hindu community, the feeling among the Sikh community was echoed by Sardar Hukum Singh who observed: 'While others got states for their languages, we lost even our language' (quoted in Brass 1974: 320). The Hindu–Sikh divide was evident in the conflicting assertions about the status of Punjabi as a dialect or a distinct language as also about what its script should be (Sarhadi 1970: 211). In a comparative mode, the movement asking for the reorganisation of Punjab on linguistic basis can be viewed within the wider context of the nationwide movement of linguistic groups seeking statehood as well as the assertion of the demand for a 'self-determined political status' for the Sikhs within the Union (Anand 1976: 263; Nayar 1968).

Socio-political Cleavages
in a Dual Community Province

Besides the factors just mentioned, the growing cleavage between the Hindu and Sikh communities could be explained in terms of the exodus of the Muslims that made post-colonial Punjab essentially a dual community province. Hindus and Sikhs were now the two communities competing for political and economic supremacy.

Table 4.1
Religious Profile of Legislators of Punjab, 1972–2002

Year	Total Members	Hindus	Sikhs
1972	104	28 (27.0)	75 (72.1)
1977	117	31 (26.5)	85 (72.6)
1980	177	32 (27.3)	84 (71.8)
1985	117	31 (26.5)	85 (72.6)
1992	117	36 (30.7)	78 (66.6)
1997	117	26 (22.2)	88 (75.2)
2002	117	36 (30.7)	79 (67.5)

Source: CSDS Data Unit.
Note: Figures in parentheses indicate percentages.

The rural–urban divide also played a role, as since the pre-partition days the Hindus were an urban-based community and the Sikhs were rural residents. The contradiction between Hindus and Sikhs also had an objective class basis related to the factor of economic dominance. Traditionally, the landed peasantry came from Sikh community, especially the Jat Sikhs, whereas the Hindus, especially upper caste Khatris, Aroras and Baniyas dominated trade, commerce, moneylending, and service sector. Such a division was reflected in the social basis of the political parties in colonial Punjab. The Sikh landlords along with Muslims supported National Unionist Party founded in 1923. Widely known as the 'Junker party', it even succeeded in forming the first elected government by defeating the Muslim League in the 1937 provincial elections with the support of the Khalsa National Party. The support base for the Congress in pre-partition Punjab thus primarily remained limited to the urban Hindus. Electoral institutions, introduced in the form of the Montague–Chelmsford Reforms of 1919 and the Government of India Act of 1935, served the colonial interest by accentuating competition for political power among the communities (Kumar 2004a: 1515).

Once the agitation for a separate state began, the Hindu–Sikh distinctions were further accentuated. To reiterate, the rejection of Punjabi as mother tongue by the Hindus actually forced the Akali Dal to take a more sectarian path. It was this ethno-religious identity-based politics that found expression in the form of the Anandpur Sahib resolutions in the 1970s and later in the form of the autonomist/secessionist movement in the decade of the 1980s.[1]

In terms of geopolitics, post-partition Punjab consists of three regions, i.e., Majha, Doaba and Malwa. As for the rural–urban divide, the geographical area of Punjab is 503,300 hectares, of which 70.28 per cent is rural and 29.72 per cent is urban. Further, 36.93 per cent of the population is Hindu and 60.75 per cent are Sikhs. These socio-geographic regions with their distinct histories and traditions reflect internal social, cultural and political cleavages among the people of Punjab (Deol 2000: 2–4).

---

[1] The core of Akali demands relating to the political, economic and social relationship between the centre and the state of Punjab are to be found in the Anandpur Sahib Resolutions adopted by the working committee of the Akali Dal in October 1973. The resolution incorporated seven objectives aimed at establishing the 'preeminence of the Khalsa through creation of a congenial environment and a political set up' (Kumar 2005: 4). These were: (*i*) the transfer of the federally administered city of Chandigarh to Punjab; (*ii*) the readjustment of the state boundaries to include certain Sikh-majority Punjabi-speaking territory, presently outside but contiguous to Punjab; (*iii*) the demand for autonomy to all the states of India with the centre retaining jurisdiction only over external affairs, defence and communications; (*iv*) introduction of land reforms in the form of land ceiling by raising it to 30 acres instead of the prevailing 17.50 acres as well as the subsidies and loans for the peasantry as also the measures to bring about heavy industrialisation in Punjab; (*v*) the enactment of an all-India Gurudwara Act to bring all the historic gurudwaras under the control of the SGPC; (*vi*) protection for the Sikh minorities living outside the state; and (*vii*) reversal of the new recruitment policy of the centre under which the recruitment quota of Sikhs in the armed forces from 20 per cent to 2 per cent. The working committee of Akali Dal added two new demands to the Anandpur Sahib Resolutions in February 1981 after which a set of 45 demands were submitted to the centre in September in the same year. The first one was with regards to the halting of reallocation of available waters of riparian Punjab to non-riparian states as under the federally regulated arrangements, 75 per cent of the river waters of Punjab were being allocated to other states. The second demand was for the recognition of Sikh personal law (Deol 2000: 101–3; Pettigrew 1995: 5).

Caste Cleavages

Besides religious contestation for political power just recounted, in the post-1966 Punjab, there was a change in the sociological origin of the political leadership especially within Akali Dal during the Punjabi Suba movement. The Akali leadership, until the 1962 elections, came primarily from the urban upper caste Khatri Sikhs, while the majority of the Sikhs lived in the rural regions. The widening and deepening of democracy in the electoral sense with passing decades, along with the economic empowerment of the rich farmers in the wake of the Green Revolution, transformed the leadership structure within the Sikh community. The emergence of Sant Fateh Singh as the top leader of SAD, a Jat in place of Master Tara Singh, an upper caste Khatri who was described as 'Bhapa' and a representative of urban Sikhs symbolised this trend. Since then, the political leadership of the Sikh community as well as SAD has been dominated by Jat Sikhs, the numerically strong peasant caste. It holds true even for the Congress.[2] The dominance of Jat Sikh community is discernable in the following data as regards the social profile of the legislators elected since the reorganisation of Punjab. Rapid social mobilisation, economic development, party competition and factionalism have, however, also led to political division within the Jat Sikh community. Significantly, Congress has had sizable support

---

[2] The political and economic rise of the Jats began in the early 17th century and the consolidation came after the formation of the Sikh Misls in the later part of the 18th century, especially after the establishment of the Sikh empire by Maharaja Ranjit Singh, a Jat Sikh. In the 19th and 20th centuries, they were recognised by the British colonial regime as the premier agricultural community in Punjab. The other castes, for instance, the Tarkhans, were classified as non-agriculturists and therefore technically unable to buy land under the Alienation of Land Act of 1900. Dubbed as part of Punjab's 'martial race', the Jat Sikhs comprised almost half of the British Indian army as early as in 1914. Between 1885 and 1947, the Britishers irrigated approximately four million hectare in the Doabs, turning a virtual wasteland into the greatest revenue generating and most prosperous and commercially productive agricultural area. These 'squares of land' from the canal colonies were granted to the Jat Sikhs, recognised as the 'agriculturists' and not to the landless 'menial' castes. The colonial regime ensured that the emergent canal colonies replicated the social order of the villages of eastern and central Punjab from where the settlers had migrated. These canal colonies thus fortified the existing social structure of the rural Punjab (as also the structure of the British rule).

within the Sikh community along with Akali Dal. The Jat Sikhs, for instance, averaged 37.47 per cent among the Congress MLAs elected between 1967 to 1992. The dominance of the Jat Sikhs has in fact diminished the political role of other castes among the Sikhs namely the mercantile upper castes Khatris, Aroras and Ahulwalias; artisan castes, like the Tarkhans, the Ramgarhias, the Rais and the Lohars (carpenter and ironworkers), Chimbas (tailor), Labnas and Kumhars (potters); and the Dalit castes, like the Chamars (tanners) and Chuhras or Balmikis (sweepers), also called Mazhabis and Ramdasias, thus creating internal cleavages within the Sikh community (Singh 1984: 42).

Besides the observance of caste hierarchy, the class division between the land-owning Jats and mostly landless Tarkhans and the Scheduled Castes people working as the retainers/tenants or agricultural labour, has been a major source of the internal cleavages in the Sikh community. Scheduled Castes account for around 31 per cent of the total population of Punjab, which is far above the all-India average (16.32 per cent), with the highest concentration in the Jalandhar district. Twenty-nine Assembly seats are reserved for them. The Sikh Scheduled Castes, called the Mazhabi Sikhs, have of late been developing their own distinct cultures of deprivation with new religious faiths and symbols of identity that reflect their alienation from the institutionalised Sikh religious structures (Juergensmeyer 1979: 255–62). In electoral terms, it is reflected in the emergence of Bahujan Samaj Party (BSP) as a third alternative, albeit a distant one, besides the Akali Dal–BJP and Congress–CPI alliance since the 1992 Assembly elections.

II

Socio-economic Profile of MLAs

The changes in the territorial boundaries of Punjab, as outlined earlier, pose serious methodological problems for any meaningful longitudinal comparison of the state's legislative elite. When the first Legislative Assembly elections were held in 1952, Punjab consisted of the present state of Haryana and some parts of Himachal Pradesh. Pepsu was a separate state. At the time of the second Assembly elections in 1957, the state of Pepsu had been merged with Punjab. Territorial boundaries remained the same during the 1962 Assembly elections. Reorganisation of the state brought changes. Thus, during the course of the first four Assembly elections, the number of constituencies, their index numbers and territoriality underwent changes. Delimitation of constituencies undertaken in 1971 came into effect only during the 1977 Assembly elections. Finally, the total strength of the house was fixed at 117. Hence the paper undertakes the study of the six assemblies formed during 1977–2002, and presents socio-economic profile of people's representative (MLAs) in the Punjab Assembly.

Age

The Punjab Assembly during the period 1977–2002 seems to have fewer young representatives. In fact, their number has declined compared to 1977. As against this, the number of older representatives has slowly increased. Thus, the overwhelming majority of representatives are of middle age (Table 4.2).

Table 4.2
Age Group of Legislators in Punjab, 1977–2002

Age Group	1977	1980*	1985*	1992	1997*	2002
25–35	11 (9.4)	6 (5.1)	11 (9.4)	11 (9.4)	8 (6.8)	8 (6.8)
36–45	27 (23.1)	33 (28.2)	31 (26.5)	39 (33.3)	23 (19.7)	26 (22.2)
46–55	45 (38.5)	38 (32.5)	40 (34.2)	39 (33.3)	41 (35.0)	38 (32.5)
56–65	26 (22.3)	30 (25.6)	23 (19.7)	19 (16.3)	30 (25.6)	34 (29.1)
66 and above	4 (3.4)	5 (4.3)	10 (8.5)	9 (7.7)	12 (10.3)	11 (9.4)
All	113 (96.6)	112 (95.7)	115 (98.3)	117 (100)	114 (97.4)	117 (100)

Source: CSDS Data Unit.
Note: *Information on age not available for the rest of the MLAs.
Figures in parentheses indicate percentage.

Gender

A mere glance at the list of members elected in the seven assemblies reveals very low level of representation of women. What is important to note is the fact that there has been no significant change over last three decades. Despite rising political awareness of women and their growing political participation in politics, the PLA continues to be a bastion of men. The unchanging pattern of women's dismal representation is definitely not conducive for healthy democracy.

Table 4.3
Women Legislators in Punjab, 1977–2004

Year	Total Members	Number of Women MLAs
1977	117	3 (2.6)
1980	117	6 (5.1)
1985	117	4 (3.4)
1992	117	6 (5.1)
1997	117	7 (6.0)
2002	117	8 (6.8)

Source: CSDS Data Unit.

Note: Figures in parentheses indicate percentage.

Education

From the point of view of educational background of MLAs, Punjab appears to show a remarkable change over the years. It is evident from Table 4.4 that during last three decades, more and more educated people are getting elected to the house. As a consequence, there has been a constant decline in the proportion of less educated representatives of the people. For an example, while the proportion of those educated up to secondary level has decreased from 41.9 per cent in 1977 to 26 per cent in 2002, those of highly educated has risen to about 69 per cent in 2002 from 35 per cent in 1977. It is satisfying to note that people in Punjab are getting well-educated leaders elected to the House, although it is altogether a different matter as to how best well-educated representatives provide leadership and fulfill the aspirations of people.

Table 4.4
Educational Profile of Legislators in Punjab, 1977–2002

Education of MLAs	1977	1980	1992	1997	2002
Non-literate	5 (4.3)	5 (4.3)	–	3 (2.6)	–
Middle pass	20 (17.1)	20 (17.1)	5 (4.3)	6 (5.1)	9 (7.7)
Matriculation	49 (41.9)	32 (27.4)	44 (37.6)	40 (34.2)	26 (22.2)
Graduate and above	41 (35.0)	54 (46.2)	68 (58.1)	65 (55.6)	81 (69.2)
Others	2 (1.7)	6 (5.1)	–	3 (2.6)	1 (.9)

Source: CSDS Data Unit.

Note: Figures in parentheses indicate percentage; data not available for 1985 PLA.

Caste

While ascertaining the caste of legislators, a problem arose in the case of quite a few Sikh MLAs as instead of using their surnames (which could help in ascertaining their castes), they use their village names, viz. Barnala, Badal, Talwandi, etc. The practice is in accordance with the basic tenets of Sikhism, which does not recognise the caste system. Due to problems like these, this chapter refers only to the figures about the caste origins of the legislators (not all of them though) in the assemblies formed in 1977, 1992, 1997 and 2002.

Table 4.5 reports caste profile of legislators from 1977 to 2002. It shows that intermediate castes — mostly Jats — from the class of peasant proprietors have been dominating the PLA for years. However, the proportion of the MLAs belonging to upper castes has witnessed ups and downs throughout the period between 1977 and 2002. In 1992, the number of upper caste MLAs was as high as 32. In the next election (1997), it dropped down to 18, the lowest ever since 1977. By contrast, the Jats have never been less than about 36 per cent and have reached 52 per cent once in 1997. As for the representation of Dalits, the proportion of SC legislators has been the same and not prone to temporal variation, mainly because seats for SC are reserved in the Assembly.

Occupation

Punjab Legislative Assembly has always been dominated by the agriculturists except for the year 1997. With this, the dominance of

Table 4.5
Caste Profile of Legislators in Punjab, 1977–2002

Caste Groups	1977	1992	1997	2002
Upper Caste	21 (17.9)	32 (27.4)	18 (15.4)	23 (19.7)
Intermediary Caste	56 (47.9)	46 (39.3)	61 (52.2)	42 (35.9)
OBC	4 (3.4)	6 (5.1)	4 (3.4)	4 (3.4)
SC	29 (24.8)	29 (24.8)	29 (24.8)	29 (24.8)
Others/Not Ascertained	7 (6.0)	4 (3.4)	5 (4.2)	19 (16.2)

Source: CSDS Data Unit.
Note: Figures in parentheses indicate percentage; data not available for 1985 PLA.

agriculturists among the legislators confirms the presence of landed peasantry as a politically significant constituency in a reorganised Punjab. As against this, the proportion of political activists, which was 12 per cent in 1977, appears to have stabilised around 6 per cent. The number of professionals among the MLAs has also been on the decline over last three decades. However, it seems that businessmen are slowly getting into politics and making their presence felt. It is quite surprising that in the 2002 Assembly election, the businessmen accounted for slightly less than one-third of the total members elected to the Assembly compared to less than one-fifth in the past elections. A closer look at Table 4.6 suggests that although the share of businessmen in the Assembly has been increasing, it is at the expense of those who are non-agriculturists. Hence, growing influence of businessmen is a not a challenge to the dominance of agriculturists.

Table 4.6
Occupational Profile of MLAs in Punjab, 1977–2002

Occupation	1977	1980	1985	1992	1997	2002
Agriculturalists	51 (43.6)	51 (43.6)	37 (31.6)	51 (43.6)	15 (12.8)	54 (46.2)
Social Workers	6 (5.1)	11 (9.3)	7 (6.0)	15 (12.8)	60 (51.3)	9 (7.6)
Professionals	17 (14.5)	12 (10.3)	24 (20.5)	22 (18.8)	13 (11.1)	12 (10.3)
Political Activists	14 (12.0)	13 (11.1)	6 (5.1)	8 (6.8)	5 (4.3)	7 (6.0)
Businessmen	17 (14.5)	18 (15.5)	27 (23.1)	19 (16.2)	19 (16.2)	33 (28.1)
Others	12 (10.3)	12 (10.3)	16 (13.7)	2 (1.8)	5 (4.3)	2 (1.8)

Source: CSDS Data Unit.
Note: Figures in parentheses indicate percentage.

Conclusion

In Punjab, societal factors such as religion, caste, region and language combine differently in different elections to produce contrasting electoral outcomes and also determine the nature of the political elite (Kumar 2004b: 5441). Over the last one-and-half decades, a virtually bipolar party system has come to stay in the state like in most of the Indian states, as political power has alternated between the SAD and the Congress and their respective allies. As for the sociological origin of the legislative elite, however, it has remained homogeneous in the sense that it continues to consist primarily of well-educated legislators, who are mainly from the dominant peasant caste of the Jats, be they Sikhs or Hindus, and are mostly farmers, businessmen or professionals. Whereas the other backward classes are marginally represented among the legislators, the percentage of Scheduled Caste legislators has hardly exceeded beyond the statutory reservation provided for them. Minorities like Muslims and Christians find almost no legislator from their communities.

Despite the region specific nature of electoral politics and the emergence of distinct identities, however, emerging trends in state electoral politics do reveal certain commonalties across the country (Kumar 2003: 3145). Politicisation and mobilisation of the 'old, received, but hitherto dormant identities', like the Dalits, women and the backward classes is arguably the most significant among them (Nigam and Yadav 1999). Now, when in rest of the country aspirations of the lower castes are increasingly being articulated, accommodated and represented, how far can Congress and the Akali Dal manage to ignore these aspirations as evidenced in episodes like Talhan (Kumar 2004a: 1520)? Just as there has been a shift in the electoral politics in post-militancy Punjab — politico-economic issues have replaced ethno-religious ones — the political parties will have to adopt a new social profile.[3]

---

[3] After prolonged dithering, the SAD has finally opened its door not only to Hindus, but more significantly, has given wide representation to Dalits, women, minorities and backward classes. The new-look SAD organisation has as many as 33 Dalits, 18 Hindus, 16 women, six Muslims and two Christians (Dhaliwal 2005: 1). This development should be viewed in response to both the alienation of the Dalits and minorities from Congress as well as the increasing assertion of the marginals, evidenced in the creditable performance of BSP in the 2004 Lok Sabha elections especially in the Doaba region, besides certain parts of Malwa such as Firozepur. A resurgent BSP is making an attempt to widen its political base on the lines of Uttar Pradesh and Madhya Pradesh models as evinced in the fact that it offered tickets to non-Dalits, mostly OBC, in as many as seven Lok Sabha seats.

References

Akbar, M. J. 1985. *India: The Siege Within*. London: Harmondsworth.

Anand, J. C. 1976. 'Punjab: Politics of Retreating Communalism', in Iqbal Narain (ed.), *State Politics in India*, pp. 262–98. New Delhi: Meenakshi Prakashan.

Brass, Paul. 1974. *Language, Religion and Politics in North India*. Cambridge: Cambridge University Press.

Deol, Harnik. 2000. *Religion and Nationalism in India: The Case of Punjab*. London: Routledge.

Dhaliwal, Sarbjit. 2005. 'New Look SAD Opens Door to Hindus', *The Tribune*, 18 April.

Juergensmeyer, Mark. 1979. 'Cultures of Deprivation: Three Case Studies in the Punjab', *Economic and Political Weekly*, 14 (7–8): 255–62.

Kumar, Ashutosh. 2003. 'State Electoral Politics: Looking for the Larger Picture', *Economic and Political Weekly*, 38 (30): 3145–47.

———. 2004a. 'Electoral Politics in Punjab: Study of Akali Dal', *Economic and Political Weekly*, 39 (14–15): 1515–20.

———. 2004b. 'Punjab: In Search of New Leadership', *Economic and Political Weekly*, 39 (51): 5441–44.

———. 2005. 'Anandpur Sahib Resolutions', in Sabyasachi Basu Ray Chaudhury, Samir Kumar Das and Ranbir Samaddar (eds), *Indian Autonomies: Keywords and Key Texts*. Calcutta: Sampark.

Nayar, Baldev Raj. 1968. 'Punjab', in Myron Weiner (ed.), *State Politics in India*, pp. 435–502. Princeton: Princeton University Press.

Nigam, Aditya and Yogendra Yadav. 1999. 'Electoral Politics in Indian States, 1989–99', *Economic and Political Weekly*, 34 (34–35): 2391–92.

Oberoi, Harjot. 1994. *The Construction of Religious Boundaries: Culture, Identity and Diversity in the Sikh Tradition*. Delhi: Oxford University Press.

Pettigrew, J. J. M. 1995. *The Sikhs of Punjab: Unheard Voices of State and Guerilla Violence*. London: Zed Books.

Sarhadi, Ajit Singh. 1970. *Punjabi Suba: The Story of the Struggle*. Delhi: UB Kapoor and Sons.

Singh, Gopal. 1984. 'Socio-Economic Bases of the Punjab Crisis', *Economic and Political Weekly*, 7 January.

5

Towards Jat Empowerment in Rajasthan

Christophe Jaffrelot and *Cyril Robin*

In contrast to Bihar, Madhya Pradesh and Uttar Pradesh, Rajasthan's politics appears to be more elitist because of the persisting subaltern position of the Other Backward Classes (OBC) from 1952 to 2003. Indeed, the proportion of the OBC MLAs in the Rajasthan Vidhan Sabha increased from 3.2 to 8.5 per cent only.

This state of things can be explained by the caste composition of the state which is characterised by a high degree of fragmentation and demographic weight of the upper castes as well as the dominant castes. In contrast to what happened in western and southern India, the political trajectory of the princely states, in spite of the *Praja Mandals* and the *Kisan Sabhas*, have also played a part in the making of a conservative political elite after independence, on the side of the Congress as well as that of the Opposition. Certainly, the caste composition of the state Assembly has changed a lot between the first state election of 1952 and that of 2003, as evident from the social profile of their MLAs. But the real winners are the Jats, who were regarded as a dominant caste till their 'reclassification' as OBC in 1999. Changes are much more limited, however, so far as the caste composition of the state government and the party apparatus of the BJP and Congress are concerned.

The Upper Caste Domination: Fragmentation, Numbers and Land-ownership

According to the Census, the population of Rajasthan was divided between 393 castes and tribes in 1931 and only nine of these castes and tribes were constituted by more than 300,000 persons, a good indication of a very important fragmentation.

The upper castes and the Jats were represented in the largest number of regions in the state and constituted 30 per cent of the population whereas the two most important OBC castes, the Gujjars and Malis,

Table 5.1
Size of the Castes in the Rajputana States, 1931

Size	Number of Castes
300, 000 and more	9
100, 000 – 299, 999	13
50, 000 – 99, 999	20
10, 000 – 49, 999	54
Less than 10, 000	297
TOTAL	393

Source: Census of India, 1931.

constituted only 8 per cent of the total. The majority of the 85 OBC castes were made up of very small entities spread all over the state (mainly artisan castes or castes engaged in agriculture or animal husbandry). This heterogeneity has prevented the OBC from developing a sense of solidarity.

At the state level, the upper castes represented 20.6 per cent of the population (7.6 per cent Brahmins, 7.4 per cent Mahajans and 5.6 per cent Rajputs) while the Jats represented the single largest group with 9.2 per cent of the population. The Chamars, the largest caste in U.P., formed the fourth largest caste in Rajasthan with 6 per cent only. According to Census 2001, the Scheduled Castes formed 17.2 per cent of Rajasthan's population. The Scheduled Tribes (12.6 per cent of Rajasthan's population in the year 2001) principally comprised

Table 5.2
The Principal Castes of Rajputana (by regions)

Castes	Population (%)	Regions
Jat	9	Bikaner, Jodhpur, Shekhawati, Jaipur, Matsya
Brahmin	8	Matsya, Jaipur, Bikaner, Kota, Udaipur
Mahajan	7	Jaipur, Jodhpur, Bikaner
Rajput	6	Jodhpur, Bikaner, Udaipur
Chamar (SC)	6	Matsya, Jaipur, Kota, Bikaner
Bhil (ST)	6	Udaipur, Banswara
Meena (ST)	5	Matsya, Jaipur, Kota, Udaipur
Gujjar (OBC)	5	Jaipur, Matsya, Kota
Mali (OBC)	3	Matsya, Jaipur, Kota, Jodhpur
Kumhar	3	Matsya, Jaipur, Udaipur, Bikaner

Source: Census of India, 1931.

two important groups — the Bhils and the Meenas. The Bhils constituted a significant share of the population of the Banswara and Dungarpur districts, the Meenas were present in large numbers in Alwar, Jaipur, Kota and Udaipur districts.

Regarding land, the central feature of the land tenure system of princely states in Rajasthan was a hierarchical system of ownership. In the state, two main types of land tenure prevailed: *khalsa*, crown lands under the direct rule and control of the central *darbar* (eminent owner of the lands in the state), and *jagir*, estates of varying value and size controlled by the Maharaja's subordinate *sardars* (Sisson 1979: 24). The landlords were mainly Rajputs, and due to lack of formal right of occupancy in *jagir* areas, non-Rajputs tenants (mostly from the Jat community) were subordinated to the Rajput rulers (Saxena 1996: 127) and did not have independent access to land. Moreover, the other feature of land-ownership was the right to political–juridical administration.

In the early 20th century, after several centuries of unquestioned Rajput hegemony, Jats-led peasant uprisings against *jagirdari* system surfaced (Narain and Mathur 1990: 20).

The Over-representation of Upper Castes in the Congress Party

The Impact of the Conservative Princely States

Before its integration in the Indian Union, most of the territory of Rajputana — except for the Ajmer area — was made of princely states which were not under the direct administrative control of the British. As a consequence, their population largely remained insulated from the mainstream of social and politico-economic changes emanating from British India. In fact, by maintaining the political identity of the Rajput rulers, the special relationship between the British and these princely states strengthened their political power.[1] Besides, as the Working Committee of the Indian National Congress declared that 'the responsibility and burden of carrying on the struggle within the

---

[1] Prior to 1949, Rajasthan had not been under a common administration.

States must necessarily fall on the States' people themselves' (quoted in Sharma 1962: 1291), the Congress did not want directly to undertake political activity in the Princely States. As a result, organisations like Praja Mandals and Lok Parishads were set up only in the late 1930s. This is one of the reasons why, in spite of the abolition of the princely states, after 1947, the former maharajas continued to play a major role in state politics. As a result, some dethroned rulers successfully entered the election arena in 1951–52. For instance, Hanuwant Singh of Jodhpur, Karni Singh of Bikaner and Brajendra Pal Singh, eldest son of the ruler of Karauli, defeated Congress candidates (Mathur 1967). The results of the elections, therefore, spurred the Congress leaders to co-opt many ex-rulers and to give them tickets in spite of ideological differences, so that their influence could electorally benefit them. Subsequently, the Congress leaders persuaded Maharaja Harish Chandra of Jhalawar to join them and contest the Assembly elections on a party ticket from Jhalawar. Maharaja Harish Chandra won the election and was inducted in the state government in 1960. Other members of royal family sup-ported the Congress; this includes the Maharaja of Kota, Maharaja Brajendra Pal Singh of Karauli, Narain Singh of Masuda Thikana and Bhim Singh of Mandawa Thikana.

The Caste Structure of the Political Protest Movements

In this part of the country, the Congress party found its origin in movements of social and political protest that developed in the Rajputana states prior to independence, as the Praja Mandals and the Kisan Sabhas, which were not systematically elite-oriented. Certainly, the Praja Mandals were elite-dominated. Their protest movements started in the 1920s and were principally concerned with demands regarding public policy, the establishment of accountable governments and civil liberties. Almost all these movements originated and focused their activities in the capital cities, which were the major centres of communication and also the primary centres of higher education. As a result, the leaders of these movements belonged almost exclusively to urban areas and came from the social elite, as it is evident from the Table 5.3.

Besides, most of the leaders were recruited from the upper castes — Brahmins, Mahajans and Kayasthas — who had received some education

Table 5.3
Recruitment of Praja Mandal Cadres in Rajputana (%)

Places of Recruitment	1919–30	1931–36	1937–41	1942–46
Capital City	62	50	45	44
District Town	38	36	40	44
Village	–	14	15	12
TOTAL	(N=13)	(N=14)	(N=42)	(N=18)

Source: Sisson (1972: 62).

in English-medium schools, had long traditions of participation in state affairs and had become associated with the movements of social reform and the nationalist movement in British India.

As it emerges from Table 5.4, the lower castes and Muslims were absent from the leadership of these movements. Even though the recruitment varied over time, the upper castes always over-dominated the Praja Mandals: Brahmins and Mahajans represented more than 60 per cent of the leadership of this organisation between 1919 and 1946.

Unlike these two castes, there was limited recruitment from the Rajputs. Indeed, 'with few exceptions Rajputs rejected the aims and political style of the Praja Mandals, although some young Rajputs educated in the British Provinces were attracted to these movements as nationalist organizations'. Moreover, the presence of Rajputs in the Praja Mandals was in areas 'which did not have a long tradition of conflict between Rajput lord and peasant caste tenant' (Sisson 1972: 64).

Yet, political mobilisation was not exclusively an urban phenomenon in the Rajputana states. Important peasant movements developed

Table 5.4
Political Generation and Caste Mobilisation in Rajasthan (%)

Castes and Communities	1919–30	1931–36	1937–41	1942–46	TOTAL
Brahmin	85	62	46	26	47
Rajput	–	–	4	6	4
Mahajan	8	23	38	35	32
Kayastha	8	8	6	3	6
Jat	–	8	6	23	10
Scheduled Castes and Scheduled Tribes	–	–	–	3	1
Muslims	–	–	–	3	1
TOTAL	(N=13)	(N=13)	(N=52)	(N=31)	(N=109)

Source: Sisson (1972: 62).

in these areas and were concerned with changes in rural society. The Kisan Sabhas, which did not start as a political organisation but were the outgrowth of a social reform movement within the Jat community, originated in the 1920s, and developed specifically in those areas of Rajputana where Jats constituted the predominant rural caste and where the Rajputs, the landed aristocracy, were also found in large numbers (Sisson 1972: 74). Indeed, this organisation moved towards struggles against the Rajput-dominated *jagirdari* system (*ibid.*: 71) and the feudal order that regulated the land relations between the different peasant groups in the countryside of the Rajputana states.

The association of the Praja Mandals and Kisan Sabha leaders resulted from the Congress' effort to develop a wider base of political support even before 1947. The sense of group identity of those two milieus continued and was transferred to the Congress before and after independence as many Praja Mandal and Kisan Sabha leaders became active in Congress affairs in several princely states of the Rajputana. As a result, though the Praja Mandals and the Kisan Sabha in the Rajputana had limited success in achieving their aim and were not mass organisations, they represented new organisations in the conservative princely states, and the different castes that constituted the leadership of these movements, i.e., the upper castes and the Jats, dominated the sociology of the Rajasthan Congress after its formation in 1946. These two categories constituted 58.7 per cent of all the Congress MLAs between 1952 and 2003: the Jats represented the single largest group with 20.2 per cent; the Brahmins formed 14.9 per cent of the total and the Rajputs, 11.6 per cent. This over-representation of the Jats is a specific feature of the Rajasthan Congress in comparison with the subordinated position of the Jats in the structure of the Congress in other states of the Hindi belt. Correlatively, the OBC only represent 5.7 per cent of the Congress MLAs, a strong indication of the significant degree of conservatism of the caste structure of the party. The Congress system, and its clientelistic 'vote-bank' politics, has thus played a very significant role in the over-representation of the upper castes in Rajasthan's politics.

The Jana Sangh and the Swatantra Party: A *Savarna*-dominated Opposition

Whether it is the Jana Sangh or the Swatantra Party, all the most important opposition parties until 1980 were characterised by a caste composition over-dominated by the upper castes. In each of these parties, the upper castes represented more than 40 per cent of the MLAs over the period 1952–72.

From 1952 to 1962 elections, the Bharatiya Jana Sangh (BJS), the political arm of the RSS, never won more than 8.5 per cent of the state Assembly seats. In the 1967 elections, among the 22 seats captured by the BJS, the Rajputs and the Baniyas respectively represented 31.8 and 22.7 per cent of the party MLAs. Therefore, with 63.6 per cent of upper caste MLAs, the BJS was much more conservative than the Congress party in which the upper castes 'only' represented 45.6 per cent. As a result, the members of the lower castes constituted less than 10 per cent if we put the Jats and other OBC together, only 4.5 per cent for the main OBC.

The Swatantra Party, which was founded in 1959 and was the most important opposition party in the 1960s, was also over-dominated by upper castes. This party developed an ideology opposed to Nehru's socialism and stood for 'protection of democracy and individual freedom, which, it alleged, were threatened by Congress' (Kamal 1967: 506). Such ideas were bound to have an impact upon those who were disgruntled with the Congress rule, wooing at the same time elements of conservatism, traditionalism, feudalism and capitalism. Thus, the Swatantra Party was dominated by industrialists and former members of the princely class like Maharani Gayatri Devi of Jaipur, Maharajkumar Jai Singh of Jaipur, Maharawal Lakshman Singh of Dungarpur or Raja Man Singh of Bharatpur. Some Rajput jagirdars, who had at some time shifted from the Congress party, had also joined the Swatantra, for e.g., Man Singh of Mahar Thikana, Man Dhata Singh of Geejgarh Thikana or Devi Singh of Mandawa Thikana.

As a result of this mobilisation, the Swatantra Party emerged as the second largest party after the 1962 and the 1967 elections. Successfully exploiting the mass appeal of the ruling princes, the party won 36 seats out of 176 in 1962 and 50 seats in a house of 184 in 1967, posing serious challenge to the Congress party. Owing to the support of the Rajput princes and jagirdars, the upper castes were over-represented in the Swatantra Party, especially the Rajputs who represented 24.7 per cent of the party's MLAs.

The second largest single group in the Swatantra Party was the Scheduled Castes, with 30.9 per cent of the MLAs, which suggests that this party adhered to the conservative 'coalition of extremes'

Table 5.5
Castes and Communities of Bharatiya Jana Sangh (BJS) and
Swatantra Party MLAs in Rajasthan, 1952–72 (%)

Castes and Communities	BJS	Swatantra Party
Upper Caste	**62.7**	**43.2**
Brahmin	10.2	8.2
Rajput	28.8	24.7
Baniya/Jain	22.0	8.2
Kayastha	1.7	2.1
Intermediate Castes	**5.1**	**5.2**
Jat	5.1	5.2
OBC	**8.5**	**7.2**
Gujjar	6.8	6.2
Yadav	–	1.0
Mali	1.7	–
Scheduled Castes	**13.6**	**30.9**
Scheduled Tribes	**5.1**	**11.3**
Meena	–	1.0
Other	–	10.3
Religious Minorities	**1.7**	**1.0**
Muslim	1.7	1.0
Unidentified	**3.4**	**1.0**
TOTAL	100.1	99.8
	(N=59)	(N=97)

Source: Survey by authors.

pattern, which tended to marginalise the backward castes. As a whole, the opposition parties never constituted an electoral alternative for the lower castes.

The Unachieved Democratisation: A Conservative Two-party System

While Rajasthan's politics has developed along the bipartisan pattern with the Indian National Congress and the Bharatiya Janata Party dominating the state political scene, these parties rely mainly on the upper castes. However, they have gradually become more open to the non-'twice born' castes in the 1990s.

The Congress: A More and More Jat-oriented Party

Three caste groups have traditionally constituted the mainstays of the Congress MLAs: the upper castes, the Scheduled Castes and the Jats.

Table 5.6
Evolution of Caste and Community of the Congress MLAs in Rajasthan, 1952–2003 (%)

Castes and Communities	1952	1957	1962	1967	1972	1977	1980	1985	1990	1993	1998	2003
Upper Castes	**51.3**	**47.0**	**45.5**	**45.5**	**42.1**	**32.5**	**31.9**	**35.8**	**22.0**	**32.5**	**31.4**	**32.1**
Brahmin	22.0	24.4	20.0	17.8	13.8	5.0	11.9	16.1	6.0	10.4	9.9	14.3
Rajput	6.1	12.6	14.4	14.4	14.5	12.5	11.1	12.5	2.0	11.7	11.9	7.1
Baniya/Jain	19.5	9.2	7.8	11.1	11.7	12.5	8.2	4.5	8.0	9.1	8.0	8.9
Kayastha	3.7	0.8	2.2	2.2	1.4	2.5	0.7	1.8	2.0	–	0.7	1.8
Khatri	–	–	–	–	–	–	–	–	4.0	–	0.2	–
Sindhi	–	–	1.1	–	0.7	–	–	0.9	–	1.3	0.7	–
Intermediate Castes	**15.9**	**17.7**	**23.3**	**16.7**	**17.2**	**40.0**	**20.7**	**14.3**	**26.0**	**29.9**	**18.5**	**28.6**
Jat	15.9	17.7	22.2	16.7	17.2	40.0	20.7	14.3	26.0	29.9	17.2	28.6
Bishnoi	–	–	1.1	–	–	–	–	–	–	–	1.3	–
OBC	**3.6**	**2.4**	**4.4**	**2.2**	**5.6**	**2.5**	**7.4**	**8.1**	**12.0**	**5.2**	**6.7**	**9.0**
Gujjar	–	–	–	1.1	2.1	2.5	3.0	2.7	4.0	1.3	2.0	3.6
Yadav	2.4	0.8	1.1	–	1.4	–	2.2	0.9	2.0	1.3	2.0	3.6
Mali	–	0.8	1.1	–	1.4	–	2.2	3.6	4.0	1.3	0.7	1.8
Kumhar	–	–	–	1.1	0.7	–	–	–	–	–	–	–
Mirwa	–	–	–	–	–	–	–	0.9	–	–	–	–
Other	1.2	0.8	2.2	–	–	–	–	–	2.0	1.3	2.0	–

Scheduled Castes	19.5	21.0	14.4	13.3	17.9	12.5	16.3	17.9	14.0	7.8	20.5	8.9
Scheduled Tribes	4.9	7.6	10.0	15.5	11.7	2.5	12.6	18.8	16.0	16.9	13.3	8.9
Meena	–	–	1.1	2.2	–	–	5.2	–	2.0	1.3	6.0	1.8
Other	4.9	7.6	8.9	13.3	11.7	2.5	7.4	18.8	14.0	15.6	7.3	7.1
Religious	4.9	4.2	2.2	6.6	4.2	10.0	7.4	5.4	8.0	7.8	8.6	8.9
Minorities												
Muslim	3.7	3.4	2.2	4.4	3.5	5.0	6.7	4.5	6.0	5.2	7.3	7.1
Sikh	1.2	0.8	–	2.2	0.7	5.0	0.7	0.9	2.0	2.6	1.3	1.8
Unidentified	–	–	–	–	1.4	–	3.7	–	2.0	–	1.3	3.6
TOTAL	100.1	99.9	99.8	99.8	100.1	100.0	100.0	100.3	100.0	100.1	100.3	100.0
		(N=82)	(N=119)	(N=90)	(N=90)	(N=145)	(N=40)	(N=135)	(N=112)	(N=50)	(N=77)	(N=56)

Source: Survey by authors.

Among the upper castes, the Brahmins represent 14.9 per cent and the Rajputs 11.6 per cent of the Congress MLAs from 1952 to 2003.

After the 1952 elections, the leaders of the Congress party increasingly wooed the Rajput community. The co-option of Rajputs contradicted the ideology of the party, but played a pivotal role in establishing its domination over the state. Symmetrically, the Congress party played into the Rajputs' hands thus allowing them to keep and reinforce their social and political power.

The second largest social category among the Congress MLAs is the Scheduled Castes, which suggests that the Congress followed in Rajasthan the same 'coalition of extremes' pattern as in Uttar Pradesh. Indeed, the Scheduled Castes represented 16.4 per cent of the Congress MLAs between 1952 and 2003 and had reached 20.5 per cent in the state elections of 1998. However, these large proportions are largely due to the reservation system and the Congress has clearly not tried to promote Dalit leaders in Rajasthan.

The Jat group is really the element of singularity of the Congress in Rajasthan. Whereas in all the other states of the Hindi belt the party obliterated this group, the Jat MLAs represented 22.2 per cent of the Congress MLAs in 1962; 40 per cent in 1977 — a very atypical year — and 30 per cent in 1993. The over-representation of Jats in the Congress party can be explained by their role in the freedom movement and by the fact that the leaders of the Congress party encouraged the presence of Jats in its organisation in order to enlarge its support base in the rural areas. Therefore, those elected from the Jat community numerically constitute the first caste in the Congress party, ahead of the Brahmins and the Rajputs since the 1970s.

The Bharatiya Janata Party: The Upper Caste Hegemony

The caste structure of the BJP MLAs has always been dominated by the upper caste members. Their share has decreased after 1980 but it has remained higher than that of the Congress party. Until 1985, they constituted more than 50 per cent of the MLAs. In 2003, they were still 36.7 per cent, as against 32.1 per cent on the side of the Congress.

Within the category of the upper castes, we can observe some significant differences. During the first four elections, the Rajput and Baniya MLAs were the two leading groups. The significant weight of the

Rajputs reflected their effort to maintain an important public role as well as the strategy of the Jana Sangh which was keen to co-opt members of a community likely to challenge the Congress supremacy. Nevertheless, from 1972 onwards, the presence of the Brahmins increased till the 1980 elections, when they constituted 31.3 per cent of the Hindu nationalist MLAs and 50 per cent of the elected upper castes.

Table 5.7
Caste and Community of the Bharatiya Janata Party MLAs
in Rajasthan, 1980–2003 (%)

Castes and Communities	1980	1985	1990	1993	1998	2003
Upper Castes	**62.6**	**55.3**	**45.3**	**43.9**	**37.5**	**36.5**
Brahmin	31.3	23.7	16.3	13.3	3.1	8.3
Rajput	9.4	7.9	8.1	16.3	18.8	15.8
Baniya/Jain	18.8	21.1	17.4	13.3	9.4	10.8
Khatri	–	–	–	–	3.1	–
Arora	3.1	2.6	1.2	1.0	–	0.8
Sindhi	–	–	2.3	–	3.1	0.8
Intermediate Castes	–	**7.9**	**4.7**	**11.2**	**21.9**	**12.5**
Jat	–	5.3	4.7	11.2	18.8	12.5
Maratha	–	2.6	–	–	–	–
Bishnoi	–	–	–	–	3.1	–
OBC	**6.3**	**15.7**	**11.8**	**6.1**	**18.7**	**8.3**
Gujjar	6.3	10.5	3.5	4.1	3.1	6.7
Yadav	–	–	–	–	3.1	–
Mali	–	–	4.7	1.0	–	0.8
Kumhar	–	2.6	1.2	–	3.1	–
Nai	–	–	1.2	1.0	–	–
Other	–	2.6	1.2	–	9.4	0.8
Scheduled Castes	**18.8**	**10.5**	**19.8**	**26.5**	**9.4**	**22.5**
Scheduled Tribes	**12.5**	**5.2**	**15.1**	**12.3**	**12.6**	**15.0**
Meena	12.5	2.6	8.1	9.2	6.3	8.3
Other	–	2.6	7.0	3.1	6.3	6.7
Religious Minorities	–	**2.6**	**2.4**	–	–	**0.8**
Muslim	–	2.6	1.2	–	–	0.8
Sikh	–	–	1.2	–	–	–
Unidentified	–	**2.6**	**1.2**	–	–	**4.2**
TOTAL	100.2 (N=32)	99.8 (N=38)	100.3 (N=86)	100.0 (N=98)	100.1 (N=32)	99.8 (N=120)

Source: Survey by authors.

The 1993 elections show a significant resurgence of the Rajput MLAs and a decline of the Brahmin representation. Moreover, we can observe that the increased presence of those returned from the Rajput community was linked to a rise in the number of BJP MLAs in the Legislative Assembly. Another explanation for the lion's share of the Rajput's representation is the development, since the beginning of the 1990s, of a new mobilising strategy of the 'Sangh Parivar' at large in terms of a 'Rajputisation' of Hindutva (see Jenkins 1998).

The Non-empowerment of the Other Backward Classes

The decrease of the percentage of the upper caste MLAs — from 60 per cent to 33 per cent — in Rajasthan from 1952 to 2003 occurred in four stages: the elections of 1957, 1972, 1980 and 1990, in each of which the upper caste MLAs experienced more or less a significant fall in their representation. The trend has not been linear since the year 1990, for in 1993, the upper castes regained their level of 1980 but this was a short-lived comeback due to the electoral success of an upper caste-dominated BJP.

However, the decline of the upper caste MLAs did not benefit the OBC. Whereas the share of the upper castes decreased by 27 percentage points, the proportion of the OBC only increased by 5.3 percentage points from 3.2 to 8.5 per cent from 1952 to 2003. The position of the OBC MLAs was marginalised by the leaders of the main political parties in comparison with the share of the OBC in the population of Rajasthan.

In fact, the category of MLAs that principally benefited from the erosion of the upper castes is that of the Scheduled Tribes. While they represented the smallest share of MLAs (along with the OBC) in 1952, the percentage of the ST MLAs increased by 11.9 percentage points from 3.1 to 15 per cent between the years 1952 and 2003. Within this category, the Meenas, who represent the single largest group in the districts of Alwar, Jaipur, Sawai Madhopur and Kota, increased their share of MLAs from 0.5 to 7 per cent from 1952 to 2003. Two main reasons explain the increasing presence of ST in the Assembly: (*i*) the growing number of ST constituencies from one in 1951, 15 in 1957, 17 in 1962, 21 in 1967 to 24 from 1977 onwards; and (*ii*) the increasing number of election of ST candidates in general constituencies with a maximum of six in 2003.

Table 5.8

Evolution of the Distribution of the Caste and Community of the MLAs in Rajasthan, 1952–2003 (%)

Castes and Communities	1952	1957	1962	1967	1972	1977	1980	1985	1990	1993	1998	2003	TOTAL
Upper Castes	**61.0**	**46.6**	**47.2**	**46.8**	**41.8**	**41.0**	**36.0**	**38.0**	**30.9**	**36.5**	**30.9**	**33.0**	**41.1**
Brahmin	16.8	18.2	14.2	15.8	13.6	11.5	13.5	16.5	10.6	11.5	9.1	10.0	13.4
Rajput	30.5	17.0	19.3	15.8	14.1	12.5	11.5	11.5	8.1	14.0	12.2	12.5	15.0
Baniya/Jain	12.1	9.7	11.4	13.6	12.5	14.5	10.0	8.0	10.1	10.0	7.6	9.0	10.7
Kayastha	1.6	1.1	1.7	1.6	1.1	1.0	0.5	1.0	0.5	–	0.5	0.5	1.0
Khatri	–	–	–	–	–	0.5	–	–	1.0	–	0.5	–	0.2
Arora	–	–	–	–	–	0.5	0.5	0.5	0.5	0.5	–	0.5	0.3
Sindhi	–	0.6	0.6	–	0.5	0.5	–	0.5	1.0	0.5	1.0	0.5	0.5
Intermediate Castes	**15.8**	**16.5**	**16.5**	**13.6**	**15.8**	**14.5**	**19.0**	**16.5**	**18.7**	**21.0**	**20.3**	**18.5**	**17.3**
Jat	15.8	16.5	15.9	13.6	15.8	14.5	19.0	16.0	18.7	21.0	18.8	18.5	17.1
Maratha	–	–	–	–	–	–	–	0.5	–	–	–	–	–
Bishnoi	–	–	0.6	–	–	–	–	–	–	–	1.5	–	0.2
OBC	**3.2**	**4.0**	**6.2**	**3.2**	**7.0**	**7.0**	**6.0**	**8.0**	**10.0**	**6.0**	**8.5**	**8.5**	**6.11**
Gujar	1.6	1.1	3.4	2.2	3.3	4.0	3.0	3.0	3.0	3.0	2.0	5.0	2.9
Yadav	1.6	1.1	1.1	0.5	1.6	1.5	1.5	1.5	2.0	1.0	2.5	1.0	1.4
Mali	–	0.6	0.6	–	1.6	–	1.5	2.0	3.0	1.0	0.5	1.0	1.0
Kumhar	–	–	–	0.5	0.5	–	–	0.5	0.5	–	0.5	–	0.2
Nai	–	–	–	–	–	–	–	–	0.5	0.5	–	–	0.1
Mirwa	–	–	–	–	–	–	–	0.5	–	–	–	–	–
Latar	–	–	–	–	–	0.5	–	–	–	–	–	–	–

(*Table 5.8 continued*)

(*Table 5.8 continued*)

Castes and Communities	1952	1957	1962	1967	1972	1977	1980	1985	1990	1993	1998	2003	Total
Charan	–	0.6	–	–	–	–	–	–	–	–	–	–	–
Bujac	–	–	–	–	–	0.5	–	–	–	–	–	–	–
Other	–	0.6	1.1	–	–	0.5	–	0.5	1.0	0.5	3.0	1.5	0.7
Scheduled Castes	**11.1**	**19.9**	**17.0**	**16.8**	**16.3**	**16.5**	**17.5**	**17.0**	**18.2**	**18.0**	**17.8**	**16.5**	**16.9**
Scheduled Tribes	**3.1**	**8.6**	**9.7**	**11.4**	**11.4**	**12.0**	**13.0**	**13.5**	**14.2**	**13.5**	**14.2**	**15.0**	**11.8**
Meena	0.5	0.6	0.6	2.7	1.1	5.0	6.5	7.0	7.1	7.5	7.1	7.0	4.5
Other	2.6	8.0	9.1	8.7	10.3	7.0	6.5	6.5	7.1	6.0	7.1	8.0	7.3
Religious Minorities	**4.3**	**2.9**	**1.7**	**4.4**	**4.4**	**6.5**	**5.5**	**5.0**	**6.0**	**4.0**	**7.1**	**3.0**	**4.6**
Muslim	3.2	2.3	1.7	3.3	3.3	4.5	5.0	4.0	4.0	2.5	6.1	2.5	3.6
Sikh	1.1	0.6	–	1.1	1.1	2.0	0.5	1.0	2.0	1.5	1.0	0.5	1.0
Unidentified	**1.1**	**1.7**	**1.7**	**3.8**	**1.6**	**2.5**	**3.0**	**1.0**	**1.0**	**1.0**	**1.0**	**5.5**	**2.2**
TOTAL	99.6	100.2	100.0	100.0	98.3	100.0	100.0	99.0	99.9	100.0	99.8	100.0	100.01
	(N=190)	(N=176)	(N=176)	(N=184)	(N=184)	(N=200)	(N=200)	(N=198)	(N=198)	(N=200)	(n=197)	(N=200)	(N=2303)

Source: Survey by authors.

The Jats as OBC?

In addition to the Meenas, the other real beneficiaries from the decline of the upper castes were the Jats who had always been prominent in the post-independence Congress party because of their leading role in the Kisan Sabhas. After independence, with the introduction of popular elections and the development of a party system, the Kisan Sabhas receded in the background as a socio-political movement and their members were largely absorbed in the Congress system. From this time, the Jats rapidly expanded their scope of participation in the Congress party. They were especially successful in the areas where Jat political activity before independence had been intense, particularly, in the districts of Jhunjhunun, Sikar, Nagaur, Barmer, Ganganagar and Churu.

In the first state elections of 1952, the Jat MLAs represented the third largest single group in the Vidhan Sabha with 15.8 per cent of the total, after the Rajputs (30.5 per cent) and the Brahmins (16.8 per cent). Then, the political weight of the Jats steadily increased. From the 1962 elections onwards, they constituted the second largest single group of MLAs with 15.9 per cent after the Rajputs (19.3 per cent) in 1962. They became the first from 1972 (15.8 per cent) onwards. However, till 1977, the share of the Jat MLAs did not significantly increase: they profited by the decline of the upper caste share, especially that of the Rajputs which decreased by 18 percentage points.

In the late 1980s, with the increasing importance of reservations in favour of the 'backwards', the Jat leaders perceived the benefits of playing the game of quota politics too. They put pressure on the state governments for having the Jats recognised as part of the OBC. In Rajasthan, the Congress party supported their demand. But after the election of Ashok Gehlot, a Gujjar, as Chief Minister in 1998, the Congress government contented itself with appointing a commission to examine the claim of the Jats. The leaders of the Jat community immediately accused the Congress of buying time. During the Lok Sabha election campaign of 1999, the BJP wooed them by assuring that the party would integrate the Jats into the OBC category if the party was voted to power. As a result, 65 per cent of the Jats voted for the BJP, which won 16 out of the 25 seats.[2]

---

[2] Source: Centre for the Studies of Developing Society Data Unit.

Table 5.9

Evolution of Jat MLAs in the Vidhan Sabha, the Indian National Congress and the BJS/BJP in Rajasthan (%)

Year	1952	1957	1962	1967	1972	1977	1980	1985	1990	1993	1998	2003
Vidhan Sabha	15.8	16.5	15.9	13.6	15.8	14.5	19.0	16.0	18.7	21.0	18.8	18.5
Congress	15.9	17.7	22.2	16.7	17.2	40.0	20.7	14.3	26.0	29.9	17.2	28.6
BJS/BJP	12.5	0	0	4.6	12.5	0	0	5.3	4.7	11.2	18.8	12.5

Source: Survey by authors.

Since October 1999, the Jats of Rajasthan have been classified in the OBC category, whereas they are a more dominant caste than OBC; the inclusion of Jats was nothing else but a symptom of vote bank politics. Since the castes which comprise the OBC are economically, educationally and numerically weaker than the Jats, the share of the OBC has artificially increased in the realm of political representation without castes like Gujjars or Yadavs being able to rise to power. While there are 269 OBC castes across Rajasthan, the benefits of reservations mainly go to the Jats simply because of their number and socio-economic status. For instance, in a recruitment drive for the Rajasthan Administrative Service in the year 2001, 85 seats were reserved for OBC and 79 of these were bagged by the Jats (Diwanji 2003). Thus, the Jats have well cornered most of the quotas reserved for the OBC, even though many of them may be part of the elite groups.

The Upper Caste Domination over the Party Apparatus and the Government

The Party Apparatus: A Position of Influence for the Upper Castes

While the upper castes lost ground in the Legislative Assembly, they remain in control of the party apparatus in the Congress as well as in the Bharatiya Janata Party. As evident from Table 5.11, the upper castes are much more well-represented in the Pradesh Congress Committee and in the BJP State Executive in the year 2005 with 44 and 53.2 per cent of the members than in the state Assembly. In addition, among the upper caste in the Congress and in the BJP, the Brahmins represent the largest group respectively with 21.4 and 22 per cent whereas they only constitute the third largest group in the Legislative Assembly with 10 per cent.

On the Congress' side, the expected over-representation of the upper caste seems to be the specific feature within the party apparatus. Indeed, the 'pre-independence patterns of social representation have persisted in state-level party institutions. Caste Hindus ... have constituted the vast proportion of representatives elected to the Pradesh Congress Committee since its founding in 1946' (Sisson 1972: 131). Thus, with 9.8 and 4.3 per cent respectively, both the Scheduled Castes and the Scheduled Tribes are under-represented in the state level Congress organisation. Moreover, the other noteworthy point is still the large under-representation of the OBC with 5.8 per cent of the Pradesh Congress Committee (PCC).

Unlike the Congress, the BJP is characterised by the significant presence of OBC in the party apparatus. With 13.4 per cent, this category represents the second largest group in the BJP state executive.

One even finds in the BJP state apparatus, one Gujjar as vice-president and two Malis as state secretaries. However, the fragmentation of the OBC category weakens its political position within the party apparatus

Table 5.10
Major Castes and Communities of the Pradesh Congress Committee Members, the BJP State Executive Members and the MLAs in Rajasthan, 2005 (%)

Castes and Communities	BJP	INC	Vidhan Sabha
Upper Castes	**53.2**	**44.1**	**33.0**
Brahmin	22.0	21.4	10.0
Rajput	11.3	9.2	12.5
Baniya/Jain	13.4	6.1	9.0
Kayastha	2.7	1.2	0.5
Mahajan	1.1	3.4	–
Other	2.7	2.8	1.0
Intermediate Castes	**11.8**	**17.7**	**18.5**
Jat	11.8	17.7	18.5
OBC	**13.4**	**5.8**	**8.5**
Gujjar	4.8	0.3	5.0
Mali	1.6	1.5	1.0
Yadav	0.5	0.9	1.0
Other	6.5	3.1	1.5
Scheduled Castes	**10.8**	**9.8**	**16.5**
Scheduled Tribes	**6.0**	**4.3**	**15.0**
Meena	2.7	3.7	7.0
Bhil	1.1	–	–
Other	2.2	0.6	8.0
Religious Minorities	**1.6**	**11.9**	**3.0**
Muslim	0.5	10.4	2.5
Sikh	1.1	1.5	0.5
Unidentified	**3.2**	**6.4**	**5.5**
TOTAL	100.0	100.0	100.0
	(N=186)	(N=327)	(N=200)

Source: Survey by authors.

as in the Legislative Assembly. Moreover, with the Jats being classified as OBC, the other castes of this group — Gujjar, Mali, Yadav, etc. — could be excluded from the heart of the decision-making process.

So far as the Congress apparatus is concerned, the proportion of Jats as office bearers reaches as high as 22.5 per cent! This strong representation seems to prove that this community is a political force to be reckoned with. Nevertheless, the decision of Sonia Gandhi to remove Narayan Singh (a Jat) from his position as PCC chief in April 2005 and to appoint B. D. Kalla (a Brahmin and former leader of Congress Legislative Party) has confused the policy of wooing the Jat community. Within the Congress party, there are many Jat leaders who do not understand the party's policy towards the Jat community.[3]

Table 5.11
Caste and Community of the Rajasthan Pradesh Congress Committee and BJP State Executive, 2005 (%)

Castes and Communities	INC	BJP
Upper Castes	**37.5**	**38.9**
Brahmin	15.0	16.7
Rajput	5.0	11.1
Baniya/Jain	2.5	11.1
Kayastha	2.5	–
Mahajan	10.0	–
Punjabi	2.5	–
Intermediate Castes	**22.5**	**16.7**
Jat	22.5	16.7
OBC	**7.5**	**16.7**
Gujjar	2.5	5.6
Mali	2.5	11.1
Other	2.5	–
Scheduled Castes	**10.0**	**11.1**
Scheduled Tribes	**5.0**	**11.1**
Meena	5.0	11.1
Religious Minorities	**12.5**	**–**
Muslim	10.0	–
Sikh	2.5	–
Unidentified	**5.0**	**5.6**
TOTAL	100.0	100.0
	(N=40)	(N=18)

Source: Survey by authors.

---

[3] Interview with Veevend Poonia, Secretary, Rajasthan PCC, 17 April 2005, Jaipur.

Governments: Still in the Hands of Upper Castes

The state government has always been dominated by the upper castes: between the years 1952 and 2003, they represented 46.7 per cent of the total and the Jats, 17.8 per cent.

If the upper castes' representation has steadily decreased (they represented about one-third of the governments' members in 1998), the share of the OBC has not significantly increased (from 9.1 per cent in 1952 to 11.1 per cent in 2003). Once again, the principal beneficiaries have been the Jats whose share increased by 13.1 percentage points after 1952 to reach 22.2 per cent in 2003.

However, from 1993 onwards, the formation of a BJP government coincided with a diminution of the proportion of ministers belonging to the Jat community as well as with an increase of the upper caste proportion whereas the constitution of a Congress ministry led to the opposite (see Table 5.12), a reconfirmation of the influence of the Jats within the Indian National Congress and of the upper castes, mainly Rajputs, within the Bharatiya Janata Party.

Thus, the hegemony of the upper castes and Jats is still significant at the level of the apparatus of the parties and the governments in comparison with their representation in the Vidhan Sabha. Now, the control of the party organisation remains most important, and the exercise of power, through the control of the position of the chief minister and the allocation of ministerial portfolios, are the ultimate focus of conflict within parties.

Conclusion

While we can notice a certain erosion of the upper castes' representation in the Rajasthan Assembly between the years 1952 and 2003, the share of the lower OBC among the MLAs remains very small whereas the Jats — so called OBC — literally surged. In 2003, the Jats represented the most important group in the state Assembly. The Scheduled Tribes, because of the Meenas, were the other group which experienced a significant rise too though to a much lesser extent.

The limitations of the political empowerment of the lower castes in Rajasthan — so far as the social profile of the political class is concerned — are even more pronounced when one considers other institutions

Table 5.12

Evolution of the Castes and Communities Representation in Successive Governments in Rajasthan, 1952–2003 (%)

Castes and Communities	1952	1957	1962	1967	1971	1977	1980	1985	1990	1993	1998	2003
Upper Castes	**81.8**	**50.0**	**56.5**	**53.8**	**40.0**	**62.5**	**43.2**	**33.3**	**34.0**	**43.3**	**33.3**	**40.7**
Brahmin	36.4	21.4	34.8	20.5	13.3	31.3	15.9	20.0	14.9	13.3	13.3	11.1
Rajput	9.1	7.1	4.3	10.3	13.3	12.5	6.8	6.7	10.6	20.0	10.0	18.5
Baniya	27.3	21.4	13.0	15.4	6.7	18.8	20.5	6.7	8.5	10.0	10.0	7.4
Kayastha	9.1	–	4.3	7.7	6.7	–	–	–	–	–	–	–
Sindhi	–	–	–	–	–	–	–	–	–	–	–	3.7
Khatri	–	–	–	–	–	–	–	–	2.1	–	–	–
Intermediate Castes	**9.1**	**28.6**	**26.1**	**17.9**	**26.7**	**12.5**	**9.1**	**13.3**	**27.7**	**16.7**	**26.7**	**22.2**
Jat	9.1	21.4	26.1	17.9	20.0	12.5	9.1	13.3	23.4	16.7	23.3	22.2
Bishnoi	–	7.1	–	–	6.7	–	–	–	2.1	–	3.3	–
Sirvi	–	–	–	–	–	–	–	–	2.1	–	–	–
OBC	**9.1**	**–**	**4.3**	**2.6**	**–**	**–**	**9.1**	**6.7**	**8.5**	**6.7**	**3.3**	**11.1**
Gujar	–	–	–	–	–	–	2.3	–	2.1	3.3	–	7.4
Mali	–	–	–	–	–	–	2.3	–	–	–	3.3	3.7
Yadav	9.1	–	4.3	2.6	–	–	4.5	6.7	4.3	3.3	–	–
Kumhar	–	–	–	2.6	6.7	–	–	–	–	–	–	–

(*Table 5.12 continued*)

(Table 5.12 continued)

Castes and Communities	1952	1957	1962	1967	1971	1977	1980	1985	1990	1993	1998	2003
SC	–	**7.1**	**4.3**	**12.8**	**13.3**	**18.8**	**22.7**	**20.0**	**14.9**	**20.0**	**16.7**	**11.1**
ST	–	**7.1**	**4.3**	**5.1**	**13.3**	–	**9.1**	**20.0**	**8.5**	**6.7**	**10.0**	**11.1**
Meena	–	–	–	–	–	–	2.3	6.7	4.3	3.3	–	11.1
Bhil	–	–	–	–	–	–	2.3	6.7	–	–	–	–
Other	–	7.1	4.3	5.1	13.3	–	4.5	6.7	4.3	3.3	10.0	–
Religious Minorities	–	**7.1**	**4.3**	**7.7**	**6.7**	**6.3**	**6.8**	**6.7**	**6.4**	**6.7**	**10.0**	**3.7**
Muslim	–	7.1	4.3	5.1	6.7	6.3	4.5	6.7	4.3	3.3	10.0	3.7
Sikh	–	–	–	2.6	–	–	2.3	–	2.1	3.3	–	–
TOTAL	100.0 (N=11)	100.0 (N=14)	100.0 (N=23)	100.0 (N=39)	100.0 (N=15)	100.0 (N=16)	100.0 (N=44)	100.0 (N=15)	100.0 (N=47)	100.0 (N=30)	100.0 (N=30)	100.0 (N=27)

Source: Survey by authors.

such as the composition of the government and the apparatus of the political parties. Consequently, the evolution of the political class of Rajasthan can be characterised by a transition from one conservative situation where the upper castes dominate to another which is defined by the over-representation of the dominant Jat caste.

⬦

References

Census of India, 1931. 1933. Government of India, Rajputana Agency, Nagpur.

Diwanji, Amberish K. 2003. 'The Anti-Reservation Man', 27 November. http://www.rediff.com/election/2003/nov/27akd.htm.

Jenkins, Robert. 1998. 'Rajput Hindutva, Caste Politics, Regional Identity and Hindu Nationalism in Contemporary Rajasthan', in Thomas Blom Hansen and Christophe Jaffrelot (eds), *The BJP and the Compulsions of Politics in India,* pp. 101–20. Delhi: Oxford University Press.

Kamal, K. L. 1967. 'Rightist Political Parties in Rajasthan', in Iqbal Narain (ed.), *State Politics in India,* pp. 503–10. Meerut: Meenakshi Prakashan.

Mathur, P. C. 1967. 'Princes in Rajasthan Politics', in Iqbal Narain (ed.), *State Politics in India,* pp. 596–607. Meerut: Meenakshi Prakashan.

Narain, Iqbal and P. C. Mathur. 1990. 'The Thousand Year Raj: Regional Isolation and Rajput Hinduism in Rajasthan Before and After 1947', in Francine R. Frankel and M. S. A. Rao (eds), *Dominance and State Power in Modern India: Decline of a Social Order,* vol. 2, pp. 1–58. Delhi: Oxford University Press.

Saxena, K. S. 1996. *State Politics in Rajasthan.* Jaipur: Aalekh Publishers.

Sharma, J. S. 1962. *India's Struggle for Freedom,* vol. 3. Delhi: S. Chand & Co.

Sisson, Richard. 1972. *The Congress Party in Rajasthan, Political Integration and Institution-building in an Indian State.* Berkeley: University of California Press.

6

Gujarat: When Patels Resist the Kshatriyas

Kiran Desai and *Ghanshyam Shah*

The present state of Gujarat came into existence in 1960 as a result of the bifurcation of the erstwhile Bombay state. Initially, the Gujarat Assembly was constituted of seating members of Bombay state Assembly elected from the Gujarat region that included Saurashtra and Kachchh. The first election for Gujarat Assembly took place in 1962. It then had 154 members. At present, the Assembly is constituted of 182 members.

Though this chapter presents a broad changing socio-occupational and demographic profile of the Members of the State Legislative Assembly, the focus is on the social profile of two major parties of the state, i.e., the Congress and the Jana Sangh/Bharatiya Janata Party (BJP), as in the last 11 assemblies. This is with a view to understand the social base of political parties and the changing nature of social context of the state's politics. The Congress ruled the state for most part of the period and it is still the major party. At present, however, the BJP is the ruling party. These two parties will continue to dominate Gujarat politics at least for the current decade.

This study is an explorative exercise based on the volumes of *Who's Who* of the Members of the State Legislative Assembly (MLA) of the period 1962–98 published by the state government from time to time. At the outset, let us mention the limitations of the data. One, the information related to education, birth date or age and occupation at the base of this study are not complete for all the MLAs. At the same time, neither the volumes nor any other published document give caste identity of MLAs except of those who belong to Scheduled Castes (SC) and Scheduled Tribes (ST). Thus, whatever information is available is not primarily based on self-reporting of the concerned MLAs. We have coded caste based on our caste-related inventory, which we have built over a period of time through various studies across Gujarat. Our informed speculation also played its part. Two, no scholar or political leader is likely to be familiar with the social background of all the MLAs of different regions as also of different periods. Three, surnames or family names may provide some hint or indication to speculate on the caste of a person, but *Who's Who* does not mention the surnames of all entries. Moreover, relying purely on surnames is very hazardous, as all those who have the same surname do not always belong to the same caste. Four, often social caste and political caste, more so in the case of political leaders are not necessarily the same. Social caste is confined to social relations, marriage network and inter-dining relationship. This is confined to *jati* or sub-subcaste where internal hierarchy is not visible. Political caste is a larger and contextual category changing from time to time. Persons of different *jatis*, sometimes of different hierarchical order, share same caste identity in political sphere. As a result, caste identity changes with changing context. For instance, a Bareeya was Bareeya in the early 1950s. He became Rajput in the late 1950s and early 1960s. He identified as Kshatriya in the late 1960s and early 1970s. But then he once again preferred to be recognised as Bareeya. Because the Socially and Educationally Backward Castes Commission appointed by the Government of Gujarat identified them in 1976 as one of the Backward Castes. That provided them certain benefits in education and employment. In this situation, the question is: which code we should give to such a person when our exercise is located in 2004? For our purpose we used the OBC list prepared by the state government for identifying the OBC caste. This list includes poor peasant castes such as Bareeya, Khant, Patanvadiya, Koli, etc. Therefore, by convention, we have adopted the official categories as they were at that time of elections to classify the MLAs as OBC, SC or ST.

However, we should note that the Bareeyas identify themselves as 'Kshatriya' as synonymous to 'Rajput' in order to build alliance in political arena and also to get higher status in social sphere. But 'Rajput' in our coding scheme falls in the category of upper caste, *dwija*. Rajputs do not get benefits, which are offered to OBC by the state. It may also be mentioned that overall economic and educational condition of Rajputs is not strikingly different than Kolis. But social status accompanying myths, which are constructed on glorification of past, tell a different story. This means, social categories are constructed by people and scholars, depending upon their objectives at particular points of time. The caste category coded by us is not definative and should be taken with caution. Moreover 'not ascertained' cases have to be ascertained.

Thus, what follows is a tentative and broad scenario. Initially we planned to collect and verify this information with the help of other informants in different districts. But because of financial and human constraints we have not been able to fulfil our intention.

Social Structure of Gujarat

More than 84 per cent of the population of Gujarat has been identified as Hindus. Around 9 per cent are Muslims. Around 3 per cent are Jains, Parsees and Christians together. Hindus are divided into numerous *jatis*. For our analysis, we clubbed them into four categories: upper castes, middle castes, Other Backward Castes and Dalits or Scheduled Castes. Most of Hindus (as also Jains) believe that the Jains are Hindus too. Both have a close social relationship. In fact, among the Jains and Hindu Baniyas, inter-marriage relationship is not uncommon. We have therefore not coded Jains as a separate social category but included them amongst upper castes. Besides the four categories just mentioned, a separate category of Adivasis or Scheduled Tribes also has been included.

Baniyas, Brahmins, Rajputs constitute the major upper castes. We have also included some other castes such as Luhana, Brahmkshatriya, Bhatias, etc., who are primarily non-peasant castes and whose higher social status is by and large acknowledged and accepted by society. Baniyas constitute nearly 3 per cent of the population. Their presence can be seen almost in each and every part of the state and a majority of them live in urban areas. They occupy leading positions in business and industry. Brahmins, comprising 4 per cent of the population, form the single largest group in white-collar jobs and amongst high-rung professionals such as doctors, engineers, architects, etc. A few Brahmins and Baniyas, around 4 to 5 per cent, live in hand-to-mouth condition, working as manual labourers in organised and unorganised sectors in urban areas. A good many of them, however, hold leading positions in employees' organisational activities such as labour unions. Brahmins continue to enjoy hegemony in educational institutions, literature, media and other spheres of public life and assume responsibility to be torchbearers in society articulating, producing and reproducing cultural values, idioms and goals.

Rajputs, traditionally rulers and army men, constitute 5 per cent of the population. Though traditionally they occupy a high status, their position as a forward caste is ambivalent. Their cultural practices and economic condition are different than that of Baniyas and Brahmins. A majority of them are not well off. Nearly one-fifth of them are labourers in farm and non-farm sectors. Their educational level is relatively low, similar to that of the backward castes. Moreover, they have marriage ties with the Kolis and several tribes who are considered low in social hierarchy.

The single largest middle caste is of Patidars, a peasant caste. Traditionally, they were known as Kanbis who elevated their status in the 20th century and came to be known as Patidars. A majority of them are landholders with middle or large sized holdings. In urban areas, a sizeable number of them are in business (small and big); they work as professionals mainly as medical doctors, engineers, architects, lawyers and also have white-collar jobs in private and public sectors. They constitute the single largest social group among the Gujarati non-resident Indians (NRI) in North America and Europe. They have followed many of the cultural practices of Baniyas and upgraded their social position from middle caste to upper caste. In Saurashtra, a subregion of the state, their sudden rise was met with stiff opposition especially by Darbars or Rajputs who until then held higher status than Kanbis. But land reforms measures in post-independence era under the leadeship of Baniya and Brahmin elite in Saurashtra changed the situation dramatically as Kanbis who used to till Darbars' lands in fact became owners and elevated their status as a result (Shah 2002b). The Rajputs could not tolerate this sudden change of fortune, and the tension between the two communities often culminated into violent clashes. Baniyas and Brahmins too were upset over the changed status of Patidars as their hegemony was severely jeopardised. But their progress could not be blocked by any as they in fact grew from strength to strength in terms of their economic condition. Also their numerical strength, 13 per cent of the population, has proved as deterrent against any such move.

All the upper and middle castes together occupy three-fourths space of the middle class. They constitute more than 95 per cent of the affluent class owning big industries and business firms in the region. Except a few, most of the Rajputs in their present economic condition are, for all practical purposes, closer to Other Backward Castes (OBC).

The government of Gujarat identified 82 castes in 1976 as 'socially and educationally backward castes'. They are also known as Other Backward Castes (OBC) who constitute nearly 40 per cent of the population. Among the OBC a majority, nearly 65 per cent, belong to different segments of the Kolis. A large number of them are poor peasants and agricultural labourers. In urban areas they are labourers in various activities of formal and informal sectors, mainly of the latter type. According to a survey in the mid-1980s, as many as 35 per cent of the Koli families, as against 8 per cent of Baniyas and Brahmins, were completely illiterate. The Thakors, Patanvadias, Bareeyas, Khants, etc., of the central Gujarat region were clubbed as Kolis by the British government, an identification which has never been accepted by the people themselves. They instead call themselves 'Kshatriyas'. Their process of *sanskritisation* as Kshatriyas began by the beginning of the 20th century. The Kolis of Saurashtra also have an identical nomenclature and those of south Gujarat are recognised as Koli Patels.

Scheduled Castes, traditionally called untouchables, and now known as Dalits, form nearly 7 per cent of the population. In rural Gujarat, they are still being discriminated against because of the practice of un-touchability and they do not have access to several spheres of public domain (Desai 1976, Shah 2000). A majority of them are agricultural labourers and poor peasants. Their proportion in government jobs, thanks to the reservation system and their collective assertion, has considerably enhanced during the last three decades.

Adivasis or Scheduled Tribes constitute 14 per cent of the population. Traditionally, they depended on forest products and worked as wage labourers for their livelihood. Though a large number of them cultivate land, a good many of them do not legally own land. They are poor peasants and they mainly make the two ends of the day meet by working as farm as well as non-farm labourers. As forest resources are getting depleted and they are losing land as well as forced to being uprooted from their motherland for so-called development projects, they are further marginalised and have become the main losers in the fast developing market economy. Despite reservations, their proportion in higher rungs of various governmental jobs remains insignificant.

Caste-based Political Mobilisation: The Making of Kshatriyas

The Congress party that led the freedom struggle had overwhelming majority in the first election of the Bombay state as also in Saurashtra and Kachchh assemblies. But its majority was substantially reduced in the second general elections in 1957 as the party faced opposition from the Maha Gujarat Janata Parishad (MGJP), which spearheaded the movement for a separate Gujarat state. MGJP was a coalition of socialists, communists and independent liberals. The Swatantra Party advocating the *laissez faire* theory came into existence in 1959. Bhailalbhai Patel, the leader of the Lok Paksh in 1952 that opposed land reforms, was the main leader of the Gujarat Swatantra Party. The party won 26 seats out of 154, i.e., 17 per cent in the 1962 elections. It improved its position in the 1967 elections by winning as many as 67 seats out of 168 seats. The Swatantra Party changed the caste dimensions of politics in Gujarat. Bhailalbhai Patel had evolved a 'grand strategy' known as *Paksh*, 'P' for Patidar and 'ksha' for Kshatriya — an electoral alliance between the Kshatriya and the Patidars. The Swatantra Party openly allied itself with the Gujarat Kshatriya Sabha (GKS), the caste organisation of the Rajputs and the Kolis, and gave party tickets to the Kshatriyas generously (Shah 1975).

The Congress party also hobnobbed with GKS since 1952, but did not accept all its demands. In fact, the Patidar members of the party prevented the Kshatriyas from enrolling as party members as they were reluctant to share power with them. But when the party lost its majority of the Assembly seats for the first time in 1962 from the GKS stronghold Kheda district in central Gujarat region, it realised that it could no longer take the Kshatriyas for granted. After 1962, the party became more liberal in offering party tickets to the Kshatriyas in the elections. As the GKS was allied with the Swatantra Party, the Congress recruited influential local Kshatriya leaders into the party, and sponsored a parallel Kshatriya organisation, particularly, of the Koli Kshatriyas. As against seven in 1962, 15 Kshatriyas (Kolis and Rajputs together) from central and north Gujarat were given assembly tickets by the Congress in the 1967 elections.

In 1969, the Congress party split into Congress (Organisation) and Congress (Ruling). The former was led by Morarji Desai and the latter by Ms. Indira Gandhi, which later came to be known as Congress (Indira). Initially, the majority of the members of the Congress in Gujarat sided with Congress(O). The Congress(I) negotiated with the GKS and promised to form the Backward Castes Commission to ensure OBC reservations in government jobs and also other benefits (Shah 1990). Relatively pro-poor and pro-backward caste leaders of the Gujarat Congress joined Congress(I). With the 'garibi hatao', slogan, the Congress(I) won 140 out of 168 seats in the 1972 state Assembly election. Congress(O) got 16 seats. However, in 1974, the party experienced a severe jolt as due to an unprecedented protest movement against its government, focusing mainly on an issue of corruption, the popularity of the Congress(I) declined. The state Assembly was prematurely dissolved and fresh elections took place in 1975. The Congress lost power, and United Front (UF), later named as the Janata Party, came into power. Jana Sangh was one of the constituents of the UF. In terms of castes, Patidars dominated the Janata Party. The Congress, which already had a support base among the Kshatriya and deprived groups, opted for a different strategy to regain power. It formed an alliance called KHAM — an alliance among the Kshatriyas (K), the Harijans (H), the Adivasis (A) and the Muslims (M) — and distributed party tickets among the members of these social groups generously in the 1980 elections. The party won the election handsomely on its new social plank. It conspicuously excluded Patidars from the leadership and also from the ministry. A Kshatriya became the chief minister of Gujarat. He was later replaced by an Adivasi in 1985.

During the 1980s, the BJP raised the issue of Ram temple in Ayodhya. A series of communal riots took place in Gujarat between 1985 and 1994. Besides arousing communal sentiments, the BJP followed the Congress strategy of wooing the backward castes as well as Dalits and Adivasis. It also sponsored Kshatriya Sabha and gave large numbers of party tickets to political leaders of various OBC (Shah 1991). This political process got reflected in the caste composition of the MLAs of this period.

In the later part of the last decade of 20th century, the BJP made a significant move by removing Keshubhai Patel as chief minister and installing Narendra Modi, a hard-core RSS leader, in his place. The change of leadership took place as a consequence of BJP's defeat in the Assembly by-elections and panchayat elections. The leadership considered these debacles as the last straw on camel's back, and hence, put into action an unrefined *hindutva* agenda through Modi. Modi lost no time in implementing the Sangh Parivaar's ideology, polarising society on communal (religious) lines as the post-Godhra holocaust has shown (Shah 2002a). The state Assembly was prematurely dissolved to arrest communal passions in the Assembly elections. The BJP along with its upper and middle caste base consolidated its inroad among the OBC and Adivasis. It won two-thirds majority in the 2002 and 2007 elections (Patel 2003).

II

Caste Composition of MLAs

Table 6.1 shows that the overall proportion of upper castes — mainly Brahmins, Baniyas, Rajputs, etc. — has sharply declined in the state Assembly from 34 per cent in 1962 to 14 per cent in 2007. If we exclude Rajputs from upper castes, the decline in proportion would go down from 30 per cent in 1962 to nearly 12 per cent in 1998.

The position of intermediary castes, mainly Patidar, has declined slightly during the 1980s and 1990s. The decline was around 2 per cent, from 27 per cent in 1962 to 22 per cent in 1998. They have not only regained their strength in the last two elections but reached an unprecedented level in 2007. The OBC, both peasant and artisan castes who are around 40 per cent, have conspicuously improved their strength in the state Assembly from a mere 8 per cent in 1962 to 34 per cent in 2007. Their rise began from the mid-1960s with the success of the KHAM alliance formula propagated by the Congress and reached its pinnacle in 1980s as the BJP also followed the same strategy of wooing Kshatriyas, Dalits and Adivasis, although excluding the Muslims. The numerical strength of the OBC somewhat declined in 1990s and regained in the early 2000s. Perhaps, however, this decline may not be real if we probe further into our 'non-ascertained' category, which is a very large percentage.

The proportion of Muslim MLAs in Gujarat Assembly has declined from 5 per cent in 1962 to 2 per cent in the last Assembly of 2007. The seats for Scheduled Castes and Scheduled Tribes are kept reserved in the state Assembly. Since the mid-1960s, one to two SC persons have been getting elected from non-reserved constituency. This however needs to be probed further. As Table 6.1 shows, in 1967, 12 per cent

Table 6.1
Caste of MLAs in the State Assemblies of Gujarat, 1962–2007

Caste/ Communities	Years										
	1962	1967	1972	1975	1980	1985	1990	1995	1998	2002	2007
Upper Castes	53 (34)	68 (40)	50 (30)	50 (27)	39 (21)	44 (25)	45 (25)	38 (21)	38 (21)	36 (20)	25 (14)
Middle Castes	41 (27)	35 (21)	39 (23)	49 (27)	38 (21)	39 (21)	45 (25)	44 (24)	41 (22)	46 (25)	51 (28)
OBC	13 (8)	19 (11)	27 (16)	27 (15)	43 (24)	42 (24)	48 (26)	39 (21)	38 (21)	53 (29)	62 (34)
SC	11 (7)	11 (6)	13 (8)	16 (9)	15 (8)	15 (8)	14 (7)	15 (8)	14 (8)	13 (7)	13 (7)
ST	21 (14)	20 (12)	23 (14)	28 (16)	28 (16)	26 (14)	27 (15)	28 (15)	27 (15)	24 (13)	27 (15)
Muslims	8 (5)	4 (2)	3 (2)	4 (2)	11 (6)	8 (4)	2 (1)	1 (1)	5 (3)	3 (2)	4 (2)
Others, N.A.	7 (5)	11 (7)	13 (7)	8 (4)	8 (4)	8 (4)	1 (1)	17 (9)	19 (10)	7 (4)	–
TOTAL	154 (100)	168 (99)	168 (100)	182 (100)	182 (100)	182 (100)	182 (100)	182 (100)	182 (100)	182 (100)	182 (100)

Source: Survey by authors.

Note: Figures in parentheses indicate percentage.

of MLAs were from ST. Again, we assume that perhaps some of those who are in 'non-ascertained' category may belong to ST.

Till the 1980s, the Congress was the ruling party except in the 1975 Assembly. It was the Janata Party, which formed the government then. The majority faction of the Janata Party was of the Congress(O). In the 1960s, the Swatantra Party was the main opposition party. Its social base, particularly in rural areas, was not significantly different than that of the BJP which emerged as an important non-Congress party in the 1980s and formed the government from the 1990s onwards. In the present context, BJP is the major non-Congress political force and will remain so in the coming decade. Hence, the focus of our analysis is on the Congress and the BJP. The Congress(O) did not have a different base from that of the Congress in the early 1970s. It may be noted that the left parties, including socialists, have never become an important non-Congress political force in the state.

Tables 6.2 and 6.3 present the caste-wise break-up of the Congress and BJP MLAs. The social base of the Swatantra Party in 1962 and 1967 largely comprised the Patidars and the Kshatriyas. Later on, the BJP penetrated that base. At that time Jana Sangh had no base in Gujarat. The base of the Congress among the intermediary castes, particularly Patidars, has declined after 1972. As against this, it has improved its strength significantly among the OBC and the ST. The BJP has improved its position among the OBC but it has not been able to sustain their support. Thus, both the Congress and the BJP are trying to retain their base among the OBC. Among the Scheduled Tribes members, Congress had an edge over the BJP whose presence had slightly declined in 1995. The Congress base sharply declined among the tribal constituencies in the 2002 elections, but regained in the elections of 2007. The BJP mobilised the tribals against Muslims in the 2002 communal carnage. As Table 6.3 indicates, the BJP improved its position in tribal areas in 1995 when it had 60 per cent of the total ST MLAs. But the party again lost ground and reverted back to a subsidiary position within three years when in the 1998 elections the Congress came to have more than 60 per cent of the total ST MLAs. However, in 2002, the BJP captured the majority of the ST reserved seats thanks to the anti-Muslim communal carnage in which the BJP could mobilise the Adivasis against Muslims (Lobo and Meckwan 2003).

Table 6.2
Caste of Congress MLAs in the State Assemblies of Gujarat, 1962–2007

Caste/ Communities	Years										
	1962	1967	1972	1975	1980	1985	1990	1995	1998	2002	2007
Upper Castes	35 (31)	36 (38)	41 (29)	20 (27)	32 (23)	36 (24)	9 (27)	9 (20)	5 (9)	7 (14)	3 (5)
Middle Castes	29 (26)	20 (22)	31 (22)	7 (9)	17 (12)	29 (20)	2 (6)	7 (16)	5 (9)	5 (10)	10 (17)
OBC	7 (6)	11 (12)	22 (16)	15 (20)	37 (26)	31 (21)	12 (36)	13 (29)	14 (27)	19 (39)	25 (43)
SC	11 (10)	4 (4)	13 (9)	11 (15)	13 (9)	13 (8)	1 (3)	4 (9)	6 (11)	4 (8)	2 (3)
ST	17 (15)	14 (15)	20 (13)	15 (20)	26 (19)	25 (17)	7 (21)	9 (20)	16 (30)	10 (21)	15 (25)
Muslims	8 (7)	3 (3)	3 (2)	4 (5)	11 (8)	8 (5)	2 (6)	–	4 (8)	3 (6)	4 (7)
Others, N.A.	6 (5)	5 (5)	10 (7)	3 (4)	5 (3)	7 (5)	–	3 (7)	3 (6)	1 (2)	–
TOTAL	113 (100)	93 (99)	140 (100)	75 (100)	141 (100)	149 (100)	33 (100)	45 (100)	53 (100)	49 (100)	59 (100)

Note: Figures in parentheses indicate percentage.

Table 6.3

Caste of the Jana Sangh and BJP MLAs in the State Assemblies of Gujarat, 1967–2007

Caste/ Communities	Jana Sangh			BJP						
	1967	1972	1975	1980	1985	1990	1995	1998	2002	2007
Upper Castes	1 (100)	1 (33)	8 (44)	2 (22)	3 (27)	18 (27)	26 (21)	32 (27)	29 (22)	22 (19)
Middle Castes	–	1 (33)	6 (33)	5 (56)	4 (36)	19 (28)	36 (30)	34 (29)	41 (31)	38 (33)
OBC	–	1 (33)	8 (44)	6 (67)	8 (72)	32 (48)	52 (43)	53 (45)	34 (26)	35 (30)
SC	–	–	–	–	–	6 (9)	11 (9)	8 (7)	9 (7)	11 (9)
ST	–	–	1 (6)	1 (11)	–	6 (9)	15 (12)	8 (7)	14 (11)	11 (9)
Muslims	–	–	–	–	–	–	–	–	–	–
Others, N.A.	–	1 (33)	–	–	–	–	12 (10)	15 (13)	4 (3)	–
TOTAL	1 (100)	4 (100)	18 (100)	9 (100)	11 (100)	67 (100)	121 (100)	117 (100)	131 (100)	117 (100)

Note: Figures in parentheses indicate percentage.

The number of Muslim MLAs is significantly less vis-à-vis their proportion in the total population of the state. As seen earlier, over a period of time, their number in the Assembly has declined and at one time in 1995 there were no Muslim MLAs at all. It should be noted that all Muslim MLAs, except in 1967, have been elected from the Congress party. The Swatantra Party had one Muslim MLA in 1967. But the BJP so far does not have any representation from the Muslim community.

III

Some Other Demographic Indicators of MLAs

Gender

The sex ratio in Gujarat is in favour of the male. There are 937 women per 1000 males. The proportion of females has been declining continuously in the last five decades. This speaks of the adverse status of women in the Gujarat society. Hence, it is not surprising that this social phenomenon gets reflected in gender representation in the state Assembly. As Table 6.4 shows, the proportion of female MLAs has never gone beyond one-tenth of the total in any Assembly. It was highest, 8.2 per cent in 1985 and lowest in 1995, i.e., 1.1 per cent. If we take

Table 6.4
Distribution of MLAs of Gujarat by Gender, 1962–2007

Year	Males	Females	TOTAL
1962	142 (92)	12 (8)	154 (100)
1967	161 (96)	7 (4)	168 (100)
1972	160 (95)	8 (5)	168 (100)
1975	178 (98)	3 (2)	181 (100)
1980	177 (97)	5 (3)	182 (100)
1985	167 (92)	15 (8)	182 (100)
1990	177 (97)	4 (2)	182 (100)
1995	180 (99)	2 (1)	182 (100)
1998	178 (98)	4 (2)	182 (100)
2002	170 (93)	12 (7)	182 (100)
2007	170 (93)	12 (7)	182 (100)
TOTAL	1860 (96)	84 (4)	1945 (100)

Note: Figures in parentheses indicate percentage.

into account all the female MLAs elected in the last nine assemblies so far, most of them, nearly 85 per cent, belong to the Congress party. On the other hand, the BJP had a rather meagre representation of females among its MLAs in various assemblies till 2002. However, in 2007, BJP had 11 females as against only one among the Congress MLAs. As a matter of fact, till the Assembly of 1995, the non-Congress parties had only one female representative, i.e., in the 1975 Assembly. In 1995, BJP secured 121 seats, but all were males. Only in the 1998 Assembly, it had three female members out of its total strength of 117.

Taking the eleven assemblies together we find that female MLAs from the upper castes are in overwhelming majority. Four out of every 10 female MLAs come from the topmost layer of social order. Barring a few exceptions, most of them are Brahmins (Table 6.5).

Table 6.5
Distribution of Female MLAs of Gujarat according to Social Categories,
1962–2007

Social Group	Number
Upper Castes	33 (39)
Middle Castes	14 (17)
OBC	6 (7)
SC	9 (10)
ST	14 (17)
Muslims	8 (10)
TOTAL	84 (100)

Note: Figures in parentheses indicate percentage.

Occupation

The information on occupation in the *Who's Who* of the MLAs is very sketchy. For instance, details on occupation like agriculture do not inform us regarding the extent of ownership of land or the nature of land with regards to the irrigation facility, i.e., whether it is irrigated or non-irrigated. The most misleading category of occupation is 'social service' or 'social work' or 'political worker'. It does not give us any idea of their economic status. In the first two assemblies of 1962 and 1967, MLAs who had reported social service and political activism as their main occupation comprised the largest group (see Table 6.6). Interestingly, the group of political activists shows considerable decline

Table 6.6
Distribution of MLAs of Gujarat according to their Occupations, 1962–98

Occupation	1962	1967	1972	1975	1980	1985	1990	1995	1998
Social Workers	35 (23)	53 (31)	45 (27)	28 (15)	20 (11)	26 (14)	12 (7)	20 (11)	13 (7)
Political Activists	55 (36)	29 (17)	9 (5)	11 (6)	–	10 (5)	–	3 (2)	–
Agriculturalists	22 (14)	13 (8)	1 (1)	75 (41)	100 (55)	69 (38)	96 (53)	71 (39)	90 (50)
Professionals	17 (11)	31 (19)	44 (26)	36 (20)	29 (16)	25 (14)	27 (15)	26 (14)	38 (21)
Businessmen	5 (3)	1 (1)	1 (1)	16 (9)	17 (9)	30 (16)	22 (12)	46 (25)	25 (14)
Others+*	20 (13)	41 (24)	68 (40)	16 (9)	16 (9)	22 (12)	25 (14)	16 (9)	16 (9)
TOTAL	154 (100)	168 (100)	168 (100)	182 (100)	182 (100)	182 (99)	182 (100)	182 (100)	182 (100)

Source: Figures in parentheses indicate percentage.
Note: * This composite category primarily includes teachers and ex-government employees.

in its proportion in subsequent assemblies. Its existence since 1967 is marginal. Although the category of 'social service' has not wiped out or become trivial as political activism, it has become less significant in later assemblies. It seems that in the initial stage, those who took active part in politics had to put on the facade of social service in accordance with prevalent moral values. But with the passage of time and with the growth of real politic, values have undergone a changed and people's perceptions about politics and politicians have changed too. The other two categories which have shown change are the agriculturalists and the businessmen. The proportion of agriculturalists has observed an upward swing from the 1975 Assembly onwards. Till 1972, the agriculturalist MLAs were not more than 14 per cent. Their proportion has increased three-fold in the 1975 Assembly. The category of businessmen, which has been a single digit figure in its proportion till 1980, has shown a jump in its percentage in the later assemblies. By and large, the presence of professionals has remained steady over a period of time. It has not ascended beyond 25 per cent. The category of 'Others' mainly included teachers and ex-government employees.

Tables 6.7 and 6.8 present MLAs of the two main parties of Gujarat by their major occupations. As Table 6.7 shows, social workers, political activists and professionals were the main occupations found amongst Congress members till 1972. But from 1975 onwards, agriculturalists have become a dominating force. The professionals have maintained their steady position in the party over subsequent assemblies. The strength of agriculturist MLAs of BJP has slowly increased from 18 per cent in 1985 to 41 per cent in 1998. At the same time, the party has a larger number of traders and professionals than the Congress party in all the assemblies.

Education

Table 6.9 presents educational background of MLAs. It shows that over a period of time educational level of the members has risen. In the last three assemblies, more than 50 per cent of the MLAs are graduates. Their proportion has gone up from 36 per cent in 1962 to 56 per cent in 1998. On the other hand, the MLAs with middle level education have declined from 33 per cent in 1962 to 12 per cent in 1998. There is not much difference in the level of education between the Congress and BJP members (Tables 6.10 and 6.11).

Table 6.7
Occupation-wise Distribution of MLAs of Indian National Congress in Gujarat, 1962–98

Occupation	1962	1967	1972	1975	1980	1985	1990	1995	1998
Social Workers	27 (24)	31 (33)	38 (27)	11 (15)	20 (14)	25 (17)	3 (9)	5 (11)	4 (7)
Political Activists	41 (36)	9 (10)	7 (5)	5 (7)	–	9 (6)	–	–	–
Agriculturalists	15 (13)	9 (10)	1 (1)	36 (48)	72 (51)	54 (36)	20 (61)	23 (51)	34 (64)
Professionals	11 (10)	17 (18)	40 (28)	16 (21)	25 (18)	19 (13)	5 (15)	8 (18)	6 (11)
Businessmen	3 (3)	1 (1)	1 (1)	3 (4)	11 (8)	24 (16)	3 (9)	7 (16)	5 (9)
Others+*	16 (14)	26 (28)	53 (39)	4 (5)	13 (9)	18 (12)	2 (6)	2 (4)	4 (8)
TOTAL	113 (100)	93 (100)	140 (101)	75 (100)	141 (100)	149 (100)	33 (100)	45 (100)	53 (100)

Note: * This composite category primarily includes teachers and ex-government employees.

Figures in parentheses indicate percentage.

Table 6.8
Occupation-wise Distribution of MLAs of Bharatiya Janata Party in Gujarat, 1967–98

Year	1967	1972	1975	1980	1985	1990	1995	1998
Social Workers	–	1 (32)	3 (17)	–	–	4 (6)	14 (12)	9 (8)
Political Activists	–	–	–	–	1 (9)	–	3 (2)	–
Agriculturalists	–	–	2 (11)	4 (44)	2 (18)	23 (34)	39 (32)	48 (41)
Professionals	1 (100)	2 (68)	7 (39)	1 (11)	4 (36)	17 (25)	16 (13)	29 (25)
Businessmen	–	–	4 (22)	2 (22)	3 (27)	11 (16)	35 (29)	20 (17)
Others+*	–	–	2 (11)	2 (22)	1 (9)	12 (18)	14 (12)	11 (9)
TOTAL	1 (100)	3 (100)	18 (100)	9 (99)	11 (99)	67 (99)	121 (100)	117 (100)

Note: * This composite category includes mainly teachers and ex-government employees.

Figures in parentheses indicate percentage.

Table 6.9

Education among MLAs of Gujarat, 1962–98

Year	1962	1967	1972	1975	1980	1985	1990	1995	1998
Illiterate	–	8 (5)	2 (1)	3 (2)	–	–	–	–	–
Middle Pass	50 (33)	51 (30)	40 (24)	49 (27)	59 (32)	36 (20)	31 (17)	31 (17)	22 (12)
Matriculation	38 (25)	24 (14)	41 (24)	60 (33)	52 (29)	63 (35)	50 (27)	52 (29)	54 (30)
Graduate and above	56 (36)	78 (46)	80 (48)	64 (35)	68 (37)	82 (45)	96 (53)	95 (52)	101 (55)
No information	10 (6)	7 (4)	5 (3)	6 (3)	3 (2)	1 (1)	5 (3)	4 (2)	5 (3)
TOTAL	154 (100)	168 (99)	168 (100)	182 (100)	182 (100)	182 (101)	182 (100)	182 (100)	182 (100)

Note: Figures in parentheses indicate percentage.

Table 6.10

Education among Congress MLAs of Gujarat, 1962–98

Year	1962	1967	1972	1975	1980	1985	1990	1995	1998
Illiterate	–	5 (5)	–	2 (3)	–	–	–	–	–
Middle Pass	36 (32)	29 (32)	32 (23)	22 (29)	45 (32)	31 (21)	5 (15)	6 (13)	8 (15)
Matriculation	32 (28)	11 (12)	30 (21)	25 (33)	38 (27)	50 (34)	9 (27)	12 (27)	13 (24)
Graduate and above	40 (35)	45 (48)	75 (54)	24 (32)	56 (40)	67 (45)	18 (55)	25 (56)	30 (57)
No information	5 (4)	3 (3)	3 (2)	2 (3)	2 (1)	1 (1)	1 (3)	2 (4)	2 (4)
TOTAL	113 (99)	93 (100)	140 (100)	75 (100)	141 (100)	149 (101)	33 (100)	45 (100)	53 (100)

Note: Figures in parentheses indicate percentage.

Table 6.11

Education among BJP MLAs of Gujarat, 1967–98

Year	1967	1972	1975	1980	1985	1990	1995	1998
Illiterate	–	–	–	–	–	–	–	–
Middle Pass	–	1 (33)	–	–	–	–	–	–
Matriculation	–	–	2 (11)	3 (33)	2 (18)	6 (9)	20 (17)	12 (10)
Graduate and above	–	1 (33)	8 (44)	3 (33)	4 (36)	19 (28)	33 (27)	36 (31)
No information	1 (100)	1 (33)	8 (44)	3 (33)	5 (46)	39 (58)	66 (54)	66 (56)
	–	–	–	–	–	3 (5)	2 (2)	3 (3)
TOTAL	1 (100)	3 (99)	18 (99)	9 (99)	11 (100)	67 (100)	121 (100)	117 (100)

Note: Figures in parentheses indicate percentage.

Age

Table 6.12 gives the distribution of MLAs by age. As expected, a majority of the members belong to the middle age, between 36 and 55 years, in all the assemblies. The Gujarat Assembly has never had more than 4 per cent of very old MLAs, with more than 65 years of age. However, their proportion has increased from 2 per cent in the 1960s to nearly 4 per cent in the 1990s. In comparative terms, the proportion of younger members has strikingly declined nearly to half, from around 15 per cent in the first two assemblies to 8 per cent in the last three assemblies. By and large, this pattern is found in both the parties, the Congress and the BJP; the former, however, has a strikingly larger number of old members than the BJP. No such difference is found among the members of the younger age group. In 1990, the Congress had more members of the younger age group than the BJP. But it was not so in the next Assembly in 1995. Then, in 1998, both the parties have almost the same proportion of younger members.

Overview

Over the last few elections, the social composition of the Gujarat Assembly has changed. The proportion of upper caste MLAs has declined and the percentage of MLAs from the OBC has increased, particularly in the 1970s and early 1980s. The position of the middle caste MLAs has not changed substantially. Representations from the Muslim community have remained insignificant. The Congress evolved the strategy to co-opt the OBC leaders. The BJP has followed the same strategy successfully with its hindutva ideology. It has not only excluded Muslims but made them 'others', adversary of the Dalits, Adivasis and OBC. Women representatives have very little space in the Assembly. A majority of the MLAs are the cultivators though the sizes of their landholdings are not known. The BJP has more MLAs who are from the trading community. On one hand, the number of college-educated MLAs has increased during the last four decades. But, on the other, the number of young MLAs has not increased.

Table 6.12

Distribution of MLAs of Gujarat according to Age Group, 1962–98

Age (years)	1962	1967	1972	1975	1980	1985	1990	1995	1998
25–35	25 (16)	23 (14)	25 (15)	19 (10)	16 (9)	24 (13)	18 (10)	11 (6)	14 (8)
36–45	44 (29)	48 (29)	64 (38)	62 (34)	72 (40)	50 (27)	63 (35)	78 (43)	66 (36)
46–55	53 (34)	59 (35)	54 (32)	70 (38)	60 (33)	64 (35)	66 (36)	52 (29)	67 (37)
56–65	14 (9)	26 (15)	20 (12)	23 (13)	25 (14)	34 (19)	22 (12)	33 (18)	29 (16)
More than 65	3 (2)	2 (1)	4 (2)	3 (2)	4 (2)	3 (2)	7 (4)	7 (4)	5 (3)
No information	15 (10)	10 (6)	1 (1)	5 (3)	5 (3)	7 (4)	6 (3)	1 (1)	1 (1)
TOTAL	154 (100)	168 (100)	168 (100)	182 (100)	182 (100)	182 (100)	182 (100)	182 (100)	182 (100)

Note: Figures in parentheses indicate percentage.

Table 6.13

Distribution of Congress MLAs of Gujarat according to Age Group, 1962–98

Age (years)	1962	1967	1972	1975	1980	1985	1990	1995	1998
25–35	17 (15)	9 (10)	22 (16)	12 (16)	14 (10)	21 (14)	5 (15)	2 (4)	4 (7)
36–45	33 (29)	22 (24)	54 (39)	17 (23)	54 (38)	43 (29)	6 (18)	14 (31)	12 (23)
46–55	40 (35)	41 (44)	41 (29)	33 (44)	48 (34)	49 (33)	15 (46)	17 (38)	23 (43)
56–65	12 (11)	15 (16)	19 (14)	10 (13)	20 (14)	27 (18)	3 (9)	9 (20)	10 (19)
More than 65	1 (1)	1 (1)	3 (2)	2 (3)	3 (2)	3 (2)	2 (6)	3 (7)	3 (6)
No information	10 (9)	5 (5)	1 (1)	1 (1)	2 (1)	6 (4)	2 (6)	–	1 (2)
TOTAL	113 (100)	93 (100)	140 (101)	75 (100)	141 (99)	149 (100)	33 (100)	45 (100)	53 (100)

Note: Figures in parentheses indicate percentage.

Table 6.14
Distribution of BJP MLAs of Gujarat according to Age Group, 1967–98

Age (years)	1967	1972	1975	1980	1985	1990	1995	1998
25–35	–	–	2 (11)	–	1 (9)	7 (10)	9 (7)	10 (8)
36–45	–	1 (33)	13 (72)	5 (56)	2 (18)	29 (43)	53 (44)	50 (43)
46–55	–	1 (33)	3 (17)	3 (33)	6 (55)	22 (33)	31 (26)	38 (33)
56–65	–	1 (33)	–	–	1 (9)	7 (10)	23 (19)	17 (14)
More than 65	–	–	–	1 (11)	–	–	4 (3)	2 (2)
No information	1 (100)	–	–	–	1 (9)	2 (3)	1 (1)	–
TOTAL	1 (100)	3 (99)	18 (100)	9 (100)	11 (100)	67 (99)	121 (100)	117 (100)

Note: Figures in parentheses indicate percentage.

References

Desai, I. P. 1976. *Untouchability in Rural Gujarat*. Bombay: Popular Prakashan.

Lobo, Lancy and Jayanti Meckwan. 2003. *Shosan Ane Atamkni Agamao Adivasio* (Gujarati). Vadodara: Centre for Culture and Development.

Patel, Priyavadan. 2003. 'Gujarat: Hindutwa Mobilisation and Electoral Dominance', *Journal of Indian School of Political Economy*, 15 (1–2): 123–42.

Shah, Ghanshyam. 1975. *Caste Association and Political Process in Gujarat*. Bombay: Popular Prakashan.

———. 1990. 'Caste Sentiments, Class Formation and Dominance in Gujarat', in Francine Frankel and M. S. A. Rao (eds), *Dominance and State Power in Modern India*, vol. 2, pp. 59–114. Delhi: Oxford University Press.

———. 1991. 'Tenth Lok Sabha Elections: BJP's Victory in Gujarat', *Economic and Political Weekly*, 26 (51): 2921–24.

———. 2000. 'Hope and Despair: A Study of Untouchability and Atrocities in Gujarat', *Journal of Indian School of Political Economy*, 12 (374): 459–71.

———. 2002a. 'Contestation and Negotiations: Hindutva Sentiments and Temporal Interests in Gujarat Elections', *Economic and Political Weekly*, 37 (48): 4838–43.

———. 2002b. 'Caste and Land Reforms in Gujarat', in Ghanshyam Shah and D. C. Sah (eds), *Performance and Challenges in Gujarat and Maharashtra: Land Reforms in India*, vol. 8. New Delhi: Sage Publications.

Part III

The Reign of Dominant Castes in the Deccan

7

Maharashtra or Maratha Rashtra?

Rajendra Vora*

Social Context

The state of Maharashtra came into existence in May 1960. The Marathi-speaking districts of the Bombay Province, the Central Provinces, Berar and the princely state of Hyderabad were grouped together to form today's Maharashtra. These areas are now known as regions of the state as follows: Vidarbha (Marathi-speaking districts from the Central Provinces and Berar), Marathwada (the districts from the Hyderabad state), western Maharashtra (the districts from the Bombay Province), and Konkan (coastal districts from the Bombay Province). The social composition of Maharashtra reflects the structure of society as it is found in these regions. One has to make rough estimates on the basis of the data of the 1931 Census of these regions to understand the caste composition of the state as a whole.

The picture which emerges after this statistical exercise (Table 7.1) suggests that Maharashtra society has a peculiar composition wherein the peasantry caste of Maratha, that is, the Kunbis account for nearly 31 per cent of the total population. No other caste comes numerically anywhere near the Maratha–Kunbi. In no other state is there a caste-cluster as large as that of the Maratha–Kunbi. Between the two, Kunbis account for about 7 per cent of the population, and although they belong to the category of intermediate castes, they are listed as one of the Other Backward Castes by the Backward Classes Commission in 1980. Traditionally, the Kunbis were considered inferior to the Marathas who always claimed the Kshatriya status. The distinction between the two however, had become un-important during the non-Brahmin movement of 1920s, especially in western Maharashtra. Many of the Kunbis wanted to be identified as Marathas and hence were enumerated

---

* I thank Suhas Palshikar, Nitin Birmal, Dinesh Thite and Prakash Pawar for their help in analysing data.

Table 7.1
Distribution of Population in Maharashtra, 1931

	Population	Percentage of Total Population
Total Population	20, 918, 503	100.00
Twice–born Castes		
Brahmins	815, 930	3.90
Kshatriyas	211, 204	1.00
Vaishyas	354, 481	1.69
Upper Shudras		
Agari	246, 535	1.17
Ahir	9, 278	0.04
Kurub	231, 015	1.10
Bhoyar	19, 045	0.09
Darzi	82, 949	0.39
Gowari	126, 675	0.60
Gujjar	7, 115	0.03
Hajam	108, 474	0.51
Gurav	10, 513	0.05
Hatkar	40, 177	0.19
Kharva	18, 287	0.08
Koli	243, 636	1.16
Koshti	136, 222	0.62
Mahratta and Kunbi	6, 526, 173	31.19
Kasar	10, 924	0.05
Mana	51, 914	0.24
Mehra	998, 887	4.77
Pardhan	68, 119	0.32
Waddar	13, 160	0.06
Marwari	32, 487	0.15
Sunar	99, 193	0.47
Telega	47, 130	0.22
Sutar	92, 997	0.44
Yadava	151, 518	0.72
Lower Shudras		
Kumbhar	136, 739	0.65
Kammar	127, 159	0.60
Teli	317, 609	1.51
Bairagi	18, 281	0.08
Bedar	40, 137	0.19
Vanjari	143, 555	0.23
Bahai	68, 257	0.32
Binjhwar	4, 154	0.01
Dhimar	157, 808	0.75
Kalar	68, 222	0.32
Nai	17, 728	0.08

(*Table 7.1 continued*)

(*Table 7.1 continued*)

	Population	Percentage of Total Population
Julahi	37, 196	0.17
Kalal	15, 975	0.07
Others	**2, 370, 555**	**11.33**
Scheduled Castes	3, 445, 330	16.47
Scheduled Tribes	1, 229, 875	5.87
Muslims	1, 486, 382	7.10
Christians	280, 196	1.33
Other Minorities	243, 205	1.10

Source: Lele (1990: 116–17).

as Marathas by the census. However, the Kunbis of Vidarbha and Konkan where their proportion is greater are known as Kunbis even today. The Maratha population is more than 31 per cent in western Maharashtra and Marathwada. The Lingayats, the Gujjars and the Rajputs are three other important castes which belong to the inter-mediate category. The Lingayats who hail from north Karnataka are found primarily in south Maharashtra and Marathwada while Gujjars and Rajputs who migrated centuries ago from north India have settled in north Maharashtra districts.

The upper castes, composed mainly of the Brahmins, constitute around 4 per cent of the total population. While Brahmins are found in all the districts of the state, the Saraswats and Prabhas, the two other literary castes of this category, are in significant number only in Mumbai city.

The third important category is that of the Other Backward Castes who roughly account for 27 per cent (excluding Kunbis) of the total population of the state. The OBC of Maharashtra, comprise peasantry castes such as Mali, Dhangar and Vanjari, and artisan castes like Shimpi, Teli, Sutar, Koshti, etc. Between the two, the peasantry castes are greater in number and each of these peasantry caste is concentrated in cer-tain districts. The Malis (gardeners) have pockets in five districts of western Maharashtra and one district of Vidarbha while the Dhangars, a shepherd community, have their pockets in a few districts of western Maharashtra and Marathwada. The Vanjaris, originally a nomadic com-munity which has taken to farming, are found in two districts of western Maharashtra and one district of Marathwada. Telis have settled in three districts of Vidarbha. The Agaris have pockets in north Konkan while the Lewas are concentrated in north Maharashtra. The artisan castes of the OBC category are scattered in all districts of the state.

Next to the Marathas and the Kunbis are the Mahars so far as the size of their population is concerned. They account for nearly 8 per cent of the total population. It is the most numerous caste among the Scheduled Castes in Maharashtra and has embraced Buddhism under the leadership of Dr Babasaheb Ambedkar (1891–1956) in 1956. The majority of the Mahars have migrated to the urban areas and taken to education. They are more advanced than the Mangs and the Chambhars who are still tied down to their traditional occupations in the villages. Lately, many from these two communities are entering into the modern sector. According to the 1991 Census, the population of Scheduled Castes is 11.09 per cent of the total population of the state.

Maharashtra has large tracts of tribal population which accounts for 9.27 per cent of the total population. These tracts fall into north Konkan, north Maharashtra and Vidarbha regions. Most of the tribes would call themselves non-Hindus and follow tribal religions. The process of 'Hinduisation' and conversion to Christianity is going on although on a small scale.

Among the non-Hindu communities, the most significant is the Muslim community which constitutes around 9.3 per cent population in the state. Although Muslims are dispersed in various towns and villages, there are areas and cities where their population has got a decisive say. Besides Muslims, three religious minorities which should be taken into account are Christians (1.3 per cent), Jains (1.5 per cent) and Parsis (0.1 per cent). While Christians are found in white-collar jobs in the urban areas, the Jains and Parsis are known for their contribution to trade and industry. In case of Maharashtra, the other minorities category also includes non-Maharashtrians who would come to roughly 1 per cent of the population and include Sindhis, Gujaratis, Marwaris, south Indians and north Indians who have settled in Maharashtra, principally in cities like Mumbai. Thus, the proportion of all communities in other minorities category would constitute about 4 per cent (Christians, Jains, Parsis and non-Maharashtrians taken together).

This character of Maharashtrian society has markedly influenced the political process in the state. It should, however, be borne in mind that the Marathi-speaking people were conscious that they belong to Maharashtra since the medieval period even though the linguistic state came into being only in 1960. The politics in colonial period also had Maharashtra as a reference point. The post-1960 politics of Maharashtra is, therefore, a continuation of what had happened earlier.

Political Context

Modern politics began in Maharashtra around the 1850s in the form of political associations floated by the English-educated class composed of upper castes and business communities of Mumbai. By the 1870s, the centre of politics had shifted to the city of Pune when Pune Sarvajanik Sabha (Pune Public Association) was formed by the Brahmins with the support of the aristocratic classes. The Pune Sarvajanik Sabha and similar associations from the city of Mumbai played a crucial role in the formation of the Indian National Congress in 1885 at Mumbai. During the phase of moderate nationalism (1885–1905), the Congress was controlled by the English-educated class composed of the upper castes and business communities belonging to Pune and Mumbai. The extremist nationalism (1895–1917) took politics to smaller towns and moderately educated classes. Masses were drawn into politics to some extent through Ganapati festival (since 1894, when public celebration of the festival became popular) and moblisation during the Hindu–Muslim riots. Only in the Gandhian phase did the masses directly participate in politics in great numbers. However, the Congress organisation was still dominated by the Brahmins.

It was Satya Shodhak Samaj ('Truth Seeking Association') founded in 1873 by Mahatma Phule (1827–90) which challenged the Brahmin dominance in politics of Maharashtra. This challenge was converted into a non-Brahmin party when the representative institutions were introduced by the Morley–Minto reforms of 1919. When the nationalist movement entered into the phase of mass politics, N. V. Gadgil (1896–1966), a Brahmin leader from Pune, initiated the process of bridging the gap between the Brahmins and non-Brahmins. Convinced by the changing social character of the Congress, Keshavrao Jedhe (1896–1959) and his non-Brahmin party entered the Congress in 1932. But the Congress organisation remained under the control of the Brahmin leadership and Gujarati Baniyas even after independence. Therefore, some of the non-Brahmin leaders chose to break away from the Congress and formed new parties such as the Peasants and Workers Party (PWP) in 1948.

Another challenge to Brahmin domination came from the Dalits. Dr Babasaheb Ambedkar organised the Dalits in 1920s to demand representation in legislative councils and also to overthrow the upper caste dominance. In 1930s, he asked for separate electorates for Dalits. Mahatma Gandhi went on to fast to oppose this demand. Finally

Dr Ambedkar signed the Poona Pact in 1932 with Gandhi and accepted reservation of seats instead of separate electorates. In 1936, he formed the Independent Labour Party and tried to establish links between factory workers and the Dalits. This experiment did not succeed and Dr Ambedkar went back to his original position to have a separate party of the Dalits by forming the Scheduled Castes Federation (SCF) in 1942. The Federation was transformed into the Republican Party of India (RPI) in 1956.

There were two important trends in the politics of pre-independence Maharashtra besides the formation of these major parties: the Left politics was represented by the communists and the socialists and the *hindutva* orientation was expressed by the Hindu Mahasabha led by V. D. Savarkar (1883–1966) and the Rashtriya Swayamsevak Sangh (RSS) formed by Maharashtrian Brahmins in 1925 at Nagpur.

The post-independence politics reflects these trends and orientations. In the first general election held in 1952, the Congress party captured 269 out of 315 Vidhan Sabha seats and 40 out of the total of 45 Lok Sabha seats. The PWP with 14, the SCF with one, Kisan Kamgar Paksha (a splinter of the PWP) with three, and the Socialist Party (SP) with nine won 27 Vidhan Sabha seats and two Lok Sabha seats (one each by PWP and SCF) (Kogekar 1956: 42–43). The Samyukta ('composite') Maharashtra movement brought together opposition parties and various caste leaders together for the common purpose of creating the Marathi-speaking state. The State Reorganisation Commission rejected the demand for Samyukta Maharashtra and instead recommended a bilingual state combining the Gujarati and Marathi-speaking population in 1956. Resentment and anger spread among the opposition parties. They formed an alliance called the Samyukta Maharashtra Samiti (SMS) to fight the 1957 elections with the purpose of defeating the Congress party which in turn had welcomed the bilingual state. The anger of the people was reflected in the elections especially in western Maharashtra where the movement was very strong. The Congress could win only 136 seats in the Marathi-speaking areas while the SMS captured 131 (Sirsikar 1976: 220–39). The Congress, however, formed the government under the leadership of Y. B. Chavan with the support from Gujarat and Vidarbha. In the elections to Lok Sabha, the SMS won 22 as against 19 of the Congress. This success of the SMS convinced the centre that a Marathi-speaking state must be created soon. Thus, Maharashtra came into being in May 1960. Y. B. Chavan became the Chief Minister of the new state. The first task which he took upon himself was to strengthen the organisation of the Congress and elevate its status in the minds of the people.

The constituent parties of the SMS developed internal differences soon. They lost the purpose for which they had come together. The 1962 elections were held in this background. The Congress party emerged victorious by winning 41 out of 44 Lok Sabha seats and 215 out of 264 Vidhan Sabha seats. The PWP won 15, the Praja Samajwadi Party (PSP) got nine, the RPI won three and the SP won one seat while as many as 15 independent candidates got elected. The Congress improved its position in a big way compared to its performance in 1957 basically due to Y. B. Chavan's efforts and abilities; therefore, the choice of Chavan for the post of chief minister was obvious. But in October 1962, Chavan went to Delhi to join Nehru's Cabinet as the defence minister. Subsequently, the Vidarbha leader Marutrao Kannamwar was appointed as the chief minister. Due to his sudden death in 1964, another Vidarbha leader V. P. Naik, a Vanjari (OBC), was chosen by Chavan to lead the state. The 1967 elections were held under Naik's leadership. The Congress which suffered a great defeat in eight states in north could come to power in Maharashtra though with a reduced strength. The party captured 37 seats out of 45 in the Lok Sabha and 202 seats out of 270 in the Vidhan Sabha; the opposition parties could win 51 seats. PWP won 19, CPI won 10, CPI(M) won one, Samyukta Socialist Party won four, RPI won five, PSP won eight, Bharatiya Jana Sangh (BJS) won four and independents won 16 seats. V. P. Naik was chosen to lead the government again. After the 1969 split, the Congress party of Maharashtra went with Indira Gandhi.

In the mid-term elections of 1971 to Lok Sabha the Congress managed to win 43 seats out of 45 in the state. The PSP and the RPI won one seat each. The Indira Gandhi wave had helped the Congress. In the 1972 Vidhan Sabha elections, Congress came out victorious again. The party won 222 seats out of a total of 271. The opposition could capture only 25 seats (PWP with seven, BJS with five, CPI with two, CPI(M) with one, SP with three, RPI with two, others with five) while the independents won 23. The Shiv Sena (SS) (founded in 1966) had emerged as a party of the Marathi-speaking population of Mumbai city during late-1960s and had contested the Vidhan Sabha election for the first time.

V. P. Naik had to struggle hard to become the Chief Minister. His government had to face the agitation organised around the issue of the development of the Marathwada region. Forces opposing Naik became so strong that he had to resign. S. B. Chavan, a Maratha leader from Marathwada, was made Chief Minister. He defended the Congress fortress during the difficult times of Emergency (1975–77).

Anti-Emergency agitation received a good response in the state. The opposition got united for the first time after Samyukta Maharashtra movement. In the 1977 elections to Lok Sabha, the Janata Party (alliance of the opposition) captured 19 seats out of the total 48 and other parties got 10, while the Congress could win only 20, the lowest ever figure for the party. When the Congress party split in 1978, Y. B. Chavan and other important Maratha leaders went with the Congress (Reddy). The Vidhan Sabha elections were held in February 1978. The Janata Party won 99 while the Congress (Reddy) won 69 and the Congress (Indira) won 62 seats. Other parties got 30 seats among themselves (CPI with one, CPI(M) with nine, Forward Block with three, PWP with 13, RPI with four) and independents won 28. The Congress parties joined hands in forming the government. The chief ministership went to Vasandada Patil, a Maratha leader from western Maharashtra, and Nasikrao Tirpude, a Dalit leader from Vidarbha, was made Deputy Chief Minister. But the Patil government could not continue in power for long. Sharad Pawar left the government with his 38 followers and formed the Progressive Democratic Front (PDF) with the support of the Janata Party and other opposition parties. The first non-Congress government came to power in July 1978 under the leadership of Pawar, the Congress leader. Taking into consideration the changing political scenario, the Congress (Reddy) leaders decided to join the Congress (Indira) in 1979. The 1980 Lok Sabha election results reflected the enhanced strength of the Congress (Indira). The party captured 39 seats out of 48. Impressed by this performance, a number of MLAs from the ruling PDF started seeking shelter under the Congress (Indira) umbrella. The PDF was dissolved in February 1980. Sharad Pawar joined the Congress (Urs) on the eve of the Vidhan Sabha election. The elections were held in May 1980. The Congress (Indira) secured majority (186 seats) while Congress (Urs) got 47 seats. Other parties secured 45 (BJP won 14, Janata Party got 17, CPI won two, CPI(M) won two, PWP won nine, RPI won one) and independents captured 10 seats

(Vora 1982: 10–23). Indira Gandhi who had emerged victorious throughout the country insisted that the chief ministership should go not only to a non-Maratha but to a Muslim leader. A. R. Antulay was chosen as the leader of the Congress (Indira) party in the Vidhan Sabha. The transformation taking place in the politics convinced Y. B. Chavan that he should join Indira's party by resigning his membership of Congress (Urs). Indira Gandhi made him wait for nearly five months to give him membership to her party. Sharad Pawar decided to remain in the Congress (Urs). A. R. Antulay tried to marginalise the Maratha bosses and directly appealed to the masses by starting innovative schemes. But the idea of collecting funds for Indira Trust and the cement quota scandal went against him. When the High Court verdict proved him guilty he had to go in 1982. In his place, Indira Gandhi put Babasaheb Bhosale, an unimportant Maratha from western Maharashtra. But soon he had to go too because of opposition from within the party. Indira Gandhi had no option but to appoint Vasantdada Patil, the Maratha stalwart of western Maharashtra, as Chief Minister of the state in February 1983.

In the 1984 Lok Sabha elections, the Congress secured 43 seats, the Congress of Sharad Pawar could win only two seats. However, the performance of Congress(I) in the Vidhan Sabha elections was not up to the mark. It secured only 162 seats. The Congress captured 54 seats and other parties got 53 seats (BJP with 16, Janata Party with 20, PWP with 13, CPI with two, CPI(M) with two seats). After the elections, Vasantdada Patil became the Chief Minister without any serious controversy. But when he realised that Sharad Pawar was to join his party and was trying to topple him, he resigned and handed over the charge to Shivagirao Nilangekar, a Maratha from Marathwada. However, Nilangekar could not continue for long and in his place in March 1986 S. B. Chavan was brought in. He remained at the helm of affairs till June 1988 when Sharad Pawar was chosen for that post by Rajiv Gandhi. Pawar had entered the Congress(I) in 1986. The party could secure 28 seats out of the total of 48. In the 1989 Lok Sabha elections, the BJP won 10 seats while Janata Dal secured five, Shiv Sena won four and CPI got one seat. During these elections, the BJP and Shiv Sena had formed an alliance on an experimental basis. In the elections to Vidhan Sabha of 1990, however, the alliance acquired more significance and confidence. The results indicated that the hindutva alliance was the serious contender for power in the state and the Congress days were numbered. The alliance secured 94 seats (BJP with 42 and SS with 42) and while the Congress could win only 141, the Janata Dal got 24. Other parties got 15 (PWP with eight, CPI with two, CPI(M) with three, Congress(S) with one, RPI with one) and independents with 14. The 1991 Lok Sabha elections showed the same pattern. The Congress won 38 seats and the BJP–Sena alliance got nine and CPI(M) got one seat. In June 1991, there was a change of guard again. Pawar who had become Chief Minister in June 1988 went to Delhi to join the cabinet of Rajiv Gandhi and in his place Sudhakar Naik, a Vanjari (an OBC) from Vidarbha was brought in. Pawar came back in February 1993 and remained as Chief Minister till the 1995 elections. The hindutva mobilisation and demolition of the mosque in December 1992 radically changed the political scenario in Maharashtra. The riots in Mumbai after the demolition of the mosque mobilised the public opinion in favour of the hindutva parties.

The 1995 elections reflected this change and produced the expected results. The Congress was defeated for the first time in a decisive manner and that too by the real non-Congress forces, namely, the BJP–SS alliance. The Congress could win only 80 seats as against 138 seats of the alliance (BJP with 65 and SS with 73 seats). The Congress rebels captured 35 seats. Other parties secured 27 seats (Janata Dal with 11, PWP with six, CPI(M) with three and others with 11) and independent got five while two seats went to the BJP rebels and one to the SS rebel. The alliance formed the government with the support of the Congress rebels. Shiv Sena leader Manohar Joshi, a Brahmin from Mumbai city, was chosen for the post of chief minister (Vora and Palshikar 1996: 87). The alliance government on the one hand consolidated its Hindu support structure and on the other hand destabilised the Congress support base in the rural areas. In the Lok Sabha elections of 1996, the Congress could win only 15 seats and the alliance secured 33 (BJP with 18 and SS with 15) (Palshikar and Deshpande 1999: 21). However, the Congress improved its position in the 1998 Lok Sabha elections by winning 37 seats along with its allies (Congress with 33 and RPI with four) The BJP–SS alliance could win only 10 seats (BJP with four and SS with six) while one seat went to the PWP. The Congress regained its confidence due to this victory and was in a better position to fight the 1999 Vidhan Sabha election with one proviso, namely, that the party was split again. Sharad Pawar quit the party on the issue that an Italian person (Sonia Gandhi) laid claims to the post of the prime minister of India, and formed the Nationalist Congress Party (NCP) in June 1999.

The Congress vote got divided due to this split. The NCP secured 58 seats while the Congress could win only 77. The BJP–SS alliance managed to get 125. Other parties among themselves got 17 (PWP with five, SP with three, CPI(M) with two, Bharatiya Republican Paksha with three, RPI with one, Janata Dal (Secular) with two and Gondwana Ganatantra Party with one seat). The independents won as many as 13 seats. After the elections, the Congress and the NCP formed a front along with other smaller parties and independents, and came to power. Vilasrao Deshmukh (from Congress), a Maratha from Marathwada, became the chief minister and Chhagan Bhujbal (from NCP), a Mali (OBC) from Mumbai was made the Deputy Chief Minister. The Congress party which had remained out of power for five years was able to form the government with the help of the NCP and other parties.

However, due to factional struggles, Deshmukh had to vacate the post of the chief minister in 2003 for Shushilkumar Shinde, a Dalit leader (a cobbler, Hindu) from western Maharashtra. Bhujbal also had to resign from his position because of his alleged involvement in the stamp paper corruption scandal. In his place, the NCP brought Vijaysinh Mohite-Patil, a Maratha leader belonging to the sugar lobby of western Maharashtra. It was thus a shift from Maratha and OBC to the Dalit and Maratha combination.

Soon the new team had to face the voters in the Lok Sabha elections of 2004. The BJP-led National Democratic Alliance (NDA) was in power at the centre. The Congress under the leadership of Sonia Gandhi had decided to join hands this time with other parties to defeat the NDA. In Maharashtra, the party formed an alliance with the NCP and the RPI (Gawai and Athawale factions) to contest the elections against the BJP–SS alliance. The BJP–SS alliance secured 25 seats (BJP with 13 and SS with 12) while the Congress and its allies got two seats less than the alliance (Congress with 13, NCP with nine and RPI (Athawale) with one seat). However, in the Assembly elections held after only four months, the Congress allies emerged as the single largest group with 146 seats and came to power (Congress with 69, and NCP with 71 and other allies with six seats). The other allies included three of the CPI(M) supported by the Congress, one of the RPI (Athawale) with whom the Congress had a seat adjustment and two independents. The BJP–SS alliance secured 119 seats (BJP with 54, SS with 62, other allies with three seats) (Palshikar and Yadav 2004: 12). The Congress and its allies took a long time to form the government due to differences between the Congress and the NCP. Finally, a compromise was arrived and Vilasrao Deshmukh (the Maratha leader from Marathwada) of the Congress assumed the office of Chief Minister while the NCP leader R. R. Patil (a Maratha from western Maharashtra) was chosen as the Deputy Chief Minister.

This overview of electoral politics of the state brings out the fact that Maharashtra, since its formation, till 1977, was a typical case of a dominant party system or the 'Congress system'. Even when the Congress party suffered defeat in 1967 in eight states in north because of the unity of the parties in opposition, it still managed to come to power in Maharashtra. The opposition parties could not come anywhere near it. In 1978, however, the opposition front was able to capture power. But, again, this was possible largely due to the defection of the Sharad Pawar faction from the Congress and this government in fact came to be headed by Pawar. The Congress regained its strength after the 1980 elections and remained in power till 1995. But our quick survey shows that Maharashtra never experienced the stability of a dominant party system since 1975 even though the Congress was in power. Indira Gandhi had started undermining the Maratha power from 1971–72 onwards. This strategy indirectly encouraged factionalism and opportunism in the party and produced instability of the worst kind while adversely affecting the performance of the party. Sharad Pawar's impatience has also given moments of instability to the Congress. The rise and growth of the Shiv Sena and the BJP, as hindutva forces, hastened the decline of the Congress during the 1990s. The electoral politics since the year 1990 suggests that the state has developed a system resembling a bi-party system and has come a long way from the one-party dominance. The politics of Maharashtra has entered the era of competition between two coalitions — the Congress and the hindutva.

This chapter intends to investigate whether these changes in the party system has altered the social profile of the members of the Legislative Assembly in any radical manner and whether Maharashtra has experienced any real transfer of power.

Caste and Communal Composition of MLAs

The survey of the caste and communal composition of the Members of the Legislative Assembly (MLAs) since the formation of Maharashtra to the elections held in 2004 indicates that in more than 40 years their social composition has almost remained the same (Table 7.2). The ups and downs in the caste or communal categories is only marginal and the changes are not very substantial.

Upper Castes

The upper castes in Maharashtra comprise the traditional literary castes — the Brahmins, the Saraswats and the Prabhus. Their proportion to the total population seems to be around 4 per cent if we go by the 1931 Census. The upper castes were at the helm of affairs during the colonial period because of their control over English education. Maharashtra was the first part of India where the Brahmin dominance was challenged by the non-Maratha elites as early as the year 1873.

However, the Brahmins continued to control politics till almost 1950. After the formation of the Marathi-speaking state of Maharashtra, the position of upper castes became insignificant so far as electoral politics was concerned. The Brahmins formed 80 per cent of the Maharashtra Pradesh Congress Committee (MPCC) executives in 1936 while there were none at all in 1966 (Sirsikar 1976: 222). Even as they were maginalised from the Congress politics, the politics of opposition parties was dominated, in many ways, by the upper castes. The party organisation of the BJP, the Shiv Sena and the socialist or the communist parties was also controlled by the upper castes till recently. The Congress strategy during Indira Gandhi days was congenial to the upper castes to a certain extent. After the riots triggered in rural areas due to the assassination of Mahatma Gandhi by a Maharashtrian Brahmin in 1948, the Brahmins had to migrate to the urban areas. Land reforms were another factor why the Brahmins were forced to leave villages. This is the reason why we find that the upper caste MLAs come principally from urban and semi-urban areas.

The average number of upper caste MLAs from the 1962 to the 2004 elections has been 14. The Congress party in its attempt to combine diverse social forces accommodated a number of upper caste leaders. The opposition parties and especially the hindutva parties seem to have

Table 7.2

Caste and Communal Composition of MLAs in Maharashtra, 1967–2004

Castes and Communities	1967	1972	1978	1980	1985	1990	1995	1999	2004
Upper Castes	**16 (5.9)**	**18 (6.6)**	**20 (6.9)**	**15 (5.2)**	**14 (4.8)**	**13 (4.5)**	**12 (4.1)**	**8 (2.7)**	**10 (3.4)**
Brahmin	11 (4.0)	15 (5.5)	10 (3.4)	10 (3.4)	10 (3.4)	9 (3.1)	9 (3.1)	7 (2.4)	6 (2.0)
Saraswat	2 (0.7)	1 (0.3)	8 (2.7)	3 (1.0)	3 (1.0)	1 (0.3)	0	1 (0.3)	0
Prabhu	3 (1.1)	2 (0.7)	2 (0.6)	2 (0.6)	1 (0.3)	3 (1.0)	3 (1.0)	0	4 (1.3)
Intermediate Castes	**116 (43.1)**	**117 (43.1)**	**118 (40.9)**	**123 (42.7)**	**113 (39.2)**	**129 (44.7)**	**131 (45.4)**	**124 (43.0)**	**129 (44.7)**
Maratha	105 (39.0)	105 (38.7)	104 (36.1)	106 (36.8)	109 (37.8)	116 (40.2)	115 (39.9)	109 (37.8)	116 (40.2)
Lingayat	6 (2.2)	7 (2.5)	6 (2.0)	8 (2.7)	6 (2.0)	7 (2.4)	7 (2.4)	7 (2.4)	4 (1.3)
Gujar	0	1 (0.3)	1 (0.3)	1 (0.3)	1 (0.3)	1 (0.3)	1 (0.3)	3 (1.0)	1 (0.3)
Rajput	1 (0.3)	2 (0.7)	3 (1.0)	3 (1.0)	2 (0.6)	1 (0.3)	3 (1.0)	2 (0.6)	4 (1.3)
Kohli	1 (0.3)	1 (0.3)	0	0	0	1 (0.3)	2 (0.6)	0	0
Komti	1 (0.3)	0	0	0	0	0	2 (0.6)	1 (0.3)	2 (0.6)
Kalar	1 (0.3)	0	0	2 (0.6)	2 (0.6)	0	2 (0.6)	0	0
Yalmar	0	0	1 (0.3)	0	0	0	1 (0.3)	0	1 (0.3)
Savaji	0	0	1 (0.3)	0	1 (0.3)	1 (0.3)	0	0	0
Wari	0	0	1 (0.3)	1 (0.3)	1 (0.3)	1 (0.3)	0	1 (0.3)	0
Lodhi	0	0	1 (0.3)	1 (0.3)	0	0	0	0	0
Somvanshiya Kshatriya	1 (0.3)	1 (0.3)	0	1 (0.3)	0	1 (0.3)	1 (0.3)	1 (0.3)	1 (0.3)
OBC	**60 (22.3)**	**58 (21.4)**	**67 (23.2)**	**57 (19.7)**	**71 (24.6)**	**75 (26.0)**	**67 (23.2)**	**68 (23.6)**	**69 (23.9)**
Kunbi	29 (10.7)	25 (9.2)	22 (7.6)	20 (6.9)	25 (8.6)	24 (8.3)	23 (7.9)	32 (11.1)	23 (7.9)
Dhangar	3 (1.1)	4 (1.4)	4 (1.3)	2 (0.6)	5 (1.7)	5 (1.7)	4 (1.3)	4 (1.3)	2 (0.6)
Mali	2 (0.7)	3 (1.1)	8 (2.7)	6 (2.0)	7 (2.4)	11 (3.8)	3 (1.0)	4 (1.3)	6 (2.0)

Vanjari	2 (0.7)	3 (1.1)	4 (1.3)	4 (1.3)	4 (1.3)	4 (1.3)	5 (1.7)	6 (2.0)	5 (1.7)
Banjara	2 (0.7)	3 (1.1)	1 (0.3)	2 (0.6)	3 (1.0)	3 (1.0)	1 (0.3)	1 (0.3)	3 (1.0)
Teli	9 (3.3)	6 (2.2)	7 (2.4)	6 (2.0)	3 (1.0)	4 (1.3)	6 (2.0)	5 (1.7)	6 (2.0)
Lewa	3 (1.1)	4 (1.4)	3 (1.0)	2 (0.6)	4 (1.3)	4 (1.3)	4 (1.3)	3 (1.0)	5 (1.7)
Bhandari	1 (0.3)	0	1 (0.3)	0	0	2 (0.6)	3 (1.0)	1 (0.3)	2 (0.6)
Padmasali	1 (0.3)	1 (0.3)	1 (0.3)	0	0	0	1 (0.3)	0	1 (0.3)
Sonar	0	2 (0.7)	1 (0.3)	2 (0.6)	1 (0.3)	1 (0.3)	0	1 (0.3)	0
Nhavi	1 (0.3)	1 (0.3)	1 (0.3)	1 (0.3)	1 (0.3)	1 (0.3)	1 (0.3)	0	1 (0.3)
Koshti	0	1 (0.3)	2 (0.6)	2 (0.6)	2 (0.6)	2 (0.6)	1 (0.3)	0	0
Agari	3 (1.1)	3 (1.1)	7 (2.4)	5 (1.7)	8 (2.7)	8 (2.7)	6 (2.0)	6 (2.0)	7 (2.4)
Powar	3 (1.1)	1 (0.3)	0	0	2 (0.6)	1 (0.3)	1 (0.3)	1 (0.3)	1 (0.3)
Shimpi	1 (0.3)	0	0	1 (0.3)	0	1 (0.3)	1 (0.3)	0	0
Gurav	0	0	0	0	0	0	1 (0.3)	0	1 (0.3)
Gandli	0	0	0	0	1 (0.3)	1 (0.3)	0	1 (0.3)	1 (0.3)
Bari	0	1 (0.3)	0	0	1 (0.3)	0	1 (0.3)	0	0
Garudi	0	0	0	0	1 (0.3)	1 (0.3)	1 (0.3)	0	0
Parkhi	0	0	1 (0.3)	1 (0.3)	0	0	0	0	0
Beldar	2 (0.7)	0	0	0	0	0	1 (0.3)	1 (0.3)	0
Yadav	0	0	0	1 (0.3)	0	0	0	0	0
Vadar	0	0	0	0	1 (0.3)	0	0	0	0
Gowari	0	0	0	0	0	1 (0.3)	1 (0.3)	0	0
Koli	0	0	3	2 (0.6)	2 (0.6)	1 (0.3)	0	0	1 (0.3)
Gawali	0	0	1 (0.3)	0	0	1 (0.3)	1 (0.3)	1 (0.3)	3 (1.0)
Tambat	0	0	0	0	0	1 (0.3)	1 (0.3)	1 (0.3)	1 (0.3)

(*Table 7.2 continued*)

(Table 7.2 continued)

Castes and Communities	1967	1972	1978	1980	1985	1990	1995	1999	2004
SC	15 (5.5)	15 (5.5)	18 (6.2)	18 (6.2)	18 (6.2)	18 (6.2)	18 (6.2)	18 (6.2)	18 (6.2)
SC (from General Constituencies)	0	0	0	0	0	0	0	0	5 (1.7)
ST	16 (5.9)	16 (5.9)	22 (7.6)	22 (7.6)	22 (7.6)	22 (7.6)	22 (7.6)	22 (7.6)	22 (7.6)
Muslim	8 (2.9)	12 (4.4)	11 (3.8)	14 (4.8)	10 (3.4)	7 (2.4)	8 (2.7)	12 (4.1)	11 (3.8)
Other Minorities	25 (9.2)	18 (6.6)	24 (8.3)	35 (12.1)	26 (9.0)	21 (7.2)	21 (7.2)	28 (9.7)	24 (8.3)
Not Ascertained	13 (4.8)	17 (6.2)	8 (2.7)	4 (1.3)	14 (4.8)	3 (1.0)	9 (3.1)	8 (2.7)	0
TOTAL	269 (100)	271 (100)	288 (100)	288 (100)	288 (100)	288 (100)	288 (100)	288 (100)	288 (100)

Source: Data collected and compiled by the Department of Politics, University of Pune.

Note: Figures in parentheses indicate percentages.

attracted many upper caste leaders into their organisation. Prabhus play an important part in the Shiv Sena while Brahmins are in leading positions in the BJP. There are six constituencies from where a Brahmin candidate has been elected consecutively through last three elections, and out of these, six have been won by the BJP and the Shiv Sena have won in five.

Intermediate Castes

This category comprises 12 castes of which the Marathas are the most significant because it is a dominant caste in Maharashtra. In nine elections (1967 to 2004), the number of Marathas elected to Vidhan Sabha has been in the range of 104 to 116, the average being 108. The Congress is the main vehicle of the Marathas; however, the number of Marathas remains the same even when the Congress is in trouble. In the 1978 elections, for instance, out 104 Maratha MLAs, only 59 belonged to the Congress party while 28 Marathas were elected as Janata Party candidates, 12 as independents, three as the PWP and two as CPI candidates. When the Congress party splits, typically, the Marathas get divided into two camps and contest elections on tickets from both the Congress parties. They did this in 1978, 1980, 1985 as also in 1999 and 2004. In the 1980 elections, 58 Marathas were elected as Congress(I) candidates and 29 as the Congress (Urs) ones, thereby making the number of the Congress Maratha MLAs a total of 87. In 1985, out of the total of 81 Marathas, 54 belonged to the Congress(I) while 27 belonged to the Congress(S). When a non-Congress party makes a decided bid for power it has to take into account the aspirations of the power-seeking Marathas. The Marathas, in turn, are also very accommodative. When they realise that the Congress is not going to help them, they approach the other parties for tickets. The rise and growth of the BJP–Shiv Sena alliance in Maharashtra politics can be ascribed to the way this alliance has attracted the Maratha leaders to its fold. In the year 1990, 31, and in the years 1995, 1999 and 2004, 44 Maratha MLAs came from the alliance. One of the reasons why the Congress could not come to power in 1995 was the challenge posed by its rebel candidates. In all, 35 rebels were elected of whom 23 were Marathas. After the elections, they formed the Maharashtra Development Front and supported the BJP–Shiv Sena alliance (Vora and Palshikar 1996: 88). It is observed that western Maharashtra and Marathwada send more

Marathas to the Vidhan Sabha than what other regions send. As seen earlier, the proportion of the Maratha population in these two regions is greater and there are many constituencies in these two regions where the Marathas decide the verdict of the election.

Among other intermediate castes, the Lingayats, the Rajputs and the Gujjars are politically more important than the others. These castes have pockets of influence and their candidates are elected from the constituencies which fall into these pockets. Except the Marathas, no other intermediate caste carries any weight in the politics of the state and non-Maratha castes of this category do not have any collective identity as such, though each caste has its own political space.

Other Backward Castes

The most significant of all the OBC castes is Kunbis. In fact, the Kunbis belong to the intermediate caste category and form the part of the Maratha–Kunbi caste-cluster. The average number of the Kunbis elected to the Vidhan Sabha in the last nine elections is 25. If we go by regions, we find that all the Kunbis are elected from either Vidarbha or Konkan, and between the two regions, Vidarbha is their citadel because out of an average of 25 Kunbis, only four are elected from Konkan and the rest come from Vidarbha. There are eight constituencies in Vidarbha from where a Kunbi candidate has been consecut. ely elected in the 1990, 1995 and 1999 elections.

The OBC category came into vogue after the Mandal Commission used it. Prior to that, many of the castes that later came to be identified as OBC were considered part of the Bahujan Samaj — a broad category comprising all non-Brahmins. After the publication of the Backward Classes Commission's report, some scattered and feeble attempts were made by the OBC to put forward their demand for the reservation of jobs in the government. Shetkari Sangathana, the farmers' organisation of Sharad Joshi tried to recruit many OBC into its fold during the 1980s. The Shiv Sena while entering into the rural areas mobilised the OBC to some extent. Similarly, the BJP made decided efforts to seek the support of the OBC. The OBC party — the Bahujan Mahasangh — formed in 1993 in Vidarbha tried to combine into its fold the Dalits and the OBC. However, it has failed to make any substantial impact on the political process of the state. The Congress party gave prominence to some OBC leaders within its organisation as a response to the attempts made by the opposition to exploit the anti–Maratha feelings. During the 1980s and 1990s, many OBC leaders came to acquire important positions within their respective parties or in the government.

If we take into account the elections from 1967, the average number of the OBC elected to the Vidhan Sabha comes to 40 (excluding the Kunbis). Table 7.2 shows that the number of OBC MLAs went up from the 1978 elections. This rise in their number after 1978 can not merely be ascribed to the politics of the 'Mandalisation'. The rise of the OBC could be traced to the anti–Maratha strategy employed by Indira Gandhi and her faithful followers like A. R. Antulay during the 1980s. From 1990 onwards, we see that the OBC are shifting to the BJP–Shiv Sena alliance. In 1978 it was the Janata wave which brought more OBC to the Assembly. The PWP is another party which consistently gives tickets to the OBC and an observation of what constituencies they come from and the caste they belong to shows that they are the Agaris of north Konkan. The break-up of seats according to the various castes in the OBC category shows that the Mali, the Vanjari, the Dhangar, the Agari, the Teli, and the Lewa are the important OBC of Maharashtra. They have been able to secure three to seven seats between 1978 to 1995. There are around 26 constituencies from which OBC MLAs are elected and 14 out of these are from Vidarbha. It must be noted that the even though the number of OBC MLAs went up after 1978, it did not affect the total strength of the Marathas. In some states of the north, the rise of OBC has adversely affected the prospects of the intermediate castes. This has not happened in Maharashtra. An OBC candidate of the BJP or Shiv Sena gets elected by defeating an OBC candidate of the Congress but not the Maratha candidate of the Congress because the Maratha constituencies are as good as reserved for the Marathas.

Scheduled Castes

In the 1967 and 1972 elections there were 15 reserved constituencies for the Scheduled Castes and from 1978 onwards that number has gone to 18. As discussed earlier, the Dalit castes, mainly the Mahars of Maharashtra, entered politics in the 1920s under the leadership of Dr Ambedkar. The RPI was formed by Dr Ambedkar in 1956 with the hope that it will become the main vehicle of not only the Dalits but also of all down-trodden groups and classes. But his dream was never realised. In fact, what we see from Table 7.3 is the decline of the RPI over last 30 years or so. The SC reserved seats go to the Congress party and lately they have been going to the BJP or the Shiv Sena rather than to the RPI. From 1990 onwards, the hindutva parties have been able to secure around eight seats. The main gainer is the BJP. The BJP and the Shiv Sena have taken the advantage of the political and social gap between the Mahar and other Dalit castes. The Mahars who are more politicised and are more advanced have been able to enter the power arena while others are deprived of such opportunities. Again, the Mahars are now Buddhists while the other Dalits are Hindus. The hindutva parties have been able give a Hindu identity to them.

The Dalit candidates are sometimes elected from general constituencies too. From 1972 to 1995, one or two Dalits were elected from the general constituencies. In the year 1999 that number went up to four.

Scheduled Tribes

Maharashtra has large tracts of tribal population and during the early years of the East India Company the tribals revolted against the foreign rulers. But in the post-independence era, the tribals have not developed any significant political organisation, nor have they made an effective demand for their own autonomous state. They have generally supported the party in power and most of the time it was the Congress. In the 1990s, the BJP and the Shiv Sena have replaced the Congress in this context. The communist parties have been organising the tribals for over last 40 years and they have been, therefore, able to win some tribal constituencies especially in the Thane district of Konkan region. Table 7.4 gives the party-wise distribution of the Scheduled Tribe constituencies. In some cases, the tribal candidates get elected from the unreserved/general constituencies too, but this figure does not go beyond one or two.

Muslims

As mentioned earlier, the Muslim population is quite large in Maharashtra, but their politics is not very successful. It has always remained a dependent factor. In 34 constituencies, the Muslim population is around 15 to 20 per cent and in five of these it is more than 20 per cent. In Mumbai city alone the Muslims can tilt the balance in

Table 7.3

SC (Reserved) MLAs in Maharashtra (party-wise distribution), 1967–2004

Election Year	1967	1972	1978	1980	1985	1990	1995	1999	2004
Congress	9 (60.0)	12 (80.0)	6 (33.3)	15 (83.3)	15 (83.3)	9 (50.0)	3 (16.6)	7 (38.8)	4 (22.2)
BJP	0	–	–	–	1 (5.5)	3 (16.6)	8 (44.4)	6 (33.3)	5 (27.7)
Shiv Sena	0	–	–	–	–	1 (5.5)	4 (22.2)	3 (16.6)	4 (22.2)
Janata*	–	–	2 (11.1)	–	–	1 (5.5)	–	–	–
CPI/CPI(M)	1 (6.6)	–	1 (5.5)	–	–	1 (5.5)	–	–	–
PWP	0	–	2 (11.1)	1 (5.5)	2 (11.1)	2 (11.1)	–	–	–
RPI	5 (33.3)	2 (13.3)	4 (22.2)	1 (5.5)	0	1 (5.5)	–	–	–
NCP	–	–	–	–	–	–	–	–	4 (22.2)
BSP	–	–	–	–	–	–	–	–	1 (5.5)
Independents	–	1 (6.6)	3 (16.6)	1 (5.5)	–	1 (5.5)	3 (16.6)	2 (11.1)	–
TOTAL	15	15	18	18	18	18	18	18	18

Source: Data collected and compiled by the Department of Politics, University of Pune.

Note: Figures in parentheses indicate percentages.

*The pre–1986 entries refer to Janata Party and the following years to Janata Dal.

Table 7.4

ST (Reserved) MLAs in Maharashtra (party-wise distribution), 1967–2004

Election Year	1967	1972	1978	1980	1985	1990	1995	1999	2004
Congress	11 (68.7)	13 (81.2)	12 (54.5)	19 (86.3)	15 (68.1)	10 (45.5)	7 (31.8)	10 (45.5)	6 (27.2)
BJP	–	1 (6.2)	–	–	1 (4.5)	5 (22.0)	5 (22.0)	4 (18.1)	4 (18.1)
Shiv Sena	–	–	4 (18.1)	–	–	2 (9.0)	3 (13.6)	4 (18.1)	2 (9.0)
Janata*	–	–	3 (13.6)	1 (4.5)	2 (9.0)	3 (13.6)	–	–	–
CPI/CPI(M)	–	–	1 (4.5)	2 (9.0)	2 (9.0)	2 (9.0)	1 (4.5)	2 (9.0)	2 (9.0)
Others	3 (18.7)	1 (6.2)	2 (9.0)	–	–	–	1 (4.5)	2 (9.0)	–
Independents	2 (12.5)	1 (6.2)	–	–	2 (9.0)	–	5 (22.0)	–	1 (4.5)
NCP	–	–	–	–	–	–	–	–	7 (31.8)
TOTAL	16	16	22	22	22	22	22	22	22

Source: Data collected and compiled by the Department of Politics, University of Pune.
Note: Figures in parentheses indicate percentages.
   *The pre-1986 entries refer to Janata Party and the following years to Janata Dal.

10 constituencies. They play an important role in five districts of Vidarbha, and their candidates generally win from towns like Bhivandi, Malegaon and Aurangabad. In nine elections since 1967, the average number of Muslims elected is 10. Muslim candidates are generally elected on the Congress ticket. In 1978, the Muslims supported the Janata Party because the Congress had antagonised them during the Emergency (1975–77). In 1980, A. R. Antulay, who was the main decision-maker within the Congress party in Maharashtra, had given tickets to 18 Muslims out of which 13 were elected. In the last seven elections to the Vidhan Sabha, the Muslims have won four or more times from five constituencies and thrice from three constituencies. Thus, it can be shown that there are around eight constituencies from where Muslim MLAs are sent to the Vidhan Sabha. The Muslim League (ML) and the Samajwadi Party of Mulayam Singh have some presence only in the city of Mumbai.

Other Minorities

In this category, we include Christians, Jains, Parsis and other non-Maharashtrians. This is a group of communities which are considered as minorities on account of their religion or their language. And therefore, this group acquires significance in cosmopolitan cities such as Mumbai. They are politically important because the average number of them who are elected as representatives to the state legislature is 25. Their proportion in the population is about 4 per cent. As in the case of the Muslims, the main party on which the other minorities depend is the Congress, but lately, the BJP has made dent into this community with its appeal of hindutva. Since many of them are from Gujarat or north India where hindutva has made great impact, the BJP finds it easier to seek their allegiance. The Shiv Sena which began its political career as the party of the Marathi people has also sought the support of the non-Marathi people especially after 1990 when the party took a decided hindutva turn.

Caste and Communal Profile of Parties

In the preceding section we analysed the caste and communal composition of the MLAs from 1967 to the present. Since a majority of the

MLAs belong to the political parties and represent their party line in the Vidhan Sabha, it would be worthwhile to prepare the caste and communal profile of the important parties. In Maharashtra, there are only three such parties — the Congress, the BJP and the Shiv Sena.

The Congress party in Maharashtra is a hold-all party which gives multiple castes and communities a share in power. Since the days of the freedom movement, the party comprised two social factions. The first had its base in the cosmopolitan city of Mumbai and another belonged to rural Maharashtra with its dominant Marathas. Y. B. Chavan combined these two trends from 1956 onwards and developed the composite character of the party through his inclusive strategy. His category of 'Bahujan Samaj' brought together the Marathas and Kunbis, the rich and poor Marathas as also the non-Maratha backward castes under the roof of the Congress. He, in fact, went beyond this category and co-opted, into the fold of his organisation, the Dalits, non-Maharashtrians and Muslims. He made it a point to bridge the gap between the Brahmins and the Marathas by giving the Brahmins a due share in cultural power and establishing rapport with the Brahmin businessmen. And all this was done without affecting the Maratha dominance. In fact, his inclusive strategy was basically meant to keep the Maratha power unchallenged. But by early 1970s, Chavan's model started developing cracks. Indira Gandhi's populist strategy challenged the Maratha power and started giving share to the non-Marathas, to the minorities, to the upstarts having no base, to the backwards or the Brahmins. Indira Gandhi's intervention made it difficult for the Maratha bosses to get hold of higher power positions. It divided the Congress Marathas but in no way did it lessen the number of Maratha MLAs.

The real challenge to the Congress Marathas came in 1995 in the form of the BJP–Shiv Sena alliance which instituted the government having its roots in the urban areas with a Brahmin chief minister (Vora 1996: 173). With the 1999 elections, the balance, it seems, has restored in favour of the Congress Marathas. Table 7.5 depicts this hold-all character of the Congress party. It also shows how the party offered tickets to the OBCs even before anyone had heard of this category. The Congress tickets allocation has remained a very complex exercise in which caste or community pockets are identified to issue tickets to the candidates belonging to that category. While doing so, care is taken to maintain an almost constant number of Marathas.

Table 7.5

Congress Party MLAs in Maharashtra: Caste and Community Profile, 1967–2004

Castes and Communities	1967	1972	1978	1980	1985	1990	1995	1999 (C+NCP)	2004 (C+NCP)
Upper Castes	10 (4.9)	12 (5.4)	–	8 (3.4)	6 (2.7)	3 (2.1)	2 (2.5)	1+0 (1.2+0)	6+2 (6.72+2.7)
Intermediate Castes	88 (43.3)	100 (44.9)	70(53.3)	102 (43.7)	89 (41.2)	75 (53.1)	44 (55.5)	23+38 (26.2+71.6)	23+37 (31.8+52.1)
Maratha	80 (39.4)	91 (40.9)	59 (45.0)	87 (37.3)	81 (37.5)	68 (48.2)	40 (50.0)	17+35 (20.0+66.0)	20+37 (27.7+52.1)
Other Intermediate Castes	8 (3.9)	9 (4.0)	11 (8.3)	15 (6.4)	8 (3.7)	7 (4.9)	4 (5.0)	5+3 (6.2+5.6)	3+0 (4.1+0)
OBC	44 (21.6)	51 (22.9)	35 (26.6)	46 (19.6)	55 (25.4)	29 (20.5)	18 (24.4)	22+5 (27+9.3)	15+15 (20.8+21)
Kunbi	22 (10.8)	24 (10.8)	13 (9.9)	17 (7.2)	21 (9.7)	11 (7.8)	5 (6.2)	13+2 (16.0+3.7)	6+4 (8.3+5.6)
Non-Kunbi	22 (10.8)	27 (12.1)	22(16.7)	29 (12.4)	34 (15.7)	18 (12.7)	13 (16.2)	9+3 (11.0+5.6)	9+11 (12.5+15.4)
SC	9 (4.4)	12 (5.4)	6 (4.5)	15 (6.4)	15 (6.9)	9 (6.3)	3 (3.7)	5+3 (6.1+5.6)	4+4 (5.5+5.6)
ST	11 (5.4)	13 (5.8)	12 (9.1)	19 (8.1)	15 (6.9)	10 (7.0)	7 (8.7)	6+5 (7.4+9.4)	6+7 (8.3+9.8)
Muslims	5 (2.4)	11 (4.9)	2 (1.5)	13 (5.5)	8 (3.7)	4 (2.8)	2 (2.5)	9+0 (11.0+0)	6+4 (8.3+5.6)
Other Minorities	11 (5.4)	16 (7.2)	4 (3.0)	25 (10.7)	19 (8.7)	11 (7.8)	4 (5.0)	12+2 (14.8+3.7)	12+2 (16.6+2.8)
Unidentified	25 (12.3)	7 (3.1)	2 (1.5)	5 (2.1)	9 (4.1)	0	0	5+0 (6.1+0)	0+0 (0+0)
TOTAL	203	222	131	233	216	141	80	82+53 = 135	72+71 = 143

Source: Data collected and compiled by the Department of Politics, University of Pune.

Note: Figures in parentheses indicate percentages.

The BJP has improved its performance in recent decades in Maharashtra. Its parent body, the RSS, was formed in Maharashtra in 1925. The main ideologue of the Hindu Mahasabha which had close links with the RSS was V. D. Savarkar, a Maharashtra Brahmin. The BJP since its beginning in the form of Bharatiya Jana Sangh in 1951 was a party which had its base among the higher castes and trading communities of the urban areas. But in mid-1970s, it was again in Maharashtra that the social character of the party began to change because of co-option of the backward castes leaders. And when the BJP thought that it was in a position to capture power with the help of the Shiv Sena it gave space also to the Marathas. The other minorities supported the BJP in its earlier days but lately, especially with the decline of the Congress, these communities have turned to the BJP in a major way. The BJP attracts them to its pro-hindutva agenda which is more expansive than the narrow Marathi politics. The party woos the Hindu Dalits by giving them the cause to take pride, it also tries to 'Hinduise' the tribals while giving them election tickets (Table 7.6).

The Shiv Sena is a Mumbai-based party which was formed to further the cause of the Marathi people in the city. But since 1980s, the party has adopted the hindutva stance which was in a dormant form in its initial phase. The party has successfully reached the rural areas by mobilising the OBC in the first instance and then recruiting the younger Marathas or the disgruntled Marathas into its organisation. The Shiv Sena is emerging as another Maratha party if we go by the number of Marathas elected on its ticket in the last four elections to the Vidhan Sabha. It has also opened its door to the non-Marathi leaders (Table 7.7).

Conclusion

In sum, the Marathas from the intermediate caste category and the Kunbis from the OBC group, who together constitute the Maratha–Kunbi caste-cluster, dominate the Vidhan Sabha in Maharashtra. While they roughly account for 31 per cent of the population, they claim about 45 per cent seats. Their strength in the Vidhan Sabha from 1967 to the present has remained in the range of 125 to 140. Their main instrument in power politics is the Congress party. The Maratha–Kunbis captured the Congress organisation around 1960 when

Table 7.6
BJP MLAs in Maharashtra: Caste and Community Profile, 1967–2004

Castes and Communities	1967	1972	1978	1980	1985	1990	1995	1999	2004
Upper Castes	**1 (2.5)**	**2 (4.0)**	–	**5 (35.0)**	**5 (31.0)**	**5 (11.9)**	**5 (7.6)**	**5 (8.9)**	**5 (8.9)**
Intermediate Castes									
Maratha	1 (2.5)	1 (2.0)	0	2 (14.2)	4 (2.5)	7 (16.6)	11 (16.9)	12 (21.4)	11 (19.6)
Other Intermediate Castes	0	0	0	0	0	2 (4.7)	5 (7.6)	2 (3.5)	5 (8.9)
OBC	**1 (2.5)**	**1 (2.0)**	–	**1 (7.1)**	**2 (12.5)**	**8 (19.0)**	**9 (13.8)**	**9 (16.0)**	**12 (21.4)**
Kunbi	–	–	–	–	–	5 (11.9)	7 (10.7)	10 (17.8)	4 (7.1)
SC	–	–	–	–	**1 (6.2)**	**3 (7.1)**	**8 (12.3)**	**6 (10.7)**	**6 (10.7)**
ST	–	**1 (2.0)**	–	–	**1 (6.2)**	**5 (11.9)**	**5 (7.6)**	**4 (7.1)**	**4 (7.1)**
Muslims	–	–	–	–	–	–	–	–	–
Other Minorities	–	–	–	**6 (42.0)**	**3 (18.7)**	**7 (16.6)**	**14 (21.5)**	**9 (16.0)**	**7 (7.1)**
Unidentified	**1 (2.5)**	**0**	**0**	**0**	**0**	**0**	**1 (1.5)**	**0**	**2 (3.5)**
TOTAL	4	5	0	14	16	42	65	56	56

Source: Data collected and compiled by the Department of Politics, University of Pune.

Note: Figures in parentheses indicate percentages.

Table 7.7
Shiv Sena MLAs in Maharashtra: Caste and Community Profile, 1967–2004

Castes and Communities	1967	1972	1978	1980	1985	1990	1995	1999	2004
Upper Castes	–	1 (100.0)	–	–	–	5 (9.6)	6 (8.2)	2 (2.6)	4 (6.4)
Intermediate Castes									
Maratha	–	–	–	–	–	24 (46.0)	33 (45.0)	31 (44.0)	33 (53.0)
Other Intermediate	–	–	–	–	–	2 (3.8)	2 (2.7)	4 (5.7)	3 (4.8)
Castes									
OBC									
Kunbi	0	–	–	–	–	3 (5.7)	7 (9.5)	7 (10.0)	6 (9.6)
Non–Kunbi	1 (100.0)	–	–	–	–	11 (21.0)	11 (15.0)	9 (13.0)	8 (12.0)
SC	–	–	–	–	–	1 (1.9)	4 (5.4)	3 (4.3)	4 (6.4)
ST	–	–	–	–	–	2 (3.8)	3 (4.10)	4 (5.7)	2 (3.2)
Muslims	–	–	–	–	–	1 (1.9)	1 (1.3)	1 (1.4)	0
Other Minorities	–	–	–	–	–	2 (3.8)	2 (2.7)	4 (5.7)	1 (1.6)
Unidentified	–	–	–	–	–	1 (1.9)	4 (5.4)	4 (5.7)	1 (1.6)
TOTAL	1	1	–	–	–	52	73	69	62

Source: Data collected and compiled by the Department of Politics, University of Pune.

Note: Figures in parentheses indicate percentages.

the Marathi-speaking state came into existence and paved the way for power by offering party tickets to the non-Marathas. Therefore, the question of OBC revolt never came up in the state. As and when there was resentment among the well-to-do sections of the OBC, some of their leaders were given the important positions. Chhagan Bhujbal (an OBC), an important leader of the Shiv Sena, was welcomed by the Congress Marathas to join their party and he was made the Deputy Chief Minister of the Congress front government in 1999. The Dalits did revolt in 1970s but their leaders were co-opted and domesticated by the Congress Marathas within a short span of time. The interventions by Indira Gandhi made things difficult for the Marathas but they took a submissive position and tried to maintain their hold. The waves in the electoral politics in north did not affect the Maratha power in any substantial way. This is evident from the fact that the Marathas have managed to hold on to power. In 1978, their government fell because of the revolt of the Maratha faction led by Sharad Pawar and not due to any external factor. When the hindutva wave reached the state the Marathas joined hands with the leaders of the BJP or the Shiv Sena. Their strength in the Vidhan Sabha remained almost the same in the 1995 elections which brought the hindutva alliance to power. In 1999, and again in 2004, the Congress Marathas regained power.

The social composition of the MLAs of Maharashtra has not changed radically even over a period of more than 40 years. Almost all major castes and communities get represented in the Vidhan Sabha from their respective pockets of influence. The Maratha–Kunbis have been able to maintain their strength which is disproportionate to their population by accommodating other castes and communities, surmounting the difficulties by sometimes taking a submissive posture or sometimes by showing exceptional patience. This empirical fact does not necessarily mean that the rich Maratha peasants are in a position to frame public policy favouring the farm sector. If one goes by the proportion of irrigation, agricultural productivity or rural development, Maharashtra, in fact, ranks very low in relation to the other major states. The contibution of the agricultural sector to the state income has declined compared to the industrial and the service sector. Maharashtra is one of the most industralised and urbanised states and is known for attracting foreign direct investment. Maratha politics with its accommodative strategy is alright when it comes to seeking a position of power in the government, but when it is a question of framing economic policies these power-holders are relegated to the secondary status either because of the pre-eminence of the industrial and urban lobby or because of the hegemonic ideas of industrialisation or globalisation projected as panacea.

References

Kogekar, S. V. 1956. 'Bombay', in S. V. Kogekar and R. L. Park (eds), *Reports on the Indian General Elections: 1951–52*. Bombay: Popular Book Depot.

Lele, Jayant. 1990. 'Caste, Class and Dominance: Political Mobilisation in Maharashtra', in Francine Frankel and M. S. A. Rao (eds), *Dominance and State Power in Modern India: Decline of a Social Order*, vol. 2. Delhi: Oxford University Press.

Palshikar, Suhas and Rejeshwari Deshpande. 1999. 'Maharashtra: Electoral Competition and Structures of Domination', Occasional Paper Series II (1). Department of Politics and Public Administration, University of Pune, Pune.

Palshikar, Suhas and Yogendra Yadav. 2004. 'The NCP Emerges in its Own Right', *The Hindu*, 24 October, p. 12.

Sirsikar, V. M. 1976. 'Maharashtra: Politics of Linkage Elites', in Iqbal Narain (ed.), *State Politics in India*, pp. 220–39. Meerut: Meenakshi Prakashan.

Vora, Rajendra. 1982. 'Rajkaran', in V. Hardikar and S. Dastane (eds), *Maharashtra*. Pune: Dastane Ramchandra and Co.

———. 1996. 'Maharashtra: Shift of Power from Rural to Urban Sector', *Economic and Political Weekly*, 21 (2–3): 171–73.

Vora, Rajendra and Suhas Palshikar. 1996. *Maharashtratil Sattantar*. Mumbai: Granthali.

8

Legislators in Karnataka: Well-entrenched Dominant Castes

Sandeep Shastri

A study of the social profile of the legislators in Karnataka affords an opportunity for a meaningful estimation of the dynamics of electoral politics in the state in particular and an in-depth assessment of the forces and factors that have shaped the course and direction of Karnataka politics in general. This chapter is based on the interpretation of the data collected on the social profile of those elected to the Karnataka Legislative Assembly. An ideal backdrop to this analysis would be an overview of the caste 'mix' in Karnataka, the nature of political competition in the state and the defining character of its politics.

It is important to record that Karnataka (earlier referred to as Mysore) was classified as a 'Part B' state after independence. Prior to independence, it was a princely state. With the reorganisation of states on linguistic lines in 1956, the boundaries of the then Mysore state were re-drawn to include the Kannada-speaking areas. The enlarged state had four principal regions: (*a*). Old Mysore region (formerly a part of the princely state of Mysore), (*b*) Hyderabad–Karnatak region (formerly a part of the territory of the Nizam of Hyderabad), (*c*) Bombay–Karnatak region (formerly part of the Bombay Presidency of British India), and (*d*) Old Madras region (formerly part of the Madras Presidency of British India) and Coorg. For the purpose of electoral analysis, the Old Madras and Coorg regions are normally re-christianed as Coastal Karnataka, by adding one district from the Bombay–Karnatak region.

The social profile of Karnataka indicates some patterns which are similar to those at the national level even while pointing to certain distinctive characteristics. More than 85 per cent of the state population are Hindus. Most important among the religious minorities in the state are the Muslims, who account for nearly 12 per cent of the population. This community is spread across the state. Christians account for nearly 2 per cent of the population and are largely present in the coastal areas. The other religious minorities account for the remaining 1 per cent of the population.

Table 8.1
Caste and Religious Composition of Karnataka

Religious Community	Caste	Percentage of State Population*	Percentage of State Population**
Hindus		**85.5**	
	Upper Castes		3.5
	Lingayats		15.3
	Vokkaligas		10.8
	Other Backward Castes		32.5
	Scheduled Castes		16.7
	Scheduled Tribes		6.7
Muslims		**11.6**	
Christians		**1.9**	
Other Minorities		**1.0**	
TOTAL		100.0	85.5

Source: Author's fieldwork.
Note: * Drawn from Census 2001 data.
      ** Based on figures in the Chinnappa Reddy Commission Report on Backward Classes. Even in the earlier report, the percentage of those belonging to the different castes was more or less the same.

The caste factor profile of the state is distinct in significant ways and caste considerations have played a crucial role in the electoral politics of the state. The Lingayats and Vokkaligas are considered the dominant castes and have been the major players in state politics. Both the Lingayats and Vokkaligas are land-owning communities in rural Karnataka. The traditional stronghold of the Lingayats has been the Bombay–Karnatak and Hyderabad–Karnatak regions while the Vokkaligas are a major force in the Old Mysore region. The Other Backward Classes — which account for more than one-third of the state's population — have attempted to emerge as a major political force ever since Devraj Urs (the first Backward Caste leader to become Chief Minister of Karnataka from 1972 to 1979) sought to unite them and break the hegemony enjoyed by the dominant castes. Since the late 1970s, the Other Backward Castes (OBC) have had a powerful impact on the electoral outcomes and their representation in the legislature and state council of ministers has increased (Shastri 1995; Shastri and Latha 2008; Shastri and Vinod 1990). The important OBC (in numerical terms) include the Kurubas (shepherds) and the Idigas (toddy tappers).[1]

The history of representative legislative institutions in the state can be traced back to the days when Mysore was a princely state. In 1881, the then Maharaja agreed to the formation of a Mysore Representative Assembly. However, during the initial years, it was a wholly nominated body. In 1891, a section of the members were elected and the size of the elected component progressively increased with the passage of time. With independence and the adoption of the Indian Constitution, the first general elections to the Mysore Legislative Assembly were held in 1952. Given the fact that the state then consisted of largely the areas under the former princely state of Mysore, the strength of the Assembly

---

[1] It is important to dwell at some length on the classification of castes in Old Mysore/ Karnataka. The Upper Caste category is mainly composed of the Brahmins. The concept of 'Backward Castes' has a long history of use in India. It is normally used to refer to those caste groups who have historically been denied opportunities to equip themselves and thus have failed to benefit from education or acquiring wealth and status in society. In the princely state of Mysore, as early as in 1921, the term 'Backward' was defined as 'all communities other than Brahmins, who are not now adequately represented in the public service' (quoted in Galantar 1978: 1812). With the organisation of the Backward Castes in Old Mysore, the major land-owning communities among the Backwards — Lingayats and Vokkaligas — gradually organised themselves and benefited significantly from the non-Brahmin movement in the state. Gradually, the two castes, both in terms of their political influence and economic power, came to acquire the status of dominant castes. With the government offering preferential treatment to the Backwards in opportunities in both educational institutions and government jobs, the question of who all constitute the Backward Castes became a zone of much controversy. Several commissions have been appointed in Mysore/Karnataka in this regard. It is important to note that all these commissions have recommended that either one or both the dominant castes be excluded from the category of Backwards. Such recommendations have immediately evoked an adverse reaction from the affected dominant caste. While preparing the list of Backward Castes, the government has always succumbed to the pressures from the dominant castes and continues to allow them to be a part of the Backward Castes basket. Thus, in this chapter, the term 'OBC' refers to the non-dominant Backward Castes. The term 'OBC' does not include the Scheduled Castes and Tribes as they are listed separately.

was relatively small, with just 99 members. With the re-organisation of the state, the strength of the Assembly rose to 208. In 1967, the Assembly strength increased to 216 and has remained at 224 ever since 1973, when the 31st Constitutional Amendment froze the number of Assembly constituencies till 2002. The Old Mysore region accounts for half the Lok Sabha and Assembly constituencies in the state. A quarter of the Lok Sabha and Assembly seats are in the Bombay–Karnatak region and the rest of the seats are distributed in the Hyderabad–Karnatak and Coastal Karnataka regions. During the period 1952–2001, 11 elections to the Karnataka Legislative Assembly have been held. The state has witnessed a relatively high turnout of voters in successive elections and the electoral process has been, by and large, free and fair. The legislative assemblies have enjoyed relative stability of tenure and were dissolved prematurely on only four occasions.

It is also significant that Karnataka was considered a safe 'Congress bastion' till 1983 as the party had never tasted defeat in either the Lok Sabha or Assembly elections here. In the first six Assembly elections (1952–78), the Congress party was elected to power with a clear mandate, on all occasions save one (i.e., 1967), a two-thirds majority (see Figure 8.1). During this period, the Congress party's performance in the Lok Sabha elections in the state was even more spectacular; it secured more than 90 per cent of the seats on all occasions, save two (88 per cent in 1957 and 66 per cent in 1967; for details, see Cheluva Raju et al. 1983; Shastri and Vinod 1991; Shastri 1994: 390–92). Even when the Congress performed poorly at the national level (especially in 1977), the performance of the party in the state remained creditable. The party's monopoly over power in the state ended in 1983. In the Assembly elections held that year, the Congress party was defeated and the Janata Party formed a minority government. The Janata Party returned to power with a clear majority in the Assembly elections held in 1985. Subsequently in 1989, the Congress party secured a two-thirds majority in the Assembly and was in power for five years, making way for the Janata Dal, which secured a majority in the 1994 elections. Once again in the 1999 elections, the Congress was able to win a majority of the seats and formed the government. In all the 11 Assembly elections held, save one (i.e., 1983), the voters of Karnataka have ensured that either the Congress party or the Janata Party/Dal secured a clear majority.

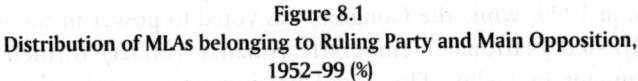

Figure 8.1
Distribution of MLAs belonging to Ruling Party and Main Opposition,
1952–99 (%)

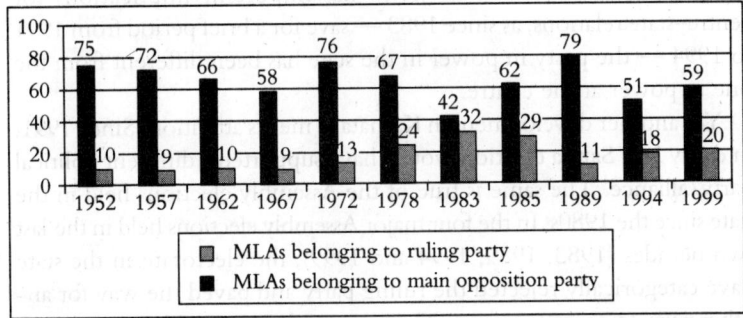

Source: Prepared by author.

In the Lok Sabha elections in the state, the Congress continued to win a majority of the seats till 1996. In 1996 and 1998, it had to concede the majority of the seats to the Janata Dal and the BJP/Lok Shakti alliance respectively. It has re-asserted its dominant position in the state in the 1999 Lok Sabha elections by winning a majority of the seats in the state. After more than three decades of Congress monopoly, Karnataka clearly witnesses the emergence of a competitive party system in the last two decades of the 20th century (for details, see Shastri 1999a).

Another trend that can be discerned in Karnataka is that when it comes to who should come to power in the state, voters here have acted differently as compared to the national electorate. This assumes even greater relevance with the emergence of a competitive party system. It is also reflective of the maturity of the Karnataka voters and their capacity to differentiate between national and state elections/issues. In 1978, the Karnataka electorate emphatically endorsed the claims of the Congress even as the Janata Party was in power at the centre. In 1983, though the Congress was in power at the centre, it was voted out of power in the state. In 1985, the Assembly elections were held in the backdrop of the Congress sweep at the national level. The Karnataka voter, however, voted the Janata Party back to power. In the 1989 Assembly elections (Lok Sabha and Assembly elections were held simultaneously), the Congress formed the government in Karnataka while the Janata Dal-led National Front came to power at the national level. In 1994, even as Narasimha Rao headed a Congress government in Delhi, the voters in the state preferred the Janata Dal as the ruling party.

Again, in 1999, while the Congress was voted to power in the state, the BJP-led National Democratic Alliance (NDA) formed the government in Delhi. This trend has important implications for centre–state relations, as since 1983 — save for a brief period from 1991 to 1994 — the party in power in the state has been different from the one in power at the centre.

Yet another development in Karnataka merits attention. Since 1991, in every Lok Sabha election, voters have supported a different political party/alliance. The same is true of the Assembly elections held in the state since the 1980s. In the four major Assembly elections held in the last two decades (1983, 1989, 1994 and 1999), the electorate in the state have categorically rejected the ruling party and paved the way for another party to come to power. The message the voter wished to convey, especially to the ruling party (both the one voted out and the one voted in), is categorical: non-performance and intra-party squabbles will not find favour (see Shastri 1999b).

It is also interesting to note that the electoral contest in Karnataka has generally involved two major formulations, with the third force being rarely favoured by the voters. If in 1978, the Congress (Brahmananda Reddy) was rejected as a third force, the same fate awaited the Janata Party (JP) in 1989, the Karnataka Congress Party in 1994 and the Janata Dal(S) in 1999. In every election, the two major political formulations have cornered more than 70 per cent of the votes polled. Karnataka appears to be clearly heading towards a bipolar alliance system.

The Karnataka electorate has also not endorsed the claims of regional parties, either in the Lok Sabha or Assembly elections. Till the late 1960s, the electoral competition in the state was largely between the Congress on the one hand and the Socialist Party/Swatantra Party on the other. After the Congress split in 1969, the two factions of the Congress were the principal political forces in the state. With the formation of the Janata Party in 1977, it became the main opposition party. Subsequently, the Janata Party/Dal and the BJP have emerged as crucial players in the electoral politics of the state along with the Congress party. Though, regional parties have occasionally been formed, they have had limited electoral success (for details, see Patil and Shastri 1994). Devraj Urs floated the Kranti Ranga in the 1980s but the party later merged with the Janata Party. Bangarappa formed the Karnataka Congress Party but this party largely played the role of a spoiler (for the Congress) in the 1994 Assembly elections (see Shastri 1995). It subsequently merged with the Congress. The Karnataka Rajya Raitha Sangha (KRRS) has also achieved limited electoral success in Karnataka winning two seats in 1989, one seat in 1994 and drawing a blank in 1999. While the Lok Shakti did emerge in Karnataka in 1998, evidence clearly points to its limited role and the advantage it derived from the alliance with the BJP (see Shastri 2000).

Thus, over the past five decades, electoral politics in the state has witnessed major changes, the most important being the movement from a one party-dominant system to a competitive party system, paving the way for the possible emergence of a bipolar alliance system. Its implications for state politics and, more specifically, the composition of the Legislative Assembly have been far reaching.

I

This chapter attempts a multi-track analysis of the social profile of the state Legislative Assembly since 1952. A comparative assessment of the membership of the legislature from the perspective of key social indicators is also undertaken.

This analysis of the social background of the Karnataka legislators is undertaken from several perspectives. The pattern in terms of representation to the dominant, forward and non-dominant Backward Castes is analysed. Further, only representation to Dalits and Muslims is assessed. Given the fact that only two seats in the Assembly are reserved for Scheduled Tribes, a separate assessment of Scheduled Tribe representatives is not undertaken here.

As mentioned earlier, the Lingayat and Vokkaliga communities are considered as the dominant castes in the state. Even though they together constitute just 26 per cent of the state population (Lingayats: 15.3 per cent and Vokkaligas: 10.8 per cent), they have always enjoyed a majority in the Legislative Assembly. In most of the assemblies, their majority has been significant, rising to over 60 per cent of the House in 1985 and 1994 (see Table 8.2; also Figure 8.2).

Within the dominant castes, the Lingayat community accounts for a larger number of legislators when compared to the Vokkaligas, except in the first Assembly elected in 1952. Given the fact that the Bombay–Karnatak region and Hyderabad–Karnatak region (in which the Lingayat community has a significant presence) was not a part of the state in 1952,

Table 8.2
Caste Profile of the Members of the Karnataka Legislative Assembly, 1952–99 (%)

	Percentage of Population*	1952	1957	1962	1967	1972	1978	1983	1985	1989	1994	1999	Average (AVG)	Standard Deviation (STD)
Lingayats (L)	15.3	17.7	30.9	29.1	38.5	30.2	31.2	32.4	35.3	35.6	35.5	35.7	32.0	5.6
Vokkaligas (V)	10.8	40.6	19.9	26.6	20.0	22.9	21.4	25.1	25.1	19.2	24.6	24.1	24.5	5.9
Dominant Castes (L+V)	26.1	58.3	50.8	55.8	58.5	53.2	52.6	57.5	60.4	54.8	60.2	59.8	56.5	3.3
Forward Castes	3.5	9.4	10.0	9.1	8.8	7.7	9.8	8.2	7.3	5.8	5.2	5.4	7.9	1.8
Other Backward Castes	32.5	7.3	13.1	14.1	11.2	12.6	13.0	13.0	10.1	13.9	12.8	12.5	12.1	2.0
Scheduled Castes	16.7	22.9	16.2	15.6	17.1	17.6	15.3	17.4	15.9	16.3	16.6	16.6	17.0	2.1
Scheduled Tribes	6.7	0	1.6	1.5	1.0	2.4	2.8	1.5	1.9	2.8	1.9	1.9	1.7	0.8
Muslims	11.6	1.0	5.2	3.0	2.4	5.4	6.1	1.0	4.4	5.8	2.8	4.0	3.7	1.8
Other Minorities	2.9	1.0	3.1	1.0	1.0	2.0	0.5	1.5	0	0.5	0.5	0.5	1.1	0.9

Source: Author's fieldwork.

Note: * Based on the figures in the Chinappa Reddy Commission Report on Backward Classes. Even in earlier reports, the percentage of population of various castes was more or less the same.

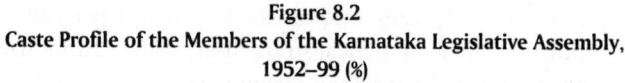

Figure 8.2
Caste Profile of the Members of the Karnataka Legislative Assembly,
1952–99 (%)

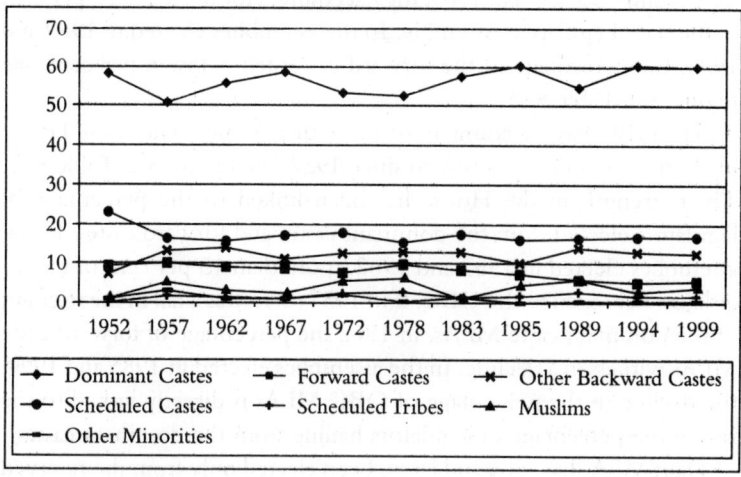

Source: Prepared by author.

the Lingayats account for only 18 per cent of the House. On the other hand, more than 40 per cent of the legislators in the first Assembly were from the Vokkaliga community. In the subsequent assemblies (except 1962), the Lingayats have accounted for more than 30 per cent of the legislators. The Vokkaligas have, since 1957, constituted nearly 20 per cent of the House. While an overwhelming majority of the legislators from the Vokkaligas community have been elected from the Old Mysore region, a significant segment of the Lingayat legislators have been returned from Northern Karnataka (Bombay–Karnatak and Hyderabad–Karnatak regions). The significant presence of the dominant castes in all assemblies is clear from the fact that the average (AVG) for the dominant castes across the assemblies is 56.5 per cent and the Standard Deviation (STD) is 3.3. However, when taken separately, there seems to be a significant fluctuation in the strength of the two communities with the STD being 5.6 for the Lingayats and 5.9 for the Vokkaligas. The comparative strength of the dominant castes in the House witnessed a marginal decline in the assemblies elected in 1972 and 1978. This development is linked to the efforts of Devraj Urs (who was the Chief Minister for much of the period of the two assemblies) to unite the OBC and to offset the political power wielded by the dominant castes.

While the forward castes account for less than 4 per cent of the state's population, their numerical strength in the legislature has been significantly higher. Till 1989, they accounted for more than 7 per cent of the state Legislative Assembly. In the assemblies elected in 1989 and 1994, the percentage of the forward castes fell below 6 per cent (see Figure 8.2/Table 8.2).

The OBC have accounted for more than 10 per cent of the House in all the assemblies constituted since 1957 (see Figure 8.2/Table 8.2). Their strength in the House has been linked to the percentage of legislators elected from the dominant castes and forward castes. In the assemblies elected in 1957 and 1962, more than 13 per cent of the legislators belonged to the OBC. If in 1957 there was a fall in the strength of the dominant caste MLAs, in 1962 the percentage of forward caste MLAs witnessed a decline. In the assemblies elected in 1985 and 1994, the decline in the percentage of OBC MLAs is directly linked to the rise in the percentage of legislators hailing from the dominant castes.

Dalit MLAs have, by and large, been elected only from the reserved constituencies. As a result their strength in the House is in the range of 16 to 18 per cent (see Figure 8.2/Table 8.2).

The Muslims constitute the largest religious minority in the state and account for nearly 12 per cent of the population. The percentage of Muslims MLAs elected has never been more than 6 per cent (Figure 8.2/Table 8.2). There is a tremendous variation across assemblies with regard to the percentage of MLAs belonging to the Muslim community. The average percentage of Muslims across assemblies is 3.7 per cent, while the STD is 1.8.

An analysis of the social profile of the members of the Legislative Assembly in Karnataka points clearly to the fact that a majority of the legislators have hailed from the dominant castes. On the other hand, the OBC have been under-represented in successive legislative assemblies. The minorities — especially the Muslims — have also had a marginal presence in the Assembly.

II

This section attempts a party-wise analysis of the social profile of the legislators. For the purpose of analysis, only the Congress party, Janata Party/Dal and the Bharatiya Janata Party (BJP) are considered. In view of the fact that no meaningful analysis of the membership profile of legislators from the major non-Congress formulations in the pre-1978 period is possible, it has not been included in the study.

In most of the assemblies, there is only a marginal difference in the percentage of the dominant castes in the House and in the ruling party (see Figure 8.3/Table 8.3). The average for the dominant castes in the ruling party and the legislature as a whole, across the assemblies, is more or less the same: 56.5 per cent in the case of the House and 56.8 per cent in the case of the ruling party. However, a deeper analysis shows specific variations across assemblies. A gradual increase in the percentage of those from the dominant castes in the ruling party is noticed in the first three general elections held after the reorganisation of the state (1957, 1962, 1967). In fact, in the 1967 elections, the percentage of those from the dominant castes in the ruling party was higher than their (dominant castes) percentage in the House. The assemblies constituted in 1972 and 1978 witness a significant fall in the percentage of dominant caste legislators in the ruling party. This decline in the percentage of dominant caste legislators is steeper in the ruling party as compared to the House. As mentioned earlier, this development is linked to the efforts of Devraj Urs to reduce the influence and role of the dominant castes in Karnataka politics. In the 1983 and 1985 elections, the dominant caste component in the ruling party registered a phenomenal increase. This is linked to the social base of the Janata Party and its increased dependence on the dominant castes. It is also important to note that the troika of leadership in the Janata Party in those days (Hegde, Deve Gowda and Bommai) hailed from the forward and dominant castes. A similar trend is noticed in 1994, when the Janata Dal came to power and in 1999 when the Congress returned to power. The fluctuation in the percentage of the dominant castes in the ruling party across the assemblies is clear from the STD for the dominant castes in the ruling party, which is 6.6, while the STD for the dominant castes in the House as a whole is 3.3, though their average is more or less the same (see Table 8.3).

It is also relevant to note that the percentage of legislators in the Congress party who have hailed from the dominant castes has been in the 48 per cent–60 per cent range, with an average of around 55 per cent (see Figure 8.3). It goes up to a record 73 per cent in 1994. In this election, the party was relegated to the third position, behind the Janata Dal

Table 8.3

Caste Profile of the Members of the Karnataka Legislative Assembly: Dominant Castes (%)

	1952	1957	1962	1967	1972	1978	1983	1985	1989	1994	1999	AVG	STD
MLAs belonging to dominant castes	58.3	50.8	55.8	58.5	53.2	52.6	57.5	60.4	54.8	60.2	59.8	56.5	3.3
Ruling party MLAs belonging to dominant castes	58.1	48.2	50.8	59.5	49.1	50.4	62.2	68.9	55.3	61.1	61.4	56.8	6.6
Congress MLAs belonging to dominant castes	58.1	48.2	50.8	59.5	49.1	50.4	57.3	44.6	55.3	72.7	61.4	55.2	7.9
Janata Party/ Dal MLAs belonging to dominant castes	–	–	–	–	–	64.9	62.2	68.9	77.3	61.1	67.8	67.0	5.9
BJP MLAs belonging to dominant castes	–	–	–	–	–	–	43.8	50.0	50.0	52.6	57.5	50.8	5.0

Source: Author's fieldwork.

Figure 8.3
Caste Profile of the Major Political Parties in the Karnataka
Legislative Assembly: Dominant Castes (%)

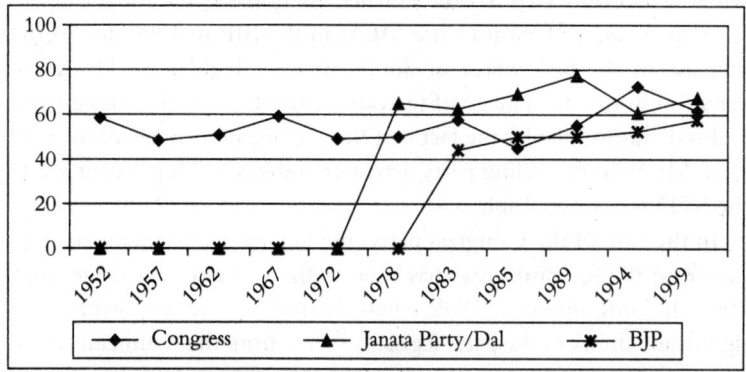

Source: Prepared by author.

and the BJP. Most of the party nominees from the non-dominant Backward Castes were defeated and the social profile of the party MLAs in this Assembly is significantly in favour of the dominant castes.

The social profile of the Janata Party/Dal MLAs clearly reveals the major share of those from the dominant castes. Whether in power or in the opposition, more than 60 per cent of the party's legislators hail from the dominant castes (see Figure 8.3). In the case of the BJP, half of its legislators have hailed from the dominant castes. It registered a significant increase in the 1999 poll.

In the first three assemblies (those elected in 1952, 1957 and 1962), the percentage of ruling party members who belonged to the forward castes was significantly higher than their (forward castes') percentage in the House. For the first time, in 1967, the percentage of forward caste MLAs in the ruling party fell below their relative strength in the House. This can be attributed to the increase in the percentage of dominant caste MLAs in the ruling party. In the Assembly elected in 1978, the percentage of ruling party MLAs from the forward castes was 2 per cent lower than their strength in the House as a result of the rise in the percentage of non-dominant Backward Caste MLAs in the ruling party. In the assemblies constituted after 1983, the percentage of forward caste MLAs in the ruling party has been considerably lower than their relative strength in the House. This is largely due to the fact that a significant chunk of the BJP MLAs (since 1983) have hailed from the forward castes. The only exception for the BJP was in 1985, when it had only two MLAs. Further, there has been a slight dip in the percentage of forward caste MLAs in the BJP in 1999 due to the increase in the percentage of dominant caste legislators. The sharp variation in the percentage of forward caste MLAs in the ruling party is also demonstrated by the fact that the average percentage of forward caste MLAs in the ruling party across assemblies is 6.9 per cent while the STD is 3.4 (see Table 8.4).

In the case of the Congress party, the percentage of members who hail from the forward castes has been in the 7–9 per cent range since 1967. It came down in 1989 when the party came to power and a significant chunk of the party legislators were from the dominant castes. The percentage of Congress legislators from the forward castes registered a sharp increase in 1994. This was when the party was relegated to the third position in the Assembly. In numerical terms, the number of legislators from the forward castes remained more or less unchanged and the percentage difference is due to the sharp fall in the number of Congress legislators from 1989 to 1994 (see Figure 8.4). It must be noted that with the party returning to power in 1999, there is again a fall in the percentage of forward caste legislators in view of the increase in percentage of legislators from among the dominant castes.

In the case of the Janata Party, the percentage of MLAs from the forward castes has been significantly high in 1978 and 1989. In 1978, the Janata Party included those who had come from the Jana Sangh and later formed the BJP. In 1989, the number of Janata Dal legislators was just a little over 10 per cent of the strength of the Assembly. While in real terms, the number of legislators from the forward castes had not significantly reduced, the sharp fall in the total number of legislators accounted for this trend.

The fact that the BJP has been a forward caste party is also endorsed by the social profile of its legislators. The party has a significantly high percentage of legislators from the forward castes. The only exception was in 1985 when the party had only two legislators (see Figure 8.4).

The percentage of MLAs belonging to the OBC witnessed a gradual increase till 1978 and since then their percentage has more or less re-mained unvaried (see Table 8.5). This trend of gradual increase is noticed

Table 8.4

Caste Profile of the Members of the Karnataka Legislative Assembly: Forward Castes (%)

	1952	1957	1962	1967	1972	1978	1983	1985	1989	1994	1999	AVG	STD
MLAs belonging to forward castes	9.4	10.0	9.1	8.8	7.7	9.8	8.2	7.3	5.8	5.2	7.9	8.1	1.6
Ruling party MLAs belonging to forward castes	9.5	11.7	10.6	8.3	8.1	7.8	4.4	6.2	4.4	2.8	2.3	6.9	3.4
Congress MLAs belonging to forward castes	9.5	11.7	10.6	8.3	8.1	7.8	9.3	9.1	4.4	12.1	2.3	8.2	2.9
Janata Party/Dal MLAs belonging to forward castes	–	–	–	–	–	14.0	4.4	6.2	9.1	2.8	0	6.1	4.9
BJP MLAs belonging to forward castes	–	–	–	–	–	–	43.8	0	25.0	21.1	17.5	21.5	15.7

Source: Author's fieldwork.

Figure 8.4
Caste Profile of the Major Political Parties in the Karnataka
Legislative Assembly: Forward Castes (%)

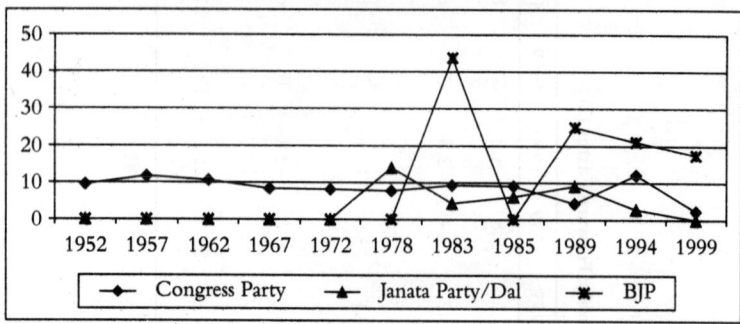

Source: Prepared by author.

in the ruling party here and the caste profile of individual political parties is analysed. The fact that the Janata Party/Dal had a high percentage of members from the dominant caste is reflected in the relatively lower percentage (as compared to the Congress) of legislators from the OBC. In recent years, a higher percentage of BJP legislators too hail from the OBC. The party has been fielding a larger number of candidates from the OBC in recent elections.

It is significant that in all the assemblies since 1962, the percentage of Dalit MLAs in the ruling party is much higher than their relative strength in the House. This implies that the election results in the re-served constituencies appear to favour the party that emerges as the ruling party. This also explains the decline in the percentage of Dalit MLAs in the Congress and the Janata Party/Dal when it sits in the opposition.

The percentage of legislators from the dominant religious minority — the Muslims — is significantly low when compared to the percentage of the religious community's population in the state. Across parties, it is noticed that the percentage of Muslim legislators is significantly lower in the Janata Party/Dal as compared to the Congress. This also explains that when the Congress has been relegated to the opposition, the percentage of Muslim legislators has registered a sharp fall. There has never been a Muslim legislator from among those elected on the BJP ticket.

Table 8.5

Caste Profile of the Members of the Karnataka Legislative Assembly: OBC (%)

	1952	1957	1962	1967	1972	1978	1983	1985	1989	1994	1999	AVG	STD
MLAs belonging to OBC	7.3	13.1	14.1	11.2	12.6	13.0	13.0	10.1	13.9	12.8	12.1	12.1	2.0
Ruling party MLAs belonging to OBC	8.1	8.1	11.7	11.4	11.2	14.9	6.7	7.0	13.8	8.3	12.1	10.3	2.8
Congress MLAs belonging to OBC	8.1	8.1	11.7	11.4	11.2	14.9	17.3	16.1	13.8	6.1	12.1	11.9	3.5
Janata Party/Dal MLAs belonging to OBC	–	–	–	–	–	5.3	6.7	7.0	9.1	8.3	14.3	8.5	3.2
BJP MLAs belonging to OBC	–	–	–	–	–	–	6.3	0	33.3	13.2	10.0	12.6	13.0

Source: Author's fieldwork.

Table 8.6

Caste Profile of the Members of the Karnataka Legislative Assembly: Dalits (%)

	1957	1962	1967	1972	1978	1983	1985	1989	1994	1999	AVG	STD
Dalit MLAs	16.2	15.6	17.1	17.6	15.3	17.4	15.9	16.3	16.6	16.6	16.5	0.8
Dalit MLAs in ruling party	11.7	17.4	20.7	18.0	17.0	20.0	16.3	17.9	21.3	16.7	17.7	2.7
Dalit MLAs in Congress	11.7	17.4	20.7	18.0	17.0	16.0	14.3	17.9	6.1	16.7	15.6	4.1
Dalit MLAs in Janata Parry/Dal	–	–	–	–	12.3	20.0	16.3	4.5	21.3	14.3	14.8	6.1
Dalit MLAs in BJP	–	–	–	–	–	5.9	0	0	10.5	15.0	6.3	6.6

Source: Author's fieldwork.

Table 8.7

Caste Profile of the Members of the Karnataka Legislative Assembly: Muslims (%)

	1957	1962	1967	1972	1978	1983	1985	1989	1994	1999	AVG	STD
Muslim MLAs	5.2	3.1	2.4	5.4	6.1	1.0	4.4	5.8	2.8	4.0	4.0	1.7
Muslim MLAs in the ruling party	3.7	4.6	2.6	6.8	7.8	1.1	1.6	6.9	2.8	4.5	4.2	2.3
Muslim MLAs in the Congress	3.7	4.6	2.6	6.8	7.8	0	10.7	6.9	2.9	4.5	5.1	3.1
Muslim MLAs in the Janata Party/ Dal	–	–	–	–	3.5	1.1	1.6	0	2.8	3.8	2.1	1.5
Muslim MLAs in the BJP	–	–	–	–	–	0	0	0	0	0	0	0

Source: Author's fieldwork.

III

An examination of the professional background of the legislators elected reveals an interesting pattern. Agriculturists and professionals (mostly lawyers) account for more than 65 per cent of the legislators elected (see Table 8.8/Figure 8.5). With the passage of time, the number of legislators who are agriculturists by profession has registered a steady increase. The standard deviation of 11.02 and an average of 46.2 per cent indicate the sharp variation in numbers across assemblies. Till 1978, lawyers accounted for one-third of the legislators. In later years their numbers have witnessed a decline. The variation in the number of lawyers elected to different assemblies is quite significant, though not as skewed as in the case of agriculturists. The average number of lawyers elected to each Assembly is 31.17 per cent and the STD is 6.2. A very small percentage of legislators have identified themselves as social workers. It has varied from nearly 2 per cent in the Assembly elected in 1983 to just over 7 per cent in the Assembly that was formed in 1985. The average across assemblies is 4.7 per cent, with a STD of 1.7.

A significant number of legislators called themselves political workers in the initial years. In the first Assembly (elected in 1952), one-fourth of the legislators were political workers. The number declined to 11 per cent in 1957 and 9 per cent in 1962 and 1967. It has further declined in subsequent years. There is tremendous variation in the percentage of political workers in each Assembly, with an average of 7.9 per cent and a significant STD of 6.3. In the first few decades after independence, many of the elected legislators may have called themselves political workers because of their involvement in the freedom movement and continued their involvement in public life after independence as legislators. The sharp decline in the number of political workers and an increase in the number of agriculturists and lawyers among legislators in subsequent years could be because most of those who entered public life in the 1960s and 1970s did not require to be 'full- time' political workers and retained their identities in their respective professions.

It is interesting to note that till the late 1980s very few legislators identified themselves as businessmen. Since 1989, over 10 per cent of the legislators have stated their profession to be business. This could be linked to the changing economic climate in the country in the light of economic reforms and privatisation as a result of which it is no longer

Table 8.8
Professional Background of Legislators: Karnataka Legislative Assembly (%)

	1952	1957	1962	1967	1972	1978	1983	1985	1989	1994	AVG	STD
Agriculturists	26.47	31.67	40.25	42.86	50.00	49.01	57.97	47.93	55.61	60.27	46.2	11.0
Social Workers	2.941	3.333	5.031	6.044	6.818	4.95	1.932	7.373	4.673	3.653	4.7	1.7
Political Workers	23.53	10.83	9.434	8.791	5.682	5.941	6.28	4.608	2.336	1.37	7.9	6.3
Professionals	41.18	33.33	35.22	34.62	32.39	32.67	27.54	31.8	23.36	19.63	31.2	6.2
Businessmen	2.941	1.667	6.918	4.396	2.841	4.95	2.415	4.608	11.21	10.5	5.2	3.3
Others	2.941	0.833	3.145	3.297	2.273	2.475	3.865	3.687	2.804	4.11	2.9	0.9

Source: Author's fieldwork.

Figure 8.5
Professional Background of Legislators: Select Indicators (%)

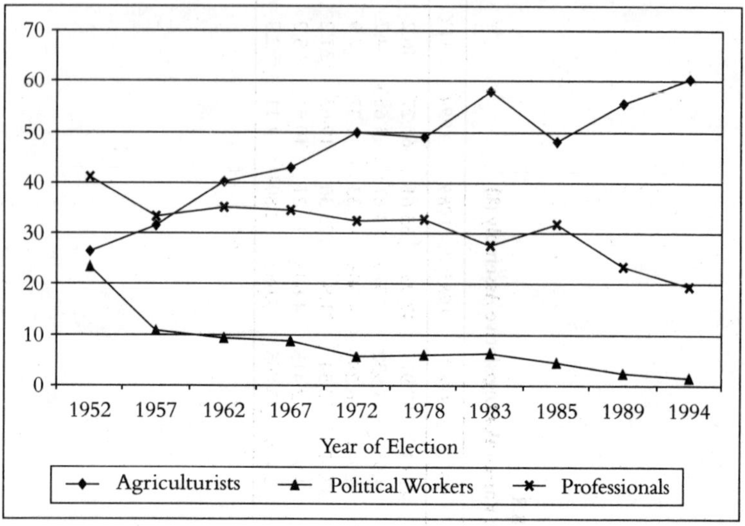

Source: Prepared by author.

a 'taboo' for a politician to be identified as being a businessman. The sharp variation in the number of businessmen among the legislators in successive assemblies, can be clearly gleaned from the fact that, overall, businessmen account for 5.2 per cent of the legislators and the STD is as high as 3.3.

It also emerges that the trends with regard to the variations in the profession of members of successive assemblies is also reflected in the composition of the ruling party (see Table 8.9), with the averages and standard deviations in both cases being more or less identical.

The Karnataka Legislative Assembly has had very few women members. Women have never accounted for more than 9 per cent of the House and since 1972 this has fallen to less than 5 per cent (see Table 8.10). In spite of the fact that Karnataka took the lead in providing for women's reservation in local bodies in 1985 itself — much before the 73rd Amendment to the Constitution (which mandated 33 per cent reservation for women in local bodies) was passed — political parties have taken little initiative to ensure that a larger number of women candidates are given party tickets to contest elections. Since 1978, in the Legislative Assembly elections to the state legislature, not more than

Table 8.9

Professional Background of Ruling Party Legislators: Karnataka Legislative Assembly (%)

	1952	1957	1962	1967	1972	1978	1983	1985	1989	1994	AVG	STD
Agriculturists in Assembly	26.407	31.607	40.25	42.806	50.00	49.01	57.907	47.903	55.601	60.207	46.20	11.004
Agriculturists in Ruling Party	25.903	26.803	34.65	44.203	45.80	49.602	51.702	49.205	53.001	65.405	44.605	12.303
Social Workers in Assembly	2.941	3.333	5.031	6.044	6.818	4.95	1.932	7.373	4.673	3.653	4.675	1.742
Social Workers in Ruling Party	3.704	4.878	4.95	8.654	6.87	3.759	1.149	5.97	5.422	4.545	4.99	2.007
Political Workers in Assembly	23.503	10.803	9.434	8.791	5.682	5.941	6.28	4.608	2.336	1.37	7.881	6.252
Political Workers in Ruling Party	18.502	15.805	12.87	7.692	4.58	6.015	6.818	3.731	2.41	1.818	8.031	5.782
Professionals in Assembly	41.108	33.303	35.22	34.602	32.309	32.607	27.504	31.80	23.306	19.603	31.107	6.186
Professionals in Ruling Party	48.105	48.708	37.62	30.707	37.40	32.303	31.802	35.007	22.809	20.00	34.408	9.307
Businessmen in Assembly	2.941	1.667	6.918	4.396	2.841	4.95	2.415	4.608	11.201	10.50	5.245	3.320
Businessmen in Ruling Party	0	2.439	7.921	4.808	3.053	6.767	2.273	2.985	13.205	6.364	4.986	3.779
Others in Assembly	2.941	0.833	3.145	3.297	2.273	2.475	3.865	3.687	2.804	4.11	2.943	0.941
Others in Ruling Party	3.704	1.22	1.98	3.846	2.29	1.504	5.682	2.985	3.012	0.909	2.713	1.449

Source: Author's fieldwork.

Table 8.10
Women Legislators in Karnataka (%)

Year of Election	1952	1957	1962	1967	1972	1978	1983	1985	1989	1994
Men	97	91	91	93	95	97	99	95	96	96
Women	3	9	9	7	5	3	1	5	4	4

Source: Author's fieldwork.

4 per cent of the party-sponsored candidates have been women (Shastri 1995: 57–58). It is also noticed that in all the elections (except in 1983 and 1985) more than 70 per cent of the women legislators belonged to the ruling party.

A review of the educational profile of the legislators shows that a majority of them are graduates. In the first Assembly, more than 80 per cent of the legislators were graduates (see Table 8.11/Figure 8.6). The percentage declined in the subsequent years and registered an increase again since the 1980s. The marginal decline in the number of graduates among the legislators in the 1960s could have been caused by the fact that many of those involved in politics in that period had sacrificed the opportunity for higher studies in order to participate in the freedom movement.

Legislators whose educational record shows that they have completed matriculation account for around one-fourth of the legislators elected. Their strength has ranged from 15 per cent in the House elected in 1952 to 29 per cent in the 1983 Assembly.

The number of legislators who had only completed middle school accounted for around 10 per cent of the House in the 1960s and 1970s. Their number sharply declined since the 1980s. This trend is linked to yet another development. The 1960s and 1970s saw an increase in the number of legislators from the OBC and the Dalits. These social groups had limited access to education. In the years after independence, the reservation policy in the field of education and greater access to educational facilities had permitted those from the disadvantaged social groups to enroll in educational institutions in larger numbers. As a result, in the 1980s and 1990s there is a decline in the number of legislators who had only passed middle school. It is also noticed that there is tremendous variation across assemblies in the percentage of those who were middle school pass. While the average is 8.98 per cent, the STD is as high as 4.9.

Table 8.11

Educational Background of Legislators: Karnataka Legislative Assembly (%)

	1952	1957	1962	1967	1972	1978	1983	1985	1989	1994	AVG	STD
Middle School Pass	3.774	10.803	20.905	10.509	9.146	9.948	8.29	5.882	4.902	5.446	8.98	4.90
Matriculation	15.009	28.303	22.30	25.808	26.202	26.108	28.50	28.403	23.004	21.209	24.50	4.20
Graduates and above	81.103	60.803	56.706	63.503	64.603	63.807	63.201	65.609	72.006	73.207	66.60	7.10

Source: Author's fieldwork.

Figure 8.6
Educational Background of Members of Karnataka Legislative Assembly (%)

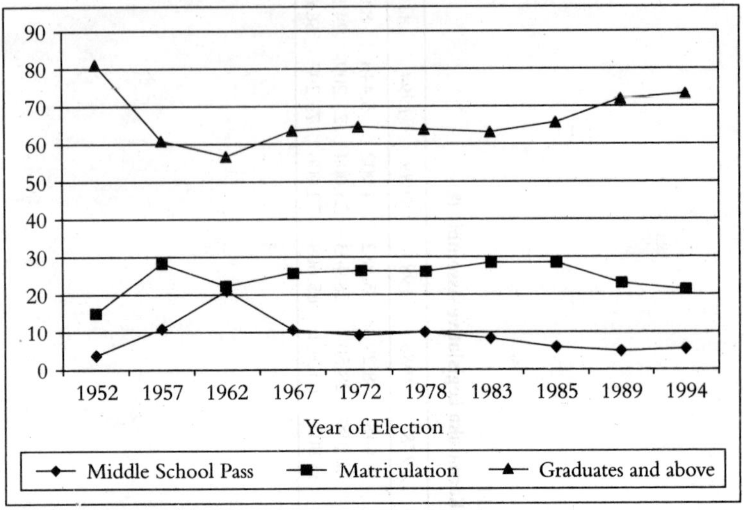

Source: Prepared by author.

Certain clear trends can be discerned with regard to the education level of the legislators in the ruling party as compared to the entire House. In the Assembly elected in 1962, the percentage of graduates among the ruling party legislators was significantly higher than their overall percentage in the House. On the other hand, the percentage of ruling party legislators who had only completed their middle school and matriculation was marginally lower as compared to their relative strength in the House. However, in the following Assembly (elected in 1967), there was a reversal of this trend. The percentage of graduates in the ruling party was significantly lower than their relative strength in the House. A higher percentage of legislators from among the opposition parties and independents were graduates as compared to the entire House. In the Assembly elected in 1978 too, the percentage of ruling party legislators who were graduates was significantly lower as compared to the percentage of graduates in the House. The percentage of graduates from among the MLAs of the principal opposition party — the Janata Party — was significantly higher.

In the assemblies elected in 1983 and 1985 (when the Janata Party formed the government), the percentage of graduates from among the ruling party was much higher as compared to their percentage in the House. However in the Assembly elected in 1994 (when once again the Janata Dal came to power), the percentage of ruling party legislators who had only completed middle school was significantly higher as compared to their percentage in the House.

Table 8.12

Age of Legislators: Karnataka Legislative Assembly (%)

	1952	1957	1962	1967	1972	1978	1983	1985	1989	1994	AVG	STD
25–35	33.3	25.2	20.4	12.4	13.8	13.4	11.4	14.6	10.5	9.35	16.4	7.63
35–45	42.4	30.5	29.3	44.1	37.4	33.7	25.9	33.0	35.9	36.9	34.9	5.66
46–55	24.2	32.8	37.6	29.9	34.5	37.1	35.3	31.1	29.7	32.2	32.5	4.0
More than 56	0	11.5	12.7	13.6	14.4	15.8	27.4	21.4	23.9	21.5	16.2	7.79

Source: Author's fieldwork.

A scrutiny of the age profile of the legislators in Karnataka shows that while one-third of the legislators are from the 36–45 age group, another one-third fall in the 46–55 age category. The youngest (less than 35) and the oldest age group (more than 56) account for the remaining one-third. While there has been a steady decline in the percentage of the younger generation of legislators (less than 35 age group) on the one hand, there has been a gradual increase in the percentage of those in the 56 and above age bracket, on the other. These two age groups have seen the maximum variation across assemblies. The average for the less than 35 age group is 16.4 per cent with a standard deviation of 7.63 while the average for the more than 56 age group is 16.2 per cent with a standard deviation of 7.79. This trend indicates that the number of younger legislators entering the House is declining while those of the older age group is on the rise. Experience appears to have more staying power than youth and fresh blood.

The age profile of the ruling party legislators reveals certain distinct trends. In the assemblies elected in 1962, the percentage of ruling party legislators who were below 35 years, was significantly lower than their strength in the House. A higher percentage of young legislators were in the opposition parties. The percentage of ruling party legislators who were about 46 years of age was much higher than their percentage in the House. The same trend continued in the Assembly elected in 1967. This can be explained in terms of the higher percentage of first-time legislators in the non-Congress parties and among the independents.

Figure 8.7
Age Profile of Legislators: Karnataka Legislative Assembly

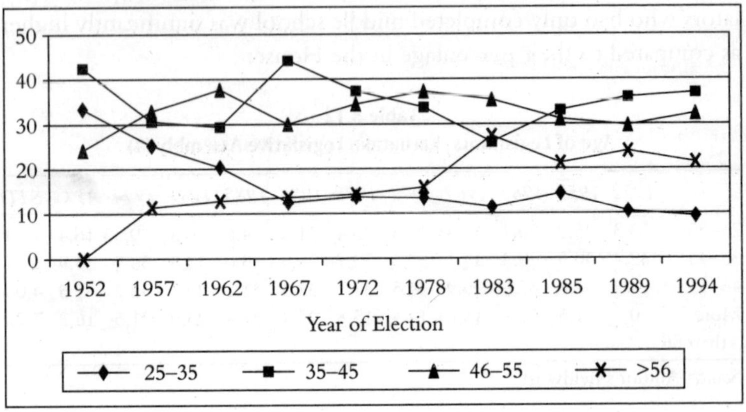

Source: Prepared by author.

Most of these legislators who were making their maiden entry into the House belonged to the younger generation.

In the Assembly elected in 1972, the percentage of ruling party legislators in the younger age group (less than 35) is significantly higher than their overall percentage in the House. A large number of ruling party legislators has been elected for the first time and this explains the high percentage of ruling party members in the younger age group.

In the assemblies elected in 1983 and 1985 (when the Janata Party came to power), the percentage of ruling party legislators who were above 46 years was much higher as compared to their percentage in the House. This was due to the fact that a significant number of those elected on the Janata Party ticket were either elected to the House on earlier occasions too or had been in the electoral fray for several years before actually winning an election. However, in the 1994 elections (when the Janata Dal came to power), the percentage of ruling party legislators who were below 35 years of age was marginally higher than their overall strength in the House.

IV

The sociological profile of Karnataka legislators is also mirrored in the composition of the Council of Ministers. In the years after the re-organisation of the then Mysore state, the Council of Ministers formed by the first three Chief Ministers — Nijalingappa, Jatti and Veerendra Patil (1957 to 1971) — saw more than half the ministers belonging to the dominant castes (also references to the ministry in Karnataka unless specifically stated are drawn from Shastri and Latha 2003). In the ministries formed under the chief ministership of Devraj Urs, the dominant castes accounted for only 37 per cent of the ministers. Even though the dominant castes accounted for half the ruling party legislators during this period, the Chief Minister ensured that their strength in the ministry was drastically reduced. On the other hand, the OBC accounted for 28 per cent of the Urs ministry. The percentage of the dominant castes in the ministry once again registered an increase with the Janata Party coming to power. In the Hegde (1983–88) and Bommai ministries (1988–89), the dominant castes accounted for more than 40 per cent of the ministers. The same trend continued in the Council of Ministers formed by the Congress chief ministers (1989–94) and those belonging to the Janata Dal (1994–99) (see Shastri and Vinod 1990, 1995).

It is also interesting to note that in the Council of Ministers formed by Nijalingappa, Jatti and Veerendra Patil, the dominant castes accounted for at least three of the five senior-most ministers. In the first phase of the chief ministership of Devraj Urs (1972–77), at least two of the five senior-most ministers were from the dominant castes. In his second term as Chief Minister (1978–82), not even one of the five senior-most ministers hailed from the dominant castes. In later years, in most of the ministries, at least two of the five senior-most ministers have been from the dominant castes.

In the Councils of Ministers formed till 1989, the forward castes accounted for more than 9 per cent of the ministry. Since 1989, they have made up less than 5 per cent of the ministry (Shastri 1990; Shastri 1995). This has been due to the increased representation accorded to the OBC and the Dalits. In the case of the representation given to the OBC in the Council of Ministers, it is clearly evident that it is registering a steady increase. If in the Nijalingappa and Jatti ministries, the OBC made up 11 per cent of the ministry, their strength rose to 16 per cent in the Veerendra Patil ministry and touched 28 per cent in the Urs ministry. In the governments formed since the 1980s, the OBC have constituted at least 22 per cent of the ministry. Till the 1960s, Dalits constituted around 10 per cent of the Council of Ministers. Since the 1970s, their strength in the ministry has risen to over 17 per cent. In the 1990s, it has touched 20 per cent.

In the Council of Ministers, the representation given to minorities has not been uniform. In some ministries, their representation has been as low as 5 per cent and they have at times accounted for 12 per cent of the ministry. In the 1990s, the representation to the minorities in the ministry has been in the range of 8 to 10 per cent.

The display of 'tokenism' by political parties, on issues relating to women's representation, is also reflected in the formation of the Council of Ministers in the state. Never has the Cabinet had more than one women minister and in most cases women have accounted for less than 8 per cent of the Council of Ministers. Even in the distribution of portfolios, women have mostly been given welfare related ministries and have rarely been assigned core or development ministries. The Karnataka experience clearly shows that the argument made by political parties that reservation for women in the local bodies would, as a natural corollary, result in a larger number of women moving on to state and national politics, does not stand the test of experience. Active participation by women in the process of governance has essentially been limited to local government. The decision-makers within political parties have sidelined women aspirants for the party ticket for elections to the Legislative Assembly on the grounds that their 'winnability' would be adversely affected, and also due to the pressure of local forces and the impact of local tactics.

If the professional background of the ministers is taken into account it is noticed that the percentage of lawyers has witnessed a slight fall in successive ministries while the number of agriculturists has been registering a sharp increase. It is also of crucial significance that lawyers and agriculturists taken together, account for 80 per cent of the ministers in all the ministries formed in Karnataka.

V

The analysis of the social and political profile of legislators of the Karnataka Legislative Assembly, as undertaken in the preceding sections, point out clear trends and patterns.

The voters in Karnataka have, over the years, demonstrated their political preference in a definitive and unambiguous way. A clear mandate has been given by the voters in every election. The Assembly elected in 1983 was clearly a 'House in transition' and was dissolved within two years of its constitution making way for a new Assembly in which the Janata Party had a clear majority. The House has also witnessed a relative stability in its tenure.

The role of the dominant castes in Karnataka politics is strikingly mirrored in the composition of the Assembly. The two dominant castes — the Lingayats and the Vokkaligas — have accounted for half the legislators ever since the reorganisation of the state in 1957. This is in spite of the fact that they account for around a quarter of the population of the state. The forward castes, too, have a higher percentage of representation in the legislature when compared to their share of the state population. This skewed representation of the dominant and forward castes has been at the cost of the OBC. Though the OBC account for over 30 per cent of the state's population, their strength in the legislature has never crossed 14 per cent. The study also reveals a significant variation in the percentage of dominant caste/forward caste legislators in the ruling party. Though Devraj Urs attempted to organise the OBC under his leadership, he was only able to marginally reduce their percentage in the ruling party and in the House. It must be, however, stressed that Urs attempted to limit the influence of the dominant and forward castes by according those who belonged to these social groups a reduced role and position in the Council of Ministers. However, since the 1980s, the dominant castes have re-asserted their position in state politics, and this is apparent both from the composition of the Assembly and of the Council of Ministers.

References and Select Bibliography

Cheluva Raju, K. H., R. L. M. Patil, Sandeep Shastri and M. J. Vinod. 1983. *Karnataka Assembly Elections: A Post Election Survey*. Bangalore: Bangalore University.

Galanter, Marc. 1978. 'Who are the Other Backward Classes? An Introduction to a Constitutional Puzzle', *Economic and Political Weekly*, 13 (43–44): 1812–28.

Government of Karnataka. 1977. *25 Years of Elections in Karnataka 1952–77*. Bangalore: Department of Personnel and Administrative Reforms (DPAR).

———. 1983. *Election Statistics of General Elections 1983*. Bangalore: DPAR.

———. 1985. *Election Statistics of General Elections 1985*. Bangalore: DPAR.

———. 1993. *Election Statistics of General Elections 1989*. Bangalore: DPAR.

———. 1994. *10th Karnataka Legislative Assembly: Details Results*. Bangalore: DPAR.

Government of Karnataka. 1996. *Election Statistics of General Elections 1996*. Bangalore: DPAR.

———. 1998. *Election Statistics of General Elections 1998*. Bangalore: DPAR.

———. 1999. *Election Statistics of General Elections 1999*. Bangalore: DPAR.

Patil, R. L. M. and Sandeep Shastri. 1994. 'Karnataka: A Profile of Major Issues and the Electoral Scene', *Indian Journal of Political Science*, 55 (3): 241–50.

Shastri, Sandeep. 1994. 'Elections to the Lok Sabha from Karnataka (1952–1991): An Analysis of the Voting Pattern and Electoral Behaviour', *Indian Journal of Parliamentary Information*, 30 (47): 7–19.

———. 1995. *Towards Explaining the Voters Mandate: An Analysis of the Karnataka Assembly Elections 1994*. Bangalore: Vinayaka Publishers.

———. 1999a. 'Emergence of Bi-Polar Alliance System in Karnataka', *Economic and Political Weekly*, 34 (34–35): 2440–48.

———. 1999b. 'Beyond Vital Statistics', *Deccan Herald* (Bangalore), 22 October.

———. 2000. Electoral Politics in Karnataka in the 1990s: An Overview. *Karnataka Journal of Politics*, 1 (1): 55–71.

Shastri, Sandeep and M. J. Vinod. 1991. 'Dynamics of Electoral Politics: A Case Study of the Karnataka Assembly Elections 1989', *Indian Journal of Social Science*, 4 (3): 287–406.

Shastri, Sandeep and Mary Latha. 2008 (forthcoming). 'Politics of Ministry Making in Karnataka', *Karnataka Journal of Politics*.

9

Two Dominant Castes: The Socio-political System in Andhra Pradesh

*Anne Vaugier-Chatterjee**

M ore than 60 years after independence, the Indian political class still relies on caste identities to organise its power at the local, state and central level. The question asked almost 40 years ago in Rajni Kothari's pioneering study on caste and politics in India: 'What form is caste taking under the impact of modern politics and what form is politics taking in a caste-oriented society?' has not lost its relevance, and the importance of the subject hardly needs to be argued (Kothari 1970).

This chapter focuses on the political elite of Andhra Pradesh, looking at the sociological background of the elected members of the 10 successive legislative assemblies since independence for which extensive data has been collected.[1] This is not a totally unexplored ground. The role of caste in Andhra politics has indeed been a subject of inquiry for many decades for both Indian and foreign scholars. In this process, naturally, divergent views have been expressed. One view is that caste — and caste alone — is the main factor in the politics of the state. Another is that the influence of caste has to be balanced by a number of other factors at play which relativise its importance in the political arena.[2]

No extensive empirical research has, however, been carried out so far on legislators in Andhra Pradesh. To my knowledge, the only endeavour in this regard was made by a political scientist from Andhra Pradesh,

---

* The ideas expressed in this chapter are the author's own and not of the organisation she belongs to.
[1] The data presented here are for the years 1957, 1962, 1967, 1972, 1978, 1983, 1985, 1989, 1994 and 1999. No *Who's Who* were, however, available before 1972.
[2] Selig Harrison's analysis (1956) on caste and politics in Andhra Pradesh was representative of the first school of thought. His tendency to oversimplify the political game by over-emphasising the caste factor was criticised by several scholars. Among them, Elliot (1970) and Srinivas (2000) share this view, as also G. Ram Reddy in his general observations on caste and state politics in India.

who, in 1972, took the fourth Assembly (1967–72) as a case-study (see Kistaiah 1972). This is the first baseline study covering all assemblies since independence following G. Ram Reddy's analysis of the political evolution of Andhra Pradesh up to the mid-1980s, looking into the three tiers of governance (Reddy 1989).

The present chapter is mainly based on the data published in the *Who's Who* of the Vidhan Sabhas, available from 1972 onwards. For the first three assemblies (1955, 1962 and 1967), we relied on other sources, namely, the lists available at the Legislative Assembly and the district records. The process of the collection of data itself seemed to support the divergent views on the subject referred to above, that is, though caste is a very present and dominant factor in the social and political fabric of Andhra Pradesh, the scarcity of records on the subject may indicate that its political institutionalisation may not be as powerful as in the northern states of India.

Contours of the Social Context of Andhra Pradesh

Before going into the caste profile of the political class of Andhra Pradesh, we should briefly survey the broad caste and communal composition of the state. The five-fold stratification of society that one sees elsewhere in India also prevails in the state. Reliable data on the caste composition of the population is not available after Census 1931 except for the Scheduled Castes. So the figures presented here have been obtained by projections of the 1931 data and can only be taken as estimates.

Among the upper castes, the Brahmins constitute a minority, only 3 per cent of the population of the state. Occupying important posts in the British administration, they dominated the political scene before independence and till the mid-1950s. The Vaishyas, traditionally engaged in trade and business, constitute another 3 per cent. The Kshatriyas, called Rajus in Andhra Pradesh, are a mere 1 per cent and geographically confined to the northern and central coastal region.

The dominant intermediary castes are the most important social group. They are mainly represented by the agricultural caste of Reddys, Kammas, Velamas and Kapus. Their economic and educational advancement in the early 20th century has enabled them to challenge the Brahmin dominance in the cultural and political spheres. While

Table 9.1
General Caste and Community Composition of Andhra Pradesh

Category	Caste/Community	Estimated Percentage of Total Population
Upper Castes	Brahmin	3
	Vaishya	3
Intermediate Castes	Kamma	5
	Reddy	8
	Raju	1
	Velama	3
	Kapu	9
Backward Classes	OBC	36
Lower Castes	SC	16
Scheduled Tribes	ST	6
Others	Muslims	8
	Others	2
TOTAL		100

Source: Survey by author.

the Reddys (about 8 per cent of the population), spread out throughout the state, are predominantly in the southern Andhra districts, the Rayalaseema and the Telangana areas, the Kammas are concentrated in the deltaic region covering the districts of Nellore, Chittoor, Anantapur and Khammam. The Kammas of coastal Andhra spearheaded the anti-Brahmin movement from the 1920s onwards. The Reddys and the Velamas of the Telangana region were landlords and pillars of a feudal order. In coastal Andhra, a large number of zamindars were Velamas.

Another significant social group is that of the Kapus (also known under different names such as Telaga, Naidu, Balija, Munnuru Kapu). Their position in the social hierarchy epitomises the struggle between the intermediary castes and the OBC.[3]

The Other Backward Classes (OBC), comprising between 38 and 46 per cent of the population, are an important component of the state's population. Out of the 50 odd Backward Castes listed by the government, the major ones identified among the regional political

---

[3] G. Ram Reddy (1989) notes that in Andhra Pradesh, the Kapus who are considered for-ward in certain districts of coastal Andhra (east Godavari, west Godavari, Krishna and Guntur), as well as in most districts of Rayalaseema are considered to belong to the backward castes in Telangana.

elite are the Yadava, Gowda, Thoorpu Kapu, Kalinga, Padmasali, Boya and Besta.

These castes have been classified into four groups by the government for reservations in education and employment (see Government of India 1993).[4] Their numerical strength and collective political and economic interests have become increasingly visible in the last two decades. Some assert that they are in a position today to challenge the social dominance of the traditional land-owning castes in the rural areas.

The Scheduled Castes (SC), constituting 15.5 per cent of the population, have also emerged as a politically significant group. The two most numerous ones, the Malas and the Madigas, are present all over the state. Madigas are numerically more (55.2 per cent) than the Malas (44.8 per cent), but the latter are better placed in terms of education, employment and political power.[5]

Andhra Pradesh also has an important tribal population of 6 per cent, largely concentrated in the forest areas. Last but not the least, the Muslims count for about 8 per cent of the population. They are found mainly in the Telangana and the Rayalaseema regions.

Previous research on the parliamentarians of Andhra Pradesh, published in the mid-1980s, has shown how, both in the period before and after independence, the so-called ' politics of accommodation' followed by the Congress party ensured the continuity of the dominant groups (see Weiner 1967). It was noted at that time that accommodation and co-option were achieved despite sharp economic differences within the forward castes and despite the increasing politicisation of the back-ward and lower castes (see Reddy and Sharma 1979: 26–33).[6] The extension of patronage by the dominant castes (who possessed state power) to leaders of disadvantaged groups encouraged competition among the latter and prevented them from combining to establish a new unified political formation with a view to implementing structural changes.

---

[4] Please note that the term used for 'OBC' in Andhra Pradesh is 'Backward Classes' (BC).

[5] For an anthropological presentation of Malas and Madigas in Andhra Pradesh, see Rao (1998).

[6] It should be mentioned here that the classical caste division made in Andhra Pradesh is between Forward Castes and Backward Castes. The Forward Castes comprise the Brahmin, Kapus, Kamma, Reddys, Komati, Kshatriya, Velama, while the Backward Castes are those that are classified as OBC.

The heterogeneous composition of the state, clearly trifurcated between the Andhra, the Telangana and the Rayalaseema regions, is also
one among the factors put forward to explain this resistance to change.

Political History

The present state of Andhra Pradesh was formed in November 1956
by merging the nine Telengana districts of the Hyderabad state with
the four Rayalaseema districts and the seven Circar districts of the erstwhile Andhra Pradesh (Andhra at that time was only three years old.
In 1953, the Telugu-speaking districts of the Madras Presidency were
carved out of it after an agitation by the Telugu-speaking people for a
separate state of their own).

As in other Indian states, the political system of Andhra Pradesh is
characterised by the interplay of four factors: caste, faction, party and
region. The political space is divided into three main regions: Andhra,
Rayalaseema and Telangana — all Telugu-speaking, historically
developed entities with distinct characteristics that provide three sub-
arenas within the state. Two major parties have dominated the political
landscape of Andhra Pradesh so far, i.e., the Congress party and the
Telugu Desam Party (TDP).

The politics of Andhra Pradesh remained a Congress bastion till
1983. In the first five assemblies (1955–57, 1962, 1967, 1972 and 1978),
the Congress was voted to power with a clear mandate. The members
of the first Assembly (1955–62) were allowed a seven-year term (that
is to say in 1957, elections were conducted in the newly added region
of Telangana alone and then the 1962 general elections were held for
the state as a whole). Despite the powerful presence of the Communist
Party in Telangana, the Congress majority, in the state as a whole,
increased year after year. On the eve of the 1962 general elections,
only the Congress party, the Communist Party and the Swatantra Party
were represented in the House. In 1962, in the third Assembly, the
Congress won 177 out of 300 seats, but because of defections from the
Swatantra Party and the Independents it increased its strength to 215.
The same process was at play in the fourth Assembly (1967–72) where
the Congress party started with 165 seats and finally ended up with 230
seats out of a total of 287. In the fifth Assembly (1972–78), the Congress
won 219 seats at the beginning and finished with 243 of 287 seats (by
then of course, the Indian National Congress had split).

In the sixth Assembly, the Congress(I) got an absolute majority and the other Congress suffered defeat. Also, for the first time, a second party, the Janata Party was recognised officially as an opposition party in Andhra Pradesh.

After 25 years of unchallenged Congress rule, the TDP, a regional party founded in 1982, reigned over the state politics from 1983 onwards (except for a few years between 1989 and 1994), and is still in power today. The TDP, elected in a landslide victory in 1983, came back to power in 1985, was defeated in 1989, re-elected consecutively in 1994 and 1999, and lost the 2004 state Assembly elections. In 2004, a strong anti-incumbency wave brought the Congress party back to power in a landslide victory. As in most other Indian states, politics in Andhra Pradesh thus evolved from a one-party dominant system to a competitive two-party system.

There have been other players on the Andhra Pradesh political scene whose presence though less steady over the period considered here, still needs notice. The Communist Party was well entrenched in Andhra Pradesh even before the creation of the state in its present form. The party came into existence in the 1930s, formed essentially, but not exclusively, by members of the Kamma community. Till the late 1930s, it did not work as a proper party but propagated its ideology among the agriculturists. It was actually during the war that, with the support of the British, it could build up its strength. Banned by the Nizam in 1946, they entrenched themselves in a few districts like Nalgonda, Warangal and Khammam in the Telangana region and formed parallel governments in rural areas.

They later spearheaded the movement in favour of linguistic states and became central actors in the politics of Andhra Pradesh by 1953. In the newly created Andhra, the Communist Party of India (CPI) formed the main opposition in the Legislative Assembly. However, unlike in West Bengal and Kerala, belying all predictions, the CPI could never form a government in Andhra Pradesh. In the early 1950s, it had become a powerful force in state politics, second only to the Congress party. Though it was hoped that it would gain further strength in the mid-term elections in 1955, the adoption of a socialist programme by the Congress and the formation of a separate state for Andhra took away much of its emotional appeal. Further, the terrorist activities of some of them in the Telangana region alienated sections of the electorate.

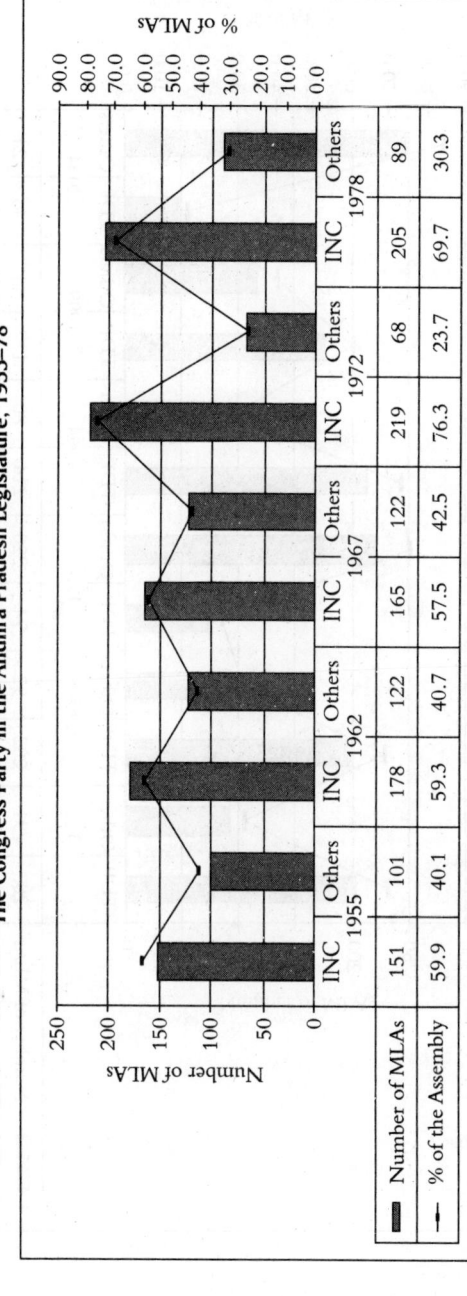

Figure 9.1
The Congress Party in the Andhra Pradesh Legislature, 1955–78

	1955		1962		1967		1972		1978	
	INC	Others	INC	Others	INC	Others	INC	Others	INC	Others
Number of MLAs	151	101	178	122	165	122	219	68	205	89
% of the Assembly	59.9	40.1	59.3	40.7	57.5	42.5	76.3	23.7	69.7	30.3

Source: Prepared by author.

Figure 9.2
The Telugu Desam Party in the Andhra Pradesh Legislature, 1983–2004

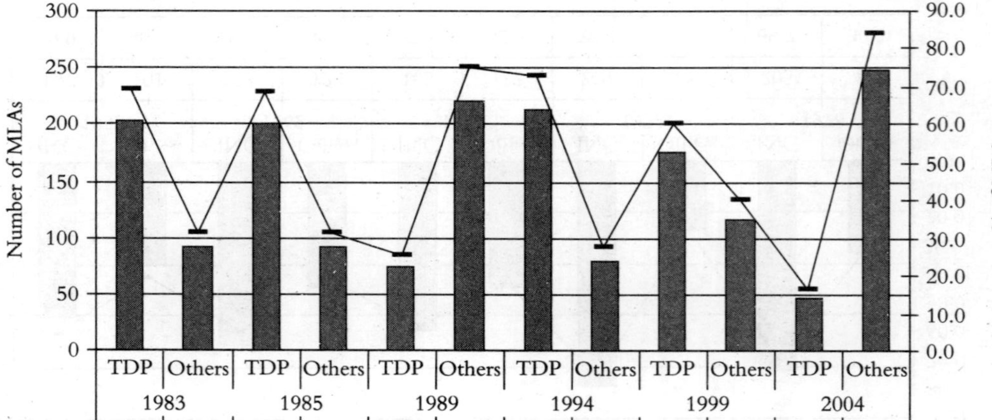

	1983 TDP	1983 Others	1985 TDP	1985 Others	1989 TDP	1989 Others	1994 TDP	1994 Others	1999 TDP	1999 Others	2004 TDP	2004 Others
Number of MLAs	203	91	202	92	74	220	214	80	177	117	46	248
% of MLAs	69.0	31.0	68.7	31.3	25.2	74.8	72.8	27.2	60.2	39.8	16.0	84.0

Source: Prepared by author.

The strongholds of the CPI in Andhra Pradesh are still today the districts of Nalgonda, Guntur, Krishna and Khammam in the Telangana and the coastal Andhra regions. However, from 1969 onwards, its strength has rapidly declined in the state. This can be explained by both the progressive disappearance of ideological distinction between the Congress and the Communist parties as also factionalism and splits within the communist group.

The Swatantra Party was as short-lived in Andhra Pradesh as in the other states of India. Its forerunner, the Krishikar Lok Party (KLP), in the early 1950s before the formation of Andhra Pradesh, represented one-tenth of the Assembly with 15 representatives out of a total of 140. In the first Assembly elections in 1955, it scored rather well, winning 22 seats of a 140-strong Assembly. The Swatantra Party emerged in Andhra Pradesh in 1959 but could not attract a single member from the Congress. In 1962, it contested for more seats (140) out of a 300-member Assembly but won only 19, thus declining marginally. In 1967, it won 29 of 287 seats. Basically reduced to a single leader, N. G. Ranga, it suffered from an over-personalisation of power.

The Muslim minority (8 per cent of the total population of the state) has played a significant role in certain parliamentary constituencies, particularly urban ones since 1956. The most influential Muslim party was, and still is, the Majlis-e-Ittehadul-e-Muslimeen (MIM) which started out in the 1930s as a religious organisation for preserving unity among different Muslims and symbolised eventually the traditionalist urban political identity of Hyderabad's Muslims. In 1949, the Majlis was dissolved to be revived almost a decade later under the leadership of Abdul Wahib Owaisi who constituted the All-India Majlis-e-Ittehadul Muslimeen (MIM) in 1958.

Over two decades (1962–78), the MIM managed to increase its strength from one to three MLAs. In 1985, it had four seats, all in the Telangana region, and maintained its number in 1989 even though a new majority party came to be in the Assembly. In the two assemblies in 1994 and 1999, the MIM maintained its hold in Hyderabad even though it was challenged by another Muslim formation, i.e., the Majlis Bachao Tahreek (MBT). Sociologically, the Majlis representatives are from the highly educated Muslim upper classes. The legacy of Owaisi is still present in the state, the power having been taken over by his descendants.

The last group that deserves mention here is the Telangana Praja Samithi (TPS). This is a regional party within the state, a sub-regional manifestation of regionalism as it were, the activities of which were confined to the Telangana region. It added a new dimension to the already complex structure of Indian politics by rejecting both region and language as the basis of political reorganisation, insisting on the significance of a historical identity alone as the only criterion of a political existence. The existence of TPS was ephemeral. It emerged as an agitation in 1969 and was transformed on the eve of the Lok Sabha elections. The recent revival of the Telangana separatist movement, instrumental in the downfall of the TDP in the 2004 elections, might make it a force to reckon with in the coming decade.

Caste/Party Realignments in Andhra Pradesh since the 1950s

As in other Indian states, the political leadership of the nationalist movement, spearheaded by the Congress, was provided by the Brahmins in Andhra Pradesh. Though the Brahmins are numerically a very small minority — about 3 per cent of the state's population — they were, until the early 1950s, heavily represented in most political parties, particularly in the Congress and the Communist parties. But within a decade after independence, the political leadership was taken up by the intermediary land-owning classes, the Reddys and the Kammas. Indeed in that crucial decade, even if the leadership of the Congress party was in the hands of the Brahmins, the latter did not act as a homogeneous group. By following their individual trajectories, they helped to jeopardise the consolidation of their power as a group.

This evolution appears clearly in the general tables on the caste background of the MLAs. One notices therein a steady decrease in the number of upper castes, in particular the Brahmins, in the composition of the 10 successive legislative assemblies that were formed between 1957 and 1999. The decline of their presence is particularly noticeable from 1978 onwards (see Figures 9.3 and 9.4).

Overwhelmingly represented in the first two assemblies of 1957 and 1962, the Brahmins thereafter rapidly became less present in the political arena. The dominance of the upper castes reached its peak in 1962. Political interest obviously preceded economic interest (Bernstorff 1998).

Figure 9.3
Average Representation of Andhra Pradesh MLAs (caste-wise), 1955–2004

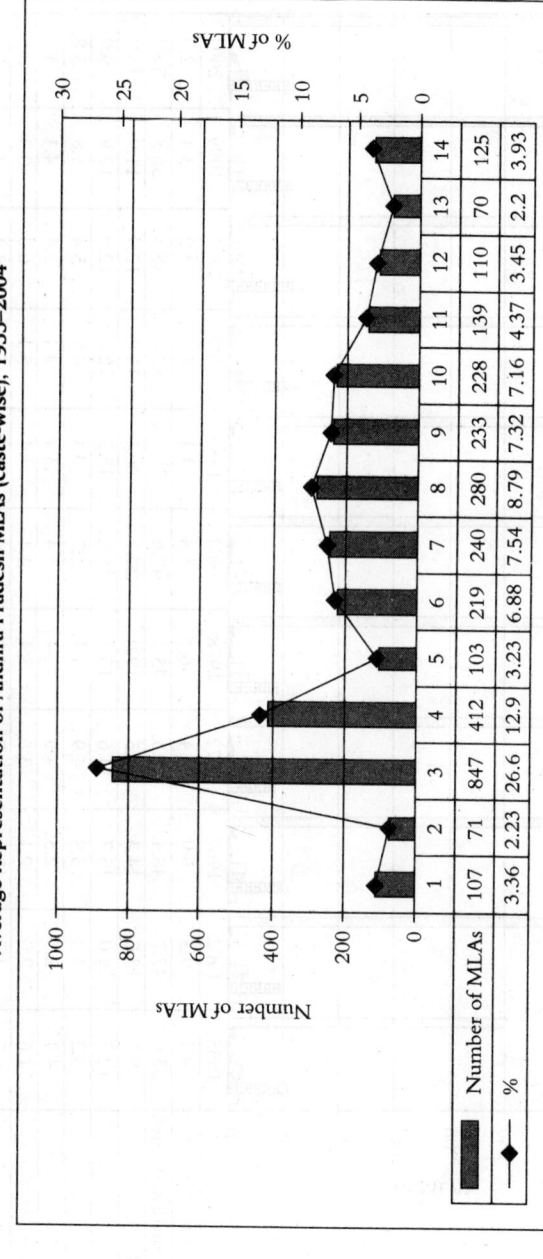

	1	2	3	4	5	6	7	8	9	10	11	12	13	14
Number of MLAs	107	71	847	412	103	219	240	280	233	228	139	110	70	125
%	3.36	2.23	26.6	12.9	3.23	6.88	7.54	8.79	7.32	7.16	4.37	3.45	2.2	3.93

Source: Prepared by author.

Note: 1 = Brahmin; 2 = Vaishya; 3 = Reddy; 4 = Kamma; 5 = Raju; 6 = Other Peasant Proprietors; 7 = Peasant OBC; 8 = Other OBC; 9 = Mala; 10 = SC; 11 = ST; 12 = Muslim; 13 = Others; 14 = NA.

Figure 9.4
Caste Composition of Andhra Pradesh Assemblies, 1955–2004

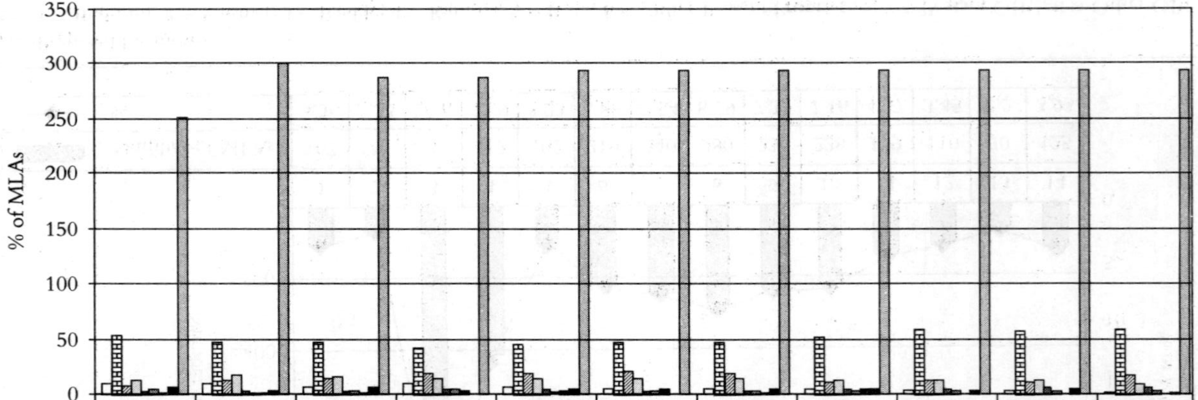

	1955	1962	1967	1972	1978	1983	1985	1989	1994	1999	2004
Upper Castes	9.1	9.3	5.9	9.4	6.1	4.8	4.4	4.4	3.2	3.4	2.0
Intermediate Castes	53.6	47.7	48.4	42.5	45.2	47.6	46.9	52.0	58.5	56.8	59.2
OBC	8.7	13.0	14.3	19.5	19.0	20.7	20.1	11.9	12.9	11.9	18.3
SC	12.7	18.0	15.7	14.6	15.3	15.6	15.3	12.6	12.9	12.9	9.9
ST	3.2	4.0	3.8	4.9	4.4	2.7	3.1	4.8	5.4	5.8	5.8
Muslims	4.4	2.3	2.5	4.9	2.4	3.4	3.4	4.1	3.4	4.1	3.4
Others	1.6	2.0	2.1	3.5	3.4	4.4	1.4	5.1	0.3	0.3	0.0
NA	6.7	3.7	7.3	0.7	4.2	0.8	5.4	5.1	3.4	4.8	1.4
TOTAL	252	300	287	287	294	294	294	294	294	294	294

Source: Prepared by author.

Table 9.2
Disaggregated Caste Composition of Andhra Pradesh Assemblies since 1955 (%)

Caste	1955	1962	1967	1972	1978	1983	1985	1989	1994	1999	2004
Brahmin	5.6	7.3	4.9	6.3	3.7	2.0	1.7	1.7	1.7	1.4	1.0
Vaishya	3.6	2.0	1.0	3.1	2.4	2.7	2.7	2.7	1.4	2.0	1.0
Reddy	34.9	27.7	25.1	22.0	24.1	25.9	22.8	28.9	26.2	23.8	32.3
Kamma	6.7	12.7	13.2	12.5	14.6	16.0	16.3	5.1	16.0	16.7	11.6
Raju	5.6	1.7	3.5	3.5	4.8	2.4	2.7	3.7	3.1	2.7	2.4
Other Peasant Proprietors	6.3	5.7	6.6	4.5	1.7	3.4	5.1	14.3	13.3	13.6	12.9
Peasant OBC	3.2	6.7	7.0	12.2	8.5	10.9	9.2	6.1	6.1	10.5	11.3
Other OBC	5.6	6.3	7.3	7.3	10.5	9.9	10.9	5.8	6.8	1.4	7.0
Mala	7.5	6.0	5.9	3.8	11.6	12.2	10.5	3.7	11.9	7.1	0
Other SC	5.2	12.0	9.8	10.8	3.7	3.4	4.8	8.8	1.0	5.8	9.9
Other ST	3.2	4.0	3.8	4.9	4.4	2.7	3.1	4.8	5.4	5.8	5.8
Muslims	4.4	2.3	2.4	4.9	2.4	3.4	3.4	4.1	3.4	4.1	3.4
Others	1.6	2.0	2.1	3.5	3.4	4.4	1.4	5.1	0.3	0.3	0
NA	6.7	3.7	7.3	0.7	4.1	0.7	5.4	5.1	3.4	4.8	1.4
TOTAL	100.1	100.1	99.9	100.0	99.9	100.0	100.0	99.9	100.0	100.0	100.0
	(N=252)	(N=300)	(N=287)	(N=287)	(N=294)	(N=294)	(N=294)	(N=294)	(N=294)	(N=294)	(N=294)

Source: Survey by author.

To evaluate the presence of Brahmins partywise, in 1962, 60 per cent of the elected Brahmins belonged to the Congress party and 20 per cent to the CPI. The remaining 20 per cent were equally divided between the Independents and the Swatantra Party. If one looks at the regional break-up, the Brahmins elected to the Assembly mainly belonged to the coastal Andhra region. In 1962, the Brahmins constituting a mere 3.4 per cent of the Congress elected members were in perfect accord with their share in the population of the state. That proportion was more or less maintained in 1967 when they represented 3 per cent of the elected members of the Congress party. This Brahmin dominance also had an impact on party affiliations. It has been argued that in reaction, members of the Kamma and the Reddy castes joined the Communist Party, aptly referred to by Selig Harrison as the 'Kamreds' (quoted in Khan 1969). The first notable decrease in the Brahmin share to 3.3 per cent of the Assembly seats was in 1972. It was then that the effort to democratise the political sphere bore tangible fruits.

If we take a look at the sociological background of the Legislative Assembly members of Andhra Pradesh over a decade (1962–72), there seems to be no radical change in the caste composition of the Assembly. In 1967, the upper castes and the intermediary castes represented 55 per cent of the MLAs, and the Reddys with 25 per cent were the single largest caste in the legislature, way ahead of the Kammas who formed 11.8 per cent. One of the advantages that the Reddys had (and still have) in the struggle for political dominance in Andhra is that they are distributed in all three regions of the state. This gives them an edge over the Kammas who form the second largest caste group but are mainly concentrated in the Circar districts, have a little base in Rayalaseema, and none in the Andhra region.

A general observation that can be made regarding the decade between 1962 and 1972 is that in the upper caste category, the share of Brahmins and Vaishyas declined. Within the dominant intermediary castes, the share of the Velmas and the Kammas increased at the expense of the Reddys. The latter had held 37.7 per cent of the seats in the 1962 Assembly and only 27.7 per cent in 1972. In the 1970s on the whole the most visible trend was the transfer of power from the upper to the intermediary castes (see Figure 9.5).

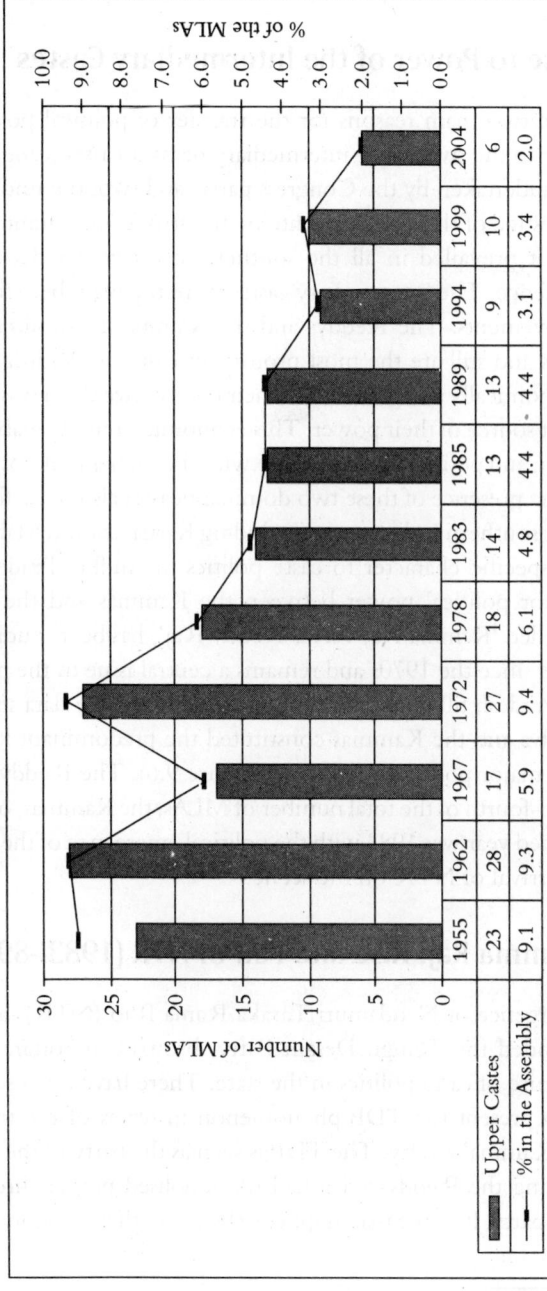

Figure 9.5

Representation of the Upper Castes in the Andhra Pradesh Assemblies, 1955–2004

	1955	1962	1967	1972	1978	1983	1985	1989	1994	1999	2004
Upper Castes	23	28	17	27	18	14	13	13	9	10	6
% in the Assembly	9.1	9.3	5.9	9.4	6.1	4.8	4.4	4.4	3.1	3.4	2.0

Source: Prepared by author.

The Rise to Power of the Intermediary Castes

There are two main reasons for the transfer of political power from the upper to the two major intermediary peasant castes. One, the land reforms undertaken by the Congress party, and two, the undermining of the prestige of the Brahman elite by the strong anti-Brahmin sentiments that prevailed in all the southern states in the decades after independence. The intermediary castes were the main beneficiaries of these movements. The Reddys and the Kammas in Andhra were in the 1950s and still are the most prominent castes in Andhra Pradesh, both economically and politically. Their control over land was the most important source of their power. This economic strength enabled them to bargain, and politically, to mediate with the higher ranks of the hierarchy. The presence of these two dominant castes also to be found in a few other southern Indian states (including Karnataka and Maharashtra) gives its specific character to caste politics in Andhra Pradesh.[7] The struggle for political power between the Kammas and the Reddys, aptly labelled 'Kamma Raj versus Reddy Raj', has been studied at the local level since the 1970s and remains a central issue in the politics of Andhra Pradesh till today. Uptil the late 60s, available data shows that the Reddys and the Kammas constituted the predominant leadership in all the major political parties (see Figure 9.6). The Reddys formed about one-fourth of the total number of MLAs, the Kammas, one-sixth. A watershed year was 1983 with the political emergence of the Kammas and the arrival of NTR on the scene.

The Kamma Raj: Rise and Fall of NTR (1983–89)

The emergence of Nandamuri Taraka Rama Rao (NTR), a Kamma who founded the Telugu Desam Party, brought important changes in the nature of caste politics in the state. There have been several attempts to present the TDP phenomenon in terms of the traditional 'Reddy–Kamma' rivalry. The TDP is seen as the party of the Kammas antagonising the Reddys who had monopolised power through the Congress party. It is true that in spite of the rise of their economic power

---

[7] See Chapter 8 on Karnataka and Chapter 7 on Maharashtra in this volume.

Figure 9.6

Representation of Two Main Castes within the Major Parties in the Successive Assemblies of Andhra Pradesh, 1955–2004

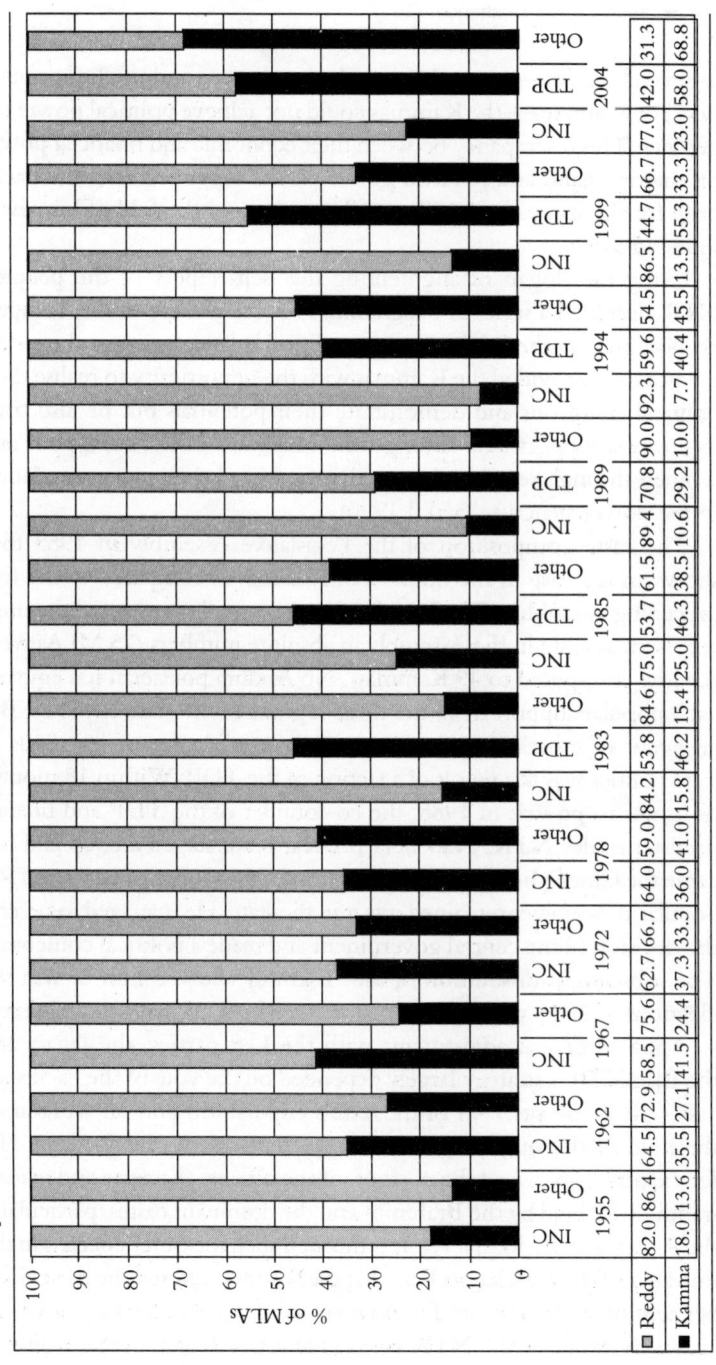

Source: Prepared by author.

in several sectors — agriculture, industry, cinema and the liquor business, for example — the Kammas could not achieve political power for decades. This discrepancy between their economic and financial power on the one hand and political power on the other provides the backdrop for the success of NTR in rallying them in the fold of his newly founded party.

Using the slogan of augmenting the 'self-respect of the people', NTR unfolded a series of programmes for the welfare of the Telugus. By doing so, he altered the existing political balance amongst the castes. He not only provided the Kammas with the opportunity to realise their political ambitions and demonstrate their potentials but he also tried to create a support base amongst the backward castes, rural poor and women through several schemes that facilitated their accommodation in the power structure (Vakil 1990).

The caste composition of the Legislative Assembly in 1983 thus shows an increase in the number of Kammas as compared to the five preceding assemblies. The Reddys, however, still constituted the most represented caste in the Assembly in absolute numbers (75 MLAs were Reddys as opposed to 49 Kammas). No Andhra politician has enjoyed such popular support in all the three regions of the state as NTR. But an event of critical importance in the consolidation of his status in state politics was the revolt of a faction of the TDP. Within 18 months of its rise to power, in 1985, the co-founder of the TDP and finance minister under NTR, Nadendla Bhaskar Rao, staged a coup and became the Chief Minister with the support of the Congress party. NTR's popularity however remained intact in the state. He managed to reverse the decision of the central government and made a political comeback. The subsequent dissolution of the Assembly allowed him to win the elections of 1985 with a huge majority. (The TDP bagged 202 seats.)

Apart from seat adjustments with the Left parties, the Janata and the BJP, NTR's strategy largely depended on the vote of the backward castes (40 to 50 per cent of the state's population) and on weakening the hold of the other dominant castes, particularly the Reddys. He, for example, abolished the posts of village officers (*karanam* and *munsif*) traditionally held by the Brahmins and the dominant castes, particularly the Reddys, at the local level. It is through such measures effected in the third tier of the Panchayati Raj, that the Reddys suffered the most. Fifty per cent of the local posts, for instance, were reserved for the backward classes by order of the NTR government (see Kohli 1988). A glance at the caste background of the Congress and TDP MLAs in the 1985 Assembly highlights the major changes in their social background.

Table 9.3
Caste Affiliation of INC MLAs, 1955–99 (%)

Caste	1955	1962	1967	1972	1978	1983	1985	1989	1994	1999	2004
Upper Castes	11.9	7.3	5.5	7.3	6.3	6.7	6.0	5.5	–	2.2	3.3
Intermediate Castes	51.0	46.1	48.5	40.6	43.9	35.0	52.0	53.6	76.9	65.6	60.8
OBC	6.0	9.6	13.3	21.0	17.6	31.7	20.0	11.6	7.7	13.3	17.4
ST and SC	16.6	26.4	21.8	22.8	21.5	21.7	12.0	18.2	11.5	13.3	16.3
Muslims and Others	14.6	10.7	10.9	8.2	10.7	5.0	10.0	11.0	3.8	5.6	2.2
TOTAL	101.0	101.0	100.0	99.9	100.0	101.0	100.0	99.9	99.9	100.0	100.0

Source: Survey by author.

In 1983, if we look at the TDP caste membership, an important section of those elected belonged to the backward castes. Foremost in importance are the intermediary caste groups. There is very little representation from the upper castes. Apparently, the selection of the candidates was made according to the numerical strength of a particular caste in a particular region and was not specifically confined to the Kamma caste.

Table 9.4
Caste Affiliation of TDP MLAs, 1983–2004 (%)

Caste	1983	1985	1989	1994	1999	2004
Upper Castes	4.9	4.5	4.1	3.7	2.3	0.0
Intermediate Castes	52.2	47.5	59.5	57.5	55.9	47.0
OBC	18.7	21.8	12.2	18.2	11.9	33.0
ST and SC	17.7	19.3	16.2	17.3	21.5	20.0
Muslims and Others	6.4	6.9	8.1	3.3	8.5	0.0
TOTAL	99.9	100.0	101.0	100.0	101.0	100.0

Source: Survey by author.

The TDP seemed to have a strategy to effect an alliance between dominant caste groups and backward classes. It, therefore, depended heavily on the numerical strength of these groups in contrast to the Congress(I)'s dependence on the traditionally separate associations of upper caste groups on the one hand, and the SC and ST on the other.

Tables 9.3 and 9.4 for the year 1985 show that the power structure in terms of recruitment of the MLAs is tilted in favour of the upper and intermediary castes. The Reddys constitute the largest group with 24.83 per cent, followed by the Kammas with 17 per cent. Clubbed together, the Velamas, Kapus, Rajus, Brahmins and Vaishyas represent 15 per cent. Among the lower castes, the backward classes account for a mere 19.72 per cent followed by the SC (13.6 per cent) and ST (4.76 per cent).

Party-wise speaking, the data reveals interesting trends. Among the 202 TDP legislators, the Kammas with 20.70 per cent and the Reddys with 18.8 per cent dominate. The Kapus and Velmas come next with 5.95 per cent and 5.44 per cent respectively. The remaining 6 per cent is shared by the Vaishyas, the Brahmins, the Kshatriyas and the Muslims.

Among the lower caste groups, the Backward Classes (BC) constitute 21.72 per cent of the MLAs followed by SC with 15.36 and ST with 3.46 per cent. In other words, nearly 40 per cent of the elected representatives belong to lower caste groups. However, on the whole, as a single caste group, the Kammas dominate the legislative presence of the TDP.

In contrast, the Reddys dominate Congress(I) with 45.80 per cent of the party MLAs. The higher castes constitute 25.55 per cent of them. Interestingly, the representation of BC and SC in the Congress(I) party appears to be lower than in the TDP (BC constitute 18.4 per cent, SC 6.1 per cent). The ST are slightly better represented than in the TDP with 4.1 per cent.

A look at the Left parties confirms that their recruitment is in favour of high dominant castes. Hence, representation in the legislature as a whole is still dominated by the upper and intermediary castes. All parties irrespective of their ideology reflect the same trend. The data reveals that lower castes have not received their due share in political representation. Although BC constitute 50 per cent of the population, no party has accommodated them with anything that remotely resembles proportionate representation. The power structure is thus more or less confined to the same elite.

NTR's popularity eroded rapidly as suspicions of nepotism and casteism grew. There were a few incidents of caste violence between Kapus and Kammas, particularly in the coastal districts. After the murder of a Congress member of the Kapu community in Vijaywada, in 1988, the Kapus went on a rampage, attacking the Kammas especially in the

Krishna district. The Kamma–Kapu antagonism created a new dimension in the caste politics of the state. These caste divisions definitely damaged the TDP and accelerated its downfall.

The 1989 elections saw the return of the Congress to power after a gap of seven years. In the four subsequent years, however, the state had no less than three chief ministers. Further, within the Congress party, the dominance of the Reddys became more pronounced. Like NTR during 1983 and 1989, the Reddy chief ministers were accused of promoting the interests of their own caste alone. The shifting of the Kapus' vote in favour of the Congress was regarded as one of the crucial factors in the defeat of the TDP in 1989. The Congress was successful in forging a caste alliance against the TDP which gathered together the Brahmins, the Vaishyas, Reddys, Kapus and the SC. This array of caste forces allowed the Congress to win with a two-thirds majority.

Other reasons often suggested for the downfall of NTR are the extreme centralisation of power during his tenure and his clashes with leaders of other castes. In 1988, a major clash occurred when he dropped a respected leader of the Kapu community — Mudragada Padmanabham — from his ministry. The latter successfully rallied together the backward classes — in particular, the prosperous Kapu community, under his leadership in the rich delta districts of the Godavari. It had been the vote banks of the TDP since its foundation in 1982. In December 1988, the murder of V. M. Ranga, an important Kapu and Congress leader who was on a hunger strike at the time, resulted in violent clashes between the Kapus and the Kammas in the coastal districts of Krishna, Guntur and west Godavari. NTR's lack of drive in bringing the killers to book further alienated the backward castes. Finding it easy to cohere, they then came together under the leadership of Padmanabham.

The phenomenon of casteism has grown even more during the last decade. M. N. Srinivas has pointed out that even the communists select candidates with a social base that is in the local dominant caste. It has even been alleged, and reasonably so, that caste-ties supersede party-affiliations. NTR, for instance, supported CPM and CPI candidates that belonged to his caste (Kumar 1994: 161*ff*.).

Against this background, the 1994 elections to the Assembly witnessed a realignment of caste groups. Caste coalitions formed by the Reddys, the SC, the Brahmins and the Vaishyas continued to support the Congress. Apart from the Kammas, its traditional supporter, the TDP was supported by the Reddys, the Kapus, the Backward Classes and the SC. The TDP literally swept the polls capturing 217 seats, leaving the Congress with just 25 seats. In the coastal region, the TDP won 105 seats out of 133 (the Congress party secured only 10). In Telangana, the TDP won 69 seats out of 107, the Congress, six (its lowest score ever). In the Rayalaseema region, the TDP secured 40 seats compared to the 10 of the Congress party. The TDP even established its presence in the SC/ST reserved constituencies. It won 28 out of a total of 39 SC constituencies (the Congress won two, its allies — the CPI and CPM — got four and five seats respectively). All the 14 ST seats were won by the TDP and its allies.

There does not seem to be any remarkable shift in the caste composition of the MLAs after the 1994 elections. As before, the Reddys and the Kammas were over-represented. About 26 per cent of the representatives are Reddys (whereas they constitute only 6 per cent of the population). Similarly, about 16 per cent are Kammas, whereas they form only 4 per cent of the population. The proportion of backward caste MLAs remains more or less the same, i.e., very low when compared to their population. They have only 38 seats whereas they constitute 46 per cent of the population of the state. Due to the policy of reservations, the share of the ST and the SC is in proportion to their numbers.

It is widely thought that the BC started to vote in large numbers for the TDP in the early 1980s not because it was representative of a particular community but because they reacted to Indira Gandhi's strategy of wooing the SC. Nevertheless, the TDP was still perceived as the political party of the Kammas, both because of its caste leadership and the presence of NTR's family members in it.

The last 10 years of political activity in Andhra Pradesh however cannot merely be reduced to the Kamma–Reddy rivalry. The growing Dalit assertion at the all-India level is notable in Andhra Pradesh as well. This has added a new dimension to caste politics. As in the other states, a number of legislative and other measures have been taken up, such as land reforms and reservations in education and employment. These have brought about significant changes in the socio-economic and political structure of Andhra Pradesh.

Andhra Pradesh has seen two different patterns of treatment of its OBC. In the Telugu-speaking part of the Madras Presidency, the Brahmin-dominated pattern was the rule. In the regions of the erstwhile Hyderabad state, the situation was different. Since Hyderabad had a Muslim ruler, Brahmins did not dominate its bureaucracy (Yadav 1994: 150–52). After the two regions were united, the state government formulated a unified pattern of reservation for the OBC in the state services and in education. This government order was however struck down by the state High Court in 1966 on the ground that the OBC list was drawn up solely upon the caste criterion whereas social and educational backwardness should also have been taken into account. A sub-committee appointed by the state government produced a new list of 112 OBC communities which, too, was rejected. These developments led to the appointment of the First Backward Classes Commission for Andhra Pradesh. Applying the caste-cum-occupation criteria, it identified 92 castes as OBC and recommended that 30 per cent of jobs and seats in professional colleges be reserved for them. The state government accepted all the recommendations except for the upper limit for reservations — which it brought down from 30 to 25 per cent. This was in addition to the 18 per cent already in place for the SC and ST. This made a total of 43 per cent of reserved seats which the high castes challenged in the court in 1972. The matter was then brought to the Supreme Court.

In 1971, Indira Gandhi's slogan of more power to the weaker sections led to an effort to mitigate the existing imbalances in political representation, in effect, to reduce the high caste representation and find suitable backward classes candidates. The new thrust by the central leadership of the Congress party did change the face of the Assembly, 50 per cent of which was occupied by newcomers. The number of legislators from under-represented categories, namely women and Muslims, also increased. But the actual number of members of the backward classes did not really go up.

The 1980s marked a turning point with the TDP encouraging the OBC to ask for more benefits. This led to the appointment of the Second Andhra Pradesh Backward Classes Commission. The Commission recommended an enhancement of their reservations in respect of jobs to 44 per cent. NTR implemented this decision in 1983. The gain for the OBC was naturally contested by the upper castes. The

Andhra High Court later struck down the government's decision on the grounds that reservations of more than 50 per cent was against the Constitution. Consequently, the government reverted to the earlier limit of 25 per cent reservations which is still in force today.

It would not be out of place to recall here that Damodaram Sanjeevaiah, the second Chief Minister of Andhra Pradesh (1960–62), was the first Harijan to become Chief Minister anywhere in India. However, his policy of reservations for Harijans in the administration and his welfare measures in favour of the weaker sections angered the upper castes. The Reddys and the Kammas united to overthrow him in 1962. The backward castes thus still had some distance to go before they could find an effective political voice.

There is a noticeable increase in the representation of the Backward Classes after the TDP came to power even though in relative terms it still remains feeble. In the 1985 Assembly, less than 20 per cent of the members were from the BC. The 1989 Assembly and the subsequent legislatures continue to represent them poorly. Their standing in the Assembly is hardly commensurate with their population.

As earlier studies have shown, efforts made by political parties to accommodate BC have been dearly paid for in that they have never failed to alienate members of the intermediary castes (Reddy 1993). Moreover, the inclusion of Kapus on the BC list on the eve of Assembly elections alienated the BC from the Congress party and largely explained the victory of the TDP in 1994.[8]

As has been noted, since the early 1990s, the growing antagonism between the dominant Reddys and the Dalits strengthened the 'Dalitisation' process in Andhra. At this point of time, the BSP had opened a wing in Andhra Pradesh and used this base for its mobilisation. In the 1994 Assembly elections, though they could not win a single seat, they created a political base at the local and state level of government, and could be a force to reckon with in the future (see Ilaiah 1995; also Suri 1996: 308–14).

---

[8] In Andhra Pradesh, the nomenclature of castes varies from region to region. Thus, whereas in Telangana, the Kapus are treated as a Backward Class under the name 'Munnuru Kapu', in Visakhapatnam, Vizianagaram and Srikakulam, they are treated as Backward Class under the name 'Turupu Kapus'. In other parts of coastal Andhra, however, they are considered as a Forward Caste.

Educational and Occupational Background of the Political Class in Andhra Pradesh

The educational background of the Assembly members is an important variable, reflecting both the process of recruitment of the elite and its attitude. We have resorted to the party/education as well as the caste/education cross-tables to establish the correlation between the level of education and the adhesion to a single party, as well as to verify the more obvious links between caste and education.

According to the 1967–72 Assembly data, though there were no illiterates in the Andhra Pradesh Assembly, about 24 per cent of the MLAs were educated only up to the primary level. Nearly a half of that percentage came from the SC and the ST. About 15 per cent of the entire Assembly studied up to matriculation. Thirteen per cent belonging to all sections had completed their education up to Secondary School Leaving Certificate. What is significant is that these educational levels cut across caste lines. Contrary to popular belief, the backward caste MLA is not necessarily uneducated only by virtue of its social origin.

Intermediate and diploma holders represent about 13 per cent. Those who studied up to the college level but left without a degree constitute a small percentage of 4 per cent. Most of these belong to the upper caste category. Thirty per cent of the MLAs are graduates/postgraduates. However, a significant number of Andhra Pradesh's legislators have high educational qualifications. This category includes specialists in medicine, engineering and law.

From 1967 onwards, right through till 1999, one notices that the BJP, although a marginal presence in the Assembly, has been far ahead of the other parties in terms of the educational qualification of its members. The caste factor could be one possible explanation of this trend. Most BJP MLAs belong to the upper caste category, a comparatively better educated elite.

On the whole, there is not much difference between the TDP and the Congress party in terms of educational qualification. Both parties have a sizeable number of MLAs in the category of graduate and above. The elected members of the MIM traditionally come from the educated Muslim elite. The representatives of the MBT come from the same background and are highly educated.

The data indicates a marked disparity in educational levels between the sexes. The proportion of women in the pre-matriculation groups is higher than that of men. Amongst graduates and postgraduates, the percentage of women MLAs is higher. Till the 1999 Assembly, no woman MLA had any professional qualification whereas this category comprised 25 per cent of the male MLAs.

On the whole, the data clearly indicates the emergence of a reasonably well-educated political elite. This trend can perhaps have an impact on the overall development process in that a highly educated elite would tend to perceive and orient the political system from a different perspective.

Amongst the indicators of social status, one of the most significant is occupation. A glance at the data pertaining to the professional background of the legislators indicates that the majority of them are agriculturists and professionals. The figures relating to the two main parties, the Congress party and the TDP show that most elected representatives are agriculturists. This may, however, need to be looked into more carefully because most of the respondents who declare agriculture as their main occupation are involved in other trades. The emergence of a rich entrepreneurial class from the rich peasant Kamma caste has been the subject of previous studies (see Upadhya 1988).

Men elected from the sector of agriculture are four times more numerous than women. There has however been a gradual decrease in the number of legislators with an agriculturist background over the years. The same observation can be made in the case of women, i.e., more than a fourth of the women elected in 1978 had declared agriculture as their occupation. This percentage had dwindled by half in the 1989 Assembly. One obvious explanation is that the presence of women in agriculture is limited due to the absence of landholdings for them. Moreover, an important percentage of women without occupation have been elected in the last assemblies of 1994 and 1999. This is also due to the political strategy, common to all states, to select women for their husbands' vacant posts.

About 20 per cent of the MLAs are lawyers. The legal profession has traditionally provided many statesmen and politicians in India. However, very few of the women MLAs belong to this category. There was only one woman lawyer in the 1983 Assembly. Most women MLAs are in the teaching profession.

Figure 9.7

Educational Profile of the INC and TDP Representatives in Andhra Pradesh, 1972–94

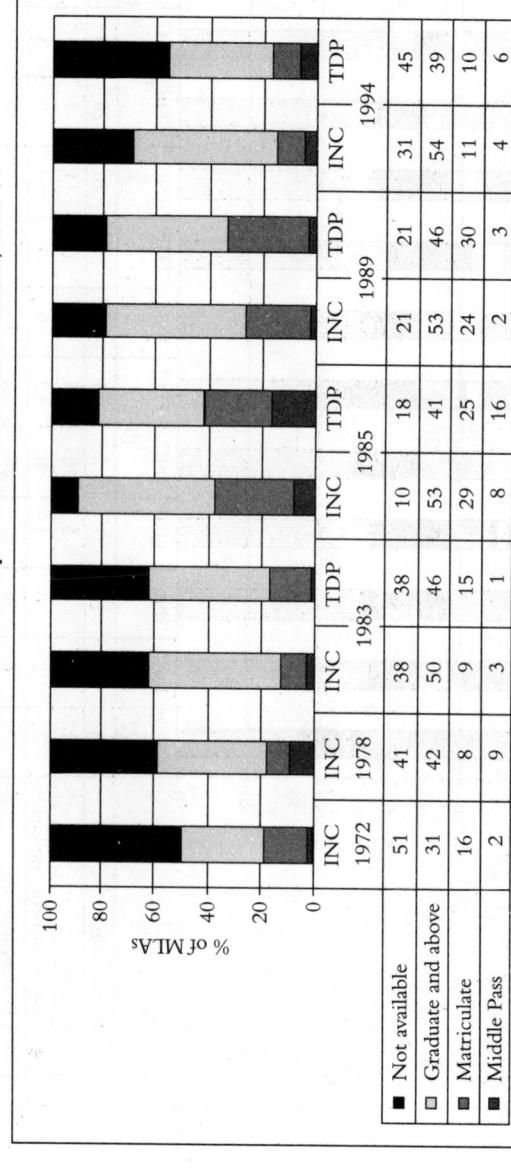

	INC 1972	INC 1978	INC 1983	TDP 1983	INC 1985	TDP 1985	INC 1989	TDP 1989	INC 1994	TDP 1994
Not available	51	41	38	38	10	18	21	21	31	45
Graduate and above	31	42	50	46	53	41	53	46	54	39
Matriculate	16	8	9	15	29	25	24	30	11	10
Middle Pass	2	9	3	1	8	16	2	3	4	6

Source: Prepared by author.

Figure 9.8
Occupational Profile of INC and TDP Representatives in Andhra Pradesh, 1972–2004

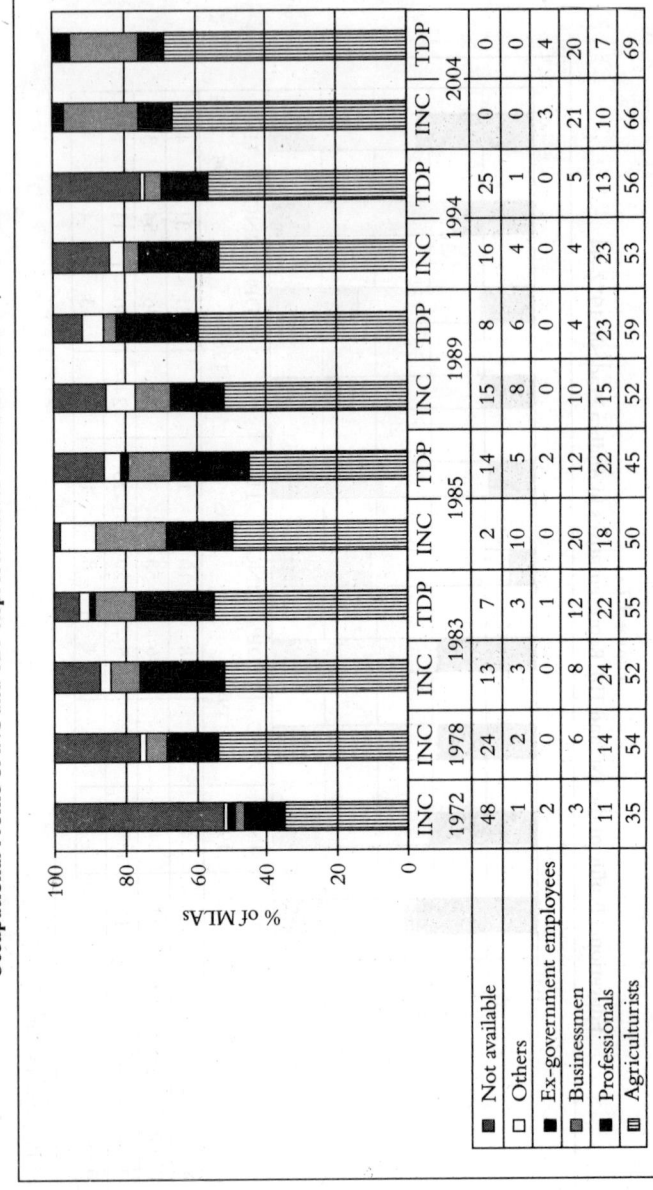

	INC 1972	INC 1978	INC 1983	TDP 1983	INC 1985	TDP 1985	INC 1989	TDP 1989	INC 1994	TDP 1994	INC 2004	TDP 2004
Not available	48	24	13	7	2	14	15	8	16	25	0	0
Others	1	2	3	3	10	5	8	6	4	1	0	0
Ex-government employees	2	0	0	1	0	2	0	0	0	0	3	4
Businessmen	3	6	8	12	20	12	10	4	4	5	21	20
Professionals	11	14	24	22	18	22	15	23	23	13	10	7
Agriculturists	35	54	52	55	50	45	52	59	53	56	66	69

Source: Prepared by author.

The composition of the successive Andhra governments is an indicator of the evolution of the political class, and mirrors the evolving profile of the legislature. As per the figures available from secondary sources, it appears that the Brahmins have seen their position gradually and steadily decline since 1956. They constituted 23 per cent of the cabinet in 1956, 10.3 per cent in 1972 and a mere 4.2 per cent in 1985. The Reddys similarly declined in the 1970s and never really regained their position. The Kammas, on the other hand, have consistently increased. The position of the Backward Castes is in inverse proportion to that of the Reddys. When the Reddys influence wanes, the Backward Castes gain; they lose ground when the Reddys come back to the fore. The SC have made consistent though relatively little progress. The ST have had minimal representation in most cabinets. The Muslims have varied from 3 to 9 per cent (see Figure 9.9 with aggregated categories) (see Reddy 1996).

Conclusion

This chapter has outlined the main features of the interplay of caste and politics in Andhra Pradesh. It has attempted to show that the intermediary castes — the Reddys and the Kammas — seem to be well-entrenched and ascendant. The upper castes, in contrast, have declined considerably over the past few decades but nevertheless are still represented in the Assembly. The backward classes have become more visible but still have some distance to travel. Their standing in the Assembly is hardly commensurate with their share in the population and the general picture is very different from that of the northern states.

We can also conclude that caste alliances in Andhra Pradesh obey certain patterns that are unlikely to change. While the Reddys, for example, may ally with the Kammas within the TDP, the Kammas are and will remain a closed group. The extreme personalisation of politics also explains the sudden rise of a particular caste on the political scene. Each leader promotes his or her own caste, clearly a national characteristic. This trait can be verified in Andhra Pradesh from the 1980s onwards both with successive dominant castes, the Brahmins, the Reddys, the Kammas and across all parties. We have also touched upon the rise of NTR. He undeniably changed the balance of power within the state

Figure 9.9
Caste Composition of the Executive in Andhra Pradesh, 1956–92 (%)

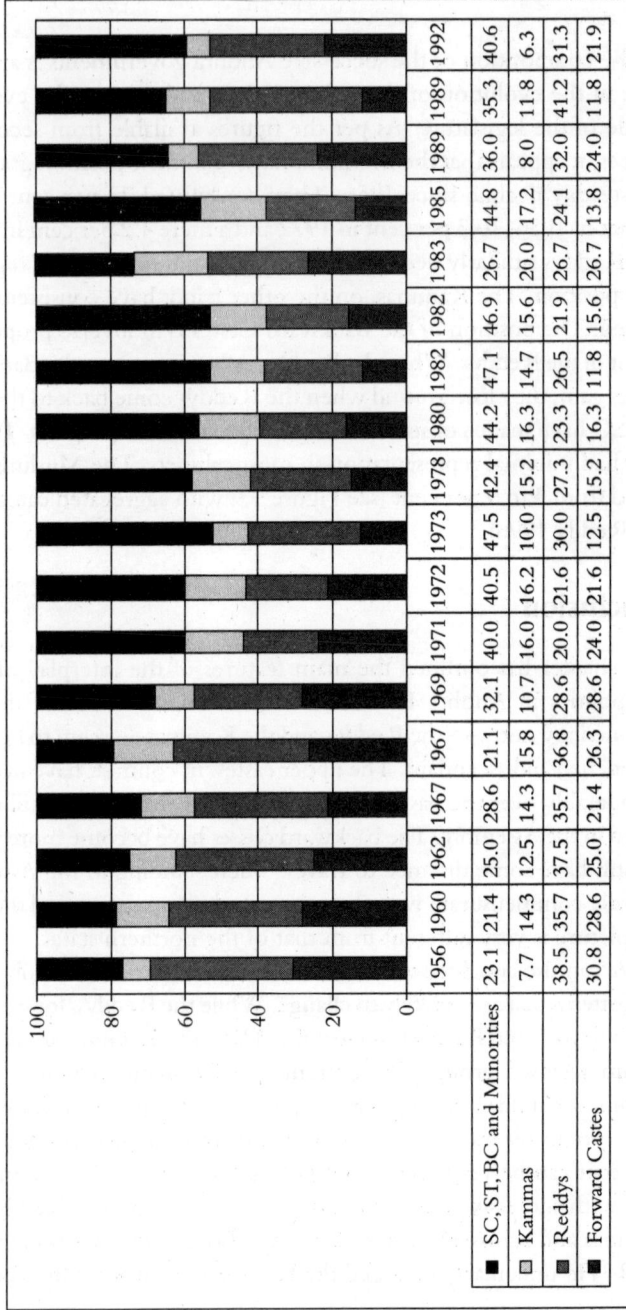

	1956	1960	1962	1967	1967	1969	1971	1972	1973	1978	1980	1982	1982	1983	1985	1989	1989	1992
SC, ST, BC and Minorities	23.1	21.4	25.0	28.6	21.1	32.1	40.0	40.5	47.5	42.4	44.2	47.1	46.9	26.7	44.8	36.0	35.3	40.6
Kammas	7.7	14.3	12.5	14.3	15.8	10.7	16.0	16.2	10.0	15.2	16.3	14.7	15.6	20.0	17.2	8.0	11.8	6.3
Reddys	38.5	35.7	37.5	35.7	36.8	28.6	20.0	21.6	30.0	27.3	23.3	26.5	21.9	26.7	24.1	32.0	41.2	31.3
Forward Castes	30.8	28.6	25.0	21.4	26.3	28.6	24.0	21.6	12.5	15.2	16.3	11.8	15.6	26.7	13.8	24.0	11.8	21.9

Source: Prepared by P. Satyanarayana.

significantly and brought the Kammas to the position of dominance that they hold today.

We have also noted that neither the educational profile of the MLAs nor their occupational background has changed radically over the past decades. Further, there is a striking similarity in the social background of the representatives of the TDP and the Congress. One reason for this characteristic, of course, is that most TDP MLAs are ex-Congressmen. Lastly, one may add that obtaining more data could contribute to further analysis, particularly in regard to the presently less visible caste groups.

Yet, quantitative analysis does not entirely reflect reality. As we have seen, the rise of the backward classes in Andhra Pradesh has not necessarily been translated into seats in the Assembly. It is, however, only logical that in the wake of their economic development, their assertion on the political scene will grow. The process may be taking longer than in northern states. Indeed, the 2004 Assembly elections in Andhra Pradesh which resulted in the ousting of the ruling TDP have not challenged the so-called 'two dominant castes equation' by bringing back the Reddy-based Congress party to power.

❖

References and Select Bibliography

Bernstorff, Dagmar. 1998. 'Eclipse of Reddys' Raj? The Attempted Restructuring of the Congress Party Leadership in Andhra Pradesh', in Dagmar Bernstorff and Hugh Gray (eds), *The Kingmakers, Politicians and Politics in Andhra Pradesh*, pp. 21–46. New Delhi: Har-Anand Publications.

Ellliot, Carolyn, M. 1970. 'Caste and Faction among the Dominant Castes: The Reddys and Kammas of Andhra', in Rajni Kothari (ed.), *Caste in Indian Politics*, pp. 129–71. New Delhi: Orient Longman.

Government of India. 1993. 'The OBCs Accepted by the Central Government for its Civil Posts and Services, w.e.f. 8 September 1993', *The Gazette of India Extraordinary*, 13 September. New Delhi: Ministry of Law, Justice and Company Affairs.

Gupta, S. K. 1985. *Scheduled Castes in Modern Indian Politics: Their Emergence as a Political Power*. New Delhi: Munshiram Manoharlal.

Harrison, Selig. 1956. 'Caste and the Andhra Communists', *The American Political Science Review*, 50 (2): 378–404.

Ilaiah, Kancha. 1995. *Caste or Class or Caste-class: A Study in Dalitbahujan Conciousness and Struggles in Andhra Pradesh in 1980s.* New Delhi: Centre for Contemporary Studies, Nehru Memorial and Museum Library.

Kaviraj, Sudipta. 1999. *Politics in India.* Delhi: Oxford University Press.

Khan, Rasheeduddin. 1969. *Political Participation and Political Change in Andhra Pradesh.* Mimeograph. Hyderabad: Osmania University.

Kistaiah, M. 1972. 'Social Background of the Members of Andhra Pradesh Legislative Assembly', *Journal of Constitutional and Parliamentary Studies.*

Kohli, Atul. 1988. 'The NTR Phenomenon in Andhra Pradesh: Political Change in a South Indian State', *Asian Survey*, 28 (10): 991–1017.

Kothari, Rajni. 1970. *Caste in Indian Politics.* New Delhi: Orient Longman.

Koteswara Prasad Rao. 1996. 'Politics in a Non-Congress State: The Case of Andhra Pradesh', in Verinder Grover and Ranjana Arora (eds), *Encyclopedia of India and Her States*, vol. 7, pp. 48–65. New Delhi: Deep & Deep.

Narayana Rao, K. V. 1973. *Emergence of Andhra Pradesh.* Bombay: Popular Prakashan.

Prasanna Kumar, A. 1994. *Andhra Pradesh Government and Politics.* New Delhi: Sterling Publishers.

Rao, N. Sudhakar. 1998. *The Structure of South Indian Untouchable Castes: A View*, in Ghanshyam Shah (ed.), *Cultural Subordination and the Dalit Challenge*, vol. 2, pp. 74–96. New Delhi: Sage Publications.

Reddy, G. Ram. 1979. *The Government and Politics in Andhra Pradesh.* New Delhi: Sterling Publishers.

———. 1989. 'The Politics of Accommodation: Caste, Class and Dominance in Andhra Pradesh', in Francine R. Frankel and M. S. A. Rao (eds), *Dominance and State Power in Modern India: Decline of a Social Order*, pp. 265–321. Delhi: Oxford University Press.

Reddy, G. Ram and D. Ravindra Prasad. 1996. 'Recruitment to the Council of Ministers in Andhra Pradesh', in Verinder Grover and Ranjana Arora (eds), *Encyclopedia of India and Her States*, vol. 7, pp. 66–79. New Delhi: Deep & Deep.

Reddy, G. Ram and B. A. V. Sharma. 1979. *State Government and Politics in Andhra Pradesh.* New Delhi: Sterling.

Reddy, K. Madusudhan and P. Satyanarayana. 1984. *Andhra Pradesh Politics.* Hyderabad: South India Publications.

Reddy, G. Krishna. 1993. 'Backward Classes and Political Power Structure in Andhra Pradesh'. Unpublished PhD dissertation. Osmania University, Hyderabad.

Shah, Ghanshyam. 2001. *Dalit Identity and Politics*, vol. 2. New Delhi: Sage Publications.

Sharma, B. A. V. and K. Madhusudhan Reddy. 1982. *Reservation Policy in India.* New Delhi: Light and Life Publishers.

Srinivas, M. N. 1987. *Dominant Castes and Other Essays.* Delhi: Oxford University Press.

———. 2000. *Caste in Modern India and Other Essays.* New Delhi: Viking.

Srinivasulu, K. and P. Sarangi. 1999. 'Political Realignments in Post-NTR Andhra Pradesh', *Economic and Political Weekly*, 34 (34–35): 2449–58.

Suri, K. C. 1996. 'Caste Politics and Power Structure in India: The Case of Andhra Pradesh', in Subrata Mukherjee and Sushila Ramaswamy (eds), *Political Science Annual*, pp. 299–316. New Delhi: Deep & Deep.

Upadhya, Carol. 1988. 'The Farmer-Capitalists of Coastal Andhra Pradesh', *Economic and Political Weekly*, 22 (27): 1376–82 and 22 (28): 1433–42.

Vakil, F. D. 1990. 'Patterns of Electoral Performance in Andhra Pradesh and Karnataka', in Richard Sisson and Ramshray Roy (eds), *Diversity and Dominance in India Politics: Changing Bases of Congress Support*, vol. 1, pp. 249–75. New Delhi: Sage Publications.

Weiner, Myron. 1967. *Party Building in a New Nation: The Indian National Congress.* Chicago: University of Chicago Press.

Yadav, K. C. 1994. *India's Unequal Citizens: A Study of Other Backward Classes.* New Delhi: Manohar Publications.

Part IV

Tribal States?

10

Jharkhand: Between Tribal Mobilisation and the Rise of the OBC

Cyril Robin

The Jharkhand state, following the enactment of the Bihar Reorganisation Bill 2000, was carved out of Bihar in November 2000 after 80 years of struggle led by several tribal-based organisations and political parties.[1]

It was expected that the political identity of the new Jharkhand Legislative Assembly should have been dominated by a large number of Scheduled Tribes. Certainly, since they are mainly elected from reserved constituencies, Scheduled Tribes MLAs represent the largest group in the Jharkhand Legislative Assembly since year 2000. But, as this chapter will attempt to demonstrate, the sizeable presence of the OBC challenges the grasp of the tribals over Jharkhand politics.

If many movements fought for the rights of the tribals, the first organisation that pressed its demand for a separate state for the Adivasis to the Simon Commission was the Chhotanagpur Unnati Samaj in 1928.[2] Its main objectives were the upliftment of Chhotanagpur from its backwardness and the social, political and economic improvement of the Adivasis' conditions. But, 'in the same age-old British tradition, the demand of the tribals to separate Chhotanagpur from Bihar was rejected' (Tirkey 2002: 60).

In the elections held in January 1937, several organisations — the Chhotanagpur Unnati Samaj (CNUS), the Kisan Sabha (KS) and the Chhotanagpur Catholic Sabha — struggling for the upliftment of Chhotanagpur from its backwardness and for the social, political and economic improvement of the Adivasis' conditions fielded their

---

[1] Jharkhand, literally meaning 'forest region', consists of the 18 districts of undivided Bihar, and represents 25.3 per cent of the total population and 45.85 per cent of total land area came into existence on 15 November 2000.

[2] The Indian Statutory Commission, also referred to as the Simon Commission, constituted by seven members of the British parliament, was nominated in 1927 to study constitutional reforms in India.

own candidates for the polls. As a result, 'the Congress swept the polls defeating the candidates fielded by the CNUS and the KS. All the reserved seats were captured by the Congress' (*ibid.*: 61). This electoral fragmentation among Jharkhand's organisations already revealed the divisions that existed within the Jharkhand movement, mainly between the Christian tribals and non-Christian tribals.

Nevertheless, in the aftermath of this political defeat, tribal leaders closed their ranks. In 1938, they united and were constituted into a single organisation called the Adivasi Mahasabha (AM) (*ibid.*: 62). The AM succeeded in bringing Santhals, Hos, Oraons, Mundas, Kharias, Christian and non-Christian tribals together. It did well in the following municipal election in February 1938 since a majority of its MLAs got elected. From 1939 onwards, the primary goal of the AM leaders became the achievement of a separate state of Jharkhand. In order to strengthen their demand, the AM needed to obtain more support from the Sadaans who had settled in Jharkhand permanently.[3] Finally, it was decided in 1950 to rename the Adivasi Mahasabha as the Jharkhand Party in order to extend the membership to non-Adivasi residents of the Chhotanagpur and Santhal Pargana region (Tirkey 2002: 74).

On the eve of the general elections of 1952, the Jharkhand Party and its leader, Jaipal Singh, were highly popular. As a result, the tribal-dominated party won 32 seats of which 25 seats were from the Scheduled Tribes reserved constituencies, five seats were from the general and two were from the Scheduled Castes reserved constituencies.[4] Thereafter, the Jharkhand Party represented the second largest party in the first state Assembly and became the main opposition party. For the first time, the movement for a separate Jharkhand state was strongly represented by a political party gathering Christian and non-Christian tribals together.

In 1953, the Jharkhand Party had the opportunity to cash in on its electoral success. The party leadership submitted two memoranda to the States Reorganisation Commission (SRC) for the creation of a Jharkhand state. But, in 1956, the SRC report only recommended the constitution of a development board for Chhotanagpur and Santhal Pargana regions. In the opinion of the members of the SRC, as a

---

[3] The term 'Sadaan' refers to permanent non-tribal settlers in the region of present Jharkhand.

[4] Out of these five general seats, four were won by Santhals and one by a Kurmi.

minority (only a little more than one-third of the total population of the Chhotanagpur Division and Santhal Pargana), the only Adivasis were not in a position to claim for the creation of the Jharkhand state (Tirkey 2002: 86).

As the Jharkhand Party failed in its demand for a separate state, the regional identity of the region was challenged, the tribal population was disillusioned and the popularity of the Jharkhand Party declined among the tribals.

In spite of this setback to the SRC, the Jharkhand Party maintained its 32 seats in the 1957 Bihar Vidhan Sabha elections. Nevertheless, out of these 32 seats, 23 were STs as against the 26 in 1952. This decrease in the number of ST candidates elected under the Jharkhand Party banner reflected the apparent resentment of the tribal population toward the failure of the Jharkhand Party.

After the 1957 elections, because of the growing struggle between the leaders of the Jharkhand Party, the Jharkhand movement started eroding.[5] The share of the Jharkhand Party in the Bihar Vidhan Sabha declined from 9 per cent to 6 per cent between 1952 and 1962. Due to internal divisions amongst the leadership, this social and political weakening led to its merger with the Congress party in 1963.

Till the end of the 1970s, factionalism within the Jharkhand movement prevented it from maintaining a sizeable and homogeneous presence in the Bihar Legislative Assembly. For instance, in the 1972 elections, three parties — the Hul Jharkhand headed by Seth Hembron and Justin Richard, the All India Jharkhand Party and the Jharkhand Party headed by N. E. Horo — represented the Jharkhand movement and could only secure seven seats out of 318.

From the late 1970s, the Jharkhand Mukti Morcha (JMM) could have appeared as the party capable of revitalising the Jharkhand movement. Indeed, the association of the erstwhile Sonot Santhal Samaj ('Pure Santhal Society') movement led by Shibu Soren with the Shivaji Samaj led by Binod Bihari Mahato, an organisation struggling against the backwardness of the Kurmi/Mahato peasant community, and the Marxist Coordination Committee of A. K. Roy, a militant trade union

---

[5] Interview with Theodore Kiro, 26 July 2005, Ranchi.

leader in the colliery of Dhanbad, led to the formation of the JMM and added a new dimension to the Jharkhand movement.[6]

As a consequence of the militant activities of these leaders among mine workers in Dhanbad and the Santhal peasants, the party 'gradually gained a stronghold in Singbhum, Santhal Parganas and Dhanbad' (Roy 2003: 75) and linked into one organisation, the workers with peasants as well as the tribals with non-tribals. However, as a result of this geographical distribution, the electoral support of the Jharkhand Mukti Morcha is smaller than it was in the early 1950s for the Jharkhand Party.

As evident from the following maps, the JMM is mainly confined to the Santhal Parganas region and in the south-east of Jharkhand (Singbhum region) whereas the Jharkhand Party was well represented in the southern parts of the state and in the Santhal Parganas region.

As an outcome of this geographical distribution, the representation of the tribes within the Jharkhand Mukti Morcha is largely dominated by the Santhals. Unlike the JMM, the Mundas, Oraons and Hos were more represented within the Jharkhand Party in spite of the sizeable presence of the Santhals, as evident from Table 10.1.

In addition, although the JMM is characterised by a definite tribal identity — mainly due to the presence of Santhal MLAs (with 62.4 per cent of Scheduled Tribes MLAs in the period 1980–2005 — the share of the non-tribals is more significant than in the Jharkhand Party. As the upper castes are totally marginalised, these JMM non-tribal MLAs are principally represented by OBC.

But, in terms of castes and communities, this larger representation has not enabled the JMM to increase the electoral attractiveness of the Jharkhand movement and the number of MLAs as compared to the Jharkhand Party. Indeed, till the creation of Jharkhand, the JMM never got more than 4 per cent of the valid votes as against 8 per cent for the Jharkhand Party and, with regard to the number of MLAs, the JMM never won more than 19 seats in the Bihar Assembly as against 30 for the Jharkhand Party. Moreover, because of a scam in the early 1990s and

---

[6] A. K. Roy did not merge his Marxist Coordination Committee with the Jharkhand Mukti Morcha (JMM) nor did Binod Bihari Mahato. Both were members of the CPI(M) District Committee and influenced the JMM ideologically (see Tirkey 2002: 106).

Map 10.1
Caste and Tribe of the MLAs of the Jharkhand Party in 1952 and of the
Jharkhand Mukti Morcha in 2005 in Jharkhand

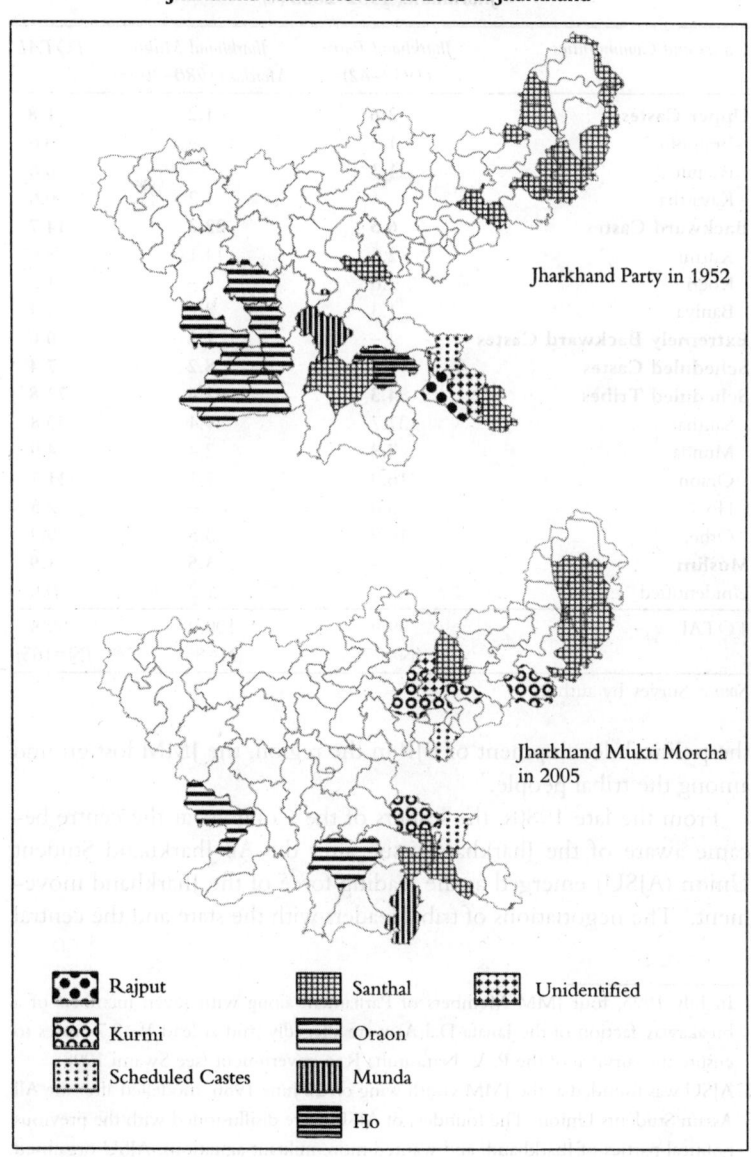

Source: Copyright with author.

Table 10.1
Caste and Community of the MLAs of the Two Main Parties of
Jharkhand, 1952–2005 (%)

Castes and Communities	Jharkhand Party (1952–62)	Jharkhand Mukti Morcha (1980–2005)	TOTAL
Upper Castes	**2.6**	**1.2**	**1.8**
Brahmin	1.3	–	0.6
Rajput	1.3	–	0.6
Kayastha	–	1.2	0.6
Backward Castes	**6.5**	**22.3**	**14.7**
Kurmi	2.6	14.1	8.6
Koeri	2.6	–	1.2
Baniya	1.3	8.2	4.9
Extremely Backward Castes	**–**	**1.2**	**0.6**
Scheduled Castes	**6.5**	**8.2**	**7.4**
Scheduled Tribes	**84.3**	**62.4**	**72.8**
Santhal	37.7	49.4	43.8
Munda	7.8	2.4	4.9
Oraon	16.9	7.1	11.7
Ho	5.0	–	2.5
Other	16.9	3.5	9.9
Muslim	**–**	**3.5**	**1.9**
Unidentified	–	1.2	0.6
TOTAL	99.9	100.0	99.8
	(N=77)	(N=85)	(N=165)

Source: Survey by author.

the political development of BJP in the region, the JMM lost ground among the tribal people.[7]

From the late 1980s, the leaders of the Congress at the centre became aware of the Jharkhand issue after the All Jharkhand Student Union (AJSU) emerged as the leading force of the Jharkhand movement.[8] The negotiations of tribal leaders with the state and the central

---

[7] In July 1993, four JMM Members of Parliament along with seven members of a breakaway faction of the Janata Dal(A) were allegedly paid at least Rs 8.7 crores to ensure the survival of the P. V. Narasimha Rao government (see Swami 1998).

[8] AJSU was founded as the JMM youth wing on 22 June 1986, modelled after the All Assam Students Union. The founders of AJSU were disillusioned with the previous political parties of Jharkhand, and wanted more militant agitations. AJSU organised general strikes and a campaign to boycott the Lok Sabha elections in 1989.

government from 1986 to 1994 led to the constitution of the Jharkhand Area Autonomous Council (JAAC) in 1994 that granted a measure of autonomy to the region, but fell far short of the demand for statehood. Besides, due to the creation of the JAAC and of the constant rivalries among the tribal leaders of the regional parties, the Jharkhand movement lost much of its momentum. Undoubtedly, the Jharkhand parties failed to build up a strong and united movement for statehood to Jharkhand and their political credibility was undermined, thereby creating a leadership vacuum which the BJP filled. In 1988, 'the Bihar unit of the BJP adopted for the first time a resolution demanding a Vananchal state comprising 18 districts' (Chaudhuri 1998: 40).

In the year 2000, since the Bihar legislative elections were held in February 2000, the new Jharkhand Legislative Assembly did not lead to new elections.

Due to the Scheduled Tribes reserved constituencies, the STs represented 35.8 per cent of the total seats in the new Assembly. As a consequence, the political identity of the new Jharkhand state seemed to be dominated by the tribals. But, as evident from Table 10.2, the OBC representatives who constituted 27.2 per cent of the Vidhan Sabha challenged this political identity.

With regard to the political parties, the ST represented the largest group in all the main organisations. But, the party, or pre-poll alliance, that won the biggest number of ST seats was not a party from Jharkhand. Indeed, the BJP-led alliance (NDA) won 15 out of the 28 ST reserved seats whereas the candidates of the Jharkhand Mukti Morcha — the tribal-dominated party leading the Jharkhand movement — only gained in seven ST reserved constituencies. Besides, unlike the JMM MLAs over-dominated by the Santhals, the ST candidates of the NDA came from the three more numerous tribes: Santhal, Munda and Oraon. As a consequence, the NDA was more represented in the ST reserved constituencies than the pro-tribal parties of Jharkhand, as evident from Map 10.2. However, unlike the INC and the JMM, the BJP led-NDA was not characterised by an overwhelming number of ST as the OBC representatives constituted 33 per cent and the upper caste 20 per cent against 38 per cent for the ST. Moreover, in the Babulal Marandi government, 40 per cent of the ministers belonged to the ST and 30 per cent to the OBC.

Table 10.2
Caste and Community of Jharkhand MLAs, 2000 (%)

Castes and Communities	Vidhan Sabha	BJP+*	INC	JMM	RJD
Upper Castes	17.2	21.0	18.2	–	11.1
Brahmin	1.2	–	9.1	–	–
Bhumihar	2.5	5.0	–	–	–
Bengali	1.2	–	–	–	–
Rajput	11.1	13.0	9.1	–	11.1
Kayastha	1.2	3.0	–	–	–
Backward Castes	23.4	18.0	9.1	8.3	33.3
Yadav	8.6	5.0	9.1	–	33.3
Kurmi	6.2	8.0	–	8.3	–
Koeri	4.9	5.0	–	–	–
Baniya	3.7	–	–	–	–
Extremely Backward Castes	3.7	8.0	–	–	–
Scheduled Castes	9.9	5.0	–	16.7	55.6
Scheduled Tribes	35.7	39.0	54.6	58.3	–
Santhal	13.6	8.0	–	58.3	–
Munda	4.9	10.0	–	–	–
Oraon	8.6	13.0	18.2	–	–
Ho	3.7	–	27.3	–	–
Other	4.9	8.0	9.1	–	–
Religious Minorities	7.4	3.0	18.0	8.3	11.1
Muslim	6.2	–	18.0	8.3	11.1
Sikh	1.2	3.0	–	–	–
Unidentified	2.5	3.0	–	8.3	–
TOTAL	99.8	97.0	99.9	99.9	111.1
	(N=81)	(N=40)	(N=11)	(N=12)	(N=9)

Source: Survey by author.
Note: * BJP+: Bharatiya Janata Party, Janata Dal (United) and Samata Party.

For the first state elections in Jharkhand in 2005, the JMM, allied with the Indian National Congress, secured 17 out of the 81 Assembly seats and became the leader of the opposition in the state Assembly. In comparison with the year 2000 elections, if the number of JMM candidates elected in the ST constituencies of the Santhal Pargana (north-east part of Jharkhand) decreased, the party won seats in the ST constituencies of the southern region of Jharkhand, as evident from Map 10.3. As a result, the JMM succeeded in adding five seats, out of which three were won by members of the Kurmi caste.

On its side, the BJP–JD(U) alliance won 36 seats with 30 for Bharatiya Janata Party (two seats less than in year 2000) and six for the

Map 10.2
Distribution of Political Parties after the Creation of Jharkhand in 2000

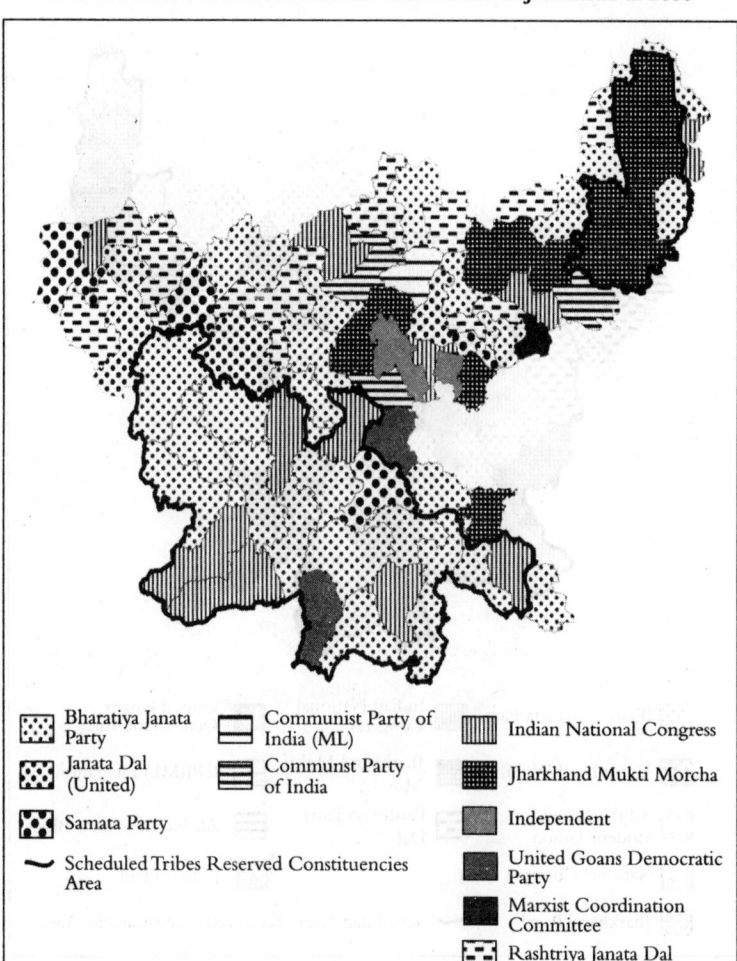

Bharatiya Janata Party

Janata Dal (United)

Samata Party

Scheduled Tribes Reserved Constituencies Area

Communist Party of India (ML)

Communst Party of India

Indian National Congress

Jharkhand Mukti Morcha

Independent

United Goans Democratic Party

Marxist Coordination Committee

Rashtriya Janata Dal

Source: Copyright with author.

JD(U) (three seats more than in year 2000) respectively. The heavy losses of the NDA are located in the ST constituencies, mainly in the Oraon belt which is in the south-west part of Jharkhand (see Map 10.3). However, the increase of OBC candidates returned under the BJP banner by four MLAs minimised the setbacks in the ST-reserved seats.

Map 10.3
Distribution of Political Parties in Jharkhand, 2005

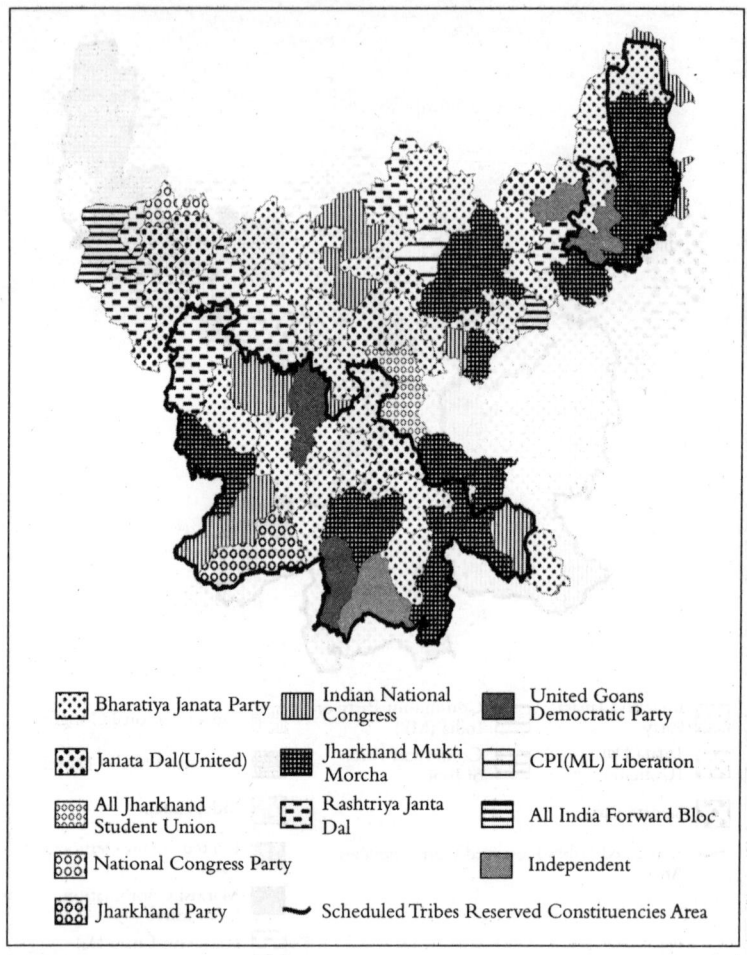

Bharatiya Janata Party	Indian National Congress	United Goans Democratic Party
Janata Dal(United)	Jharkhand Mukti Morcha	CPI(ML) Liberation
All Jharkhand Student Union	Rashtriya Janta Dal	All India Forward Bloc
National Congress Party		Independent
Jharkhand Party	Scheduled Tribes Reserved Constituencies Area	

Source: Copyright with author.

Although the ST MLAs represent the largest group in the Jharkhand
Legislative Assembly with 37 per cent, yet they do not constitute a
homogeneous group as they belong to at least four tribes — Santhal,
Oraon, Munda and Ho — and are divided amongst several parties,
primarily the Bharatiya Janata Party, the Jharkhand Mukti Morcha and

the Indian National Congress (see Table 10.3). Moreover, it is interesting to note that the STs are not represented in the same way in the
political parties. If the Santhals and the Oraons have a sizeable presence
within the JMM and the INC, the Mundas constitute the largest ST
group in the BJP–JD(U) alliance.

Further, 94 per cent of the ST MLAs won from a reserved constituency. Out of the 28 reserved seats for Scheduled Tribes, the
Bharatiya Janata Party and the Jharkhand Mukti Morcha won 10 seats
respectively.

Because of these reserved seats, the tribals are therefore quantitatively
well-represented in the Jharkhand Legislative Assembly. In addition,

Table 10.3
**Caste and Community of the MLAs
in Jharkhand Legislative Assembly, 2005 (%)**

Castes and Communities	Vidhan Sabha	BJP–JD(U) Alliance	INC–JMM	RJD
Upper Castes	**11.0**	**11.2**	–	**42.9**
Bengali	1.2	–	–	–
Bhumihar	4.9	5.6	–	14.3
Rajput	4.9	5.6	–	28.6
Backward Castes	**28.4**	**36.2**	**19.2**	**14.3**
Yadav	9.9	11.1	3.8	14.3
Kurmi	14.8	16.7	15.4	–
Koeri	1.2	2.8	–	–
Baniya	2.5	5.6	–	–
Extremely Backward Castes	**2.5**	–	–	**14.3**
Scheduled Castes	**11.1**	**16.7**	**7.7**	**14.3**
Scheduled Tribes	**37.0**	**27.8**	**53.8**	**14.3**
Santhal	16.0	8.3	30.8	–
Munda	7.4	13.9	3.8	–
Oraon	9.9	5.6	15.4	–
Ho	1.2	–	3.8	–
Other	2.5	–	–	14.3
Religious Minorities	**3.7**	**2.8**	**7.7**	–
Muslim	2.5	–	7.7	–
Sikh	1.2	2.8	–	–
Unidentified	6.2	5.6	11.5	–
TOTAL	99.9 (N=81)	100.3 (N=36)	99.9 (N=26)	100.1 (N=7)

Source: Survey by author.

at the upper echelons of politics level, with three portfolios and the chief minister's position for Arjun Munda (BJP), the ST represent the main 'group' and account for 40 per cent of the ministers.

As regards the Other Backward Classes (OBC), their proportion in the Vidhan Sabha is quite significant with an increase from 19 seats in the year 2000 to 22 seats in the year 2005. This strong representation (29.7 per cent) is mainly due to the social profile of the BJP–JD(U) alliance in which the OBC representatives form the largest group with 36.1 per cent and represent 50 per cent of all the backward caste MLAs. Moreover, this sizeable presence of the OBC in the Legislative Assembly is all the more noteworthy as they do not enjoy any reserved seats at this level in a so-called tribal state.

Within this category, the Kurmis, whose number rose from five to 11 between the years 2000 and 2005, constitute 13.6 per cent of all the MLAs, i.e., the second largest group after the Santhals (16 per cent).[9] Among them, four are BJP representatives (Kurmis are the largest caste represented with 16.7 per cent in the BJP–JD(U) alliance), four from the JMM, two for the JD(U) and one for the AJSU. This distribution of the Kurmis indicates that none of the political parties can avoid nominating Kurmis for the Jharkhand elections and, as a legacy of the politics in Bihar, the backward castes represent an important electorate in Jharkhand. In addition, the gain of the Kurmis mainly occurred in constituencies held by upper caste members till the year 2005.[10]

As a consequence, the Jharkhand political scenario tends to be more and more polarised between the tribals versus the non-tribals (mostly the backward castes). Undoubtedly, the tribal identity of the state can be challenged.

---

[9] The Kurmis of Jharkhand are Sadaans, and form an economically powerful class (see Upadhyay 2002).

[10] These constituencies are: Gomia, Bermo, Jamshedpur West and Ichagarh — all located in the eastern region of Jharkhand.

References

Chaudhuri, Kalyan. 1998. 'Carving out a Vananchal State', *Frontline*, 23 May, 15 (11): 40–41.

Roy, Amit. 2003. 'Second Phase of Jharkhand Movement', in R. D. Munda and S. Bosu Mullick (eds), *The Jharkhand Movement: Indigenous Peoples' Struggle for Autonomy in India*, pp. 73–77. Copenhagen: International Work Group for Indigenous Affairs (IWGIA) and Bindrai Institute for Research, Study, and Action (BIRSA).

Swami, Praveen. 1998. 'The Givers and the Tackers', *Frontline*, 25 April, 15 (9): 22–24.

Tirkey, Agapit. 2002. *Jharkhand Movement: A Study of its Dynamics*. New Delhi: All India Coordinating Forum of the Adivasi/Indigenous Peoples (AICFAIP).

Upadhyay, R. 2002. 'Jharkhand: March to Extreme Tribalism?', *South Asia Analysis Group*, 9 August, Paper no. 506.
Available at http://www.southasiaanalysis.org/papers6/paper506.html.

11

Tribals, OBC, Reformist Movements and Mainstream Politics in Chhattisgarh

Samuel Berthet

The name 'Chhattisgarh' refers to a specific region organised around 36 forts or administrative headquarters. The first mention to this is found in a manuscript of the 14th century. It principally included the region of the Mahanadi and the Seonath basins, and neither Koriya and Surguja districts which belong to the eastern part of Vindhyanchal Baghelkand (Singh 1995), nor the districts of Kanker, Bastar and Dantewara were included in Dandakaranya region. The anthropological survey led by Ajit Danda in 1977 included the districts of Shadol, Mandla and Balaghat but not the Bastar region (Danda 1977). This was based on the mother tongue of the inhabitants, since Chhattisgarhi is recognised as a specific dialect of Sanskrit origin. The distinct character of Chhattisgarh's culture was first raised as a political issue in the beginning of the 20th century by a few politicians such as Khubchand Baghel (1900–69) and Thakur Pyare Lal Singh (1891–1954) in the 1940s and 1950s, and then again in 1967, when Baghel formed the Chhattisgarh Bhratra Sangathan for a separate state.[1] The predominant feeling among the politicians in Chhattisgarh was that the elite from Indore and Bhopal were foreign to them and their interest. But it did not take the shape of either an articulated or a mass movement. By the late 1970s, the trade union movement led by Shankar Guha Neogi, namely, the Chhattisgarh Mukti Morcha (CMM) also put forth Chhattisgarh's identity both on a social and environmental basis for special focus is typically given to regional claims in the literature of the leftist trade union

---

[1] Hailing from an agricultural background, Dr Khub Chand Baghel, a freedom fighter from the Congress party and early promoter of Chhattisgarh, joined the Kisan Mazdoor Praja Party (KMPP) after independence, just like Thakur Pyare Lal Singh. Baghel was elected to the Vidhan Sabha in 1951 and 1957 and then was returned to Rajya Sabha as a nominee of the Congress party, courtesy his old friend D. P. Mishra, Chief Minister in 1965.

movement (CMM 1998). The movement indeed gained some sympathy among the intellectuals and generated a social workers network at the grass-root level, but it did not evolve into a broad regional movement nor demanded statehood.

On 1 November 2000, Chhattisgarh was carved out of India's largest state, Madhya Pradesh. It now consists of 16 districts: Bastar, Bilaspur, Dantewara, Dhamtari, Jashpur, Kanker, Kawardha, Koriya, Mahasamund, Raigarh, Raipur, Rajnandgaon, Surguja, Durg, Jangjir Champa and Korba. Except for the last three districts, all share borders with other states. The state is surrounded by Maharashtra, Andhra Pradesh, Orissa, Bihar, Jharkhand, Uttar Pradesh and Madhya Pradesh. This location situates Chhattisgarh at the junction of the northern, southern and eastern regions of the peninsula, and hence the state bears their diverse influences. The population is estimated to be approximately 20,796,000 inhabitants, the main part being rural (79.92 per cent), just a little less than Haryana. It covers an area of 135,000 square kilometers, ranks ninth in terms of the size of the surface included within its borders, and therefore does not deserve the reputation of a 'small state'. Chhattisgarh has 90 Assembly constituencies and sends 11 members to the Lok Sabha. The state is one of the richest in mineral resources.

During the British Raj, Chhatisgarh was declared as a separate Commissionery with its headquarters at Raipur in 1854. Later, it had two revenue divisions, one with Raipur as its headquarter, the other one being Bilaspur. The rest was formed by princely states. Those princely states were mainly inhabited by tribes. Raipur and Bilaspur are in the central part of the state where the rivers Mahanadi and Seonath flow. The Chhattisgarhi dialect which originates from the plains is close to the Hindi spoken in Oudh. Like Madhya Pradesh, Chhattisgarh remains a collection of various subregions. The new state presents a wide spectrum in terms of both ethnic and linguistic diversities. The main sociological characteristics include: first, the presence of the important OBC community representing nearly half of the total population and the tribal community accounting for almost one-third of the population. Nonetheless, Chhattisgarh is often introduced as a tribal state because it has the highest percentage of Scheduled Tribes in the tribal belt. Another reason for the identification of the state with its ST communities is the cultural influence of the tribal people which prevailed for centuries, even in the plains. The SC communities, representing 11.4 per cent of the population, complete the picture.

Being composed by princely states in almost two-thirds of their territory, Chhattisgarh was only very partially integrated with the national political arena. A patronage relationship entrenched in the local context remained, and still remains, very strong. The northern region was marked by a strong sense of emulation and competition between Christian and Hindu missionaries. The central plains of Chhattisgarh carried a strong tradition of reformist movements, whereas Bastar in the south was certainly one of the latest to be integrated into the national political fold. The overall picture that remains of the political class of Chhattisgarh is therefore dominated, on the one hand, by local context and kinship, and on the other hand, by the ruling party's ability to co-opt local leaders with not much national-level or even state-level ambition, except a few apparatchik, mainly Brahmins outside of Chhattisgarh, such as the Shukla dynasty and Motilal Vora. To the decline of this sociological class inherited from the traditional leadership of Congress has succeeded the rise of a local political class, also belonging to the upper castes, with a notable number of them having direct affiliation with the RSS, for instance, Dr Ramen Singh and Dilip Singh Yudev, and another important branch represented by the Baniya class, namely, Aggrawal. Nevertheless, it is worth noticing that Arjun Singh, who is from a Baghel Rajput family from the nearby region of Rewa, has been instrumental in undermining the Shukla–Vora stronghold.

A Composite State in Search of its Identity

The top guns of the Congress in Chhattisgarh have had their share in the Madhya Pradesh political arena through their various tenures as chief ministers: Ravi Shankar Shukla was the Chief Minister from 1947 till his death on 31 December 1956; Shyam Charan Shukla from 1969 to 1972, 1975 to 1977 and 1989 to 1990; and Motilal Vora from 1985 to 1988, and again in 1989. Raja Naresh Chandra Singh, a Gond tribal ruler of Sarangarh state, was also Chief Minister for a brief period in 1969. Such regular access to the highest position at least until 1989 certainly contributed to a state of affairs which would annihilate the desire to demand a separate political entity. Other explanations for this are: (a) Chhattisgarh does not have a strong organic community-based lobbying capacity; most of its politico-administrative and economic elite either come from outside or are settled there for not more than two or three generations; (*b*) the region remains highly composite in terms of the socio-cultural background, even in the Indian context. The creation of the new state has to be analysed in fact as one on the verge of the change in the sociological composition of the political elite and the relative decline in the role of the leaders from Chhattisgarh at the state level as they could neither access the post of chief minister after 1989, nor at the central level.[2]

The genesis of the movement for a separate state can be traced back to 1967, when Dr Baghel formed the Chhattisgarh Bhratra Sangathan (loosely translated as 'brotherhood association'). He travelled throughout India, met with the people of Chhattisgarh working in tea gardens, jute mills, steel plants, public sector undertakings, and tried to galvanise them into one whole. Pawan Deewan was his most ardent supporter and perhaps the most promising young leader at that time. The Chhattisgarh *asmita* or identity was given a big thrust by Arjun Singh, Chief Minister from 1980 to 1985. He provided the official momentum for the promotion of Dalit and tribal local icons like Guru Ghasidas, Veer Narayan Singh and Sunder Lal Sharma. He also set up the Chhattisgarh Development Authority, and thus gave an official recognition to the specific needs of the state. But the question of the creation of the state really received a new impetus after being taken up by national parties, first by the BJP, and then the Congress.

A small movement appeared in order to first articulate the demand. An independent group of intellectuals of the Chhattisgarh Asmita Sangathan (CAS) (Chhattisgarh Self-respect Forum) met in 1994 in order to support the creation of the state. They were led by Mannulal Yadu, a linguist and a representative of the OBC community in Chhattisgarh. The son of Ravi Shankar Shukla, V. C. Shukla, a former Union minister under Indira Gandhi, who was by then sidelined by the Congress, joined the CAS in 1999. It evolved into the Chhattisgarh Rajya Sangharsh Morcha (CRSM). An alliance between dominant castes could be seen during this stage, but V. C. Shukla's move in favour of the creation of Chhattisgarh would be better understood as a late attempt to revive his political career. His brother, S. C. Shukla, a former chief minister

---

[2] Ravi Shankar Shukla and V. C. Shukla both, however, accessed important positions at the national level. This could be compared with the decline of the political elite from Uttaranchal in the state of Uttar Pradesh.

himself, had expressed his reservation against it till the late 1990s. The support of the leader of the OBC, Mannulal Yadu, is more significant than V. C. Shukla's, since the OBC form about half the total population of Chhattisgarh and are under-represented.[3]

Basic Approach to the Different Vote Banks

Chhattisgarh had mainly two sociological specificities: an important OBC and ST population, about 50.34 per cent and 32.46 per cent of the total respectively, and a quite marginal upper caste community of less than 4 per cent. Another important sociological aspect of Chhattisgarh is constituted by the various movements which, from the 18th century onwards have either begun or spread there, such as the Kabirpanth and Satnam, and deeply influenced the sociological pattern of the state, especially the Dalit communities which form about 12.2 per cent of the population.

On 1 November 2000, the MLAs of the Assembly constituencies belonging to the new politico-administrative entity formed the Vidhan Sabha of Chhattisgarh, and Ajit Jogi became the first Chief Minister. A tribal chief minister for a tribal state — it seemed that the history of tribal political empowerment was in the making. Things were, of course, more complicated. The identity of Ajit Jogi is itself a blend of the various prominent sociological elements in the state. If we look back at his ascendants we find that one of his grandmothers was a tribal (from the Kanwar community) who married a Christian. On the other side, we find affiliation to the Satnami community, a reformist sect which emerged from a Dalit community towards the end of the 19th century. Different religious affiliations within the same family, which by that time had numerous members, were common among communities at the bottom of the social pyramid who tried to have a wider access to various opportunities of social recognition and elevation.

In an obvious attempt to target both the SC and the ST vote banks, the Congress National Committee and the then Madhya Pradesh Chief Minister, Digvijay Singh, decided to back Ajit Jogi — an IAS and former District Magistrate in four districts of Madhya Pradesh between

---

[3] The rivalry between V. C. Shukla and Digvijay Singh should also be taken into account.

1973 to 1986 — against the self-declared candidate, V. C. Shukla, son of R. S. Shukla, the former Union minister. Digvijay Singh's support of Jogi followed Arjun Singh's strategy of challenging the Shukla in their own stronghold by playing the Chhattisgarh card against the non-Chhattisgarh Brahmin.

Jogi held important responsibilities in the central apparatus of the Congress but was a relatively unknown political figure in Chhattisgarh. He was introduced as a tribal representative in a state which had 34 of its 90 seats reserved for the ST. The links of Jogi with the Satnami community, a very influent community among the SC who have 10 reserved seats in the Vidhan Sabha, added to its potential capacity to attract large sections of the new state electorate. The former District Magistrate's own political skill and his knowledge of the administrative apparatus were also deciding factors. But the Congress' calculation happened to fall short of people's expectations, at least temporarily. The Congress was defeated after the first elections for the State Assembly in December 2003. This setback was confirmed in the general elections of 2004, the BJP managing 50.075 per cent of the voters in the four reserved constituencies (Bastar: 47.26 per cent, Kanker: 49.52 per cent, Raigarh: 50.75 per cent, and Surguja: 52.77 per cent).

Jogi was not known as a tribal leader in the political scene before he became CM, even if he may later have gained this status. This way of co-opting or designating leaders in order to target specific vote banks is one of the Congress' most used tactics in Madhya Pradesh. It worked until a contender came in the position to attract a decisively wide spectrum of the society and to co-opt local notables himself, which the BJP eventually managed to do from the 1990s onwards. Tribal leaders such as Arvind Netam, Nand Kumar Sai, Sohan Potai or Baliram Kashyap started to join the BJP. Can the rise of the BJP be interpreted as the political empowerment of the ST?

The creation of the state itself has been analysed in the first instance as the result of the policy of the BJP to target the OBC support (Venkatesan 2000), a rising sociological class in the aftermath of the Mandal Commission, notably in the Hindi belt to which Chhattisgarh is said to belong, in spite of the fact that it is also described as a tribal state. The momentum gained by Chhattisgarh's demand can be perceived as concomitant with the rise of the OBC in Madhya Pradesh.

If the result of the BJP's firm implantation in Chhattisgarh can be seen as the result of its electioneering strategy, this political shift of the electorate is indeed concomitant to the same move in Madhya Pradesh. It underlines two facts:

(a) the early establishment of a strong network through RSS and its various outfits like the Akhil Bharatiya Vanvasi Kalyan Ashram (ABVKA) created in Jashpurnagar in 1952 by R. K. Deshpande and M. H. Ketkar and the rapid growth of this network in the recent years which eventually contributed in helping the BJP to win all the four seats reserved for ST (Bastar, Kanker, Sarguja and Raigarh parliamentary constituencies) during the 1999 and 2004 Lok Sabha elections; and

(b) the limits of the Congress policy of patronisation which created an illusion of presence but actually did not translate into grassroot social and political democratisation, and therefore left areas wide open for parallel networks to take roots.

The social background of the Members of Parliament and Members of Legislative Assembly in Chhattisgarh from 1952 to 1998 has been analysed in Christophe Jaffrelot's study of Madhya Pradesh from which the new state has been carved out (see, in particular, Chapter 3 of this volume), as also in the comparative study of Madhya Pradesh and Uttar Pradesh (Jaffrelot and Zérinini-Brotel 2004). The main issue, therefore, is to detect if there is any specificity in the social background of the political representatives of Chhattisgarh. Two main difficulties matching up with each other in complexity can be outlined here. In a similar manner as that of the creation of Madhya Pradesh in 1956, the creation of the new state has not been preceded by a regionalist movement which could have provided a base for the study of both its leaders and its mass supporters. Moreover, the political picture of Chhattisgarh is an almost entirely bipolar one, no political party really being in a position to interfere in the duel between the BJP and the Congress. For the 2003 Vidhan Sabha elections, the two parties put together a total of 75.67 per cent of the voters, with 39.26 per cent and 36.71 per cent respectively for the BJP and the Congress, the rest being scattered among other parties. Only the BSP managed two seats for a total of 6.94 per cent. The two main national parties increased their total share during the 2004 Lok Sabha elections with 47.78 per cent and 40.16 per cent of the total voters, for a combined total of 87.94 per cent — the highest combined total of the states.

The spectrum for the statistical analysis of the social composition of the MLAs in Chhattisgarh is rather narrow if we consider that out of 90 MLA seats, the attribution of 44 seats is stable and that change can therefore be observed only on the basis of the remaining 46 non-reserved seats. The most significant evolution is the rise of the share of OBC in the Vidhan Sabha from 8.5 to 23.34 per cent, a confined rise when compared to the total OBC population, and a relative decline of the upper castes from 36.5 to 24.4 per cent, a figure still largely exceeding the total population of upper castes. The relevance of the analysis of the composition of the executive committee and of the ranks in the government is therefore crucial.

The Various Patterns of the Sociology of the Political Class in Chhattisgarh

From 1962 to 1980, the sociological profile of the MLAs in Chhattisgarh has undergone changes to reach a configuration very similar to the present.[4] From a dominance of the upper castes, who in spite of their very limited number — less than 4 per cent — accounted for more than one-third of the Vidhan Sabha, the present figure gives a picture where OBC and upper castes are in direct competition, both having almost an equal share of the 50.5 per cent of non-reserved seats in the new state of Chhattisgarh. From 1980 to 2003, there have been some variation, upper castes regaining prominence, particularly during the 1990 election which sealed the first victory of the BJP in the state. To the relative decline in the share of the upper castes correspond the inroads of the OBC in the Chhattisgarh politics, from 8.5 per cent in 1962, to 22.2 per cent in 1980 and 23.4 per cent in 2003. The analysis sometimes put forward about the rise of the OBC in Chhattisgarh, which occurred at an early stage compared to the rest of Madhya Pradesh, could seem to be confirmed here. But this study of the sociological profile of the members of the Congress and BJP executive committee and of the composition of the two first governments show the continuing domination of the upper castes over the politics of Chhattisgarh. The examination of the profile of the MLAs in Chhattisgarh has, of course, to take into

---

[4] The data available for 1957 contains too many unidentified MLAs to be considered here.

account the importance of the reserved seats — 44 out of 90. With 34 seats, the ST have the biggest share, hence providing a justification for Chhattisgarh to be called a 'tribal state'. As a matter of fact, one can observe that the new majority has been formed thanks to the results in the tribal constituencies. But this crude mathematical reality translates neither into the political apparatus, nor into the attribution of the policy-makers' posts.

While the ST dominated in the State Assembly (40 per cent), the upper castes and OBC take almost an equal share of seats with 25.55 per cent and 23.33 per cent respectively. The SC share is of 11.1 per cent. Both SC and ST candidates are typically elected only to the seats reserved to them. The situation is different in the state executive committees of the two largest parties where upper castes dominate with 40 per cent for the BJP and 33.67 per cent for the Congress, with OBC in the second position with 32 and 22.44 per cent respectively in the two parties. Unlike in the Vidhan Sabha, the ST come only in the third position with 21.33 per cent in the BJP and 19.38 per cent in the Congress state executive committee. The SC are in the fourth position in the BJP with 4 per cent, and fifth in the Congress where they are preceded by other communities clubbed together (Muslim, Jain, Christian and Satnami) but with a more important share of 8.16 per cent. Therefore, both parties follow a similar pattern, with the Congress state executive committee reflecting the social spectrum of Chhattisgarh in a slightly broader way. But the long-time ruling party has lost what was considered its traditional vote bank, even if this conception of tribal electorate as one affiliated to the Congress is, by largely, mistaken, and its co-option policy has been challenged. Moreover, its state executive committee spectrum narrows at the decision-making level as it appears in the sociological composition of the MLA group from the Congress.

The overall picture shows different vote banks increasingly splitting up in almost equal share between the two main parties, the BSP remaining to be added in the case of the SC (two of the 10 seats reserved for SC in the 2003 polls, against six for the BJP and two for the Congress). [5] The BSP vote represents only 4.4 per cent, but was

---

[5] This observation is based on electoral results, CSDS exit polls and projections by the leaders of the different communities.

quite significant in the Bilaspur region (Kumar and Yadav 2003) where the Satnamis are concentrated. But even the BSP electoral results have worsened as compared to previous elections. Though the upper castes are still over-represented, when compared to the demographic composition of the state, the inroads of OBC in the state politics is confirmed by their share both at the level of the party organisation and at the level of the State Assembly. The data for the year 2003 shows that OBC are still in the second position, after the upper castes, at the party level. But in the Assembly they hold an almost equal share. As far as the ST are concerned, their strong presence in the Lok Sabha through the reservation policy does not translate at the party level where their number is proportionally almost half.

The composition of the upper caste groups is different in the two parties: Brahmins overwhelmingly dominate the Congress (60.60 per cent of the upper castes among the state executive members, 58.3 upper castes among the upper castes MLAs and 60 per cent of the upper castes among the state ministers). In the BJP, the Kshatriyas dominate Brahmins in the state executive committee (43.3 per cent against 40 per cent, and 6.6 per cent for the Baniyas) while the Baniyas dominate at the government level: five out of nine MLAs (55.55 per cent), three Brahmins (33.33 per cent) and one Kshatriya (11.11 per cent). Baniyas have a decisive share at the top command with Lakhi Ram Aggarwal, former Rajya Sabha member considered to be the party's godfather, his son Amar Aggarwal, Finance and Industry Minister, and Brij Mohan Aggarwal, Home Ministry. Based on a small number, this figure nevertheless corroborates the long-run analysis of the sociological composition of the political class in Madhya Pradesh (see Chapter 3 of this volume). At the same time, the Brahmin–Baniya rivalry described by Girish Kumar (2006) appears better defined in the case of Chhattisgarh as an association of Brahmin–Rajput for the Congress as opposed to a Brahmin–Baniya dominated elite for the BJP. This goes along with another analysis proposed by Jaffrelot relevant to the case of Chhattisgarh regarding the traditional ruling aristocracy. The royal families clubbed in the Ram Rajya Parishad (RRP) got three parliamentary tickets in 1952. The Congress successfully integrated them by co-opting the former candidates of the RRP which, in turn, fell apart.

The sociological profile of the BJP is, in itself, very informative about the on-going attempts of upper castes to reach a compromise.

Table 11.1
Caste Background of the Congress MLAs in Chhattisgarh, 1957–2003 (%)

	1957	1962	1967	1972	1977	1980	1985	1990	1993	1998	2003	Average Percentage
Upper Castes	**34**	**46**	**37**	**43**	**29**	**28**	**27**	**41**	**30**	**32**	**28**	**34**
Baniya/Jain	10	4	7	6	6	6	4	–	4	4	3	6
Brahmin	13	21	20	29	14	14	13	27	19	13	14	17
Kayastha	1	4	2	–	–	–	–	–	–	–	–	1
Khatri	–	–	–	–	–	–	1	–	–	–	–	0
Rajput	10	17	8	8	9	8	9	9	7	15	11	10
OBC	**1**	**8**	**12**	**11**	**29**	**24**	**20**	**25**	**25**	**15**	**29**	**17**
Agharia	–	–	–	–	–	–	–	–	–	–	5	0
Baghel	–	–	2	2	3	1	1	–	2	–	–	1
Bairagi	–	–	–	1	–	1	–	–	–	–	–	0
Jaiswal	–	2	2	–	–	1	3	5	–	–	–	1
Kurmi	–	2	3	2	6	8	5	5	7	8	8	5
Mali	–	–	–	–	–	–	1	5	2	–	–	1
Pankha	–	–	–	–	–	1	1	–	2	–	–	1
Teli	–	–	2	2	3	3	3	5	6	6	8	3
Weaver	–	–	–	–	3	–	–	–	–	3	3	0
Yadav	1	–	–	–	–	1	1	–	2	–	–	1
Others	1	4	3	3	11	8	5	5	4	–	5	4
SC	**16**	**19**	**19**	**14**	**14**	**12**	**9**	**9**	**9**	**6**	**11**	**13**

ST	33	21	20	32	29	35	40	27	35	44	30	32
Kanwar	–	–	2	–	3	1	3	–	4	–	3	1
Others	33	21	19	32	26	33	37	27	31	44	24	31
Others	1	2	2	2	–	–	1	–	2	4	3	1
Muslim	1	2	2	2	–	–	1	–	–	4	3	1
Sikh	–	–	–	–	–	–	–	–	2	–	–	0
Unidentified	14	4	10	–	–	1	–	–	–	–	–	3
TOTAL	99.9	100	100	102	101	100	97	102	101	101	101	100
	(N=70)	(N=48)	(N=59)	(N=65)	(N=35)	(N=78)	(N=75)	(N=22)	(N=54)	(N=48)	(N=37)	(N=591)

Source: Data concerning years 1957–2000 are collected by Christophe Jaffrelot; data concerning the elections in 2003 are by author.

Table 11.2
Caste Background of the BJP MLAs in Chhattisgarh, 1980–2003 (%)

	BJS			Janata Party		BJP					
	1962	1967	1972	1977	1980	1980	1985	1990	1993	1998	2003
Upper Castes	**20.0**	**11.0**	**10.0**	**32.0**	–	–	**25.0**	**25.5**	**23.0**	**28.0**	**18.0**
Brahmin	20.0	11.0	10.0	–	–	–	8.0	7.8	13.0	8.0	6.0
Baniya/Jain	–	–	–	9.5	–	–	8.0	9.8	7.0	14.0	12.0
Rajput	–	–	–	19.0	–	–	8.0	5.9	3.0	3.0	–
Sindhi	–	–	–	4.0	–	–	–	2.0	–	3.0	–
Intermediary Castes	**40.0**	–	–	2.0	–	–	–	–	–	–	–
Maratha	40.0	–	–	2.0	–	–	–	–	–	–	–
OBC	**20.0**	**10.0**	**10.0**	**7.5**	–	**16.5**	**16.0**	**12.0**	**17.0**	**23.0**	**22.0**
Teli	20.0	10.0	10.0	5.5	–	16.5	–	–	7.0	11.0	4.0
Yadav	–	–	–	2.0	–	–	–	–	–	6.0	2.0
Kurmi	–	–	–	–	–	–	–	2.0	–	–	–
Bairagi	–	–	–	–	–	–	–	–	–	–	2.0
Fishermen	–	–	–	–	–	–	16.0	6.0	10.0	3.0	2.0
Weavers	–	–	–	–	–	–	–	–	–	–	2.0
Others	–	–	–	–	–	–	–	4.0	–	3.0	10.0
SC	**20.0**	–	**10.0**	**7.5**	–	–	**17.0**	**13.5**	**20.0**	**14.0**	**8.0**
ST	–	**78.0**	**70.0**	**41.5**	**100.0**	**83.5**	**42.0**	**47.0**	**37.0**	**31.0**	**50.0**
Sikhs	–	–	–	**2.0**	–	–	–	**2.0**	**3.0**	**6.0**	**2.0**
Muslims	–	11.0	–	–	–	–	–	–	–	–	–
Unidentified	–	–	–	7.5	–	–	–	–	–	–	–
	(N=5)	(N=9)	(N=10)	(N=53)	(N=1)	(N=6)	(N=12)	(N=51)	(N=30)	(N=36)	(N=50)

Source: Author's fieldwork.

This compromise lies in giving room to the numerically dominating groups in order to obtain electoral gains, strengthen their position both at the state and at the central level, and remaining at the top. The government which came out of the first elections in the new state is indicative of this trend. Another element observed by Jaffrelot relevant here is the attempt of the Congress to forge an alliance between the upper castes and the ST. It was translated in the composition of the Ajit Jogi government, but not at the party level where the ST share is still below their total percentage in the population and even below their share in the BJP. And comparatively, the OBC have also a more significant share in the BJP than in the Congress.

Table 11.3
Caste of the State Executives of the BJP in Chhattisgarh, 2003

	Number	*Percentage*
Upper Castes	**30**	**40.0**
Brahmin	12	16.0
Kshatriya	13	17.3
Baniya	5	6.6
OBC	**24**	**32.0**
ST	**16**	**21.3**
SC	**3**	**4.0**
Others	**2**	**2.2**
Muslim	1	1.1
Sikh	1	1.1
TOTAL	75	100.0

Source: Author's fieldwork.

The analysis of the sociological profile of the MLAs and the political history of Chhattisgarh shows the necessity to reconsider the notion of Chhattisgarh as a 'stronghold' of the Congress, particularly with regards to the tribal areas. The *modus operandi* of co-option by the Congress without long-term and articulated political empowerment of the population is certainly one of the main reasons for the shift of tribal vote to the BJP. The success of the Hindu nationalists and its allied organisations — the RSS, the VHP, the ABVKA and others — took shape through a long-run networking at the grass-root level.

Table 11.4
Caste of the State Executives of the Congress in Chhattisgarh,
until February 2004

	Number	Percentage
Upper Castes	36	**36.7**
Brahmin	20	20.5
Kshatriya	3	3.0
Baniya	13	13.2
OBC	22	**22.5**
ST	19	**19.5**
SC	8	**8.1**
Satnam	1	1.0
Others	12	**12.2**
Muslim	8	8.0
Sikh	3	3.0
Christian	1	1.0
Unidentified	1	**1.0**
TOTAL	98	100.0

Source: Author's fieldwork.

A State Dominated by Non-tribal

The sociological analysis of the politics and ST political representatives is made difficult by the variety of communities and subcommunities and the rather limited scope of analysis offered by the dominating anthropological approach. A first attempt to draw the bases of a typology was made by Surajit Sinha (1962), and not much has been written since then. The various effects of the 'rajputisation' of tribal communities in central India has become a structuring, but uneven, pattern for tribal sociology, specially in Chhattisgarh. The endeavour of tribal leaders to identify themselves, or even to associate, with Rajput lineages has undergone a trend of reversal after independence, when Rajput status became of less political interest. After independence, the strategies of tribal movement began to be shaped according to the reservation policy. It may lead to confusion regarding the status of some Gond/Rajput (Raj gond) families, who shifted back to their tribal status after 1947 for benefiting from the reservation system. However, this question is of lesser relevance for the princely state of Bastar whose, former ruler was clearly identified with a royal lineage from present Andhra Pradesh.

The Congress party has a legacy of antagonistic relationships with tribal populations, which is in conflict with the view that tribal regions are its stronghold. Recently, poll results repeatedly challenged this pre-conceived idea routinely repeated in the press. Areas dominated by tribal communities were largely under princes' rule, and therefore some clientelistic arrangement remained in force during the British rule. After independence, the princes and the Adivasis found a common ground against the intrusion of the central government which resulted in the deprivation of their customary rights without any interesting prospect in return. This alliance led to early regional movements in tribal areas of Orissa, Chhattisgarh and Hyderabad.[6] The tumultuous relationships between Pravir Singh Deo, descendant of the princely family of Bastar, and the Congress are indicative of these difficulties in sustainably inte-grating the tribal areas into the party's fold. The Congress gave Deo a ticket for the 1957 elections, and the prince and his nominees helped the party to get a huge majority (Sundar 1997). But a period of turmoil began between the prince and the Congress which eventually led Pravir Singh to create his own party, the Adivasi Seva Dal. He led the tribal protest against deprivation of their traditional rights, especially those regarding the land. The Congress ST candidates dropped by half, from 23 in 1957 to 10 and 12 in 1962 and 1967 respectively. In 1965, gov-ernmental measures meant to solve the food penury provoked a further critical deprivation for peasants in Bastar; meanwhile the Malik Makbuja case, the Bastar forest scandal, disclosed the corruption of the adminis-tration. The conflict between the population of Bastar and the central gov-ernment eventually ended in 1966 in a very violent repression, leaving many dead, including Pravir Singh, the latter under the most suspicious circumstances.

The Hindu nationalist parties made their political inroads into the tribal vote bank during the 1967 elections — seven out of their nine candidates elected in Chhattisgarh were ST. Hindu nationalist parties banked on the reaction against Congress misadministration in tribal

---

[6] Questions and conflicts arose before independence, for instance, with the Jharkhand movement that began in the 1920s. The next decade saw a growing conflict between princes and zamindars on one side and the Congress elite on the other. In princely states, the degree of penetration of the Congress was low. When it took over the reins of the government, there are some instances where resistance of the princes and the tribal communities found common ground and combined, for example, in western Orissa. Hence, as early as 1948, Orissa saw the emergence of a regional party, namely, the Ganatantra Parishad (see Banerjee 1984: 375).

areas much before they started expanding their socio-religious network in the 1990s. Having stressed upon the use of Hindu rituals and attributes, Parvir Singh Deo paved the way for further neo–Hindu movements. After his death, Baba Bihari Das gained popularity as Pravir Singh's reincarnation. He headed a sect set up on the pattern of classical *bhagat* (reform and classical) movements in India (Sunder 1997: xxiv). It included typical brahminical rules like wearing the *kanthi* (tuft), the prohibition of alcohol and meat which stand opposed to tribal culture. Such movements which occurred among the untouchables in Chhattisgarh by the second half of the 19th century and took place a century later in the tribal areas indicate a similar move towards the first phase of political integration through reformist movements, implying, in turn, an acculturation or even a deculturation process. After the death of Pravir Singh, the Congress party stood by its usual method and co-opted the prince's self-proclaimed avatar during the 1972 elections. All its candidates were elected, but no indication of taking up the issue of tribal empowerment could be traced. Meanwhile, the disappearance of the traditional ruler led to a relative decline of the tribal leadership traditionally affiliated with the prince, mainly the Bhatra community, whereas the Gonds started to play a major role. A more integrated tribal leadership was in the making with Mahendra Karma, who came from a dynasty of tribal chiefs into the political arena through the 'classic' students' union channel.

In 1994, the first significant symptom of this political integration reflecting the national pattern was perceived in the political divide during the demonstrations supporting or opposing the application of Schedule VI. While the Communist Party of India (Marxist) supported the demonstration, the tribal Congress leaders were divided and the BJP was opposed to it. Among the prominent leaders, Mahendra Karma (then Independent) was against it while Arvind Netam (then Congress) supported it. The extension of the Panchayat Act in 1996 to the Schedule V area ended the debate. But the on-going democratic decentralisation process, even if it remained incomplete and imperfect, was soon shaken by the opposition of Naxalites, who spread from Andhra Pradesh into the region in the 1980s and became a major factor. The extreme leftists stopped the local electoral process and thereby prevented the functioning of the Panchayat Raj. Shyamlal's conclusion about tribal leadership in Rajasthan that today 'tribal leadership has, by and large, become part of all Indian politics and wider leadership of the state and the country' (Shyamlal 2000: 171) appears relevant in the case of Chhattisgarh. But there is little indication so far as that the integration of ST into the national political arena is leading to the tribal communities' empowerment. And, the creation of Chhattisgarh, introduced as a step forward in the recognition of these communities, has not provided any guarantee towards change.

Chhattisgarh has the largest percentage of reserved seats for ST in any Vidhan Sabha of the Indian peninsula. The 34 reserved seats for ST out of a total of 90 account for 37.77 per cent.[7] When elected MLAs of the Madhya Pradesh Vidhan Sabha formed the new State Assembly, among the Congress MLAs, almost 48 per cent were tribal (23 out of 48). A representative of the ST community was chosen against the representatives of the Congress upper caste aristocracy, such as S. C. Shukla, former Madhya Pradesh CM; his brother and former Union Minister V. C. Shukla; and Motilal Vora, another former CM. An ST candidate coming to power, preferred to the local tribal leader, Arvind Netam, and moreover, winning over three Brahmins — what could look like a sign of tribal empowerment was actually rather a symbol overshadowing a more complex reality. Only three years later, the Vidhan Sabha elections of 2003 restored the power balance where ST did not have a predominant share of the power in the state. Their share in the new BJP government was slightly superior to Jogi's in appearance (36 per cent against 34.5 per cent), but the Baniyas and, the Brahmins held the key posts in the cabinet, where the ST were now only three in number, while there were six in the Jogi government, including the chief minister.[8] The first elected Vidhan Sabha of Chhattisgarh produced a government where ST were under-represented, in terms of key posts, although the BJP owed its success to the tribal constituencies, with 50 per cent of its MLAs elected in those constituencies (25 MLAs out of 50). The under-representation of ST among the high apparatus of the BJP can be

---

[7] In contrast, Jharkhand has 34.5 per cent reserved seats for the ST, Orissa has 23 per cent, Madhya Pradesh has 17.8 per cent, Gujarat has 14.25 per cent, Rajasthan has 12 per cent, West Bengal has 5.7 per cent, and Andhra Pradesh has 5 per cent of them.

[8] The ST ministers included Ram Vichar Netam, the SC, ST, Backward and Minority Development Minister and Nankim Ram Kanwar, Minister of Rehabilitation and Agriculture, Animal Husbandry, Fisheries, Cooperatives, Law and Legal Affairs.

corroborated at different points: the government, the executive committee (21.33 per cent) but also its leadership. Among its three prominent leaders, Raman Singh, Dilip Singh Judeo and Ramesh Bais, none belongs to the ST and the possibility of a deputy speaker representative of the ST has been strongly opposed by the party's apparatus.

Table 11.5
Social Composition of the 2003 Vidhan Sabha

	BJP		Congress	
	Number	Percentage	Number	Percentage
Upper Castes	9	18.0	13	35.2
OBC	11	22.0	9	24.3
SC	4	8.0	4	10.8
ST	25	50.0	10	27.0
Muslims	–	–	1	2.7
Sikhs	1	2.0	–	–
TOTAL	50	100.0	37	100.0

Source: Author's fieldwork.

Table 11.6
Sociological Composition of the First Government of Chhattisgarh

Ajit Jogi Government (2000–03)		
	Number	Percentage
Upper Castes	**10**	**38.5**
Brahmin	6	23.0
Kshatriya	3	11.5
Baniya	1	3.8
OBC	**3**	**11.5**
ST	**9**	**34.5**
SC	**2**	**7.7**
Satnami	1	3.8
Others	**2**	**7.7**
Muslims	2	7.7
TOTAL	26	99.9

Source: Author's fieldwork.

One of the reasons for the tribal allegiance to the BJP during the elections in 2004 is the disappointment felt by ST regarding the previous government. Jogi's action, indeed, did not break away from the traditional coercive line of action of the state against tribal livelihood. The most illustrious case is the controversial consultation of the Gram Sabhas

Table 11.7
Sociological Composition of the Second Government of Chhattisgarh

Raman Singh Government (2003–04)		
	Number	*Percentage*
Upper Castes	**4**	**22.0**
Brahmin	3	16.5
Baniya	1	5.5
OBC	**5**	**28.0**
ST	**7**	**39.0**
SC	**1**	**5.5**
Others	**1**	**5.5**
Sikh	1	5.5
TOTAL	18	100.0

Raman Singh Government (2004–)		
	Number	*Percentage*
Upper Castes	**4**	**28.4**
Brahmin	3	21.4
Baniya	1	7.0
OBC	**3**	**21.4**
ST	**5**	**36.0**
SC	**1**	**7.0**
TOTAL	13	92.8

Source: Author's fieldwork.

in Nagarnaar, Amaguda, Kasturi and Maganpur (Bastar) regarding a steel plant project. In spite of the disapproval of the project by the local population, its implementation was carried on, thanks to alleged false documents. The Congress already had a rather long legacy of antagonistic relations with tribal communities in Chhattisgarh. As a consequence, the BJP, thanks to the numerous outfits of the Sangh Parivar, was in a position to bank efficiently on people's disenchantment, particularly in Bastar. Its position at the central government also helped it in attracting frustrated tribal leaders through the well-established clientelistic *modus operandi*. But this alliance of some tribal leaders with the BJP did not coincide with the rise of a new ST elite or a pro-Adivasi politic.

If the use of reservations as a means for democratic inclusion is not disputed, its ability to support political empowerment still remains doubtful. The steady decline of the tribal independent MLAs from five out of seven reserved seats in the 1952 elections (see Election Commission of India 1951: 4–10), and 10 in 1962 to zero at present can be interpreted as a symptom of this integration into the fold of mainstream politics. It confirms Virginius Xaxa's assertion that the main effect of the reservation is the integration into mainstream politics through the divide of tribal leaders along party lines (2005). In Chhattisgarh, Arvind Netam has joined the BJP, Mahendra Karma, the Congress, while CPI(M) has a small but significant presence in tribal areas.

The reservation policy has led to the integration of the ST in the mainstream politics but has not led to their empowerment. In the Congress and BJP party apparatus, the ST account for 19.32 and 21.33 per cent respectively, a significantly lower share compared to the 37.7 per cent reserved seats in the Vidhan Sabha. It is worth noticing that the ST appear to be slightly more represented in the BJP apparatus.

After more than half a century of independent political history, the tribal political consciousness has not yet assumed the form of a distinctive movement either through a specific party or within the existing parties of Chhattisgarh. While adjacent tribal regions have both specific political organisations like the Gondwana Ganatantra Party in Madhya Pradesh, and the Jharkhand Mukti Morcha in Jharkhand, which have articulated the force behind the tribal movement for the last eight decades, there is no similar movement in the new 'tribal' state.[9] The presence of tribal representatives in Congress as well as in the BJP remains merely part of their vote-banking strategy. BJP has the advantage of a wider and more efficient network at the local level and can also rely upon the disillusionment of the ST population towards the former ruling party. The delay of their political empowerment could end the hopes of finding a solution to pending tribal issues through a common community-building process and may encourage schismatic alternatives to arise or existing ones, like the Naxalite movements, to further develop.

The Paradoxical Effect of Reformist Movements: Dalit Identity and its Dilemma in Chhattisgarh

The two national parties — the Congress and the BJP — had an equal number of SC representatives, four each, while the other two seats had been won by the BSP. In the general elections of May 2004, the

---

[9] In Jharkhand, the JMM proved its importance once again winning four seats during the 2004 Lok Sabha elections.

BJP candidates were elected on both the reserved seats for SC. Besides being considered as a tribal state, Chhattisgarh is also generally viewed as a backward state. But, at the first glance, its political scene does not bear such a mark. A second general remark is that the Congress, despite its legacy of association with the representative of the SC community, through the Satnami, does not have a hold on this vote bank nowadays.

Having a high proportion of low castes, and with the new trade roads keeping it away from modern infrastructure development (Mc Eldowney 1980), Chhattisgarh gained the reputation of a 'backward state' during the 19th and the 20th centuries. But because of flourishing reformist movements, the Dalits are perceived as one of the main components of the identity of Chhattisgarh (Shukla 1995). Their total population is estimated above 12.2 per cent. The new state has 10 out of 90 seats reserved for the SC in the Vidhan Sabha. However, though it may seem contradictory, the part of SC in the political arena of the new state appears to be quite marginal, except for the Satnami which is one of the groups which has been most effectively involved in reformist movements.

Chhattisgarh has a long record of anti-untouchability movements at least since the Middle Age. Kabirpanth, Raedasis, Ramnam and Satnam are the main movements which recruited their devotees among low castes and untouchables, articulating the refusal of the discriminatory status given to them by rejecting the mediation of Brahmin and mimicking their habits. Through the brahminical mimesis (refusal of any polluting action such as consumption of alcohol, meat, etc.), they eventually favoured the integration of the Chhattisgarh society into the brahminical fold.

One of the first major identified reformist movements is the Kabirpanth. The devotion to Kabir was well spread in Chhattisgarh by the 18th century. The Kabirpanth cuts across many castes, and therefore acts as a strong linking factor in the Chhattisgarh region.[10] The 19th century saw two other reformist movements in the region: the

---

[10] The figure for the numeric strength of the Kabirpanthis varies in different accounts — from 100 thousand to 30 per cent of the total population (roughly 7 to 8 million), though the latter seems exaggerated. Kabirpanthis in Chhattisgarh are traditionally attached to the Panika community (Singh 1998). It certainly is well represented by a community almost entirely attached to the devotion of Kabir through centuries and sympathisers who come from diverse sociological backgrounds.

Satnam and the Ramnam; both originated from the Chamar community in Chhattisgarh. The Satnam Panth, the second most important social movement in Chhattisgarh, was created by Guru Ghasidas in the
second half of the 19th century and spread in the context of an increasing economic pressure caused by the social exploitation due to
British land settlements and the expansion of the Malguzari system.
The movement caught up with the nationalist movement when
attempts were made to recast it on a Hindu or a Christian pattern. The
Ramnam movement emerged almost simultaneously. It also appears
as an attempt to free people from social subordination, but through a
total identification and appropriation of the Hindu legacy. Those
movements stemmed from the encounter with a brahminical–baniya
order establishing its dominance over society, through the British administration. Eventually, they acted as a transitional phase leading to
the integration of the Chhattisgarh society into the mainstream Hindi
belt society. The strong social commitment of the leaders of the Indian
nationalist movement in Chhattisgarh can be seen from that perspective. Those movements laid down a platform for a mediation between
untouchables and the upper castes. Not only was the commitment of
Gandhi against untouchability to find echoes in Chhattisgarh, in fact,
some local leaders had preceded him in this direction. And when
Gandhi went to Raipur in 1933, he acknowledged that a pioneer of
his social commitment was the social reformer Pandit Sunderlal Sharma
(1881–1940), promoter of the untouchables' cause through his support
of the Satnam movement.

Naindas and Ajordas, two leaders of the Satnami Mahasabha, headed
to the Kanpur session of the Indian National Congress with a five-
member delegation. There, they were given recognition of their status
by Jawaharlal Nehru. Close links existed between the Satnami community and the upper caste politicians at that time. Various achievements resulted from the inroads made by the Satnami community into
national politics. Ratriram, President of the Satnami Mahasabha, often
became the representative of the oppressed class to the Central Province
Legislative Council. The division inside the community threatened to
widen after the set-up of the All India Scheduled Caste Federation in
1942. Some prominent leaders joined the movement led by Ambedkar

while the Satnami Mahasabha stood by the Congress' side. However, the Ambedkar movement did not take roots in Chhattisgarh, whereas in the first Assembly of the Central Provinces, the Satnami Mahasabha had one of his leaders, Guru Agamdas Agarmandas, elected as MLA and after the 1952 elections, for the first Lok Sabha (1952–57); his wife, Srimati Minimata Agamdas, too became an MP. She was re-elected twice in the Bilaspur–Durg Raipur SC reserved seat (1957–67) and then elected in the fifth Lok Sabha (1971–77) in the Janjgir reserved seat. Satnamis' political role persisted with one of its sympathisers, Keyur Bushan, MP from Raipur from 1980 to 1991.

The SC always retain a minimal presence in each government, usually equal or inferior to the total percentage they represent in the population. This presence is, by and large, the monopoly of the Satnami community. Split in various subbranches, it has shown a certain autonomy towards the Congress, some of the representatives openly supporting the BJP in 2004. Nevertheless, the presence of SC is still higher in the Congress party apparatus (8.6 per cent) compared to the BJP (4 per cent); in Ajit Jogi's government it was higher too (7.7 per cent) compared to the first Raman Singh government (5.5 per cent). The reshuffle of the latter has readjusted the balance as 7 per cent of the ministers are from the SC community, which means one minister out of a total of 12.

Integrated and channelised, the Dalit movement took a regional dimension which made the connection with the national scene either unnecessary or difficult. This may be one of the reasons why the Bahujan Samaj Party has had till now a relatively limited support base, with only seven elected MLAs since 1990. If no party can really claim to have control over the SC vote bank in Chhattisgarh today, BJP has made significant inroads in this group by winning four out of 10 reserved seats for SC in the 2004 Vidhan Sabha polls. The NCP did not contest the 2004 Lok Sabha elections, and therefore did not take any share in the traditional Congress vote bank. Nevertheless, the BJP domination over this group has been confirmed, both of its candidates being elected in the two parliamentary constituencies reserved for SC. The shift of the representatives of the Satnami community, such as Vijay Guru, leader of the Satnami Mahasabha or the Satnami Samaj, from supporting the Congress to the BJP is also significant (see *Hitavada* 2004).

A Constant Trend for an Unfinished Agenda: The Assertion of Backward Classes

The share of the OBC among the MLAs elected from Chhattisgarh has been in constant rise from 1962 to 1980, from 8.5 to 22.2 per cent. Thereafter, it has undergone a certain stagnation to reach its higher percentage ever in the last Vidhan Sabha elections with a total of 23.4 per cent and subsequently the lowest percentage ever for upper castes. Is it the result of the assertion of the OBC population through the Chhattisgarh identity? The answer may be more complex. Starting from a point where the backward communities are dramatically under-represented in the early-1960s, it would be more appropriate to see in this augmentation, a readjustment or a rise skilfully contained by the upper castes in a state where they account for half of the population. The promotion of OBC identity has been one of the instruments to attack the stronghold of Brahmins dominating Chhattisgarh's political arena, namely the Shuklas and Motilal Vora, by rivals such as the Congress leader Arjun Singh who was Chief Minister from 1980 to 1985. If the BJP could underplay this political component to access to the power in 1990, they had to integrate it in order to come to power in Chhattisgarh for the first ever election to elect a separate Vidhan Sabha in 2003. Significantly, the BJP has a higher number of OBC MLAs (11 equivalent to 52.38 per cent of its representatives elected in the general seats) compared to the upper caste MLAs (nine amounting to 42.85 per cent), and a significantly higher percentage of OBC MLAs as per its total number of MLAs than compare to the Congress (37.5 per cent). The OBC have also a larger representation in the BJP apparatus at the party level (32 per cent against 22.4 per cent for the Congress) as well as at the government level (29.4 per cent in the Raman Singh government against 11.5 per cent for Ajit Jogi).[11] If the history of the

---

[11] This figure has been modified after the first reshuffle of the Raman Singh government with the implementation of the 91st Amendment to the Constitution. Apart from three ST ministers and two ministers from the general category, Poonam Chandrakar, Minister of State attached to the chief minister, belonging to the OBC community, and Transport, Industry and Commerce Minister Rajinder Pal Singh Bhatia, from the Sikh community, were asked to resign. This confirms that in spite of the overall changing equilibrium, the high command of the executive power remains in the hand of upper caste ministers, with a strong influence of the Brahmin and the Baniya communities.

new state appears as one where the OBC are regaining their hold (in a state where, if we exclude the tribal areas, they occupy a prominent position), one should not forget that as in the case of the ST, the OBC community do not have a specific political platform and that their assertion is incorporated within the frame of the two major national parties' apparatus in the state primarily controlled by the upper castes.

The sociological composition of Chhattisgarh's population is dominated by backward classes. The OBC communities are estimated between 48 and 51 per cent of the total population. Kabirpanth movement, whose members are numerous among OBC, notably among Panikas, is partly a cultural expression of this sociological component, even if Kabirpanth movement attracts people from other sociological groups as well. The recent renaming of Kawardha district as 'Kabirdham' under Ajit Jogi's government is the symptom of the political representatives' attempt to attract the OBC vote bank in Chhattisgarh. It is noteworthy that the former Kawardha district is also an area traditionally associated with tribal history, such as that of Baigas and Gonds, which has clearly been bypassed.

In Chhattisgarh, the two major OBC groups are the Telis (Sahu) and the Ahirs (Yadav, Yadu, etc.) with 9 and 8 per cent respectively of the total backward population. Panika (identified by anthropological studies as water-carriers), Mali (gardeners), Kurmi (an agrarian community) and Kenwat (a fishermen community) also have a significant share (circa 3 per cent each). Other groups, composed mainly by craftsmen, fishermen and small agrarian communities (Kamlar, Dhobi, Lohar, Lodhi, Kosta, Nai, Dhimar, Kumhar, Bairagi, Sonar, Ghosai and Darji) altogether account for almost 9 per cent. The rest of the OBC population is formed by people belonging either to the Muslim or to the Christian community. The fragmentation of the OBC community in former Madhya Pradesh is therefore also relevant in the new state. Although Yadavs and Telis, and to a certain extent Kurmis, have an important position, unlike Bihar and Uttar Pradesh, no other community forms a dominating community through land-owning or contracting activities. Kurmis represent 33.93 per cent of the OBC MLAs elected from 1962 to 2003; Telis, 22.37 per cent. From 1977 onwards, the Yadavs have a share fluctuating from 14 per cent to 5 per cent. Kurmi and Teli MLAs together represent one-third of the present Vidhan Sabha. But there is still no overall dominance of any one group upon the others. None of them hold a deciding vote share in any constituency.

Table 11.8
OBC MLAs in Chhattisgarh, 1962–2003

Community	1962 (%)	1967 (%)	1972 (%)	1977 (%)	1980 (%)	1985 (%)	1990 (%)	1993 (%)	1998 (%)	2003 (%)
Agharia	0	0	0	0	0	0	0	0	0	10
Baghel*	0	13	11	7	5	6	0	6	0	0
Bairagi	0	0	0	0	5	6	8	0	0	0
Fishermen	0	0	0	0	5	11	8	0	0	5
Jaiswal	14	13	11	7	5	11	8	0	0	0
Kurmi	14	38	22	14	35	22	8	33	53	19
Mali	0	0	0	0	0	6	8	6	0	0
Panika	0	0	0	0	5	6	0	6	0	0
Teli	14	13	33	29	10	22	31	33	27	14
Dewangan	0	0	0	0	0	0	0	0	0	10
Yadav	0	0	0	14	5	6	8	6	13	5
Others	57	25	22	29	30	22	31	11	7	38
Total OBC MLAs	(N=7)	(N=8)	(N=9)	(N=14)	(N=20)	(N=18)	(N=13)	(N=18)	(N=15)	(N=31)
Total Number of MLAs	83	82	84	90	90	90	90	90	90	90
Total OBC MLAs (%)	8.5	9.8	10.7	15.5	22.2	20	14.5	20	16.7	23.4

Source: Data concerning years 1957–98 are collected by Christophe Jaffrelot; data concerning the year 2003 are by author.

Note: * Baghel, as presented here as a category, can be classified either as Kurmi Satnami or Thakur.

The gradual rise of OBC in Madhya Pradesh observed by Jaffrelot since 1980 (see Chapter 3 of this volume) is corroborated by its current firmly established place in the new state, at least at the level of the Legislative Assembly. The OBC had a share of only 8.5 per cent of the total number of the MLAs elected in the Assembly constituencies of Chhattisgarh in the Vidhan Sabha of Madhya Pradesh in 1962. It has increased to 23.33 per cent in 2003. The rise of the OBC population in the political arena of Chhattisgarh has been constant between 1957 and 1980 (from 8.5 to 22.22 per cent). The major rise of OBC MLAs occurred during the 1977 elections (from 10.71 per cent in 1972 to 19.55 per cent in 1977). This election was marked by a setback for the Congress with Kailash Joshi of Janata Party becoming Chief Minister. The rise of the OBC in Chhattisgarh was first linked to the alternative to the Congress rule. It anticipated the trend at the state level in Madhya Pradesh, when in 1980, Arjun Singh grounded the political dominance of the Congress by widening the OBC share. By 1980, it had already reached the present figure of about one-fourth of the Vidhan Sabha. The assertion of low castes in Chhattisgarh has therefore occurred at an early stage compared to that of the rest of Madhya Pradesh and this has somehow confirmed the importance of the OBC factor in the new state political identity. The Chhattisgarh political arena has either influenced the general evolution of the Congress policy in Madhya Pradesh — through political leaders such as S. C. Shukla, maybe as a part of a general electioneering strategy — or it has foreshadowed it.

The OBC position at the forefront of the promotion of the identity of Chhattisgarh is corroborated by the action of personalities such as Khubchand Baghel, Bisahu Das Mahant or Mannulal Yadu. Besides the cultural factor, their hold on Chhattisgarh land through the Malguzari system is described as one of the reasons of their endeavour to regain authority over the 'outsiders', people belonging to upper castes who immigrated to Chhattisgarh along with the British administrators and had the upper hand over the political arena after independence (Venkatesan 2000). As in the rest of Madhya Pradesh, the hold over the political arena by upper castes in Chhattisgarh just after independence (at least 32.53 per cent of the MLAs from Chhattisgarh in the 1957 Vidhan Sabha) was reinforced by the Congress policy of co-option of princes and local notables, but the low castes nevertheless started to assert their presence as early as the second Vidhan Sabha elections in 1962.

Table 11.9
Upper Caste MLAs, 1962–2003

Community	1962	1967	1972	1977	1980	1985	1990	1993	1998	2003	TOTAL
Baniya/Jain	2	5	4	7	5	4	7	4	7	7	52
Brahmin	12	14	21	15	12	11	15	15	9	10	134
Kayastha	3	1	–	–	–	–	–	–	–	–	4
Khatri	–	–	–	1	–	1	–	–	–	–	2
Rajput	13	6	6	6	6	8	7	6	8	5	71
Sindhi	–	–	–	–	–	–	1	–	1	–	2
Total Upper Caste MLAs	30	26	31	29	23	24	30	25	25	22	265
Total Number of MLAs	83	82	84	90	90	90	90	90	90	90	879
Percentage	36.15	31.7	36.9	32.2	25.5	26.7	33.3	27.8	27.8	24.4	30.14

Source: Survey by Christophe Jaffrelot.

However, it would perhaps be simplistic to sum up the relation between OBC and upper castes in Chhattisgarh as an opposition between a local elite and a dominant group from the Hindi belt; a readjustment has occurred and there is a game of balance of power between the upper castes and OBC. The OBC factor may grow in the years to come in the new state, their share in the political arena still remaining largely inferior compared to the total of the population they represent. Moreover, they are yet to reach the top level of the political apparatus. Neither in the Ajit Jogi government nor in Raman Singh's did they hold prominent functions. But none of the two dominant parties can afford not to consider them as a major political component.

Conclusion

The bipolar character of Congress versus BJP in the tribal areas of Chhattisgarh may be interpreted in two ways. It can be perceived as the result of a late integration into the mainstream arena of a region which was dominated by princely states before 1947. It may be also seen as the result of the still unachieved political empowerment of the people of the new state of Chhattisgarh, specially the ST, which resulted in the inability to create a specific political movement. This difficult and unachieved integration of the ST is contradictory to the identity of the state commonly introduced as 'tribal'. The high percentage of reserved seats for ST did not imply the emergence of a dominant tribal political class in Chhattisgarh. A tribal representation was allowed by the Congress apparatus in the context of this alliance between the extremes, tribal leaders having no real chance to challenge the dominance of upper castes at the decision-making level anyway. Therefore, this space given to the tribals may be understood as a way to counterbalance the rise of the OBC more than as a support given to tribal political empowerment. The composite social structure of the population, even within the ST communities, has certainly a role in making it difficult for an endogen and unitary political movement to emerge.

Gradually, the patronisation policy of the Congress has been challenged when the BJP happened to be in a position to propose an alternative to the two main social components of Chhattisgarh, the OBC and the ST. A 'caste equilibrium management', wherein the different communities would get some degree of representation, is now in force within a structure where the balance of power has not fundamentally changed. And, at present, the various social groups are scattered across the two parties, with a stronger hold of BJP in the ST vote bank, but with no real forefront leaders from this category of population being given a prominent role. The political prospect relies on the question as to for how long the upper castes will manage to counterbalance the political rise of the OBC and the ST, one against the other, in order to remain at the top positions. The statistical and general analysis tends to prove that the ST remain a privileged target for vote-banking strategies, their rise being easier to confine to subregional responsibilities in the margin of the Chhattisgarh territory.

Appendix: Vidhan Sabha 2003

Sociological Representation in the General Seats

	Number	Percentage
Upper Castes	**22**	**49.57**
Brahmins	10	21.33
Kshatriyas	5	13.04
Baniyas/Jains	7	15.20
Other Backward Classes	**21**	**45.65**
Scheduled Tribes	**1**	**2.17**
Scheduled Castes	**0**	**0**
Others	**2**	**4.34**
Muslims	1	2.17
Sikhs	1	2.17
TOTAL	46	101.73

Source: Author's fieldwork.

General Sociological Composition including Reserved Seats (90 seats)

	Number	Percentage
Upper Castes	**22**	**23.28**
Brahmins	10	11.11
Kshatriyas	5	4.40
Baniyas/Jains	7	7.77
Other Backward Classes	**21**	**23.33**
Scheduled Tribes	**35**	**38.88**
Scheduled Castes	**10**	**11.11**
Others	**2**	**1.33**
Muslims	1	
Sikhs	1	
TOTAL	90	97.93

Source: Author's fieldwork.

Party-wise Sociological Background of MLAs in the General Seats

	BJP		Congress	
	Number	Percentage	Number	Percentage
Upper Castes	9	**42.85**	15	**52.49**
Brahmins	3	14.28	7	29.16
Kshatriyas			5	20.83
Baniyas/Jains	6	28.56	3	12.5
Other Backward Classes	11	**52.38**	9	**37.5**
Scheduled Tribes	0	**0**	1	**4.6**
Muslims	0	**0**	1	**4.6**
Sikhs	1	**4.76**	–	
TOTAL	21	99.9	26	99.19

Source: Author's fieldwork.

Party Share on the Reserved Seats

Number of BJP MLAs Elected on ST Reserved Seats	Percentage of the Total of 35 Seats	Congress MLAs Elected on ST Reserved Seats	Percentage of the Total of 35 Seats
25	71.4	10	28.5

Number of BJP MLAs Elected on SC Reserved Seats	Percentage of the Total of 10 Seats	Congress MLAs Elected on SC Reserved Seats	Percentage of the Total of 35 Seats	BSP MLAs Elected on SC Reserved Seats	Percentage of the Total of 10 Seats
6	60	2	20	2	20

Source: Author's fieldwork.

References and Select Bibliography

Baker, D. E. U. 1979. *Changing Political Leadership in an India Province: The Central Provinces and Berar (1919–1939)*. Delhi: Oxford University Press.

Banerjee, K. 1984. *Regional Political Parties in India*. Delhi: B. R. Publishing Corporation.

Chhattisgarh Mukti Morcha. 1998. *Nawan Bharat bar Nawan Chhattisgarh* (Chhattisgarhi). Raipur.

Danda, A. K. (ed.). 1977. *Chhattisgarh: An Area Study*. Calcutta: Anthropological Survey of India.

Dube, Saurabh. 1998. *Untouchable Pasts: Religion, Identity, and Power Among a Central Indian Community, 1780–1950*. Albany: State University of New York Press.

Election Commission of India. 1951. *Statistical Report on General Election, 1951, to the Legislative Assembly of Madhya Pradesh.* New Delhi: Government of India.

Hitavada, The. 2004. 'Satnami Samaj Favours BJP', 15 April.

Jaffrelot, Christophe and Jasmine Zérinini-Brotel. 2004. 'Post-Mandal Politics in Uttar Pradesh and Madhya Pradesh', in Rob Jenkins (ed.), *Regional Reflections, Comparing Politics Across Indian States*, pp. 139–74. New Delhi: Oxford University Press.

Kumar, Girish. 2006. *Local Democracy in India: Interpreting Decentralization.* New Delhi: Sage Publications.

Kumar, Sanjay and Yogendra Yadav. 2003. 'Understanding the Chhattisgarh Vote', in *The Hindu*, CSDS–*The Hindu*, 11 December.

McEldowney, Philip. 1980. 'Colonial Administration and Social Developments in Middle India: The Central Provinces, 1886–1921'. PhD dissertation, University of Virginia.

Mishra, Neeraj. 2002. 'Numbers Game', *India Today*, 26 October.

Prakash, Amit. 2003. *Jharkhand.* New Delhi: Orient Longman.

Shukla, Hira Lal. 1995. *Chhattisgarh Rediscovered.* New Delhi: Aryan Books.

Shyamlal. 2000. *Tribal Leadership.* Jaipur: Rawat Publications.

Singh, K. S. 1998. *All India's Communities.* New Delhi: Oxford University Press.

Singh, R. L. (ed.). 1995. *India: A Regional Geography.* Varanasi: National Geographic Society of India.

Sinha, Surajit. 1962. 'State Formation and Rajput Myth in Tribal Central India', *Man in India*, 42: 35–80.

Sundar, Nandini. 1997. *Subalterns and Sovereigns: An Anthropological History of Bastar, 1854–1996.* New York: Oxford University Press.

Venkatesan, V. 2000. 'Chhattisgarh: The Quiet Arrival', *Frontline*, 19 August, 17 (17), http://www.hinduonnet.com/fline/fl1717/17170370.htm.

Xaxa, Virginius. 2005. 'Electoral Reservations for the Scheduled Tribes: The Legitimation of Domination', in S. Tawa Lama-Rewal (ed.), *Electoral Reservations, Political Representation, and Social Change in India: A Comparative Perspective.* Delhi: Manohar.

Part V

Where the Upper Castes Resist

12

The Resilient *Bhadralok*: A Profile of the West Bengal MLAs

*Stéphanie Tawa Lama-Rewal**

The data evaluated here come from two main sources: the *Who's Whos* published by the West Bengal Legislative Assembly (WBLA), presenting the biodata of MLAs; and interviews focusing on the identification of the caste/community of MLAs, since this information is not available in the *Who's Whos*. But these data are limited both in their availability and reliability.

As far as the biodata are concerned, out of the 13 assemblies elected in West Bengal between 1952 and 2001 (1952, 1957, 1962, 1967, 1969, 1971, 1972, 1977, 1982, 1987, 1991, 1996 and 2001), three *Who's Whos* for the years 1952, 1967 and 1971 were missing.

Moreover, in the available *Who's Whos*, especially before 1977, the biodata of some MLAs were missing; this is the case in up to 58 per cent of biographical notes in the 1972 edition. From 1977 onwards however the proportion of missing notes gradually decreased from 26 to 6 per cent in 1996. The missing information accounts for the proportion of the 'Not Ascertained' category, which can be quite high in some tables for information that depends exclusively on the *Who's Whos*, such as education and occupation.

Even data which are provided in the *Who's Whos* are fraught with problems. They are sometimes quite ambiguous (for instance, when 'agriculture' or 'social work' are given as occupation); they obviously reflect the subjective choice of the MLA as to what he/she wants to project of his/her personality, and they include a number of errors. In spite of all these shortcomings, however, the data provided in all the

---

*I am very grateful to Mr Sabyasachi Sen and Mr Bhagwat Dutta for their help in the collection of the data presented here.

Who's Whos published by the WBLA constitute a very rich source of information, of which only a part will be analysed here.

As far as the identification of the caste of MLAs is concerned, this information proved extremely difficult to obtain. Given the eminently local nature of caste, interviews with local people were both the only and the best source of information on this subject. But the party cadres whom I first contacted invariably pretended not to know the caste of their MLAs, and I had to finally rely on a limited number of informants (officials of the WBLA, local representatives) for this crucial question. Furthermore, informants had doubts regarding the *jati* of a large number of MLAs, and categorically asserted that there was no such thing as caste among Muslims. As a consequence, most tables in this chapter refer to caste categories rather than *jatis*, in order to stick to the more accurate information, and Muslims are treated as one category.

Lastly, OBC proved to be particularly problematic as a category, since the Left Front government has always been extremely reluctant towards caste-based reservations, which it views as an obstacle to class consciousness. The Left Front government in fact refused to answer the Mandal Commission queries and to identify OBC on the basis of caste, arguing that poverty and low standards of living were better indicators of backwardness than caste (Bhattacharya 1997: 105). Yet, several communities, both Hindu and Muslim, regularly claim OBC status and the afferent benefits.[1] Moreover, many of those *jatis* identified as OBC by my informants (albeit with some hesitation) were actually included among 'Middle Castes' in Census 1931. I finally chose to club OBC together with intermediary castes in order to adhere as closely as possible to the categories considered as relevant by the actors themselves.

In order to get a clearer idea as to who is in which caste category, it is useful to bear in mind that upper castes comprise, mainly, the Brahmins (traditionally, priests and scholars), Kayasthas (scribes) and Vaidyas (doctors); intermediary castes include Aguris and Mahishyas (both peasant proprietors), and OBC such as Telis (oil pressers), Goalas, Ahirs (cowherds), Mahatos (peasants), Malakars (garland-makers) and Malis (fishermen). Scheduled Castes include mostly Bagdis (agricultural labourers and fishermen), Bauris, Namasudras, Rajbanshis, Pods

---

[1] Today, OBC in West Bengal are entitled to a reservation of 5 per cent of the seats in educational institutions.

(cultivators), Sunris (wine-sellers) and Sattars (servants); Scheduled Tribes include Santhals, Majhis, Mundas, Oraons, Rais, Limbus, and Mahlis.

The often-heard statement that 'caste is irrelevant in West Bengal politics' actually constitutes as much a methodological dilemma as the starting point of this analysis. How far does this declaration, expressed by people from all parties, be it the Congress, the CPI(M) or the more recent Trinamul Congress, stand verified by the data collected? It can indeed be observed *in situ* that politicians — party cadres, elected representatives — pretend not to know the caste of their colleagues, nor even their own, beyond categories such as upper castes or Scheduled Castes.

Bengal is known to have been at the margins of the territory of brahminical Hinduism in ancient India; mass conversions to Islam further weakened the hold of caste on social relations, and finally, reformist Hindu sects contributed to the particular role of caste in Bengal's society (Kohli 1992: 395). As a result, untouchability does not have the same meaning here as in the Hindi belt, and relations between different castes are not as rigid, even though caste hierarchy is certainly present.

One has to keep in mind here the rough break-up of the population of West Bengal in terms of caste/community. According to Census 1991, Muslims constituted 23.6 per cent of the population, Scheduled Castes 23.6 per cent and Scheduled Tribes 5.6 per cent. As far as the other categories are concerned, one has to rely, as in other states, on the figures provided by the last census taking caste into account, which was in 1931. In the area today known as West Bengal, the proportion of upper castes was then about 6 per cent of the population and that of intermediary castes about 35 per cent (Chatterjee 1998: 72). The projection of figures dating back to 70 years is particularly hazardous in West Bengal because of the massive entry of Hindu refugees which resulted from the partition in 1947. According to Partha Chatterjee, however, 'the present proportions are not likely to be vastly different, except for a probable increase in the upper caste Hindu proportions in the districts of 24 Parganas, Nadia, Jalpaiguri and Cooch Behar, following partition and migration from the districts of eastern Bengal' (*ibid.*: 73). If one considers this increase as accounting for the gap in the figures just recounted, then the proportion of upper castes would be about 10 per cent today.

Table 12.1
Estimated Caste/Community Composition of West Bengal, 1931 and 1991
(% of the total population)

	1931	1991
Upper Castes	5.7	10.0
Middle Castes/Intermediary Castes	35.1	35.0
Depressed Classes/Scheduled Castes	17.4	23.6
Tribes/Scheduled Tribes	7.8	5.6
Muslims	27.9	23.6

Sources: Chatterjee (1998); Vijayan Unni (1998).

Background: West Bengal's Politics since Independence

In the struggle for independence, Bengal was both at the forefront — the Swadeshi movement, the first mass movement of Indian national-ism, originated as reaction to the first attempt by the British to partition the province of Bengal in 1905 — and at the margin, since Bengali nationalism always remained wary of Hindi–India domination (Kohli 1990: 392). Bengal's specificity also included the radicalism of its elite's involvement in the nationalist movement through 'revolutionary terrorism', and the difficulty of the Congress party to come to power. Indeed, prior to independence, electoral politics in Bengal was dom-inated by the Muslims (who were then the majority community), through the Krishak Praja Party of Fazlul Huq and then through the Muslim League.

Bengal was partitioned for the second time in 1947, which means that it was reduced to one-third of its size. It ceased to be a Muslim-majority region because of the transfer of Hindu population from east Pakistan, and lost its Muslim political elite. According to Kohli, the Congress, which came to power after independence, lacked deep electoral roots from the very beginning (1990: 407). It nevertheless won an absolute majority in the Assembly elections of 1952, 1957, 1962, as elsewhere in India. The opposition, comprising mostly the Left parties, was then unable to overcome the major weakness of constant internecine quarrels. In 1964, the Communist Party split into two — the smaller, Moscow-oriented Communist Party of India, or CPI, and the larger, Beijing-oriented Communist Party of India (Marxist), or CPI(M).

From 1967 to 1977, West Bengal experienced economic crisis, political violence, governmental instability and state repression on an unprecedented scale. In 1966, a food crisis (following the drought of the past two years) erupted, which was felt particularly strongly in Calcutta, and the Left parties successfully mobilised the population against the government on this issue. The Congress split, with Ajoy Mukherjee founding his own Bangla Congress Party (BCP). In the 1967 elections, the Congress failed to get a majority, and the Bangla Congress then joined an array of small Left parties (of which the CPI(M) was the most important) to form the United Front government. The United Front's rule was marked by economic and political chaos. Left parties did not want to crush peasant rebellions such as the ones that erupted in Naxalbari in 1967 (led by a radical section of the CPI(M)) nor workers protests. As a result, strikes multiplied, the Naxalite movement developed into urban terrorism and President's rule was soon imposed by the centre. Mid-term elections were organised in 1969, and once again, a United Front government came to power. Once more, political and economic chaos ensued, and President's rule was imposed for a second time in 1970. Following the 1971 mid-term elections, a new coalition government was formed, this time around the Congress, but it resigned after a few months and President's rule was imposed for the third time. After her victory in the war against Pakistan in 1971, Indira Gandhi used her new popularity to crush the Naxalites, and the Congress won massively in the 1972 elections, even though communists always contested the validity of this election.

In 1977, the end of the Emergency was marked in West Bengal by a massive victory of the Left Front, who went on to win an absolute majority of seats for the next five elections.[2] Since then, the Congress has continued to weaken under the weight of factionalism,[3] which ultimately took the form of a split initiated by the Youth Congress leader of Calcutta, Mamata Banerjee, who formed her own Trinamul Congress ('Congress of the roots') in 1997 proceeding to become the

---

[2] In 1977, the Left Front consisted of the CPI(M), the Forward Bloc (FBL), the Revolutionary Socialist Party, the Forward Bloc (Marxist), the Revolutionary Communist Party of India and the Biplabi Bangla Congress. Later, the CPI also joined it.

[3] By 'Congress', I mean the main Congress party, i.e., the Congress (Ruling) in 1969, and the Congress (Indira) since 1978.

second political force in the state in the Lok Sabha elections of 1998 and 1999, and then in the Assembly elections of 2001.

One can, thus, distinguish three main phases in the political history of the state: the years of Congress dominance (1952 to 1967), the years of turmoil (1967 to 1977), and the years of Left Front dominance (1977 till today). However, even though the Left Front enjoyed a sixth consecutive victory in the 2001 Assembly elections, one must mention that Mamata Banerjee's political outfit has proved itself an important, albeit fluctuating, political force. The quick succession of elections at the centre (in 1999), at the municipal level (in 2000) and at the state level (in 2001) were marked by an unexpected rise of the Trinamul Congress; but the same series of elections five years later were marked by a huge defeat of the new party, which nevertheless remains the most vocal opposition to the Left Front.

Caste/Community Identity of MLAs in West Bengal

The most immediately striking feature of Figure 12.1 presenting the caste/community composition of the WBLA over the last 50 years, is in fact that of the consistent over-representation of upper castes. Even though the importance of upper castes in the WBLA fluctuates between 37.5 per cent (in 1972) and 50 per cent (in 1957) of all MLAs, it remains

Figure 12.1
Caste/Community Composition of the WBLA, 1952–2001

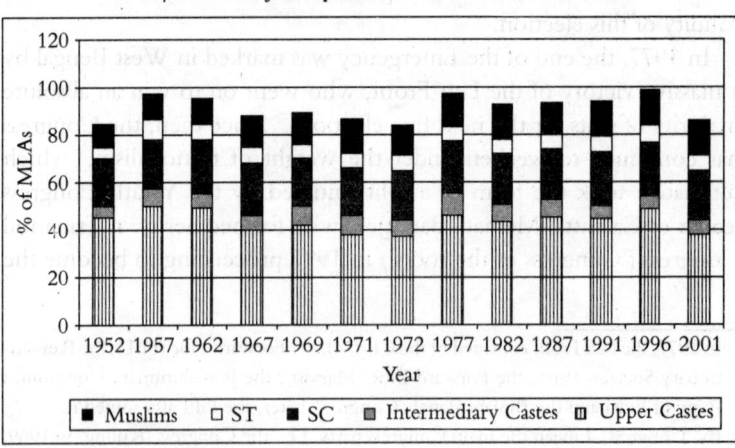

Source: Prepared by author.

consistently out of proportion with their demographic importance. They are relatively less dominant during the 'turbulent decade' from 1967 to 1977. This can be attributed to two reasons: (*i*) the prominence of the Bangla Congress, born from a split in 1967, and often called a *kulak* party because of its relatively higher proportion of intermediary and lower castes; and (*ii*) the fact that in 1972 a large number of members of the Left cadres, who were overwhelmingly upper caste, were in jail following state repression of the Naxalite movement. But the higher position (a rise from 45.4 to 50 per cent) of upper caste MLAs in the three assemblies dominated by the Congress (1952, 1957 and 1962) as well as in the six assemblies dominated by the Left Front (an increase from 45.9 per cent in 1977 to 49 per cent in 1996, with a significant decrease to 37.8 per cent in 2001, however), testifies to the over-representation of upper castes in these two political forces, a theme that will be further explored.

Table 12.2 focuses on the *jatis* which make up the upper castes. These appear to be composed almost exclusively of Brahmins (who make up 49.1 per cent of all upper caste MLAs over the whole period) and Kshatriyas (50 per cent), with Vaidyas (1.5 per cent) coming a distant third.

The proportion of the Scheduled Castes, accounting for 19.7 per cent (in 1952) to 21.1 per cent (in 2001) of MLAs, closely reflects their demographic weight since most of them are elected from reserved constituencies whose number is precisely proportional to their population, as shown in Figure 12.2a, which presents the number of SC MLAs in reserved and general seats over the years.

The same can be said of the Scheduled Tribes, whose number oscillates between 5 per cent (in 1952) and 6.5 per cent (in 2001) of MLAs, with a relative peak in 1957 (8.3 per cent), which is very conspicuous in Figure 12.2b, but for which I have not found an explanation.

Out of the remaining categories, it is obvious that intermediary castes and, to a lesser extent, Muslims are largely under-represented. The former oscillate between 4.6 per cent (in 1952) and 6.1 per cent (in 2001) of all MLAs, and their importance in the WBLA is a case of trendless fluctuation, the only constant being their weak presence, notwithstanding a peak in 1977 (9.5 per cent) reflecting a rare instance of the impact of the central scene on the state politics, where the Janata Party (JNP) was voted to power after the end of the Emergency. Lastly, Muslims account

Table 12.2
Upper Caste MLAs in West Bengal, 1952–2001

	1952	1957	1962	1967	1969	1971	1972	1977	1982	1987	1991	1996	2001
Brahmins	50	59	52	65	58	60	59	66	68	64	62	71	60
Kayasthas	54	66	70	38	58	41	46	69	58	69	70	71	50
Vaidyas	4	0	1	8	0	6	0	0	0	0	0	1	0
Other Upper Castes	0	1	1	1	1	0	0	0	1	0	0	1	0
Total Upper Caste MLAs	108	126	124	112	117	107	105	135	127	133	132	144	110
Total Number of MLAs	238	252	252	280	280	280	280	294	294	294	294	294	294

Source: Survey by author.

Figure 12.2a
SC MLAs in Reserved and General Seats in West Bengal, 1952–2001

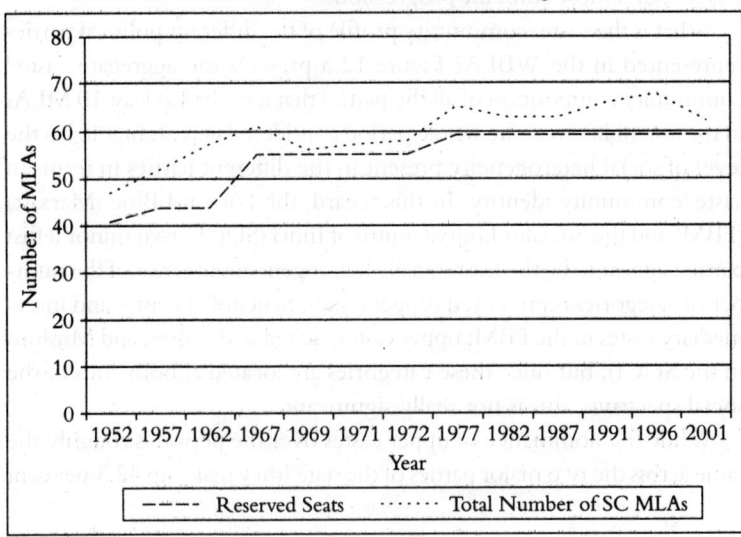

Source: Prepared by author.

Figure 12.2b
ST MLAs in Reserved and General Seats in West Bengal, 1952–2001

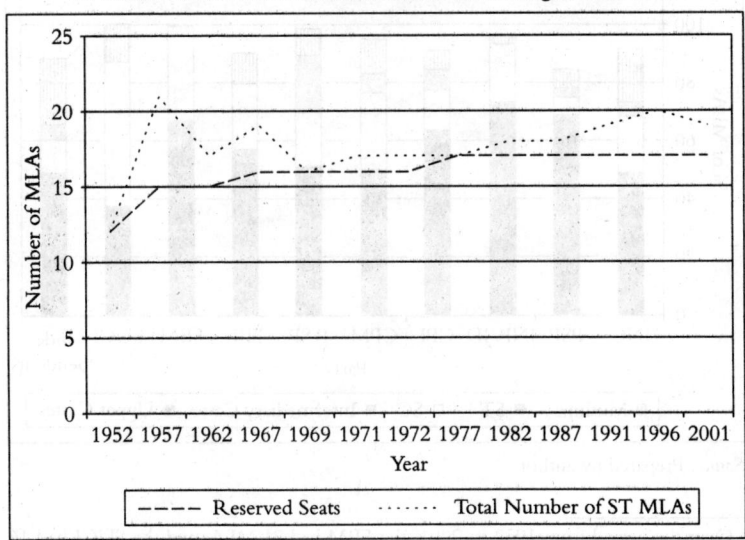

Source: Prepared by author.

for 9.7 per cent of MLAs in 1952, and to 14.3 per cent in 2001, through a slow but almost constant progression.

What is the caste/community profile of the different political parties represented in the WBLA? Figure 12.3 presents the aggregate caste/community composition of all the parties that have had at least 10 MLAs in the assemblies over the whole period considered here. It highlights the level of social heterogeneity present in the different parties in terms of caste/community identity. In this regard, the Forward Bloc (Marxist) (FBM) and the Socialist Unity Centre of India (SUCI), two minor leftist parties, appear to be the least socially heterogeneous in terms of the number of categories represented (upper castes, Scheduled Castes and intermediary castes in the FBM; upper castes, Scheduled Castes, and Muslims in the SUCI), but since these categories are located at both ends of the social spectrum, this is not really significant.[4]

While the dominance of upper castes over the period is roughly the same across the two major parties of the state (they make up 42.3 per cent

Figure 12.3
Caste/Community Composition of Parties in the WBLA, 1952–2001

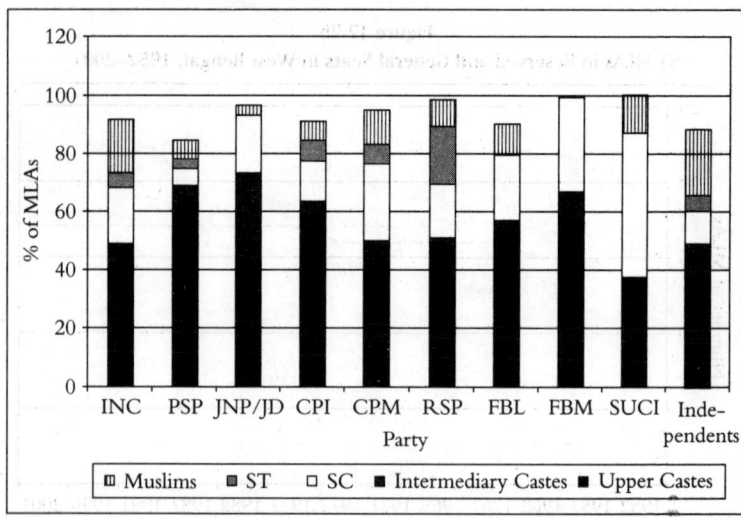

Source: Prepared by author.

[4] Over the period from 1952 to 2001, the FBM had 21 MLAs and the SUCI had 16 MLAs.

of Congress MLAs, and 43 per cent of CPI(M) MLAs), it is generally more pronounced in the Left parties: 62.5 per cent of upper caste MLAs in the Praja Socialist Party (PSP) (which however disappeared from the WBLA in 1972), 58.5 per cent in the CPI, 57.1 per cent in the FBM and 52.1 per cent in the FBL.

Not surprisingly, the Janata Party/Janata Dal has the largest proportion of intermediary castes (30 per cent), but even there upper caste MLAs are the most numerous (43.3 per cent).

The Scheduled Castes are comparatively better represented in the FBM (33.3 per cent) and in the SUCI (50 per cent). The Revolutionary Socialist Party (RSP) proves to have the largest proportion of Scheduled Tribes MLAs (20.1 per cent out of a total of 134 MLAs). This is consistent with the known fact that the Left Front has tended to attract the majority of votes from these two categories since 1977.

Lastly, the Congress has the largest proportion of Muslim MLAs (18.2 per cent) among all parties; however, Muslim MLAs are even more numerous among independents (22.7 per cent), which points to a problem in their political representation, a point to which I will later return.

In order to understand the evolution of the caste/community composition of the WBLA over time we can now focus on the two main political parties of the state since independence, i.e., the Congress and the Communist Party. The caste/community identity of the MLAs of the Indian National Congress (INC) since 1952 is presented in Table 12.3, that of the CPI/CPI(M) in Table 12.4. In the latter case, figures up to 1962 are those of the CPI, and figures concerning the period after the 1964 split concern the CPI(M).

A comparison of Tables 12.3 and 12.4 suggests that the respective sociological evolutions of the two parties are closely linked. The year 1977 appears as pivotal, when the Congress started having fewer Scheduled Castes (from 21.3 per cent in 1952 to 10 per cent that year), but more Muslims (with a record proportion that year of 55 per cent Muslim MLAs), while the proportion of upper castes among its MLAs reached a low 25 per cent before starting a continued ascent. At the same moment, the CPI(M) started having fewer upper castes (from an all-time high of 63 per cent in 1957 to 44.9 per cent in 1977), but more and more Scheduled Castes (from an all-time low of 8.7 per cent in 1957 to 25.3 per cent in 1977) among its MLAs.

Table 12.3

Caste/Community Identity of the Congress MLAs, 1952–2001 (% of the total number of the party's MLAs)

	1952	1957	1962	1967	1969	1971	1972	1977	1982	1987	1991	1996	2001
Upper Castes	44.7	44.1	47.1	37.8	23.6	33.0	34.3	25.0	38.8	50.0	55.8	58.5	30.8
Intermediary Castes	4.0	7.2	5.7	4.7	12.7	9.7	7.9	0	8.2	5.0	4.7	3.6	7.7
SC	21.3	26.3	25.5	18.9	21.8	19.0	21.8	10.0	8.2	7.5	2.3	12.2	15.4
ST	5.3	7.9	5.7	9.4	12.7	7.0	5.1	0	0	2.5	0	0	3.8
Muslims	13.3	13.8	12.7	15.0	23.6	18.0	13.4	55.0	32.7	22.5	27.9	23.2	38.5
Not Ascertained	11.3	0.7	3.2	14.2	5.5	14.6	17.8	10.0	12.2	10.0	9.3	2.4	3.8
TOTAL	(N=150)	(N=152)	(N=157)	(N=127)	(N=55)	(N=103)	(N=216)	(N=20)	(N=82)	(N=40)	(N=43)	(N=82)	(N=26)

Source: Survey by author.

Table 12.4

Caste/Community Identity of the MLAs of the CPI/CPI(M), 1957–2001 (% of the total number of the party's MLAs)

	1957	1962	1967	1969	1971	1977	1982	1987	1991	1996	2001
Upper Castes	63.0	62.0	53.5	52.5	43.4	44.9	42.0	43.3	43.1	45.2	33.6
Intermediary Castes	6.5	6.0	4.7	8.7	8.0	8.4	8.0	6.9	5.3	6.4	4.9
SC	8.7	14.0	20.9	20.0	23.0	25.3	26.4	25.7	27.7	29.3	26.6
ST	10.9	10.0	–	2.5	4.4	7.3	8.0	7.0	6.4	7.6	9.1
Muslims	4.3	6.0	9.3	7.5	10.6	12.9	11.5	12.8	11.7	10.8	12.6
Not Ascertained	6.5	2.0	11.6	8.8	10.6	1.1	4.0	4.3	5.9	0.6	0
TOTAL	(N=46)	(N=50)	(N=43)	(N=80)	(N=14)	(N=178)	(N=174)	(N=187)	(N=188)	(N=157)	(N=143)

Source: Survey by author.

Tables 12.5a and 12.5b will help to correct these observations by showing the distribution of the MLAs of each caste/community among these two parties over time. These tables underline the shifts that took place over the years, especially concerning the Scheduled Castes who were present in massive numbers in the Congress from 1952 till 1962, and similarly so in the CPI(M) from 1977 onwards. The 'turbulent decade' truly appears here as one of transition in the party affiliations of the different castes/communities. The astonishing figures of 1972 have to be read keeping in mind that a large part of the Left leadership was then in jail, following state repression of the Naxalite movement. Scheduled Tribes too seem to have deserted the Congress in favour of the CPI(M) *en masse*. Lastly, these tables show that if Muslims were indeed largely with the Congress until 1962, they have been attaching themselves to other parties since then, and have become much more present in the CPI(M) (42.9 per cent of them were with CPI(M) in 2001).

The figures presented so far, taken together, point to a number of specific features of the West Bengal political scene.

First, there seems to be no caste/community-based vote bank since most caste/communities are represented in most of the political parties. The changing distribution of Scheduled Castes, Scheduled Tribes and Muslims among the main parties follows roughly the decline of the Congress and the rise of the CPI(M)-led Left Front in the state.

Second, upper castes have been largely dominating the WBLA from 1952 till today. This fact is well known. As Atul Kohli put it 13 years ago, 'radical, conservative or reformist, modern Bengali politics has been dominated by an upper caste, well-off, educated minority' (Kohli 1990: 367). Several explanations can be suggested.

One, no party in West Bengal has been able to challenge the upper caste domination of state politics. The only relatively significant parties which did not share this feature of a strong presence of upper castes among their MLAs were shortlived ones: the Kisan Mazdoor Praja Party disappeared from the WBLA after the 1952 elections (it merged with the much more upper caste-dominated Praja Socialist Party), while the Bangla Congress, born out of a split from the Congress in 1965, lived only through three elections: 1967, 1969 and 1971. 'The rise and fall of this party clearly showed the electoral non-viability of a distinctly *kulak* party vying for provincial power' (Chatterjee 1998: 82).

Table 12.5a

Proportion of Congress MLAs within Each Caste/Community (% of the total number of MLAs in each caste/community category)

	1952	1957	1962	1967	1969	1971	1972	1977	1982	1987	1991	1996	2001
Upper Castes	62.0	53.2	59.7	42.9	11.1	31.8	70.5	3.7	15.0	15.0	18.2	33.3	7.2
Intermediary Castes	54.5	57.9	60.0	37.5	30.4	47.6	89.5	0	25.0	13.6	16.7	21.4	11.1
SC	68.1	76.9	70.2	39.3	21.4	33.3	81.0	3.1	6.3	4.8	1.5	14.7	6.5
ST	66.7	57.1	52.9	63.2	43.8	41.2	64.7	0	0	5.6	0	0	5.3
Muslims	87.0	77.8	71.4	50.0	34.2	43.9	78.4	26.8	37.2	23.7	27.9	43.2	23.8

Source: Survey by author.

Table 12.5b

Proportion of CPI/CPI(M) MLAs within Each Caste/Community (% of the total number of MLAs in each caste/community category)

	1952	1957	1962	1967	1969	1971	1972	1977	1982	1987	1991	1996	2001
Upper Castes	13.9	23.0	25.0	20.5	35.9	45.8	5.7	59.3	57.5	60.9	61.4	49.3	43.2
Intermediary Castes	14.3	18.8	20.0	12.5	30.4	42.8	6.3	53.6	63.6	59.0	62.5	71.4	38.9
SC	12.8	7.7	12.3	14.8	28.6	45.6	6.9	69.2	73.0	76.2	78.8	67.6	61.3
ST	0	23.8	29.4	0	12.5	29.4	5.9	76.5	77.8	72.2	63.2	60.0	68.4
Muslims	0	7.4	10.7	10.5	15.8	29.3	5.4	56.1	46.5	63.2	51.2	38.6	42.9

Source: Survey by author.

Why is that so? The social structure of West Bengal is historically characterised by the relative weakness of those lower castes who were at the forefront of the construction of political identities on the basis of caste in many other states. According to Partha Chatterjee:

> Muslim conversion has a great deal to do with the rather unique caste structure in Bengal, because a very substantial bulk of the peasantry, who would otherwise have formed the middle castes, became Muslim. In many respects, both before and after partition, the Muslim landowning peasantry in both halves of Bengal have behaved much like the dominant peasant middle castes in other parts of India, but because of religious 'communalism', this has taken completely different ideological and organisational forms in undivided and later divided Bengal (1998: 74).

Moreover, the *jatis* pertaining to intermediary castes are characterised in the state by their great fragmentation: 'with the exception [of the Mahishyas, the Sadgops, the Goalas and the Kurmis in South Western Bengal], none of the other [middle] castes numbered more than 3 per cent of the population in any district' (*ibid.*).

Two, the dominance of the Left since the 1970s has probably reinforced the hold of upper castes on the political leadership in three ways: (*i*) the Bengali communist cadres are typically recruited among an elite; (*ii*) the practice of democratic centralism does not favour a quick turnover of the leadership; (*iii*) the communists have typically ignored caste (as well as gender, for that matter) in their analysis of social relations, since class is traditionally the privileged category in their ideological framework, and they have worked instead on the construction of a multi-class alliance to support them; they have succeeded to the extent that middle and small farmers (who often constitute the bulk of OBC in other Indian states) have been supporting the Left Front ever since it came to power and started implementing land reforms.[5]

Caste, then, is not an issue, yet it certainly is a strong political resource in West Bengal politics. Why is this fact never discussed in the state? Caste movements in fact did exist in colonial Bengal, one of the most prominent being that of the Namasudras, which however vanished in the 1940s

---

[5] This might be changing though: in 2001, the proportion of upper castes among CPI(M) MLAs was only 33.6 per cent.

'when new identities emerged and new alignments were made in anti-cipation of an imminent transfer of power' (Bandyopadhyay 1997: 9). Since then, two main movements have pitted the rural landless poor against the (often) upper caste landlords: the Tebhaga movement in 1946, mostly composed of Scheduled Castes (Rajbanshis, Namasudras) and Muslims; and the Naxalite movement born in 1967, mostly ani-mated by Scheduled Tribes (Santals) and Scheduled Castes. But both movements took place outside the sphere of electoral politics, were relatively shortlived, and ignored castes on behalf of revolution.

Is this situation changing? Two relatively recent developments de-serve to be mentioned here. First, Mamata Banerjee — whose Trinamul Congress (TMC) has become, since 1998, the second political force in the state notwithstanding the fact that her support is largely limited to the Kolkata region — publicly supported Muslims' demands for job reservations, thus exposing herself to accusations of blatant commu-nalism. Even though this particular move may have to do with her difficulties in reconciling her participation in the coalition headed by the Hindu Right at the centre and her need of the support of Muslim voters in the state, it nevertheless points to the near possibility for the caste/community factor to become an issue in West Bengal. However, a closer look at the caste/community composition of the TMC exposes the rhetorical dimension of Banerjee's demand: 53.3 per cent of the party's MLAs belong to the upper castes and only 3.3 per cent of them are Muslims.[6]

Second, and more importantly, in the last two decades, at least one political movement has relied on the assertion of a caste-based identity: the Kamtapuri movement, by which Rajbanshis, claiming to be indi-genous to the north Bengal region, demand a separate state composed of the five northern districts where they — now listed as a Scheduled Caste in the West Bengal government — are concentrated. The move-ment started in the 1970s, concentrated mostly in the rural areas, especially the tea plantations of Jalpaiguri and Cooch Behar, and lived through a succession of re-creations, until it came back strongly in 1998 under the leadership of the Kamtapur People's Party, and developed in

---

[6] The sudden rise of the TMC might actually explain the noticeable change in the caste/community profile of Congress MLAs; it is, in fact, likely that the TMC has attracted a large number of the former Congress upper caste MLAs.

other districts of north Bengal (parts of Darjeeling and north and south Dinajpur) through militant actions.[7]

Another ethnic movement is the Gorkhaland movement led by Subash Ghising and his Gorkha National Liberation Front (GNLF) which demanded in the 1980s that Darjeeling become a separate state. After four years of agitation, the creation of the Darjeeling Gorkha Hill Council in 1986 was achieved as a compromise between the Left Front government and the GNLF. In 2000, the demand for statehood re-emerged, issued by former members of the GNLF who by then had begun calling themselves the Gorkhaland Liberation Organisation.

Are these movements reflected in the sociological profile of the WBLA? A region-wise break-up of the caste/community composition of the Assembly will perhaps answer this. Figure 12.4 shows that, as expected, the local concentration of some castes/communities is reflected in the identity of the MLAs of the four main regions. Thus, 59.4 per cent of all intermediary caste MLAs come from the south western region,

Figure 12.4
Caste/Community Distribution of MLAs by Region in West Bengal, 1952–2001

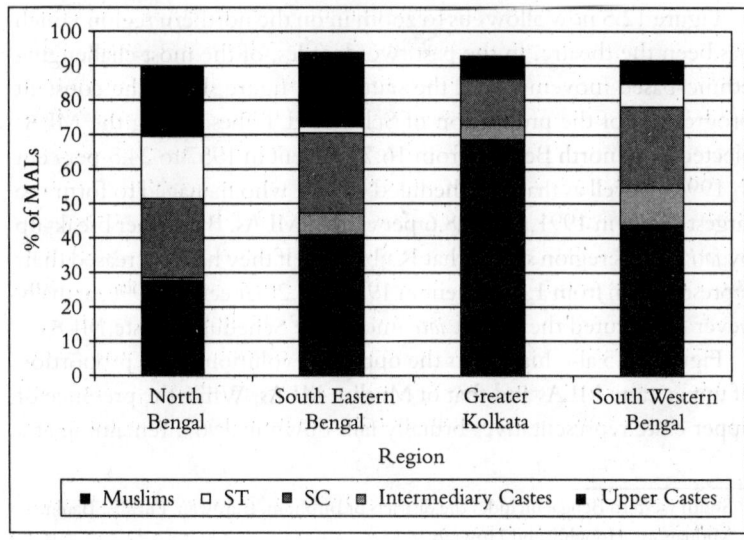

Source: Prepared by author.

---

[7] Cooch Behar is the Indian district with the highest proportion of Scheduled Castes, i.e., 51.8 per cent (Source: *Census of India* 2001).

especially from the districts of Midnapore, Hooghly and Howrah, where Mahishyas, who are the largest caste of peasant proprietors in Bengal, are often the dominant caste.[8] Again, 53.6 per cent of all Scheduled Tribe MLAs come from the northern region, especially from the districts of Jalpaiguri and Darjeeling.[9] And, 44.1 per cent of Muslim MLAs are elected from the south eastern region, especially Nadia, Murshidabad and the 24 Parganas.[10] The second region electing a relatively large number of Muslims is the north, as we will later see. The importance of Scheduled Caste MLAs is roughly constant in all regions, except in Kolkata where they are comparatively less numerous. There, upper caste MLAs are the most dominant (they form 68.5 per cent of MLAs elected in Greater Kolkata), while they are the least present in the north. The fact that 28.3 per cent of upper caste MLAs come from Greater Kolkata indeed suggests that the state capital retains its historical hold over the countryside. We have, here, an illustration of the well-known 'continued domination by an upper caste Hindu and predominantly urban middle class in virtually every sphere of organised political ... life in the state' (Chatterjee 1998: 23).

Figure 12.5 now allows us to zoom in on the northern region which has been the theatre, in the past two decades, of the most challenging ethnic-based movements of the state. This figure shows the constant progression of the proportion of Scheduled Tribes among the MLAs elected from north Bengal (from 16.7 per cent in 1957 to 24.5 per cent in 1996) as well as that of Scheduled Castes, who managed to form the largest group in 1991, with 28.6 per cent of MLAs. But a finer break-up by *jati* for this region shows that Rajbanshis, if they have increased their representation from 1.5 per cent in 1952 to 8.2 per cent in 1996, actually never constituted the largest *jati* among the Scheduled Caste MLAs.

Figure 12.5 also highlights the opposite evolution of the proportion of upper caste MLAs and that of Muslim MLAs. While the presence of upper caste representatives brutally falls down in 1967, remaining at a

---

[8] South western Bengal includes the districts of Birbhum, Burdwan, Purulia, Bankura, Midnapore, Hooghly and Howrah.

[9] The northern region encompasses the districts of Cooch Behar, Jalpaiguri, Darjeeling, north Dinajpur, south Dinajpur and Malda.

[10] The south eastern region includes the districts of Murshidabad, Nadia, North 24 Parganas and South 24 Parganas.

Figure 12.5
Caste/Community Identity of MLAs Elected from the
North Bengal Region, 1957–66

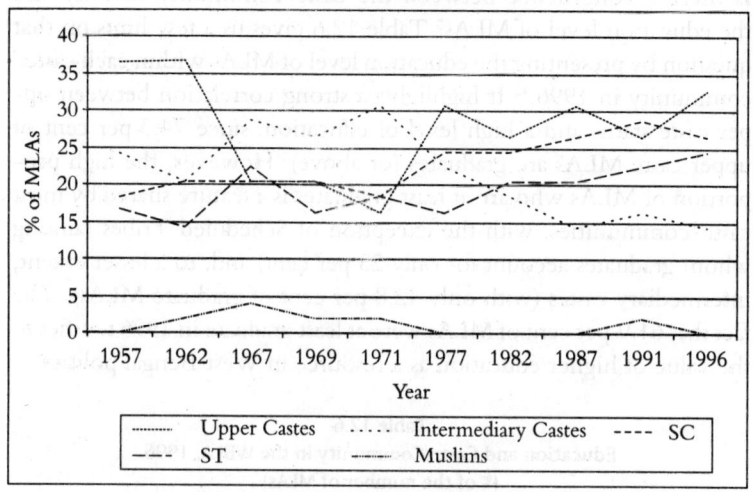

Source: Prepared by author.

relatively low level until 1977, the proportion of Muslim MLAs follows an exactly reverse course, with a peak at 30.6 per cent in 1971. This is a clear reflection of the concentration of upper caste MLAs in the Left Front parties and of the strong presence of Muslims in the north Bengal Congress (22.2 per cent of Congress MLAs are Muslims in 1967, 26.1 per cent in 1969, 30.6 per cent in 1971). In 1996, however, upper caste MLAs regain their formerly dominant position in the region, since they form, that year, 32.7 per cent of the total number of north Bengal's MLAs.

Are *bhadraloks*, then, still in power in today's West Bengal? These 'respectable people', an urban elite enjoying the multiple privilege of upper caste status, English education and employment in the higher professions, have been dominating the public life of Bengal since the 1930s.[11] In order to test the hypothesis of their persistent domination in the state Assembly, one must now compare the caste/community variable in the WBLA with those of education and occupation.

---

[11] *Bhadraloks* in fact dominated Bengal's public life since the end of the 19th century, but at that time they were mostly landlords.

Looking for the *Bhadralok*

Is there a congruence between the caste/community identity and the education level of MLAs? Table 12.6 gives us a few hints on that question by presenting the education level of MLAs within each caste/community in 1996.[12] It highlights a strong correlation between upper caste status and a high level of education, since 74.3 per cent of upper caste MLAs are graduates (or above). However, the high proportion of MLAs who are at least graduates is a feature shared by most caste/communities, with the exception of Scheduled Tribes (among whom graduates account for only 25 per cent) and, to a lesser extent, intermediary castes (with only 42.8 per cent of graduate MLAs). The fact that 61.9 per cent of MLAs were at least graduate in 1996 testifies to the value of higher education as a resource in West Bengal politics.

Table 12.6
Education and Caste/Community in the WBLA, 1996
(% of the number of MLAs)

	Non-literate	Middle-level Pass	Matriculate	Graduate and above	Not Ascertained	TOTAL
Upper Castes	0	4.9	14.6	74.3	6.3	(N=144)
Intermediary Castes	0	21.4	21.4	42.8	14.3	(N=14)
SC	0	25.0	22.1	50.0	2.9	(N=68)
ST	0	15.0	55.0	25.0	5.0	(N=20)
Muslims	2.3	6.8	22.7	65.9	2.3	(N=44)

Source: Survey by author.

The third criterion defining the bhadralok status, i.e., occupation, must now be considered. Figure 12.6 shows the caste/community composition of each occupational group present in the WBLA for the period 1957–96.

It is important to underline here the ambiguities of the data on occupation that are provided in the *Who's Whos*. 'Social worker' is a very vague category; it tells us more about the value attached by MLAs themselves to social work as a proof of commitment to people's welfare, than about

---

[12] Unfortunately, owing to the large number of missing biographical notes in the *Who's Who*, it is not possible to make comparisons of the relationship between caste/community identity vis-à-vis education levels over time.

Figure 12.6
Occupation and Caste/Community in the WBLA, 1957–96

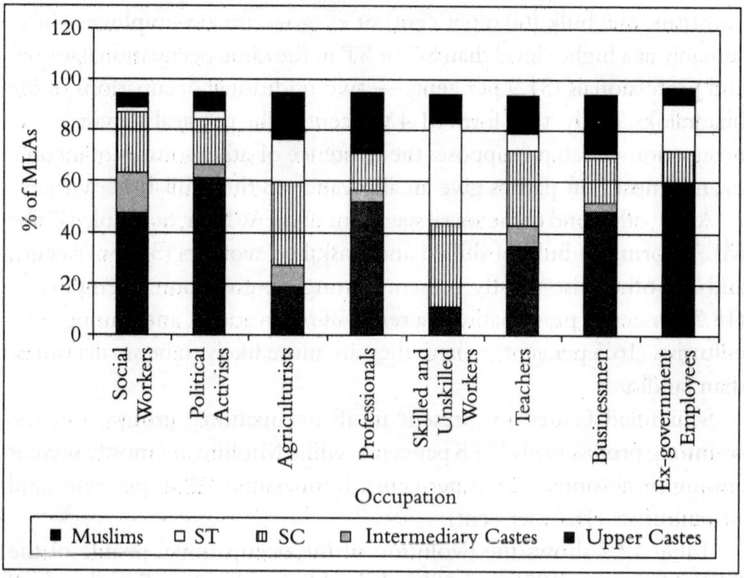

Source: Prepared by author.

their actual occupation. The category 'Agriculturists', too, can recover very different realities. Indeed, the caste break-up within this group suggests that (*i*) upper caste agriculturists (18.9 per cent) may roughly represent the number of landlords; (*ii*) intermediary caste agriculturists (8.6 per cent) may represent peasant proprietors; and (*iii*) agriculturists among the Scheduled Castes (32.5 per cent), Scheduled Tribes (16.5 per cent) and Muslims (18.1 per cent) may represent small farmers. Because categories such as those of agriculturists, as also of businessmen and ex-government employees, can recover very different realities, one is hard put to derive any conclusion from the data concerning the occupation of MLAs. A comparison of these data with those concerning caste and community, however, gives us some clues as to their interpretation.

Looking at Figure 12.6, one would notice the fact that upper castes are largely present among most occupation groups, except workers (skilled and unskilled) and agriculturists; this is consistent with the earlier observation that as far as education is concerned, upper caste MLAs are the most educated ones, and tends to confirm our tentative equation of upper caste MLAs with bhadraloks, since eschewing manual work is one of the defining features of bhadraloks. Indeed, upper caste MLAs constitute the bulk (60.6 per cent) of ex-government employees (presumably at a higher level than SC or ST in the same occupational group) and professionals (51.9 per cent) — two traditional occupations of the bhadraloks. Lastly, they form 61.4 per cent of the political activists — an occupation which presupposes the existence of other sources of income even if most Left parties give an allowance to their full-time workers.

At the other end of the social spectrum of the WBLA, Scheduled Tribe MLAs form the bulk of skilled and unskilled workers (38.9 per cent), and are otherwise mostly present among ex-government employees (18.2 per cent), presumably as a result of reservations, and among agriculturists (16.5 per cent), where they are more likely to be small farmers than landlords.

Scheduled Castes are present in all occupational groups, but less so among professionals (13.8 per cent), while Muslims are mostly present among professionals (23.8 per cent), businessmen (22.6 per cent) and agriculturists (18.1 per cent).

Table 12.7 shows the evolution of the occupational profile of the WBLA between 1957 and 1996. It highlights the rise of teachers and that of political activists, both linked to the ascension of the Left Front. It also shows the simultaneous decline of professionals and agriculturists, two occupational groups which dominated the Assembly when the Congress was in power, i.e., until 1969.

Table 12.7
Occupational Profile of the WBLA, 1957 and 1996
(% of the total number of MLAs for each year)

	1957	*1996*
Social Workers	8.3	10.5
Political Activists	10.7	26.2
Agriculturists	20.2	6.1
Professionals	26.6	8.8
Skilled and Unskilled Workers	0.4	0.7
Teachers	6.7	35
Businessmen	7.1	5.1
Ex-government Employees	0.8	2.7
Not Ascertained	19.0	4.1
TOTAL	(N=252)	(N=294)

Source: Survey by author.

Taken together, the broad trends, observed as far as caste/community identity, education level and occupation are concerned, suggest one thing about the classes represented in the WBLA. Scheduled Tribe MLAs, combining a relatively low level of education, an under-representation among professionals (0.6 per cent) and an over-representation among workers (38.9 per cent), seem to occupy the last rank in the social scale of the WBLA. As far as other categories are concerned, however, the inherent ambiguities of several categories of occupation prevent us to establish any definite correlation between caste/community and class.

Gender in the WBLA

Table 12.8 presents the proportion of women among the MLAs of those parties (including 'Independents') which had at least one female MLA over the whole period considered — thus leaving out 20 all-male parties, including the Janata Party/Janata Dal, the Revolutionary Socialist Party, the Jana Sangh, the Marxist Forward Bloc, the Praja Socialist Party, the Samyukta Socialist Party, the Kisan Mazdoor Praja Party and the Indian Gorkha League (parties which had at least 10 MLAs over that period).

Table 12.8
Gender Composition of Parties with At Least One Female MLA, 1952–2001
(% of the total number of MLAs in each party)

	Male	*Female*	*TOTAL*
INC	96.4	3.6	(N=990)
CPM	94.0	6.0	(N=1121)
CPI	96.0	4.0	(N=229)
FBL	96.6	3.4	(N=188)
Independents	95.8	4.2	(N=119)
BCP	97.0	3.0	(N=33)
SUCI	93.7	6.3	(N=16)
GNLF	75.0	25.0	(N=8)
RSP	99.3	0.7	(N=134)
TMC	93.3	6.7	(N=60)

Source: Survey by author.

Leaving aside the Gorkha National Liberation Front, which can boast of 25 per cent women MLAs because two out of its eight representatives are women, it appears that the Trinamul Congress is relatively more favourable to women (who make up 6.7 per cent of the party's MLAs), followed by the SUCI (6.3 per cent) and the CPI(M) with 6 per cent, a somewhat better figure than the Congress' 3.6 per cent. But all figures remain abysmally low, especially compared to the strength of the women's fronts attached to Left parties, particularly the CPI(M)'s All India Democratic Women's Organisation.

Who are the women who still make it to the WBLA? Table 12.9 presents the caste/community of MLAs of both sexes for the whole period. It shows that upper castes are even more over-represented among women than among men MLAs. This suggests that social prestige might compensate handicaps linked to gender (women generally have a more limited access to political resources such as time, money and contacts). The second largest group is that of Scheduled Caste women, which fits with the known fact that women's economic activity and social mobility in this social group is relatively less restricted. Finally, the under-representation of Muslims among women MLAs is not surprising, since traditional gender roles in the Muslim community make it particularly difficult for women to carry out a political activity.

Table 12.9
Gender and Caste/Community in the WBLA, 1952–2001
(% of the total number of MLAs within each caste category)

	Upper Castes	Intermediary Castes	SC	ST	Muslims	TOTAL
Male	43.7	6.6	21.9	6.3	13.5	(N=2929)
Female	61.8	9.2	11.5	6.9	6.1	(N=131)

Source: Survey by author.

Finally, Table 12.10 presents the evolution of the proportion of women in the two major parties in the WBLA over the years. Here again the Congress and the CPI/CPI(M) often seem to follow opposite courses. While the proportion of female MLAs in the Congress reaches an all-time high (7.6 per cent) in 1962, it simultaneously goes down to 2 per cent in the CPI. On the contrary, from 1977 onwards, the number of women MLAs in the CPI(M) slowly picks up, while women disappear altogether from the Congress between 1971 and 1991, with an exception of 1972 (when there were four women out of 216 MLAs).

Two visible trends need to be commented upon. First, the 'turbulent decade' (1967–77) was obviously not women-friendly. This may well

Table 12.10

Women MLAs in the Main Parties, 1952–2001 (% of the total number of MLAs in each party)

	1952	1957	1962	1967	1969	1971	1972	1977	1982	1987	1991	1996	2001
INC	2.0	5.3	7.6	4.7	1.8	0	1.9	0	0	0	4.7	3.7	11.5
CPI/CPI(M)	3.6	2.2	2.0	4.7	2.5	2.7	0	0.6	2.9	4.4	9.0	10.8	9.8
All Parties	1.7	4.0	5.2	3.6	2.5	1.8	2.1	1.4	2.7	4.4	7.1	7.1	8.2
TOTAL	(N=4)	(N=10)	(N=13)	(N=10)	(N=7)	(N=5)	(N=6)	(N=4)	(N=8)	(N=13)	(N=21)	(N=21)	(N=24)

Source: Survey by author.

have to do with the level of political violence experienced in the state at that time. Second, if post-independence Congress displayed a greater openness to women, it lost this quality from 1967 onwards (notwith-standing a sudden increase in the number of women MLAs in 2001 to about 11.5 per cent), while the CPI(M) had a fast expanding propor-tion of women (17 out of 140 MLAs in 1996). This must be connected to the recent attempts by the communist party to question its traditional analytical framework and compensate for its past neglect of Scheduled Castes and women as such. Indeed, in the special conference held by the CPI(M) in 2000 in Kerala to update its party programme, two of the major innovations were the recognition of the legitimacy of the struggles waged by Dalits and women: the party then officially recognised that the fight for the abolition of the caste system is an important part of the movement for people's democracy, and that the movement for women's equality is an integral part of the movement for social emancipation (*Frontline* 2000).

The Caste/Community Composition of West Bengal Cabinets

The Legislative Assembly is obviously only one site of the state's polit-ical leadership. In order to have a more complete view of the sociological profile of this leadership, one would have to take into account also the political personnel at the district level, especially in West Bengal, where the Left Front used institutions of local self-government as early as in 1978 to grow strong roots in the countryside. While such an end-eavour goes beyond the scope of the present study, I would like to conclude this review of the sociological profile of West Bengal MLAs by comparing it with that of West Bengal ministers on one variable: the caste/community identity.

Table 12.11 shows the caste/community composition of the council of ministers of the West Bengal cabinet from 1952 to 2001. A compari-son with Table 12.3 highlights interesting contrasts between the repre-sentation of caste/communities in the Assembly and in the cabinet.

The domination of upper castes is generally even more pronounced in the cabinet than in the Assembly, particularly since 1977, with a peak (81.8 per cent) in 1982. The elite character of the Left leadership is strongly visible here.

Table 12.11
Caste/Community Composition of the Cabinets of West Bengal, 1952–2001
(% of the total number of ministers)

	1952	1957	1962	1967	1969	1972	1977	1982	1987	1991	1996	2001
Upper Castes	**50.0**	**41.7**	**42.8**	**61.1**	**60.7**	**42.8**	**73.9**	**81.8**	**72.7**	**71.0**	**67.6**	**51.5**
Brahmins	14.3	16.7	28.6	38.9	32.1	7.1	39.0	36.4	40.9	41.9	45.9	30.3
Kayasthas	35.7	25.0	14.3	22.2	28.6	35.7	34.8	45.4	31.8	29.0	21.6	21.2
Intermediary Castes	**35.7**	**41.6**	**50.0**	**22.2**	**17.9**	**14.3**	**17.4**	**13.6**	**9.0**	**6.4**	**8.1**	**6.0**
SC and ST	**0**	**0**	**0**	**11.1**	**10.7**	**14.3**	**0**	**0**	**9.0**	**3.2**	**13.5**	**18.2**
SC	–	0	0	–	–	–	–	–	9.0	3.2	10.8	15.1
ST	–	0	0	–	–	–	–	–	0	0	2.7	3.0
Muslims	**14.3**	**16.7**	**7.1**	**5.6**	**10.7**	**28.6**	**8.7**	**4.6**	**9.0**	**16.1**	**10.8**	**18.2**
TOTAL	(N=14)	(N=12)	(N=14)	(N=18)	(N=28)	(N=14)	(N=23)	(N=22)	(N=22)	(N=31)	(N=37)	(N=33)

Sources: Kohli (1990: 374) for the years 1952 to 1982; *West Bengal Legislative Assembly Who's Who of Members* for the years 1987 to 1996; the official website of the government of West Bengal for 2001.

Note: Only the members of the Council of Ministers are taken into account here.

One can also observe a simultaneous rise of upper castes and decline of intermediary castes in West Bengal cabinets. Indeed, intermediary castes are generally much more represented in the cabinet than in the Assembly. Their presence is actually roughly proportional to their demographic weight in 1952, and it increases until 1962, when they are the dominant group in the council of ministers; one might read in this fact the importance of the 'kulak' following of Ajoy Mukherjee. But the proportion of intermediary castes in the cabinet then slowly declines, and since 1982 it has been at par with their presence in the Assembly.

While Scheduled Castes and Scheduled Tribes were not at all represented in the cabinet in the Congress years, their presence suddenly increased during the years of turmoil.[13] Then they disappeared altogether in the two first governments of Left Front, and they have been increasingly represented since 1987. The pure and simple absence of any Scheduled Tribe minister from 1977 to 1996 confirms the weakness of Scheduled Tribes as a group in the Assembly, while the substantial increase in the number of both Scheduled Caste and Scheduled Tribe ministers in the cabinets formed in 1996 and 2001 testifies to the realisation by the Left parties that Dalits have to be taken into account.

Muslims are slightly more present in the cabinet than in the Assembly in the first two legislatures, and are largely over-represented in the Congress government of 1972. Apart from these three years, however, they are generally even more under-represented than in the Assembly.

The 2001 cabinet is actually marked by a visible effort to bring more balance in the social composition of the council of ministers: while upper castes are notably less dominant (even though they remain the largest group), Scheduled Castes, Scheduled Tribes and Muslims are clearly given a bigger place. This might be a sign that Left Front parties are seriously questioning the traditionally elite character of their leadership.

Conclusion

This analysis of the sociological profile of West Bengal MLAs along four variables –– caste, education, occupation and gender — in spite of

---

[13] These two categories were clubbed together by Kohli (1990).

the many uncertainties inherent in the data presented, highlights a few political resources, some changes and some permanent features.

First, upper caste status is definitely an important political resource in West Bengal, and so is higher education.

Second, the main changes in the sociological profile of the WBLA over the years concern the rise of some occupations — teachers, political activists — and the fall of others — agriculturists and professionals. Moreover, women's presence has been increasing from 1977 onwards, albeit slowly. Also, Scheduled Castes and Scheduled Tribes have massively shifted their loyalties from the Congress to the Left Front during the 'turbulent decade', which was therefore a period of transition. Muslims too started leaving the Congress in the 1970s, but since then about one-third of them have remained with this party while two-thirds have joined the Left Front.

Third, the under-representation of Muslims and of intermediary castes is one of the main permanent features of the WBLA. This is not likely to change because: (*i*) the assertion of Muslim identity as such is taboo in a region whose past was marked by communalism in its most violent form; (*ii*) intermediary castes remain fragmented in most regions of the state; and (*iii*) the Left Front government has always strongly resisted the demand for reservations for the OBC.

Last, and concomitantly, the over-representation of upper castes, graduates, teachers and political activists among MLAs suggest that bhadraloks are still in power in the West Bengal Assembly.

⬦

References and Select Bibliography

Bandyopadhyay, Sekhar. 1997. *Caste, Protest and Identity in Colonial India: The Namasudras of Bengal, 1872–1947*. Richmond: Curzon.

Bhattacharya, M. 1997. 'Reservation Policy: The West Bengal Scene', in V. A. Pai Panandiker (ed.), *The Politics of Backwardness: Reservation Policy in India*, pp. 183–219. New Delhi: Konark Publishers.

Broomfield, J. H. 1968. *Elite Conflict in a Plural Society: Twentieth Century Bengal*. Berkeley: University of California Press.

Census of India, 2001. 2001. New Delhi: Government of India.

Chatterjee, Partha. 1998. *The Present History of West Bengal*. Delhi: Oxford University Press.

Duyker, Edward. 1987. *Tribal Guerrillas: The Santals of West Bengal and the Naxalite Movement*. Delhi: Oxford University Press.

Franda, M. 1971. *Radical Politics in West Bengal*. Cambridge: MIT Press.

Frontline. 2000. 'Continuity and Change', 17(22), 10 November.

Kohli, Atul. 1990. 'From Elite Activism to Democratic Consolidation: The Rise of Reform Communism in West Bengal', in F. Frankel and M. S. A. Rao (eds), *Dominance and State Power in Modern India: Decline of a Social Order*, vol. 2, pp. 367–415. Delhi: Oxford University Press.

———. 1992. *Democracy and Discontent: India's Growing Crisis of Governability*. Cambridge: Cambridge University Press.

Kothari, R. 1991. *Caste in Indian Politics*. New Delhi: Orient Longman.

Owens, R. and A. Nandy. 1976. 'Organizational Growth and Organizational Participation. Voluntary Associations in a West Bengal City', in D. B. Rosenthal (ed.), *The City in Indian Politics*. Faridabad: Thomson Press (India) Ltd.

Sanyal, Hitesranjan. 1971. 'Continuities of Social Mobility in Traditional and Modern Society in India: Two Case Studies of Caste Mobility in Bengal', *The Journal of Asian Studies*, February, 30(2): 315–39.

Vijayan Unni, M. 1998. *State Profile 1991 India*. New Delhi: Controller of Publications.

Weiner, M. and J. Field (eds). 1976. *Electoral Politics in the Indian States: Impact of Modernization (Studies in Electoral Politics in the Indian States)*. Delhi: South Asia Books.

13

Socio-Economic Background of Legislators in Kerala

G. Gopa Kumar

The major argument of this chapter is that Kerala's society has become more democratic and polyarchical as a consequence of the socio-economic policies it pursued over more than 150 years in which the forces of modernisation including social reformers, Christian missionaries, the communist movement and traditional monarchs have contributed significantly at various historical junctures. If the famous Hindu saint Swami Vivekananda described Kerala as a 'lunatic asylum' during the close of the 19th century, today the state has become one of the most progressive units in the country. Modern Kerala abolished feudalism, implemented land reforms successfully, and established a wide network of public distribution system and primary health centres throughout the state. Kerala also succeeded in implementing decentralisation reforms, achieving 0 per cent population growth rates, and eradicated illiteracy. Today, Kerala tops in health standards for both men and women; it has the lowest rates of infant mortality and dropout in primary schools besides the lowest incidence of child labour. On the whole, the establishment of civil society in modern Kerala is in fact a combined effect of history and modernity. The achievement of independence in 1947, the formation of the state in 1956 and the electoral victory of Community Party in 1957 further hastened the process. The evolution of coalition politics is also another manifestation of the pluralist nature of the society and political system. The experience of development in Kerala has shown that even without adopting the western capitalist model, society can indeed grow rapidly. Indeed, the state is internationally noted for social change and human development, although this is not matched with sound economic growth and industrial development (see George 1993 and Swamy 2003). The unusual phenomenon has baffled scholars as to how the state keeps up its high standards of living, education, health while the economic parameters are seldom encouraging. In addition to the significant history of social and political developments, the impact of Gulf remittances (known as the 'money order economy') contributed by Malayalis in the Gulf since the 1970s has also raised the lifestyles and culture of the people.

The state of Kerala, formed on the basis of linguistic consideration in the Indian Union, was born on 1 November 1956 with the integration of the erstwhile princely states of Travancore, Cochin and the British-ruled Malabar region of the Madras Province. Politically and socially, the state enjoyed several unique features. The state of Travancore, which integrated with the Indian Union in 1947, pioneered many social reforms including the abolition of slavery and removal of untouchability based on caste; it introduced western education and health reforms, and developed a scientific temperament. The traditions of princely rule accompanied by modern reforms, the impact of Christian missionaries and Hindu social reformers, the rise of militant communism during the pre-independence period, etc., have made Kerala's society a launching-pad for introducing a civil society from the background of an uneven, socially oppressed hierarchical structure. The evolution of social development and social capital could be traced from this background.[1]

Historically, by integrating Travancore and Cochin on 1 July 1949, a new state was formed called the Travancore-Cochin State. This unit actually preceded the state of Kerala. Between 1948 and 1956, there were three elections to the state legislatures (Travancore and Travancore-Cochin) but none of them could complete its tenure. Very soon, the predominance of the Congress party was shattered for the first time in India and there arose a keen contest on the basis of a multi-party system. The three major political parties during the period were the Indian National Congress, the Communist Party of India (CPI) and the Praja Socialist Party (PSP). The poor record of six governments (of these five were led by the Congress party and one by the PSP) during the period mostly discredited the Congress party. Although, there were some attempts to build up coalition governments, personal, casteist,

---

[1] A succinct analysis is made by Harris (2001) and Parayil (2000).

communal and regional rivalries did not permit the formation to gain deep roots. The poor track record of the Congress party enabled the communists to gain more credibility and appeal among the public. Once the state was formed in 1956 by the integration of Travancore, Cochin and Malabar, it was therefore convenient for the Communist Party to capture power through democratic means. Besides the anti-Congress trend that prevailed in the state, the accession of the Malabar region to the newly formed state of Kerala helped the CPI electorally to gain more seats at the expense of the Congress in the 1957 elections. At the same time, the loss of the Kanyakumari region to the state of Madras also brought electoral setbacks to the Congress party in Kerala.

In spite of the historic victory of the CPI to power in Kerala, the state politics did not witness political unity and continuity. This is partly due to the fact that constant political upheavals and disunity among parties in the state resulted in chronic instability. The Assembly is infamous for its divisions and unpredictable character which led to frequent elections and change of governments. On the whole, the state has produced 20 governments and 13 elections during the last 50 years (see Kumar 2003b: 83). Under this compelling scenario, the tradition of politics emerged as a 'life boat strategy'. However, unlike other states, the dynamics of coalition politics in Kerala helped in shaping a competitive bipolar politics within the background of a multi-party system (Kumar 2003a: 32 and Kumar 1999).

This chapter is an attempt to study the socio-economic and cultural background of legislators (Members of Legislative Assembly) in Kerala since 1957. It shows that in spite of all the progressive developments mentioned earlier, the elite groups of Kerala's society remain over-represented among the state's political personnel. The study focuses on the social profile of MLAs during the 1957–2006 period. However, the election held to the state Assembly in May 1965 is not included here — simply because the mid-term elections could not produce an Assembly. The electoral verdict, for the first time in Indian political history, became abortive; no party or coalition was able to form a government. This chapter examines as to how diverse the Kerala Assembly has become over the last 50 years. The profiling of legislators includes a range of socio-economic and demographic variables such as age, gender, education, caste and occupation.

Age Profile

The age-wise analysis of the MLAs in Kerala (Table 13.1) since 1957 brings forth the following evaluation. There has been a constant decline in the proportion of younger legislators (25–35 age group). Their proportion has come down from 26 per cent in 1957 to 7–8 per cent in the 1990s. While over the last five decades, the representation of younger legislators has considerably declined, the number of those falling in the age group 46–55 has increased about two-fold by 1996 as compared to the year 1957. The proportion of relatively older legislators has also shown considerable increase. It appears that the younger generation of leaders fails to attract and mobilise people in elections.

Table 13.1
Age Profile of Legislators in Kerala, 1957–1996

Age Group	1957	1960	1967	1970	1977	1980	1987	1991	1996
25–35	33 (26)	19 (15)	14 (11)	13 (10)	18 (13)	21 (15)	14 (10)	10 (7)	11 (8)
36–45	47 (37)	48 (38)	64 (48)	54 (41)	38 (27)	39 (28)	35 (25)	55 (39)	34 (24)
46–55	27 (21)	30 (24)	41 (31)	44 (33)	57 (41)	56 (40)	48 (34)	34 (24)	53 (38)
56–65	8 (6)	11 (9)	12 (9)	12 (9)	22 (16)	23 (16)	32 (23)	26 (19)	26 (19)
Above 65	3 (2)	3 (2)	2 (2)	1 (1)	4 (29)	1 (1)	11 (8)	15 (11)	12 (9)

Source: CSDS Data Unit, Delhi.
Note: Figures in parentheses indicate percentage. Column figures may not add up to 100 due to unavailability of information for the rest of the legislators.

Among the three major parties in the state, the Congress party tops in nominating the younger lot in the 25–35 age group. The Congress ratings presented here show an aggregate (mean) of 13 per cent followed by CPI (12 per cent) and CPM (9 per cent). For the age group 36–45, there is no significant difference among the three parties — it varies from 29 per cent for CPI to 33 per cent for the Congress. A similar pattern could be observed for the age group 46–55.

Gender

In spite of the social development for women in Kerala, the political arena presents a gloomy picture. Robin Jeffrey argues that not much space is available for women in the politics of the state (1992: 1–5). Indeed, the gender domination of males is very evident in all the political parties of Kerala and the differences between them, if any, are only marginal. Altogether, a reflection of a patriarchal nature is found in the Kerala Legislative Assembly. Nowhere in the history of Kerala Assembly, has the women's representation crossed 5 per cent even though the Panchayati Raj Institutions (PRI) Acts of 1994 initiated some concrete changes at the level of local self-governing bodies, since there exists a constitutional mandate for providing 33 per cent reservation for women in local bodies. The study conducted by Thomas Issac and Richard Franke (2000) suggests that the women recruitment to the leadership of local bodies is somewhat encouraging. It is somewhat certain that without a constitutional mandate we cannot expect a balanced representation for women in state legislature in the near future.

Educational Profile

It is well known that Kerala's record in the field of education is very good with almost complete literacy and substantial achievements in the area of higher education. As a result of wide development of education, most of the representatives are educated above secondary level (Table 13.3). In fact, the number of those who are highly educated has consistently been growing over the last five decades. In 1996, about 62 per cent of legislators were qualified as graduate and above as against 52 per cent in 1957. On the other hand, the proportion of those educated up to middle level has been falling.

Caste Profile

Unlike in other regions in India, the upper caste dominance in society and politics was challenged in Kerala since 1957 itself as evident from Table 13.4. Gradually, the proportion of upper caste legislators has declined from 49 per cent in 1957 to 38 per cent in 2001, which still reflects a massive over-representation. The falling number of upper castes has turned out to gain the middle or intermediary castes. In fact,

Table 13.2

Gender Profile of Legislators in Kerala, 1957–96

Gender	1957	1960	1967	1970	1977	1980	1987	1991	1996
Male	118 (94)	107 (85)	132 (99)	130 (98)	139 (99)	135 (96)	132 (94)	132 (94)	125 (89)
Female	5 (4)	7 (6)	1 (1)	2 (2)	1 (1)	5 (4)	5 (4)	8 (6)	12 (9)

Source: CSDS Data Unit, Delhi.

Note: Figures in parentheses indicate percentage. Column figures may not add up to 100 due to unavailability of information for the rest of the legislators.

Table 13.3

Educational Profile of Legislators in Kerala, 1957–96

Educational Level	1957	1960	1967	1970	1977	1980	1987	1991	1996
Middle Level	12 (10)	6 (5)	18 (14)	19 (14)	16 (11)	20 (14)	16 (11)	10 (7)	6 (4)
Matriculation	31 (25)	26 (21)	46 (35)	43 (32)	54 (39)	46 (33)	39 (28)	38 (27)	34 (24)
Graduate+	65 (52)	64 (51)	56 (42)	45 (34)	55 (39)	62 (44)	72 (51)	76 (54)	87 (62)

Source: CSDS Data Unit, Delhi.

Note: Figures in parentheses indicate percentage. Column figures may not add up to 100 due to unavailability of information for the rest of the legislators.

Table 13.4
Caste Profile of Legislators in Kerala, 1957–96

Caste	1957	1960	1967	1970	1977	1980	1987	1991	1996	2001
Upper Castes	62 (49)	58 (46)	56 (42)	57 (43)	73 (52)	58 (41)	61 (44)	60 (43)	56 (40)	54 (38)
Middle Castes	36 (27)	33 (26)	44 (33)	40 (30)	28 (20)	37 (26)	39 (28)	35 (25)	40 (29)	44 (31)
SC	12 (10)	3 (2)	11 (8)	11 (8)	13 (9)	15 (11)	15 (11)	13 (9)	13 (9)	15 (11)
ST	1	1	1	1	2	1	1	1	2	1

Source: CSDS Data Unit, Delhi.
Note: Figures in parentheses indicate percentage. Column figures may not add up to 100 due to unavailability of information for the rest of the legislators.

this trend began since 1957, or even earlier, as the struggles of pre-independence period already account for the increased representation of the backward classes in administration and power. Kerala was the first state to offer a high level of representation to OBC in the entire country, both in politics and administrative positions in bureaucracy. The Kerala State Public Service Commission earmarked 39 per cent representation to OBC in government jobs since 1957, and together with Scheduled Castes and Scheduled Tribes, the figure of reservation rose to 50 per cent. At the national level, this proportion was implemented only during V. P. Singh's tenure as Prime Minister in 1990, in the wake of the Mandal Commission's recommendations. At the political level, the OBC population is evenly distributed all over Kerala and hence the impact came in a uniform manner. The analysis of the caste composition of various ministries in Kerala would also support this formulation.

As a result of early dismantling of upper caste dominance, there is little temporal variation in the caste composition of the Kerala Assembly. As far as the representation of SC and ST are concerned, there is a fixed quota for them. Only occasionally, they seem to get elected beyond their fixed quota. It is the trend almost across India.

The profile of legislators by party indicates that the proportion of upper castes in the Congress has been much higher than in the Left (Table 13.5). On the other hand, the Left has had higher proportion of middle castes than in the Congress. Similarly, the representation of SC in the Left has been higher, though slightly, than in the Congress.

Religious Profile

Like many other states in India, Kerala is a multi-religious state. Hindus, Christians and Muslims are, however, the most dominant religious groups. While Hindus constitute the dominant religious group, Christians and Muslims form significant minority religious groups. In terms of representation of minority religious groups, Kerala fares better than other states. Over the years, the representation of minority

Table 13.5

Caste Profile of Legislators in Kerala (party-wise)

Party/Caste	1957	1967	1977	1982	1987	1991	1996	Mean (%)
INC								
Upper Castes	23 (56)	5 (56)	19 (50)	14 (41)	14 (42)	28 (51)	20 (54)	50
Middle Castes	11 (26)	3 (33)	8 (21)	11 (32)	9 (27)	15 (27)	10 (27)	28
SC	5 (11)	1 (11)	4 (10)	3 (9)	4 (12)	5 (9)	3 (8)	10
Left								
Upper Castes	28 (47)	31 (44)	19 (47)	17 (42)	14 (41)	13 (32)	19 (33)	41
Middle Castes	21 (35)	27 (38)	11 (27)	10 (25)	11 (32)	16 (39)	21 (36)	33
SC	7 (12)	7 (10)	6 (15)	9 (22)	3 (9)	7 (17)	8 (14)	14

Source: CSDS Data Unit, Delhi.

Note: Figures in parentheses indicate percentage. Column figures may not add up to 100 due to unavailability of information for the rest of the legislators

Table 13.6

Religious Profile of Legislators in Kerala, 1957–2006

Religion	1957	1960	1967	1970	1977	1980	1987	1991	1996	2006
Hindu	86 (68)	70 (56)	86 (65)	77 (58)	82 (59)	83 (59)	86 (61)	79 (56)	71 (51)	80 (57)
Christian	25 (20)	25 (20)	23 (17)	32 (24)	34 (24)	28 (20)	30 (21)	32 (23)	34 (24)	34 (24)
Muslim	12 (10)	19 (15)	21 (16)	15 (11)	24 (17)	28 (20)	24 (17)	29 (21)	26 (19)	26 (19)

Source: CSDS Data Unit, Delhi.

Note: Figures in parentheses indicate percentage. Column figures may not add up to 100 due to unavailability of information for the rest of the legislators.

religious groups has improved significantly. Now, the representation of religious groups seems to be almost proportionate to their share in the total population (see Table 13.6).

Occupational Profile

Legislators in Kerala come from diverse occupational/professional backgrounds. These include social work, political activism, volunteering work, farming, teaching, law, business, other professions, government employment (retired or resigned), etc.

In the Kerala Assembly, the proportion of social workers, agriculturists and businessmen has been very low. There is negligible temporal variation in their representation. Political activists have, however, dominance among the legislators. More significantly, their number has been increasing over the last five decades. Professionals constitute the other most dominant group, next only to political activists. However, it could be noted that the dominance of professionals has been on decline and this decline is more salient in recent decades. Their proportion to total number of representatives has come down from 33 per cent in 1957 to 22 per cent in 1996 (Table 13.7).

Conclusion

The study shows that no dramatic change has occurred in Kerala so far as the social profile of the Assembly members are concerned. Figures regarding caste, occupation, gender and religion did not undergo any significant transformation. The only evolution which deserves some attention may be the rise of professional politicians among Congress MLAs. While the MLAs of the Left parties have consistently been drawn from the category of political activists, this is a new development on the side of the Congress party where more and more full-time party activists are contesting elections.

Interestingly, the government of Kerala has realised the need for another kind of professionalisation of the MLAs. It has recently set up the Institute for Parliamentary Affairs with a Cabinet minister in charge of Parliamentary Affairs to instil more professionalism among the legislators. Although political parties in parliamentary democracy may

Table 13.7

Occupational Profile of Legislators in Kerala, 1957–96

Occupation	1957	1960	1967	1970	1977	1980	1987	1991	1996	2006
Social Workers	4 (3)	5 (4)	2 (2)	49 (37)	–	–	3 (2)	7 (5)	7 (5)	56 (40)
Political Activists	50 (40)	46 (36)	58 (43)	–	55 (39)	63 (45)	63 (46)	58 (41)	69 (49)	32 (23)
Agriculturists	8 (6)	4 (3)	9 (7)	17 (13)	19 (14)	8 (6)	15 (11)	11 (8)	9 (6)	3 (2)
Businessmen	2 (2)	2 (2)	2 (2)	3 (2)	6 (4)	9 (6)	5 (4)	6 (4)	2 (1)	6 (5)
Professionals	41 (33)	37 (29)	33 (25)	30 (23)	32 (23)	34 (24)	33 (24)	42 (30)	31 (22)	31 (22)
Others	21 (17)	32 (26)	29 (21)	34 (25)	28 (20)	26 (19)	21 (15)	16 (11)	22 (17)	12 (8)

Source: CSDS Data Unit, Delhi.

Note: Figures in parentheses indicate percentage.

share many perceptions and features in common, the changing scenario in society, demography and electoral politics might demand new trends to develop. Political parties are, after all, dependent variables in the socio-economic process of the society; hence, the need for specific training for developing new skills and cultivating old ones.

❖

References

George, K. K. 1993. *Limits to Kerala Model of Development*. Thiruvananthapuram: Centre for Development Studies.

Harris, John. 2001. *Depoliticizing Development: The World Bank and Social Capital*. New Delhi: Left Word Publishers.

Issac, Thomas and Richard Franke. 2000. *Local Democracy and Development*. New Delhi: Left Word Publishers.

Jeffrey, Robin. 1992. *Politics, Women and Well-being: How Kerala Became a Model?* Delhi: Oxford University Press.

Kumar, G. Gopa. 1999. 'Coalition Experiments in Kerala', *Journal of Integration Studies*, January, 5: 23–30.

———. 2003a. 'Coalition Politics at Cross-Roads in Kerala', *South Asian Politics*, 12 (7): 54–61.

———. 2003b. 'Kerala: Stable Bipolar Alignment', *Journal of Indian School of Political Economy*, 15 (1–2): 79–95.

Parayil, Govindan (ed.). 2000. *Kerala: The Development Experience: Reflections on Sustainability and Replicability*. London: Zed Books.

Swamy, Subramanian. 2003. 'An Unsustainable Model', *The Hindu*, 7 June, p. 10.

Part VI

The Domain of Proportionality

14

Himachal Pradesh: Well-established Domination of Majoritarian Upper Castes

Ramesh K. Chauhan, S. N. Ghosh and *T. R. Sharma*

With the integration of about 30 princely states of this hilly region, Himachal Pradesh came into existence on 15 April 1948 as a chief commissioner's province. When the Indian Constitution came into force on 26 January 1950, the chief commissioner's provinces (except the Andaman and Nicobar islands) became Part 'C' states. With this, Himachal also became a Part 'C' state of the Indian Union which constituted an important landmark in establishing the democratic process in the state (Verma 1995: 146–59). The former princely states had entirely undemocratic political structures; society was highly feudal and the economy extremely primitive. After the integration of these princely states into Himachal Pradesh and the first general elections in 1952, the people of Himachal Pradesh got their first representative government.

But as a result of the reorganisation of the states on linguistic basis in 1956, the very survival of Himachal Pradesh as a separate political identity was threatened; the status of Himachal Pradesh was transformed from a Part 'C' state into a 'Union Territory' under the direct control of central government. The state Legislative Assembly was dissolved and a 'Territorial Council' with limited powers was formed. As a centrally administered unit, Himachal was denied a democratic set-up; instead a scheme of diarchy was introduced. Under this scheme, the government was divided into two houses. One half was managed by the lieutenant-governor with the help of the bureaucracy and the other half by the territorial council. This arrangement continued till 1963, when a popular government was restored and the existing territorial council converted into a Legislative Assembly. It had 43 members including two nominated ones. Among the elected members, 14 belonged to the Scheduled Castes, three to the Scheduled Tribes and the remaining 24 to the general category (Government of Himachal Pradesh 1977: 73–74).

In the wake of the reorganisation of Punjab on linguistic basis in 1966, the Punjab Hilly Areas (Kangra, Kullu, Lahaul and Spiti) along with 13 Assembly seats were transferred to Himachal Pradesh. With this reorganisation not only the area but also the population of Himachal Pradesh almost doubled. Consequently, the strength of the state legislatures which was 34 in the year 1952, rose to 60 in the year 1967, and, further, to 68 in the 1972 elections.

To sum up, the period from the first general election held in 1952 to the year 1967 witnessed political instability and uncertainty. Ultimately, the people of Himachal Pradesh attained the long cherished goal of statehood on 25 January 1971, as the 19th state of the Indian Union. This study intends to focus on the changing profile of legislature of Himachal Pradesh Assembly from 1967 till the last Assembly election held in the year 2003.

Socio-economic Profile of Legislators: An Analysis

Gender Profile

Himachal Pradesh is predominantly a rural state where traditional values and ethos still prevail. As the society is patriarchal, males dominate almost all walks of life, particularly the political domain. Representation of women in the politics of the state in comparison to their male counterparts is abysmally low. The electoral experience of more than five decades has failed to make any notable difference in their representation in the state Legislative Assembly.

The strength of the legislators in the successive state assemblies from 1967 to 2003 reflects an overwhelming male dominance. Over last three decades, the women representation has remained less than 10 per cent with a maximum of six (8.8 per cent) legislators in 1998 (Table 14.1). This pattern of gender representation is, by and large, similar across political parties. Although the representation of women in the state has gradually increased, it is negligible in comparison to their size in the population. Despite the low level of participation of women in the state-level

Table 14.1
Women Legislators in Himachal Pradesh, 1972–2003

Year	Total Strength	Number of Women MLAs
1972	68	4
1977	68	1
1982	68	3
1985	68	3
1990	68	4
1993	68	3
1998	68	6
2003	68	4

Source: CSDS Data Unit.

politics, Himachal still has a higher average representation in the state legislature as compared to socially progressive Kerala and economically developed Punjab (Government of India 2003: 229–30).

Prior to 1962, there was a complete male dominance in the House as there were no women members either in the Legislative Assembly of the Part 'C' state of Himachal Pradesh from 1952 to 1956, or in the territorial council from 1957 to 1962. For the first time, in 1962, two women candidates (one elected and one nominated) entered the House. In the Legislative Assembly of 1967, there were no women members. Since 1972, though, women members are being elected to every House but their representation still remains nominal. This reflects a skewed male dominance especially in the face of the fact that with the rise in their literacy level, women's participation has substantially increased in all walks of life except politics. The predominance of male representatives is also visible in the case of the Scheduled Castes, Scheduled Tribes and Other Backward Classes categories. So far only one female representative from each of these three categories could make it to the Legislative Assembly of Himachal Pradesh.[1] Like the provision made for the higher representation of women at the grassroot level, arrangements to increase their representation are required both at state and national-level political institutions.

---

[1] The female legislator who was elected was Nirmala Devi (BJP) from the Scheduled Caste category, from Pragpur in 1998, Lata Thakur (Congress), a Scheduled Tribe candidate, from Lahaul and Spiti in 1972, and Sarveen Chaudhry (BJP), an Other Backward Class member, from Shahpur Assembly constituency in 1998.

Age Profile

The profile of the legislators in terms of age group in years indicates that from 1967 Assembly elections to 1982, the age group of 25–35 years had a relatively higher representation: 21.7 per cent in 1967, 17.6 per cent in 1972, 25 per cent in 1977, and 19.11 per cent in 1982. From 1985 onwards, however, there is a declining trend in the representation of legislatures falling in this age group. The representation of MLAs in the age group 36–45 years continued to increase till 1993. In 1967, about 28.33 per cent of MLAs belonged to this age group, which increased to 45.6 per cent in the 1985 Assembly election. The proportion of legislators in the age group 46–55 years also shows an increasing trend, though gradually (Table 14.2).

Table 14.2
Age Profile of Legislators in Himachal Pradesh, 1967–2003

Year	Total	25–35	36–45	46–55	56–65	66 +
1967	60	13 (21.7)	17 (28.3)	14 (23.3)	12 (20)	4 (6.7)
1972	68	12 (17.6)	27 (39.7)	19 (27.9)	4 (5.9)	3 (4.4)
1977	68	17 (25)	22 (32.4)	20 (29.4)	8 (11.8)	1 (1.5)
1982	68	13 (19.1)	19 (27.9)	21 (30.9)	12 (17.6)	2 (2.9)
1985	68	9 (13.2)	31 (45.6)	16 (23.5)	10 (14.7)	2 (2.9)
1990	68	4 (5.9)	26 (38.2)	20 (29.4)	15 (22.1)	3 (4.4)
1993	68	4 (5.9)	23 (33.8)	23 (33.8)	11 (16.2)	7 (10.2)
1998	68	6 (8.8)	12 (17.6)	28 (41.2)	14 (20.6)	8 (11.8)
2003	68	6 (8.8)	12 (17.6)	28 (41.2)	14 (20.6)	8 (11.8)

Source: CSDS Data Unit.
Note: Figures in parentheses indicate percentage.

Caste Profile

The profile of the legislature in terms of caste categories reveals a predominance of upper castes in the state Legislative Assembly. The Rajputs and Brahmins are the two politically dominant upper castes in the state. The Rajputs being higher in their numerical strength (28 per cent), followed by Brahmins (20 per cent), principally represent and influence the electoral politics in the state. The upper caste MLAs' representation since 1972 has remained above 60 per cent, except for the 1998 Assembly when it was 58.8 per cent. The representation of Scheduled Castes and Scheduled Tribes in the state legislature has remained proportionate to their statutory limit, i.e., 16 and three seats respectively. The OBC who constitute 10.5 per cent of the state's population have been able to increase their representation from a mere 1.7 per cent in 1967 to the maximum of 10.3 per cent in 1993 (Table 14.3).

The overall caste profile of the legislators in Himachal Pradesh since the 1967 elections reveals that there is a clear-cut dominance of upper castes in the state electoral politics. However, of late, the representation of various caste categories has come to be in proportion to their population in the state. Indeed, the average representation of legislators in terms of caste in the last nine assembly elections of the state indicates that the upper caste representation has been 64.4 per cent; the Scheduled Castes, 23.7 per cent, Scheduled Tribes, 4.5 per cent, and the middle castes, 6.2 per cent.[2]

Table 14.3
Caste Profile of Legislators in Himachal Pradesh, 1967–2003

Year	Total Number of Members	Upper Caste	OBC	SC	ST
1967	60	41 (68.3)	1 (1.7)	15 (25.0)	3 (5.0)
1972	68	46 (67.6)	2 (2.9)	16 (23.5)	3 (4.4)
1977	68	45 (66.2)	4 (5.9)	15 (22.1)	3 (4.4)
1982	68	44 (64.7)	5 (7.4)	16 (23.5)	3 (4.4)
1985	68	45 (66.2)	4 (5.9)	16 (23.5)	3 (4.4)
1990	68	42 (61.8)	5 (7.4)	16 (23.5)	4 (5.9)
1993	68	42 (61.8)	7 (10.3)	16 (23.5)	3 (4.4)
1998	68	40 (58.8)	5 (7.4)	16 (23.5)	3 (4.4)
2003	68	42 (61.8)	5 (7.4)	16 (23.5)	3 (4.4)

Source: CSDS Data Unit.
Note: Figures in parentheses indicate percentage.

Occupational Profile

The occupational profile of the legislature in Himachal Pradesh since 1967 shows the predominance of the agriculturists, followed by professionals and ex-government employees. The average representation

---

[2] The overall percentage of caste-wise representation has been determined by the number of representatives elected in all the nine elections to the State Legislative Assembly divided by the total number of seats in the State Assembly from 1967 to 2003.

in terms of occupational categories, i.e., agriculturists, ex-government employees and professionals has been 26.7 per cent, 19.7 per cent and 12.7 per cent respectively.[3] The representation of other occupations such as those of social workers and political activists has been marginal in comparison to the other major occupations just mentioned. In the 1967 Assembly, agriculturists, ex-government employees, professionals and political activists together represented 99 per cent of the MLAs. This pattern was observed in the subsequent elections till 1985, except in 1977 when the Congress was ousted from power and the Janata Party (JNP) won in a big way with a relatively higher representation of ex-government employees (33.8 per cent).[4]

Another significant change in the pattern of occupation-wise representation has been the rise of professionals (except in the year 1985) and the decline in the representation of political activists. The dominance of the agriculturists over other occupations continued through the 1990s too where a radical change has been observed in the overall (average) representation of agriculturists amounting to 60.8 per cent as against the preceding election's figure of 25.3 per cent. This change can be attributed to the fact that in order to escape the provision of income tax, the majority of the representatives opted for agriculture, since income from agriculture is exempted from taxation. The share of the MLAs from this category in the assemblies resulting from the elections held in 1990, 1993 and 1998 was 57.4 per cent, 60.3 per cent and 64.7 per cent respectively (Table 14.4). This shows a significant change. Representation of professionals and ex-government employees gradually declined during this period. It was probably because ex-government employees opted instead for agriculture/horticulture as their profession.

Education Profile

In the early years of its existence, Himachal Pradesh was one of the most backward states of India with regards to education. However, during

---

[3] The overall percentage of occupation-wise representation has been determined by the number of representatives elected in all the nine elections to the State Legislative Assembly divided by the total number of the seats in the State Assembly from 1967 to 2003.

[4] Here, teachers have been clubbed together with ex-government employees.

Table 14.4
Occupational Background of Legislators in Himachal Pradesh, 1967–2003

Year	Total	Social Worker	Political Activist	Agriculturist	Professionals	Ex-government Employees	Others
1967	60	1 (1.7)	15 (25)	19 (31.7)	11 (18.3)	14 (23.3)	–
1972	68	7 (10.3)	6 (8.8)	18 (26.5)	16 (23.5)	11 (16.2)	10 (14.2)
1977	68	8 (11.8)	5 (7.4)	14 (20.6)	14 (20.6)	17 (25.0)	10 (14.2)
1982	68	3 (4.4)	6 (8.8)	16 (23.5)	18 (26.6)	15 (22.3)	10 (14.2)
1985	68	8 (11.8)	6 (8.8)	17 (25.2)	11 (16.4)	16 (23.6)	10 (14.2)
1990	68	1 (1.5)	–	39 (57.4)	13 (19.1)	6 (8.7)	9 (13.2)
1993	68	4 (5.9)	–	41 (60.3)	12 (17.6)	3 (4.4)	8 (11.8)
1998	68	3 (4.4)	1 (1.5)	44 (64.7)	7 (10.3)	3 (4.4)	10 (14.2)
2003	68	6 (8.8)	–	32 (47.1)	11 (16.2)	2 (2.9)	17 (25.0)

Source: CSDS Data Unit.
Note: Figures in parentheses indicate percentage.

the last six decades, the state has made significant gains in literacy/ education. With the establishment of various educational institutions in the state, both at basic and higher levels, the process of expansion of education gradually picked up, and today the state is ranked the second highest after Kerala in its literacy rate. The impact of the increasing level of literacy/education is clearly reflected in the rising percentage of graduates, post-graduates and professionals in the successive assemblies of the state. In the first Legislative Assembly elected in 1952, several members were illiterate, a few were just literate and only three or four members had studied up to graduation. There was only one MLA with a post-graduate degree and one with a doctorate degree. However, after 1967, this position changed significantly; the spread of education thus began getting reflected in the legislature as well as in other walks of life (Table 14.5).

In the 1967 state Assembly elections, 26 (43.3 per cent) members were graduates or above and 21 (35 per cent) were matriculates; only 11 (18.3 per cent) members were middle-pass. The position regarding the level of literacy of the MLAs further improved in the successive legislative assemblies. In the 1972 Legislative Assembly there was not even a single member who had not studied at least up to middle standard while the number of graduates and above accounted for 31 (45.6 per cent), the matriculates were 25 (36.8 per cent) and only 9 (13.2 per cent)

Table 14.5
Educational Profile of Legislators in Himachal Pradesh, 1967–2003

Year	Total	Middle Level	Secondary Level	Graduate and Above
1967	60	11 (18.3)	21 (35)	26 (43.3)
1972	68	9 (13.2)	25 (36.8)	31 (45.6)
1977	68	8 (11.8)	23 (33.8)	37 (54.4)
1982	68	5 (7.4)	20 (29.4)	43 (63.2)
1985	68	4 (5.9)	18 (26.5)	46 (67.6)
1990	68	2 (2.9)	25 (36.8)	30 (57.4)
1993	68	3 (4.4)	12 (17.6)	53 (77.9)
1998	68	3 (4.4)	17 (25.5)	45 (66.3)
2003	68	1 (1.5)	13 (19.1)	53 (77.9)

Source: CSDS Data Unit.
Note: Figures in parentheses indicate percentage.

were middle-pass. In 1977, when the Janata Party came to power, the percentage of graduates and above rose to 37 (55.4 per cent) (an increase of over 9 per cent from 1972), followed by the matriculates with 23 legislatures (33.8 per cent), whereas the middle-pass MLAs were only eight (11.8 per cent). In the 1982 Assembly elections as many as 43 (63.2 per cent) MLAs were graduates and above, followed by 20 (29.4 per cent) matriculates; the remaining five (7.4 per cent) legislators were middle-pass. This trend of a rise in the number of graduates and above in the successive legislative assemblies, which began in 1967, continued in the 1985 elections. Here the legislators belonging to the highly educated category increased to 67.6 per cent with 46 members. The remaining 18 (26.5 per cent) MLAs were matriculates, followed by those who had studied up to the middle standard constituting 5.9 per cent with four representatives. Although in the 1990 Assembly the number of MLAs in the category of graduates and above decreased slightly with 39 (57.4 per cent), correspondingly, the strength of matric-pass MLAs increased to 25 (36.8 per cent). In the 1993 mid-term elections to the state Assembly, the number of MLAs qualified as graduates and above rose again to 53 (77.9 per cent) followed by the matriculates who were 12 in number (17.6 per cent). The 1998 elections further reflect the dominance of highly educated MLAs in the state Assembly with 45 (66.2 percent) MLAs with a graduate degree or above and 17 (25 per cent) matriculates. As far as the Legislative Assembly elected in 2003, the profile of legislatures in terms of education is more or less similar to the state Legislative Assembly of 1993. Here too, 53 (77.9 per cent) MLAs are graduates or above and 13 (19.1 per cent) are matriculate.

Conclusion

Changes have been few in Himachal Pradesh so far as the social profile of the MLAs is concerned. Upper castes being in majority in the state population have retained power in the Assembly. Except for one Scheduled Castes candidate who won from an unreserved constituency in 1967, no other Scheduled Castes candidate could win the state Assembly election from an open seat.[5] This makes it quite clear that representation of the lower castes has remained confined to statutory limits. In the upper caste category, Rajputs rule the roost in the electoral politics of the state due to their proportionately higher population and traditional ruling background.

Since Himachal is a rural society, agriculture/horticulture has remained the main occupation of the people in the state and of the MLAs. Other than agriculturists, a significant presence of representatives has been from ex-government employees and professionals due to their effective role in the state's electoral politics. In the recent Assembly elections, an increase in the representation of legislators from business community indicates a change towards the increasing influence of money power in electoral politics.

The most significant change has been observed in the overall educational profile of the legislators in the successive assemblies of the state. Drastic improvement and expansion in education/literacy has raised political consciousness and has led to a qualitatively better participation in the electoral politics.

A significant presence of middle-aged representatives in the legislature indicates that the relatively younger leadership has occupied the political space at the decision-making level in the highest political institution of the state.

---

[5] Hari Singh was elected from Gopalpur Assembly constituency as an independent candidate in the 1967 elections.

Except for gender and caste, the other socio-economic profile of legislators indicates a gradual and visible change over these years in the state Legislative Assembly of Himachal Pradesh. Since different major castes have now come to be represented almost in proportion to their total population in the state, it is the dismal representation of women which has still miles to go better representation.

◈

References and Select Bibliography

Government of Himachal Pradesh. 1977. *A Statistical Analysis of General Elections to House of the People, State Legislative Assembly (1977)*. Shimla: Financial Commissioner and Chief Electoral Officer.

Government of India. 2003. 'Gender Empowerment', *Himachal Pradesh Development Report*. New Delhi: Planning Commission.

Sharma, R. 1977. *Party Politics in a Himalayan State*. New Delhi: National Publishing House.

Sharma, T. R. 1999. 'Local Configurations and National Parties in Himachal Pradesh', *Economic and Political Weekly*, 34 (34–35): 2467.

Verma, V. 1995. *The Emergence of Himachal Pradesh: A Survey of Constitutional Developments*. New Delhi: Indus Publishing Company.

15

Changing Face of Delhi's Politics: Has it Changed the Face of the Political Representatives?

Sanjay Kumar

The politics of Delhi especially in the 1990s has undergone a remarkable change. Though surrounded by states like Rajasthan, Haryana and Punjab, where caste plays a very important role in state politics, in Delhi, although caste has its own role, in recent times, it is class that has come to occupy a dominant role in the electoral politics of the state. But this is not the tone of Delhi's politics still for it continues to be perceived in terms of the old language of the Jat and Punjabi vote. The question is: what resulted in the changing pattern of politics in Delhi? Has the pattern of vote politics also made a difference in the character of the political representatives?

Over the years, Delhi has witnessed enormous demographic changes. The population, which was 1,744,072 in 1951, has crossed the 10 million figure. The city witnessed nearly a 90 per cent increase in the population between 1941 and 1951, which, is largely credited to influx of refugees after partition. The population of Delhi has also increased at a rapid rate during the last decade. This is primarily due to large-scale migration to the city from other states of the country. While the migration to this city is not a new phenomenon, its pace has certainly picked up during the last decade. The large-scale migration has changed the whole character of the city. Delhi no more remains a city of the native *Delhiwala*. As per the 1991 Census, 60.6 per cent of Delhi's population is constituted of those who are born in Delhi while 39.4 per cent of the city's population comprise the migrants. Even among those who are born in Delhi and are treated as natives according to the Census, there is a large section of population which consists of the second or third generation migrants. While the Census may not account for this, the HT–CSDS Delhi survey estimated that the native Delhiwalas comprise nearly 21 per cent and the rest are migrants, considering all those whose ancestors come from outside Delhi as migrants.[1]

If we look at the regional pattern of migration we find that as per the 1991 Census, 80 per cent of the migrants come from the north Indian states comprising Bihar, Uttar Pradesh, Punjab, Haryana and Rajasthan. The west accounts for 3.5 per cent, the south for 3.4 per cent and the east and north-east account for 2.9 per cent of the migrants in Delhi. Besides this, there are migrants from Pakistan and a few other countries as well. The migrants from U.P. account for 45.9 per cent, Haryana, 11.9 per cent and Bihar, 7.2 per cent of the total migrants in Delhi. The HT–CSDS survey indicates that the number of migrants from Bihar has increased over 100 per cent during the past five years. Though migrants from Bihar account for 7.2 per cent, during 1993–98, 18 per cent of the migrants came from Bihar.

Large-scale migration, especially from Bihar and eastern Uttar Pradesh during the past decade, has changed whole profile of Delhi considered to be a city of the rich in the past. Most of these migrants from Bihar and U.P. consist of unemployed youth who have come to the city looking for jobs. These youths, either uneducated or in some cases with only basic education, find it very difficult to get a decent job and finally settle down in *jhuggis* or slums engaging in petty businesses or very low occupations. Most of these migrants have been reduced to the poor class and have added to the city's population in big numbers during the past decade. As per the HT–CSDS survey, Delhi consists of nearly 24.8 per cent poor as compared to only 10.2 per cent who belong to the rich class.[2] Their sheer numerical strength and more or less similar

---

[1] The HT–CSDS survey focuses on the socio-political opinions and attitudes of the people living in the city of Delhi. With a sample size of 12,311 this is probably the biggest survey undertaken in any city of the world. The survey began two months before the 1998 Assembly elections in Delhi, and was carried out in 1400 locations spread across all the 70 Assembly constituencies of Delhi. The survey was undertaken by the Centre for the Study of Developing Societies, Delhi and sponsored by the *Hindustan Times* wherein the findings of the survey were subsequently published.

[2] The 'poor' are defined as those who do not possess any consumer durables such as televisions, refrigerators, two-wheeler vehicles like scooters, etc., and earn less than Rs 5,000 a month. On the contrary, the 'rich' are those who possess sought after consumer durables like colour televisions, air conditioners, cars, etc., and have a monthly income of more than Rs 20,000.

problems faced by them has resulted into organising these people. With their social profile somewhat different from the others in Delhi, political parties have started adopting various means to woo these urban poor people, generally migrants, for their vote during elections. So with the changing social and economic profile of the city of Delhi, the urban poor has really turned out to be a crucial vote bank in the elections.

The regional pattern of the settlements in Delhi shows that nearly 59 per cent of the city's population lives in the East Delhi and the Outer Delhi areas. The population in these two regions has especially witnessed rapid growth during the past decade largely due to large-scale settlement of migrants. Similarly, nearly 65.2 per cent of Delhi's poor live in these two regions. It is also important to note that these two regions are also two political units comprising two biggest Lok Sabha constituencies. Outer Delhi has 2,926,563 and East Delhi has a total of 2,264,600 strong electorate. Since these two Lok Sabha constituencies account for 41 out of 70 Vidhan Sabha constituencies, these become politically more dominant as compared to other Lok Sabha constituencies of Delhi.

Over the years, the two major political contenders, the Congress and the BJP, have competed among themselves for the vote of different sections of society. It is generally believed that the BJP has a strong base among voters belonging to the upper caste especially among the Punjabi Khatri community. The party is also considered to be the first choice of Sikh voters. In contrast, it is widely believed that the Congress party has a strong presence among the voters belonging to the OBC or the Dalits. But with changing economic profile, this traditional vote bank theory does not seem to hold too strong. The findings of the survey in fact indicate that the economic class of the voters, irrespective of their caste, is one of the determining factors in voting choices.

Table 15.1
Voting Pattern of Different Communities: Assembly Elections 1998

Party	Punjabi Khatri		Other Upper Castes		OBC		Dalit		Sikh	
	Rich	Poor	Rich	Poor	Rich	Poor	Rich	Poor	Rich	Poor
Congress	22.8	33.9	23.3	43.7	41.7	45.7	47.1	59.8	27.3	43.3
BJP	47.3	43.8	47.8	36.3	41.7	31.1	20.6	16.9	36.4	36.7

Source: HT–CSDS Delhi Survey 1998.

Fewer among the poor Punjabi Khatri voters voted for the BJP as compared to those belonging to the rich economic class. Similarly, among voters belonging to other upper castes, nearly 48 per cent of those from the rich economic class voted for the BJP while only 36 per cent among those belonging to the poor economic class voted for the BJP. Among those upper castes voters who are low in economic status, nearly 44 per cent voted for the Congress. On the contrary, among the rich voters belonging to the OBC, the vote for both Congress and BJP is equally divided, and it is only among the poor OBC voters that the support for the Congress is higher as compared to the BJP. It is widely believed that after the Sikh massacre in Delhi following the assassination of Indira Gandhi, large number of Sikhs voted for the BJP. But the survey indicates that even among the Sikhs, large numbers of those who belong to the poor economic class voted for the Congress. It should be noted that among the poor Sikh voters, the majority voted for the Congress and fewer among them voted for the BJP. These findings go on to prove that, although the caste factor may still be the dominant theme of politics in Delhi, class has started to play an important role in its politics. During the last decade there has also been a shift in the focus of political parties from caste to class, especially when one-fourth of the voters owe allegiance to a single class. This is not to say that caste is no more the focus of political parties; those basic social blocks owing allegiance to caste still play their role.

While Delhi witnessed enormous change in the social and economic profile of the voters, can we assume that the social and economic profile of the elected representatives also changed? While the official results from the Election Commission do tell us the story of who won from which constituency or which party won how many seats, it helps little in understanding the social or economic profile of the elected representatives. The economic status of an individual is something very difficult to quantify, but the social status of the individual, i.e., the caste to which he/she belongs is a topic of objective analysis. In the following discussion, I have attempted to analyse the social profile of the elected representatives in Delhi.

Before we look into the social profile of the elected representatives in Delhi, however, it would be useful to have a look at the social profile of different Assembly constituencies of Delhi in terms of caste domination. While it is common to talk about the Jat domination or the Punjabi Khatri domination in Delhi politics, there is no data available as to precisely which are the areas where these two dominant castes play a decisive role. Although there is no official data available on this information, the HT–CSDS Delhi survey does make an estimate of the proportion of different castes in the different Assembly constituencies of Delhi.

Table 15.2
Profile of Assembly Constituencies in Terms of Caste Domination

Caste Category	Assembly Constituencies	Number of Assembly Constituencies	Percentage of Total Assembly Constituencies
Punjabi Khatri (35% or more)	Janakpuri, Hari Nagar, Timarpur	3	4
Punjabi Khatri (20–34 %)	Jangpura, Kalkaji, Malviya Nagar, Tilak Nagar, Rajouri Garden, Madipur, Shakurbasti, Shalimar Bagh, Badli, Geeta Colony, Krishna Nagar, Vishwas Nagar, Shahdara, Wazirpur, Moti Nagar, Patel Nagar	16	23
Jat (35% or more)	Bawana	1	1
Jat (20–34%)	Najafgarh, Palam, Narela	3	4
Brahmin (20–34%)	Sarojini Nagar, Hastsal, Patparganj, Mandawali, Rohtas Nagar, Seelampur, Yamuna Vihar	7	10
Rajput Majority	R.K. Puram, Nasirpur	2	3
Dalit Majority	Gole Market, Minto Road, Delhi Cantonment, Madipur, Sahibabad Daulatpur, Sultanpur Majra, Mangolpuri, Nangloi Jat, Mahipalpur, Saket, Ambedkar Nagar, Tughlaqabad, Trilokpuri, Patparganj, Gandhi Nagar, Seemapuri, Nand Nagri, Bhalswa Jahangirpuri, Adarsh Nagar, Chandni Chowk	20	28
Muslim Majority	Babarpur, Seelampur, Quarawal Nagar, Paharganj, Matia Mahal, Ballimaran	7	10
TOTAL		59	84

Source: HT–CSDS Delhi Survey, 1998.

These are the Assembly constituencies in which one social community can play an important role in electing a political representative (MLA) on account of its numerical strength. Besides these Assembly constituencies, the Vishnu Garden Assembly constituency is dominated by the Sikh voters, which comprises nearly 44 per cent of the electorate. Muslim voters are predominant in Babarpur (26 per cent), Seelampur (67 per cent), Qarawal Nagar (25 per cent), Paharganj (33 per cent), Matia Mahal (75 per cent), Okhla (40 per cent) and Ballimaran (50 per cent) Assembly constituencies. Other constituencies could be classified as mixed type in which two or more communities have more or less similar numerical strength.

Table 15.3
Caste Profile of MLAs in Delhi (%)

Caste	1993	1998	2003
Brahmin	14	17	21
Rajput	7	7	4
Vaishya	16	6	7
Punjabi Khatri	17	16	14
Jat	9	13	9
Gujjar	6	6	7
Yadav	1	1	–
Dalit	19	20	20
Muslim	7	7	7
Sikh	4	7	7

Source: Data collected from the *Who's Who* volumes of 1993, 1998, and 2003 by the CSDS team and informal sources.

It is true that election in Delhi is always discussed in terms of the Jat vote or the Punjabi vote. But if we look at the composition of the Delhi Assembly during the elections in 1993, 1998 and 2003, we find that though these two communities are represented in the House in a fair number, it is the Dalits who constitute the biggest number of MLAs in the Assembly.

If we cast a glance at the composition of the Delhi Assembly during the 1993 Assembly elections, we find that nearly 19 per cent of the MLAs were Dalits. The proportion of the Dalit representation in the 1998 and 2003 Assembly increased by just 1 per cent, as compared to their representation during the 1993 Assembly. Nearly 19 per cent Assembly seats in Delhi (13 Assembly seats out of a total of 70 seats) are reserved for the Dalits. It is beyond doubt that at least 19 per cent of the MLAs in the House would be Dalits, but during the 1998 and 2003 Assembly elections, Shadi Ram, a Dalit by caste, got elected from the Kamala Nagar unreserved Assembly constituency, increasing the proportion of the Dalit representation by just 1 per cent. Such instances of a Dalit or an Adivasi getting elected from a general constituency are, however, very rare.[3]

The caste profile of the MLAs in Delhi during the assemblies of 1993, 1998 and 2003 indicates that the representation of the Brahmins has increased over the last decade. The Brahmins had a fair representation in the Delhi Assembly both during the 1993 and the 1998 Assembly, but this increased further in the 2003 Assembly. During the 1993 Assembly, nearly 14 per cent of the MLAs were from the Brahmin caste. The proportion of Brahmins went up to nearly 17 per cent during the 1998 Assembly, and further up to about 21 per cent in the 2003 Assembly. The Brahmins actually outnumbered both the Jats and the Punjabi Khatris in almost all the three assemblies of 1993, 1998 and 2003.

The politics of Delhi is often viewed in terms of the Jat or Punjabi dominance, but if we look at the actual representation of these two castes in the Delhi Assembly, there is nothing noteworthy. The representation of the Punjabis in Delhi Assembly has remained more or less the same in the three assemblies of 1993, 1998 and 2003. While in the 1993 Assembly they were nearly 17 per cent, their numbers went down slightly in the 1998 Assembly, and even more so in the 2003 Assembly.

The representation of the Jats in the Delhi Assembly is not as strong as it is generally believed either. Their representation has continued to fluctuate over the assemblies of 1993, 1998 and 2003. While during the 1993 Assembly, the Jat MLAs were merely 9 per cent of the total MLAs, their proportion went up to 13 per cent in the 1998 Assembly, but again went down to 9 per cent in the 2003 Assembly. Even though we hear so much about the Jat dominance in Delhi politics, they have not been able to make their presence among the state legislature in any significant way.

---

[3] In Lok Sabha, Dr B. R. Ambedkar got elected in 1952 from the unreserved constituency of Bombay North East; B. P. Maurya was elected in 1962 from the Aligarh unreserved constituency. In recent years, Prakash Ambedkar won the Lok Sabha elections of 1998 and 1999 from Akola, an unreserved seat.

Though there is very little mention of Rajput politics in Delhi, still their share among the Delhi legislature, both in 1993 and 1998, has been nearly 7 per cent. Their representation in the Assembly has remained the same during these two assembly elections, and dropped slightly in the 2003 Assembly. Similarly, the Gujjars have had a steady representation during this period. Over the assemblies of 1993, 1998 and 2003, their representation has been nearly 6 per cent.

The representation of the Vaishya community, which was sizeable during the 1993 Assembly, went down both in the 1998 and 2003 assemblies. In the 1993 Assembly, there were nearly 16 per cent MLAs who belonged to the Vaishya community. In terms of the numbers, the representation of the Vaishyas was third after the representation of the Dalits and the Punjabi Khatris in the 1993 Assembly. But the representation of the Vaishyas went down drastically in the 1998 and 2003 assemblies. One should remember that it was during the 1993 Assembly elections that BJP performed very well and won 49 seats while there was a reversal during the 1998 Assembly election. The Congress had registered an impressive victory in the 1998 Assembly election winning 49 seats while BJP could manage to win only 16 seats. The 2003 Assembly also had similar results. While Congress won 47 seats, the BJP won only 19 seats. The representation of the Vaishyas might have gone down on account of the poor performance of the BJP, both during the 1998 and 2004 Assembly elections. The Vaishya community is understood to be very close to the BJP. While it may be difficult to give any explanation for this at this point, it may be useful to examine the caste backgrounds of MLAs belonging to different political parties, which may help us understand the cause of the low representation of the Vaishya community during the 1998 and 2003 Assembly elections in Delhi.

While most of the MLAs belonging to the Scheduled Castes in the year 1993, 1998 and 2003 got elected from Scheduled Castes reserved constituencies, there was only one exception in the year 1998 and 2003. Similar trends could be noticed for the Muslim MLAs. Most of the MLAs belonging to the Muslim community did get elected from the constituencies where they have a numerical dominance. But the same story could not be narrated for the MLAs belonging to Brahmin, Punjabi Khatri or the Jat community. The Brahmins enjoy a predominant numerical strength in about 10 per cent Assembly constituencies, but in all the three assemblies — 1993, 1998 and 2003 — the proportion of

MLAs belonging to the Brahmin caste is more than what one would have expected. The data indicate that more than half of the Brahmins MLAs got elected from constituencies in which they do not form a sizeable majority. Only a few of the Brahmin MLAs got elected from the constituencies dominated by Brahmin voters.

The Assembly constituencies, in which Punjabi Khatri community has a numerical dominance, are large in numbers. There are about 19 Assembly constituencies (27 per cent of the total Assembly constituencies) in which Punjabi Khatri community constitutes a sizeable majority. But if we look at the proportion of the Punjabi Khatri MLAs in the 1993, 1998 and 2003 assemblies, we would notice that while their representation was 17 per cent in 1993, it went down to about 16 per cent in the 1998 Assembly, and further down to 14 per cent in the 2003 Assembly. The interesting point is that half of these Punjabi Khatri MLAs have been elected from Assembly constituencies where they do not form a sizeable majority.

The numerical dominance of voters belonging to the Jat community could be noticed only in four Assembly constituencies (5 per cent of total Assembly constituencies), but their representation in the Delhi Assembly in 1993 was about 9 per cent and in the year 1998 it was nearly 13 per cent. The proportion of the Jat MLAs went down again to about 9 per cent in the 2003 Assembly. This makes it very clear that a large number of MLAs belonging to the Jat community managed to get elected from the non-Jat Assembly constituencies.

Caste/Community of MLAs Across Political Parties

It is somewhat clear that the representation of the MLAs belonging to different castes/communities is not in proportion to their numerical dominance in certain Assembly constituencies. At the same time, the data also suggest that the MLA belonging to a particular community does not necessarily get elected from the constituency in which voters belonging to that particular community are numerically dominant. In order to analyse further, I have tried to examine whether MLAs of a particular community have greater affiliation to one political party, while MLAs of another community get elected under party tickets of a different political party.

Table 15.4
Caste Profile of MLAs Across Political Parties (%)

Caste	Caste Profile of Congress MLAs			Caste Profile of BJP MLAs		
	1993	1998	2003	1993	1998	2003
Brahmin	22	21	28	14	13	11
Rajput	–	6	2	10	13	11
Vaishya	7	4	2	21	12	21
Punjabi Khatri	14	12	13	21	31	21
Jat	–	12	6	8	19	11
Gujjar	–	4	4	4	–	11
Yadav	–	2	–	2	–	–
Dalit	36	29	26	16	–	11
Muslim	14	4	8	–	–	–
Sikh	7	6	9	4	12	5
	(N=14)	(N=49)	(N=47)	(N=49)	(N=16)	(N=19)

Source: See Table 15.3.

If we look at the caste profile of the MLAs belonging to the two political parties — the Congress and the BJP — we find that a large number of BJP MLAs either belong to the Punjabi Khatri or the Vaishya community, while among the Congress MLAs large numbers are Dalits as also from the Brahmin community.

If we look at the profile of the BJP MLAs during the 1993 Assembly, we find that nearly 21 per cent of the MLAs were from both Punjabi and Vaishya communities. Even if the BJP performed badly both during the 1998 and 2003 Assembly elections, the proportion of the Punjabi community among the BJP MLAs did not change very much. While in the 1998 Assembly it actually went up to 31 per cent, in the 2003 Assembly, it came down to 21 per cent; but the maximum number of BJP MLAs still belong to the Punjabi Khatri community. Large numbers of BJP MLAs also belong to the Vaishya community. Both in the 1993 and 2003 Assembly, nearly 21 per cent of BJP MLAs were from the Vaishyas. The proportion of the Vaishya MLAs belonging to the BJP went down in 1998, but still it was reasonably high. The profile of the Congress MLAs presents a picture of contrast in terms of representation of these two castes. Only one or two MLAs from the Congress belong to the Vaishya community and the proportion of Punjabi Khatris among the Congress MLAs also remained very low in all the three assemblies. The share of the Punjabi community among the Congress MLAs has been between 14 to12 per cent in the three assemblies of 1993, 1998 and 2003. Among the political representatives from the Punjabi Khatri and Vaishya communities, BJP seems to be the most popular party.

If we look at the profile of the MLAs belonging to the Congress party, we find that a large number of Congress MLAs belong to the Dalit community. Nearly 36 per cent of the Congress MLAs during the 1993 Assembly were from the Dalit community. The proportion of the Dalits among the Congress MLAs went down to 29 per cent during the 1998 Assembly and further down to 26 per cent in 2003. The proportion of Dalits among the Congress MLAs went down not because less number of Dalit MLAs got elected, but on the contrary, because the number of seats of the Congress increased manifold. The number of Dalit MLAs from the BJP is still very low. Even though the BJP won a similar number of seats during the 1993 Assembly elections as was won by the Congress during the 1998 Assembly elections, the proportion of the Dalit MLAs among all the BJP MLAs remained as low as only 16 per cent. In the 1998 Assembly, none of the BJP MLAs were from the Dalit community, while in the 2003 Assembly, nearly 11 per cent among the BJP MLAs were Dalits.

Further, if we look at the caste profile of the Congress MLAs, we find that apart from the Dalits, a large number of MLAs belong to the Brahmin community. During the 1993 Assembly, of all the Congress MLAs, 22 per cent were from the Brahmin community, while during the 1998 Assembly, of all Congress MLAs, 21 per cent were from this caste. The proportion of Brahmins among the Congress MLAs went up to 28 per cent in the 2003 House. The number of MLAs belonging to the Brahmin caste among the BJP MLAs remained as low as about 13 per cent during the 1993 and 1998 Assembly, and further down to 11 per cent in the 2003 Assembly.

The Sahib Singh factor seems to add to the Jat presence among the BJP MLAs. During the 1998 Assembly, of all the BJP MLAs, 19 per cent were from the Jat community while their proportion was a little less during the 1993 Assembly. This does not mean that there were lesser number of Jats among the BJP MLAs during the 1993 Assembly as compared to the 1998 Assembly. The fact is that the BJP had won large number of seats during the 1993 Assembly elections as a result of which the proportion of Jats among all the BJP MLAs went down drastically. The number of MLAs belonging to the Jat community among all the

BJP MLAs went down slightly in the 2003 Assembly. Of the Congress MLAs, few belong to the Jat community. Of the 14 Congress MLAs during the 1993 Assembly, there was no one from the Jat community, while during the 1998 Assembly, 12 per cent of the Congress MLAs belonged to the Jats. In the 2003 Assembly, 6 per cent of the Congress MLAs were from this caste.

If we look at the party affiliations of the Muslim MLAs in Delhi, we find that during all the three Assembly elections held in 1993, 1998 and 2003, five Muslims have managed to win elections. No Muslim MLA was elected on a BJP ticket. In the 1993 and 1998 assemblies, while two Muslim MLAs owe allegiance to the Congress party, three belong to the Janata Dal legislative group. During the 2003 Assembly election, four of the five MLAs belonged to the Congress while only one MLA belonged to Janata Dal (Secular). Similarly, if we look at the Sikh MLAs in the Delhi Assembly, we find that there were three Sikhs in the 1993 Assembly, while five Sikhs managed to win both in the 1998 and 2003 Assembly elections. During the 1993 elections, of the three Sikh MLAs one belonged to the Congress party while two were from the BJP. If we look at the 1998 Assembly, we find that three Sikh MLAs were from the Congress party, while two Sikh MLAs belonged to the BJP. In the 2003 Assembly, four Sikh MLAs owe allegiance to the Congress party while one belongs to the BJP. Most of the Rajput MLAs in Delhi belonged to the BJP party during the last three assembly elections.

Caste/Community of MLAs Across Different Regions

Any analysis of Delhi's politics would be incomplete if one does not examine the regional pattern of politics. The question is: do MLAs belonging to a particular caste/community get elected from one particular region while MLAs of certain other communities get elected from a different region.

The electoral boundaries divide Delhi into seven parliamentary constituencies, but for a more meaningful analysis, I have divided Delhi into three different political regions: Outer Delhi, East Delhi and the rest of Delhi. With this political division, we would find that there are 21 Assembly constituencies within the Outer Delhi region and

20 Assembly constituencies within the East Delhi region. These two regions also correspond to the two Lok Sabha constituencies of Delhi. There are 29 Assembly constituencies which fall in the rest of Delhi.

Table 15.5
Regional Pattern of the Caste Profile of MLAs (%)

Caste	Outer Delhi			East Delhi			Rest of Delhi		
	1993	*1998*	*2003*	*1993*	*1998*	*2003*	*1993*	*1998*	*2003*
Brahmin	19	19	19	10	15	30	–	17	17
Rajput	14	–	–	10	15	10	–	7	3
Vaishya	10	10	10	15	5	15	21	3	–
Punjabi Khatri	–	–	5	20	15	5	28	28	28
Jat	24	29	24	–	5	–	4	7	3
Gujjar	5	10	19	10	10	5	3	–	–
Yadav	–	5	–	5	–	–	–	–	–
Dalit	24	24	24	25	25	25	10	14	14
Muslim	–	–	–	5	5	5	14	14	14
Sikh	5	5	–	–	5	5	7	10	14
	(N=21)			(N=20)			(N=29)		

Source: See Table 15.3.

As mentioned earlier, though the politics of Delhi is generally discussed in terms of the Punjabi vote or the Jat vote, if one looks at the political representation of the two communities from different regions, we find that the political presence of these two communities is localised to more or less only one region of Delhi.

The Jat MLAs come entirely from the Outer Delhi region. Of all the MLAs from this region, there were 24 per cent Jats during the 1993 Assembly, 29 per cent during the 1998 Assembly and 24 per cent during the 2003 Assembly. Irrespective of their party affiliation, almost all the Jat MLAs get elected from Outer Delhi. At times, only one or two MLAs belonging to the Jat community get elected from other regions of Delhi.

If we look at the representation of the Punjabis in the Delhi Assembly, we find that most of the MLAs belonging to the Punjabi Khatri community get elected from regions other than Outer Delhi. While there are some MLAs from Punjabi Khatri community who get elected from the East Delhi region, large number of MLAs from this community get elected either from South Delhi, New Delhi, or from Karol Bagh areas. Figures from Table 15.5 make it very clear that the MLAs from Punjabi community are concentrated in only a few locations and not spread all over the city. Of all the MLAs from the region other than Outer Delhi or East Delhi, 28 per cent belong to the Punjabi community. Their representation from this area remained same during all the three assemblies 1993, 1998 and 2003. Among those elected from the East Delhi region, there are MLAs who belong to the Punjabi community, but their representation in this region is only next to the representation of the Dalits from this region. Nearly one-fourth of the MLAs from East Delhi are Dalits. Similarly, among those MLAs who have been elected from the Outer Delhi region, nearly 24 per cent are Dalits. Their proportion in this region is sizeable, but in terms of their number, they are only next to the number of Jat MLAs from this region.

Thus, there is a regional pattern in the caste profile of the MLAs elected from different regions of Delhi.

Age Profile of the MLAs

If we look at the age profile of the MLAs, we find that most of the MLAs in the 1993 and the 1998 Assembly were fairly young, but the MLA in the 2003 House were somewhat aged. While in the 1993 Assembly, nearly 50 per cent MLAs were below the age of 45 years, the proportion of young MLAs went down to 43 per cent in the 1998 Assembly and further down to only 27 per cent in the 2003 House. While the proportion of MLAs from the older age group has remained unchanged during the assemblies of 1993, 1998 and 2003, the number of MLAs between the age group of 46 to 55 years has gone up in the 1998 and 2003 assemblies. In the 1993 Assembly, only 27 per cent MLAs were in the age group of 46–55 years, but their proportion grew to 36 per cent in 1998 and to 46 per cent in 2003. Though there is not much change in the number of MLAs who are aged, the Delhi Assembly seems to have had a graying effect during the last decade.

The MLAs of the 1993 Assembly had a much younger profile as compared to the MLAs in the 1998 and 2003 assemblies. While in the 1993 Assembly, nearly 16 per cent of the MLAs were below 35 years of age, and another 33 per cent were between the age group of 36 to 45 years, in the 2003 Assembly, only 4 per cent MLAs were below the

Table 15.6
Age Profile of the MLAs (%)

Age Group	1993	1998	2003
25–35	16	9	4
36–45	33	34	23
46–55	27	36	46
56–66	21	16	19
66 and above	3	5	7
TOTAL	100 (N=70)	100 (N=70)	99 (N=69)*

Source: See Table 15.3.
Note: *Madan Lal Khurana vacated the Moti Nagar Assembly seat.

age of 35 years and only 23 per cent were between the age of 36 to 45 years. The number of young MLAs seems to have gone down steadily during these three assemblies.

The number of very young MLAs was relatively less in the 1998 Assembly. Only 9 per cent MLAs were below the age of 35 years, but 34 per cent MLAs were in the age group of 36 to 45 years and another 36 per cent MLAs were between 46 to 55 years. So, in total, nearly 80 per cent of the MLAs were below the age group of 55 years.

The figures from Table 15.7 indicate that in general the Congress MLAs share a relatively younger age profile as compared to the MLAs belonging to the BJP. In the 1998 Assembly, only 25 per cent of the BJP MLAs are below the age of 45 years, but nearly 43 per cent of the Congress MLAs in the same house are in this age group. Though the difference in the age group of Congress and the BJP MLAs was not very sharp during the 1993 Assembly, still the Congress MLAs were younger

Table 15.7
Age Profile of MLAs Across Parties (%)

Age Group	Congress			BJP		
	1993	1998	2003	1993	1998	2003
25–35	29	8	4	8	6	5
36–45	21	35	26	37	19	11
46–55	14	35	43	33	50	58
56–65	29	14	21	20	25	16
66 years or above	7	8	6	2	–	11

Source: See Table 15.3.

in their age profile. Nearly 50 per cent of all the Congress MLAs were below the age of 45 years, while of all BJP MLAs, only 45 per cent were below the age of 45 years.

The 2003 Assembly too has Congress MLAs who are much younger compared to those of the BJP. Among all Congress MLAs, 30 per cent are below the age of 45 years, but among the BJP MLAs only 16 per cent are below 45 years. While only 6 per cent of the Congress MLAs are more than 66 years of age, of all the BJP MLAs nearly 11 per cent are of such an older generation.

Educational Profile of the MLAs

An examination of the educational profile of the MLAs in Delhi (Table 15.8) shows that there has not been much change in the educational profile of the Delhi legislature during the three assemblies of 1993, 1998 and 2003. Figures suggest that the majority of the MLAs in Delhi are reasonably well educated. During the 1993 Assembly, nearly 80 per cent of all the MLAs had received college education. The proportion of the MLA's having college education or more went down to nearly 70 per cent in 1998 and 2003 assemblies, but it was still fairly high. There were very few MLAs in Delhi who had not managed to study beyond the middle school level.

Table 15.8
Educational Profile of the MLAs (%)

Level of Education	1993	1998	2003
Middle School	4	6	4
Matriculation	17	24	24
Graduate and above	79	70	70

Source: See Table 15.3.

If we look at the educational profile of the MLAs belonging to different political parties (Table 15.9), we find that, in general, the BJP MLAs are more educated as compared to the MLA's from the Congress party. In the 1993 and 1998 assemblies, more than 80 per cent of all BJP MLAs have attained higher education while, among the Congress MLAs only 65 per cent have managed to attain that level of education. It is only in the 2003 Assembly, that we find the Congress MLAs slightly

Table 15.9
Educational Profile of the MLAs Across Parties (%)

Educational Profile	Congress			BJP		
	1993	1999	2003	1993	1999	2003
Middle School	–	6	4	4	–	5
Matriculation	36	29	21	14	19	32
Graduate and above	64	65	75	82	81	63

Source: See Table 15.3.

more educated as compared to the BJP MLAs. There are very few MLAs who have attained low level of education, and this is true of both the mainstream political parties.

Conclusion

Though with few exceptions, the number of Dalits getting elected to the Delhi Legislative Assembly has not been higher than the number of seats reserved for them. But at the same time, it should be noted that their representation in the Assembly has been higher than any other community in Delhi. However, there has been hardly any focus on this fact as Delhi's politics has been traditionally characterised in terms of either Jat or Punjabi domination. Since most of the Jats and Punjabis are economically well off, they have been able to dominate Delhi's politics in the past, while due to poor economic conditions, even if numerically large, the Dalits have not been able to play an assertive role in the politics of the state.

But things have changed during the past decade. Enormous population growth, a result of rapid migration of poor people from states like Bihar and U.P. have changed the profile of the population of Delhi. There has been an enormous rise in the population of these belonging to the poor class and now they constitute a big vote bank. A unique settlement pattern, where most of these migrants stay in *jhuggi-jhonpri,* has resulted in a vote bank for political parties in these localities.

The analysis of the data also indicates that caste does not play a dominant role in Delhi's politics as even among people belonging to one particular caste/community, there is a substantial difference in the voting patterns of those belonging to different economic classes. Under this changing scenario, the political parties now hardly eye the vote bank of a particular caste; rather, they try to woo voters belonging to one particular class. In recent years, we have witnessed a constant tussle between the two main political parties — the Congress and the BJP — to woo the people living in *jhuggi-jhonpri*. To conclude, in this altered state of affairs, it may not be correct to still paint the picture of Delhi's politics in the twin colours of Jat and Punjabi politics. It is time; one must shift the focus of Delhi's politics from caste to class.

Part VII

The Tamil Exception:
The Subalternist Tradition

16

Caste and Beyond in Tamil Politics

Jean-Luc Racine

In a volume largely dedicated to the study of the caste profile of MLAs in India, a chapter on Tamil Nadu can only start with a reminder of the specificity of the state. Tamil Nadu is known for being the stronghold of the Dravidian movement which has developed a specific ideology and is not simply based upon linguistic and cultural regional identity.[1] The ideologues of the Dravidian movement have theorised the concept of 'Tamilness' in contrast to the Brahmin legacy which was supposed to have been imported in the south and imposed by aliens from the north upon the more egalitarian and secular Dravidian tradition. The purpose of this chapter is neither to reopen the debate on the origins of the Dravidian movement, nor to reassess the merits and the excesses of rewriting Tamil history in the light of such theory. It is, however, necessary to revert to this background for understanding Tamil politics in independent India for the following reasons. First, since the arrival of the Dravida Munnetra Kazhagam (DMK, literally, the 'Association for the Emancipation of Dravidians') to power in 1967, the Dravidian movement, undivided or divided, has constantly been re-elected to power. Second, the policy of emancipation has relied upon a tool used more in Tamil Nadu that in the rest of India, namely, the reservation of seats in public education and public services, not just for Dalits and Tribes, but also for the largest conglomerate of castes defined in Tamil Nadu as elsewhere in India, the 'Other Backward Classes' (OBC). Most of the MLAs in the Tamil Nadu Legislative Assembly come from these classes not, however, because of reservations, for electoral constituencies are

---

[1] The state of Madras, inheritor of the large and multilingual Madras Presidency of the British Raj, has been redefined in several steps under the framework of the reorganisation of states on a linguistic basis launched in 1953 and finalised in 1956. When the Dravidian movement came to power in 1967, the new DMK government decided to rename it 'Tamil Nadu' (the Tamil Country). Later, the name of the city of Madras was changed, and reverted to the old 'Chennai', the Tamil name by which Madras was popularly known. In 2001, Tamil Nadu's population was 62 million.

set apart only for Scheduled Caste and Scheduled Tribe candidates (SC and ST). To suggest that the social background of the lawmakers explains why they have tried to favour their communities would not however tell the whole story. The historical legacy left by the non-Brahmin movement and by its successors, the Self Respect movement and the Dravidian movement, has also contributed in defining a specific political climate in a state where, before and after 1947, the issue of reservations has for long been on the agenda of caste organisations, and on the table of policy-makers. The tactics and the strategies of the DMK and of its antithetic clone, the Anna DMK, did the rest.

Before commenting on the data available on the Tamil MLAs, one should therefore locate the assemblies in their context — historical, ideological, political. The first section of this chapter attempts to do it by paying attention to the legacy of the pre-independence movements to the specificities and complexities of caste affiliations in Tamil Nadu, and to the 40 years of supremacy of the Dravidian parties in Tamil politics, with emphasis on the issue of reservations. The second section comments on the data available on caste and class affiliations of Tamil MLAs and on other parameters, such as education, age, socio-professional status. It also pays attention to the caste strategies of political parties. The last section draws lessons from the data commented upon in Section II, and attempts to go beyond by echoing current debates on Tamil politics, particularly those related to the upper castes' apparent desertion of the political field, to populism, to the dialectics between lower castes and modernity, and to the challenges faced by Dalit politics. In the limited framework of this chapter, one hopes to offer a few insights on the relation between politics and civil society in one of the prominent states of the Indian Union.

I

The Background of Dravidian Politics in Tamil Nadu

The Historical Legacy:
From the Non-Brahmin Movement to Electoral Politics

The non-Brahmin movement was launched by non-Brahmin upper castes, active and well-trained, who decided to challenge the Brahmin supremacy which had reinforced itself under the British rule, in a phase of decisive transformation of political rule and economic development. In the beginning of the 20th century, in Madras Presidency, the supremacy of the Brahmins in education and access to positions of responsibilities was striking. The 1921 Census of India offers significant data on the access of the male population of key Tamil castes to education summarised in Table 16.1.

Table 16.1
Access to Education in Key Tamil Castes in the Madras Presidency, 1921

Caste	Male Population	Literate (%)	Literate in English (%)
Tamil Brahmins	255,976	71.50	28.20
Vellalars	1,311,309	24.20	2.37
Vanniyars	1,325,361	11.20	0.34
Paraiyars	1,143,480	3.50	0.02

Source: Irschik (1969: 16–17) and Census of India, 1921, Part I, pp. 128–29; Part II, pp. 76–78.

The consequences of such a discrepancy between Brahmins, landed upper castes (Vellalars), small peasant castes (Vanniyars) and 'depressed classes', i.e., Dalits (Paraiyars) were predictable: the control of crucial positions by Brahmins went much beyond their traditional prominence in intellectual and religious activities. Besides education and science, they were largely dominant in the administration and the judiciary. In 1912, while Brahmins were 3 per cent of the population in the Madras Presidency, they accounted for 55 per cent of deputy collectors (the second highest post in district administration); 83 per cent of the sub-judges and 72 per cent of the *munsifs* in the district courts (Irchik 1969: 14).

Such a privilege was not agreeable to the new rising elite of non-Brahmin upper castes, who were asserting themselves not just as big landlords but also as professionals in activities connected with the transformation of the economy of colonial India: lawyers, bankers and traders. Furthermore, the transformation of the British rule and the new access to elected posts of responsibility, first in the district boards, then in provincial politics, stimulated the ambitions of the non-Brahmin elite (see Washbrook 1976).[2] In December 1916, the South Indian Liberal

---

[2] For a comprehensive synthesis on the socio-political significance of the non-Brahmin and Dravidian movements, see also Washbrook (1989: 204–64).

Federation was born as the political wing of the South Indian People's Association established in November for launching a newspaper called *Justice*. The movement came to take the form of the Justice Party. It asserted itself quickly, got from the British authorities, 28 seats reserved for non-Brahmins out of the 98 seats of the Legislative Council to be elected under the Montague–Chelmsford Reforms 1919, but, in fact, won many more in the elections in 1921. With 63 representatives, the Justice Party became the key partner in the diarchy established in the Presidency, the Congress having decided to boycott the elections. The rise of the Justice Party to power was, however, fragile for two reasons. First, the rise of the nationalist movement finally gave prominence to the Congress. When it changed its line and decided to contest elections in 1937 after the promulgation of the 1935 Act ending diarchy and giving more power to provincial governments, the Congress won. Chakravarti Rajagopalachari, a Brahmin, became the head of the government in 1937. Second, a new, more radical trend emerged in the 1920s under the name of Self Respect Movement. Established in 1925 by E. V. Ramaswami Naicker, a former Congressman from a high non-Brahmin caste, the Self Respect Movement developed a new ideology based not just upon the opposition to Brahmin supremacy, but also upon the celebration of the Dravidian identity and the aspiration to social reform. The Justice Party, in decline after the rise of the Congress, was taken over by Naicker in 1938, who transformed it in 1944 into the 'Dravidian Association' — Dravida Kazhagam. The Dravida Kazhagam was no more a political party. It was a powerful tool for agitating society, promoting anti-Brahminism but also anti-Hinduism, opposing the caste system, and rethinking the future of the Dravidian people, possibly outside an independent India in future bound to be dominated by the Congress and therefore, according to Naicker, by Brahmins.

By 1933, a new organisation had emerged — the Backward Classes League. Certainly, the League opposed the Brahmin supremacy, but it also denounced the non-Brahmin upper castes, whose uplift in the administration and professional jobs was well advanced. S. Saraswathi notes: 'Thus began an alliance among the lower non-Brahmin castes who began to repeat the same charge against forward non-Brahmin leaders as these had levelled against the Brahmins in the past' (1974: 120). In 1944, the League estimated in a memorandum that in the Presidency almost two-thirds of the gazetted officers posts, the upper ranks in the administration, were cornered by the Brahmins (37 per cent of the posts) and the non-Brahmin upper castes (27 per cent), while these groups accounted for only 3 per cent and 22 per cent of the population respectively. Backward Classes, said to be half of the population, had only 2 per cent of the top officers' postings. The League, once again, asked for special reservations according to the estimated share of each group in the total population. This would have given 50 per cent for Backward Classes, 22 per cent for 'Forward non-Brahmins', 14 per cent for 'Depressed classes', 7 per cent for Muslims, 4 per cent for Christians, and 3 per cent for Brahmins (Saraswathi 1974: 120–22).

In a way, the non-Brahmin movement and the Justice Party had by then played their role of promoting the uplift of the non-Brahmin upper castes. But once this process was on, the struggle for the emancipation of the Backward Classes was bound to assert itself. This was perfectly understood by the Dravida Kazhagam (DK), and put in practice by a new organisation rooted in the Dravidan movement philosophy, the Dravida Munnetra Kazhagam.

In 1949, at a time when the Constituent Assembly was finalising the parliamentary regime bound to govern independent India, younger leaders of the DK, not always happy with the personal style of functioning of Naicker, decided to establish a new organisation, the Dravida Munnetra Kazhagam (DMK), led by C. N. Annadurai. However, Periyar ('the Great Man'), as Naicker came to be known, was still recognised as the leading figure of the Dravidian movement, its ideological point of reference. If the DMK was softer than the DK in demonstrations against Hinduism, it did retain much from its parent organisation in terms of Dravidian identity and anti-caste discourse.

The DMK did not enter electoral politics immediately. As late as 1954, it was still playing with the rhetorics of separatism (it changed its discourse on this point during the Indo-China war of 1962, when the central government threatened to ban secessionist parties). But, in fact, the core of its action was elsewhere, and much more confined to the newly carved Madras state, limited to the Tamil-speaking areas, than to the old concept of Dravida Nadu encompassing the whole of south India. On the issue of identity, the Tamil greatness and the celebration of the Tamil language were still on the forefront. The DMK agitation against the proposed promotion of Hindi, in 1965, did much for preparing its electoral success in 1967. In 1952, the party had also successfully opposed Chief Minister Rajagopalachari's scheme to develop a part-time education programme proposing that children from the working classes have apprenticeship within their family: a scheme attacked by the DMK on the grounds that it was a way to perpetuate the connection between caste and professional status. Rajagopalachari resigned in 1954, and significantly, the Congress party brought K. Kamaraj as Chief Minister, the first to come from a Backward Class background a Nadar.

Sociologically, the DMK contended to represent not just the non-Brahmin elite, but all Tamils, including the lower castes and the Dalits. A part of its success came from its social programme of emancipation of the Backwards, as also from its unique capacity to mobilise the medium of films as a way to disseminate its ideology through popular cinema. Agitators and authors, Annadurai and his successor Karunanidhi, were also screenplay writers, and they understood that if publishing books and debating upon Tamil cultural legacy and social reform was important, there was only one place where Tamils of all castes, literate or non-literate, men and women, could sit under the same roof, side by side, to share a story with a message: the cinema hall. One would not appreciate the impact of the Dravidian parties and their chief ministers without giving to the medium of films their due. If leaders of the DMK were scriptwriters, the leaders of the breakaway All India Anna Dravida Munnetra Kazhagam (AIADMK) — M. G. Ramachandran and Jayaram Jayalalitha — were film stars before entering politics.

Two political developments helped the DMK to enter electoral politics: the decline of the Communist Party of India (CPI), and the short-lived appearance of caste parties in the Madras state. The CPI and its affiliated trade unions had been very active in the Madras Presidency in the late 1940s, and the party did well in 1952 in the elections to the first Legislative Assembly of the large Madras state. With 62 MLAs out of 375, it came second behind the Congress. But the repression of agitations by the government, and the redefinition of the Soviet policy, which decided, in 1951, to support Nehru's regime and its new policy of non-alignment, weakened the CPI. In 1957, it got only four MLAs in the new Madras state. There was thus a space left for the DMK which bagged 50 seats out of 205 in its first appearance in the Assembly elections in 1962.

The second parameter is related to the emergence, in 1951, of the Tamilnadu Toilers' Party launched by Vanniyar politicians, for the benefit of their caste, the largest standard peasant caste settled north of the Kaveri river, said to account today for 12 per cent of the entire population of the state and for about one-third of the population of the northern districts.[3] Soon a split occurred, when a group launched the Commonweal Party. In 1952, the two Vanniyar parties did pretty well, bagging 25 seats. Rajagopalachari called the leader of the Commonweal Party to join the government. A few years later, in a similar move, Kamaraj nominated the leader of the Toilers' Party as a minister. Both the Vanniyar parties were finally dissolved into the Congress. Frustrated, the DMK leadership, who had extended support to these parties in 1952, discovered that the Vanniyar politicians had ultimately served the Congress party in power. The lesson was not lost: the DMK, which had already developed a large sociological basis, transcending specific castes, entered electoral politics. It did succeed, and for two or three decades, caste parties in Tamil Nadu were no more relevant.

The Caste Structure in Tamil Nadu

As in many parts of India, the four-fold varna paradigm of the Sanskrit tradition does not apply well in Tamil Nadu. As we have seen, Brahmins are conspicuous, more by their impact on society and culture, and their heavy presence in professions related to law, education and administration, than by their mere numbers. A strong anti-Brahmin movement, coupled with access to high education, contributed to the migration of a number of highly qualified Tamil Brahmins outside Tamil Nadu (and sometimes even outside India), but not to the point of weakening their importance in elite circles, except in politics.

---

[3] These estimates of the Vanniyar population are borrowed from Radhakrishan (2002). In 1921, the detailed Census of castes and communities gave for the then south Arcot district (a stronghold of the Vanniyars and from where present leader S. Ramadoss hails from), a precise figure of 31.34 per cent of Vanniyars. At that time, in this district, Dalits were 26.53 per cent; landed castes of various status above the Vanniyars were 13.53 per cent; Brahmins, 1.53 per cent; trading castes, 3.32 per cent; artisans of various status, 5.82 per cent; cattle breeders, 4.19 per cent; other low castes of service, 3.74 per cent. Tribals were 1.70 per cent; non-Hindus were 5.66 per cent; and unidentified castes, 1.85 per cent of the total population.

At the other end of the traditional hierarchy, outside the pale of the varnas, Dalits are clearly identified as well, and in much greater numbers: 19 per cent of the population in Tamil Nadu is labelled as 'Scheduled Castes' by the 2001 Census (the figure for India is 16.3 per cent). The best known amongst Tamil Dalits are the Paraiyars, settled in the northern districts of the state, and the Pallars, settled in the southern districts. Most of them, in both cases, are agricultural labourers.

In between, however, the picture is much more blurred. Despite the existence of great Tamil dynasties a millennium ago, the Kshatriyas are insignificant in numbers, and subjected to question. Inheritors of the Maratha rulers who established themselves in a few strategic places in the 18th century would be accepted as genuine Kshatriyas. Local dynasties may have tried to graduate to Kshatriya status in some cases but for the rest, 'Kshatriya' would be a reference invented in the 19th century by imaginative genealogists rewriting the history of their caste in order to upgrade its status, at a time when, under the British rule, the assertiveness of competitive caste power was enhanced by the new opportunities offered by local elections. A case in point is offered by the Vanniyakula Kshatriyas, supposed to be from a divine lineage, and who are in fact Vanniyars.

The categorical concept of Vaishyas, similarly, is not one that is often used. The highest trading castes would rather use the local title of 'Chettiars', which includes various groups, some of them speaking Telugu, such as the Komuttis. Most of them are, however, Tamil Chettiars of various status, the Nattukottai Chettiars being a class by themselves, of rich families of bankers who modernised the financial economy of the Madras Presidency under the British rule, expanded their networks up to Burma and, eventually, asserted their status by receiving nobility titles by the Crown while fully playing their role as leading patrons of the arts and knowledge. Sir Raja Annamalai Chettiar (1881–1948) offers the most prominent example of such a profile. A member of the Legislative Council of the Madras Presidency, then thrice elected to the Council of State set up by the Montague–Chelmsford Reforms, he was one of the founders of the Indian Bank and one of the directors of the Imperial Bank of India. A benefactor of the Nataraja temple at Chidambaram, he founded, close to this sacred town, the secular Annamalai University in 1929, and was, in 1943, the founder of the prestigious Music Academy of Madras, the Tamil Isai Sangam. By contrast, some trading low castes would use 'Chettiar' as a title in order to enhance their low rank: this is the case in some fishermen castes of the Coromandel Coast.

The least we say about the so-called Shudras is the best, for this is probably the most confused concept related to caste structure in Tamil Nadu. Some old classifications include castes of extremely diverse status under this varna from service castes, traditionally low ranked (barbers, washermen), to castes of small peasants (Vanniyars, Gounders) and castes who raised their low status since a century or so, such as the Nadars — who gave to Tamil Nadu its first 'Backward Class' chief minister, the well-respected Congressman K. Kamaraj — or the Thevars who include many subcastes, labelled as 'criminal castes' by the British (they were 'denotified' after independence) but now asserting their power. To add to the confusion, some classifications enter, in the Shudra varna, castes with a long history of high status, such as the Reddiyars (a landlord caste of Telugu origin, who are generally the powerful patrons of local temples served by Brahmin priests) or Vellalars (a landlord caste, a large number of whose members urbanised themselves in the 20th century and entered new professional occupations, as urbanised Brahmins did). Just as in the 19th century some Vanniyar ideologues redefined their caste as Vanniyakula Kshatriya, the leadership of the Dalit Pallar caste has more recently renamed the caste as 'Devendrakula Vellalar'. In both cases, a high non-Brahmin reference was invoked, without in fact confusing anybody.

In a way, 'Shudra' has now become more a militant concept than a reference in daily life. The word has been used in different ways, from Ambedkar (1947) himself (*Who were the Shudras?*) to Kancha Ilaiah (1996) (*Why I Am Not a Hindu: A Sudra Critique of Hindutva Philosophy, Culture and Political Economy*). In 1982, A. N. Sattanathan, who had earlier been the Chairman of the first Backward Classes Commission set up in 1969 by the DMK government, thus commented upon the arrival of the DMK to power: 'the rule of the Sudras had begun' (1982: 24).[4] But Shudras, as Sattanathan recognised, are a very diverse category. This is

---

[4] After the election of 1962, 'the DMK was firmly in power . . . the rule of the Sudra has begun . . . the succession from Brahman dominance first passed on to the higher castes among non-Brahmans, who again formed only a small percentage of the total population . . . the succession is already passing from the higher caste non-Brahmans to the more numerous backward class non-Brahmans . . . We have yet to wait and see how fast the succession passes down to the leadership of the lower classes in the Sudra fold and then to the scheduled castes' (Sattanathan 1982: 24–26).

why Kancha Ilaiah makes a clear distinction between those he refers to as 'neo-Kshatriyas', the 'Shudras upper castes', i.e., castes of power and status who are neither Brahmin, nor Kshatriya, nor Vaishya, and the 'Dalitbahujans', the Scheduled Castes and Other Backward Classes, characterised as 'people and castes who form the exploited and suppressed majority' (Ilaiah 1996: vii–ix). In contrast, an active Tamil Dalit intellectual, Ravikumar, recently used the term in a much more divisive perspective, resolutely contrasting Dalits to Shudras. Referring to 'Vanniyars designated as a Most Backward Class' as 'the main per-petrators of atrocities against Dalits in the northern districts (of Tamil Nadu)', he celebrated 'the fearless war against the shudra repression' initiated by Tamil Dalits during the 1990s (Ravikumar 2005). We have to keep these contradictions in mind for interpreting caste politics and its electoral dimension.

To sum up, beyond the militant categorisations, a sociological per-spective sensitive to the historical dynamics which transformed Tamil society from the 19th century onwards is more relevant than the four-fold varna paradigm for understanding the competitive politics at play for decades. After all, it is now 45 years that M. N. Srinivas underlined this:

> The varna scheme refers at best only to the broad categories of the society and not to its real and effective units. The categories of shudra subsume in fact the vast majority of non-Brahminical castes which have little in common . . . The shudra-category spans such a wide structural and cultural gulf that its sociological utility is very limited . . . In peninsular India, there are no genuine Kshatriyas and Vaishyas . . . The varna model has been the case of misinterpretation of the caste system (1962: 65).

Another major difficulty is to be recognised before analysing the data available on Members of the Legislative Assembly. The caste structure in Tamil Nadu, as everywhere, cannot be reduced to 'caste' as such — the *jati*. Not only are all castes subdivided in many subcastes, locally rooted, and considered unequal in status; in fact, the practice of as-suming a title to nominate a group, and the use of high caste titles by groups of low status adds greatly to the confusion. Chettiar, we have noted, could refer to anything, from the elite banking communities of Nattukottai Chettiar to the groups of Chettiar listed as OBC, such as the Karpura Chettiar or the Kasukkara Chettiars, or to some other subgroups listed as Most Backward Classes, such as the Kongu Chettiars from Coimbatore, the Kuruhini Chettiar, the Sozhia Chettiar, etc. The same could be said of Vellalar, who, at the top, could belong to elite non-Brahmin castes, while some subgroups using the Vellalar title are listed as OBC, such as the Kaniyala Vellalar, the Kudikkara Vellalar, the Nangudi Vellalar, not to forget the Dalit Devendrakula Vellalar mentioned earlier. Village barbers who are also musicians are called Isai Vellalar as well. On the one hand, broad caste names are misguiding up to a point for they could be used by subgroups of very different status. On the other hand, the struggle for getting access to reservations and the continuous expansion of the OBC administrative category have, in fact, resulted in listing, in this major conglomerate, subgroups of very different status. In the reality of Tamil social life, there is little in common indeed between, say, the peasants of Gounder caste and the Kaikkolar weavers, who would enjoy, in the traditional social perceptions, a much more respectable image than, for instance, the folk dancers Dommaras or the nomadic tribe of Lambadis. All of them, however, are listed under the single category as OBC.

The intricacies of the nomenclature of the old castes, subcastes and subgroups, and the ambiguity of the administrative category of 'OBC' should never be forgotten, for they define a first set of limitations to the exercise we undertake here. This is because, first, these categories, both the traditional ones (the castes and their subcastes) and the more recent administrative ones (the Backward Classes), do not always provide clear-cut indications about the real social position of the groups they incorporate. Second, a more accurate analysis of the dialectics between caste politics and social change based upon the personal profiles of MLAs would require more than their caste affiliation: their family background and their real socio-economic status would offer decisive information. This would require a research work of a much more ambitious scope than the present one. Third, 'caste' is too polysemous a word for not calling for caution when interpreting social change and political dynamics. If caste is indeed a key parameter in Tamil politics as it is in Indian politics as a whole, politics is not guided only by caste consideration, and the dialectics between caste affiliation and social dynamics are not confined to competitive politics. While sections of Backward Classes have seized the opportunity offered by electoral politics for promoting their emancipation and their empowerment (this is precisely the meaning of 'munnetra' in the names of the Dravidian parties), elite castes have developed alternative strategies for maintaining their socio-economic position without being greatly represented in the Legislative Assembly. On the other hand, Dalits who have successfully entered electoral politics in mainstream parties are not necessarily in tune with the militancy of the leadership of Dalit parties, not to mention the stand of more radical Dalit intellectuals.

Another point deserves attention: the reluctance of the Dravidian leadership to comment upon their own caste background. It is of course consistent with an anti-caste philosophy (we observe the same reluctance in Communist leaders all over India). Official biographies never mention it. Laudatory books avoid the topic as well. C. N. Annadurai, who comes from a weaver caste, appears in a volume collecting his speeches in the parliament as 'the son of middle-class parents', born 'at the hand-loom town of Kanchipuram' (Ramachandran 1975: xvii). An early panegyric of Karunanidhi presents him as the son of 'a scholar and a pandit', 'born of ordinary peasant stock, in a little village' (Swaminathan 1974: 21). He is said to be, in fact, from a most backward caste of Thanjavur district. The caste of M. G. Ramachandran, a Malayalee from Kerala, born in Sri Lanka, has always been irrelevant; much more important was the story of his life, from poverty at childhood to stardom and chief ministership. The caste of Jayalalitha — a Brahmin — has also been irrelevant for her political career at the top of AIADMK.

In short, the role of caste in politics is an important subject (although sometimes caste is a politically incorrect topic) but it cannot be confined to determinist labels ascribed to politicians. These methodological and structural limitations duly noted, it remains, however, useful to analyse the data available on MLAs, for it provides significant information on major social groups at the state level besides offering material for a comparative inter-states perspective.

The Political Scenario in Tamil Nadu after 1967: Forty Years of Dravidian Parties' Pre-eminence

The most striking fact in Tamil Nadu since 1967 is the sustained pre-eminence of the Dravidian parties. The victory of the DMK, in 1967, was testimony to the strength of a party which has been able to build upon a strategy relying upon complementary legacies. On the one hand, the DMK drew from the non-Brahmin movement and its political tool, the Justice Party, run, as we have seen, by an elite of non-Brahmin professionals of high castes. On the other hand, it owes its specificity to the Self Respect Movement of Periyar, playing on the rewriting of Tamil history and focusing on both the exaltation of Tamil identity and a progressive agenda, supposed to be part of an antique tradition later on weakened by the northern Brahmin–Baniya supremacy. From the Self Respect Movement, the DMK inherited an ideology (some would say, a rhetoric) open to all popular castes and classes; from the Justice Party, it borrowed the strategy of electoral politics, but with a difference, for the times after independence were no more those of the elite monopolies. Universal franchise and the quick expansion of competitive politics, in a state where the Congress hegemony was soon challenged, defined new parameters which helped the politicisation of the common citizen to take deep roots. Most importantly, successful mass agitations and a decisive involvement in popular media helped the DMK to develop a strong network of local cadres in villages, towns and cities. This strategy gave the movement such strong popular roots that despite the major split of 1977, which gave birth to the new Anna Dravida Munnetra Kazhagam (ADMK, later AIADMK), Dravidian parties remain till today the cornerstone of politics in Tamil Nadu.[5]

The Pre-eminence of the Dravidian Parties

From the first victory of the DMK in 1967 till today, the Dravidian parties (the DMK and the AIADMK in addition to, marginally small breakaway parties) have so far established their supremacy in the Tamil Nadu Legislative Assembly. From 59 per cent of the seats in 1967, they raised their share to 79 per cent in 1971, and got respectively 76, 71, 67, 77, 70 and 75 per cent of the seats in the six following elections reviewed in detail here. In 2001 and 2006, they got 70 per cent of the seats (Table 16.2). Since 1977, the DMK and the AIADMK are certainly arch-rivals, but their acute divide, so important for tactical politics in Tamil Nadu, does not really benefit third parties. At the most, it compels

---

[5] The party's name was, first, Anna Dravida Munnetra Kazhagam, with reference to Annadurai, the founder of the DMK. Later, during the Emergency, it added 'All India' to its denomination in order to appear as a national party. Its political constituency remained, however, confined to Tamil Nadu.

the DMK and the AIADMK to search for allies, but their partners have never come close to the first rank. The complete routing of one of the two leading parties benefits the other Dravidian party of common ideological lineage, rather than the non-Dravidian parties. From 1984 to 1996, the DMK and the AIADMK have successively risen and fallen in a strikingly symmetrical way, the losses of one becoming the gains of the other. The most significant examples of such dramatic swings were the 1991 elections (AIADMK with 164 seats, DMK with two) followed by the 1996 poll (DMK with 173, AIADMK with four). This is less due to decisive shifts in popular appreciation than to the electoral pattern — uninominal votes cast in a single poll — which explains why seats gained by each party are not always representative of the respective strength of these parties, for the 'first past the post' principle gives the constituency to the candidate who is ahead, leaving no space for others.[6]

Equally significant is the fact that the two big traumas which resulted in massive victories for the Congress party in the Lok Sabha — the assassination of Indira Gandhi in 1984 and the assassination of Rajiv Gandhi in 1991 — benefited the Congress in Tamil Nadu only marginally. Certainly, its best scores since 1967 were reached on these occasions (62 seats in 1984; 60 in 1991), but not at the expense of the Dravidian parties. If the DMK paid the price for being in power at the time of the assassination of Rajiv Gandhi — killed by the Sri Lanka Liberation Tigers of Tamil Eelam (LTTE) during an electoral meeting in Tamil Nadu — the AIADMK registered, as per compensation, its best performance ever till then, with 164 MLAs: 82 per cent of the members of the Assembly.

Factionalism and personal rivalries have resulted in additional splits within the Dravidian movement. Some new-born parties have been short-lived. Some have gained a space for themselves, such as the Marumalarchi Dravida Munnetra Kazhagam (MDMK, literally, the Association for the Renovation of the Dravidian Emancipation) launched by V. Gopalswamy, alias Vaiko, in 1994. It is too early to guess if the Desiya Murpokku Dravida Kazhagam (DMDK or the National Progressive Dravidian Association) launched by film star Vijayakanth

---

[6] This explains why in the Assembly elections of 2001, for instance, the two key parties had very contrasting results despite securing almost the same number of votes: with 8.8 million votes, the AIADMK got 132 MLAs; with 8.6 millions, the DMK got only 31.

in 2005 will last for long. Amongst DMDK candidates, Vijayakanth alone has been elected, but the party got almost three million votes in the state. For a comprehensive assessment of the strength of the Dravidian parties in the Assembly, one has to take these small parties into account (listed in Table 16.2, as 'Other DMK').

This resilience of the Dravidian parties can be explained only by the grip they developed on the electorate despite the accusations of corruption and nepotism that their respective leadership regularly charge against each other. Many factors are at play here, one of them being that the 'estranged brothers', linked by a common proclaimed ideology, seem to offer the electorate an alternate choice 'within the family', when voters want to teach a lesson to those in power, and return the incumbent party to the opposition. Charisma is also essential. In a noted study on Tamil politics, M. S. S. Pandian (1992) has analysed in detail how the image of M. G. Ramachandran, who broke away from the DMK for launching the ADMK, has gained from his legendary status as film star in Tamil Nadu, and from the kind of popular characters he used to perform. Both his former leader Muthuvel Karunanidhi, against whom he rebelled, and his partner in films and inheritor in politics, Jayaram Jayalalitha, have charisma on their own as well. Jayalalitha, as M. G. Ramachandran's most prominent partner on screen, stands as the epitome of the Tamil heroine (despite being a Brahmin born in present Karnataka), as also a shrewd and resolute politician able to come back after crushing defeats. Karunanidhi reinforces his strength as the closest disciple of the DMK founder and first non-Congress Chief Minister C. N. Annadurai (1967–68); he also derives his image as the big old man of Dravidian politics. Karunanidhi never lost an election since he entered electoral politics, and has been elected no less than 11 times to the Tamil Nadu Legislative Assembly. After the elections of 2006, he became, at 82, chief minister for the fifth time, 37 years after his first nomination at this post in 1969. His activity as a writer has always added to his status as well.

However, neither the leaders' charisma nor the very strong networking of the Dravidian parties across the state — which largely accounts for the deep politicisation of the Tamil electorate — can alone explain the continuous leadership of the Dravidian parties. The political programme of these parties is obviously essential as well as the way they conduct popular politics. The anti-Brahmin dimension of the Dravidian ideology and the celebration of the 'unique' greatness of the Dravidian civilisation

Table 16.2

Strength of Parties in the Tamil Nadu Legislative Assembly, 1967–2006

	Congress	DMK	AIADMK	'Other DMK'	Communists (CPI+CPM)	Independent	Others	TOTAL	Share of 'Dravidian Parties' (%)
1967	50	138	–	–	13	7	26	234	58.97
1971	15	184	–	–	8	8	19	234	78.63
1977	27	49	129	–	17	1	11	234	76.06
1980	30	38	128	–	21	8	9	234	70.94
1984	62	24	133	–	7	3	5	234	67.09
1989	26	151	27	3	18	5	4	234	77.35
1991	60	2	164	–	2	1	5	234	70.94
1996	39	173	4	–	9	1	8	234	75.64
2001	30	31	132	–	11	5	25	234	69.78
2006	34	96	61	7	15	1	20	234	70.08

Source: Data collected by Professor G. Koteswara Prasad, Department of Politics, University of Madras.

Note: 'Congress' refers to all successive denominations of the Congress party which played a role in Tamil Nadu, including formations such as the Indian National Congress Organisation (NCO) in 1967 and the Tamil Manila Congress (TMC) in 1996.

'Other DMK' refers to parties which broke away from either the DMK or the AIADMK, while keeping the Dravidian ideology, such as the MGR-ADMK in 1989 and, in 2006, the MDMK and the DMDK.

'Others' with particular relevance in specific assemblies include: Swatantra Party: 20 MLAs in 1967; Swatantra Party: six MLAs and Forward Block: seven MLAs in 1971; Janata Party: 10 MLAs in 1977.

would not have paid such dividends if the DMK and the AIADMK had not conducted a decisive social engineering in Tamil Nadu. The identity factor — 'Tamilness' — was played (and overplayed) very much, and its relevance is certainly not lost today as it gives pride and a sense of belonging, particularly to large segments of the population who conduct their entire life in the confines of Tamil Nadu. However, the way both the AIADMK and the DMK compromised with their ideology, by allying themselves with the Bharatiya Janata Party for challenging each other better in Tamil Nadu, has not really affected their popularity, as if pragmatism in all-India politics was acceptable, and good relations with the centre positive, provided that the political machinery on the ground serving OBC (and secondarily, Dalits) was still running as before.[7] The best example of such a logic was the ability of Jayalalitha, in 1994, to get the support of all national parties for preserving the existing level of reservations in Tamil Nadu at 69 per cent albeit the Supreme Court had ruled that the limit of reservations be 50 per cent. This was again a key precondition she raised before her party joined the BJP-led National Democratic Alliance Government in 1998.

Dravidian Parties and the Reservation Policy

If the politics of Tamil identity is the brand-mark of the Dravidian movement, the politics of reservation has been its most efficient tool for remaining in power. Tamil Nadu has been at the forefront of the reservation movement, which has a long history dating back to the first half of the 19th century when, in the Madras Presidency, diverse groups and associations sent petitions to the British Raj representatives who partially obliged. The strength of the Non-Brahmin movement, the emergence of the Self Respect Movement, and the multiple petitions addressed to the government for decades by caste associations (including the Adi-Dravida Mahajana Sabha for Dalits) gave momentum to the idea at a time when Ambedkar (amongst others) pleaded for reservations for 'Depressed Classes' — the Dalits. In 1919, two years after the release

---

[7] AIADMK was a member of the first coalition government led by the BJP and run by A. B. Vajpayee in 1998. When the Prime Minister refused to follow Jayalalitha in her political vendetta against Karunanidhi too far, then Jayalalitha in fact withdrew her support, and the central government fell. This resulted in new general elections, with a new polarisation: AIADMK allied with the Congress, and DMK with the BJP.

of the non-Brahmin manifesto, came the first significant victory: an Act reserved 28 seats for non-Brahmins out of the 98 elected seats in the Madras Legislative Council.[8] In 1927, quotas were introduced in public services for all groups of castes and communities, the 'non-Brahmin Hindus' being the best endowed.[9] In 1935, 30 seats out of 215 were allotted for Scheduled Castes (the new name given to the 'Depressed Classes') in the legislature. Their share in public service rose to 14.3 per cent in 1947 when a new Government Order redefined the quota policy, also making a distinction between 'forward non-Brahmin Hindus' and 'backward non-Brahmin Hindus'.[10]

After independence, the reservation policy was bound to change, as the Constitution was considering reservation for Scheduled Castes only on a temporary basis. The Dravida Kazhagam was on the forefront of the struggle for preserving the Government Order of 1947 against negative judgements passed by the High Court of Madras and the Supreme Court of India. Finally, in 1951, the first Amendment to the Constitution defined the framework for a compromise. The Congress government of Madras, led by P. S. Kumaraswamy Raja, reintroduced reservations on public services and government educational institutions, but on a new pattern: there were no longer quotas for all groups. Sixty per cent of the seats were for open competition, 25 per cent were for 'socially and educationally backward classes', 15 per cent for SC/ST. Despite protests from many 'backward' quarters, the Congress stuck to that line, particularly after absorbing, in its fold, the leadership of the Vanniyar parties set up in the early 1950s.

After arriving in power, the DMK was bound to go beyond what competing groups had got for themselves under the British rule and under Congress governments. In 1969, the DMK government set up a Backward Classes Commission which recommended increasing the existing reservation of 25 per cent for Backward Classes, and to identify Most Backward Classes to make special provisions for them. In 1971,

---

[8] In Tamil Nadu, key studies on reservations, past and present, owe much to P. Radhakrishnan. See, in particular, Radhakrishnan (1996), as also other references to his works at the end of this chapter.

[9] The calculation ran by 'units of 12 appointments': on 12 appointments, non-Brahmins got five; Brahmins, Muslims, Anglo-Indians/Christians got two each; and others (including the Depressed Classes) got one (Radhakrishnan 1996: 114).

[10] The new calculation ran by units of 14 appointments (ibid.: 121), with six for forward non-Brahmin Hindus; two each for backward non-Brahmin Hindus, Brahmins and Scheduled Castes; one for Muslims and one for Anglo-Indians/Christians.

Karunanidhi partly followed this recommendation. While reservations for Scheduled Castes and Scheduled Tribes rose to 18 per cent, reservations for Backward Classes rose from 25 to 31 per cent. The total was still below 50 per cent.

In 1979, M. G. Ramachandran, Chief Minister of the first AIADMK government, decided to implement another recommendation of the Commission with regards to the 'creamy layer', in other words, the effective beneficiaries of reservation (a minority amongst the Backward Classes) which might be dropped from the list on the basis of economic criteria. But soon after a Government Order had defined the category to be removed from the list (this included families with income above Rs 9,000 a year), the defeat of the party at the Lok Sabha election of 1980 was received as a strong negative signal. The government withdrew its order, and to make its message clear to the electorate, increased the reservation for OBC to 50 per cent, the total reservation being therefore raised to 68 per cent, much above the prescribed limit. The case was brought to the Supreme Court of India which ordered the Tamil Nadu Government to revise its policy but to no avail. In 1990, the DMK government of Karunanidhi added 1 per cent for the Scheduled Tribes, withdrawing them from the SC–ST list, the SC keeping the previous quota of 18 per cent for themselves. The total reservations thus rose to 69 per cent. In November 1992, a Supreme Court ruling confirmed that reservations should be confined to 50 per cent. The following year, Jayalalitha being Chief Minister, the Tamil Nadu government got a bill passed unanimously at the Assembly for preserving the 69 per cent quota. This being done, Jayalalitha asked the central government, run by the Congress, its ally in Tamil Nadu, to support the bill. The government of Narasimha Rao obliged, 'in view of the importance and sensitive nature of the matter' and after getting the 'general consensus' of the leaders of political parties in July 1994. With the President of India's assent, the AIADMK government passed the Tamil Nadu Act 45 of 1994, which was included in the Ninth Schedule of the Constitution, by the 66th Amendment voted by the Indian parliament the following month.[11] The AIADMK could then present itself as the party which

---

[11] See the 'Statement of Objectives and Reasons' released by the central government in 1994 before the 66th Amendment of the Constitution was passed by the parliament, http://indiacode.nic.in/coiweb/amend/amend76.htm (accessed 10 October 2006).

not only raised the level of reservations much above the normal limit, but who could also protect this gain by getting consensus at home and decisive support from New Delhi against the Supreme Court ruling. Consequently, the reservations in Tamil Nadu since the 1990s stand as follows:

Table 16.3
Reservations in Government Educational Institutions and Public Services in Tamil Nadu, 2006

Category	Population (million)	Percentage of Population	Share of Reservation (%)
Backward Classes	28.79	46.14	30
Most Backward Classes (MBC)	10.87	17.43	(MBC+DC: 20)
Denotified Communities (DC)	2.14	3.44	
Scheduled Castes	11.85	19.00	18
Scheduled Tribes	0.65	1.04	1
Others	8.07	12.95	0
TOTAL	62.37	100.00	69

Source: Government of Tamil Nadu (2005). Population figures are from the *Census of India, 2001*.

The gratitude of the electorate was not strong enough, however, for preventing the debacle of the AIADMK in the 1996 Assembly election. However, no one has questioned the expansion of reservations conducted by M. G. Ramachandran and Karunanidhi and supported by Jayalalitha. The introduction of subcategories (Most Backward Classes and Denotified Communities) has not changed the general pattern of reservations, but it has met specific concerns. Rather than implementing a 'creamy layer' policy, as recommended by the Second Backward Classes Commission set up on the suggestion of the Supreme Court in 1982, the introduction of the MBC category was supposed to put up with the concentration of benefits of reservations in favour of some specific groups. Such a decision was obviously easier to implement than the family approach supposed to be followed for the fair identification of the 'creamy layer'. The identification at a very detailed level of precisely located 'Denotified Communities', a mix of subcastes and subtribes of low status, some of them having been classified as 'criminal castes' by the British, was supposed to meet demands from the ground, from the most backward of the backwards, but not defined as Scheduled Castes or Scheduled Tribes.[12]

Such detailed listings unravel one of the intricacies, (or the paradoxes) of the reservation policy. While caste (negative) discrimination is not allowed by the Constitution, the expansion of reservation beyond Dalits has necessarily led the government to revert to the pre-independence practice of caste identification, conducted this time at the very level of small subcastes located in just one or two districts — which is more precise, in fact, than the caste identification conducted by the Census of India before independence. It appears, therefore, that Tamil politics plays the caste factor at two different levels. On the one hand, at the level of the state where strategic political discourses are elaborated, categories are aggregative and large: SC, ST and OBC (and secondarily, MBC). These large categories may easily be subdivided into key castes which demographically dominate Tamil Nadu subregions (Vanniyars, Gounders, Thevars, etc.), but strategically, the mega-categories — Dalits and OBC — are decisive: they are supposed to blur the reality of (local) caste politics. This however is not always the case, for, on the other hand, local parameters may not always conform to the theory of caste vote banks. We may, therefore, observe very different political practices. If for local reasons, MLAs have built up a solid base, a caste may offer a strong vote bank to a party as the Thevars do for the AIADMK, for instance in the southern districts. On the contrary, in the northern districts, the Vanniyars vote for a number of parties, not just for the Pattali Makkal Katchi born out of the Vanniyar Sangam. In such a configuration, the point for all parties is not to miss the Vanniyar vote when they present candidates in districts where Vanniyars are a major caste.

II

Political Parties and the Politics of Caste and Class

The basic data used in this section is a compilation of detailed information collected and coded by the CSDS for eight successive elections to the

---

[12] The Government of Tamil Nadu has published three lists, revised in 1997 and still valid today: one for 142 Backward Classes, one for 41 Most Backward Classes, one for 68 Denotified Communities. Each list identifies what anthropologists would call subcastes or subtribes. Available at www.tn.gov.in/department/bcmbc.htm.

Legislative Assembly in Tamil Nadu from 1967, the year the DMK arrived in power, to 1996, 30 years later. In addition, we shall use some data of a different nature related to the elections to the Assembly held in 2001 and 2006. Despite the limitations underlined earlier, the analysis of the available caste cross-tabulations offers interesting insights when compared with other parameters.

The data available for eight elections held since 1967 was originally tabulated in 14 categories of castes and communities, which will be reduced to five here, for sake of clarity:

(*i*) The 'upper castes' category does not specify who, besides Brahmins, are listed as non-Brahmin upper castes. They generally include the traditional landlord castes mentioned earlier: particularly, Reddiyars and Vellalars, many of them also being professionals.

(*ii*) Chettiars and Mudaliyars raise a more difficult problem. We have already noted that many Chettiar subcastes listed as 'Other Backward Classes' are from a modest background. Similarly, if the caste name of Mudaliyars suggests a high social status (*mudal* in Tamil means 'the first'), all of them are not in leading positions. We have clubbed the two together, between the upper castes and the OBC, because electoral sociology suggests that amongst MLAs, many Chettiars and Mudaliyars come, not from the lowest groups which may have appropriated this title, but from well-established communities of traders and businessmen which would be recognised, in fact, as part of the non-Brahmin upper castes.

(*iii*) In Table 16.4a, 'Peasants and OBC' may include the traditional peasant castes (Gounders and Vanniyars) as well as Nadars, Thevars and those listed as 'Other OBC'. This is by far the largest social conglomerate in Tamil Nadu, whose official list of 132 groups is utterly confusing, mixing groups of very diverse status, including nomadic tribes. Furthermore, it would make sense to distinguish between OBC, and Most Backward Classes who are now listed separately from OBC. The available election data, however, do not distinguish the MBC from OBC.

(*iv*) Scheduled Castes mostly include Paraiyars from the north of Tamil Nadu, and Pallars from the southern districts. In our data, Scheduled Tribes are listed from 1984 onwards (they account only for 1 per cent of the population of Tamil Nadu). Before that, the category 'Others', from 1967 to 1984, appears to have included them. The number of MLAs from Scheduled Tribes is, in any case, very limited.

(v) Religious minorities are subdivided between Muslims and Christians.[13] The data list them separately, albeit some of them appear as OBC in administrative listings. Here again, the politics of reservation explains why groups of theoretically high status according to Islamic tradition, such as Sheikhs and Syeds, have asked for being listed as OBC.

Castes, Communities and MLAs

A detailed survey of the data available from 1967 to 1996, once aggregated in the five categories as listed, provides significant results (Table 16.4a).

First, the dominance of 'Peasants and OBC' is striking. It has fluctuated between 155 and 133 MLAs along the years, the average number

Table 16.4a
Main Caste and Community Groupings in the Tamil Nadu
Legislative Assembly (by numbers), 1967–96

	Upper Castes	Chettiyars and Mudaliars	Peasants and OBC	SC–ST	Religious Minorities	Total MLAs
1967	7	35	155	29	8	234
1971	3	41	144	34	12	234
1977	4	38	138	44	10	234
1980	4	44	135	43	8	234
1984	6	37	133	46	12	234
1989	7	21	144	42	20	234
1991	5	24	146	48	11	234
1996	2	25	145	43	19	234
TOTAL	38	265	1140	329	100	1872
Average (%)	2	14	61	17.57	5.34	100

Source: Data collected by Professor G. Koteswara Prasad, Department of Politics, University of Madras.

---

[13] Other minorities in Tamil Nadu do not aggregate to more than 1.5 per thousand of the population, according to the 2001 Census. These non-Christian, non-Muslim minorities include Sikhs, Jains, Buddhists and 'others'. Almost one per 1000 of the population (59,000 out of 62.4 million) has not declared any religion.

for the eight assemblies being 141 (61 per cent).[14] Amongst this major group, a few castes are particularly important. The Vanniyar small peasants from the northern districts and the Gounders, their equivalent in the Salem–Coimbatore area (some Vanniyars from the northern districts are also called Gounders) provide the largest groups of MLAs. From the south, Nadars, originally toddy-tappers, and Thevars, stigmatised by the British, are the most prominent by their numbers and their upward mobility. They are mostly peasants today.

Second, in contrast, the share of the upper castes, small in 1967 (seven MLAs) has further plummeted (two in 1996). Their average share of seats, for eight successive elections, stands at a meagre 2 per cent, less than what is estimated to be their share in society. In between, Chettiars and Mudaliyars are much better endowed, but their share has reduced: after getting between 35 and 44 seats from the 1960s till the 1980s, they stand between 20–25 seats after 1989.

Third, the Scheduled Castes–Scheduled Tribes group has seen its share increasing noticeably. With 30 MLAs in 1967, it rises consistently to above 40 after 1977. The group is, for decades now, the second in strength at the Assembly, even if we aggregate the upper castes and the Chettiars–Mudaliyars. The key to the SC–ST success in elections rests on one word: reservations, as 36 seats are reserved for SC in the Assembly, and three for ST. It must be noted, however, that at each election since 1977 the group has won a few more seats than those reserved, a testimony to the growing assertiveness of the Dalits. This being said, the game is not so easy for Dalit militants. In the 2006 elections, the Dalit Panthers of India got just two seats from the north of the state, and the Puthiya Tamilagam drew a blank, despite the activism of its leader S. Krishnaswamy in the southern districts. Most Dalits elected to the Assembly are, therefore, not members of Dalit parties.[15]

---

[14] From 1967 to 2006, the number of MLAs elected to the Tamil Nadu Legislative Assembly has not changed; it has been 234 all along these decades.

[15] The southern districts of Tamil Nadu are known for the acute competition between Thevar peasants, listed as MBC but locally powerful, and Dalits. In village politics, this competition has gone to the extent of murders of elected Dalits by Thevars, or strong pressure to compel elected members of local bodies to resign. See Viswanathan (2004) for a documented analysis of the recent acts of violence against the Dalits in Tamil Nadu, and Gorringe (2004) for an in-depth study of the emerging Dalit engagement in politics.

Fourth, from 1967 to 1996, the share of the religious minorities has fluctuated between eight and 20 MLAs, but the trend was upward during the 1980s and 1990s. Muslims have been often present in greater numbers (12 in 1989, 11 in 1996) than Christians (never above eight between 1967 and 1997).[16] This does not exactly reflect their strength in Tamil Nadu, where Muslims and Christians account for 5.6 per cent and 6.1 per cent respectively of the total population according to Census 2001. If Muslims are often under-represented in the Assembly, Christians are always under-represented. This does not mean that these communities have no political relevance. Jayalalitha shared the concern of the BJP about conversions from Hinduism to minority religions: her position has not been forgotten by many members of these creeds. On the other hand, the DMK tries consistently to retain the Muslims, who vote more for the major parties than for the Tamil Nadu Muslim League. In 2006, the number of Muslim MLAs went down to four, which did not prevent the new DMK government to include two Muslim ministers, and to prepare, in August 2006, a bill for extending reservations to Muslims and Christians in all educational institutions and employments.

The same data, aggregated not by numbers of MLAs but by percentages of MLAs belonging to some significant castes and communities tells the same story, but in a slightly different way (see Table 16.4b, where the main categories are defined in a way to facilitate the comparison with data collected in other states and presented in other chapters of this volume). In Table 16.4b we have aggregated the upper castes, the Mudaliyars and the Chettiyars. Their relative decline is visible and shared, albeit unequally, by all subgroups. For OBC, the trend stands out in more contrast. On the whole, they lose four points in 30 years (from 66.3 per cent of the MLAs in 1967 to 62 per cent in 1996), but they remain by far the most important category in the Assembly. Amongst them, the Vanniyars, the largest caste in 1967, remains so 30 years later, with an even larger score, while the Thevars and the Nadars from the south regress slightly. On the other hand, the decline of the Gounders (their data include also a few Lingayats) is striking and continuous. As some Vanniyars in Tamil Nadu are also called Gounders, a case by case

---

[16] The Tamil Nadu Legislative Assembly has, besides its 234 elected members, a single nominated member from the Anglo-Indian community, supposed to be Christian.

Table 16.4b
Main Caste and Community Groupings in the Tamil Nadu Legislative Assembly, 1967–96 (%)

Castes and Communities	1967	1971	1977	1980	1984	1989	1991	1996
Upper Castes	**17.9**	**18.8**	**17.9**	**20.5**	**18.4**	**11.9**	**12.4**	**11.6**
High Castes	3.0	1.3	1.7	1.7	2.6	3.0	2.1	0.9
Mudaliyars	5.1	8.5	3.4	8.5	6.0	5.1	3.0	4.3
Chettiyars	9.8	9.0	12.8	10.3	9.8	3.8	7.3	6.4
OBC	**66.2**	**61.6**	**59.0**	**57.7**	**56.9**	**61.5**	**62.4**	**62.0**
Thevars	13.7	11.5	10.3	12.4	12.0	12.8	12.4	12.8
Gounders	17.1	15.0	15.0	15.0	12.4	13.7	10.7	10.3
Vanniyars	19.7	16.7	16.2	16.7	17.5	18.8	22.6	22.6
Nadars	6.4	6.0	6.4	5.1	5.6	4.7	6.4	5.6
Others	9.4	12.4	11.1	8.5	9.4	11.5	10.3	10.7
Scheduled Castes	**12.0**	**14.5**	**18.0**	**17.1**	**18.4**	**17.9**	**20.1**	**17.9**
Pallars	9.0	10.7	10.3	9.8	11.1	4.7	11.1	6.4
Paraiyars	3.0	3.8	7.7	7.3	7.3	13.2	9.0	11.5
Muslims	1.3	3.8	1.3	0.9	1.3	5.1	0.4	0.4
Christians	2.1	1.3	3.0	2.6	2.6	3.4	2.1	4.7
Other	0.4	–	0.9	1.3	2.6	–	2.6	3.4
TOTAL	99.9	100.0	100.1	100.1	100.2	99.8	100.0	100.0
	(N=234)	(N=234)	(N=234)	(N=234)	(N=234)	(N=234)	(N=234)	(N=234)

Source: Data collected by Professor G. Koteswara Prasad, Department of Politics, University of Madras.

enquiry would be needed in order to clarify if a part of the Gounders' decline is not due to a change of affiliation, some of them, particularly in the Vanniyar belt in northern Tamil Nadu, having possibly declared themselves as Vanniyars, and no more as Gounders.

In contrast to the other large categories, the Dalits, as noted earlier, have clearly improved their political ambit from 12 per cent in 1967 to 18 per cent or more after 1984. The share of religious minorities, with the exception of 1989, has grossly remained between 4 and 5 per cent after 1971, with the Muslims fluctuating more than the Christians. To sum up, Tables 16.4a and 16.4b show that higher castes have lost a part of their power in the Assembly while Dalits have improved their lot. In between, the OBC supremacy remains unassailable, despite a slight overall decline, as the most numerous amongst OBC, the Vanniyar small peasants, assert themselves with force.

The Caste Strategy of Political Parties

After the absorption of Vanniyar parties by the Congress in the 1950s, Tamil Nadu did not have, for long, what can be labelled as caste-based parties, i.e., parties openly created by caste associations. This can be explained by the philosophy of both the Congress and the DMK. The Congress was supposed to be representative of all Indians, from Dalits to Brahmins, as also religious minorities. The DMK was supposed to be representative of all Dravidians, excluding Brahmins. Furthermore, its strong anti-caste ideology could not, in theory, lend itself to play caste politics. Ideology was also at play here, for in the heroic days of the 1950s and early 1960s, when the young DMK was opposing the Congress, its programme was not confined to the safeguard or the recovery of Dravidian identity. It had a strong social dimension as well; it spoke of land reforms and the rights of the poor. It is not by chance that one of the sons of M. Karunanidhi, born in 1953, and now number four in the government, has been named Stalin.

Dravidians Parties and Caste Politics

However, upon entering elections, politics drove the DMK (and later, the AIADMK) to play intense caste politics, but with a difference: the focus was on OBC and Dalits as a whole, and not specific castes. To play the card of local castes under the OBC at the time of identification of the party candidate was mere electoral calculus; the Dravidian parties, at the state level, do not represent specific castes, but, principally, the OBC–MBC–Dalit combine, with a strong premium for the more numerous OBC/MBC, who are also better represented amongst their cadres. While the official ideology of the AIADMK is not really different from the ideology of the DMK, the two parties have a slightly different social base, the AIADMK having usually a stronger constituency amongst the most deprived, though with local exceptions. But the OBC vote bank is decisive for the two parties.

An analysis of four significant Assembly elections shows how all key parties have resolutely played the OBC card. In 1967 (Table 16.5a), the Congress and the DMK had 64 per cent and 63 per cent of their MLAs respectively from this group. Even the Swatantra, supposed to be the party of industrialists in favour of a liberalised economy, banked on the OBC as well: they accounted for 60 per cent of its representatives. In 1984 (Table 16.5b), the winner, the AIADMK, had 61 per cent of OBC in the Assembly (and 22 per cent of Dalits) while the Congress got 52 per cent and the DMK 46 per cent. In 1991 (Table 16.5c), the Congress raised its share of OBC to 72 per cent, while the great winner, the AIADMK, stood at 60 per cent (with 22 per cent of Dalits), while the DMK was routed. In 1996 (Table 6.5d), in an opposite

Table 16.5a
Main Party and Caste Groupings in the Tamil Nadu Legislative Assembly, 1967

	Upper Castes	Chettiyars and Mudaliars	Peasants and OBC	SC–ST	Religious Minorities	Others	Total MLAs
Congress	3	5	37	1	4	–	50
	(6.0)	(10.0)	(64.0)	(2.0)	(8.0)	–	–
DMK	1	21	90	23	3	–	138
	(0.7)	(15.2)	(63.1)	(16.7)	(2.1)	–	–
Swatantra	1	4	13	2	0	–	20
	(5.0)	(20.0)	(65.0)	(10.0)	–	–	–
Communists	1	4	7	1	0	–	13
	(7.7)	(30.7)	(53.8)	(7.70)	–	–	–
Others	1	1	8	1	1	1	13
	(7.7)	(7.70)	(61.5)	(7.70)	(7.70)	(7.70)	–
TOTAL	7	35	155	28	8	1	234
	(3.00)	(14.90)	(66.40)	(12.00)	(3.40)	(7.70)	–

Source: Data collected by Professor G. Koteswara Prasad, Department of Politics, University of Madras.
Note: Figures in parentheses indicate percentage.

Table 16.5b
Main Party and Caste Groupings in the Tamil Nadu Legislative Assembly, 1984

	Upper Castes	Chettiyars and Mudaliars	Peasants and OBC	SC–ST	Religious Minorities	Total MLAs
Congress	2	15	32	11	2	62
	(3.2)	(24.2)	(51.6)	(17.7)	(3.2)	–
AIADMK	1	18	81	29	4	133
	(0.8)	(13.6)	(60.8)	(21.8)	(3.1)	–
DMK	1	4	11	4	4	24
	(4.2)	(16.7)	(45.9)	(16.7)	(16.7)	–
Communists	2	0	3	2	0	7
	(28.5)	–	(42.8)	(28.5)	–	–
Others	0	0	6	0	2	8
	–	–	(75.0)	–	(25.0)	–
TOTAL	6	37	133	46	12	234
	(2.6)	(15.8)	(56.9)	(19.7)	(5.2)	–

Source: See Table 16.5a.
Note: Figures in parentheses indicate percentage.

Table 16.5c
Main Party and Caste Groupings in the Tamil Nadu Legislative Assembly, 1991

	Upper Castes	Chettiyars and Mudaliars	Peasants and OBC	SC–ST	Religious Minorities	Total MLAs
Congress	0	6	43	7	4	60
	–	(10.0)	(71.7)	(11.7)	(6.6)	–
AIADMK	5	16	98	37	7	164
	(3.0)	(9.8)	(59.9)	(22.5)	(4.2)	–
Others	0	2	5	3	0	10
	–	(20)	(50)	(30)	–	–
TOTAL	5	24	146	47	11	234
	(2.1)	(10.3)	(62.4)	(20.5)	(4.7)	–

Source: See Table 16.5a.
Note: Figures in parentheses indicate percentage.

Table 16.5d
Main Party and Caste Grouping in the Tamil Nadu Legislative Assembly, 1996

	Upper Castes	Chettiyars and Mudaliars	Peasants and OBC	SC–ST	Religious Minorities	Total MLAs
TMC	0	5	25	5	4	39
	–	(12.8)	(64.0)	(12.9)	(10.2)	–
DMK	2	19	105	34	13	173
	(1.2)	(11.0)	(62.0)	(19.7)	(7.5)	–

(Table 16.5d continued)

(*Table 16.5d continued*)

	Upper Castes	Chettiyars and Mudaliars	Peasants and OBC	SC–ST	Religious Minorities	Total MLAs
Communists	0	1	6	2	1	10
	–	(11.1)	(66.6)	(22.2)	(11.1)	–
Others	0	2	5	3	0	10
	–	(20.0)	(50.0)	(30.0)	–	–
TOTAL	2	26	135	42	17	231
	(0.9)	(10.7)	(62.4)	(20.5)	(4.7)	–

Source: See Table 16.5a.
Note: Figures in parentheses indicate percentage.

scenario, the victorious DMK had 62 per cent of OBC (and 20 per cent of Dalits), the Congress had 64 per cent of OBC and 13 per cent of Dalits, and the AIADMK was routed.

If all key parties broadly play the card of caste affiliation (the Communists, perhaps, less than others), the way they play it would deserve a much more detailed analysis, for the data provided here offers only large categories aggregating many castes. The strategy of the main parties, which present candidates in most constituencies, must obviously be based upon a more precise matrix which takes into account a number of local factors. The weight of the most numerous caste in each constituency has to be appreciated and drawn upon, but the basic rule of cajoling the leading local caste (in term of voters at least) suffers exceptions or inflexions.

First, in reserved constituencies, all parties have to select a Dalit candidate (or a tribal one, in three constituencies). True, in these reserved constituencies, the Dalit population is generally large, but not always the largest. Second, parties have to take note of the strongholds of their competitors. The DMK leaders know well that Thevars, in the south vote more for the AIADMK than for them, or that the Pramallai Kallars have been long ago politicised by a local leader affiliated to the Forward Block, and generally remain faithful to this party (Headley 2006). Third, and more generally, the personal profile of politicians is decisive, and can make a difference — the most obvious example being Jayalalitha herself, a Brahmin at the helm of a major Dravidian party. More commonly, the personal factor explains why a key local politician might hope to bring along his/her vote bank after leaving a party for joining a new one. Fourth, in the context of expanding coalition politics, the main parties have to make concessions to their partners while allocating party tickets, and they usually leave aside constituencies that are expected to be won by the latter. Caste affiliation cannot be the key of all political strategies when nominating a candidate or while defining political strategies, but clearly, in elections to the Legislative Assembly, caste arithmetics remain a major parameter. In elections to the Lok Sabha, the rationale could be a little more flexible: the Congress has thus no hesitation to nominate a well-known Brahmin in his traditional constituency, such as Mani Shankar Aiyer, who became a minister in the central government.

Parties take care of caste in their own organisation as well, for nominations in the party hierarchy can be read also (but not only) through a caste matrix. For instance, when the DMK General Council met in June 2003, it nominated, under the party old guard, President M. Karunanidhi and the General Secretary K. Anbazhagan, three deputy general secretaries. One was M. K. Stalin, Karunanidhi's son. The second was Parithi Illamvazudhi, a Dalit. The third was Sarguna Pandian, a Nadar lady. A new post of Principal Secretary was offered to S. Duraimurugan, a Vanniyar. OBC from the north (Vanniyars) and from the south (Nadars) as well as Dalits and women could thus be considered as represented in the top leadership of the party.

The Pattali Makkal Katchi and the Vanniyar Caste

Despite the claim of the Dravidian parties to offer political opportunity to most castes and communities, caste parties have nevertheless re-appeared in Tamil Nadu. The most significant of them is the Pattali Makkal Katchi (PMK or the Workers People Party) launched in 1987 by Dr Ramadoss, the leader of the Vanniyar Sangam, a Vanniyar association founded in 1980. The Sangam has forcefully revived, since the 1980s, the tradition of Vanniyar activism (from the days of the Vanniyakula Kshatriya Maha Sangam), but in a different context. Backward Classes, on paper, were then certainly endowed with 50 per cent reservations, the Vanniyar Sangam argued, but in fact only a few Backward Castes cornered most of the benefits of this quota.[17] The Sangam was thus asking for specific reservations for Vanniyars, as much as 20 per cent. The agitation led by Ramadoss, himself a medical practitioner from a small town in

---

[17] Radhakrishnan (1996: 130) notes that in 1980–82, 34 communities out of the 222 Backward Classes in Tamil Nadu accounted for more than three-fourths of OBC students admitted to professional courses like engineering, medicine and law.

South Arcot district, the stronghold of the Vanniyar belt, was powerful and multifaceted. It culminated, in 1987, in a violent one-week road blockade, which left 20 dead and massive destruction, where Dalits were targeted as much as the government. In 1988, while Tamil Nadu was under President's Rule after political instability followed M. G. Ramachandran's death, Ramadoss threatened to ask Vanniyars to boycott the coming Assembly elections, which were postponed. Soon after returning to power, the DMK stuck a deal: if it rejected reservations for a specific caste, it did set apart, from the total OBC reservations, 20 per cent for the new MBC category, the Vanniyars accounting for about half of them.

Twenty years after its creation, the PMK has delineated a space for itself in Tamil politics, and has perfectly used its bargaining power for getting its pound of flesh — including central ministers' berths — in the context of coalition politics. The irony is that the PMK succeeded in its strategy of getting a part of the power cake without monopolising the votes of the Vanniyar caste, which has been, since 1967, without any exception, the caste that is most represented in the Assembly (Vanniyars are supposed to account for approximately 12 per cent of the population of Tamil Nadu). Unsurprisingly, most of the MLAs of the PMK are Vanniyars, but in small numbers. The party got only one MLA in 1991 (the AIADMK got 33 Vanniyars, and the Congress got 18 out of a total of 53 Vanniyars at the Assembly). It got four MLAs in 1996 (the DMK got 40 Vanniyars, the Tamila Manila Congress got six out of 53 Vanniyars again). The PMK understood quickly that there is a gap between successful agitations by a caste association and their political dividends. Despite a long tradition of clashes between Vanniyars and Dalits, the PMK leadership decided after the disappointing electoral results in 1991 to open the party to Dalits and Muslims. It had candidates in seats reserved for Dalits, and nominated a Dalit Central Minister, Dalit Ezhumalai, in the Vajpayee government. But the strategy, which paid off in the case of the Bahujan Samaj Party in Uttar Pradesh did not work so well for the Pattali Makkal Katchi in Tamil Nadu, for the main parties had, for long, cultivated their Vanniyar caste base, and had tried to answer the challenges raised by the Vanniyar Sangam agitations.[18]

---

[18] This explains as well as to why the Bahujan Samaj Party failed to develop itself in Tamil Nadu. In the 2006 elections to the Legislative Assembly, it presented 164 candidates, and drew a blank with only 0.79 per cent of the votes.

Nevertheless, the PMK was able to define a niche for itself in the state politics and to draw the attention of the media as often as possible.[19] Ramadoss, who does not compete for electoral seats or ministerial postings himself, knows how to negotiate PMK's influence, not just in Tamil Nadu, but on the national scene as well. In the fluid context of fragile coalition politics in parliament, the PMK has extracted a heavy price for offering its support to the government. In the 2004 general elections, out of 39 Tamil MPs, the PMK got five candidates elected to the parliament from the Vanniyar belt (one of them, a Dalit in a re-served constituency). This modest number did not prevent the party to get two central ministers, one of who, the Minister of Health, was the son of the PMK founder.

Dalit Parties

The case of Dalit parties in Tamil Nadu deserves attention as well. All-India Dalit parties such as the Republican Party of India have never made inroads in the state. Local activists, on the other hand, have strongly protested against atrocities targeting Dalits. The first noticeable Tamil Dalit party to emerge out of the Pallar caste and its Devendra Kullar Vellala association was the Puthiya Tamilagam (the New Tamil Land), led by K. Krishnaswamy. If the party and its leader made a name for themselves for mobilising Dalits about their rights, the Puthiya Tamilagam did not expand to the north of the state where another party took the lead, the Dalit Panthers of India (Viduthalai Siruthaigal, in Tamil), led by T. Thirumavalavan. As in the case of the PMK, the cap-acity to launch agitations has not always generated immediate political dividends. First, because, as for Vanniyars, the mainstream parties had already cornered a large part of the Dalit votes, and, as noted before, the quota for Scheduled Caste candidates in the Assembly has been used, for long, by all parties. Dalit parties have to face specific challenges as well. The Dalit parties have been able to get the cooperation of some other parties in their agitations against injustice and atrocities: the CPI(M), for instance, has supported K. Krishnaswamy's struggle. So did the Tamil Manila Congress after the Manjoali tea estate incident when 11 Dalits

---

[19] The PMK regularly expresses its sympathy for the cause of the Sri Lankan Tamil insurgents, the Liberation Tigers of Tamil Eelam (LTTE). In 2002, it raised the issue of a separate state for Vanniyars, drawing adverse comments from all quarters.

and four Muslim workers died in a police action, in 1999, in Tirunelveli district. But joining hands with the DMK or the AIADMK is an uncertain strategy, because opportunism prevails and electoral agreements are fragile (the DMK, who supported them in 2001, accepted neither the Puthiya Tamilagam nor the Dalit Panthers in its coalition for parliament elections in 2004 once the more powerful Vanniyar-based PMK had joined it). The choice to politicise Dalits more radically is not an easy one, and not easy to implement either. In a way, the debate between Dalit intellectuals is valid for politicians as well: should integration in the mainstream be a model, or should Dalits evolve their own ways and means, against a system which remains oppressive?

Education, Age, Socio-professional Categories and Gender

The Educational Background

The general expansion of education in Tamil Nadu since independence translates itself, unavoidably, in the world of politics. The percentage of 'middle pass' MLAs (with barely primary education) has gone down from 38.5 per cent in 1967 to 12.4 per cent in 1996. The percentage of matriculates has slightly gone up from the end of the 1970s onwards, reaching 41 per cent in 1996. More significant is the rise of the 'graduates and above' category, which has risen from 29 per cent in 1967 to 43.2 per cent in 1996 (it was 59 per cent in 1991).

Table 16.6
The Rise of the Educational Background of MLAs in Tamil Nadu, 1967–96

	Middle Pass	Matriculates	Graduates and Above	N.A.	TOTAL
1967	90	71	68	5	234
	(38.50)	(30.30)	(29.10)	(2.10)	
1984	50	87	93	4	234
	(21.40)	(37.20)	(39.70)	(1.70)	
1996	29	96	101	8	234
	(12.40)	(41.00)	(43.20)	(3.40)	

Source: Data collected by Professor G. Koteswara Prasad, Department of Politics, University of Madras.
Note: Figures in parentheses indicate percentage.

On the one hand, the rise of the educational level of Tamil MLAs is testimony to the general elevation of the Backward Classes, in a state where reservation for education has been a major political stake. On the other hand, the rise is not such that the standard cliché about the majority of MLAs would become outdated. For Tamils with high education background, MLAs remain generally poorly educated with an academic training which cannot compete with the educated elite of highly trained professionals or top bureaucrats of the Indian Administrative Service, or those at the helm of key state administrative departments or even the district administration. There is, of course, a caste/class bias in this judgment, which is not specific to Tamil Nadu. This state of affairs, in any case, does not seem to be a major handicap in the road to economic dynamism, as Tamil Nadu is amongst the best ranked states in India in this field.

A glance at the 13 Tamil MPs who joined the Manmohan Singh government in 2004 might offer an additional perspective here. Be they Congress members, DMK parliamentarians or PMK MPs, most of them have a BA, a BSc or an LLB (many having the LLB degree in addition to the BA or the BSc). Two have an MBA (one among them is Finance Minister Palaniappan Chidambaram, with his degree from Harvard), one has an MBBS; Mani Shankar Aiyer alone represents the top profile of the all-India elite (Doon School, St. Stephen's College in Delhi, and Cambridge University). Most of these Tamil ministers at the centre have however been educated in Tamil Nadu.

The Age Structure of the Assembly

The rise of the educational background of MLAs in Tamil Nadu has not changed the age structure of the Legislative Assembly very much (Table 16.7). About two-thirds of the Assembly has been consistently constituted by MLAs in the age group of 36–55 years (66.2 per cent in 1966; 67.3 per cent in 1984: 64.5 per cent in 1996, against 70.5 per cent in 1991), and key parties stick usually to the line (70.8 per cent of DMK MLAs in 1989; 69.5 per cent of AIADMK MLAs in 1991 and 73.5 per cent of Congress MLAs in 1991 were in this age group). But the young MLAs, below 36, are less common than before (from one-fourth to one-tenth between 1966 and 1996), while the older group is growing (from 7.3 per cent in 1966 to one-fourth — 24.4 per cent — in 1996).

The 'greying' of the elected representatives is more accentuated in the DMK (12.7 per cent of MLAs below 36 and 25.5 per cent of MLAs above 55 years in 1996) than in the AIADMK (20.1 per cent of MLAs below 36 and 8.5 per cent of MLAs above 55 years in 1991).

Table 16.7
Age Groups of MLAs in the Tamil Nadu Legislative Assembly, 1967–96

	25–35	36–45	46–55	56–65	66+	N.A.	TOTAL
1967	62	99	56	14	3	0	234
	(26.50)	(42.30)	(23.90)	(6.00)	(1.30)	–	–
1984	52	85	72	18	5	2	234
	(22.20)	(36.50)	(30.80)	(7.70)	(2.10)	(0.90)	–
1991	39	120	45	24	3	3	234
	(16.70)	(51.30)	(19.20)	(10.30)	(1.30)	(1.30)	–
1996	25	75	75	46	11	2	234
	(10.70)	(32.10)	(32.10)	(19.70)	(4.70)	(0.90)	–

Source: See Table 16.6.
Note: Figures in parentheses indicate percentage.

It testifies to the aging of the DMK leadership, but also to its political longevity despite splits and factionalism. The top leadership of Dravidian parties is in a way representative of this fact, with a generational gap between Karunanidhi, born in 1928, Jayalalitha, born in 1948, and Vaiko, the MDMK leader, born in 1944.

The Socio-professional Background of the MLAs

As mentioned earlier, 61 per cent of the MLAs, between 1967 and 1997, have come from what we labelled as 'Peasants and OBC'. It is, therefore, not surprising to find a majority of 'agriculturists' amongst them: 52 per cent on an average for eight successive assemblies, with a peak at 58 per cent in 1977 and a low at 38 per cent in 1991 (Table 16.8). Professionals account for 22 per cent for the 30 years under record here, with a pretty regular figure from 1967 to 1989, and irregular data thereafter (34 per cent in 1991 against 16 per cent in 1996). This low 1996 figure is not sufficient to conclude that professionals are less interested than before in joining politics even if the trend is not confirmed by more recent data. The third group, 'businessmen', stands at 14 per cent on an average and rises to 21 per cent in 1996. Two other groups are poorly represented: the 'social workers and political activists' with a declining trend and a combined average of 4 per cent, and the 'teachers and ex-government servants' with a poor 3 per cent (other categories, coupled with 'no information', account for another 4 per cent).

One should be careful in interpreting such figures for obvious reasons. Many full-time politicians may present themselves as agriculturists if they own land, and the category of 'activists' is probably underestimated.

Table 16.8
Socio-professional Categories of MLAs in the Tamil Nadu
Legislative Assembly, 1967–96

	Activists	Agriculturists	Professionals	Business-men	Teachers and Ex-government Servants	Others and N.A.	Total MLAs
1967	17	126	46	26	10	9	234
	–	(54)	(20)	(11)	–	–	–
1971	9	125	52	32	12	4	234
	–	(53)	(22)	(14)	–	–	–
1977	12	136	40	32	7	7	234
	–	(58)	(17)	(14)	–	–	–
1980	12	125	50	26	10	11	234
	–	(53)	(21)	(11)	–	–	–
1984	6	130	51	28	7	12	234
	–	(55)	(22)	(12)	–	–	–
1989	13	113	52	34	8	14	234
	–	(48)	(22)	(15)	–	–	–
1991	9	90	79	36	11	9	234
	–	(38)	(34)	(15)	–	–	–
1996	6	124	38	50	7	9	234
	–	(53)	(16)	(21)	–	--	–
TOTAL	84	969	408	264	72	75	1872
	(4)	(52)	(22)	(14)	(3)	(4)	(100)

Source: See Table 16.6.

Note: 'Activists' refer to MLAs defined as social workers and political activists. Percentages in columns are given only for the three main categories. The last line shows the average share of each category after aggregating the eight assemblies.

Figures in parentheses indicate percentage.

Among the 'professionals', lawyers are usually leading. 'Businessmen' is also an unclear concept. It may encompass very diverse activities, and relate to very different financial assets. Big business is certainly less present in the Assembly than traders of various shades. More striking is the very weak presence of teachers and ex-government officers: the spheres of education and administration seem not prone to enter active politics.

An analysis of the socio-professional background of MLAs of the leading parties in successive assemblies does not provide clear cut information about specific privileged links between classes and parties (Table 16.9). In 1967, the Congress had proportionally more agriculturists than the DMK (two-thirds against one-half respectively), a fact which could perhaps be testimony to the old grip of the Congress party

Table 16.9
Socio-professional Status of MLAs of Leading Parties in Five Tamil Nadu Legislative Assemblies, 1967–96

Year and Party	Total MLAs	Agriculturists	Professionals	Businessmen
1967 DMK	138	70 (51)	32 (23)	18 (13)
1967 INC	50	33 (66)	10 (20)	4 (8)
1977 ADMK	129	72 (56)	26 (20)	21 (16)
1977 DMK	49	29 (59)	7 (14)	10 (20)
1984 ADMK	133	83 (62)	32 (24)	10 (8)
1984 INC	62	35 (56)	14 (23)	8 (13)
1991 ADMK	164	61 (37)	62 (38)	21 (13)
1991 INC	60	26 (43)	13 (22)	14 (24)
1996 DMK	173	90 (52)	28 (16)	39 (22)
1996 TMC	39	20 (51)	7 (18)	11 (22)

Source: See Table 16.6.

Note: Rounded percentages in parentheses indicate the share of the category as compared to the total number of MLAs of the party.

TMC: Tamil Manila Congress (Moopanar).

on the rural elite. Its poor share of businessmen could be explained by
the impact of the Swatantra Party, led by C. Rajagopalachari, who had
left the Congress in 1959 as Nehru's economic policy was not liberal
enough for him. Later on, the Swatantra being dead, the Congress seems
to have recuperated a part of the 'businessmen', but only a part of them,
for a good reason. The long hegemony of the Dravidian parties has
unavoidably enabled the DMK, apparently more than the AIADMK,
to build up interest groups amongst businessmen and professionals.
On the field, it is confirmed that in the districts, if not always in the
Madras elite circles, the peasant castes as well as those eager to benefit
from the new power structure developed after 1967 have joined the
Dravidian parties in great numbers: in 1997, there is practically no difference in between the DMK and the Tamil Manila Congress in the
socio-professional background of their MLAs.

Castes, Communities and Classes: How the Electorate Voted in 2006

From an additional perspective, we may consider the electorate of key
parties as well. The leading Chennai-based newspaper, *The Hindu*, has
published polls conducted during the Assembly elections of 2006. The
validity of this type of data may be discussed, but the opinions collected,
within a margin of uncertainty, nevertheless illustrate interesting trends

on the vote pattern of castes, communities and classes. In the context of the prevailing coalition politics, the data is offered not for the DMK and the AIADMK as such, but for the alliances that they have built up. The leadership of the two parties is such, however, that the sociological image offered may be roughly valid for the key parties themselves (Table 16.10).

Table 16.10
Distribution of Votes Among Castes, Communities and Classes in the Legislative Assembly of Tamil Nadu, 2006

Categories	DMK Alliance (%)	AIADMK Alliance (%)	Other Parties (%)
Caste and Community			
Upper Castes	44	42	14
Naidus	43	45	13
Gounders	45	38	17
Vanniyars	50	37	12
Nadars	42	39	19
Thevars	38	48	13
Other OBC	44	42	14
Dalits	41	43	17
Tribals	50	32	19
Muslims	50	36	14
Christians	54	31	17
Others	46	35	19
Economic Status			
Rich	49	36	15
Middle	46	38	16
Lower	42	43	15
Poor	44	42	13

Source: Compiled by author from information based on *The Hindu* (2006: 14), tables 5 and 6.
  DMK alliance = DMK+Congress+PMK+Communists (CPI and CPI(M))
  IAIDMK alliance = AIADMK+MDMK+Dalit Panthers+Janata Dal(S)
  Others = DMDK+Bharatiya Janata Party+Bahujan Samaj Party+Others

A few observations need to be made before interpreting Table 16.10. First, the two alliances have cornered 85 per cent of the votes (44.73 per cent for the DMK coalition; 40.06 per cent for the AIADMK coalition), and once again, the share of votes is no indication of the share of seats won (the DMK alone got 26.45 per cent of the votes, and bagged 96 seats, while the AIADMK, with 32.64 per cent of the votes, bagged only 61 seats). Second, the national parties which have not joined any of the Dravidian alliances have registered a setback. The BJP, with 2.02 per cent of the votes got no seats. The BSP too failed to make any inroads with 0.79 per cent of the votes. The DMDK launched by film star Vijayakanth did much better, with 8.38 per cent of the votes (but just one seat). The electorate below 25 years voted for it more resolutely (16 per cent in this age group) than other age groups.

The most important lesson to be drawn from Table 16.10 is probably the way upper castes, the rich and the middle income group now vote for Dravidian parties in general, and for the DMK in particular. In 2006, the DMK alliance won most of its supporters from among the poor income group, but not very significantly. The AIADMK is generally considered as having a greater mandate amongst the poor. It did not click this time, and this may explain why the AIADMK lost. Jayalalitha has also clearly paid the price for her position against conversions: Muslims gave 14 percentage points more votes to the DMK than to the AIADMK, and Christians voted 23 points more. The presence of the PMK in the DMK coalition has helped it, clearly overtaking the AIADMK alliance, amongst Vanniyars and Gounders. On the other hand, Thevars have remained faithful to Jayalalitha (an advance of 10 points). The lead of the AIADMK has been confirmed amongst Dalits (Dalits mostly from the north, in addition to what the Dalit Panthers ally brought; i.e., only 1.29 per cent of the votes). Nadars and other OBC, on the other hand, have favoured the DMK alliance. On the whole, the caste or community vote bank divide is strong in six cases, with the DMK alliance leading clearly amongst the peasant castes of Vanniyars and Gounders, the tribals and religious minorities. The attractiveness of the two alliances remained more balanced at the extremes (upper castes and Dalits, with just a difference of two points). Finally, beyond their competition, the Dravidian parties remain clearly the focal points around which both the choices of the electorate and the strategy of other parties are structured.

Gender

Women's opinion is vital for Tamil politicians, for women's vote is only slightly less than men. During nine elections (1971–2006), their participation rate has been, only once, 8 percentage points below the men's average (61.6 per cent against 69.4 per cent in 1980). It stands generally between 4 to 5 points below the men's rate, and has oscillated between 56.8 per cent in 2001 and 72.4 per cent in 1984 (Table 16.11). But women are clearly in minority in politics, as they are in government (there are three women out of 31 ministers in the 2006 DMK government; there were, again, three out of 24 ministers in Jayalalitha's previous government). Their participation in active politics is, however, on a rising trend, with ups and downs: from no candidate in the Assembly elections in 1971 to 156 candidates in 1996 and 2006; from two MLAs in 1977 to 32 in 1991; 25 in 2001; 22 in 2006. The type of 'protection populism' (Arun Swamy quoted in Harris 2001: 4) deployed by the AIADMK, particularly by M. G. Ramachandran, had an impact on women voters, particularly the generalisation of the free midday meals in all schools, a scheme quickly labelled as unproductive populism till the World Bank praised it for its twin impact of child nutrition and school attendance amongst poor families. Jayalalitha has cultivated this legacy. The figure of 'Amma' (the Mother) impressed the women electorate, not just by her being the first woman chief minister, and a strong leader, but also by specific schemes well advertised, such as police stations run only by women. More interestingly, the reservation of one-third of the seats for women in village panchayats certainly encourages a culture of political participation among women. Prominent people may have used it, in the beginning, by having their wives or daughters file nomination as candidates, but subsequently, genuine women candidates from diverse backgrounds have decided to compete on their own. The empowerment of women, whatever its shortcomings, explains partly why the fertility rate is one of the lowest amongst Indian states.

Table 16.11
Women Electorate and Women MLAs in Tamil Nadu, 1971–2006

	Women Voting (%)	*Women Candidates*	*Women Elected*
1971	69.60	0	0
1977	59.10	24	2
1980	61.60	17	5
1984	72.40	46	8
1989	69.00	78	9
1991	61.70	102	32
1996	64.70	156	9
2001	56.80	112	25
2006	68.75	156	22

Source: Compiled by author from data from Election Commission of India (1971–2006). Key Highlights of General Election to the Legislative Assembly of Tamil Nadu.

The development of Self Help Groups, in which women are a majority, is another testimony to this growing assertiveness, which is not restricted to the middle class.[20]

III
Social Change, Caste and Modernity

The data analysed in the previous section is clear, at least, on two points: (*i*) the political power is in the hand of a majority of OBC politicians; (*ii*) the upper castes are no more a force to reckon with in the Tamil political arena. They account between 1 and 3 per cent of the MLAs. Jayalalitha is not a key political figure in Tamil Nadu because she is a Brahmin, but because she was an unequalled cine star when she was the screen partner of M. G. Ramachandran and because she has asserted herself as a true political leader, able to mobilise voters for victories and to overcome defeats.

Brahmins, OBC, Education and Politics

In the years following independence, upper castes in general and Brahmins in particular were still prominent in the political life of the Madras state. The leading figure was C. Rajagopalachari, who had been Chief Minister first in 1937, had been close to Gandhi, had served as the last Governor General of India and as Home Minister in the Nehru government after the death of Sardar Patel. As Chief Minister of the Madras state for a second time in 1952, he led a government largely dominated by upper castes.[21] With the access of the DMK to power, the political supremacy of the Brahmins was challenged, and by and large they deserted the field of politics. A substantial section of the upper castes

---

[20] For a larger perspective on women and politics in India, see Basu (2005).

[21] Rajagopalachari's government in 1952 included 15 ministers. Of them, six were Brahmins, one was from a princely family, two were Reddiyars (landlords from high caste), and three were from other good castes (Naidu, Naicker and Nair). Only one could be listed as OBC. When Rajagopalachari resigned after the DMK campaigned against the education policy of the government, said to preserve caste legacies, the Congress government sent a strong signal by appointing a Backward Class Nadar, K. Kamaraj, as Chief Minister. Despite this, the government set up by Kamaraj was still dominated by upper caste ministers, many of them having previously served under Rajagopalachari.

did the same. If landlords were eager to keep their influence in villages, the urbanised upper castes/middle class chose to assert themselves in other field of activities where they were already influential.

In Tamil Nadu, as in other Indian states, it is fashionable today in some upper caste circles to deride the access of the OBC to power, to lament on the negative effect of the constant expansion of reservations 'at the cost of merit', and to criticise the way popular politics is conducted. Populism and blatant opportunism, not to mention corruption, are seen as the sad ingredients of mass politics. The upper middle classes are said to vote less than the common man. Upper castes in general and Brahmins in particular have certainly retreated from politics, but they have not disappeared from the stage of power. They have, for long, invested in spheres where education is the key, and such a trend has been confirmed by recent developments, be it the rise of the knowledge economy, the growth of media professions and the opportunities offered, abroad or in India, by globalisation.

However, the long rule of the Dravidian parties has not disconnected non-Brahmins from this trend. Besides prestigious institutions (the Indian Institute of Technology and the Anna University in Chennai), the proliferation of Colleges of Technology in Tamil Nadu owes a lot to the thirst for higher education amongst OBC. If upper castes are still in commanding positions in the field of culture and in the media, their monopoly is now over. Both the DMK and the AIADMK have developed not just a powerful film industry (Chennai studios are only second to Bollywood), they also control their own press, and their own TV channels (Sun TV for the DMK, Jaya TV for the AIADMK). If education is seen more than ever as a key to social mobility, education plus politics can only enhance this. While M. Karunanidhi remains faithful to Tamil Nadu, his nephew Murasoli Maran, Rajya Sabha member from 1967, was for decades the DMK man in New Delhi, and ended his career as a noted Central Minister for Trade in the Vajpayee government. He was, in fact, a prominent player at the launch of the Doha round at the WTO. If Maran's background was typical of the DMK leadership (his family name has been de-sanskritised, he wrote film-scripts and was editor of the flagship of the DMK press, *Murasoli*), his son's background has been different: Dayanidhi Maran is an alumni from the elite Loyola College of Madras, and has been appointed, at 38, a Cabinet Minister in the Manmohan Singh government, with the portfolio of Information Technology. Ambumani Ramadoss, Health Minister in the same government, symbolises, for the Vanniyar PMK, what Dayanidhi Maran symbolises for the Dravidian politics: the emergence of a new generation of heirs who are in tune with the present dynamics of change transforming India at the highest political level.

Although Tamil Nadu has been on the forefront of reservation politics for long, the expansion of reservations remains a crucial issue, precisely because the rising lower middle class of intermediate castes is eager to get diplomas and jobs. It is no surprise, therefore, that the DMK and the PMK are pressing their Congress partner at the centre to push through the project of extending reservation to all institutions of higher education and to expand reservations for Muslims and Christians, not to forget the old promise of selecting one-third of seats for women in the parliament.

Interestingly, the movement for education and professional status, which push OBC on the tract followed for long by the upper castes, does not prevent some upper caste professionals from thinking afresh about politics. A new party was registered just before the Assembly elections in Tamil Nadu in 2006: Lok Paritran, launched by highly educated young professionals (some of them Brahmins), alumni from top Indian Institutes of Technology eventually trained also in the United States. Lok Paritran was able to present seven candidates, on an agenda focused on jobs for everyone and opposing corruption (in interviews, his President, Tanmay Rajpurohit, 28, declared that they had to launch a new party to escape from the ruling practices of 'gerontocracy, ploutocracy and kleptocracy'). The candidates polled a total of 30,000 votes, and made a (small) mark against some established DMK and AIADMK politicians in two constituencies. Lok Paritran may or may not last, but it was largely commented upon in the (English-speaking) media as a refreshing departure from the past, or as a promise for the future: for once, educated upper caste youngsters were not simply opposing reservations or confining themselves to non-political voluntary associations.[22]

More importantly, the supremacy of the Dravidian parties in 10 successive assemblies, their political agenda and their style of governance

---

[22] For a recent enquiry on Brahmins, see Chuyen (2004), particularly Chapters 4 and 5, focused on Tamil Brahmins.

raise significant questions which have been debated by analysts during the past few years.

Jobs, Self-respect and Populism

The non-Brahmin movement, and later the constant pressure for more reservations have been seen as a quest for benefits by victims of the established structure of power, and rightly so. But Geetha and Rajadurai (1998) are right as well to remind what the Self Respect movement has brought to many Tamils: a 'new structure of feeling' which 'can never be reduced to ... the material interest of a class'; 'an existential foreboding about the powers and possibilities of human thought and action', 'the need to address questions of caste' and to 'reinscribe politics within quotidian acts'. If one accepts this vision of Periyar as really 'the great man' who challenged resolutely the existing order, how are we to assess those who present themselves as his inheritors?

The political supremacy of the Dravidian parties is now long enough for assessing what they have really delivered. The question, today, is less related to the end of separatism than to the relative weakening of the ethnic parameter, the social agenda of populism and the type of politicisation of the citizens in Tamil Nadu. The works of Narendra Subramanian (1999) and Arun Swamy (1998 and 2003), and the comments spelled out by John Harris (2001), offer, here, ample material for theoretical debates on the various forms of populism — the 'paternalist populism' (*ibid.*: 11) of M. G. Ramachandran which won many votes from Dalits and from women to the AIADMK, and the 'assertive populism' (*ibid.*) which all Dravidian parties relied upon as a way of political mobilisation. Interestingly, populism is today challenged by the proponents of economic liberalisation, and severely condemned by liberal economists who blame populist politics for budget deficits, one of the structural weaknesses of the Indian economy. That does not prevent the present DMK government to implement a policy which allows rice to be sold in 'fair price shops' at Rs 2 per kilogram (an electoral promise), to waive massive cooperative loans granted to farmers, to offer free electricity to weavers, etc. But 'Dravidian politics' is not always, for that matter, benevolent. The DMK and the AIADMK have been more than once prone to authoritarianism, opposed to trade unions, and have selectively distributed state patronage to clients rather than to all citizens. The glass is therefore half-empty or half-full. On the whole, the socio-economic parameters and the Human Development Index (HDI) of Tamil Nadu are above the national average: the state ranking for HDI was seventh in 1981, third in 1991, third again in 2001 behind Kerala and Punjab; Tamil Nadu is one of the most dynamic states in India in terms of national or foreign investments. But this relative good position does not prevent the state to illustrate also what Barbara Harris-White and S. Subramanian (1999) have called 'illfare', in order to counter a sense of complacency on issues related to health care, employment generation, social security and development.

Dalit Politics, Caste and Modernity

In such a complex context, marked by a growing empowerment of the lower castes but also by increasing social divides, the future of Dalit politics holds probably the key of this century-old massive and multifaceted movement which, under colonial rule and after independence, has animated Indian society. Tamil Nadu, in a way, has anticipated a number of trends that north India has developed later on, and this explains why the Mandal controversy has been much more discreet in the south. Today, the blogs of anti-reservationists (from India or from the diaspora) keep the flame alive, but internet is no substitute to massive street agitation. Arun Swamy wrote about 'the absence of mass political violence in South India' (1998), and about what he called the 'sandwich tactics' (Swamy 2003: 1) by which, historically, 'have-a-lots succeeds in allying with have-nothings against the have-a-littles' (Harris 2001: 4). I wonder if this model is still valid today, not just because the old Congress strategy has evaporated for long, but also for additional reasons. The DMK and the AIADMK have privileged, in theory, the intermediate castes and the poor — in fact, the OBC more than the Dalits. The upper castes and the dominant classes might have grumbled against their populist policies, but it served them indirectly. The political stability of Dravidian government has shun away social revolution long ago, and the bourgeoisie could safely extract itself from active politics. As David Washbrook noted about M. G. Ramachandran's attitude, 'if the price of political stability is 25 paise a day for a Midday Meal, it would be the height of folly to stop paying it' (1989: 262). At that cost, the elite could agree with welfare economy. Is this still valid in the new political economy of India?

Whatever could be the liberal doctrine behind the transformation of Indian economy since 1991, the coalition politics leaves room for manoeuvring for chief ministers who wish to carry on 'protection populism', as illustrated by the DMK Manifesto 2006.

However, 'protection populism' is not a full substitute to popular aspiration for empowerment. It is here that the contradictions of the system may develop, with the growing assertiveness of Dalits, who account for 19 per cent of Tamil Nadu's population. Old domination was based upon the submissive status of the Dalits. In the new context, tensions and violence arise not so much from their submission but from their progress on the road to emancipation. Dalits' empowerment is opposed eventually by intermediate castes, the most documented example being the Thevars' opposition to Pallars' entry in local elections, which led to events largely commented upon, from the killing of Dalit panchayat president of Melavalavu in 1997, to the pressure put on elected Dalits to resign, not to forget the occurrence of violence and intimidation in day to day life or in election times. More ingrained in tradition is the opposition to Dalits against pulling the deity's chariot in the Kandadevi temple festival.

Such issues, which are not specific to Tamil Nadu, raise decisive questions for the future of Indian society and politics. It is easy to label struggles of lower castes asking for increased reservations as communal or outdated. One may rightly deride the type of moral order the Vanniyar-based PMK and the Dalit Panthers of India (DPI) plead for when they organise protests against film stars who smoke and drink on screen or who talk about pre-marital sex — the more so, when we know the history of tensions between Vanniyars and Dalits.[23] It is also easy to despise the way the Pudhiya Tamilagam and the DPI try to find a political space for themselves by negotiating with various mainstream parties. But it is essential to understand that the agitations conducted by the Pudhiya Tamilagam against aggression and oppression of Dalits, and for Dalit rights, give an added value to the action conducted by dozens of Dalit associations across the state, precisely because this is a political

---

[23] In October 2005, PMK and DPI launched a campaign of public protest against actress Khushboo who was supposed to have defamed Tamil women by stating that 'no educated man would expect his (bride) to be a virgin', in an interview to a Tamil magazine. See AFP release, 6 October 2005, http://news.sawf.org/Bollwood/3243.aspx (accessed 9 July 2008).

party and that key struggles cannot be led just by what is sometimes labelled as civil society, associations and NGOs. Laws are prepared and voted by politicians, and imposing the respect of law depends greatly on the political will of those in power. Dalit parties might be weak, divided, prone to politicking eventually. They, however, introduce a new element in the political stage.

The Dravidian movement has developed an anti-caste philosophy. It has encouraged civilian inter-caste marriages, just as the DMK, back to power in 2006, tried to reintroduce a bill for opening the job of *archakas* (temple priests) to all castes. But on the other hand, the expanding politics of reservation and the quest for vote banks of local castes and communities have inscribed caste afresh in politics, at a time when the aspiration for social mobility is widespread, too widespread for everyone accepting to play the game individually. Is caste modern when Dalit political agitations can be interpreted as an aspiration to 'democratize democracy' as Hugo Gorringe (2005: 50) suggests in his documented study? Were the Dalit Panthers of India right when, in the beginning, they proposed to boycott elections? M. S. S. Pandian has underlined, in a recent study, 'the disenchantment of the Indian modern (even in its Marxist incarnation) with the language of caste' (2002: 19). Is caste pushed outside modernity by the nation-state, and by the credo in the 'common good', asks Pandian, and suggests that the 'modern civil society, in its invocation of modernity … continues to resist the articulation of lower caste politics' (*ibid.*: 20), concluding that in fact, 'being one step outside modernity is indeed being one step ahead of modernity' (*ibid.*: 21).

Today, in Tamil Nadu, in elections to the Legislative Assembly as well as in elections to panchayats, the question is no more confined to the upper castes/backward castes divide, long after the Brahmin/non-Brahmins issue has been solved. What is at stake really is the role and the future of the caste parties, and particularly the Dalit parties, which appeared as a result of the shortcomings of Dravidian politics. If one may draw lessons from the PMK history, Dalit parties, locally entrenched in specific districts, might just become, if they grow in strength, new pressure groups playing politics and getting the benefits of power for their leadership and their cadres. If vivified by the assertiveness of social movements, they may perhaps become more than that, and bring tangible results for their community, knowing, however, that Dalits, just as Vanniyars, don't vote only for caste parties, and that in any case, electoral arithmetics calls for alliances and coalitions. The Dravidian movement has been on the forefront of the non-Brahmin ascendancy and of reservation politics, when compared to north India. It remains to be seen if, in the beginning of the 21st century, caste politics as illustrated in north India will be replicated in Tamil Nadu or not.

References and Select Bibliography

Ambedkar. B. R. 1947. *Who were the Shudras? How they Came to be the Fourth Varna in the Indo-Aryan Society*. Bombay: Thacker & Co.

Barnett, M. R. 1976. *The Politics of Cultural Nationalism in South India*. Princeton: Princeton University Press.

Basu, A. 2005. 'Women, Political Parties and Social Movements in South Asia', Occasional Paper 5, United Nations Research Institute for Social Development (UNRISD), Geneva.

Census of India, 1921. 1922. Part I and Part II, vol. 13. Madras: Government Press.

Census of India, 2001. 2001. New Delhi: Government of India. Available at www.censusindia.gov.in.

Chuyen, G. 2004. *Who is a Brahmin? The Politics of Identity in India*. New Delhi: Manohar Publications.

Election Commission of India. 1971–2006. *Statistical Report on General Elections to the Legislative Assembly of Tamil Nadu*. New Delhi: Government of India.

Geetha, V. and S. V. Rajadurai. 1998. *Towards a Non Brahmin Millennium: From Iyothee Thass to Periyar*. Calcutta: Samya Publishers. Available at http://www.tamilnation.org/books/Caste/geetha.htm (accessed 9 July 2008).

Gorringe, H. 2005. *Untouchable Citizens: Dalit Movements and Democratisation in Tamil Nadu*. New Delhi: Sage Publications.

Government of India. 1994. 'Statement of Objectives and Reasons', New Delhi, http://indiacode.nic.in/coiweb/amend/amend76.htm (accessed 10 October 2006).

Government of Tamil Nadu. 1997. Backward Classes and Most Backward Classes and Denotified Communities Lists, Chennai. Available at www.tn.gov.in/department/bcmbc.htm.

Government of Tamil Nadu. 2005. *Policy Note 2005–06*. Chennai: Backward Classes and Minorities Welfare Department.

Harris, J. 2001. 'Populism, Tamil Style: Is it Really a Success?', *Working Paper Series, 1–15*, Development Studies Institute, London School of Economics and Political Science. Available at http://www.lse.ac.uk/collections/DESTIN/pdf/WP15.pdf.

Harris-White, B. and S. Subramanian. 1999. *Illfare in India: Essays on India's Social Sector in Honour of S. Guhan.* New Delhi: Sage Publications.

Headley, Z. 2006. 'Les Voleurs d'Indra'. Unpublished PhD dissertation, École des Hautes Études en Sciences Sociales (EHESS), Paris.

Ilaiah, K. 1996. *Why I Am Not a Hindu: A Sudra Critique of Hindutva Philosophy, Culture and Political Economy.* Calcutta: Samya Publishers.

Irschik, E. 1969. *Politics and Social Conflict in South India: The Non-Brahman Movement and Tamil Separatism, 1916–1929.* Berkeley: University of California Press.

Pandian, M. S. S. 1992. *The Image Trap: M. G. Ramachandran in Films and Politics.* New Delhi: Sage Publications.

———. 2002. *One Step Outside Modernity: Caste, Identity Politics and Public Sphere.* Amsterdam/Dakar: SEPHIS-CODESRIA.

———. 2006. *Brahmins and Non-Brahmins: Genealogies of the Tamil Political Present.* New Delhi: Permanent Black.

Radhakrishnan, P. 1990. 'Backward Classes in Tamil Nadu: 1872–1988', *Economic and Political Weekly*, 25(10).

———. 1996. 'Backward Class Movements in Tamil Nadu', in M. N. Srinivas (ed.), *Caste: Its Twentieth Century Avatar*, pp. 110–34. New Delhi: Penguin.

———. 2002. 'The Vanniyar Separatism', *Frontline*, 17–30 August. Available at http://www.frontlineonnet.com/fl1917/19170400.htm.

———. 2006. 'Affirmative Action through Usurpation: OBC Reservation and the Tamil Nadu Model', *South Asian Journal*, July–September, 13. Available at http://www.southasianmedia.net/Magazine/Journal/13obc-reservation.htm.

Ramachandran, S. (ed.). 1975. *Anna Speaks at the Rajya Sabha 1962–1966.* Madras: Orient Longman.

Ravikumar. 2005. 'Iyothee Thass & the Politics of Naming', *The Sunday Pioneer*, 28 September. Available at www.countercurrents.org/dalit-ravikumar280905.htm.

Saraswathi, S. 1974. *Minorities in Madras State: Group Interests in Modern Politics.* Delhi: Impex India.

Sattanathan, A. N. 1982. *The Dravidian Movement in Tamil Nadu and its Legacy.* Madras: University of Madras.

Srinivas, M. N. 1962. *Caste in Modern India and Other Essays.* Bombay: Media Promoters & Publishers Pvt. Ltd.

——— (ed). 1996. *Caste: Its Twentieth Century Avatar.* New Delhi: Penguin.

Subramanian, N. 1999. *Ethnicity and Populist Mobilization: Political Parties, Citizens and Democracy in South India.* New Delhi: Oxford University Press.

Swaminathan, S. 1974. *Karunanidhi: Man of Destiny.* New Delhi: East-West Press.

Swamy, A. R. 1998. 'Parties, Political Identities and the Absence of Mass Political Violence in South India', in Atul Kholi and Amrita Basu (eds), *Community Conflicts and the State in India.* New Delhi: Oxford University Press.

———. 2003. 'Consolidating Democracy by Containing Distribution: "Sandwich Tactics" in Indian Party Competition, 1931–96', *India Review*, 2(2): 1–36.

Tamil Nadu Legislative Assembly. 'The State Legislature: Origin and Evolution'. Available at www.assembly.tn.gov.in/history/history.htm.

The Hindu. 2006. 'How Tamil Nadu Voted', 19 May.

Vaasanthi. 2006. *Cut-Outs, Caste and Cine Stars: The World of Tamil Politics*. New Delhi: Penguin.

Viramma, J. Racine and J. L. Racine. 2002. *Viramma: Life of a Dalit*. New Delhi: Social Sciences Press.

Viswanathan, S. 2004. *Dalits in Dravidian Land: Frontline Reports on Anti-Dalit Violence in Tamil Nadu, 1995–2004*. Pondicherry: Navayana Publishing.

Washbrook, D. 1976. *The Emergence of Provincial Politics: The Madras Presidency, 1870–1920*. New York: Cambridge University Press.

———. 1989. 'Caste, Class and Dominance in Modern Tamil Nadu: Non-Brahminism; Dravidianism and Tamil Nationalism', in F. Frankel and M. S. A. Rao (eds), *Dominance and State Power in Modern India*, vol. 1, pp. 204–64. Delhi: Oxford University Press.

About the Editors

Christophe Jaffrelot is Research Director, Centre National de la Recherche Scientifique (CNRS), and Director, Centre d'Études et de Recherches Internationales (CERI), Sciences Po, Paris where he teaches South Asian politics. His recent publications include *Dr Ambedkar and Untouchability: Analysing and Fighting Caste* (2005), *India's Silent Revolution: The Rise of the Lower Castes in North India* (2003) and *The Hindu Nationalist Movement and Indian Politics: 1925 to 1990s* (1996). He has co-edited *Patterns of Middle Class Consumption in India and China* (2008) with Peter van der Veer and *The BJP and the Compulsions of Politics in India* (1998) with Thomas Blom Hansen.

Sanjay Kumar is Fellow, Centre for the Study of Developing Societies (CSDS), Delhi. His research interest is in electoral politics, and he specialises in Survey Research Techniques. He has been the National Coordinator for three national electoral surveys (National Election Study 1998, 1999 and 2004) conducted by the CSDS, and has also been the country coordinator from India for the 'State of Democracy in South Asia' (SDSA) study conducted in the five South Asian countries of India, Pakistan, Bangladesh, Sri Lanka and Nepal. Apart from extending professional guidance to various institutes and researchers in designing surveys and analysing survey data, he has authored various research reports, and contributed to a number of edited volumes, research journals and newspapers.

Notes on Contributors

Samuel Berthet is a historian and Research Coordinator for the Europe South Asia Maritime Heritage project under Jawaharlal Nehru University (Asia Link programme), Delhi. His interests primarily focus on Indian federalism and, in particular, Chhattisgarh as a case study of a new emerging state.

Ramesh K. Chauhan is Associate Professor, Department of Political Science, Himachal Pradesh University, Shimla where he teaches International Politics, Nationalism and Nation-Building. His publications include *Punjab and Nationality Question in India* (1994); and the co-authored volume *South Asia Today* (2005). Presently, he is working on the politics of globalisation and the future of nation-states.

Kiran Desai is Associate Professor at the Centre for Social Studies, Surat. His main research interests have been the working class, communal relations, the Gandhian method and urbanisation. He is a member of the editorial board of *Arthat*, a Gujarati journal issued by the Centre for Social Studies, Surat; and is co-author of *The Pardi Annakhed Satyagraha: Adivasi Assertion for Rights* and *Child Labour in Diamond Industry*.

S. N. Ghosh is Associate Professor, Department of Psychology, Himachal Pradesh University, Shimla. His current research interest is interdisciplinary study of social phenomena, utilising the principles of behavioural science. He has been a visiting faculty at the Albert Einstein College of Medicine, Yeshiva University, New York, and is at present actively involved in conducting cross-cultural studies in preventive and intervention research.

Ashutosh Kumar is Reader in Indian politics at the Department of Political Science, Panjab University, Chandigarh. He has earlier taught at the University of Delhi and Jammu University; he was Visiting Fellow at the International School of Social Sciences, University of

Tampere, Finland, and at the Centre for Democracy and Development, Lagos, Nigeria. He has been associated with the Lokniti network, CSDS, Delhi as Coordinator for Punjab. Dr Kumar is the author of *Political Economy of the State in India* (1993); and has co-edited *Burning Issues in Jammu & Kashmir Politics* (1999); *Politics of Autonomy in Jammu and Kashmir* (1998); and *Globalisation and Politics of Identity in India* (forthcoming).

G. Gopa Kumar is Professor and Head, Department of Political Science, University of Kerala, Trivandrum. He teaches comparative and international politics. His early specialisation was in the politics of Kerala; his doctoral dissertation was on 'The Congress Party in Kerala Since 1967', and he has published several books and articles. He served as Visiting Professor at the University of Calgary, Canada and Claremont Graduate University, California. He has coordinated several election studies in Kerala since 1996 conducted by the CSDS, Delhi.

Stéphanie Tawa Lama–Rewal is CNRS Research Fellow in Political Science at the Centre for the Study of India and South Asia, Paris, currently on deputation at the Centre de Sciences Humaines, New Delhi. Her recent publications include *Electoral Reservations, Political Representation and Social Change in India: A Comparative Perspective* (2005). She has co-authored *Democratization in Progress: Women and Local Politics in Urban India* (2005). Her main research interests are the political representation of groups, local democracy, and urban governance in India.

Jean-Luc Racine is Senior CNRS Fellow, the Centre for South Asian Studies, École des Hautes Études en Sciences Sociales (EHESS), Paris, and Fellow, Asia Centre, Paris. He teaches South Asia geopolitics at the Institut Français de Géopolitique, University Paris 8; and Indian political economy at EHESS. He also heads the International Programme for Advanced Studies run by the Fondation Maison des Sciences de l'Homme, Paris, in cooperation with Columbia University.

Cyril Robin received his PhD from the Institute of Political Studies, Paris. His dissertation deals with the rise of the Other Backward Classes on the political scene in Bihar (1952–2005). He is currently affiliated to the Centre of International Studies and Research, Institute of Political Studies, Paris as Research Fellow, and is based at the Centre de Sciences Humaines, New Delhi since October 2004.

Ghanshyam Shah is retired as Professor, Jawaharlal Nehru University, and is former Director, Centre for Social Studies, Surat. He is author and editor of several books; among them are: *Social Movements in India* (2004); *Caste and Democratic Politics* (2004); *Dalit Identity and Politics* (2002); and *Public Health and Urban Development* (1997).

T. R. Sharma is retired as Professor of Political Science, Panjab University, Chandigarh. He served as Honorary Coordinator at the Centre for Defense and National Security Studies at the University. Till recently, he was Fellow, Indian Institute of Advanced Study, Shimla. He has authored *Relevance of Marxism in the Contemporary World* (1990) and *Communism in India: The Politics of Fragmentation* (1984). Some of his co-edited volumes include *Maharaja Ranjit Singh: Ruler and Warrior* (2005); *New Challenges of Politics in the Indian States*; and *India's Security and Strategic Interests in Mid-West and Central Asia* (forthcoming).

Sandeep Shastri is a political scientist and Director of the International Academy for Creative Teaching (*i*ACT), Bangalore. He is a visiting Adjunct Professor at the University of California at Berkeley and in the Faculty of Education at the University of California Berkeley. He has published widely, and is associated with several international research bodies in the field of political science and education. These include the Comparative Study of Election Systems, World Values Survey, Institute of Public Integrity and the International IDEA project on Civic Education.

Anne Vaugier-Chatterjee is currently Political Adviser, Delegation of the European Commission to India. A postgraduate from the Institut d'Études Politiques, Paris, she holds a PhD in political science from the École des Hautes Études en Sciences Sociales, Paris and headed the Political Science department at the Centre de Sciences Humaines, New Delhi between 1998 and 2002. Apart from having regularly contributed to French newspapers, she has published a number of papers in academic journals on various political and social issues and is the author of two books: *Education and Democracy in India* (2004) and *Histoire Politique du Pendjab de 1947 a nos jours* (2001).

Rajendra Vora (Late) was a political scientist based in Pune. He was Lokmanya Tilak Professor of Politics at the University of Pune until his retirement in 2006, and was involved in a research project on Muslim politics in India. He co-edited *Region, Culture and Politics in India* (2006); and *Indian Democracy: Meanings and Practices* (2004); and was the editor of *Socio-Economic Profile of Rural India* (2005). He is author of *The Struggle against Mulshi Dam: A Non-Violent Movement in Colonial India* (forthcoming).

Jasmine Zérinini works for the French government and is posted in Paris. She was previously Research Fellow, Centre de Sciences Humaines, Delhi between 1996 and 1999 where she carried out a research project on the Indian National Congress party's evolution since independence in Uttar Pradesh. She also co-led, with Anne Vaugier-Chatterjee, a programme on the sociology of MLAs.